WORKS ISSUED BY
THE HAKLUYT SOCIETY

———

THE VOYAGE OF GEORGE VANCOUVER, 1791–1795

VOLUME III

SECOND SERIES
NO. 165

HAKLUYT SOCIETY

Plate 36. Joseph Whidbey.

GEORGE VANCOUVER

A Voyage of Discovery
to the
North Pacific Ocean
and Round the World
1791–1795

With an Introduction and Appendices

VOLUME III

EDITED BY

W. KAYE LAMB

THE HAKLUYT SOCIETY
LONDON
1984

ISBN 0 904180 19 0
0 904180 16 6 (set of four volumes)

Printed in Great Britain by the
University Press, Cambridge

Published by the Hakluyt Society
c/o The Map Library,
British Library Reference Division
London WC1B 3DG

CONTENTS

v

ILLUSTRATIONS

† Indicates engravings reproduced from a set of the 1798 edition of *A Voyage of Discovery* in the British Library (1889 R 42), by permission of the Library. Original captions, where retained, are indicated by quotation marks.

PLATES

SKETCH MAPS

All base maps by Michael E. Leek

CHAPTER V.

Departure of Lieutenant Broughton for England—Progress towards the Sandwich Islands—Fruitless Search for the Islands of Los Majos—Arrive at Owhyhee—Visited by the Chiefs—Anchor in Karakakooa Bay—Land the Cattle—Regulations adopted—Account of two English Seamen residing on the Island—Capture of the Schooner Fair American—Character of some of the leading Chiefs.

THE preceding chapters brought to a conclusion the various occurrences of our voyage to the end of 1792; the beginning of the following year was not marked by any thing of very particular moment. Senr Quadra's benevolent disposition encouraged me again to obtrude on his goodness by requesting some black cattle and sheep, for the purpose of establishing a breed of those valuable animals in the Sandwich islands. A dozen, being as many as we could possibly take on board, were immediately provided, consisting of four cows, four ewes, two bulls, and two rams.[1] The prospect we had of a good passage to those islands induced me to lay myself under this additional obligation, hoping by such an importation, to accomplish at once the purpose I had in contemplation; which, if effected, could not fail of being highly beneficial, not only to the resident inhabitants, but also to all future visitors.

Notwithstanding that I was extremely anxious to get away from Monterrey that the further objects of our pursuit might re-commence, and that we might be no longer the cause of Senr Quadra's detention, yet, with our utmost labours and exertions, it was not until Sunday the 6th that the several charts, drawings, letters, and other documents were in readiness to be transmitted to England.[2]

[1] Oddly enough, Vancouver's notes or recollections were at fault here; later references show that there must have been seven cows and four rams on board. He states that one cow, a bull, two ewes and three rams died during the voyage (p. 801); that a cow and a bull, both in very poor condition, were sent ashore before the *Discovery* reached Kealakekua Bay (p. 806), but that at the bay itself the 'remaining live stock' landed there consisted of 'five cows, two ewes and a ram'. (p. 812).

[2] These included: a covering letter dated 13 January 1793; 19 charts and sketches, including Baker's chart of the Northwest Coast and Broughton's chart of the Columbia River, as well as copies of nine Spanish charts (eight provided by Quadra and one by Galiano); 27 drawings by John Sykes and 12 by H. Humphrys; a report on the 'state and condition' of the *Discovery* and *Chatham*; and (in Vancouver's words) 'a copy of my Journal, from our departure from Falmouth to the end of the year'. The letter, lists of the charts and drawings, and the report on the ships are in P.R.O., Adm. 1/2629, ff. 44–50v.

After this, having no further occasion for our establishment on shore, the tents, observatory, instruments, and every other article were reshipped, it being my full determination to sail with the land wind the following evening, Monday the 7th: in the interval I was honored on board with the company of Sen^{rs} Quadra, Caamano, the commandant of the Presidio with his lady, and most of our Spanish friends.

In the course of the afternoon a very material alteration took place in the weather, for the first time since our arrival in this bay. The wind blew a hard gale from the S.E. attended with heavy squalls and torrents of rain. In addition to this another circumstance concurred to detain us some time longer. The armourer of the Chatham, a most industrious and excellent workman, found an opportunity in the course of the day, with one of the Chatham's best marines, to absent themselves. The abilities and generally good conduct of the armourer, made his loss a matter of no small consequence, especially as there was no other person in our little community that was competent to fill his post.[1] The only mode to be pursued for their recovery, was to make a proper and formal application to Senr Quadra, and to Senr Arguello, the commandant of the Presidio. In consequence of this, these gentlemen took similar steps to those which on a former occasion had recovered a seaman belonging to the Discovery, who had attempted to make his escape.[2] The better to insure

Most of the charts and drawings are now in the keeping of the Hydrographer of the Navy, but the whereabouts of the copy of Vancouver's journal (if it is still in existence) is unknown.

[1] James Etchinson is entered in the muster roll as Armourer's Mate, not Armourer. The marine was James Landon. The Spaniards returned them to the Chatham at Monterey on 4 November 1794. In his letter to the Admiralty, Vancouver states that Etchinson's desertion 'from his use and abilities' was 'the greatest loss we could sustain in any one man'. Manby was convinced that the Spaniards had enticed him to desert: 'The greatest cordiality existed between the Dons' and ourselves, 'till a day or two previous to taking leave, Two men from the Chatham deserted one of them the Armourer, a very ingenious Mechanic, he had done a great many Jobs for the Spaniards, who we found out had inticed him away, with a promise of forty Dollars per month, scouting parties were sent in every direction for three days, but without effect, which obliged us to give up the pursuit'. – Manby, letters, January. Bell at first shared Manby's suspicions, 'but the exertions the Spaniards made to recover [the men] did away the Suspicions aforementioned, at least as far as related to the Spanish Officers.' – January.

[2] The reference is to the attempted desertion of James Bailey. Menzies describes it in some detail: 'We this day learnd that James Baily...had travelled out to the Mission of Carmillo, & having got within that sanctuary, claimed the protection of the Reverend Fathers, which he so far obtaind, that they waited on Captain Vancouver to intercede for his pardon, but finding that would not be granted, the only mitigation they procurd was a promise that he should not be punishd whilst the ship remained at Monterrey, & next day a Serjeant with a party of Marines went out privately to the Mission where he was given up to them & brought on board as a prisoner. He remained in irons till we went to sea & was then punishd at two different times with six dozen lashes each time, tho we cannot help thinking that a mitigation of this severe punishment at the instigation of the Worthy Fathers would have been equally efficacious & a more creditable procedure, especially as we did not find that the severity of treatment in this case had prevented others from deserting before departure.' – December 18.

success in this instance, a reward of twenty-five dollars for each of the deserters was offered to the soldiers, who were dispatched in every direction in search of them. The like sum was offered by Senr Quadra, by the commandant, and by myself, to any person who would deliver them up, or who should be the cause of their being taken. The loss we had thus sustained, and the active exertions making to repair it, would at any rate have induced me to wait a few days for the event of our researches. The S.W. and southerly winds with succeeding calms continued, however, to prevent our sailing until Sunday the 13th, when in the morning the regular sea-breeze from the N.W. prevailed.

During this interval no tidings had been gained of the absentees, and the soldiers who had been sent in quest of them returned unsuccessful. Senr Quadra evidently felt much distressed that so unfortunate an occurrence should take place just on the eve of our separation, and issued orders, that on their being apprehended they should be imprisoned; that they might be forwarded to me at Nootka, during any period of our remaining in these seas. And as a proof that these people had absconded without the knowledge, privity, or encouragement of any of the Spanish officers, he very obligingly offered to replace the armourer by substituting the only smith in this establishment; who, being reported to be a very good workman, was an artificer of too much importance, to persons in our situation, to be hastily declined. With great reluctance, and though contrary to my wishes, I was induced to accept the advantage of so friendly an offer, to which the urgency of the case alone could have obliged me to assent.[1] He was accordingly received on board the Chatham, and Senr Quadra's vessels as well as our own being in readiness to depart, it was agreed we should sail together, so long as our southern course answered the purpose of our respective routes, that we might continue as long as possible to benefit from each other's society.

We now waited only for the favourable land breeze to take our departure. I consigned to the charge of Mr. Broughton the dispatches I had prepared, with orders, as far as it might depend upon himself, not to lose a moment's time in repairing to England; and I directed my first lieutenant, Mr. Puget, to take upon him the command of the Chatham, during the absence of Mr. Broughton.[2]

[1] José de los Santos, aged 27, joined the Chatham on January 13. He was 'brought on board under Guard' and 'was obliged to serve much against his Inclination', but someone with his qualifications was 'indispensably necessary'. – Puget, January 14.

[2] 'On this occasion I have not superseded Lieut! Broughton in the command of the Chatham, but have appointed my first lieutenant, Mr. Puget, to take upon him that charge during Lieut! Broughton's absence, or until their Lordships' pleasure shall be known.' – Vancouver to Stephens, 13 January 1793. Vancouver praised Broughton, recommended him for the command of any ship the Admiralty might propose to send to the Pacific to join the Discovery and Chatham, and expressed the hope that 'his well executing the service now entrusted to his charge will be the means of recommending him to their Lordships' further protection and favor.' Puget celebrated his promotion by beginning a new volume of his personal log, and he appended to the first volume an estimate of the distances travelled from 4 January 1791, the day he joined the Discovery at Deptford, to 14 January 1792,

The night was perfectly calm; about nine o'clock on Monday morning the 14th, a light breeze sprung up from the eastward, with which the Discovery weighed; but, as neither the Chatham nor any of the Spanish vessels were able to move, we waited for them off point Pinos, this we passed at the distance of two or three miles, and had soundings from 38 to 55 fathoms, black sand and muddy bottom.

The next morning we found ourselves more to the southward, and further from the shore than we expected; the wind blew a fresh breeze from the land, and we stood to the northward in quest of our friends. The Chatham joined us about nine o'clock, when our situation afforded a good opportunity of making such observations as were required to prove the rate of the chronometers. At noon the latitude was found to be 36° 23'; Kendall's chronometer shewed 238° 18'; Arnold's No. 14, 238° 7½'; No. 176, 238° 10¾', and Earnshaw's pocket watch, 238° 3'. In this situation the southernmost land in sight bore by compass S. 56 E.; and an apparently detached piece of land like a small island, S. 72 E.; and point Pinos N. 31 E. This point, according to our observations made on shore at Monterrey, is situated in latitude 36° 38', longitude 238° 22'; from which it appeared that the chronometers, since they had been taken on board, had acquired the following errors, (viz.) Kendall's 13', Arnold's No. 14, 2' 30"; Arnold's No. 176, 5' 45", to the east of the truth. Earnshaw's pocket watch appeared to be correct. By these observations Kendall's had acquired the greatest error, and Earnshaw's had gone perfectly right. The great regularity of Kendall's hitherto made it difficult to account for this sudden alteration, which could be attributed to nothing but the change that had taken place in the climate on their being removed from the shore to the ship. The thermometer was found daily to vary at the observatory between mid-day and the evening, from about 72° to 40°; the excess was more as it would sometimes rise to 76°, and fall to 31°; but this did not frequently

the day he left her at Monterey. The reference to Point Menzies (far inland, on Burke Channel) indicates that the distance travelled by some (perhaps all) of the boat excursions was included. Text of the table follows:

This Book Contains Miles run by the Log

From the Downs to Falmouth	392·6
Falmouth to Teneriffe	1920·6
Teneriffe to Cape Good Hope	5701
Cape of Good [Hope] to New Holland	5119
New Holland to New Zealand	2344
New Zealand to Otaheite	4241·2
Otaheite to the Sandwich Islands	3895·2
Oneehow to Cape Flattery NW America	2902·6
Survey of De Fuca's Streights	1824·0
From Point Menzies to Nootka	492·6
Nootka to Francisco	1777·4
Francisco to Monteray	94·6
	30703·0

[The total is incorrect; it should be 30704·8.]

happen, though early in the mornings it was not unusual to find the little wells we had dug skimmed over with thin flakes of ice, and the ground covered with hoar frost. On board the ship, the mean temperature of the air in which they were kept was between 54 and 60 degrees. This opinion appeared to be particularly corroborated in the instance of Kendall's watch, which evidently went nearly at its Nootka rate during our passage from thence to Monterrey; but on its being there landed, the increase and continuation of the cold appeared soon to accelerate its motion from that of gaining $11\frac{1}{4}''$ to $18\frac{1}{2}$ per day. On allowing its rate of gaining at Nootka, from the time of its last coming on board at Monterrey, it was found to agree very nearly with the longitude of point Pinos, as affixed to it by our observations; and as I am perfectly satisfied of the accuracy of our observations, the difference can surely be attributed to no other cause, than that the best of these delicate pieces of mechanism are not yet, with all the ingenious and valuable improvements that have been made on them, able to withstand, for any length of time, the transitions and vicissitudes of different climates. Mr. Arnold's two watches on board the Discovery, being of later date by some years than Mr. Kendall's, appear to have continued their rate of going more correctly, but even these felt the effect of their altered situation; Mr. Earnshaw's was the newest, and was the least sensible of the change in the climate to which it was removed. Future experience may however enable me to form other conjectures, which may tend to elucidate more fully a subject of so much importance to nautical science.

In resuming the narrative of the proceedings it is necessary to state, that the longitude shewn by the chronometers will in future be inserted according to the Monterrey rate, until an opportunity may offer of making further observations.

We remained off point Pinos until the evening; when, being joined by our Spanish friends, we directed our course to the southward with so light a northerly breeze, that by noon of Wednesday the 16th we had only reached the latitude of 36°, the land bearing by compass from N. 20 E. to S. 83 E. the nearest shore N.E. distant about 4 leagues.

The Active brig considerably outsailed our little squadraon, and the Aransasu, the worst sailer of the whole party, was by sun set nearly out of sight astern. As neither Senr Quadra nor myself wished to experience the least delay, we agreed to avail ourselves of the favourable gale from the north, and without waiting for Senr Caamano in the Aransasu, to make the best of our way. By Friday the 18th at noon we had reached the latitude of 32° 30', longitude 239° 14', and and variation of the compass 12° eastwardly.

From this station the tracks we each had to pursue began to diverge, so that by continuing together we should not only have drawn each other from the proper line of direction, but, in consequence of the superiority which the Active had in point of sailing, have necessarily occasioned a further detention to Senr Quadra; who, with Mr. Broughton, and such of our Spanish friends as could be spared from the brig, honored me with their company to partake of a parting dinner.

The wind blew a gentle breeze from the north; the serenity of the sky and smoothness of the sea, prolonged my pleasure on this occasion until near midnight; when we exchanged our mutual good wishes, and bad our friends of the Active farewel. Amongst all that valuable society, there was but one friend who we could reasonably hope and expect to see again, whilst the prospect of never again meeting Senr Quadra and our other friends about him, was a painful consideration.[1] To the feelings of those perusers of this journal who have experienced moments like this, I must appeal. Their recollection will enable them to conceive the sensations which, inspired by the grateful recollection of past kindnesses, occurred in thus bidding adieu to Senr Quadra; who was the main spring of a society that had produced us so much happiness, who had rendered us so many essential benefits, and whose benevolence and disinterested conduct had impressed our minds with the highest esteem and veneration. On reaching the Active, our friends took their leave; we saluted them with three cheers, which they cordially returned; and we each pursued our respective voyages with all sail set.

Nothing worthy of notice occurred until Monday the 21st; when Joseph Murgatroyd, one of the carpenter's crew, was in the space of about a quarter of an hour from the time he had been last seen missing. He was last observed opening the gun-room ports, and whilst so employed, had probably been induced to seek his own destruction by contriving to let himself down into the sea; since it was scarcely possible he could have met his fate there by accident. An experiment was afterwards made, by much smaller men than himself, to force themselves out of the port-holes, which was not accomplished without great difficulty and trouble; it was however pretty evident that he must have perished that way, as he was never seen to come out of the gun-room: add to this, that as he was a good swimmer, as the wind blew only a gentle breeze, with a smooth sea, and as every thing was very quiet upon deck, it is natural to conclude, that if he had fallen overboard, the accident must have been immediately known, and that he most likely would have been preserved.[2]

The weather continued dark and gloomy, with frequent showers, until noon of Wednesday the 23d; when the atmosphere became less loaded and more pleasant; the observed latitude at this time was 25° 54′, the longitude,

---

[1] Vancouver had in fact seen Quadra for the last time. This remark must have been made in the light of later events. Quadra was not at Monterey when Vanvouver called there in November 1793, and he died in Mexico City on 25 March 1794.

[2] No reason for this suicide was known, 'except that he had been severely punishd some months before for a theft he had committed, the guilt & shame of which might have preyd on his mind, especially as he was always observed to be of a gloomy religious cast. He had formerly workd at one of our Dock Yards in the River.' Menzies, January 21. The logs show that he had received 36 lashes on 4 August 1792.

by Kendall's chronometer, 237° 37′. Our progress was so slow, that on the 24th we had reached only the latitude of 24° 50′. The true longitude, deduced from subsequent observations, and corrected back to our quitting the coast, was at this time 236° 14′. Kendall's chronometer shewed 236° 53′; Arnold's No. 14, 236° 27′; No. 176, 236° 31′; Earnshaw's 236° 19′; and Arnold's, on board the Chatham, 236° 8′: from whence it appeared, that their respective errors continued nearly in the same ratio as our observations had shewn the day after we quitted Monterrey.

The wind, though favorable between the N.N.E. and N.N.W. was light, and frequently sunk into a calm, attended with a heavy rolling sea from between west and N.W.

In consequence of my intention to determine the existence or non-existence of a cluster of islands, described in the Spanish charts as lying between the 19th and 21st degrees of north latitude, and between the 221st and 225th degrees of east longitude,[1] I had been induced to steer a very easterly course; but, suspecting that the light winds we had experienced were occasioned by our vicinity to the continent, we steered a more westerly course during the two last days, with the hope of meeting a fresher trade wind. In this I was disappointed, for instead of having a more favorable breeze, the wind veered round to the west and S.W. and so continued until Saturday evening the 26th, when our latitude was 22° 10′, the true longitude 236° 23′.

To this station the variation had gradually decreased to 8°; and for some days past we had regularly been affected by a current setting us to the south, at the rate of seven or eight miles per day; particularly during the preceding twenty-four hours we had been set twelve miles further south than the log shewed.

In the course of the day some tropic birds were about the ship; and after a few hours calm in the evening, a light breeze sprang up from the S.E. which gradually veered round to the N.E. yet the N.W. swell still continued to be very heavy.

The N.E. wind, proving to be a steady trade wind, soon increased to a fresh gale, attended with pleasant weather. On Monday morning the 28th, being nearly in the latitude assigned to the easternmost of the islands before mentioned, the Chatham was sent by signal to look out on the larboard beam. At noon our observed latitude was 21° 12′, true longitude 234° 39′, and the variation of the compass 5° 34′ easterly: Kendall's chronometer shewed the

---

[1] The names given to the islands on old charts vary; Vancouver refers to them as the islands of Los Majos. Unknown to him, La Pérouse had made a systematic search for the islands in 1786. He concluded that some Spanish ship had sighted the Sandwich (Hawaiian) Islands and placed them on the chart about 10° too far E. E. W. Dahlgren disputed this thesis in a monograph entitled *Were the Hawaiian Islands Discovered by the Spaniards before Their Discovery by Captain Cook in 1778?* (Stockholm, 1916). This was considered a conclusive denial of the Spanish claim, but doubts linger. See Bern Anderson, *Surveyor of the Sea* (Seattle, 1960), pp. 128–34.

longitude to be 235° 22', Arnold's No. 14, 234° 59', Arnold's No. 176, 235° 1', and Earnshaw's 234° 48'. The north-westerly swell still continued to be very heavy.

On Thursday the 31st, we passed through a large quantity of the medusa villilia, like those which, in our way to the north the preceding spring, we had found occupying a much larger space in the ocean; these extended only a few leagues in the direction we were steering, and were by no means so numerous.

The trade wind varying between the E.N.E. and N.N.E. increased to a fresh gale, and brought with it squally and unsettled weather, with some passing showers of heavy rain. Having nearly reached the situation assigned to the islands we were in quest of, though without any of the usual indications of the vicinity of land, I yet judged it expedient to reduce our sail at night to prevent the possibility of passing any land that might exist in the neighbourhood. Our latitude at sun-set 19° 54', longitude 227° 42'. This and several following nights were passed in such a manner, as that the point of view a-head in the evening, and that a-stern the next morning, should meet in the same horizon unless intercepted by land, though even very moderately elevated. Thus we continued to proceed in search of these islands at night; and in the day time, spreading as wide as our signals could be plainly discerned.

The weather being delightfully serene and pleasant enabled us on the 3d of February to make the following observations for the longitude.

Sets of distances of the ☾ and ☉ taken by

Eight	Myself,	224° 14' 43"
Seven	Mr. Baker,	224 21 51
Eight	Mr. Whidbey,	224 19 30
Six	Mr. Orchard,	224 11 20
Eight	Mr. Ballard,	224 25 32

In all 37 sets, which gave the mean longitude at noon — 224 18 35

The true longitude deduced from these and subsequent observations I considered at this time to be — 224 2

The observed latitude was — 19 53

Kendall's chronometer on allowing the Nootka rate, from the time of its removal at Monterrey to the ship, shewed the longitude to be — 224 21

According to its Monterrey rate — 225 13 30

Arnold's No. 14, by ditto — 224 28 15

Ditto No. 176, by ditto — 224 27 16

Earnshaw's — 224 9

The variation of the compass 5° 16′ eastwardly. At this juncture we were passing over the position assigned in a chart I had received from Senr Quadra, to the center of the easternmost of the islands in question. Messrs. Portlock and Dixon also had searched for them to no purpose;[1] but as the track of these navigators seemed to have been on the northern side, our's was directed along the southern side of this supposed cluster of islands, until Wednesday the 6th, when the latitude at noon was observed to be 19° 19′, the true longitude 219° 49′.

During this search the trade wind, having been moderate between the S.E. and N.E. attended with tolerably pleasant weather, afforded us during the day time a constant, extensive and distinct view all around, but no indication of them, nor of the vicinity of land, was discovered; nor had I in any of my passages across this ocean, which have been many, ever passed over so vacant a space, as since our departure from the coast of New Albion. No bird, fish, or other object occurred to attract our attention, beside two tropic birds, one booby, about as many petrels, and three or four porpoises; these and our little consort excepted, the heavens and the ocean gave uninterrupted limits to our sight. The latter however caused us great inconvenience, by means of a very heavy and irregular swell, chiefly from the N.W. which gave the ship such a labouring uneasy motion, as to render the transacting of all sedentary business almost impossible. At the close of day there was no appearance of these islands so far as could be seen a head, and as we had now passed some distance to the westward, I concluded they could have no existence in the neighbourhood of the spot assigned to them, and for that reason I relinquished any further search, and made the best of our way to Owhyhee.

On this occasion it is but just to observe, that the Spanish sea officers have no faith[2] in the existence of these islands; the only authority which they are acquainted with for their insertion in the Spanish charts, is their having been so found in a chart of the Pacific Ocean, constructed many years ago by an old pilot who had frequently passed between South America and the Philippines, and whose skill and observation had acquired him much reputation and credit in his profession: but as the spot in which they were placed was totally out of his path, it was generally believed by the Spanish officers that *he* had laid them down from the authority of others.[3]

---

[1] Portlock gives a short account of his search in May 1786 in his *Voyage Round the World* (London, 1789), pp. 56–7; Dixon makes only a brief reference to the matter in *A Voyage Round the World* (London, 1789), p. 49.

[2] Misprinted 'have faith' instead of 'have no faith' in the second edition.

[3] Menzies notes that a chart 'was receivd from Sr. Quadra before we left Monterrey, & which was the production of the oldest Pilot they have on this Coast, & as he was with Sr. Quadra at Monterrey we had an opportunity of enquiring of him more particularly on whose authority these Islands had crept into their Charts; he said that he knew of no authority for them, nor did he ever hear the name of any person that saw them it was reported to him that they were first discovered by some Vessel coming from China to Mexico, but this is very improbable from their situation being so far out of the usual track of Vessels coming from that quarter, & it is not at all likely that any one would

The variation in the afternoon had been observed to be 5° eastwardly. The trade wind blew only a gentle breeze, and so continued until Friday the 8th, when we had a fine fresh gale; but were reduced to our topsails for the purpose of keeping company with the Chatham. The observed latitude on Monday the 11th was 19° 34', and the true longitude 207° 20'; the fresh gale continued from about the N.E., the weather squally with thick mist and much rain. We however made a tolerable progress till two the next morning, Tuesday the 12th, when, not wishing with such uncertain weather to run our observations too close, we hauled to the wind under an easy sail to wait for day-light, when we again made sail; and at nine in the forenoon saw the east end of Owhyhee, bearing by compass S. 60 E. distant seven leagues.

My intention was, that Mr. Puget in the Chatham should examine the coast of this island, from its east point southward round to Karakakooa bay;[1] whilst we were employed on the survey of its shores in the opposite direction. By these means the whole coast of the island would be ascertained, with all its bays, harbours, or roadsteads; and every other information that circumstances could admit of, would thus be acquired. The Discovery was brought to, for the purpose of communicating these directions to Mr. Puget; after which we separated and pursued our respective courses.

The observed latitude at noon was 19° 40'; at this time the east point of Owhyhee bore by compass S. 30 W., at the distance of seven miles, and was placed, by our chronometers according to Kendall's per Nootka rate, in the longitude of 205° 40½'; by the Monterrey rate 206° 49'; Arnold's No. 82, on board the Chatham, per Nootka rate, 205° 45'; per Monterrey rate 205° 18'; Arnold's No. 14, per Monterrey rate, 205° 41' 30"; No. 176, by the same rate, 205° 31' 30"; Earnshaw's per Monterrey rate, 205° 13' 30"; and my own last lunar observations brought forward, by Earnshaw's watch, 205° 19' 13". This point is placed by Captain Cook in 205° 6', which being esteemed by me to be the true longitude shews the errors of the several chronometers during this passage.[2]

Our course was now directed towards the north-eastern point of this island,[3] which forms the eastern point of a very deep bay.[4] Into this we steered, as far as was prudent, to avoid being imbayed, as the wind blew a fresh gale directly on the shore; and though we were sufficiently near its southern parts to see the surf break with great violence, yet so dense was the haze in which the land was enveloped, that it was impossible to distinguish any object on shore. A low projecting point was indistinctly seen, where the breakers appeared to fall back from their northern direction; beyond this point they were not visible from the deck, until we drew near to the northern side of

persevere in so low a Latitude against the prevailing direction of the Trade Wind.' – 3 February.

[1] Kealakekua Bay.
[2] Cape Kumukahi, the E point of the island of Hawaii, is in lat. 19° 31' N, long. 154° 49' W (205° 11' E).
[3] Leleiwi Point.　　　　　　　　　　[4] Hilo Bay.

the bay; here we brought to, about four o'clock, within two miles of the north-eastern point, in the hope of seeing some of the natives, but being disappointed, we made sail off the shore, and plied during the night. The next morning, Wednesday the 13th, with a fresh gale at E.S.E., we sailed along the N.E. side of Owhyhee, within two or three miles of its shores; these were firm and compact, terminating mostly in steep rocky cliffs, with a few small indented bays, rendered easily accessible to their canoes by the sandy beaches that bounded them. From the rugged rocky cliffs, many streams of water fell, and discharged themselves into the ocean.

The country, in this point of view, had a very dreary aspect; perfectly uncultivated, and nearly destitute of habitations; those which were observed were small, and thinly scattered at great distances from each other. As we advanced to the westward, the population and cultivation seemed to increase, and to keep pace with each other. About nine o'clock, a canoe was seen coming towards the ship from one of the small bays; we immediately brought to, in the hope that others would follow her example, but we were again disappointed.

On the arrival of our visitors they gave us to understand, that a general taboo had prevented the inhabitants coming off to us; they however had ventured to trespass on the interdiction, at the hazard of suffering death, should their transgression be ever known to any of the priests or chiefs. The taboo had now existed some days, and in the course of a day or two more would cease. These people further informed us, that *Tamaahmaah* [1] was then residing at Karakakooa, and that hogs, and the other refreshments of the island, were prohibited from being disposed of to European or American visitors, under penalty of death, for any other commodities [2] whatever than *arms and ammunition*.

This is the baneful consequence arising from the injudicious conduct of unrestrained commercial adventurers, who have thought proper to furnish these people, naturally a warlike and daring race, with a large assortment of arms and ammunition, [3] not only rendering them, by these means, a formidable nation; but by thus absurdly and profusely out-bidding each other,

[1] Kamehameha.

[2] Misprinted 'for any commodities' in the second edition.

[3] Vancouver probably had the *Butterworth* and her companion ship specifically in mind. Bell comments: 'We were not surpriz'd at the Native's demand for Guns, when we learnt that Mr. Stewart Master of the Jackall and Mr. Brown of the Butterworth had given ToMaiha Maiha and other chiefs of the Island no less than 30 Muskets in barter for refreshments, this is a most shameful trade, and calls loudly for a stop to be put to it.' – February. Menzies regretted that the natives had not been 'kept without the use of those destructive weapons that have been so industriously dispersed amongst them and which serve to stir up their minds with a desire of conquest, ruin and destruction to their fellow creatures.' He foresaw a day when the natives would 'become more daring and insolent in their behaviour, more exorbitant in their demands for refreshments, and by their overpowering numbers and stratagems will become too formidable for any single vessel to encounter or venture amongst them.' – February 20.

bringing the generality of other European commodities into contempt and low estimation. Our visitors, however, regardless of the taboo, disposed of their cargo, consisting of one hog, two or three fowls, some roots, and bread-fruit, seemingly much to their satisfaction, for some iron; with which they returned to the shore.

Towards noon we arrived off a part of the northern side of Owhyhee, where the coast is composed of a cluster of remarkably high, steep, rugged and romantic cliffs, discharging from their naked summits many rapid cataracts into the ocean.[1] The rushing of these impetuous torrents down the black barren surface of the rocky cliffs, contrasted with the enchanting, cultivated, and populous country to the east and west, and behind this dreary frontier, for a considerable distance up the sides of the lofty mountains, on approaching them in the offing, present a very beautiful and picturesque appearance. Nearly in the centre of these cliffs is a tolerably deep small bay,[2] much resembling, in appearance and in most other respects, the bay in the island of St. Helena; but, unfortunately, seemed too much exposed to the sea, and the generally prevailing winds, to be an eligible situation for shipping. Off the western extremity of these cliffs lie some rocky islets, at a little distance from the land. Westward from these cliffs, the surf was observed to break with great violence near the shore, which was then within two miles of us; at this moment we suddenly arrived in seven fathoms water, the west point of the island lying S. 70 W., at the distance of nine miles. The trade wind blew a strong gale, attended by a very heavy, confused, irregular sea, probably occasioned by the violence of the wind, and an uneven bottom. As this appearance extended all the way to the west end of the island, on finding ourselves in soundings of seven fathoms we hauled a little off the shore, and did not again reach the bottom; though at the rate we were then going we were not likely to have gained soundings, in much deeper water.

The western part of the land, from this situation, falls in a gradual descent from the base of the mountains, and forms an extensive plain towards the water-side, which seemed to be in a state of high cultivation, and abounded with the habitations of the natives. We passed the west point at the distance of about a league, close on the verge of the agitated water; this I suspected to arise from a very sudden decrease in its depth, but could not ascertain the fact, as the wind blew with too much violence, and the agitation of the sea was too great, to venture on a more minute examination, either with the ship or the boats; and as the adjacent shores afford no shelter for vessels, there can be no necessity for approaching within a league of them.

Having passed this point, situated by our corrected survey, in latitude 20° 18′, longitude 204°,[3] we hauled into Toeaigh bay, and at seven o'clock

---

[1] Waipio, Waimanu, Waikaloa, Hanokane and Polulu streams all rush down deep valleys into the sea within a distance of only about 10 miles.

[2] Waimanu Bay seems a likely identification.

[3] Upolu Point; its correct position is lat. 20° 16′ N, long. 155° 22′ W (204° 08′ E).

anchored about seven miles to the south of the point above mentioned,[1] in 41 fathoms water, brown sandy bottom, with small pieces of coral.

The night proved very boisterous, attended with very heavy gusts and flurries of wind directly off the land: in one of these, about three in the morning of Thursday the 14th, we drove from the bank, but as it was my design to acquire every information that could be obtained respecting this bay, the anchor was weighed, and we turned up into it, against a very strong S.E. gale.

As the day advanced, it moderated, and the weather became serene and pleasant. The adjacent shores, forming the north-western part of the bay,[2] seemed to be very fruitful, whilst the number of habitations indicated them to be well peopled; yet none of the natives ventured near us. As we considered the taboo to be at an end, I began to be apprehensive that the shyness of the inhabitants originated from some more serious cause; about ten o'clock however a canoe was seen paddling towards the ship; we immediately brought to, and on her coming alongside, we were informed by those in her that they belonged to *Kahowmotoo*;[3] who was then residing at a village, on an estate of his, in the bottom of the Bay, named Toeaigh; off which there was good anchorage, and excellent water easily to be procured. These people, without the least hesitation, said that the reason of our not having been visited before was, that the whole of the island was under a very strict taboo, that prohibited the inhabitants from using their canoes, or quitting the shore by any other means; but that the rank and consequence of their master *Kahowmotoo*, authorized him to dispense with the restrictions on the present occasion; as he entertained hopes that the vessel in sight was the same in which his favourite servant *Terehooa*[4] had embarked; he had therefore sent them to make the necessary inquiries, and in case his expectations should be confirmed, a present of a hog and some vegetables was in the canoe for *Terehooa*; whose gratitude for such a mark of remembrance was instantly testified, by the tears that flowed on his receiving the message. This was accompanied by a pressing request, that I would stand in and anchor off *Kahowmotoo*'s village, where I should be supplied with every refreshment the island afforded, as soon as the *taboo* was at an end; which had now existed four days, but would intirely cease at sun-rise the day after the next.

I had not the least objection to accept this invitation, and a breeze favouring my design we steered for the village of Toeaigh. Mr. Whidbey, who was in the cutter sounding for the best anchorage, soon made the signal for an eligible situation, where, about half past two, we anchored in 25 fathoms water on a bottom of fine brown sand and mud: the points of the bay bore by compass

[1] Kawaihae Bay; but the anchorage must have been about 17 miles S of Point Upolu, not seven miles.

[2] The North Kohala District.

[3] Keeaumoku.

[4] Kalehua is a modern spelling. He had joined the *Discovery* on her previous visit to Hawaii.

N. 36 W. and S. 31 W. the morai, which is also conspicuous in pointing out this station, N. 67 E. and the watering place at the distance of a mile and a quarter, being the nearest shore, S. 87 E. On sounding near the ship, about half a cable's length to the S.W. of us was found a very small patch of coral rocks, where the water was only 10 fathoms in depth, but increased suddenly to 20 fathoms all around it. On the opposite side, however, was clear good anchorage for near a mile, where many vessels might ride without inconvenience from the bottom, though nevertheless exposed to the violence of the winds and sea between the limits above mentioned, comprehending 113° in the western quarter.

Soon after the ship had anchored, our old acquaintance *Kahowmotoo* paid us a visit, and brought with him half a dozen very fine hogs, and a handsome supply of vegetables. Notwithstanding that I took an early opportunity to acquaint *Kahowmotoo* that arms and ammunition were still *tabooed*, who seemed much to regret the continuance of these restrictions;[1] yet it did not appear to influence his hospitality; as he assured me, that if I would remain a few days at Toeaigh, we should be supplied with every refreshment in his power to procure, and that the promise he had formerly made, should now be punctually performed.

After dinner I went with him on shore, to take a view of the watering place; it is situated in a small sandy bay, where, over a space of twenty yards of rugged rocks and stones, a fine stream empties itself, whose water is easily to be procured by landing the casks on the sandy beach, and having the water brought in small vessels to fill them; a service the natives will readily perform for a trivial reward. This made me regret the absence of the Chatham; as in the immediate neighbourhood of the water the country did not appear to be very populous, we might each have supplied our wants without being teazed and pestered with a numerous throng of the natives, whom we should most likely meet with in the more inhabited parts of the island, and which on such occasions had frequently proved very inconvenient.

Kahowmotoo strongly urged my remaining a few days at Toeaigh; where he would supply us with refreshments, and would afterwards accompany us to another place of his called Ti-ah-to-tooa,[2] lying between this bay and

[1] The *Chatham* was also meeting demands for firearms. Vancouver had explained that all the arms in both ships were owned by King George and could not be disposed of in trade. The natives were willing to sell vegetables in exchange for such items as nails and beads, but not hogs: 'we could not buy any...their cry was Muskets and Powder, – these of course they could not get, and many of them returned to the Shore with their Cargo's. After standing out in these demands for some time, preceiving we were determined not to comply with them, Red Cloth was asked for, and for a Yard of this, we purchased 10 large Hogs, at this rate all the Chiefs were eager to sell their Cargo's, and in an hour we bought as much as we could with any convenience Stow.' – Bell, 15 February. The *Discovery* had a similar experience; ultimately 'the natives became so fond of our red cloth, that they gave seven, eight & sometimes even ten Hogs for a square piece of it, & left off entirely asking for firearms & ammunition.' – Menzies, 20 February.

[2] Kaiakekua Bay, which Vancouver would visit again in February 1794.

Karakakooa. This he represented as a small bay affording good anchorage; water, according to his account, was a scarce commodity there, but all kinds of refreshments were in the greatest abundance, and were perfectly at our command. To these solicitations I in some measure consented, by promising to stay the next day, in the expectation of not only deriving some supplies for ourselves, but of procuring some provender for the cattle and sheep; which, in consequence of the inferior quality of the hay obtained at Monterrey, were almost starved. To this cause I attributed the unfortunate losses we had suffered in our passage amounting to three rams, two ewes, a bull and a cow. These were serious misfortunes, and in a great measure disappointed the hopes I had entertained, from the importation of these valuable animals into the several islands of the Pacific Ocean. Still however I flattered myself with the expectation of succeeding in Owhyhee, by leaving the remaining bull, with the rest of the cows, under the protection of *Tamaahmaah*, who I expected would meet me at Karakakooa, to receive, and insure as far as possible, the preservation of the animals I had on board. To *Kahowmotoo*, who had taken the greatest care of the goats I had presented him with on a former occasion, and of their produce since my last visit, I gave a ram, two ewes, and an ewe lamb that had been born on our passage. On his being informed that all the rest were designed for *Tamaahmaah*, he strenuously recommended their being landed at this place, it being highly necessary that they should have pasture as soon as possible, especially as *Tamaahmaah*, had very extensive possessions in the immediate neighbourhood, where, he affirmed, great care would be taken of them. I should gladly have subscribed to his judicious advice, but the shortness of our acquaintance did not authorize me to place implicit confidence in all the assertions of *Kahowmotoo*, particularly in his declarations of being the most intimate and sincere friend of *Tamaahmaah*; for should these hereafter have proved to be false, it might possibly have caused the total destruction of the animals, or have been the occasion of commotions, or other unhappy disputes. This determined me to deliver them myself into the hands of *Tamaahmaah*, for whom they were originally intended.

During the day, a gentle refreshing breeze blew into the bay from the westward; but soon after sun-set, a gale suddenly arose from the eastward, attended with very heavy gusts, and continued until day-light the next morning, Friday the 15th, when it fell calm, and the weather resumed a pleasant degree of serenity, attended as before with a gentle refreshing breeze from the westward.

This morning, agreeably to his appointment, *Kahowmotoo* came on board, for the purpose of accompanying me to his habitation on shore. His visit was rendered still more acceptable by his presenting me with sixteen very fine hogs, a large assortment of vegetables, and a supply of green food for the cattle. Arms and ammunition now ceased to be sought after, and he seemed very highly pleased and fully recompensed on receiving about two yards of red cloth, and a small piece of printed linen, with a few beads and other trivial articles for his favourite ladies. Of these he had no less than four, in the character of wives, who (he said) were waiting on shore with much anxiety to see me; and the *taboo*, though at an end as it respected some particulars, was still in force as to the women embarking in canoes; such of our female visitors, as had been induced to favour us with their company, had therefore been obliged to have recourse to swimming for that purpose.

The name of the village Toeaigh was by us extended to the bay, (which is the same that had been called by captain King Toeayahha bay,)[1] since the natives give no distinctive name to any part of the ocean that washes the shores of their islands. Such bays, coves, &c. as are so distinguished, having been named by their European visitors from the contiguous villages or districts.

Toeaigh is situated in a grove of cocoa-nut trees, just behind a sandy beach. A reef of coral rocks, extending thence about three quarters of a mile into the sea, rendered it inaccessible to our boats in a direct line, but we landed very commodiously in a narrow channel, between the reef and the shore, near the morai, to the S.E. of the beach, from whence we had about two miles to walk to the habitation of *Kahowmotoo*.

We could, I believe, have gone much further with the boats in that channel, but as the navigation was intricate and tiresome, I preferred the walk, and attended by the corporal and six marines, we proceeded along the beach; leaving the boats, properly manned and armed, in readiness to support us in case of any treacherous or hostile behaviour. These precautions however appeared to have been intirely unnecessary, as nothing but the most civil, attentive, and friendly deportment was experienced from all classes of the people. The village consisted only of straggling houses, of two classes; those appropriated to the residence of the inhabitants were small, mean, miserable huts; but the others, allotted to the purposes of shading, building, and repairing their canoes, were excellent in their kind; in these occupations several people were busily employed, who seemed to execute their work with great neatness and ingenuity.[2] In about the middle of the village is a reservoir of salt water, nearly in the centre of a large inclosure, made by walls of mud and stones. Between these walls and the reservoir the whole space is occupied by shallow earthern pans, of no regular size or shape, nor placed in any order or degree of elevation. The reservoir is separated by a bank or small portion of the sandy beach from the ocean, and had no visible communication with it, but was apparently a stagnated standing pool, covered with a muddy scum, of a yellowish green colour. This, the natives say, it always bears, and without being replenished by them from the sea constantly affords a sufficient quantity of

---

[1] Cook's own journal ends before he visited Kawaihae Bay. In King's journal the name is spelled Toe-yah-ya. Cook was in the bay early in February 1779, only a few days before his death. *Journals*, III, pp. 525–6.

[2] The chief 'shewd us a large War Canoe he was building, & askd Capt. Vancouver to give him as much English Canvas as would make a Sail for it, which was promisd him...' They also saw 'two Swivels & a Carronade, these were to be placed on his War Canoe.' – Menzies, 15 February.

excessively salt water, for supplying the numerous pans; the exposure of which to the influence of the sun, soon causes evaporation and crystallization. The crystals are then carefully taken up; and if found dirty from the cracking or breaking of the pans, which frequently want repair, or by the falling of rain whilst making, they are washed clean in sea-water and dried. This is their process in making salt, which is always white in proportion to the care bestowed in gathering it. They have large quantities, equal in colour and in quality to any made in Europe, but the crystals are much larger. The quantity of salt obtained, might be supposed, from the appearance of this salt-pond, to be produced rather from the saline quality of the surrounding earth, in which it is contained, than purely from the sea-water. Yet, its being not more than thirty yards from the sea-side, makes it probable that the oceanic water penetrates into it, through the loose sandy beach that separates it from the sea, and that the richness of the fluid may be produced from both those causes.

Paying our respects to *Kahowmotoo's* wives,[1] and inspecting this salt-pond, occupied most of our time, and claimed most of our attention, Having rendered our visit pleasant to the former, by distributing such articles as we knew they held in high estimation, we returned towards the boats, accompanied by the chief and his ladies, and attended by the natives, who conducted themselves in the most orderly and respectful manner. They brought us cocoa-nuts as we passed along, and seemed studious to afford us any little service or civility, without being the least troublesome; and strictly conformed themselves to the orders of their chief, who directed that few only should advance near us, and that the crowd should be seated at a distance, in whatever direction we should pass.

On reaching the boats, I requested that *Kahowmotoo* would accompany us on board to dinner, but in consequence of the *taboo*, I had no idea of soliciting that favour from the ladies; they however entertained very different notions, particularly *Kahowmotoo's* favorite, *Na-ma-han-na*,[2] who contended, that although the taboo prohibited their embarking in canoes belonging to Owhyhee, it could not possibly extend to the boats of those who totally disregarded their laws and restrictions. This ingenious mode of reasoning seeming to meet *Kahowmotoo's* concurrence; we soon embarked, leaving Mr. Menzies, who had been of our party, on shore, in pursuit of new vegetable productions. He returned in the evening, after receiving much hospitable civility from the natives.[3]

---

[1] The party paraded with the marines as escort 'to the Chief's residence, where we found his wife Mother & two Sisters seated on a Mat under a Canopy erected before the House, & if size & corpulency are here necessary qualifications of dignity these Ladies were certainly entitled to the highest rank, for four stouter & more masculine Dames could hardly be met with any where.' They 'expressed a curiosity of seeing the Marines go through their manual exercises, in which Captain Vancouver readily gratified them.' – Menzies, 14 February.   [2] Namahana.

[3] Menzies described the excursion: 'We were accompanied back to the Boats by the Chief & the Ladies, & as he & his wife expressed a wish of going on board with Captain

Kahowmotoo went on shore with his lady in one of our boats. On its return a message was brought from *Tianna*,[1] desiring to be informed, who we were? adding, that it we were his friends, he would make all possible haste to visit us; but, as it would be late on account of his distance before he should be able to arrive, in order that he might be admitted on board in the dark, he would carry in the bow of his canoe a large fire, as a signal by which he might be known. He accordingly arrived about four o'clock next morning, Saturday the 16th, just as we were getting under sail. In his canoe were half a dozen fine hogs, these he desired might be taken on board, and said, he had many others on the road, that would follow the ship to the southward. *Kahowmotoo*, attended by his favorite wife, agreeably to a preconcerted signal with him of firing a gun on our departure, came on board to fulfil his engagement of conducting us to *Tyea-ta-tooa*. The wind proved very variable, not only in direction but force. The weather sometimes was perfectly calm, at others we had violent gusts from the land, so that it was not until the evening that we were abreast of the south point of this bay, forming the western extremity of Owhyhee.[2] The weather continued squally, with lightning, thunder and rain. A little before it was dark, a brig and a sloop were seen in the offing. From the natives we learnt that these were the Chatham, and the Jackall trader,[3] under the orders of Mr. Brown of the Butterworth. We immediately made towards them, and as they seemed to be under little sail, soon expected to join our consort. But, to our great astonishment, next morning, Sunday the 17th, notwithstanding the night had been mostly calm, we found ourselves at least nine or ten leagues from the land, and had lost sight of both vessels. A fresh breeze from the N.E. during the morning, carried us at the rate of three or four miles an hour, directly towards the land, yet we did not appear to approach its shores; and at noon its nearest part, being about the south point of Toeaigh bay, bore E. by N. ten leagues distant. The observed latitude was 19° 42'. The north-east wind was soon afterwards succeeded by a calm.

The morning of Monday the 18th brought the two vessels again in sight, and towards noon the Chatham was sufficiently near us to receive a visit from Mr. Puget; from whom I learned, that he had traced the shores on the S.E. side of Owhyhee from its east to its south point,[4] at the distance from one to three miles of the shore, without finding any place that presented a

Vancouver I thought I might on that account travel with greater security a little way up the Country to collect Plants, & intimated my intention to the Chief; with a request that he would order two of the Natives to accompany me as guides which he readily agreed to, & gave them strict directions to obey my commands, & provide me with Victuals & Drink whenever I wishd to have any, in consequence of this last injunction they kept inquiring now & then if I was hungry or thirsty.' Menzies visited the famous Puukohola Heiau, where, after his unsuccessful revolt against Kamahameha, Keoua and 11 of his followers had been put to death in 1791. Their skulls were still 'displayd as ornamental trophies on the rail around the Morai.' – 15 February.

[1] Kaiana.   [2] Keahole Point.

[3] The *Jackal* (as the name should be spelled) was at Nootka when Vancouver sailed for California.   [4] Ka Lae (South Point).

probability of anchorage; and if soundings were to be had, they must exist upon an open coast, exposed to the prevailing winds, where so violent a surf broke on the shores, that any communication with the land, by such means as we possessed, would have been impossible. From the south point of the island, their examination was not attended with that minuteness which was necessary to determine the object I had in view. This it seems had been occasioned by baffling winds, and a current setting the Chatham some distance from the land to the northward. That part which required the most minute survey lies between the south point and Karakakooa, where some of the traders are said to have discovered a more eligible situation for the reception of shipping than Karakakooa affords; on this report I placed little reliance, but as I expected to have a future opportunity of ascertaining the fact, it was of little importance on the present occasion.[1] Mr. Puget informed me also, that I should find Karakakooa a more formidable place than I expected, as he had understood from those in the Jackall who had visited it, that it was by no means a desirable stopping place for small vessels; since *Tamaahmaah* had procured from the several traders a number of cannon, with a proper assortment of ammunition. That these cannon were planted, and in some measure protected by stone walls, thrown up by the natives along the beach in the bay before his houses; situated in the same place where the habitations of the priests were destroyed, after the unfortunate death of Captain Cook.[2]

---

[1] Puget explained in his log: 'After rounding the South Point [Ka Lae], we hauled more towards the Land to look for a Bay which Mr. Mears noticed in his Narrative, here we found a Sandy Beach close to a Bluff that rizes almost perpendicular from the Sea but on it a very heavy surf and *apparently* open to the Winds to the Southward of East. The Current prevented our getting so close in as we wished, therefore I only mention the Situation of this Bay from my Conjecture.' – narrative, February 13. Actually, Vancouver had sent Puget on a fruitless quest, due to an error in Meares's text. The abstracts of his ships' logs show that none of Meares's three ships explored the W coast of the island of Hawaii S of Kealakekua Bay, which is in lat. 19° 28′ N, but his narrative states that his anchorage in what he calls Tirowa (or Tiroway) Bay, and which he describes enthusiastically, was in lat. 19° 4′ N, or not a great distance N of Ka Lae. But this was an error, corrected in the abstract of the log of the *Iphigenia*, which placed it in lat. 19° 41′ N. – Meares, *Voyages to the North West Coast of America* (London, 1790), p. 355 and log abstract (unpaged). When Vancouver visited the bay in February 1794 he identified it firmly as Tyahtatooa (Kaiakekua) Bay, a small cove N of Kealakekua Bay. Vancouver refers to a nearby point as Kowrooa, which may have suggested Meares's name Tirowa. (See p. 1186.) Bell believed that they had seen the bay: 'we were near enough into this place to determine that it was a very unsafe Bay for Vessels to lay some time being much exposed.' – February 13.

[2] The crews of Cook's ships were so infuriated by his murder and so bent on vengeance that at times they could not be controlled: 'In every instance it was not in the power of the Officers to restrain them; & there was too little danger to make them for their own sakes obedient to orders: hence when it was only necessary to burn down some huts near the Well which afforded shelter for a few Indians that threw stones, not only these were burnt, but the whole Village, & before a boat could be sent on shore to order them on no account to burn the priests houses, they also were set on fire.' – King's journal, Cook, *Journals*, III, 562. The ships were in need of water from the well. The priests had been friendly, and King was anxious to protect them.

Calms and light baffling winds detained us in this inactive situation, which was rendered extremely unpleasant by a heavy irregular swell, and by oppressively hot sultry weather. A circumstance now occurred that contributed to make me infinitely more dissatisfied with this irksome detention from the shore. The only bull that remained, and a cow that had brought forth a dead calf, were no longer able to stand on their legs, and it was evident, that if a speedy opportunity did not offer itself for relieving them by sending them on shore, their lives could not possibly be preserved. The loss, particularly of the bull, would have been a cruel disappointment to my wishes; but as favourable circumstances often take place when least expected, so it was on this occasion.

In the afternoon of Tuesday the 19th we were visited by many canoes, though at the distance of eight or nine leagues from the land. In one of these was a chief named *Crymamahoo*,[1] half brother to *Tamaahmaah*, and chief of the district of Ahiedo. To him and to his friends I made such presents as were considered by *Kahowmotoo* highly suitable to his rank, and which were accepted with marks of great approbation and content: this induced me to hope, that by his good offices I should be enabled to get these poor animals conveyed to the shore. As his canoe was sufficiently large and roomy, I requested he would consent to their being put into it, but to my great surprise a thousand evasions and excuses were immediately started. Anxious for the future advantages these people would derive by the propagation of these animals, I probably discovered much earnestness, whilst endeavouring to prevail with *Crymamahoo* to lend me his assistance, in securing to himself and countrymen so important a benefit. This he certainly perceived, but possessing no desire to oblige, nor any patriotic zeal, he was only studious to turn my intreaties to his own particular advantage. After *Kahowmotoo* had anxiously interfered, but with the same success, I offered *Crymamahoo* (well knowing that avarice is a predominant passion with many of these islanders) a moderate recompence, only for allowing his canoe to perform this service. He instantly waved all his former objections, and the bull and cow were soon comfortably placed in his canoe, in which there were some vegetables that the bull ate, seemingly with much appetite; this gave me great pleasure, as I was now in hopes that he would soon recover by the help of proper nourishing food, which the shore abundantly supplied.

The next morning, Wednesday the 20th, we had again increased our distance from Owhyhee; but towards noon, with a light breeze from the south-westward, we made all sail for the island. As we approached we were met by several large and small canoes, laden with the several productions of the country, which were exchanged by the natives in the most honest and civil manner, for our various articles of traffic; amongst these, red and blue woollen cloths, with printed linens, seemed the commodities in the highest

[1] Kalaimanahu, chief of the district of Hamakua.

estimation. Beads and other trinkets were accepted as presents, but were considered as unworthy any return.

Amongst our numerous visitors was *Tamaahmaah's* eldest son, and presumptive heir to the sovereignty of Owhyhee. He was a boy about nine years of age; possessing a shrewd and lively appearance.[1]

In return for the presents I had made him, he presented me on leaving the ship with three or four hogs, and promised me a further supply in the morning.

By this time we had nearly reached Tyahtatooa. Mr. Whidbey was dispatched in the cutter to examine the anchorage, as in the event of its being found superior to that of Karakakooa, I purposed giving Tyahtatooa the preference for the transacting of all our material business before we proceeded to the other place, where in case of any disagreement with the inhabitants, we might be much inconvenienced by the cannon, of which they were said to be possessed.

A calm succeeded the rising of the sun. This continuing until ten in the forenoon of Thursday the 21st, we were again driven a considerable distance from the land; but a S.W. breeze then springing up, enabled us to steer towards Tyahtatooa.

About noon I was honoured with the presence of *Tamaahmaah*, the king of Owhyhee, whose approach had been announced sometime before his arrival.

Not only from Captain King's description, but also from my own memory, as far as it would serve me, I expected to have recognized my former acquaintance by the most savage countenance we had hitherto seen amongst these people;[2] but I was agreeably surprized in finding that his riper years had softened that stern ferocity which his younger days had exhibited, and had changed his general deportment to an address characteristic of an open, cheerful, and sensible mind; combined with great generosity, and goodness of disposition. An alteration not unlike that I have before had occasion to notice in the character of *Pomurrey* at Otaheite.

Tamaahmaah came on board in a very large canoe, accompanied by John Young, an English seaman, who appeared to be not only a great favourite, but to possess no small degree of influence with this great chief.[3] *Terrehoa*,[4] who had been sent to deliver the bull and cow to the king, was also of the party, and informed me that the cow had died in her passage to the island,

---

[1] This child has not been identified. He cannot have been Liholiho, afterwards known as Kamehameha II, as he was not born until 1797. It is curious that Vancouver refers to him as the heir *presumptive*.

[2] Vancouver here is paraphrasing King, who met Kamehameha in January 1779 and described him as having 'as savage a looking face as ever I saw'. But he added: 'it however by no means seemd an emblem of his disposition, which was good naturd & humorous...' – Cook, *Journals*, III, p. 512.

[3] Vancouver later describes Young's arrival in the islands and his activities there.

[4] Kalehua.

but that the bull arived safe, and was lodged in a house where he ate and drank heartily.

After the usual ceremonies and assurances of friendship had passed between *Tamaahmaah* and myself, he said that the queen,[1] with several of his friends and relations were in the canoe alongside, and requested they might be admitted on board. This was instantly granted, and I was introduced to her majesty, who we had previously understood was the daughter of *Kahowmotoo*, by his favorite wife now on board, *Namahanna*. The meeting of the daughter and her parents sufficiently indicated the relation, and the affection that subsisted between them. She appeared to be about sixteen, and undoubtedly did credit to the choice and taste of *Tamaahmaah*, being one of the finest women we had yet seen on any of the islands. It was pleasing to observe the kindness and fond attention, with which on all occasions they seemed to regard each other; and though this mode of behaviour in public would be considered as extravagant in the polished circles of society, yet to us, so far removed from the civilized world, the profusion of tenderness was very admissible, and could not be regarded without a warmth of satisfaction at thus witnessing the happiness of our fellow creatures; though so far behind us in that state of civilization, from which alone we imagine the essential comforts and happiness of life can be derived.

The sole object of this visit was to invite and intreat our proceeding to Karakakooa: to their solicitations I replied, that our boat was examining Tyahtatooa,[2] and that on her return I should determine. With this answer they were perfectly satisfied, but observed, that I should not find it so convenient as Karakakooa.

I was much pleased with the decorum and general conduct of this royal party. Though it consisted of many, yet not one solicited even the most inconsiderable article; nor did they appear to have any expectation of receiving presents. They seemed to be particularly cautious to avoid giving the least cause for offence; but no one more so than the king himself, who was so scrupulous, as to enquire when and where it was proper for him to be seated. The inhabitants, who had assembled round the ships, were by this time very numerous; on being denied their requests to be admitted on board, which was observed towards all but the principal chiefs, they remained perfectly quiet in their canoes, and in a most orderly manner carried on an honest and friendly intercourse.

The demand, amounting to clamour, for arms and ammunition, which on our first arrival seemed at that time to be so formidable an obstacle to our procuring refreshments, appeared now to be entirely done away, whilst the cordial manner in which we had been received and treated, the profusion of good things we had purchased at an easy rate, and the value attached to our

---

[1] Kaahumanu, the favourite wife of Kamahameha.
[2] Kaiakekua Bay.

articles of traffic, impressed me with a more favorable idea of the character of these people than that which had been recently given to the world.

Being determined that nothing should be wanting on my part to preserve the harmony and good understanding that seemed to have taken place between us; and having learned from Young, that our royal visitors did not entertain the most distant idea of accepting any thing from me until they had first set the example; I considered this a good opportunity to manifest our friendly disposition towards them, by presents suitable to their respective ranks and situations; in the hope that by such an early compliment I should confirm, or perhaps heighten the favorable opinion of us, that they already seemed to have imbibed. Accordingly, such articles were distributed as I knew were likely, and (as they afterward proved to be) highly acceptable to the whole party. Permission was now requested for the friends and relations, who were alongside in their canoes, to be suffered to visit the ship. I easily comprehended what was the real object of the request, which soon became evident by the behaviour of the new visitors, who, of both sexes, and different ages, instantly found their way aft, and nearly filled the cabin; until *Tamaahmaah* desired that no more should be admitted into the ship; and then demanded of me, if it were my intention to make those now on board any presents? On his being answered in the affirmative, he undertook the distribution himself, and was so œconomical as to give me several opportunities to make some addition to his dispensations,which were more bountifully bestowed on some of the men, than on the generality of the women. The ladies however were no losers on this occasion. The deficiency of *Tamaahmaah*'s attention being otherways amply supplied, produced no small degree of mirth, in which *Tamaahmaah* bore a very considerable part. This distribution being finished, and the whole party made very happy, the king, in addition to what he had before received, was presented with a scarlet cloak, that reached from his neck to the ground, adorned with tinsel lace, trimmed with various coloured gartering tape, with blue ribbons to tie it down the front. The looking glasses being placed opposite to each other displayed at once the whole of his royal person; this filled him with rapture, and so delighted him that the cabin could scarcely contain him. His ecstasy produced capering, and he soon cleared the cabin of many of our visitors, whose numbers had rendered it very hot and unpleasant. He himself soon followed, and after strutting some little time upon deck, he exposed himself in the most conspicuous places, seemingly with the greatest indifference, though in reality for the sole purpose of attracting the admiration and applause of his subjects. The acclamations that his appearance produced from the surrounding multitude were evidently gratifying to his vanity; yet his joy and satisfaction were incomplete until two in the afternoon, when Mr. Whidbey returned, and reported, that although the anchorage at Tyahtatooa seemed convenient, yet it was infinitely more exposed than any part of the anchorage at Karakakooa.

I had by this time understood that the account of *Tamaahmaah*'s cannon and fortification was entirely void of truth; and as there could be no hesitation which of the two situations to prefer, from Mr. Whidbey's representation, we steered immediately for Karakakooa.[1] *Tamaahmaah* soon became acquainted with my determination. The high degree of satisfaction he expressed on this occasion was not easily to be described, as I could not recollect in any former instance ever to have noticed sensations like his, in the countenance or behaviour of any person.

The breeze was too gentle, and the day was too far advanced to reach Karakakooa before night; when the general happiness of our party received some small degree of check.

Notwithstanding the present harmony, and the prospect of its continuance, I considered it highly important not to relax in any of the precautions I had taken on former occasions; but to be most vigilantly on our guard, and to watch with a jealous eye over the behaviour of these ambitious chiefs. Had I permitted any of them to have slept on board, which they are very fond of doing, our caution would naturally have lessened, by a continuance of their then docile behaviour, and had one been admitted to this indulgence, many others could not, without giving great offence, have been refused. Their numbers might thus have increased beyond expectation, and by distributing themselves unobserved in different parts of the ship, a favorable opportunity might have been seized, had they been so inclined, when we least expected danger, to carry any ambitious projects into execution. Having uniformly adhered to the maxim, that 'prevention is better than punishment,' I determined in no instance whatever, so far as it was in our power, to suffer the least temptation to be laid in their way, either in and about the ship, or in any of our transactions with them on shore. On this occasion however a difficulty arose, by *Kahowmotoo* having remained on board three nights successively. After explaining that this would not have happened, had not the ship been unavoidably driven to a great distance from the land, the whole party appeared pretty well satisfied, and about dark retired to the shore in

---

[1] Vancouver does not mention a visit paid to the *Discovery* by Towereroo (Kualelo), the Hawaiian youth who had travelled from England in the ship and who had been left on the island of Hawaii in March 1792, where Kaiana had promised to look after his welfare. Menzies wrote: 'He [Towereroo] now told us that soon after he landed Tamahai maiha [Kamehameha] gave him a small Plantation in consequence of his having visited England, & that by lately marrying a Chief's daughter, he had got another Plantation, on which he said there lived at least two hundred Vassals who considered him their Chief, but he was still anxious that Capt. Vancouver would buy him a little more land which would greatly add to his consequence on the Island & a double Canoe, which was all he asked for, & which I thought was very reasonable, & had no doubt but Capt. Vancouver would comply with his request, especially as the King by giving him a Plantation had already shown so much inclination to serve the Youth. He further told us that the few things he carried on shore with him when he first landed with Tianna [Kaiana], that that Chief had kept them as his own.' – Menzies, 21 February. It is not known whether or not Vancouver secured the additional land for Towereroo.

high spirits, and in extremely good humour, some of them having taken their grog and wine very cheerfully.

By seven the next morning, Friday the 22d, we were abreast of Karakakooa bay, from whence, and the adjacent shores, we were visited by a vast concourse of people,[1] who brought in their canoes the greatest abundance of refreshments, and who seemed to be as eager to exchange them for our articles of traffic, as on the first discovery of these islands. But as we were well stored with such good things, I directed that no more should be purchased until the ship was properly secured.[2] This was effected by noon; the best bower anchor lying to the S.S.W. in 22 fathoms, and the small one E.N.E. in 12 fathoms water, soft sandy bottom. The points of the Bay lying S. 5 W. and N. 87 W. distant from Kakooa[3] the nearest shore, about the length of a cable and half.

This village as already stated, we found to be the residence of *Tamaahmaah*; from whence, before the ship was well secured, eleven large canoes put off from the shore with great order, and formed two equal sides of an obtuse triangle. The largest canoe being in the angular point, was rowed by eighteen paddles on each side; in this was his Owhyhean majesty, dressed in a printed linen gown, that Captain Cook had given to *Terreoboo*;[4] and the most elegant feathered cloak I had yet seen, composed principally of beautiful bright yellow feathers, and reaching from his shoulders to the ground on which it trailed.[5] On his head he wore a very handsome helmet, and made altogether a very magnificent appearance. His canoe was advanced a little forward in the

[1] All sources agree that the natives assembled in unprecedented numbers. 'We were at this time surrounded by the greatest concourse of Natives in their Canoes & Swimming that we ever saw collected together afloat at these Islands, upon the most moderate computation we are pretty certain their number could not be short of three thousand, besides the Beeches being lin'd with vast crowds of them gazing from the shore...' – Menzies, 22 February. 'The Multitudes of the Natives who now came off to the Ships surpass'd any thing I had an idea of. The Canoes were so thick and numerous that they fairly covered the surface of the water a considerable distance all round us, – and I believe I may safely say that I might have walked over from the Chatham to the Discovery.' – Bell, 22 February. Puget estimated that there were 'between four and five thousand Indians on or in the Water.' – 23 February.

[2] The *Chatham* 'followed the Example of the Discovery in getting a number of Canoes to assist in towing us in   this many of them with pleasure complied with & in a few minutes there were repeated applications for tow Ropes...' – Puget, 23 February.

[3] On the E side of Kealalelua Bay; the town of Napoopoo is now in about the same location.

[4] Kalaniopuu, chief of Hawaii at the time of Cook's visit.

[5] Kamehameha 'told Captain Vancouver in the hearing of the Officers, that the featherd Robe he then had about him must be carefully conveyd to King George of Britannee, as it was the most valuable present he could send him, being the only one of the kind at these Islands, & the richest Robe any of the Kings of Owhyhee ever wore, but as it was on that account most solemnly Tabooed, he would not leave it on board till the day of our Sailing, when he would see it packd up himself, & he gave the strictest & most solemn injunctions that it should not be put about any person's shoulders till it was deliver'd to King George in Britannee.' – Menzies, 22 February. This cloak may be one of those now in the British Museum.

procession, to the actions of which the other ten strictly attended, keeping the most exact and regular time with their paddles, and inclining to the right or left agreeably to the directions of the king, who conducted the whole business with a degree of adroitness and uniformity, that manifested a knowledge of such movements and manœuvre far beyond what could reasonably have been expected. In this manner he paraded round the vessels, with a slow and solemn motion. This not only added a great dignity to the procession, but gave time to the crowd of canoes alongside to get out of the way. He now ordered the ten canoes to draw up in a line under our stern, whilst, with the utmost exertion of his paddlers, he rowed up along the starboard side of the ship; and though the canoe was going at a very great rate, she was in an instant stopped, with that part of the canoe where his majesty was standing immediately opposite the gangway.[1]

He instantly ascended the side of the ship, and taking hold of my hand, demanded, if we were sincerely his friends? To this I answered in the affirmative; he then said, that he understood we belonged to King George, and asked it he was likewise his friend? On receiving a satisfactory answer to this question, he declared that he was our firm good friend; and, according to the custom of the country, in testimony of the sincerity of our declarations we saluted by touching noses. He then presented me with four very handsome feathered helmets, and ordered the ten large canoes that were under the stern to come on the starboard side. Each of these contained nine very large hogs, whilst a fleet of smaller canoes, containing a profusion of vegetables, were ordered by him to deliver their cargoes on the opposite side. This supply was more than we could possibly dispose of; some of the latter he was prevailed upon to reserve; but although our decks, as well as those of the Chatham, were already encumbered with their good things, he would not suffer one hog to be returned to the shore.

The remaining live stock I had on board, consisting of five cows, two ewes and a ram, were sent on shore in some of his canoes; these were all in a healthy state though in low condition, and as I flattered myself the bull would recover, I had little doubt of their succeeding to the utmost of my wishes. I cannot avoid mentioning the pleasure I received, in the particular attention paid by *Tamaahmaah* to the placing of these animals in the canoes.[2] This business was

---

[1] 'The Scene altogether was the grandest I had ever witnessed nor could I before conceive that it was in the Power, or Capacity of Indians to conduct a Visit of Ceremony with so much good Order and Regularity.' – Puget, 23 February.

[2] Kamehameha had seen the animals on board the ship. 'The Cattle greatly delighted him, though it took some time to quiet his fears, lest they should bite him, he called them large Hogs, and after much persuasion, we prevailed on him, to go close up to them, at this instant one of the poor Animals turned his head round quickly, [which] so alarmed his Majesty that he made a speedy retreat, and run over half his retinue.' When the cattle landed 'we were a good deal diverted at seeing the terror the whole Village was thrown into, by one of the Cows, galloping along the beach, and kicking up her heels, thousands run for the Sea, and plunged in – every Cocoa-nut Tree was full in a moment, and some jumped down precipices – others Scrambled up Rocks and houses, in short not a Man would approach for half an hour.' – Manby, letters, February.

Plate 37. Kamehameha I. From the portrait by Louis Choris,
painted in 1817.

The Crater on the Summit MOUNT WORRORAY OWHYHEE.

Plate 38. 'The Crater on the Summit of Mount Worroray [Hualalai] Owhyhee.'

principally done by himself; after which he gave the strictest injunctions to his people who had the charge of them, to pay implicit obedience to the directions of our butcher, who was sent to attend their landing. At the departure of these canoes, I was unacquainted with the extent of *Tamaahmaah*'s intended compliment. In addition to his magnificent present of provisions, other canoes were now ordered alongside, from which a large quantity of cloth, mats, and other articles of their own manufacture, were delivering into the ship; but we were so much incommoded, that there was no possibility of taking care of these valuables, and on promising to receive them on a future day, the king permitted them to be returned to the shore, giving particular charge to one of his attendants, to whom they were intrusted, to be very careful of them, as they belonged to me, and not to himself.

This present, though not accompanied by the elegant entertainments that followed those made by *Fenow* and *Powlahow* to Captains Cook and Clerke at the Friendly islands,[1] was however highly worthy of a generous and noble mind; especially when the manner is adverted to, in which it was made, as a token of the sincerity of the king's wishes and desire to establish, upon a firm and permanent basis, our mutual good understanding and harmony; and possibly, in some measure, as a requital for the service I had rendered his country in the introduction of the sheep and cattle. On this score, however, I soon convinced him that I required no return; as in so doing I only complied with the directions of my sovereign, in his humane and friendly disposition towards them, by adding as much as was in my power to their comfort and happiness.

These transactions did not pass unobserved by *Kahowmotoo*, who strictly attended to every occurrence. He appeared to be much rejoiced at the introduction of the sheep and cattle on the island, yet he could not refrain from observing, that he considered it a very unequal distribution, to give all the large cattle to *Tamaahmaah*, and none to himself, *Tianna*, or other principal chiefs. In reply to these observations, I pointed out that I had already done *Tamaahmaah* an injustice, by giving him, *Kahowmotoo*, the sheep originally designed for the king. That, under this consideration, he ought to be perfectly contented; and as there was a probability of my returning, that I should endeavour to bring with me a supply of those, and very likely some other useful animals, by which I should have it in my power to oblige him, and the rest of our friends in Owhyhee. *Kahowmotoo* paid particular attention to this conversation and seemed to be tolerably well satisfied; which gave me hopes that I should be able to steer a middle course between these jealous chiefs; but whilst we were at dinner, another impediment occurred by the arrival of *Tianna*.

On his entering the cabin, I again recognized the identical *Tamaahmaah* I had known some years before, by the savage austerity and gloom that was now

[1] Finau Ulukalala, a Tongan chief, and Fatafehi Paulaho, King of Tonga. Cook describes briefly the dances offered on 20 May and 17 June 1777. *Journals*, III, pp. 109–10, 131. William Anderson, surgeon of the *Resolution*, describes them at greater length. *Ibid.*, pp. 874–8, 894–7.

diffused over the countenance of that chief. *Tianna* was nevertheless received by me with due civility and cordiality, which by the increased sullenness of the king's countenance, seemed greatly to augment his dislike to the presence of our new visitor. *Tianna* presented me with a helmet, and desired that I would order some hogs, which were in the canoes that had attended him, to be taken into the ship. These proved to be fifteen of the finest animals of this description I had ever seen at any of these islands; but, in consequence of the numbers already on board, I was under the necessity of declining them, which could only be done under a promise of receiving them, as soon as our stock on board should be exhausted. With this assurance *Tianna* was perfectly contented;[1] but it awakened the envious disposition of *Kahowmotoo*, who contended, that he was not treated with the friendship I had professed towards him, since twenty very fine hogs of his had been returned unconditionally. Whilst I was endeavouring to pacify him, by stating that I had no other intention than to accept his kind and friendly present, the instant the animals could be received on board; the king, who since *Tianna*'s appearance had sat in the most sullen silence, and had not uttered a single word, replied with some warmth, that I had no occasion for hogs, or other productions of Owhyhee, from *Kahowmotoo*, *Tianna*, or any other chief, as he had many more to supply our wants, when those which he had presented were exhausted. Under these circumstances of rivalship, it became no easy matter to ascertain and pursue a line of conduct, which should be equally agreeable and accommodating to the bountiful dispositions of these contending chiefs.

I was however fully determined on the measures to be pursued; to pay my principal court to *Tamaahmaah*, as the king of the whole island, and to treat the other chiefs with a due degree of respect and attention. And though, at first, this sort of conduct might occasion some dissatisfaction, yet I entertained no doubt that it would soon wear away.

After this discussion on the subject of pigs and poultry was brought to a conclusion, the king had a short, though serious, conversation with *Tianna*; the subject matter we did not rightly comprehend, but we understood it to respect his coming from the north-west part of the island without the king's knowledge or permission. On this being settled, some jokes passed between them, when the latter gradually resumed his usual cheerfulness, and harmony seemed to be again re-established on all sides.[2]

---

[1] Menzies had a different impression. His journal states that 'Tianna was much hurt at his present not being likewise accepted, especially as he had brought it as far as from the North West point of the Island on the former pledges of Captain Vancouver, & conceiving himself but coolly receivd, he left the Ship in a huff & carried his Hogs on shore.' – 22 February.

[2] Puget's account differs: 'We were much astonished at the appearance of Tianna whome we understood was banished to Toehi [Toeaigh, i.e., Kawaihae], & was supposed to be in Friendship with Titeree [Kahekili] the King of Mowee, to whose Party Tianna was every Day expected to join. The Meeting between him and Tomaihomaihaw [Kamehameha] was cool & reserved on both Sides in the Cabbin of the Discovery and the King plainly

Tamaahmaah understanding that I intended to erect the tents and observatory on shore, gave me the strongest asssurance that no injury nor offence should take place, provided we would subscribe to such regulations as he should point out, tending to the preservation of that harmony which so happily existed at the present moment.

In consequence of the convenience with which we could lie near to that part of the shore where the tents and observatories of the Resolution and Discovery were erected in the year 1779, on their unfortunate visit to this island, I preferred that station to any other part of the bay, for the services we had now to perform. Here those whose business required their residence on shore, would be fully protected by the ship against any surprize or attack from the natives of the country. But this situation we could not immediately occupy, as it was part of the consecrated ground of the morai,[1] which it was unlawful for us to enter during the continuance of the periodical *taboo* that was to commence this evening at sun-set, and to end at sun-rise of the 24th; during which interval there could be no communication between the shore and ship: but as soon as the interdiction should cease, the king promised to return on board, after issuing his orders and injunctions that our party should be properly received, and sufficiently guarded.

The whole of Saturday the 23d, we remained in the most perfect silence; not a canoe was seen afloat, excepting a few that went out of the Bay to take fish. This degree of quiet was a very agreeable change, and a great relief to us, having the preceding day been almost stunned by the clamour and intolerable noise of near three thousand people of both sexes, in their canoes, or swimming about the vessels. Much to their credit, however, it was in this circumstance only that their company was unpleasant; for they conducted themselves with great honesty, and in every other respect behaved with the greatest civility and good humour.

On our passage from the coast of America, we had reason to believe that the main mast was materially defective; a fish was here put on, that reached from the main deck to the upper part of the cheek, and such other repairs were undertaken as the rigging, sails, &c. required.

by his Looks disapproved of the Present being made by Captain Vancouver to Tianna – they however entered into no Conversation & in about an hours time this turbulent Gentleman took his Leave. After his Departure the King began very roundly to express his Astonishment at the Civil treatment of Tianna & seem[ed] to intimate that we favored the Rebellions Cause. As it was proper to contradict or do away [with] those suspicions to preserve our established Harmony, Tomaihomaihaw was informed, That no Party Matters would be countenanced by the Officers, yet Every Chief till he had abused our Confidence, was entitled to our Friendship, this by no means agreed with his sentiments – & he willingly would have dispensed with such a partially [impartiality?] of Conduct. In the Afternoon a few more presents totally did away with his Resentment.' – 25 February.

[1] *Morai* is a version of the Tahitian word *marae*. The Hawaiian word for a sacred place is *heiau*. The ground was adjacent to the heiau of Hikiau, a little to the N of the middle point of Kealakekua Bay. The heiau is now in ruins.

Agreeably to his promise *Tamaahmaah*, attended by Young, repaired on board immediately after sun-rise on Sunday 24th. He informed me that all the necessary directions respecting our tents, &c. were left with persons properly authorized to take charge of them, and that they might be sent on shore whenever I pleased. This was instantly done under the care of Mr. Whidbey; and soon after breakfast, accompanied by the king, Mr. Puget, and some of the officers, I went on shore with a guard of six marines to be left for the protection of our party there. I was made very happy by finding that the presence of such a guard had not been in the least necessary; as the person appointed by *Tamaahmaah*, under the immediate directions of Young who had accompanied Mr. Whidbey, had conducted himself with the greatest propriety, and had acted in every respect so very conformably to Mr. Whidbey's instructions, that a guard on shore seemed almost an unnecessary precaution. In point of dignity, however, if not of security, I considered such formalities as indispensible; but being well aware of the avidity with which muskets and ammunition were here sought after, I did not lead them into any temptation by sending on shore any spare small arms, or the field pieces, lest such a valuable booty might stimulate them to a breach of that integrity, which at present seemed to regulate all their actions. Yet, as I did not think it prudent to place unlimited confidence in the sincerity of their professions, the field pieces were mounted on the quarter deck in readiness for action, either in that situation, or to be transported to the shore at a moment's notice. The guns were all shotted, plenty of ammunition was at hand, and a small anchor and hawser laid out for a spring on the cable. Four centinels were always at their posts, with a certain number of small arms kept constantly loaded, and every man in the ship was at all times ready to fly to quarters. These precautions did not pass unregarded by *Tamaahmaah*; who, in the confidence of our friendship, instead of being displeased, or apprehending any danger from the occasion, highly applauded the measures that were taken; as they would effectually prevent the ill disposed part of his people from planning or attempting any enterprize to our prejudice. I learned from him that he had issued the strictest injunctions to prevent any offence, or cause of complaint arising from any improper conduct, or behaviour in his subjects, and that he entertained no doubt of their being punctually attended to and obeyed.

The king observed, there were persons in the neighbourhood, who were servants and vassals belonging, not only to the chiefs of the other islands who were his inveterate enemies, but also to many belonging to Owhyhee, who were not better inclined; and conceiving it to be very likely that some of these might think proper to make depredations on our property, or to insult our persons, he had taken due precaution to prevent any such mischievous design; fearing lest I might be impelled to seek such redress as would prove fatal to his person or his government, or probably to both; although he and his people might be perfectly unconcerned in the offence committed.

This conversation was urged by *Tamaahmaah* in the coolest manner, though in the most forcible language, and concluded by hoping, that I would cause such measures to be pursued for the regulation of our conduct towards them, as would avoid all possible chance of any misunderstanding. To this end he made the following requests; that I would give the most positive orders that none of our people, on any account whatsoever, should be suffered to enter their morai's, or consecrated places, or be permitted to infringe on their rights or sacred privileges; that no person should be allowed to stray about the country; and that I would scrupulously adhere to my practice of admitting none but the principal chiefs into the vessels; and that in the day time he should be frequently on board. This, he said, would deter the lawless from any improper conduct, whilst in their canoes about the vessels for the purpose of trading; that when any of our people wished to travel into the country, they should first apply to him, and he would appoint a proper person to be their guide; and a number of others in whom he could confide, to protect them, carry their baggage, and render them every service of which they might stand in need; that, under these regulations, as many of the officers and people as were inclined to make excursions, might extend their travels over the whole island, provided they committed no act contrary to the advice of their guides, and he would himself be accountable for their safety, and also for their receiving every attention of friendly hospitality; that if any of the natives were daring enough to commit any acts of fraud, or were guilty of other irregularities, the offenders should be delivered over to him; by which means a more public example would be made, and they would receive a severer punishment than he conceived it was likely I should cause to be inflicted.

Regulations so well concerted, and dictated by so much good sense and sound policy, could not fail to meet my hearty concurrence, and to insure my utmost exertions to have them duly obeyed.

These were all, *Tamaahmaah* said, which on his part he had to propose;[1] but he begged that I would make such additions to them as circumstances might hereafter require.

Convinced of the advantage, as well as the necessity, of preserving peace with these people, not only on the score of humanity, but as it respected our own present and future welfare; it became indispensibly requisite that I should leave no object unattended to, that was likely to co-operate with the judicious measures the king had concerted.

Notwithstanding that the spot on which our tents and observatories were situated, became consecrated from its vicinity to, or rather from forming a part of, the morai, yet it was very much confined, and afforded but little room for our people to act in their defence, should any sudden change take place,

---

[1] Vancouver had rejected one proposal. In order 'more effectually to carry his Regulations into Execution, he [Kamehameha] requested permission for two of his Canoes to row round the Vessels at Night, as Guard Boats, this was refused on a Supposition, that the Natives might conceive, that we were not of sufficient Power to guard ourselves.' — Puget, 23 February.

and the natives be hostilely inclined. In the event of any misunderstanding, I was by no means certain, that the sanctity of the place would render sacred the persons of our party residing within its precincts; and should they be unfortunately cut off, the loss of our instruments and chronometers would certainly follow; many important objects of our voyage, would necessarily be defeated; and consequences of a more serious nature might ensue.

These important considerations led me seriously to reflect, in what instances the precautions of *Tamaahmaah* could be strengthened. Little apprehension existed with me, except from the insatiable desire these people possessed for arms, particularly muskets and pistols.[1] These were apparently the only temptations to a breach of the subsisting cordiality and friendship. To prevent therefore any of these from being thrown in their way, by the carelessness of those who might occasionally be permitted to amuse themselves on shore, I gave directions that no one should take on these occasions any arms, excepting a small pair of pocket pistols; which were to be kept intirely out of sight, and from the knowledge of the Indians, until the moment when self-preservation, or any other absolute necessity, should call them into action. This restriction was suggested by my own experience in several instances at different islands in these seas; where I have seen even considerate officers, as well as midshipmen, when on shore with a gun, either fatigued by the heat of the climate, or disappointed by the want of game, intrust their fowling pieces to an attendant native, who would watch for a good opportunity to make off with it; or, by holding fire arms carelessly in a crowd of the natives, have them wrenched from their hands, and instantly conveyed out of sight. Amongst a much more docile race than those of the Sandwich islands, the most unpleasant consequences have followed these misadventures; not only all supplies of refreshments have been stopped, but the blood of innocent natives has been shed on being fired upon for the thief, by the companions of the person robbed; but amongst these clever, designing, resolute people, worse results were to be expected, especially if any of the dissatisfied and turbulent chiefs should chance to be concerned.

This was by no means unlikely to take place; and should they once succeed in any trifling attempt, they might, when wholly unexpected by us, in order to delay or prevent punishment, pursue their object to a fatal and serious end.

---

[1] Kamehameha had recently secured arms from William Brown, master of the *Butterworth*, and Alexander Stewart, master of the *Jackal*, her trading companion. Menzies learned this when he visited the King's house: 'At the further end of the House we observd upwards of two dozen Muskets which the King said he lately procurd in the way of traffic from Mr. Brown Master of the Ship Butterworth of London & added that they were so very bad that some of them burst on the first firing, on which account they were now afraid to fire any of them off. '– 24 February. Bell visited the King's house the next day where he 'found upwards of 30 Muskets, about six and twenty of which had been given him by Mr. Brown & Stewart, but such trash I never beheld, woe be to the man that first fires out of them!' – 25 February.

For the preservation therefore of our present happy intercourse, I deemed it expedient, and consequently directed, that the whole of these regulations should be most rigidly observed; and though they caused some dissatisfaction to inconsiderate individuals, yet for the faithful discharge of His Majesty's service entrusted to my execution, and for the security and happiness of his subjects under my command, I demanded and enforced a strict obedience to these orders, as well as those formerly issued respecting our traffic with the Indians, which were carried into execution on our first arrival.

This morning on shore I met with two sea-men, one an Irishman, who had deserted from an American trader about three months since, named John Smith;[1] the other whose name was Isaac Davis, had been unfortunately captured by these islanders in the schooner Fair American, as was noticed on our former visit to Attowai. But as the information I then received now seemed to differ materially from the truth, and as the circumstances of this transaction, together with the treatment which this poor fellow and Young have since received, reflect not less credit on themselves for their good sense and propriety of conduct, than on *Tamaahmaah* for his humanity and justice, I shall proceed to state, in the abstract, the report made to me both by Young and Davis; and as I have not any doubt of the veracity of either, their information will serve in a great degree to illustrate the different characters of some of the ruling people of these islands, and prove how requisite it is, that every precaution should be taken, by visitors to this country from the civilized world. For although I had every reason to be satisfied of *Tamaahmaah*'s abhorrence of violence and injustice, yet it did not appear that his authority was always equal to restraining the ambitious desires, that governed the conduct of many of the subordinate chiefs.

John Young was boatswain of an American snow, called the Eleanor,[2] mounting ten guns, navigated by ten Americans and forty-five Chinese, or other inhabitants of that country, and commanded by Mr. Metcalf,[3] on a commercial voyage to the coast of North-West America in the fur trade; in which pursuit Mr. Metcalf had likewise embarked his son, a youth of about eighteen years of age, in a small schooner, called the Fair American, of about twenty-six tons burthen, and navigated with five men, one of whom was Davis the mate.

---

[1] Menzies thought he was English, not Irish: 'On shore we met another Englishman namd John Smith, who had been upon the Island about three months, he landed from an American Vessel that was going to the North West Coast for Furs, on account of ill usage. He had since mostly livd with the King who made him a Chief of the Island & gave him a portion of Land to support his dignity in that capacity.' – 24 February. Bell noted that 'little was known about him, he had absconded from a Vessel call'd the *Eliza*, and I believe did not intend making any long stay here.' – February. Bell thought he had been in the islands 'about nine months'.

[2] The *Eleanora*, a brig of about 190 tons, of New York.

[3] Simon Metcalfe.

These two vessels had sailed from China, and in the year 1789 the Fair American was detained by the Spaniards at Nootka,[1] but the Eleanor came on in the autumn of that year to the Sandwich islands, and remained principally about Owhyhee during the winter.

Young stated, that in February 1790, they proceeded to Mowree,[2] where a boat belonging to the snow, with one man in her, was stolen by the natives from the stern of the vessel; and, on a reward being offered for the boat and the man, Mr. Metcalf was informed, that the former was broken to pieces, and that the latter had been killed. The bones of the man were then demanded, which, with the stem and stern-post of the boat, were carried on board the snow in about three days. The natives in the mean time had continued to trade with the crew; and after delivering up the remains of the man, and parts of the boat, they supposed the anger of those on board was intirely appeased, and demanded of Mr. Metcalf the reward he had offered. This, Mr. Metcalf replied, they should soon have, and immediately ordered all the guns to be loaded with musket balls, and nails; and having *tabooed* one side of the ship in order to get all the canoes on the starboard side, next the shore, the ports were hauled up, and the guns fired amongst the canoes. The guns between decks, being nearly upon a level with the canoes, did great execution, as did the small arms from the quarter-deck and other parts of the ship. On this occasion, Young represented that upwards of an hundred were killed, and a great many were wounded.[3]

Having thus taken such revenge as he considered equivalent to the injury received, Mr. Metcalf quitted Mowree, and returned with his vessel to Owhyhee; where, to all appearance, they were on very good terms, with the chiefs, and the inhabitants of that island.

On the 17th of March, Young had permission to be on shore until the next day, when the snow stood close in, and fired a gun as a signal for him to return on board; but, to his very great astonishment, he found the canoes all *tabooed*, and hauled up on the shore, and was informed by *Tamaahmaah*, that if he attempted to take a canoe by himself, he would be put to death, but that he should have a canoe the next day. Having no other resource, Young was obliged to submit; and in the evening he was informed, that the schooner Fair American had been captured by *Tamaahmootoo*,[4] to the southward of

[1] Metcalfe had purchased the *Fair American* at Macao and had placed his son, Thomas Humphrey Metcalfe, in command of her. She and the *Eleanora* left Macao together in June 1789, but they lost contact with one another in a storm. The *Fair American* arrived at Nootka late in October and was seized by Martinez. She was taken to San Blas, but the Viceroy ordered her release. She then proceeded to the Sandwich Islands. See Warren Cook, *Flood tide of Empire*, pp. 192–8.   [2] Maui; so spelled in both editions.

[3] The *Eleanora* was anchored off Honuaula, Maui. In Hawaiian annals the affair is known as the 'Olowalu massacre'. For details of primary sources see R. S. Kuykendall, *The Hawaiian Kingdom, 1778–1854* (Honolulu, 1938), p. 24n.

[4] Kameeiamoku, chief of Kohala. Because of the capture of the *Fair American* Vancouver would have no dealings with him, but he agreed finally to meet him when paying his last visit to the islands in 1794.

Toeaigh bay; and that Mr. Metcalf's son, and the four men composing the crew, had been barbarously murdered.

The snow remained two days off Karakakooa, firing guns, and standing in shore, as a signal for Young; but after the news was confirmed of the schooner having been captured, the king would not permit him to leave the island,[1] but behaved to him in the kindest manner; telling him that he should not be hurt, and that he should be at liberty to depart in the next ship that arrived; but that he would, on no account, allow a canoe to go off to the snow, lest his people should be killed.

Tamaahmaah, who had been on the strictest terms of friendship with Mr. Metcalf and his people, took Young immediately to his house, where he was treated with every kindness and attention.

The king, being excessively concerned, and very angry at the late inhuman business, collected a very considerable force; and, as if he intended to chastise those who should be found the perpetrators of this barbarous transaction, he sat out, accompanied by Young, on the 22d of the same month, in order to inquire into the circumstances that could have caused so great a breach of hospitality. The schooner was found in the situation already described, destitute of almost every thing that was moveable. *Tamaahmaah* demanded that the vessel should instantly be delivered up to him, that he might restore her to the proprietor Mr. Metcalf, should he ever again visit Owhyhee. This was complied with by *Tamaahmootoo*, who received from the king a very sharp rebuke for the great impropriety of his late conduct in the capture of the schooner, and his unpardonable barbarity in murdering the commander and the people; in excuse for which, he alledged he had been struck and otherways ill treated by the father of the unfortunate young man.[2]

Here they found Isaac Davis, the mate, still alive, but in a most deplorable condition. *Tamaahmaah* ordered that he should immediately be taken to his residence, and gave particular injunctions that he should receive every assistance in their power to bestow.

From Davis I learned, that he had been treated by *Tamaahmaah* and his attendants with a degree of humanity, kindness, and careful attention, that he could not have believed these people were capable of shewing.

The following is his account of the melancholy fate of the younger Metcalf and his people, on the capture of the schooner by *Tamaahmootoo*; which I have every reason to believe is a true and fair statement of that unjustifiable transaction.

'The schooner, being close in with the land, and nearly or intirely becalmed,

[1] Young was detained to prevent news of the massacre from reaching Captain Metcalfe.

[2] According to Kuykendall it was quite by chance that the *Fair American* was the victim of an attack. Kameeiamolu 'had once committed some petty offense on board the *Eleanora* for which he was struck with a rope's end by Captain Simon Metcalfe. Smarting under this affront to his dignity, Kameeiamoku is said to have sworn that he would have revenge on the next foreign ship that came his way. As fate would have it, the next ship was the tiny schooner *Fair American*, commanded by Metcalfe's son and having a crew of only five men.' – *The Hawaiian Kingdom, 1778–1854*, pp. 24–5.

she was visited by *Tamaahmootto*, a very powerful chief, who was attended by a great number of the inhabitants. Many of these, as well as their chief, made considerable presents to the young commander, and others sold their hogs and vegetables for little or nothing; and in order to ingratiate themselves further in the good opinion of Mr. Metcalf, and to gain his permission for their entering his vessel, they told him that the snow was but a little way to the westward, and that he would see his father before night.

Davis, who was at the helm, represented the impropriety of this measure to Mr. Metcalf, and said that he thought the behaviour of the natives had a very suspicious appearance; but all he could urge was to no effect; the young commander, perfectly satisfied of their friendly intentions, replied that they would do them no harm, and allowed as many as thought proper to come on board his vessel. In a few minutes he was seized by *Tamaahmootoo*, thrown overboard, and was no more seen. Davis having a pistol at hand, snapped it at the chief on his seizing his commander, but it unfortunately missed fire. He was then thrown overboard himself, and most inhumanly treated whilst in the water; the women stripped him there of his cloaths, and the men endeavoured to murder him with their paddes, being otherways all totally unarmed. But Davis being a good swimmer, and a very strong athletic man, escaped from one canoe to another before his pursuers, in order to preserve his life, which he appeared to be incapable of prolonging but for a few moments. At length, exhausted by fatigue, and the loss of blood, which had been very considerable from the wounds he had received, he was hauled into a large double canoe; and as they had no weapon or instrument with which they could put him to death, he was held with his throat across the rafter that unites the two canoes, whilst the inhuman wretches jumped upon his neck and shoulders, with the intention of thus depriving him of life, but still without effect; till, being tired with their cruelties, they ceased to persecute him.

After a short respite he recovered a little, and looking up to the most active of the party, said '*mytie, mytie,*'[1] signifying 'good;' the man, instantly replied '*arrowhah,*'[2] meaning, that he pitied him, and instantly saluted him, by touching noses, gave him some cloth, and assisted him to wipe and bind up his wounds. After this he had no other injury offered to him; on his being taken on shore he was kindly treated by *Harapy*, brother to *Kahowmotoo*,[3] who nursed him, and expressed great concern for his deplorable condition; but *Tamaahmootoo*, notwithstanding the state he was in, took him in triumph through the village, and made a jest of him.

Davis further stated, that *Tamaahmootoo* took every thing out of the schooner that he possibly could, before the arrival of the king and Young; that he was rejoiced to see the latter, and thought he had come from the snow to fetch the schooner; but when they met, and he had heard the snow was gone, and that Young had been informed of the particulars of the late cruel transaction, they were both sitting in the greatest affliction, when the king

[1] maikai, maikai.   [2] aloha.   [3] Keeaumoku.

came to them, caught them in his arms and comforted them; and said, that no one should hurt them whilst he could protect them. The king then gave directions that he should be properly taken care of, and told him he was very sorry for what had happened, but that he, Davis, should live with, and be protected by him.

After this, the king reprimanded *Tamaahmootoo* in such terms, that Davis saw tears in the eyes of the latter. *Tamaahmaah* then took possession of the schooner for the right owner.'[1]

Although there can be no possible excuse offered in vindication of the unjustifiable conduct of this turbulent and ambitious chief, yet it appears to have been almost as inexcuseable on the part of the elder Metcalf, that he should have thrown such a temptation in his way. The vessel in question had been a pleasure boat, and was lengthened at China; her gunwale was not a foot higher than that of the double canoes of this country, and being navigated and protected by five persons only, under the command of an inexperienced young man, she became not less a desirable acquisition to *Tamaahmootoo* than a prize of easy attainment. To risk therefore a vessel so circumstanced, amongst a set of Indians, whose daring and ambitious character was so well known in every corner of the civilized world, must ever be regarded as highly imprudent and inconsiderate.

John Young, who was about forty-four years of age, born at Liverpool, and Isaac Davis, then thirty-six years old, born at Milford,[2] have from this period resided intirely with *Tamaahmaah*; are in his most perfect confidence, attend him in all his excursions of business or pleasure, or expeditions of war or enterprize; and are in the habit of daily experiencing from him the greatest respect, and the highest degree of esteem and regard. Near the bay of Whyeatea the king has given them three very fine estates; and *Kahowmotoo*, who is the firm friend of *Tamaahmaah*, not only from connection, but a sincere regard, and who, from his atchievements in war and advice in council, is considered as the second chief in the island, has likewise shewn them, on all occasions, the greatest marks of friendship and respect, and has presented each with a very fine estate near the east point of the island. *Kavaheero*[3] and

[1] Davis' narrative is the only first-hand account of this episode; other accounts, such as that in Bell's journal, are obviously derived from it or directly from him.

[2] John Young became an important figure in Hawaii, and differing accounts of him have been published. It seems clear that he was born near Liverpool, England, in 1744, went to America before the Revolution, and served as a seaman on merchant ships sailing out of New York and Philadelphia. He joined the *Eleanora* in 1789 and arrived in Hawaii in March 1790. He died in 1835, having spent 45 years in the islands. He had two sons, one of whom became Minister of the Interior, and one of his daughters was the mother of Queen Emma, consort of Kamehameha II. See G. R. Carter, 'A new document of John Young', Hawaiian Historical Society *32nd Annual Report*, 1924, pp. 51–3. Less is known about Isaac Davis, who is believed to have been born in Milford, Surrey. He died in 1810, aged 52 years. See *With Lord Byron at the Sandwich Islands in 1825, Being Extracts from the MS Diary of James Macrae, Scottish Botanist* (Honolulu, 1922), p. 36.

[3] Keaweaheulu. The name is also spelled Kavahero and Cavaheero.

Commanowa,[1] who are considered the next chiefs in power and authority to the two former, have also treated them both in the most friendly manner; but neither of them could speak of *Tianna* in the same favorable terms. This chief eyes them with great jealousy, and has made some attempts on their lives; particularly on the return of Captain Colnett from St. Blas. On this occasion, Captain Colnett, understanding that there were two white men on the island, very humanely desired, by letter, that they would repair on board his vessel, and that he would afford them all the protection and service in his power.[2] Young and Davis being extremely averse to their present way of life, concerted a plan for escaping to Captain Colnett's vessel; a measure very contrary to the wishes and inclinations of *Tamaahmaah* and the chiefs of the island; lest revenge for the capture of the schooner should follow their departure, to prevent which they were always very narrowly watched, and strongly guarded, whenever any vessel was in sight.

In reply to Captain Colnett's letter Young wrote to him, and stated how he and Davis came to be on the island, what had happened with respect to the schooner, and the means that were used to prevent their escaping. This letter was sent off by one of their attendants, who, meeting *Tianna*, shewed him the letter. This *Tianna* immediately took to the king, and, in consequence of his voyage to China, and having lived so long in the society of Englishmen, persuaded the king that he could read its contents. He pretended that Young and Davis had desired Captain Colnett to get the king into his possession, and to keep him until the schooner and they were delivered up to him; and that he then should kill the king and many more of the islanders. To prevent this calamity, he earnestly advised the king to kill Young and Davis; after which, he said, no one would know any thing about them but themselves.

Captain Colnett concluding the two men were prevented by the natives from getting off to him, very kindly wrote them another letter, and said, that if they were so circumstanced, he begged they would send for any thing they wanted, and if he had it, it should be sent on shore to them. To this very kind letter Young wrote an answer, and told the man who undertook to carry it on board that the Captain would make him a handsome present for so doing. The next day the man returned, and said he was afraid to deliver the letter, as the king had given orders, that every man should be punished with death, who should carry any thing from either Young or Davis to Captain Colnett. This disappointment determined them if possible to effect their escape.

They had in their possession two muskets, with some powder and shot;

---

[1] Kamanawa.

[2] There is only one brief reference in Colnett's journal to the letters he sent to Young and Davis. He evidently heard of them on 2 April 1791, when off the SW coast of the island of Hawaii. The entry reads: 'on learning that he [Kamehameha] was to the Northward and several Europeans that had deserted their Vessels with him, I sent two notes to them, and Bore up to the N.W.' He anchored in Kailau Bay, but only remained there three or four days. Howay (ed.), *The Journal of Captain James Colnett* (Toronto, 1940), p. 213.

they loaded their pieces and sat out, but before they had got near to the water side opposite to the vessel, they were followed by a great number of the inhabitants, who, being fearful of their guns, did not molest them. Some of the natives however endeavoured to prevent their reaching a point, that was nearly surrounded by water, from whence being near to the ship, they were in hopes of effecting their purpose. In accomplishing this, Young was obliged to strike one man with the but of his piece, (for they did not like to fire) and unfortunately broke its stock. They had not long been here before the king arrived in his canoe, attended by many others. *Tamaahmaah* very dispassionately advised them to return from whence they had come; and said, that he would do any thing they could wish to render their lives more comfortable, but that he could not consent they should leave the island; assuring them that his people would rebel, and put him to death, the instant they took their departure. *Tianna*, who was present, seemed to be of a different opinion; and offered to take Young and Davis on board Captain Colnett's vessel, in his own canoe. But the king, well knowing that *Tianna* only wanted to accomplish their destruction, immediately interposed; and in the kindest and most persuasive manner requested they would on no account accept *Tianna*'s offer, but that they would return in his canoe with him. The confidence they reposed in *Tamaahmaah*, that they should be subject to no inconvenience in consequence of their attempt to escape, and the earnestness with which he solicited them to go back with him, at length had the desired effect, and they both embarked on board his canoe. Davis was in the fore part, and Young in the after part of the canoe, when they were boarded by many others; and *Tamaahmaah*, observing some violence was likely to be offered to Davis, went forward to rescue him, and to prevent any accident took Davis's musket away from him; in the mean time many of the natives fell upon Young, who received several wounds before the king could return to his assistance, who was obliged to strike several of them with his paddle before they would desist.

After this project was defeated, Young and Davis were never suffered to be both afloat at the same time until our arrival; and they were given to understand, that the escape of the one would be fatal to the other. This seemed to be a very political measure, as the interest they had in each other's happiness and welfare, and the sincere friendship and regard that subsisted between them, could not escape the observation of *Tamaahmaah*, who would readily suggest the expediency of such an interdiction. Thus have Young and Davis since remained, observing that fidelity towards each other, which the true principles of honor dictate under such circumstances.

Young and Davis had now been resident in Owhyhee nearly three years, which had afforded to each of them frequent opportunity of noticing the characters of the principal chiefs, and leading people on the island. I derived from them such information respecting the conduct of certain chiefs as may be considered important; at least to those whose pursuits may lead them into these seas.

Tianna, they represented, as possessing the most turbulent and ambitious disposition, with great activity of mind, and a thorough contempt of danger. Had his power been sufficient, or had his plots and designs been countenanced and adopted by *Tamaahmaah*, they must have proved fatal to many of the small trading vessels that have visited these islands. Ever since *Tianna* had been settled on Owhyhee with the arms and ammunition he had brought from China, his mind had constantly been directed to the seizing of every small vessel that had arrived amongst them; whilst the plans he had repeatedly concerted for such enterprizes had been seconded by his brother *Nomatahah* and *Tamaahmoottoo*,[1] and as uniformly opposed, and over-ruled by *Tamaah-maah*, *Kahowmotoo*, *Crymamahoo*, and *Cavaheero*.[2] The chief, *Commanow*,[3] was of the king's pacific party, had uniformly rejected the counsels of *Tianna*, and was adverse to his ambitious projects, excepting in one instance; that of the capture of the sloop Princess Royal. In justification however of his conduct on this occasion, he says, the reason that induced him to concur in that enterprize, was, that the Spaniards had taken the Princess Royal from the English, and therefore he thought there could be no harm in taking her from the Spaniards.[4]

Nomatahah and *Tamaahmootoo* are artful, designing, and restless characters, and have dispositions to act on all occasions of hazard, or unlawful attempt, in conjunction with *Tianna*. One single instance may serve to shew with what art their projects are designed, and with what success they are likely to be attended.

About two months before the capture of the Fair American, whilst Mr. Metcalf was lying with his snow in Karakakooa bay, it was proposed to *Tamaahmaah* by these chiefs to seize the snow, to put as many of her crew to death as they thought necessary, but to reserve a sufficient number to navigate her, and to instruct them in the management of such vessels. By this acquisition so great an advantage would be gained over the rest of the islands, as would make the conquest of them all very easy; for under the power that *Tamaahmaah* would then have, they must inevitably be reduced to subjection.

The mode proposed by *Tianna* for the accomplishment of this project was, that whilst the crew were engaged aloft in furling the sails after they had been loosed to dry, which, in consequence of the then rainy season, was a daily practice on board the vessel, these chiefs, with others on whom they could

---

[1] Namakeha, a brother of Kaiana, and Kameeiamoku, chief of Kohala, who had seized the *Fair American*.

[2] Keeaumoku, Kalaimamahu (a half-brother of Kamchameha) and Keaweaheulu.

[3] Kamanawa.

[4] There seems to be no evidence that any attempt was actually made to capture the *Princess Royal*. Presumably it would have taken place in Kailau Bay, where she spent the first days of April 1791. She had been seized at Nootka by Martinez in 1789 and, manned by a Spanish crew commanded by Manuel Quimper, was bound for Manila, whence she was to proceed to Macao, where she was to be returned to her British owners.

depend, being assembled on board for this express purpose, should murder all those who remained upon deck, and put as many of the others to death, as they considered necessary, on their coming down out of the rigging. *Tianna* reduced the success of this exploit nearly to a certainty, as he had been two or three times on board the vessel whilst her sails were furling, and saw with what ease his plan could be carried into effect.

Notwithstanding *Tamaahmaah* revolted at the idea of this barbarous scheme, and with great abhorrence rejected the proposals of *Tianna*, he very fortunately still remained in the neighbourhood. For when the projectors, instead of subscribing to the orders of their king, and abandoning their cruel design, repaired on board the vessel, *Tamaahmaah* on becoming acquainted that they were so assembled, went in person immediately on board, and ordered them out of the vessel; adding threats, that if they did not instantly comply, he would inform Mr. Metcalf of the danger that awaited him. They denied having visited the ship with any hostile intention; and Mr. Metcalf left the island without having the least knowledge of the conspiracy that had been formed for his destruction; and which had been the case also with the Princess Royal, and several other vessels, against which their plots had been equally well concerted; but, by the timely interference of *Tamaahmaah*, their barbarous projects had been defeated, and the lives of many civilized people preserved.

On this subject I had questioned both *Tamaahmaah* and *Kahowmotoo*, who confirmed the information given by Young and Davis; and in addition to it they stated to me, that in council *Tianna* was always for war and coercive measures, by which conduct he had not only incurred their disapprobation, but that *Tamaahmaah* had obliged him to quit his former residence in the neighbourhood of Karakakooa, and to retire to the northwest part of the island.

CHAPTER VI.

Transactions at Karakakooa Bay—Visit from the Widow of Terreeoboo—An Indian Sham-fight—Proposals for a general Peace amongst the Indians—Quit Owhyhee—Astronomical Observations.

HAVING now opened a friendly communication with the chiefs, and adopted measures for establishing and preserving the good understanding that had taken place between the inhabitants and ourselves, one thing only appeared necessary to make our situation perfectly comfortable: this was, to discover some means of recruiting our supply of water, which Karakakooa does not naturally furnish. On visiting the well from which the Resolution and Discovery had obtained theirs, I found that it contained but a small quantity, and this so excessively brackish, that I was fearful of its bad effects on the health of our people; and as there was no better within our reach, I applied, on Monday the 25th, to *Tamaahmaah* for his assistance to relieve our wants. The vast consumption of water by the cattle on our passage hither, made the quantity we now required very considerable, and he was for some time at a loss to devise the best means for procuring a sufficiency. At length he proposed that a certain number of his canoes, each taking one, two, or three puncheons, according to their size, should be sent to different places on this side of the island, and there be filled with water brought by the natives in calabashes to the casks at the sea side, from the little wells in their plantations.

This plan being determined upon, a dozen puncheons, by way of experiment, were put into the canoes, the destination of some of which was at that distance, that they were not expected to return in three days. Six of the casks, however, were brought back full of most excellent water the following morning, Tuesday the 26th, for which service those employed seemed amply rewarded by receiving a piece of iron about 6 inches long, and two inches in breadth, being the price fixed by the king for filling each cask, who also directed that the people of the neighbourhood should bring down water for sale; this was furnished in tolerable abundance, and they acted in this, as in other articles of traffic, with the greatest honesty and propriety of conduct.

The king spent the day in visiting the two vessels,[1] though he passed most

---

[1] This day Bell went ashore and visited the Queen: 'Her Majesty is a very handsome woman, and carries in her looks & Manners a very suitable degree of dignity....The Palace

of his time on board the Discovery, where his observation was constantly awake, and few of our most common operations escaped his notice; all his enquiries were pertinent, directed to useful objects, and calculated to obtain information that would hereafter answer some good purpose.

On missing his early visit the next morning, Wednesday the 27th, I received a message from him, that an axe and some small articles belonging to the Chatham had been stolen by the women who had been permitted to sleep on board, and who had escaped to the shore undetected. Our first knowledge of the theft was by this message from *Tamaahmaah*, who informed me that the offender, a young woman, was in custody, and that the instant the stolen goods were recovered, they should be returned to the place from whence they had been taken. This was done about breakfast time, after which he spent the remainder of the day with me, and gave me the unwelcome intelligence, that the bull for whose recovery I was so very solicitous, was dead. On this mortifying occasion I much regretted that I had not followed the advice of *Kahowmotoo*, from whose connection with the king I most probably might have relied with perfect security on his offers, of taking charge of the cattle at Toeaigh. Two of the young cows, however, appeared to be in calf; this encouraged me to hope that his loss would be repaired by one of them bringing forth a male. The finest of the two ewes, I was now informed was killed by a dog the day after the cattle were landed; whose life was instantly forfeited for the transgression.

Our plan for procuring water answered very well; the casks were taken the greatest care of, and were punctually and regularly returned; so that by this evening we had acquired eight tuns of excellent water.

On Thursday afternoon the 28th, *Kerneecuberrey*, the unfortunate widow of the late *Tereeoboo*,[1] favored me with a visit. After lamenting the death of her husband, and witnessing nearly the extirpation of his whole race, she had survived to this time in a state of captivity. Under these melancholy circumstances, she had met in *Tamaahmaah* not only a humane and generous conqueror, but a friend and a protector.

During the conflict at the revolution, he was under the necessity of using some violence to shelter her from the revenge of his nearest relations, and the fury of the mob, who loudly demanded her immediate execution, and the

---

is pleasantly situated, it consisted of 3 Houses enclosed by a Stone Wall, within a large Square. One of these Houses and the largest was the Kings it consisted but of one apartment, of about thirty feet in length & high & broad in proportion very strong, and very neatly put together...it was floor'd with many folds of Clean Cloth, with a high raised Pillow of the same all round, at the upper end was His Majestys Bed which was raised between two & three feet from the ground, composed entirely of fine Soft Cloth....The next house in size was the Queens which was very clean & covered with Matts. But as by the Laws respecting the Crown here, neither the King or Queen can enter either of the others house, the third house which is small, and situated between the two others, is their Majesty's Bed Chamber, and only made use of when they sleep together.' – Bell, 25 February.

[1] Kanekapolei, the widow of Kalaniopuu.

829

lives of all her husband's adherents. Although on my visit to these islands in the year 1779 she was then advanced in life, yet I perfectly recollected the features of her countenance. The high degree of sensibility and vivacity it then possessed, compared with her present appearance, too plainly bespoke the sorrow and dejection she had since experienced.

In a very feeble faltering voice she said, that we had been formerly acquainted, that she had come with *Tamaahmaah* to pay me a visit and see the ship, presented me at the same time with a small feathered cap, which was all she had now in her power to bestow. My name was perfectly familiar to her, but my person was so altered, that it was some time before she was quite reconciled to the change that fourteen years had produced.[1] Curiosity induced her to visit most parts of the ship; and whilst she was so engaged, a slight degree of cheerfulness seemed to obtrude, and for a moment appeared to suspend the weighty afflictions that her declining years were scarcely able to sustain. Satisfied with the surrounding objects, and gratified in her inquiries after many of the officers and some of the people of the Resolution and Discovery, I presented her with an assortment of valuables suitable to her former distinguished situation, and obtained from *Tamaahmaah* a most solemn promise in her presence, that the articles I had given her should not be taken from her by himself or any other person.

Kahowmotoo, who with a part of his family had been our constant visitors in the day time, and whose good offices had been uniformly exerted to the utmost of his ability in our service, took a very friendly leave on Friday morning the 1st of March, for the purpose of collecting such things as would be most acceptable to us after quitting Karakakooa; it being my intention to visit Toeaigh previously to my departure from this island. On this occasion I presented him with some useful articles that were highly acceptable to him, particularly a suit of sails made of old canvass for his largest canoe, and a cloak of scarlet cloth made after the fashion of that I had given to *Tamaahmaah*, but not quite so gaudily decorated.

Mr. Menzies, who had departed on Monday in pursuit of botanical researches, accompanied by one of the midshipmen of the Discovery,[2] on an excursion into the country, returned to the ship this morning. He had been attended by a guide and eight people appointed for that purpose by *Tamaahmaah*.[3] From these people he had received the greatest attention and civility, and through all the inhabited parts of the country they had passed, had been treated with the utmost respect and hospitality.[4]

---

[1] Vancouver was 22 when he visited Hawaii for the second time in 1779, with Cook.
[2] John Stewart.
[3] John Smith was also a member of the party.
[4] Menzies describes the expedition in his journal. The party travelled inland about 16 miles, in the general direction of Mauna Loa. He was much impressed by the intensive agriculture and by the forests, and foresaw Hawaii's sugar industry: 'Men of humanity industry & experienced abilities in the exercise of their art would here in a short time be

On Saturday the 2d, most of our material business being by this time accomplished, our wood and water completely replenished; and finding that on application to the chiefs a sufficient quantity of refreshments were instantly supplied, I annulled the order prohibiting a general barter, and gave permission for the purchasing of curiosities.

Accompanied by *Tamaahmaah* and some of the officers, on Sunday the 3d, I visited the three villages in this bay; and first of all the fatal spot, where Captain Cook so unexpectedly, and so unfortunately for the world, was deprived of his valuable life. This melancholy, and ever to be deplored event, the natives are at much pains exactly to represent,[1] to produce reasons for

enabled to manufacture Sugar & Rum from luxuriant Fields of Cane equal if not far superior to the produce of our West India Plantations & that without Slavery...' But from the botanical point of view his experience was exasperating; he found many trees and shrubs that were entirely new to him: 'I therefore diligently searchd for their Flowers & their Fruits in order to be able from the one either to ascertain or describe them, but few of them being at this time in bloom, my researches were in a great measure fruitless, on which account I could not help considering my situation as the most vexatious & tantalizing that a scrutinizing Botanist could ever be placed in, surrounded on all sides by new & rare objects & yet destitute of the means of obtaining a knowledge of them, by not being able to visit them at different seasons of the year'. – February 26 and 27.

[1] The chief reason advanced was an incident noted in King's journal a fortnight before Cook's death: 'We were in want of fire wood & the Captain desird us to treat with the Natives, whether or no they would not sell the Pailing round their Morai, they had often themselves taken out some of the pales, & as it had much the Appearance of being suffer'd to go to decay, we did not seem to run any risk in being look'd upon as impious to propose the purchasing of it; It was accordingly done & the Wood most readily given to us even without any demand; they were however handsomely rewarded, & this morning the launches from both Ships took it off'. – February 1, 1779. Cook, *Journals*, III, 516. The natives may have been less happy about this transaction than King believed. Some contended that it roused the hostility to Cook that led to his murder. Puget was so informed when he visited the heiau on 26 February: 'In the Afternoon I went on Shore with Davis & my Friend Terrymiki [Keliimaikai, brother of Kamehameha], where we were joined by Mr. Whidbey and the high Priest, who immediately conducted us to the Morai from which Capt King had taken the Wood, this he explained through Davis to have been the Original Cause of their Dispute with Captain Cook for at that time though sanctioned by the Chief, yet it gave great Offence to the Populace.... The Priest informed us, *they* had predicted the Death of Capt Cook from the Moment the Wood had been carried away; this appears to be their Province, for they are generally right Nine times out of Ten; however this is easily accounted for, they work the Minds of the People up to a spirit of Revenge & then foretell the sudden dissolution of a Chief for having committed some Offence against their Religion or Morais, & it is pretty certain that person will shortly be found dead. this no doubt was the Case of Capt Cook, for I am convinced it was not entirely the Events of the Morning on which he was killed, that entirely was the Cause of his Death, but the Chiefs and People were prepared to lay hold of the first Opportunity of fulfilling the predictions of the Priests incensed against him for the Circumstance of the Wood.' Beaglehole comments: 'The incident was given gratuitous importance as a cause of Cook's death in the nonsensical account by Ledyard in his "journal" pp. 136–7 [Hartford, 1783], as a "sacreligious depredation" – an account much copied by later writers.' He concludes: 'the story...seems very much a justification after the fact; and both it and Ledyard are disposed of pretty effectually by Thomas G. Thrum, "The Paehumu of Heiaus Non-

its taking place, and to shew that it fulfilled the prophecies of the priests, who had foretold this sad catastrophe. But as these are matters that require further examination, I shall defer them to future consideration.

At this place, as well as at the other villages, the inhabitants, who were very numerous, behaved with the utmost civility and decorum. It may not however be unimportant to observe, that we repaired on shore with both boats well armed, our men dressed, as was the usual practice on a Sunday, in their best attire, and with a guard of marines. Possibly our appearance had some influence on their general behaviour, though for my own part, I entertained not the least suspicion that such protection was at all necessary. The vanity of *Tamaahmaah* was however highly gratified by the parade, and he much regretted that he had not an English dress to wear upon this occasion. For this he had substituted a garment I had given him, that had not before been exposed to public view, which much attracted the notice and applause of the surrounding multitude. *Tianna*, with several other chiefs, were also present; the latter had every appearance of a cheerful and happy disposition; but the countenance of the ambitious *Tianna* could not conceal the envy he felt in not being treated with the same degree of respect that was shewn to his sovereign. His jealousy became conspicuously evident in our walk through the village, by his asking in a surly tone of voice, why I gave *that man* so many things and himself so few? This I endeavoured to explain, though possibly not intirely to his satisfaction.

Nothing worthy of notice occurred during our perambulation on shore; which, being ended, we returned on board to dinner.

Notwithstanding we had completely finished the principal business of refitting the vessels, yet as I considered the meridian of this place to have been accurately and unalterably fixed by Captain Cook and Captain King, for the better regulation of our chronometers, I much wished for the further observations of a day or two at the observatory; and having promised to give the king an entertainment with fire-works, that exhibition was fixed for Monday evening; and that he might contribute to the pleasures of the day, he proposed to have a sham-battle on shore in the afternoon, between such of his best warriors as could be assembled on so short a notice.[1]

On Monday the 4th, as soon as dinner was over, we were summoned to this review, and as *Tamaahmaah* considered all ceremonies and formalities on my part as adding to his consequence, he requested that I would be attended on shore by a guard.

We found the warriors assembled towards the north corner of the beach, without the limits of the hallowed ground. The party consisted of about an

Sacred", Hawaiian Hist. Soc., *35th Annual Report* (Honolulu, 1926), pp. 56–7.' – Cook, *Journals*, III, cxlvi, n. The *paehumu* was the enclosure round the heiau.

[1] Sham battles were staged frequently and were part of army training. Much attention was given to throwing, dodging and parrying spears.

hundred and fifty men armed with spears; these were divided into three parties nearly in equal numbers, two were placed at a little distance from each other; that on our right was to represent the armies of *Titeeree* and *Taio*,[1] that on the left the army of *Tamaahmaah*. Their spears on this occasion were blunt pointed sticks, about the length of their barbed ones; whilst, on each wing, we were to suppose a body of troops placed to annoy the enemy with stones from their slings. The combatants now advanced towards each other, seemingly without any principal leader, making speeches as they approached, which appeared to end in vaunts and threats from both parties, when the battle began by throwing their sham spears at each other. These were parried in most instances with great dexterity, but such as were thrown with effect produced contusions and wounds, which, though fortunately of no dangerous tendency, were yet very considerable, and it was admirable to observe the great good humour and evenness of temper that was preserved by those who were thus injured. This battle was a mere skirmish, neither party being supported, nor advancing in any order but such as the fancy of the individuals directed. Some would advance even from the rear to the front, where they would throw their spears, and instantly retreat into the midst of their associates, or would remain picking up the spears that had fallen without effect. These they would sometimes hurl again at the foe, or hastily retreat with two or three in their possession. Those, however, who valued themselves on military atchievements marched up towards the front of the adverse party, and in a vaunting manner bid defiance to the whole of their adversaries. In their left hand they held their spear, with which in a contemptuous manner they parried some of those of their opponents, whilst with their right they caught others in the act of flying immediately at them, and instantly returned them with great dexterity. In this exercise no one seemed to excel his Owhyhean majesty, who entered the lists for a short time, and defended himself with the greatest dexterity, much to our surprize and admiration; in one instance particularly, against six spears that were hurled at him nearly at the same instant; three he caught as they were flying, with one hand, two be broke by parrying them with his spear in the other, and the sixth, by a trifling inclination of his body, passed harmless.

This part of the combat was intended to represent the king as having been suddenly discovered by the enemy, in a situation where he was least expected to be found; and the shower of darts that were instantly directed to that quarter, were intended to shew that he was in the most imminent danger; until advancing a few paces, with the whole body of his army more closely connected, and throwing their spears with their utmost exertion, he caused the enemy to fall back in some little confusion, and he himself rejoined our party without having received the least injury.

[1] Titeeree (Kahekili), chief of Maui and other islands W of Hawaii, and his younger brother Taio (Kaeo) were two of the opponents Kamehameha would have to overcome if he were to fulfil his ambition to extend his authority to all the islands.

The consequences attendant on the first man being killed, or being so wounded as to fall on the disputed ground between the contending armies, were next exhibited.

This event causes the loss of many lives and much blood, in the conflict that takes place in order to rescue the unfortunate individual, who, if carried off by the adverse party dead or alive, becomes an immediate sacrifice at the morai. On this occasion the wounded man was supposed to be one of *Titeeree's* soldiers, and until this happened, no advantage appeared on either side; but now the dispute became very serious, was well supported on all sides, and victory still seemed to hold a level scale, until at length the supposed armies of *Taio* and *Titeeree* fell back, whilst that of *Tamaahmaah* carried off in triumph several supposed dead bodies, dragging the poor fellows, (who already had been much trampled upon) by the heels, some distance through a light loose sand; and who, notwithstanding that their eyes, ears, mouth, and nostrils were by this means filled, were no sooner permitted to use their legs, than they ran into the sea, washed themselves, and appeared as happy and as cheerful as if nothing had happened.

In this riot-like engagement, for it could not possibly be considered any thing better, the principal chiefs were considered to bear no part; and on its being thus concluded, each party sat quietly down on the ground, and a parly, or some other sort of conversation took place. The chiefs were now supposed to have arrived at the theatre of war, which had hitherto been carried on by the common people only of both parties; a very usual mode of proceeding, I understood, among these islanders. They now on both sides came forward, guarded by a number of men armed with spears of great length, called *pallaloos*.[1] These weapons are never relinquished but by death, or captivity; the former is the most common. They are not barbed, but reduced to a small point, and though not very sharp, yet are capable of giving deep and mortal wounds by the force and manner with which they are used. The missive spears are all barbed about six inches from the point, and are generally from seven to eight feet long.

The warriers who were armed with the *pallaloos*, now advanced with a considerable degree of order, and a scene of very different exploits commenced; presenting, in comparison to what before had been exhibited, a wonderful degree of improved knowledge in military evolutions. This body of men, composing several ranks, formed in close and regular order, constituted a firm and compact phalanx, which in actual service, I was informed, was not easily to be broken. Having reached the spot in contest, they sat down on the ground about thirty yards asunder, and pointed their *pallaloos* at each other. After a short interval of silence, a conversation commenced, and *Taio* was supposed to state his opinion respecting peace and war. The arguments seemed to be urged and supported with equal energy on both sides. When peace under certain stipulations was proposed, the *pallaloos* were inclined towards the ground,

[1] Pololu, a long war spear.

and when war was announced, their points were raised to a certain degree of elevation. Both parties put on the appearance of being much upon their guard, and to watch each other with a jealous eye, whilst this negociation was going forward; which, however, not terminating amicably, their respective claims remained to be decided by the fate of a battle. Nearly at the same instant of time they all arose, and, in close columns, met each other by slow advances. This movement they conducted with much order and regularity, frequently shifting their ground, and guarding with great circumspection against the various advantages of their opponents; whilst the inferior bands were supposed to be engaged on each wing with spears and slings. The success of the contest, however, seemed to depend intirely on those with the *pallaloos*, who firmly disputed every inch of the ground, by parrying each other's lunges with the greatest dexterity, until some to the left of *Titeeree's* centre fell. This greatly encouraged *Tamaahmaah's* party, who, rushing forward with shouts and great impetuosity, broke the ranks of their opponents, and victory was declared for the arms of Owhyhee, by the supposed death of several of the enemy; these at length retreated; and on being more closely pressed, the war was decided by the supposed death of *Titeeree* and *Taio*; and those who had the honor of personating these chiefs, were, like those before, dragged in triumph by the heels over no small extent of loose sandy beach, to be presented to the victorious *Tamaahmaah*, and for the supposed purpose of being sacrificed at his morai. These poor fellows, like those before mentioned, bore their treatment with the greatest good humour.

The first exhibition appeared to be extremely rude, disorderly, and ineffectual, though much dexterity was certainly shewn; but from the manner in which the *pallaloos* were managed, it would seem that they are capable of sustaining a very heavy assault.

These military exploits finished towards sun-set, and as soon as it was dark we entertained the king and a large concourse of his people with a display of fire works. *Tamaahmaah* and some of the chiefs recollected to have seen a few indifferent ones, that were fired by Captain Cook on his being visited by *Terreeoboo*; but ours, being in higher preservation, of greater variety, and in a larger quantity, were viewed by the several chiefs, who were the only persons admitted within our *tabooed* precincts, with the greatest mixture of fear, surprize, and admiration; and by the repeated bursts of acclamation from the numerous body of the inhabitants assembled on the occasion, it was hard to determine which of these passions most generally preponderated.

The following morning, Tuesday the 5th, *Cavahero*, the chief of Kowrooa,[1] who was of our party the preceding evening, informed me, that on his return home, the inhabitants of that village at first considered what they beheld as a diversion only, but from the time it lasted, and the continual clamour that they had heard, they had become very much alarmed, and suspected that some

---

[1] Keaweaheulu, a chief of Kau, in the S of Hawaii. Usually spelled Kavaheero in the first edition.

misunderstanding had taken place between us and *Tamaahmaah*; and that we were destroying him, with all his people and houses, on this side of the country. The same opinion had prevailed with most of the women who were on board the vessels, and who were not easily persuaded to believe otherwise.

These intimations afforded me an opportunity which I did not suffer to escape, to impress on their minds the very great superiority we possessed, should we ever be obliged to act towards them as enemies. The sky and water rockets, balloons, hand grenades, &c. &c. I represented to be like guns fired without shot, when designed for entertainment; but like them capable of being rendered formidable and destructive weapons, when occasion might require. Of this they seemed to entertain no doubt, and were anxious beyond measure to be provided with a few, for their protection against *Taio* and *Titeeree*. On this subject the king was so excessively pressing, that I was induced to indulge him by complying with his request. I gave to the charge of Young, who with his comrade Davis had so conducted themselves as to be intitled to our confidence, a dozen sky rockets, and half that number of effective hand grenades, for the sole purpose of *Tamaahmaah's* protection, and with the strictest injunctions, that they should never be used but with this design. I likewise exhorted them on no pretence to attend *Tamaahmaah*, or assist him, in any ambitious schemes for the conquest of the neighbouring islands; but to support him to the utmost of their power, not only in the defence of his island against foreign invasion, but in maintaining his authority against domestic insurrection.

I had embraced every opportunity, and had met with no little difficulty to convince *Tamaahmaah*, and the chiefs who had been our constant visitors, that a peaceable mode of life was infinitely to be preferred, and more conducive to their real happiness, than the continued state of warfare that had so long disgraced their islands; without any other motive that could be urged as an excuse for despoiling each other's lands, or destroying their fellow creatures, than a wild and inordinate ambition to possess themselves of each other's territories, which experience had shewn them they were incapable of retaining after conquest.

These and similar arguments I had repeatedly made use of, for the desirable purpose of bringing about a general pacification with the contending sovereigns of these islands; and had at length succeeded so far, as to induce the king, and most of the chiefs, to give the matter their serious consideration. One obstacle, however, seemed to be insurmountable. The want of confidence in all the ruling parties. Such a negociation could only take place by personal conference, and were a chief to be sent from hence to Mowee, with full powers to enter upon so desirable a business, it was alledged the people there would have no good opinion of his intentions; and, considering him as a spy, would instantly put him to death.

I endeavoured to do away this objection, by offering to take any chief so empowered on board the ship, and to tow his canoe to Mowee, where

I would protect him, and remain until the negociation was at an end. This was not considered as a sufficient protection, as the ambassador would be safe no longer than I should remain on the spot. The business however did not rest here; for being on shore the day before *Kahowmotoo*'s departure, I was solicited to attend a council of the chiefs at *Tamaahmaah*'s house. Here much was said on the subject of the peace I had so earnestly recommended. The king and several of the chiefs seemed to be well convinced of the benefits with which a peace would be attended; on this part of the discourse little was said by *Kahowmotoo* or *Tianna*, but that they were convinced that little confidence could be placed in *Titeeree*. They were however of opinion, that the best method of insuring success would be, that I should take a chief of Owhyhee to Mowee, and having shewn to *Titeeree* and *Taio* the advantages of making peace, and convinced their minds of the propriety of so doing, and of the inclination of *Tamaahmaah* to accomplish this happy object, that I should return with *Taio* to Owhyhee, where they would immediately enter heartily into the business with him, and leave all disputed points to be adjusted by me, as the mutual friend of both parties.

There was doubtless a great deal of solid sense in this mode of arguing, and probably there was no other mode so likely to have been attended with success; but I was so much pressed for time, that it was impossible for me to have made the experiment. On my stating, that the want of time put it totally out of my power to comply with this arrangement, which I should otherwise have cheerfully acceded to, some conversation, that I did not understand, passed in a low voice between the king and *Kahowmotoo*; after which the former requested, as I seemed so desirous of effecting a peace between the two islands, that I would use my endeavours when I went to Mowee to bring this matter about, and that on my return next autumn to these islands, I should visit Mowee first, and if I then found the business unaccomplished, should bring *Taio* under my protection to Owhyhee, where every thing should be adjusted and settled in the manner before proposed. To this I gave no positive answer, wishing first to know on what terms *Tamaahmaah* would agree to peace; to this it was replied, that Mowee, Morotoi, and the neighbouring islands, should be ceded to his sovereignty of Owhyhee, in right of his last conquest; and that *Titeeree* and *Taio* should remain in the quiet possession of Woahoo, Attowai, and the rest of the small islands to leeward.

This exorbitant demand I was confident would never be listened to, and I therefore declined having any thing more to do in the business, until terms should be offered that might incline the opposite party to be desirous of an accommodation.

After much conversation respecting the magnitude, population, and fertility of Owhyhee, which was stated to be equal if not superior to all the islands collectively taken, the right which *Titeeree* held in the sovereignty of Mowee and its neighbouring islands was next discussed. As the possession of these territories appeared to have been in the family of *Titeeree* for many ages, I stated that it was not likely he should easily relinquish his pretensions; and though he might be tempted to do so on certain conditions, at the moment, yet after he had re-established his power, and recruited his strength in men and canoes, there could not be a doubt but he would endeavour to re-assume the dominions of his forefathers, and then the same devastation and warfare would be again revived.

These, and other arguments to the same effect, induced the king and his counsellors to listen to the conditions I proposed. They were founded on the spirit of their original laws, and the ancient custom of governing Owhyhee and Mowee, with the islands in their immediate vicinity; at which time, according to their own account, they lived in great harmony and friendship with each other. My first proposition was, that Owhyhee should remain a separate and distinct government of itself, under the authority of *Tamaahmaah* and his heirs; that *Titeeree* and *Taio* should remain in the sovereignty of the other islands, as distinct or foreign dominions; and that the king of Owhyhee should surrender all claim or pretensions to those territories; experience having already demonstrated his inability of retaining conquered countries, without endangering his authority, and disturbing his peace at home. After due consideration, it was agreed that I should on my arrival at Mowee use my endeavours to establish a permanent peace on my own principles; and, by a letter to Young from thence, inform *Tamaahmaah* with the progress of my negociation, which they promised to conclude and ratify, if a chief, properly authorized, brought the letter from Mowee.

I avoided noticing this business whilst it was pending, in the order of my narrative, under the idea that new objections would arise from after considerations, and additional consultations on the subject; all matters however now seemed finally adjusted, and it may not be uninteresting to state the circumstances that first gave rise to this disposition towards peace, as I do not claim the merit of the thought having originated with myself.

The king and several of the chiefs solicited my assistance in the conquest they meditated of all the islands to leeward. They entertained great hopes of my concurrence from the friendship I had uniformly manifested, and from the utter abhorrence I had as uniformly expressed of the cruel and horrid murder of our countrymen at Woahoo, belonging to the Dædalus. This vessel they considered as belonging to me, and for the purpose of exciting my revenge, and inducing my compliance with their wishes, they alledged, that this lamentable outrage was committed in the presence, and by the positive order, of *Titeeree's* brother. This assertion however seemed to be intended for no other purpose than to aggravate the crime of their neighbours, and to increase our misfortune: and they were not less disappointed than surprised that, notwithstanding the forcible reasons they had urged, I peremptorily refused them any assistance. Instead of encouraging hostilities between them, I pointed out the many important advantages that would result from a friendly intercourse with each other; and recommended, that a permanent peace should be established with the inhabitants of all the islands. Still they endeavoured to prevail upon me to listen to their solicitations, and disregarding the pacific measures I had recommended, thought to influence my conduct by presenting, that Mr. Ingraham, commanding the American brig Hope, on some misunderstanding with *Tireeree* and *Taio*, had fired several shot at them as they went from his vessel to the shore; and that in consequence of this treatment, those chiefs had given directions to the inhabitants of all the islands under their authority, to kill every white man they should meet with, whether English, American, or of any other nation. What impression this intelligence might have made at any other time I cannot say, but on this occasion it did not in the least tend to affect my determination, founded on the cause of humanity, and many weighty political considerations.[1]

A general periodical *taboo* was to take place this evening, Tuesday the 5th, and as most of the chiefs our friends had disposed of such matters as they had brought for our service, they took their leave, knowing our departure was nigh, and returned to their respective places of abode; well satisfied with their visit, and intreating us to return again soon to Owhyhee.

The *taboo* demanded the removal of our tents, observatory, &c. these of course were duly received on board; and I acquainted *Tamaahmaah* that it was my intention to sail on Wednesday night, or the following morning. The king earnestly requested that we should not depart until Friday, as he should then be able to accompany us some distance along the island to the northward; but as the season was fast advancing, I entered into no engagement, but left our stay to the event of circumstances.

Tamaahmaah conceiving this might be his last visit, presented me with a handsome cloak formed of red and yellow feathers, with a small collection of other native curiosities; and at the same time delivered into my charge the superb cloak that he had worn on his formal visit at our arrival. This cloak

---

[1] Vancouver does not mention that he endeavoured at this time to persuade Kamehameha to cede Hawaii to Great Britain, a proposal he was to renew on his next visit. Menzies and Manby both refer to the matter: 'As a great number of Chiefs & Natives were collected to see these entertainments [the sham battle and fireworks], Captain Vancouver was very urgent with Tamaiha-maiha to take this opportunity of declaring himself & his Subjects together with the whole Island under the dominion of the King of Great Britain, but this he positively declined doing unless Captain Vancouver would promise to leave one of the Vessels behind at the Island to assist in defending him & his people from the inroads of their Enemies, which was certainly a very strong & reasonable argument.' – Menzies, 4 March. Manby records that after Capt. Vancouver made his proposal 'a long debate ensued, which terminated by Tomah Maha's assenting to the proposal, provided Captn. Vancouver would leave a Vessel for its protection or a force with Guns. The Chief argued the point with great reason, pointing out the imprudence of our accepting the Island without guarding it. As during our absence their inveterate Enemy, Tieteree the King of Mowee, would make his threatened invasion, perhaps with success. As could it be expected the Owhyeeans would fight with firmness for their Country, if they had imprudently given it away to those who would not protect it – this considerate reply, totally put a stop to any further proposals.' – Letters, 7 March.

was very neatly made of yellow feathers; after he had displayed its beauty, and had shewn me the two holes made in differing parts of it by the enemy's spears the first day he wore it, in his last battle for the sovereignty of this island, he very carefully folded it up, and desired, that on my arrival in England, I would present it in his name to His Majesty, King George; and as it had never been worn by any person but himself, he strictly enjoined me not to permit any person whatever to throw it over their shoulders, saying, that it was the most valuable thing in the island of Owhyhee, and for that reason he had sent it to so great a monarch, and so good a friend, as he considered the King of England.

This donation I am well persuaded was dictated by his own grateful heart, without having received the least hint or advice from any person whatever, and was the effect of principles, highly honorable to more civilized minds. The cloak I received, and gave him the most positive assurance of acting agreeably with his directions.[1]

Although *Tamaahmaah* considered himself to be amply rewarded by the different articles I had from time to time presented him with, yet, the very essential services he had rendered us, his steady friendship, and the attachment he had shewn to our welfare, demanded, I thought, some additional testimony of our general approbation. For this purpose I selected a number of useful as well as ornamental articles; amongst the latter were two cloaks similar to those I had before presented him, and a quantity of plain and coloured gartering tape; this was held in great estimation, especially when two or three sorts were sewn together to form that part of their dress called the *maro*, about three yards long, and six inches broad. The useful matters consisted of a variety of culinary utensils and implements of husbandry, with some smiths and carpenters tools. With this acquisition he was greatly delighted, and expressed much surprise at the liberality of the present.[2]

He then in the most affectionate manner took his leave, not only of myself and all the officers, but of every person he saw on deck; and requesting that I would remain until Friday morning, which however I did not think adviseable to promise, he left the ship with considerable reluctance.

---

[1] Kamehameha was evidently anxious that no other gift should seem to rival or detract from his own. This same day Menzies met Namakeha, a brother of Kaiana, whom he had known during his first visit to Hawaii. 'After making him some little presents & renewing our former friendship, he was handing me in as a present from his Canoe a long feathered Cloak, which the King observing, he immediately Tabooed it, thinking perhaps that it would lessen the value of his own presents of the same kind to Capt. Vancouver.' – 5 March.

[2] Bell provides some details: 'TaMaiha-Maiha had a high respect for the English Nation, and had a great desire to imitate us in many things, he ask'd for a Cot, and Bed to Sleep in, which were given him to his great delight, he liked our manner of Cooking, and begg'd permission for his Cook to stay on board the Discovery, and become a Student of the Captain's Cook, this was granted, and a man actually staid on board the whole time in that situation but whether he reaped much benefit or not from his Studies I cannot say, the King was supplied with all kinds of Culinary utensils, and also furnished with some plates, Knives & forks, Glasses &c.' – March.

Amongst those who had accompanied the king on this visit, were two chiefs, one named *Crymakoo*,[1] the other *Quoti*, but more commonly called *Kookinney*,[2] which in their language means *quickness*. To the care of these chiefs Mr. Whidbey and the observatory had been entrusted, with an additional guard of some natives of the order of the priesthood, each of whom strove to surpass the other in acts of service and civility. The situation that the two chiefs filled, and the superiority they possessed, afforded them more frequent opportunities than the rest of manifesting their friendly intentions, in a uniform steadiness deserving the highest commendation.

As an acknowledgment for their services and fidelity, I requested that *Tamaahmaah* would point out to me such articles as would be most worthy of their acceptance; these were presented to them, and they were highly gratified by this compliment to their integrity.

There were none of the chiefs who seemed to feel so much regret on our departure as these two young men. They had been constantly with Mr. Whidbey in the marquee, and had acquired such a taste for our mode of living, that their utmost endeavours were exerted to imitate all our ways, and they seemed so perfectly happy and pleased with our society, that they were scarcely ever absent unless when sent for by the king. Their attachment was by no means of a childish nature, or arising only from novelty; it was the effect of reflection; and the consciousness of their own comparative inferiority. This directed their minds to the acquirement of useful instruction, from those whom they acknowledged to be so infinitely their superiors. Their conversation had always for its object important information, not frivolous inquiry; and their questions were of a nature that would not have discredited much more enlightened observers. Their vivacity and sensibility of countenance, their modest behaviour, evenness of temper, quick conception, and the pains they took to become acquainted with our language, and to be instructed in reading and writing, bespoke them to have not only a genius to acquire, but abilities to profit by instruction.

It appeared to us very singular that these two young men, who were nearly allied to the most inveterate enemies of *Tamaahmaah*, should have been selected by him from the numerous train of favorites attending on his person, to be his most intimate and confidential friends. *Crymakoo*, who was about twenty-four years of age, was son to a chief of the first consequence in Mowee, and one of *Titeeree*'s principal warriors. In his early infancy he was taken under the care of *Tamaahmaah*, brought up by him and had for some years past possessed the confidence, and been the constant companion, of the king, for whose interest and prosperity he entertained the greatest regard; and in return, he was invested by his prince with an authority almost equal to his own. *Quoti*, though not possessing at this time power and authority equal to that of *Crymakoo*, yet seemed to divide with him the affection and esteem of the king. He was about the age of eighteen; and notwithstanding that he was inferior

[1] Kalaimoku.   [2] Kuakini.

in point of figure and address to *Crymakoo*, whose person and deportment excelled in a great degree any of the islanders we had seen, yet he had a very engaging manner, and a pleasing mode of conducting himself. In his intellectual endowments he seemed to possess a great superiority over *Crymakoo*. This youth was the reputed son of *Terreeoboo* by *Namahanna*, the favorite wife of *Kahowmotoo*, but report whispered that he was a much nearer relation than that of cousin to *Tamaahmaah*.

All our external business being completely finished,[1] little else remained to be done but to bend the sails, and get the vessels ready for sea; this service was performed the next day, Wednesday the 6th, when all our friends who continued or resided in the neighbourhood were in sacred retirement. This *taboo* was not observed by the lower orders of the people with the same degree of strictness as that mentioned in the preceding chapter. Many of the men were busily employed in their traffic alongside, but no woman was permitted to be afloat.

On this occasion I think it important to state, that ever since permission had been granted for a general traffic with the islanders, I had attentively watched its effect, and could not have had a better opportunity to be convinced, how absolutely requisite it is that a prohibition on a general trade, between the crews and the natives, should take place on board all European or American vessels, until the more important business, of procuring the necessary supplies of refreshments, wood and water, be accomplished. Whilst the prohibition was in force on board the Discovery, all the essential articles were brought to market, and purchased by us as fast as they could conveniently be received; and any number of hogs, or quantity of vegetables, might have been procured during that period. But no sooner were these restrictions discontinued, and our people at liberty to indulge themselves in the purchase

---

[1] Vancouver makes no mention of having had any contact with Towereroo (Kualelo), the native he had brought back to the islands in 1792. Both Bell and Menzies felt that Vancouver had treated him less than fairly both in Tahiti and Hawaii, and Puget was evidently of the same opinion. Bell wrote: 'Toweraroo had during our stay been our constant visitor, and preferr'd the Chatham to the Discovery this preference was politically ill chosen, and unlucky for him, for contrary I must own to my own expectations on our first coming in, Captn. Vancouver did nothing for him. Mr. Puget had bought him on our first arrival, a Single Canoe which he wish'd for, – and Captn. V. to make it a double one, bought him, at his request, another single one – besides this I know of nothing else he did for him, nor gave him, except a small piece of Red Cloth.' Bell continues: 'much to the honor of Mr. Puget he endeavoured, as far as lay in his power to supply this deficiency of attention, it was now too late to make any alteration in his situation, but he was desired to mention what articles he wanted, and his demand was modest. Some of every species of the Trade [goods] that was consider'd most useful to him, or that he liked was put up for him, and he was contented.' – March. On 6 March Menzies noted in his journal: 'Toomorero attended on board the Discovery most part of the day in expectation of some considerable present from Capt. Vancouver before his departure agreeable to his former promise that he should see him settled when he returnd to the Islands, but all he receivd on this occasion was half a dozen Axes & some other Trinkets of less value.'

of what at the moment they esteemed to be curiosities, than almost all our essential supplies ceased to be brought from the shore, and the few articles of that description which did appear alongside, were increased in price four or five hundred per cent.; even at that rate I endeavoured to purchase our daily consumption of water, but could not succeed. The depreciation in the value of our own commodities was also the consequence of the permission for a general trade, from the extravagant prices given by the crew in outbidding each other for insignificant articles, which were no sooner possessed than they were neglected, and often in a few days were thrown overboard.

The weather became cloudy with some rain in the afternoon, and the wind was unsteady, blowing in squalls very hard from the northern quarter. This continued all night, and in the morning of Thursday the 7th, brought a very heavy swell into the bay, that obliged us, much to the satisfaction of *Tamaahmaah* and our friends on shore, to remain stationary. Soon after sun-rise they all flocked round us with their usual affability and friendship; the king however was not, according to his general practice, amongst the earliest. A delay had been occasioned by his waiting to come off in great state in one of his largest canoes, that we had rigged for him with a full suit of canvas sails, sloop fashion, to which I had added a union jack and a pendant; but these not having been placed according to his directions, required alteration; and, that they might be quite in proper order, he cruized for some time about the bay, before he came alongside. On his arrival we found him highly delighted with his man of war, but he observed that she would make a much better appearance with a few swivels properly mounted; I agreed with him in this opinion, but the words ' *Taboo* King George' were sufficient to prevent a syllable more being urged on that subject.

Tamaahmaah, knowing my intention of visiting *Kahowmotoo* in my way to Mowee, informed me, that he had sent directions to the persons on his estates at Toeaigh to supply us with a full stock of hogs and vegetables, and any thing else the country afforded; and that he might be certain that his orders would be duly executed, he requested that Young and Davis might attend us thither; as it was impossible for him to absent himself from Karakakooa until certain ceremonies had taken place, in consequence of his having celebrated the festival of the new year in this district; and of his having transgressed the law by living in such social intercourse with us, who had eaten and drank in the company of women.

On the evening of our departure, *Tamaahmaah* was to resign himself to the strict obedience of a *taboo* that was then to commence. On this occasion, all his people who had been in commercial intercourse with us, were to lay before him the whole of the treasure they had acquired, and to render to him the customary tribute. The presents that the king himself had received would also be exposed to public view, when certain priests would perform prayers, exhortations, and other functions of their office. These ceremonies frequently continue without stopping, near half a day, and are sometimes repeated ten days successively.

On the morning of Friday the 8th, the weather being pleasant, with a gentle breeze from the land, we sailed from Karakakooa, and stood along shore to the northward; about four miles from our last station we passed a small creek, where we saw the captured schooner laid up,[1] and a house built over it to protect her from the sun. About this time *Tamaahmaah* with his queen and most of his attendants had overtaken us. I took this opportunity of resuming this unfortunate subject, and understood from *Tamaahmaah*, that it was his intention to return the schooner to Mr. Metcalf her owner. This, *Tamaahmaah* promised to do; either to Mr. Metcalf himself, or to the commander of any vessel authorized by Mr. Metcalf to receive her. Young bore witness to the king's sincerity, and said that this had been his constant language, from the moment he became acquainted with the melancholy cause of her detention. From Young we learned, that the schooner was now of little value, having nearly fallen to pieces for want of the necessary repairs.[2]

The royal party remained on board until about ten in the forenoon, when, after taking an affectionate leave of us all, and expressing the greatest concern at the shortness of our visit, they returned to Karakakooa.

With a favorable breeze from the south-west we continued our route to the northward, within about two miles of the land. Some rocks and breakers were

[1] The *Fair American*.
[2] Menzies noted that she was 'laying in a Small Cove...roof'd over with Thatch to preserve her, in order to be deliverd to Mr. Metcalf when he came to the island.' – March 7. She was evidently in better condition than Young thought. Almost a year later, when Vancouver was paying his last visit to Hawaii, Bell described a visit to her in his journal: 'we went on board the Schooner, who was lying in a Creek, to look at her. She was afloat and riding by two Anchors...We could not fail of being Struck with Surprize, at so small a Vessel having been employ'd on such a Commercial pursuit as she had been, and to have travers'd Such an immense tract of Boisterous Ocean as she had done; She was only about 33 feet Keel, and 7 or 8 feet broad. She was housed over with a Thatch work, the Same as the houses on Shore, she was coppered, and seem'd in tolerable condition, except a leak she had Sprung, when ToMaiha Maiha went thither in her to War in the Year 1791. There was nothing in her but a Small piece of Ordnance, and a few Stores of Rope Paddles &c. belonging to Kuymayamoku [Tamaahmotoo]; She was very well taken care of, being bailed dry out twice every day, and a man who went by the appellation of Captain by the Natives, slept on board of her every night, and as an additional instance of their care of her, we were informed of a circumstance that made us Smile – which was – that when it blew hard, the people of the Village to the amount of a hundred or two, collected on the Rocks, and by turns dived to the bottom, and held on the Anchors of the little Vessel whilst the hard puffs of wind lasted.' – 27 January 1794. Later in 1794 the Hawaiians evidently returned the *Fair American* to active service. In September the American trading ship *Jefferson* encountered her, commanded by a very proud native captain: 'No man could entertain a higher idea of this important station than himself, by the many airs that he had been taught to assume on account of his rank as first commander of the king's schooner.' – Quoted by Derek Pethick, *The Nootka Connection* (Vancouver, 1980), p. 197 from a copy of the journal of the *Jefferson* in the Provincial Archives, Victoria.

seen lying, about half way from the shore, off the west point of the island, and extending two or three miles from thence towards Toeaigh. To the north of these the bottom is free from rocks, where vessels may anchor, but the situation does not afford any fresh water; and it is besides objectionable, on account of its being exposed to the north winds, which, with those that blow from the north-westward, are the most violent and dangerous known in this country. Towards the evening we were pretty far advanced in the bay, where, with a moderate breeze from the land, we plied during the night.

Our friend *Kahowmotoo*, agreeably to his promise, visited us the next morning, Saturday the 9th, and presented me with twenty fine hogs, and a large assortment of vegetables; to these he was pleased to add a very handsome feathered cloak.

The servants of the king were very alert in obeying their master's orders, and brought eighty very fine hogs for the Discovery, and half that number, equally good, for the Chatham; with large supplies of vegetables for both. They behaved with the utmost decorum, and inquired if any more of these, or any other articles, would be wanting, adding, that if so, they should be immediately provided. This abundant supply was however far beyond what we could possibly require, one third being fully sufficient for all our purposes; the remainder was therefore directed to be returned to the shore.

During the forenoon we received a visit from *Tianna*, who brought as a present to me about half a dozen small ill-fed hogs, for which we had neither room nor occasion. He was not however dismissed without a farewel present, and such a one, as in my opinion he ought to have been extremely well contented with; since, on no one of his visits, which had been very frequent, excepting on the first, had he offered us any refreshments; yet he had received from me presents nearly equal to those I had made to other chiefs, who had been instrumental in supplying our wants, and anxious on all occasions to render us service. Although *Tianna* could assume no merit, either for his supplies, or services bestowed upon us, yet, such was his envious pride, that instead of being thankful for what he had not deserved, he could not refrain from expressions of dissatisfaction, that he had not been shewn the same attention and respect, and complimented with articles of similar value to those, that had been offered to *Tamaahmaah*. In short, his conversation was in so haughty a stile, and so unlike the general conduct of all the other chiefs of Owhyhee, that I was induced to request that he would return the scarlet cloak, axes, and a variety of other useful articles I had just before given him; observing, that as these things were in his opinion so inadequate to his claims, they could not possibly be worthy his acceptance. With this request however *Tianna* did not think proper to comply, but departed, affecting to be perfectly satisfied and contented, though his countenance proclaimed those designing, ambitious, and (I believe I may with justice add) treacherous principles, that apparently govern his turbulent and aspiring disposition.

Kahowmotoo, who was present, expressed the highest disapprobation of

Tianna's conduct; saying, that if any one could be dissatisfied, he had cause to complain, that such valuable presents had been bestowed on a man who had appeared totally indifferent to our welfare, and who had never even endeavoured to render us any service. This observation was extremely well timed, and was immediately followed by the most grateful acknowledgments for the valuable articles himself and family had received. These, he said, had far exceeded the utmost limits of his expectations.

I was less pleased with the gratitude of *Kahowmotoo*, than with the assurance of his being so well contented with the selection of things I had given him, as they were on our part tributes very justly due to his steady, uniform, and friendly attention.

Amongst other points of information that I collected at Owhyhee, I learned that *Tamaahmaah*, having obtained some intimation of our intended visit, had been excessively impatient for our arrival, that he might obtain an opportunity of displaying his real and true character; which he understood had been most unjustly traduced, by some of the traders who had visited this island since he had acquired its government. Instructions had been given to several of the masters of the trading vessels by their owners, directing them to be excessively cautious of, and vigilantly on their guard against, the treacherous, villainous, and designing arts of *Tamaahmaah*; these unnecessary admonitions had been explained to him; and being conscious of his own innocence, his concern was excessive, and he impatiently looked forward to an opportunity of rescuing his character from such imputations, by exhibiting his real disposition to his more candid visitors.

If what I have here had occasion to state, respecting the conduct and liberal sentiments of this chief, be not sufficient to wipe away the aspersions that have detracted from his good name, I doubt not of having yet a further opportunity of producing such facts, as will effectually accomplish that purpose.

Tianna was not ignorant of our prepossession for *Tamaahmaah's* virtues, and goodness of heart; this prompted his envy, to let no occasion escape for saying something to his prejudice and dishonour, so long as any one would listen to this favourite topic of his conversation; and it is by no means unlikely, that when he had successfully implicated the king by his artful contrivances, in his crimes and misdemeanors, he entertained the ambitious hopes to undermine our good opinion by the continual repetition of his calumnies, and to engage us to assist him in the destruction of *Tamaahmaah*, and the assumption of the government. But, on finding that his wishes for royalty and power were not to be gratified by our means, he experienced a disappointment that he had neither prudence to conceal, nor fortitude to support.

As we had now no further business at Owhyhee, we made the best of our way out of the bay; but calms and light baffling winds rendered our situation nearly stationary. This afforded some of the natives an opportunity of shewing their dexterity in catching a small kind of bonetto;[1] not only an amusing but a profitable employment. A small canoe is paddled as quick as possible by three or four people, whilst another is in the stern with a fishing rod, a very fine line, and a neat small hook; this hook passing swiftly through the water, is taken by the bonetto for a small fish, and to increase the deception, the angler is constantly throwing water about his hook with his hand, in order that it may be the less distinctly seen; so that almost the instant he throws it into the sea, it is taken by the bonetto. This mode of fishing was conducted with so much dexterity, that we saw great numbers taken, but did not observe one that had been hooked to escape. We were not only entertained with the sport, but it furnished an explanation of the general and rigid *taboo* all over the island at the time we arrived on the coast. It now appeared to have been in consequence of the season having commenced for the taking of these fish, which are exceedingly good to eat when fresh, and being caught in abundance, make a very considerable part of the food of the inhabitants when preserved and salted.

In the evening *Kahowmotoo* with all the natives took their leave, after assuring us of a continuance of their friendship, and expressing the highest satisfaction and happiness at our visit. Our two countrymen, Young and Davis, bid us also farewel with a degree of reluctance that did credit to their feelings.

It may not be improper to state in general terms, that I became perfectly convinced that the cause of these two men being left on shore at Owhyhee was not desertion, nor their own choice; nor did it arise from their having been dismissed by the commanders of vessels under whom they had served, for improper conduct and unruly behaviour; but from a series of events impossible to foresee or provide against. Their behaviour on the island had been meritorious in the highest sense of the word; supporting by their character (for they possessed nothing else) such a degree of consequence, that whilst it insured them the respect, it engaged the affections and regard, of the natives; and of no one more than of the king himself, who did not fail to listen to their counsel and advice; and I am well persuaded we had been much indebted for our very friendly and hospitable reception, as also for the orderly and civil behaviour we experienced from the generality of the inhabitants, by their attention to the instructions and example of these our countrymen.

That they might be encouraged to continue in the exercise of those virtuous principles which they had taught, I gave them a written testimonial of their good conduct;[2] and in the most serious manner enjoined them to persevere in the path that their own good understanding had pointed out; and at all times to be useful and assisting to the subjects of every civilized power, who

[1] The ocean bonito (aku).

[2] Dated 'Discovery, Toeyah Bay', 9 March 1793; printed in the appendix. Vancouver's letter is a testimonial for Kamehameha, his chiefs and his people, as well as for Young, Davis and Smith.

might resort to Owhyhee. From the king and the principal chiefs I obtained a promise of the continuance of their protection, not only to their persons, but to their property also; particularly, a large assortment of useful and necessary articles that I had given them, as well for their own comfort, and for the support of the consequence they had hitherto maintained, as for the purpose of introducing such things into use amongst the inhabitants.

I appointed to meet the king and his friends, with Young and Davis, on my return to the islands from the coast of America, in the bay between the east and north-east points of Owhyhee,[1] where I had been given to understand there was a commodious bay or port, that afforded secure and good anchorage.

The following astronomical observations made at Karakakooa, will conclude the narrative of our transactions during our stay at Owhyhee. This island we quitted about eight in the evening, and directed our course, close hauled, towards the east end of Mowee.

ASTRONOMICAL OBSERVATIONS.

On the 24th of February Kendall's chronometer shewed the longitude at the observatory to be, according to the Monterrey rate — 206° 17′ 15″

Arnold's on board the Chatham, do. — 203 39

Ditto, No. 14, ditto, ditto — 204 43 15

Ditto, No. 176, ditto, ditto — 204 10 15

Earnshaw's ditto, ditto — 203 27 30

On the 25th of February, Mr. Whidbey observed the immersion of Jupiter's first satellite, this gave the longitude, — 203 52 15

differing 7′ 45″ to the westward of the longitude by Captain Cook, and corresponding with that deduced by Mr. Bailey from two eclipses.

Latitudes of the observatory by six meridian altitudes of the sun corresponding with Captain Cook's — 19 28 12[2]

The following lunar observations for ascertaining the longitude were made for the purpose of shewing the agreement between our instruments and those of Captain Cook.

Mean of thirty-two sets taken by Mr. Whidbey, — 204 4 21

Mean of twenty sets taken by myself, — 203 52 27

Ditto sixteen sets taken by Mr. Orchard, — 203 51 52

---

[1] Hilo Bay.

[2] The correct lat. must have been about 19° 28′ 40″ N. The lat. of the bay is given officially as 19° 28′ N.

Mean of the above sixty-eight sets collectively
taken,   203 57 54[1]

But allowing the longitude, as settled by Captain
Cook, to be 204°, Kendall's chronometer in that case
appeared to be fast of mean time at Greenwich at
noon on the 4th of March,   1^h 42′ 27″ 23‴
And gaining per day at the rate of,   8 52
Arnold's on board the Chatham, fast of mean time
at Greenwich,   5 11 58 23
And gaining per day at the rate of,   35 59
Arnold's No. 14, fast of mean time at Greenwich,   1 24 20 23
And gaining per day at the rate of,   15 29
Arnold's No. 176, ditto ditto   3 42 14 23
And gaining per day at the rate of,   43 37
Earnshaw's, ditto ditto   1 22 36 23
And gaining per day at the rate of,   17 22
    The variation by four compasses in thirty-one sets
of azimuths, differing from 5° 47′ to 9° 47′, gave the
mean result,   7° 47′
    The vertical inclination of the magnetic needle,
Marked end, North face East   42° 35′
    Ditto ditto West   43 30
    Ditto South Face East   40 52
    Ditto ditto West   38 40

Mean inclination of the marine dipping needle, 41 24

---

[1] The correct long. would be about 155° 55′ 20″ W (204° 04′ 40″ E). The long. of the
bay is given officially as 155° 56′ W (204° 04′ E).

849

CHAPTER VII.

Arrive off Mowee—Particulars relative to the Murder of Lieutenant Hergest, Mr. Gooch, and others—Conversation respecting a Peace with Owhyhee—Reasons for sending the Chatham to Nootka—The Peace acceded to by the Chiefs—Information acquired by an Excursion of the Boats—Departure from Mowee.

BY day-light in the morning of Sunday the 10th of March we were well in with the eastern shores of Mowee, extending from S. 80 W. to N. 16 E. the nearest shore bore by compass N. 62 W. about a league distant. I was not certain whether the northernmost land thus seen formed the eastern extremity of Mowee or not, from the direction of the coast it so appeared, but its distance to windward of us was so great, that it would have required some time to have ascertained the fact, and as we could not accomplish the examination of both sides of the island on this occasion, I availed myself of the prevailing favorable breeze, and bore away along the coast about two miles from the shore. This took a direction S. 72 W. distant 16½ miles from hence to the south point of the island; which is according to our observations situated in latitude 20° 34′, longitude 203° 36.′[1]

Notwithstanding that the appearance of Mowee at a distance has been very accurately represented by Captain King; yet, as we had an opportunity of being better acquainted with this part of the island than those on board the Resolution or Discovery on that voyage, it may be useful to remark, that the part we were abreast of at day-light in the morning, though terminating very abruptly in the ocean, and though its surface was very uneven, had yet a verdant and fertile appearance, and was seemingly in an advanced state of cultivation. From the number of villages and distinct houses, we were led to consider it as tolerably well inhabited. This pleasant scene was shortly changed on our advancing a few miles to the westward. The face of the country became totally different, the shores and sides of the hills had no indications of being inhabited and were almost destitute of vegetable productions. They appeared to be a rude mass of naked barren rocks, broken into many deep gulleys, that extended from the mountains to the water side. Beside these, were many small circular hills that appeared to be composed either of sand or stones, and had acquired a very smooth surface of a light brown colour. Perpendicular veins

---

[1] Pohakueaea Point. Vancouver's position is very close to the official reading, lat. 20° 35′ N, long. 156° 23′ W (203° 37′ E).

separated the different strata, and descended down the mountains; these, so far as our glasses enabled us to distinguish, betokened this part of the island to have undergone some violent effects from volcanic eruptions.

We passed the south point before mentioned at the distance of about half a mile; it is formed by rugged craggy rocks, and the sea breaks at a little distance to the north west of it. On approaching these breakers we gained soundings, and suddenly decreased the depth of water from 25 to 10 fathoms rocky bottom; but, in hauling off shore, we almost instantly reached no bottom with 80 fathoms of line. Whilst in this situation, we were visited by a few of the poor natives from a small sandy cove, where they had some miserable habitations. The poverty of these people was apparent, by their bringing only a few small packages of salt to dispose of, and by their canoes being very small and out of repair. Two miles to the north-west of this point we were greatly inconvenienced by light baffling winds and calm weather, whilst without, or to the eastward of us, the trade wind blew strong. We continued to make a slow progress, and passed between Morokinney[1] and Tahowrowa.[2]

In the afternoon, we were visited by a chief in the only decent canoe we had yet seen at Mowee. From him I learned, that he was sent by *Titeeree*[3] to inquire who we were, and if we had friendly intentions towards the island. On his first question being answered, he seemed instantly to become suspicious of the motives of our visit, in consequence of the late murders at Woahoo. The reports that had been propagated respecting this unfortunate melancholy business, made me desirous of seeing *Titeeree* and *Taio*,[4] in order to obtain from them the real circumstances of this sad affair. This I communicated to the chief, and told him further, that if the offenders should prove to have been natives, those who were concerned should be given up to justice; but that neither *Titeeree* nor *Taio* should receive the least injury, if I found that they were innocent; and, as a pledge of my pacific disposition towards *Titeeree*, I returned by the chief such a present as I knew would be worthy his acceptance, and would be most likely to insure his confidence in my sincerity. I was not deficient in due acknowledgments to the messenger, in order to secure the faithful discharge of his embassy. He informed me, that the best anchorage was near the north-west part of the island, called Raheina,[5] and that if I would proceed thither, *Titeeree* would not hesitate, under this, and my other assurances of friendship, to pay us a visit. These I repeated again, and after telling him that I purposed to anchor near the spot he had pointed out, the chief departed, apparently much gratified with the execution of his commission.

Towards sun-set we passed to the south-west of Morokinney, and meeting

---

[1] Molokini Island. Spelled Morokume on the engraved chart.
[2] Kahoolawe Island. Spelled Tahoorowa on the chart.
[3] Kahekili.
[4] Kaeo.   [5] Lahaina roadstead.

there a light breeze from the N.E. we worked up into a large bay[1] on the south-west side of Mowee, lying before the low isthmus that unites the two large lofty bodies of land which compose the island. Here, about midnight, we anchored in 39 fathoms water, muddy bottom; and at day-light on Monday morning the 11th, found we had taken a station towards the eastern side of the bay. Morokinney, and the S.E. point of Tahowrowa in a line, bearing by compass S. 11 E.; the south point of Mowee S. 39 E.; the nearest shore E. by N. two miles, and the westernmost part of Mowee in sight N. 56 W.

The appearance of this side of Mowee was scarcely less forbidding than that of its southern parts, which we had passed the preceding day. The shores, however, were not so steep and rocky, and were mostly composed of a sandy beach; the land did not rise so very abruptly from the sea towards the mountains, nor was its surface so much broken with hills and deep chasms; yet the soil had little appearance of fertility, and no cultivation was to be seen. A few habitations were promiscuously scattered near the water side, and the inhabitants who came off to us, like those seen the day before, had little to dispose of.

The weather was cloudy, and the wind at the station we had taken was very unpleasant, in consequence of the trade wind from the N.E. reaching us at intervals in furious squalls, over the low land of the isthmus. A strong current setting to the S.E. at the same time, obliged us to remain at anchor, and wait for a more favorable opportunity to proceed.

About noon we had the company of a chief named *To-mo-ho-mo-ho*,[2] who said he was younger brother to *Titeeree*, and that he had come by his orders to conduct us to the best anchorage at Raheina, where *Titeeree* himself would shortly meet us. *Tomohomoho* produced a certificate from Mr. Brown of the Butterworth, recommending him as a very useful, friendly, and honest man. His canoe was a very fine one; this he requested might be towed a-stern of the ship, which he recommended should get under sail that we might arrive before dark at Raheina; but in the event of any delay, directions had been given for fires to be made in such situations, as would enable him to place the ship with security.

As the wind and weather were more settled, these requests were complied with; and thus, provided with a pilot, the Chatham and ourselves stood across the bay under double reefed topsails, until we had shut in the isthmus; when the high land intercepting the current of the trade wind, the gale was succeeded by light baffling airs. With these, and the assistance of the lights on the shores, we arrived at our destination about half past eight in the evening, when we anchored in 25 fathoms water, on a bottom of sand, stones, and coral.

The next morning, Tuesday the 12th, we discovered our situation to be in the place pointed out in our former visit to these islands by Mr. Broughton, who then mentioned another anchoring place in Mowee, a little to the

[1] Maalaea Bay.   [2] Kamohomoho.

southward of a remarkable round hill, on a sandy beach, projecting its rocky base into the sea. Its top, having the appearance of a crater, acquired the name of VOLCANO HILL.[1] It lies N. 26 W., about a league from the south point of Mowee, directly opposite to the barren and uninhabited islet of Morokinney, which lies something more than two miles from the shore of that bay. Here Mr. Broughton had found regular soundings from 25 to 15 and 7 fathoms, within half a mile of the beach, sandy bottom. The beach, about half a mile long, appeared very convenient for landing upon; but I was given to understand, by our pilot and others of the natives, that good water was not to be procured even in small quantities within a considerable distance, and that its neighbourhood was very barren and thinly inhabited.

In this roadstead we were pretty well protected by the surrounding land, excepting toward the S.S.W.; in which direction the wind seldom, if ever, blows violently. The Volcano hill bore by compass S. 54 E.; Morokinney S. 46 E.; Tahowrowa from S. 35 E. to S. 7 E.; Rannai[2] from S. 54 W. to N. 78 W.; the westernmost part of Morotoi[3] in sight N. 66 W.; and of two low projecting points of land from the shore of Mowee forming the points of the roadstead, the northernmost bore N. 26 W., distant four miles and a half; the southernmost, S. 64 E. distant five miles; and the nearest shore N.E. by E., half a league distant.

The village of Raheina is of some extent towards the north-west part of the roadstead; it seemed to be pleasantly situated on a space of low, or rather gently elevated land, in the midst of a grove of bread-fruit, cocoa-nut, and other trees; to the eastward, the country seemed nearly barren and uncultivated, and the shores were bounded by a reef, on which the surf seemed to break with so much force as to preclude any landing with our boats. In the village, the houses seemed to be numerous, and to be well inhabited. A few of the natives visited the ships; these brought but little with them,[4] and most of them were in very small miserable canoes. These circumstances strongly indicated their poverty, and proved what had been frequently asserted at Owhyhee, that Mowee, and its neighbouring islands, were reduced to great indigence by the wars, in which for many years they had been engaged.

Our native pilot seemed very proud of the confidence we had reposed on his skill, in conducting the ship to this anchorage; and that the situation he had chosen in the night now met our approbation. From the moment of

---

[1] Puu Kanaloa, on the NW side of La Perouse Bay.

[2] Lanai. Spelled Ranai on the chart.   [3] Molokai.

[4] Both Bell and Puget commented on the conduct of the native traders: 'though we traded with these people very largely, and very liberally, yet we could perceive a wonderful difference between their behaviour, and that of the people of Owhyee, some of the lower class were inclined to be insolent, and to endeavour to cheat us in the most barefaced manner, such as filling their Calabashes with Saltwater, along side, and attempting to sell it...' – 13 March. Puget commented: 'some of the lower Class were rather inclined to be insolent which receiving a proper Check in its Infancy had the desired Effect for the greatest good Order was afterwards preserved during the remainder of our Stay.' – 13 March.

his coming on board, he had pleaded the cause of *Titeree* and *Taio* with all his eloquence, and gave a positive contradiction to the reports in circulation, of the murders having been premeditated by them at Woahoo, and committed by their express orders, for the sole purpose of revenging a difference that had happened between them and Mr. Ingraham. These reports, he said, he was well aware prevailed at Owhyhee; but he denied them in the most positive terms, and asserted, that the conduct of the people at Woahoo, instead of being sanctioned by their chief, had incurred his highest displeasure; and that *Titeeree* on being informed of the event, sent immediate orders that the offenders should be put to death; and that in consequence of these orders three men, who were principally concerned, had been executed.

This led me to inquire of *Komohomoho*, if three people only had been implicated in that barbarous transaction? To this he replied, that there were three or four more considered as equally guilty; but that these had found means to escape, and had fled to the mountains, where they had eluded their pursuers for such a length of time, that any further search had been discontinued, and the offence had blown over, and was nearly forgotten.

I had understood at Owhyhee, that three of the principal offenders concerned in the murder had been put to death by the orders of *Titeeree*; and if we revert to the circumstances attending our visit in last March, several months subsequent to the dispute with Mr. Ingraham, it is more than probable, that had any such sanguinary directions, as have been already mentioned, been issued by *Titeeree*, they must have been equally in force at the time we were there, as on the arrival of the Dædalus not long after our departure. And though I must confess, that our reception at Woahoo did not impress me with the most exalted opinion of their friendly and hospitable intentions, yet, they did not appear to use any means of carrying such orders into effect; although they had frequent opportunities in the course of our walks through the plantations, where they could easily have interrupted our retreat. But, admitting that the people of Woahoo were under such injunctions, as some have pretended, and that we were indebted for our preservation to the small force that attended us, or because that day was 'taboo poory,'[1] or a day of rest and prayer; yet these arguments would be insufficient on many accounts; for they could not be reconciled with the friendly, trusty, and honorable conduct pursued by the chiefs and people on our visit to Attowai,[2] particularly on the evening of our departure. Such behaviour towards us could not possibly have been observed by a people who were under orders from their king, to kill every white man who might come within their power.

These circumstances duly considered, render it more than probable, that *Titeeree* and *Taio* were innocent of the contrivance, and not concerned in the perpetration of the murders at Woahoo.

The different mercantile people who had visited these islands since that

[1] Kapu pule in modern Hawaiian.
[2] Kauai. Spelled Atooi on Vancouver's chart.

unfortunate period, had taught the natives to apprehend the horror and detestation with which we regard unprovoked assassination. They had apprized them of the difference between our ships, and the trading vessels that had touched here for refreshments; that we acted, not from the orders of any private individual, but under the special authority of our sovereign, who had given me power to take cognizance of all such circumstances, and to requite the barbarity of the natives with the severest punishment.

No hint whatever of this nature had ever escaped my lips, since the moment I had to deplore the melancholy transaction. I was nevertheless fully determined in my own mind not to omit making every enquiry, nor to suffer the crime to pass unnoticed; and, at the same time, to pursue such measures, as might appear most likely to prevent in future such unpardonable and savage proceedings.

To the minds of the natives it now appeared a matter of great national concern; and in that point of view it was considered of such importance, as to demand from me the most particular investigation, and the most serious attention.

Being thus fortunately possessed of so much essential information from *Tomohomoho*, I considered myself to be fully provided to meet *Titeeree* on this distressful subject, especially as I had heard with great satisfaction from *Tomohomoho*, that the unfortunate commander of the Dædalus and his party had been guilty of no offence whatever, to provoke the untimely fate they had so unjustly met.

I now came to a determination of insisting with *Titeeree*, that the remaining offenders should be brought to justice: not by any measures of force in our power, but by their own means. That, on their conviction the cause of their punishment should be clearly and satisfactorily made known to the islanders, with assurances that no distance of time would in future secure any from detection, or prevent the punishment which such crimes demand.

A pusillanimous conduct on an occasion of this nature, could not fail to sink the character of Europeans into the lowest contempt; and atrocities would become more frequent, either to satisfy the passions of the avaricious or licentious, or the revenge of any individual, who might think proper to take umbrage if not indulged in every whim that his fancy might dictate; to the disgrace of human nature, and the destruction of the adventurers engaged in the commerce of the North Pacific Ocean.

In undertaking to negociate a peace on a firm and broad basis, between Owhyhee and all the contiguous islands, my views were directed to the advantage, as well as to the general happiness, of the inhabitants on all the islands. The new impressions my mind had received, tended to convince me of the important necessity for such a measure, were it only to recover the people of Mowee from the deplorable condition to which they had been reduced by an eleven years war; and, notwithstanding that they had not fought a single battle during the last two years, yet the detriment sustained by the contending parties was almost equally great. To guard their respective dominions, *Tamaahmaah* on the western parts of Owhyhee, and *Titeeree* on the eastern side of Mowee, had each assembled a large body of men. By these means, not only those parts were greatly impoverished and exhausted of supplies for the maintenance of those forces, but the inhabitants being drawn from their homes in the different districts of the country, the land was necessarily neglected, and the produce of the soil was lost for want of people to carry on its cultivation. The war, and the vast supplies that the half famished trading vessels had recently drawn from some of these islands, had left a very scanty portion for the remaining inhabitants of Mowee, and the other islands under the authority of *Titeeree* and *Taio*. This information was communicated to me by several respectable chiefs at Owhyhee, and was now fully confirmed by *Tomohomoho*, particularly as to Mowee and Morotoi; he stated these as having been the principal seats of *Tamaahmaah*'s wars, and that Rannai and Tohowrowa, which had formerly been considered as fruitful and populous islands, were nearly over-run with weeds, and exhausted of their inhabitants; nor had Owhyhee escaped the devastation consequent on her foreign and intestine disputes, which had been numerous and severe.

Every hour produced some new intelligence, to convince me of the necessity of bringing, if it were possible, to an immediate conclusion, the ambitious pretensions of these sovereigns; being now decidedly of opinion, that a continuation of such commotions would soon desolate these islands, and render them incapable of affording those abundant and excellent supplies we had constantly derived, and without which the English traders would be ill qualified to maintain the commerce of north-west America. Whereas, if peace could be happily established, and the inhabitants be prevailed upon to be satisfied, and to live in harmony and good fellowship with each other, they would readily return to their habitations, and to their former employments, of cultivating the land, and the other arts of peace. These occupations would be immediately resumed with great energy; and the ability of procuring European commodities, for the purpose of imitating our manners and fashions, by the produce of their own labour and ingenuity, would stimulate them to an industry and exertion, that would be attended with so abundant an increase of productions, as would render the supplies of these islands almost inexhaustible; especially, as the breed of black cattle, sheep, and goats, already introduced, when established under such happy circumstances, would soon greatly increase.

These ideas I communicated to *Tomohomoho*, who listened to them with the greatest attention, and expressed much pleasure in looking forward to so happy an event; and assured me, that *Titeeree* and *Taio* would gladly accede to the measures I had to propose, but that *Tahowmotoo* and *Tianna* were not to be trusted.

In the forenoon we were visited by a young man, a citizen of the American states, who said that he had deserted about three months before, from the same

American vessel that Smith (whom we found at Owhyhee) had left, in consequence of the ill treatment received from his commander. That he was now in the service of *Titeeree*, and his principal business was to visit such ships as might arrive at the island, and to order them such supplies of wood, water, and refreshments, as they might have occasion for, without their commanders having the trouble of bartering with the natives; and that on the departure of such vessels, some small acknowledgment to *Titeeree* the king only was expected. That in virtue of his appointment, he had done us the favour of issuing his directions to this effect. We afterwards found, however, that his authority as purveyor had been unjustly assumed, and that his orders were issued to no purpose.[1] He likewise stated, that he was directed by *Titeeree* to acquaint me, that he was on his way towards the ship; but that his age and infirmities prevented him from travelling otherwise than very slowly. This message made me entertain some suspicion that the king had doubts of my sincerity; and I therefore desired that *Tomohomoho* would either go himself, or send some trusty person, to dispel any groundless apprehension that *Titeeree* might be under. To this request he instantly replied, with a smile, that *Titeeree*, conscious of his own innocence with respect to the offence committed at Woahoo, would have no sort of objection to trust himself in our power; and that he, *Tomohomoho*, had received positive directions to remain with us until the arrival of the king, to prevent any improper behaviour of the natives. All this was corroborated by a chief named *Namahanna*,[2] who, with his wife, were far the handsomest couple we had seen on these islands. He was next in consequence to *Titeeree*, and possessed at that time in Mowee almost the sovereign power over its inhabitants. Of these but few visited us, who brought nothing to dispose of, excepting such articles as our people deemed curiosities. They conducted themselves with great propriety, and the little traffic that was entered into, was carried on with the greatest honesty.

On Wednesday afternoon the 13th, we were honoured with the presence of *Titeeree*, who I was given to understand was considered as the king of all the islands to leeward of Owhyhee; and that from him *Taio* derived his authority.

There seemed, however, nothing in his character or appearance to denote so high a station, nor was his arrival attended by any accumulation in the number of the natives on the shores, or in the canoes about the vessels. He came boldly alongside, but entered the ship with a sort of partial confidence, accompanied by several chiefs who constantly attended him; his age I supposed must have exceeded sixty; he was greatly debilitated and emaciated; and, from

---

[1] Bell had not been impressed: 'From this man's appearance and manners I should conceive him the most unfit man in the world to be left among those Indians, that is, under the general idea of a European being of benefit to them – for he seemed to be a very thick headed stupid fellow, and if I mistake not widely, of a very indolent disposition...' – March. Bell confirms that, like Smith, he had deserted from the American brig *Eliza*.

[2] Misprinted Tamahanna in the second edition.

the colour of his skin, I judged his feebleness to have been brought on by an excessive use of the ava. His faultering voice bespoke the decline of life; and his countenance, though furrowed by his years and irregularities, still preserved marks of his having been, in his juvenile days, a man of pleasing and cheerful manners, with a considerable degree of sensibility, which the iron hand of time had not yet entirely obliterated.

Amongst the articles I presented to *Titeeree* on this occasion, was a cloak, similar to those I had given *Tamaahmaah*; this highly delighted him; and he was also well pleased with the other presents he received. In proportion to their rank, and the situations they held, his whole suite were complimented, and all seemed well satisfied with their visit.

After a short conversation respecting the stay I purposed to make at Mowee, and islands to leeward, with other miscellaneous matters, I introduced the subject of a peace with Owhyhee, and was attended to with great earnestness; not only by the king, but by the whole of his attendants, who seemed unanimously desirous for the accomplishment of so beneficial an object, and a measure so important to their future happiness and tranquillity. They appeared to be perfectly convinced of my good intentions as a mediator; but the same want of confidence prevailed here as at Owhyhee. They all agreed, that no faith could be reposed in the integrity of the Owhyhean chiefs; and that if peace was again restored, the several chiefs who had been assembled in Mowee for their general protection, would retire to their respective islands; and Mowee and its dependencies would be again left open to the invasion of *Tamaahmaah*, whose unconquerably ambitious spirit, they said, would not allow him to neglect so favorable an opportunity. I endeavoured to combat these prejudices by every argument I could make use of, and assured them, that I firmly believed that *Tamaahmaah*, and the people of Owhyhee, were as desirous of peace as they could possibly be; that the king was sincere, and that I was convinced he would most religiously abide by such conditions as might be mutually approved. Our deliberations however drawing to no conclusion, it was agreed to adjourn the subject until the arrival of *Taio* from Morotoi, who was expected in the course of the following day.

The royal party appearing to be perfectly satisfied of our friendly intentions, I demanded of *Titeeree*, what offence had been committed by the late Mr. Hergest, and Mr. Gooch, to occasion their having been put to death? To this question they all replied, that neither of those gentlemen, nor any other person belonging to the Dædalus, had, to their knowledge, been guilty of any offence whatever. I then requested to know, what was the reason of their having been murdered without any provocation on their part; and who was the chief that gave orders for that purpose, or that was by any other means the cause of their losing their lives? This question was also answered by the solemn declaration of the whole party, that there was no chief present on that melancholy occasion; nor was any chief in the least degree concerned; but that the murder was committed by a lawless set of ill-minded men; and that the instant *Titeeree* had become acquainted with the transaction, he had ordered all those who had been principally concerned to be put to death; and in consequence of his direction, three of the offenders had suffered that punishment. I then desired to know if three people only had been concerned? The king then replied, that many were present at the time, but that only three or four more were concerned in the murder; who would likewise have suffered death, had they not found means to escape to the mountains, where they had secreted themselves for some time; but that he understood they had returned, and were now living on or near an estate belonging to *Tomohomoho.* These protestations corresponding with the evidence before related, induced me to give credit to the asserted innocence of the chiefs, and the guilt of the persons criminated by them. As punishment ought to fall on those alone, I demanded that three or four, who were known to have been principals in the horrid act, should be sought, and punished according to the heinousness of their crime; not by us, but by themselves, without the least interference on our part. And that as the punishment of the murderers might be made as public and impressive as possible, I recommended that it should take place alongside of the ship, in the presence of the natives; and that the spectators, as well as all the absent inhabitants of the several islands, under the jurisdiction of *Titeeree,* or the inferior chiefs, should be made thoroughly acquainted, that the criminals had been punished for having been guilty of murder, or for aiding and assisting therein, and for that crime only: and that in future, neither chiefs, nor private individuals, who might commit such acts of barbarity, should be excused, or escape similar punishment, be the distance of time ever so great, so long as the offending parties had life, or the English continued to visit these islands.

These propositions met not the smallest opposition, but on the contrary, much to the credit and honor of the whole party, were readily and cheerfully agreed to in every particular. This being the case, I desired that a chief might be appointed to attend us, for the purpose of carrying these resolutions into effect, and causing justice to be properly executed. After a short consultation, *Titeeree* nominated *Tomohomoho,* and invested him with due authority, not only for this function, but for the supplying of our wants, as far as the country might be able to afford.

Being desirous that a more minute survey of this side of Mowee should be made in the boats, I acquainted *Titeeree* with my wishes; and in order that thefts, or other improper behaviour, might not be experienced from the different islanders they might meet, I requested that a chief should be appointed to attend the expedition. *Titeeree* replied, that the orders he had issued were sufficient to answer every purpose; but that if I was particularly desirous of the attendance of a chief, *Tomohomoho* should undertake the charge. Matters being thus arranged, Mr. Whidbey received my directions to proceed on this service in our cutter, accompanied by that of the Chatham;[1] which took place accordingly early the next morning.

In the forenoon of Thursday the 14th, we were again favored with the

---

[1] Manby, at this time master of the *Chatham,* was in charge of her boat.

company of *Titeeree* and his party. Whilst our boats were engaged in the survey, Mr. Menzies wished to make an excursion into the country; and on his desire being made known to the king, together with mine, that a chief might be appointed to accompany him who should be answerable for the behaviour of the natives, *Tomowha*, the chief of the district, [1] with a young chief called *Tea-ow-whan-nee*, [2] were accordingly nominated for his guides and protectors.

This young chief was one of the king's sons; he appeared to be about fifteen years of age, was well made, and had a pleasing, sensible, and open countenance. If the American sailor's information could be depended upon, this young prince was invested with very considerable power and authority. Thus guarded, Mr. Menzies, with two or three of the gentlemen and the American sailor, set out, relying with confidence upon the declaration of the king, for experiencing every civility and attention they could possibly require. [3]

Titeeree, considering himself under an obligation to make some return for the handsome present he had received, brought me four small lean hogs, with a few vegetables; accompanying them with many apologies, stating that his poverty prevented him from making such acknowledgments, as his inclination directed, or his situation demanded. The present reduced condition of the island, and consequently of his wealth, had been wholly occasioned, he said, by the ravage of *Tamaahmaah*'s forces, who, not content with the vast quantity of provisions consumed during their stay in these islands, nor with loading their canoes with the productions of the soil, had laid waste the lands on all sides, broken the fences of the plantations, thrown down the banks of the little canals made for watering the crops, which were torn up by the roots; and that all the hogs, dogs, and fowls, that could not be carried away, were killed, or dispersed over the country.

Such was the deplorable account he related of the distressed situation of Mowee, and the neighbouring islands. This had hitherto so humbled and

[1] Kamauoha, chief of Lahaina.

[2] Koalaulani. Menzies gives his name as Toowhennee and states that he was 'a boy eleven or twelve years old'.

[3] Menzies described the expedition in his journal. He had hoped to cross the island, but found travelling too slow and difficult. He was much impressed by the way in which 'the rugged banks of a large rivulet' that came out of a chasm were 'cultivated & watered with great neatness & industry, even the shelving cliffs of Rocks were planted with esculent roots, banked in & watered by aqueducts from the Rivulet with as much art as if their level had been taken by the most ingenious Engineer....The indefatigable labor in making these little fields in so rugged a situation, the care & industry with which they were transplanted waterd & kept in order surpassed any thing of the kind we had ever seen before...' – 14 March. But botanically he had mixed fortune: 'I was here equally unfortunate in not finding at this season of the year many of them [the plants] either in flower or seed; what I did find however in a perfect state were quite new & undescribed by any Botanist whatever, which amply compensated any labor & fatigue & the danger to which I frequently exposed myself in collecting them.' – 15 March.

broken the spirit of the people, that little exertion had been made to restore these islands to their accustomed fertility by cultivation; and they were at that time under the necessity of collecting provisions from Woahoo and Attowai, for the maintenance of their numerous army on the eastern parts of the island. I expressed my concern for the calamitous state of his dominions, and took that opportunity of again pointing out the beneficial consequences that would result from a peace with *Tamaahmaah*; and that nothing short of this could remove or repair those serious disasters of which he so justly complained. And as I considered that the present he had brought me, though in itself small, might possibly have put him to inconvenience, I desired it might be returned; but at the same time I assured the king, that his inability to afford me a greater quantity of refreshments, would not in the least degree influence my conduct in promoting the welfare of himself and his people, or induce me to withhold such articles as would be of real utility to him.

In the afternoon we were visited by *Taio*, who presented me with a feathered cloak; and in return, amongst other valuables, I presented him with one of scarlet cloth, which in a very short time he gave to his eldest brother and sovereign, *Titeeree*. On my asking the reason for so hasty a disposal of it, he replied, that the old king was only taking care of it for *Taio*; but I afterwards understood, that it was a sort of care that would free *Taio* from any further trouble in the possession.

The day was too far advanced to enter at large on the interesting negociation I had set on foot. I briefly pointed out to *Taio* the outline of the business, and was happy to find, that the idea of a peace with Owhyhee seemed to afford him more pleasure and satisfaction, than had been expressed by any other chief to whom this proposal had been communicated. After a short conversation, he observed, that we had formerly been very great friends when I was at Attowai with Captain Cook and Captain Clerke, that he still retained a very great regard for me, and hoped we should both remain in the same sentiments towards each other. That, as a proof of the sincerity of his friendship, he had still in his possession a lock of my hair, which I had given him at that period, when at the same time I refused a similar pledge to *Enemo*, and several other chiefs, who were present on that occasion. This story, corresponding exactly with what I had heard from *Tianna* and *Enemo* the preceding year, induced me to ask where the lock of hair was? To this *Taio* replied, that it was on shore, with some other valuable testimonies of friendship, that constantly attended him in his travels or campaigns; and that he would bring it with him in the morning.[1]

---

[1] Menzies had known Taio (Kaeo) well during his previous visit to the islands: 'In him I was happy to meet an old friend to whose hospitality & kind offices I had been formerly under many obligations at a time when it was not in my power to repay him with any adequate return: To shew him however that I still entertained a gratefull sense of these obligations & his great merit, I instantly on his coming on board exposed every little treasure I now possessed to his view, & entreated him to select whatever was most gratifying or useful to him, which he did, & amongst several other things, a piece of red cloth for

The circumstance of the hair having before been frequently mentioned to me, had made me endeavour to recal the person of this former friend to my remembrance; and on recollection, I suspected that *Taio* must have been a young chief, at that time about eighteen years of age, who had made me several presents, and who had given me many other instances of his friendly attention. But, to my great surprize, on his entering the cabin, I beheld him far advanced in years, seemingly about fifty; and though evidently a much younger man than *Titeeree*, yet nearly reduced to the same state of debility. If he were in reality the person I had considered him to have been, I must have been much mistaken with respect to his age on our former acquaintance; or the intemperature of that pernicious intoxicating plant the ava, which he took in great quantities, assisted by the toils of long and fatiguing wars, have combined to bring upon him a premature old age. Notwithstanding these appearances of the decline of life, his countenance was animated with great quickness and sensibility, and his behaviour was affable and courteous. His inquiries were of the most sagacious nature, respecting matters of useful information. The shrewdness of his understanding, his thirst to acquire and wish to communicate, useful, interesting, or entertaining knowledge, sufficiently indicated a very active mind, and did not fail to impress us with a very favourable opinion of his general character. *Taio* and his party remained on board until near dark, when they took their leave for the night, carrying with them such presents as were suitable to their several ranks and situations.

The bottom of the Chatham having been examined by diving, it was discovered that some of the copper had been torn off when she accidentally got on shore, sailing out of Nootka. On this representation from Mr. Puget, I deemed it expedient that no time should be lost in replacing the copper, and having the bottom thoroughly examined, lest some more important damage might have been sustained. For this specific purpose, I gave orders that the instant her supplies of wood and water were completed, she should proceed to Nootka, and I directed Mr. Puget, on his departure from hence, to examine the north side of Morotoi; as it was my design, in visiting the other islands belonging to this group, to pass along its southern side.

The next morning, Friday 15th, my old friend *Taio* was amongst the earliest of our visitors, and brought with him the lock of hair. It was tied carefully round at the bottom, where it was neatly decorated with some red feathers, and appeared to have been well preserved, and held in some degree of estimation. The colour corresponding with that of my own, tended to prove its identity.

The preservation of this memorial exhibited a striking instance of similarity in the human mind, by shewing the same pledge of friendship that exists in

a long robe was highly acceptable to him.... When the ship Prince of Wales was at Atooi about five years ago, Taio was a great favourite both with the Officers and Crew for his kind attention & friendly behaviour towards them...' – 16 March. Menzies' friendship with Taio doubtless aided Vancouver in his negotiations for a peace settlement.

the civilized and polished states of the world, to be held equally in estimation by the untaught inhabitants of these distant regions. These customs must certainly arise from principles innate and common to the species; since, at the time that *Taio* solicited and received that token of my regard, it was not possible that he should have acquired the idea from any European or other civilized person. This was one amongst innumerable instances, that occurred in our acquaintance with the uncultivated world, which served to shew the analogy of the several passions and affections, that, under every colour, clime, or in every stage of civilization, govern the human heart.

On this occasion, I could not help feeling some internal humiliation at the superiority which the steadiness of *Taio*'s friendship had gained over me; by preserving the lock of my hair; by retaining, after an absence of fourteen or fifteen years, a perfect recollection of my name; and by recounting the various incidents, and the several acts of reciprocal kindness and friendship that had taken place in our former acquaintance. All these he seemed to remember with the greatest pleasure; but all these had been long oblitered from my memory.

I trust, that my wish to pay some tribute to *Taio*'s unshaken friendship, will be my excuse for the insertion of this otherwise unimportant subject.

In the forenoon, the king, with *Taio*, *Namahanna*, and such other chiefs as were necessary to the occasion, being assembled in the cabin, the negociation for peace was again resumed, and the subject was discussed with much warmth amongst themselves. All their arguments tended to prove, that peace was an object of their most earnest desire, but that they doubted the possibility of obtaining its blessings, because they could place no confidence in the fidelity of *Tamaahmaah*. This prejudice I endeavoured to do away by all my former arguments; and, in addition, I pointed out that peace was an object as important, and as much desired in Owhyhee as in Mowee and its dependencies: that this could not be disputed, as the king and chiefs of Owhyhee would not have solicited my interference and good offices to accomplish this happy undertaking, had they not been instigated by these weighty reasons.

Taio however was decidedly of opinion, that peace could not be obtained, unless I would return to Owhyhee; being convinced, that *Tamaahmaah* would place no reliance on any message, that should be sent from them by any of their chiefs. I told them, it was impossible for me to accede to their wishes in this respect, but that I would adopt other measures which would in effect answer the same purpose, provided they were in earnest, and would faithfully abide by the stipulations I had made with *Tamaahmaah*, and the chiefs of Owhyhee. These I had communicated to them, and in addition had recommended that they should by all means forget, if possible, but certainly forgive, all past enmities, and the occasions of them; all injuries and insults; and discourage by every effort in their power, all animosities, disputes, and wrangling, between the subjects of *Titeeree* and those of *Tamaahmaah*. And as great intemperance in the support of the question, which of these kings was the greatest and most powerful monarch, was a grievance much complained of on both sides, and had given rise to much ill blood and contention amongst the people of the different governments; it became a matter of infinite consequence, that such conversations should be immediately prohibited. When these preparatory measures had undergone due consideration, and had been adjusted by both parties, an intercourse of confidence and friendship, I alledged, would naturally take place between the present contending powers; and such measures would be then agreed upon, as would seem to be best calculated to secure a permanent good understanding, and most beneficial to their respective interests. After repeating to them the happy consequences that would result from so wise, humane and political a measure, in the same manner as I had represented them to *Tamaahmaah*, both *Taio* and *Namahanna*, but particularly *Taio*, with respectful formality, questioned me as to the sincerity of my views in thus strongly recommending these peaceful overtures. They desired to know the reason, why the advice I gave was so directly opposite to that of the several commanders, and people of the trading vessels, who for some time past had been their constant visitors? who had uniformly recommended a continuance of the war with Owhyhee; had pointed out the numerous advantages they would obtain; and had supplied them with arms and ammunition, for the express purpose of carrying that advice into execution. To these interrogatories I had no mode of replying, but by producing facts that were completely within their own knowledge and observation. I stated, that such advice did not come from friends, but from persons interested, not in their happiness and welfare, but in their own aggrandizement; who, having brought with them to these countries a large assortment of arms and ammunition, as articles of trade, would be great losers by such ventures, were the inhabitants of the different islands to remain in peace and unanimity with each other; that under the happy circumstances proposed, these engines of destruction would soon fall into low estimation; that therefore it was not surprizing, if animosity, revenge, and war were recommended, in order to enhance the value of these commodities, and by that means secure a larger supply of refreshments. That my pursuit was of a very different character they must have been well convinced, by the nature of the articles they had received, either as presents from me, or in exchange for the several productions of their country; which were such as were ornamental to their persons, or really instrumental to their welfare. That one of my most favourite objects was, to render them such services, on all occasions, as my situation could afford. Of this they would be convinced, should they think proper to adopt the pacific measures I had proposed; in which case, I would communicate their content, by writing to the Englishman residing at Owhyhee with *Tamaahmaah*. On the receipt of this, I alledged, a council of the chiefs whould be immediately assembled, and in the presence of a chief to be appointed by *Titeeree*, and entrusted with the charge of this important commission, *Tamaahmaah*, and the chiefs of Owhyhee, would solemnly agree to, and faithfully abide by the peace, on the terms already mentioned. And that further, to secure the performance of the promises made to me at Owhyhee, I would threaten to withdraw the friendship and good will I entertained towards that Island, in case the king and the chiefs should refuse to ratify their engagement.

Having thus explained to *Titeeree* and his friends, my wishes, and motives for the advancement of their happiness and welfare, I left them at full liberty either to embrace the blessings and advantages of peace, or to continue in their present calamitous state of warfare and hostility.

After a short consultation with each other, they unanimously declared for peace.

Without any solicitation on my part, *Taio* requested that, on my return to these islands, I would take him to Owhyhee, where, under my protection, he would, in person, treat with *Tamaahmaah*, in order that a lasting peace might be concluded, and an amicable intercourse established between Owhyhee and all the islands; and he desired that these his intentions might be made known to *Tamaahmaah*. This was accordingly done in my letter to Owhyhee on this subject, which was to be intrusted to a sensible and careful chief; who, impowered with sufficient authority, was immediately to proceed to Owhyhee, in order to negociate this desirable business with *Tamaahmaah*.

The execution of this embassy was allotted to a chief named *Martier*;[1] a man, whose first appearance and deportment were likely to make unfavourable impressions; but whose real character, I understood, was that of a shrewd sensible fellow; and though his countenance was ferocious, yet he was remarkable for the mildness and evenness of his disposition. In all our conferences he was a principal speaker, and from the great attention paid by *Titeeree* and *Taio* to what he said, it was evident that his abilities were in great estimation.

This favourite object being so far attained, I embraced the opportunity of a full assembly, to advert again to the inhuman murder at Woahoo. On this occasion I was stopped, rather hastily, by *Titeeree*, who observed, that that business was already settled; that they had full confidence in my assertions, and that I ought not to doubt them!

Having considered a general restoration of tranquillity to these islands, and the punishment of the criminals at Woahoo, to be matters of the first importance to the safety and interests of the commercial adventurers in this ocean, they had for some time past occupied much of my attention. The prospect of the one being happily accomplished, and of the other being executed with justice, afforded my mind no small degree of satisfaction; and as, by the survey on which our boats were employed, I should obtain a perfect knowledge of the shores of this island, the principal objects that had induced my visit hither, seemed to promise a successful termination.

As neither hogs nor other refreshments could be procured, I was anxious to quit this station. *Titeeree* and his counsellors were made acquainted that I

---

[1] Possibly Makia.

intended so to do, on the return of the boats, which were expected the next morning; when, agreeably to their earnest request, I purposed to pay them a visit on shore, whilst the ship was preparing for her departure.

They expressed much concern at the shortness of our stay, and some surprise that we should so suddenly take our leave. This I explained was occasioned by the necessity I was under to visit other distant countries, and not from any disinclination, or want of friendship for them, as they had supposed. With this reason they became perfectly satisfied, but hoped, as I could pay them only one visit on shore, that it might be deferred until Sunday morning, because the next day was *taboo poory*, and it would be impossible for them to receive us as they could wish. They eagerly intreated me to remain until that time, when they would repair to the ship and accompany me on shore. The fame of our fire-works had reached Mowee, and they added to this request an earnest desire, that their curiosity might be gratified in this respect. *Taio* in particular was very pressing in his solicitations, and as it was our first visit to these chiefs, whose friendship and good opinion I much wished to cultivate, I was induced to comply with their wishes; especially as I was now satisfied that I had sufficient time for the business I had to transact this season at the other islands, and to join the Chatham at Nootka, long before she would be ready to proceed with us to the northward.

The chiefs having succeeded in their wishes the whole party seemed excessively happy, and returned to the shore for the purpose of attending their religious ceremonies.

In the evening, Mr. Menzies with his party returned from the mountains, having received the greatest civility and attention from such of the natives as they had met with during their excursion; and the next morning, Saturday the 16th, Mr. Whidbey arrived on board, after completing the examination of the shores on this side of Mowee.

The Chatham's cutter was sent on board, and Mr. Puget, agreeably to my directions, sailed for Nootka, passing between the west end of Mowee and the east part of Morotoi.[1]

Mr. Whidbey resumed his survey round the west point of Mowee; which service he performed, and returned in the evening.

Before I close the narrative of our proceedings on this station, I shall state the result of the information obtained in Mr. Whidbey's excursion.

During the first day the boats did not advance more than seven miles along

[1] Puget describes the survey of the N shore of Molokai: 'I never witnessed so Barren and desolate an appearance as the North Side of this Island afforded....After Running about four Leagues we came off a low Rocky Point [Kahiu Point] projecting from the line of the Shore about a Mile between this Point and the East Extreme were two Places bearing some Appearance of Bays but...I am certain neither will be hereafter found to afford Anchorage for Shipping, as the NE Wind must blow directly into them....By noon we reached the West Point, perfectly satisfied of their being no safe Anchorage on this side of Morotoi...' – 17 March. U.S. *Coast Pilot 7* agrees: 'the N coast is exposed and offers very little protection.' The only traffic along it is a twice-yearly supply barge.

the shore, in a direction N. 60 E. to a place called by the natives Patoa,[1] and reached even that with much labour and difficulty; not only in consequence of the violence of the wind, which had nearly driven them from the land, but because, in their endeavours to approach the shores, the Chatham's cutter shipped some heavy seas, and was in imminent danger of being lost.[2] Patoa is represented by Mr. Whidbey as a roadstead affording good anchorage; its depth of water from 10 to 20 fathoms, sandy bottom; the former within half a mile, the latter about a mile from the shore, where there is an excellent run of fresh water, though the place is inconvenient for filling casks expeditiously, as the water takes its course amongst some rugged rocks over which large casks could not be rolled. This difficulty, however, might easily be surmounted by allowing the casks to remain on the beach, where the natives, for a very small reward, would soon fill them. The soundings from the ship were regular all the way to Patoa; a station easily found, by attending to the following description.

The large bay already noticed, lying before the isthmus,[3] has its western side formed by high rocky precipices, that rise perpendicularly from the sea. To the westward of these precipices the coast is chiefly composed of sandy beaches, and the mountains, at some distance from the shore, form two remarkable vallies, separated from each other by a high rugged mountain, seemingly detached from the rest, and approaching nearer to the beach than those to the right and left of it. The anchorage at Patoa is abreast of the easternmost of these vallies, which appeared to be fruitful and well cultivated.

The boats remained at this station until the next morning, when they proceeded along shore to the eastward, and found the same soundings until they were abreast of the rocky precipices; here they gained no ground; but,

[1] Probably Olowalu. The bearing must have been S. 60 E., not N 60 E.

[2] Manby gives a dramatic account of an incident that Vancouver passes over with this bare mention. The two boats had set out at 4 a.m.; at 8 the weather took a turn for the worse and by 11 it was blowing a hurricane. Whidbey, nearer land, was able to get ashore, but the Chatham's boat was less fortunate. 'Every Moment kept increasing my distance from the Shore in spite of all our efforts. The Crew jaded to Death by fatigue. The Boat nearly full of Water ten Miles from Land, without provision, and still blowing with astonishing rapidity [sic] fast, out to sea, at the mercy of the Elements – impresses us, with but little hopes of our preservation. In this wretched state we existed, five long hours, expecting every instant to meet, the awful moment of our destruction, by perishing in [a] Watery grave. Cheering up the timid, and applauding the Grave, occupied my time which so far succeeded, that each exerted his exhausted strength and kept the Boat from upsetting, by baling out the Water with their Hats, as each entending wave tumbled it in upon us.' Fortunately a change in the wind in the afternoon enabled them to clear the boat of water, hoist the sail and make for shore. Whidbey had given them up for lost. 'A worthy Chief Tomoutoo, brother in Law to the King received us with kindness and hospitality, stripped us of our Wet Cloathes, wrapt us in Island Cloth and so completely dried our Cloathes in an hour that we were all as well as if nothing had happen'd, all attired in our own Jackets and Trowsers. This friendly and generous Chief then served up a sumptuous repast...' – Letters, March.

[3] Maalaea Bay.

close to the shore the bottom, which was rocky, was reached with twenty fathoms of line. These precipices extend about a league from Patoa, in the line of the shore, then trend more northerly, and at the distance of about four miles join the low land of the isthmus; before this lies a reef, or rather detached patches of rocks, at the distance of near a quarter of a mile from the shore; without which the soundings are regular and good. The western side of the large bay is formed by these precipices or cliffs; its opposite shore about four miles distant, takes a north direction from the Volcano hill; the depth of the bay is there somewhat increased; the soundings on the eastern side are regular, but very rocky.

Nearly in the middle of its western side is a village, called by the natives Mackerrey;[1] off this there is anchorage in seven fathoms water, a little more than a quarter of a mile from the shore, the bottom sand and broken coral. This situation is land-locked in every direction, excepting between Tahowrowa and Rannai, where to the south-westward it is exposed about two points of the compass, but not liable I believe to much wind from that quarter. The neighbouring shores afford good landing, and, in moderate weather, the communication is easily effected; but, the neglected and impoverished state of the surrounding country offers no inducement to strangers, under its present circumstances, to make choice of it as a stopping, or resting place; though it is probably one of the best sheltered and most convenient anchorages which these islands possess. In all likelihood, good water might with little labour be procured at a small distance to the southward of the village, from the upper part of a stream that was found rushing through the loose sand composing the beach; though just below high water mark it was somewhat brackish. The inhabitants, who are generally nice in this particular, procure their water from this run at low tide. The examination of this bay being the limits of Mr. Whidbey's excursion to the eastward, he returned to the ship; from whence he continued his researches round the western point of Raheina roadstead, and found the shores bounded by a reef, which admits of only one landing place for boats, and that a very indifferent one, at the eastern part of the village. From the ship to the shore the soundings were regular, decreasing to five fathoms close to the reef, extending in general about a fourth of a mile from the beach and not exceeding that distance from the west point of the roadstead; where on the north side of that point the reef terminates. This point, with the west extremity of Mowee, which is bold and free from rocks or other impediments, forms an excellent little bay,[2] its outer points lie from each other N. 14 W. and S. 14 E. about a league asunder. The northern point is formed by a round hill close to the water side, much resembling Volcano hill, but not quite so large. This bay Mr. Whidbey esteemed the most eligible anchoring place he had seen in Mowee; the soundings, in the line of the two points, from ten to fourteen fathoms, soft, sandy bottom, regularly decreased to five

---

[1] Probably Maalaea.   [2] Honolua Bay.

fathoms close to the beach; which is protected from the ocean, and the prevailing winds, by its north point locking in with the eastern part of the island of Morotoi. It is free from rocks, shoals, or other obstacles; and affords pleasant landing and good anchorage, where vessels may lie nearly land-locked in every direction, excepting that between Rannai and Monotoi, in the western quarter. This space, however, embraces but a small extent, from whence little danger can be apprehended.

The day being too far spent prevented Mr. Whidbey from landing; but we were informed by *Tomohomoho*, that the shores of that bay afforded abundance of very excellent water. This advantage gives the bay a great preference to any other station in Mowee, especially as its ingress and egress may be effected with much ease by approaching it from the northward; as the regular trade wind may be depended upon, which without interruption or suddent gusts, blows past the bay, and enables vessels to chuse in it what station they please.

By these means a very accurate knowledge of the shores on this side of Mowee was acquired. These appeared to be more likely to afford anchorage and shelter, than those of the other islands; but, as I have already had occasion to observe, under the present impoverished state of this and the neighbouring islands, Mowee is certainly not the most desirable rendezvous for vessels employed in the commercial pursuits of this hemisphere; it is likewise necessary to add, that notwithstanding the advantages of Patoa and Mackerrey, there is great reason to suspect that the bottom at those places, as well as on all this side of Mowee, is no where good holding ground. That of the roadstead of Raheina, I am convinced, is nothing more than a very slight covering of sand, over a bed of hard coral; and the same remark seems to extend to the edge of the bank, where, in forty fathoms water, the bottom is much softer, but the declivity of the bank is such, that with a strong wind from the shore, vessels would not be able to retain their anchorage. By Mr. Whidbey's examination of the south-west part of Mowee, the soundings generally indicated the same deceitful bottom; this can only be discovered by anchoring upon it, as the lead only brings up the sand and small stones, which cover a bed of solid rock beneath, that the anchor cannot penetrate. Of this we had proof on two different days in the squalls of wind that came across the isthmus, which drove the vessels in whatever direction the wind chanced to blow, though they were riding with a very sufficient scope of cable. As we were not moored, I at first attributed this circumstance to the anchor being foul, but on heaving it up, this was not found to be the case; whilst the peak of the anchor, with the under part of the stock, were found much chafed, by their having been dragged along the hard ground.

Another inconvenience attending these two places, is the violent gusts, or rather gales of wind, that I believe constantly prevail when the trade wind blows fresh at sea; and particularly, when it is from the northern quarter. At these times it is most violent, and rushes with such fury over the isthmus, as to prevent all communication with the shore; and if my conjecture respecting the bottom be right, vessels would have great difficulty to maintain their stations.

The king, *Taio*, and the rest of the chiefs returned according to their promise to the ship, on Sunday morning the 17th; and in the forenoon, accompanied by *Titeeree*, and some of our officers in two armed boats, with a guard of marines, I paid my compliments on shore, where the landing was but indifferent.

We were received by the natives with the greatest civility and friendship. At the first view they appeared very numerous, being collected on a small space of ground; but when they were a little distributed, their number, including the children, did not exceed six or seven hundred. The king conducted us through the crowd, who made way for us, and behaved in a very orderly manner. We soon arrived at his residence. This consisted of two small shabby huts, situated in a pleasant grove of spreading trees, where we were served with cocoa nuts, and other refreshments. I requested that *Titeeree* and *Taio* would accompany us in a walk through the plantations; this they begged leave to decline, and pleaded their age and infirmities as an excuse. They however directed that *Namahanna*, *Tomohomoho*, and *Martier* should attend us, who would equally prevent the obtrusion of the curious, and render us every service.

Attended by our guard and these chiefs, we visited the cultivated parts of the plain of Raheina; these occupied no very great extent; the part bordering on the sea shore was pleasantly laid out in plantations of taro, potatoes, sugar cane, the cloth plant, &c. tolerably well shaded by spreading trees, chiefly of the bread fruit; but in point of size, or in the luxuriance of its productions, it bore no proportion to the plains of Otaheite and of the Society islands. Through these grounds little canals were cut in various directions, that supplied the several plantations with water; the whole originating from a continual spring of excellent water, sufficiently above the level to inundate every part. The taro was growing among the water, but in a very bad state of culture, and in very small quantities. To the ravage and destruction of *Tamaahmaah*'s wars, the wretched appearance of their crops was to be ascribed; of this they grievously complained, and were continually pointing out the damages they had sustained. The despoiled aspect of the country was an incontrovertible evidence of this melancholy truth. Most of the different tenements in the lands formerly cultivated, were now lying waste, their fences partly or intirely broken down, and their little canals utterly destroyed; nor was a hog or a fowl any where to be seen. By far the larger portion of the plain was in this ruinous state; and the small part that was in a flourishing condition, bore the evident marks of very recent labour.

Having extended our walk as far as our inclinations led us, and having satisfied our curiosity, we returned to the royal habitation, where we found *Titeeree* and *Taio* at dinner on raw pickled fish, and *poe taro*; that is, a mess made of the taro root, not unlike a hasty pudding. Sensible that we were not likely to relish such food, they had provided two very fine baked hogs, which were immediately set before us, but the cook having neglected to provide any vegetables, which was a more important article to us, we declined the repast, and the chiefs having finished their meal, returned with us on board.[1]

As this was likely to be the last visit of *Titeeree* and *Taio*, I presented them with a large assortment of useful tools, implements, and household utensils, with cloth, linen, some beads, and other articles of ornament. To *Titeeree* I gave also some goats; and these being the first foreign animals imported into Mowee, were regarded as a most valuable present. The inferior chiefs and attendants were not neglected on this occasion, and I had the satisfaction to find, that my liberality had exceeded their most sanguine expectations. By this time they had become well acquainted with the noble and generous conduct of *Tamaahmaah*, and our reception and treatment at Owhyhee. This they would have been happy to have imitated, had they not been prevented by the general distress of their country; but they promised to assist us on our return to the very utmost of their power and ability.

In the evening, we had a display of fire-works from the after part of the ship, to the great terror and admiration of our visitors, and their attendants on board, and of the natives of all descriptions assembled in their canoes about the ship, comprehending most probably all the inhabitants.

The exhibition being concluded, I expected to have taken leave of my Mowee friends, but the night being very dark, and a heavy surf breaking on the shore, the king and *Taio* were not much inclined to leave us, saying they should be liable to great danger in passing the reef in the dark. This circumstance induced me, though contrary to my established rule, to indulge them and the major part of their retinue with my cabin. The night was more appropriated to conversation, than to sleep. I retired to rest, but was frequently awakened, and found that their discourse was principally on the occurrences that had taken place since our arrival, and on the destructive powers of our fire-works when used in war.

The next morning, Monday the 18th, *Titeeree* departed in a very sudden manner, and without my knowledge. I became apprehensive that some accidental offence had been given him; but *Taio* assured me of the contrary, and that such was his common practice of retiring. I had indeed, before,

---

[1] Menzies gives a quite different impression of this expedition. He found that 'the whole plantation was cultivated with such studious care & artful industry as to occupy our minds & attention with a consistant gaze of admiration during a long walk through it...' Far from being unattractive, he describes how the fish offered to him at the royal residence were specially caught 'from one of the ponds near the house' and how they were cooked, his final verdict being that 'I think I never tasted fish better or more relishing, even without the aid of any sauce whatever.' – March 17.

noticed an abruptness in his leaving the ship; but on the present occasion I thought he would have shewn more respect.[1]

Taio, *Martier*, and some of the others chiefs, remained with us till we sailed. This we were prevented doing until near noon; when, with a light breeze from the westward, we put to sea, and they took an affectionate leave of us.

Thus we quitted Mowee, little benefited by the refreshments it had afforded; for although I did not choose to accept the inadequate returns of the chiefs, yet every article of this sort that was brought alongside for sale was purchased, and the whole did not amount to two days subsistence.

The mean result of our observations made between the 12th and 17th, shewed the latitude of the ship's station at Raheina roadstead, to be 20° 50', the longitude 203° 19'.[2] All further nautical information, relative to this anchorage and its immediate neighbourhood, will most probably be better obtained from the charts of the islands, than from any written description.

[1] Menzies gives a quite different explanation: 'Next morning one of the Oneehow women [passengers in the *Discovery*] missed a piece of ribbon which it was supposd some of those who had slept in the Cabin stole from her, Captain Vancouver in endeavouring to recover this trifle put himself into such a passion & threatened the Chiefs with such menacing threats that he terrified some of them out of the Ship with great precipitation; The King in particular came running into my Cabin before I knew any thing of the business & instantly jumping into his Canoe through the port hole, paddled hastily to the shore & we saw no more of him. Taio who was not so easily frightend & who was among the last that left us, was the first who told me the cause of Taiteree's sudden departure as he came into my cabin soon after to get his last present. Excepting this little fracas which I was sorry should happen for so trifling a circumstance at the time we were leaving them we enjoyd the utmost tranquility during our stay'. – March 18.

[2] A very accurate reading; the position of the roadstead is given officially as lat. 20° 52' N, long. 156° 41' W (203° 17' E).

CHAPTER VIII.

Proceed to Whyteete Bay—An Indian's Account of the Murder at Woahoo—Three of the Murderers brought on Board—Their Trial and Execution—Proceed to Attowai—Settle two Female Natives, found at Nootka—Quit the Sandwich Islands.

LIGHT baffling winds attended us, after leaving Raheina roadstead, until the evening of Monday the 18th, when we reached the channel between Mowee and Morotoi, where we met the regular trade wind blowing a pleasant gale. With this we stood to windward, and anchored for the night off the N.W. part of Mowee in 19 fathoms water, soft sandy bottom. Its shores extended by compass from N. 51 E. to S. 4 E., its nearest part bore E. by S. two miles from us, and the east point of Morotoi, N. 15 W. distant eight miles.

Early the next morning, with a pleasant breeze from the N.E., we stood over towards the east point of Morotoi, until we were within a league of the shore, which was bounded by a reef extending about half a league from it. Thus we sailed along to the westward, and saw several shallow breaks forming passages for boats, but not affording any shelter for shipping against the prevailing winds. About half a league south of the east point of Morotoi, which is situated in latitude 21° 9', longitude 203° 16',[1] lies a small barren rocky islet, called by the natives Modooeneete;[2] and from that point the shores of the inland lie S. 53 W. In this direction the land rises rather abruptly from the sea, towards the lofty mountains in the centre of the east part of Morotoi; and though the acclivity was great, yet the face of the country, diversified by eminences and vallies, bore a verdant and fertile appearance. It seemed to be well inhabited, in a high state of cultivation, and presented not only a rich, but a romantic prospect. To the westward of these cliffs, the shores terminated in the former direction by a low point of land, called by the natives Crynoa,[3] and from thence they stretch N. 85 W. eight leagues to the west point of the island. From Crynoa the country assumes a dreary aspect. The mountains, forming the eastern part of the island, gradually descend to the westward, and like those of Mowee, terminate on a low isthmus, which appears to divide the island into two peninsulas. These however bear no proportion to each other; the easternmost, which is far the largest, is composed of very high land,

---

[1] Cape Halawa, in lat. 21° 10' N, long. 156° 43' W (203° 17' E).
[2] Mokuhooniki. [3] Evidently in the vicinity of Kamalo.

but the westernmost does not rise to any elevation, beyond that of a moderate height.[1] The country from Crynoa rises from the sea by an ascent, uninterrupted with chasms, hills, or vallies. This uniform surface, on advancing to the westward, exhibited a gradual decrease in the population; it discovered an uncultivated barren soil, and a tract of land that gave residence only to a few of the lower orders of the islanders, who resort to the shores for the purpose of taking fish, with which they abound. Those so employed are obliged to fetch their fresh water from a great distance; none but what is brackish being attainable on the western parts of Morotoi. This information I had before gained from several chiefs at Mowee, and was now confirmed in it by *Tomohomoho*, who was accompanying us to Woahoo; and who also acquainted me, that along the shores of this south side, which are chiefly composed of a sandy beach, anchorage would be found on a clear sandy bottom. But as there were no projecting points for shelter, I did not think a further examination worth the time it would employ, and therefore proceeded to the bay at the west end of the island, for the purpose of seeing if, contrary to my former observations, it was commodious for the refitting of vessels, as it had been reported.

We passed within about half a league of the west point of the island, situated in latitude 21° 6′ 30″, longitude 202° 43′,[2] with regular soundings from 17 to 23 fathoms, sandy bottom. The N.W. point of the island[3] lies from the west point N. 25 E., at the distance of three leagues; between these two points a commodious bay had been stated to exist; whereas we found the whole intermediate space nearly a straight shore, composed alternately of rugged rocks and sandy beaches.

The day being too far advanced for standing over to Woahoo, we stood to windward, and anchored for the night in 19 fathoms water, sandy and bad holding ground; as the ship would not ride with less than a whole cable, although the trade wind blew but a moderate breeze. In working up, the soundings were pretty regular from 17 to 60 fathoms, fine sandy bottom; and where we anchored, within about a mile of the breakers, the west point of the island bore by compass south, distant four miles; and the north-west point N. 26 E. about the same distance. Our situation here was as close into shore as vessels can lie with safety; this side of the island being entirely open, and exposed to the north and north-west winds, which blow frequently with great violence; and to a heavy sea, that is almost constantly rolling from that quarter on the shores; and which at that time broke with so much fury, that it would have been dangerous to land even in canoes.

The country had the same dreary and barren appearance as that noticed on the south side, and I was informed it was equally destitute of water.

With a light easterly breeze, about six o'clock on Wednesday morning the 20th, we directed our course so as to sail along the north side of Woahoo.

---

[1] 'mean height' in the first edition.

[2] Laau Point, in lat. 21° 06′ N, long. 157° 19′ W (202° 41′ E).   [3] Ilio Point.

Tomohontoho objected to this mode of approach, saying, that the murderers resided near Whyteete bay, which would be the best station for us to take; for if we went to the other side, he should have a great distance to go in search of them, by which means the offenders might get intelligence of our errand, escape into the mountains, and *Titeeree* would be accused of breaking his promise. There appeared so much good sense in this precaution, and so much earnestness in *Tomohomoho* to execute the business entrusted to him, that I did not hesitate to yield to his wishes, and postponed the examination of the north side of the island till our next visit; and we proceeded to Whyteete, where we anchored about three o'clock, in ten fathoms water, occupying near our former station.

We were visited by a few of the natives in small single canoes, who brought little or nothing to dispose of. One double canoe only made its appearance. In this came James Coleman, one of the three men we found last year left by Mr. Kendrick at Attowai. This man had quitted Mr. Kendrick's employ, and had entered into the service of *Titeeree*, who had stationed him at this island in order to regulate the trade, and to assist such vessels as might touch at Woahoo for refreshments. This corresponded with what I had heard in support of *Titeeree*'s character, in contradiction to the report that had been circulated, of his having issued orders for putting to death all the white men who resided in, or who might visit, his dominions.

Coleman was accompanied by a chief named *Tennavee*,[1] and a lad called *To-hoo-boo-ar-to*.[2] The latter had made a voyage to China in some of the trading vessels, and had picked up a few English words that rendered his conversation very intelligible. These informed me, that they were sent by *Try-too-boo-ry*,[3] *Titeeree*'s eldest son, and governor of Woahoo in his absence, to inquire who we were, and to offer such supplies as the island afforded; though at present they could not boast of any abundance. They apologized for *Trytooboory*'s not coming himself, as he was ill, and not able, without much pain, to walk or sit upright.

Coleman introduced the melancholy subject of our countrymen's unhappy fate, and stated the circumstances attending it much in the same way as we had heard them at Mowee; but, for our more particular information, he referred us to *Tohoobooarto*, who, he said, was present, and would relate the whole of that transaction.

Tohoobooarto stated, that he had received much civility from Mr. Hergest and the rest of the gentlemen, on his visiting the Dædalus at Whymea bay, on the opposite side of this island; that when Mr. Hergest and Mr. Gooch were going on shore, he accompanied them in the boat, to assist as an

---

[1] Not identified.

[2] Menzies spells the name Tobeaitoo and states that he 'happened to be the very man that landed with Lieutenant Hergest & Mr. Gooch as a Guide when they were killed on the other side of the Island by the Natives.' – 20 March.

[3] Kalanikupule.

interpreter; that when they arrived at the beach, he advised Mr. Hergest by no means to land; telling him, that there was no chief present, and that it was a part of the island where a great many very bad people resided: that no attention was paid to his advice; that they went on shore, and after taking some measures, without any opposition, for procuring a supply of water, Mr. Hergest left some directions with his people; and then, still contrary to the advice of this young man, went with Mr. Gooch from the sea-side up to the habitations of the natives, who behaved to them in a friendly manner. At this time *Tohoobooarto* had left them, in order to wash himself in the fresh water, (a prevailing custom on landing after being some time at sea) and whilst the gentlemen were absent, a dispute arose at the watering place, between the natives and the people of the Dædalus, from which an affray ensued, and the Portuguese seaman was killed. That no harm or molestation had been offered, or was intended, towards those gentlemen, who were treated civilly by the people of the village, until the news of this unfortunate transaction arrived; when, to prevent revenge taking place, it was thought necessary to put to death the chiefs whom they had in their power; and that, in pursuance of this horrid resolution, Mr. Gooch was instantly killed by being stabbed through the heart with a *pahooa*; that the first blow only wounded Mr. Hergest, who, in endeavouring to make his way towards the boat, was knocked down by a large stone hitting him on the side of his head, and was then murdered in a most barbarous manner. The man who stabbed Mr. Gooch, the one who first wounded Mr. Hergest, and another who had been principally concerned at the watering place, had been, he said, apprehended by *Titeeree*'s orders, and been put to death. To assure us of his having been present and having interfered to save Mr. Hergest, he pointed out the scar of a wound in his left arm, which he said he had received on that occasion; and further added, that the man who knocked down and murdered Mr. Hergest, with two or three others materially concerned, were still living, and resided not far from our then anchorage. The former of these he had pointed out a few days before to Coleman. I inquired of Coleman, if he had ever heard this young man tell this melancholy story before? who instantly replied, that he had, and precisely as it was then related; which corresponded with the account he had received from other natives, and that he believed it to be a very true statement.

After *Tohoobooarto* had finished his account, he was questioned by *Tomohomoho*, about the residence of the offenders, who desired that he would accompany him and *Tennavee* for the purpose of apprehending the delinquents, and bringing them to justice. At first, *Tohoobooarto* declined engaging, fearing the friends and relations of the offenders would murder him; but on being assured of protection by *Tomohomoho*, he consented, and the whole party made the best of their way to the shore. I intrusted to Coleman a present of red cloth, and some other things, as a pledge of my good will and friendly disposition towards *Trytooboory*; as also an axe, and other articles, to *Tomohomoho*, which he requested to be the bearer of for the same purpose.

The next forenoon, Thursday the 21st, Coleman with *Tomohomoho* and *Tennavee* came on board. As no one appeared like a prisoner in the canoe, I inquired of Coleman if the murderers were in custody? He said, he believed they were, but did not positively know, as the business after landing the preceding evening, had been conducted by the chiefs with the most profound secrecy; that he had seen nothing of the party during the whole of the night, nor till they were about to put off from the beach, when he jumped into the stern of the canoe. The two chiefs desired I would attend them into the cabin; where, after shutting all the doors, they informed me, that the man who had murdered Mr. Hergest, with two others who had been equally active and guilty, were in the forepart of the canoe, and that no time should be lost in securing them, lest any thing should transpire, and they should again make their escape. Orders were immediately given for their being admitted into the ship, and they soon were brought into the cabin.

The chiefs now pointed out the principal offender, whose appearance corresponded with the description given by *Tohoobooarto*. One half of his body, from his forehead to his feet, was made jet black by punctuating; the other two men were marked after the same manner, but not with the same regularity. These appearances alone would not have been sufficient to have identified their persons, as we had seen many of *Titeeree*'s subjects disfigured after the same barbarous fashion; which I understood had been adopted in the late wars, for the purpose of increasing the ferocity of their appearance, and striking their enemies with terror.

Tohoobooarto was not present as a witness against the accused persons; this I very much regretted, but as there was great probability that Coleman's evidence would confirm what the chiefs had asserted, he was called in. After stedfastly surveying their persons, he pointed out the same man whom the chiefs had accused as the murderer of Mr. Hergest, but said, that he had no knowledge of the other two.

Notwithstanding Coleman's corroborative evidence, I much wished for further proof before I sanctioned their punishment; and having heard that Mr. Dobson, one of the midshipmen who came out in the Dædalus, had spoken of one of the natives, who, when alongside on that occasion, had been remarked for his insolence and improper behaviour; and who, the instant the boat with Mr. Hergest put off from the ship, had paddled hastily to the shore, where he landed, became very active in the affray, and was, in the unanimous opinion of the crew, suspected to have been the principal, if not the sole cause, of the calamity that followed; I having therefore called upon Mr. Dobson, and asked him if he had any recollection of the prisoners; he, without the least hesitation, pointed out the same man who stood accused as the person who had acted the part above described, and was ready to make oath to his identity.

These proofs, though not positive, were yet so circumstantial as to leave little doubt of this man's guilt; but as the evidence of *Tohoobooarto* would be still an additional confirmation, I desired *Tennavee* would repair to the shore and bring him on board, that the criminals might be fairly tried, and that we might have the fullest satisfaction of their guilt which the nature of the case would afford. During this interval, I ordered the prisoners into confinement, until further testimonies should be produced to criminate or acquit them.

Tomohomoho disliked much the delay of punishment, and requested that the prisioners might be immediately executed; but I persisted in the exercise of my own feelings and judgment. On questioning him concerning a fourth man, who had been implicated in the murder, he acknowledged, that there was a fourth who had been very materially concerned; but said, that all he could learn about him was, that he had been seen in the neighbourhood some months before; and as he had not lately made his appearance, it was by no means certain whether he was then on the island, or had gone to some of the others. Under all circumstances there appeared little probability of this man being taken, especially when the news of the three others being in custody should be spread abroad. This determined me not to insist upon any further search, on the conviction that it would be neither prudent nor proper to adopt any measures of force to effect an object, that want of time might oblige me to abandon and leave unaccomplished.

In the afternoon *Tennavee* returned without *Tohoobooarto*. At this I was not less concerned than surprized, and could not but consider his absenting himself as an indication of some misconduct. The two chiefs assured me I need be under no such apprehensions, as they were certain it was only the fear of revenge from the relations and friends of the delinquents that prevented his attendance. Despairing of his evidence we had only one further appeal. This was to know from *Trytooboory*, the chief of the island, if he believed these were the identical people guilty of the offence? and as his indisposition prevented him from coming on board, I desired *Terrehooa*,[1] who could not be at all interested in any event that might take place, and who had conducted himself with great fidelity during twelve months he had been on board, to accompany Coleman, and make this inquiry of *Trytooboory*. This they accordingly performed, and returned in the evening.

Terrehooa declared, that *Trytooboory* had positively pronounced that all three of the prisoners were guilty of the murder with which they were accused. This Coleman confirmed, and added, that the chief desired they might be immediately punished with death. To this declaration Coleman made oath, in the most solemn manner in the presence of myself and all the officers of the ship, who had attended the investigation in the morning; and who, having maturely considered the business, were unanimously of opinion with me, that justice demanded exemplary punishment, in order to stop, or at least to check, such barbarous and unprovoked outrages in future.

It was clearly established in the course of the examination, by the testimonies of all the natives who were questioned, that neither those two unfortunate

---

[1] Kalehua had joined the *Discovery* in March 1792.

gentlemen, nor the people in the boats, had given the least cause for umbrage. This certainly aggravated the crime. After much enquiry it did not appear that any other witnesses could be procured. And though *we* could have wished to have had more satisfactory proof of the criminality of the persons in custody, yet as they had been apprehended by their own people, accused and convicted by their own neighbours, and condemned by their own chief, it was, after the most serious deliberation and reflection, deemed sufficient to authorize the execution of the three prisoners; but as the day was too far spent it was deferred until the next morning, contrary to the wishes of the chiefs, who were very desirous of its immediately taking place. When they returned to the shore, I desired they would use their endeavours to find out and bring on board every person, that might be able to prove the innocence of the persons in custody. This injunction was treated with indifference, because they were perfectly convinced no such persons could be found. And as I wished that as many of the natives as could be collected, should witness the awful punishment that the prisoners had brought upon themselves by their barbarity, I desired also that they would make it publicly known that the execution would probably take place the next forenoon.

On Friday morning the 22nd a few of the natives were about the ship, but not so many as on the former days. After breakfast, Coleman, with *Tomohomoho* and *Tennavee*, came on board. The two latter demanded the immediate execution of the prisoners. This however was not complied with, as it was deemed right that they should again be accused by their own chiefs, in the presence of all the witnesses, of the crime with which they stood charged, in order, if possible, to draw from them a confession of their guilt, and to renew the opportunity which before had been given them, of producing some evidence in proof of their innocence. Nothing however could be extorted from any of them, but that they were totally ignorant of any such circumstances having ever happened on the island. This very assertion amounted almost to self-conviction, as it is not easy to believe, that the execution of their comrades, by *Titeeree*'s orders, for the same offence with which they had been charged, had not come to their knowledge, or that it could have escaped their recollection.

Neither myself nor my officers discovered any reason, from the result of this further examination, to retract or alter our former opinion of their guilt, or of delivering them over to their own people, to be dealt with according to the directions of their chief.[1]

Before they went from the ship, they were placed in irons on the

---

[1] Some doubt still lingers as to whether or not those executed were involved in the murders. Of those on the spot, Hewett (always critical of Vancouver) was sceptical. He threw doubt on the testimony given by Dobson, whom he characterized as 'an Indolent careless young man', and contended that it was well known ashore that Vancouver was determined to have the men concerned executed. Under those circumstances he thought it was incredible that the murderers would come on board the ship, as the accused men did, 'without the least hesitation'.

quarter-deck; where, in the presence of all the ship's company, I recapitulated the crime which they had committed, the evidence that had been adduced against them, and the condemnation of their chiefs, and stated the punishment that was now to be inflicted. All this was likewise made known to the Indian spectators who were present.

That the ceremony might be made as solemn and as awful as possible, a guard of seamen and marines were drawn up on that side of the ship opposite to the shore, where, alongside of the ship, a canoe was stationed for the execution. The rest of the crew were in readiness at the great guns, lest any disturbance or commotion should arise. One ceremony however remained yet to be performed. One of these unfortunate men had long hair; this it was necessary should be cut from his head before he was executed, for the purpose of being presented, as a customary tribute on such occasions, to the king of the island. I was shocked at the want of feeling exhibited by the two chiefs at this awful moment, who in the rudest manner not only cut off the hair, but, in the presence of the poor suffering wretch, without the least compassion for his situation, disputed and strove for the honor of presenting the prize to the king. The odious contest being at length settled, the criminals were taken one by one into a double canoe, where they were lashed hand and foot, and put to death by *Tennavee*, their own chief, who blew out their brains with a pistol; and so dexterously was the melancholy office performed, that life fled with the report of the piece, and muscular motion seemed almost instantly to cease.

If steadiness and firmness, totally devoid of the least agitation, can be considered, in the performance of such a duty, as a proof of conscious rectitude; or that the forfeiture of these three men's lives was considered as no more than what the strict principles of retributive justice demanded, it should seem that *Tennavee's* mind had been completely made up, not only as their judge, but their executioner; and that he was perfectly convinced his conduct was unimpeachable, in executing an office that justice demanded.

The whole of *Tennavee's* deportment, on this sad occasion, afforded us additional cause to believe, that the persons executed were wholly guilty of the murder, and that the chiefs had not punished the innocent to screen themselves.[1]

This public example, made so long after the crime was committed, we had reason to hope, would convince the islanders, that no intervention of time

[1] Two months later, when the *Discovery* rejoined the *Chatham*, Puget heard accounts of the executions and wrote in his journal: 'The Chiefs pressed Capt. Vancouver to hang the Men at the Fore Yard which certainly being more Conspicuous, might have more terror in its Appearance, but as he had determined only to see Justice done on the Criminals, he would acquiesce in no such Plan & insisted as they brought the Indians on board as the Offenders, it was also in their province to punish them. After some Altercation it was agreed that all three should be shot alongside by their Chiefs, which was performed next morning....' – 27 May.

would, in future, prevent justice taking its regular course; and that any one who should dare to commit such barbarities would, sooner or later, suffer punishment.

The dead bodies were taken to the shore, attended by most of the natives who were present at the execution, and who, on this occasion, observed some small degree of solemnity, by paddling slowly towards the island. When they had gained about half the distance between the ship and the shore, they stopped, and some lamentations were heard, that continued, I believe, until they were landed.

I had proposed that the dead bodies should each be hung upon a tree near the shore, to deter others from committing the like offences; but *Tomohomoho* informed me, that such spectacles would be considered as very improper, contrary to their religious rites, and would greatly offend the whole of the priesthood. That such an exposure was totally unnecessary, as all the inhabitants would become fully acquainted with every circumstance attendant on their trial and execution, and the crime for which they had justly suffered; and that he verily believed their fate would have the good effect of restraining the ill-disposed in future. I inquired of him, why so few of the natives had attended on this awful occasion? He replied, it was in consequence of the message I had sent on shore to require it. This had created suspicions, arising, he said, from the former conduct of Europeans, on disputes or misunderstandings taking place between the chiefs and the commanders. Some of these, under the pretext of re-established friendship, would prevail on many of the inhabitants to come off to their ships, where they would, as usual, enter into trade with the natives, until great numbers were assembled; the commanders then ordered them to be fired upon, which continued, without mercy, as long as any of the canoes were within shot. *Tomohomoho* stated, that two or three instances of this barbarous nature had taken place, as well by the English as the American traders, and which was the reason why my invitation had been distrusted.

The two chiefs solicited my visiting *Trytooboory*, saying, if he had not been so ill, he would have been with us during the late unpleasant business; and that he was very desirous of seeing me, that he might be better convinced of my friendship and good inclinations towards him. I should certainly have complied with this request, had there been any object whatever to attain. Although I did not entertain any apprehension for the safety of myself, or any person belonging to the ship, whilst under the protection of the chief, yet I did not consider it prudent, whilst the execution of the criminals was so fresh in the minds of the people, to throw temptations of revenge in the way of the daring and ill-disposed part of the society, by placing myself and others in their power on shore. Should my confidence, on making the trial, prove ill-grounded, I should stand self-accused, in having so unnecessarily opened the channel for a fresh effusion of blood. Their civil invitations were, for these reasons, declined, seemingly much to their mortification. I was not however at a loss to relieve them of the disappointment, provided their intentions were as pure as their professions.

As the only object the two chiefs had in view, was stated to be an interview between me and *Trytooboory*, whose indisposition, and the want of a proper conveyance, prevented him coming on board, I proposed, as the day was remarkably fine and pleasant, to make a commodious platform on a double canoe, on which he might with great ease come alongside, and then if he found himself inclined to come on board, he should be hoisted in by means of a chair, or I would converse with him on the platform, and render him any medical or other assistance. With this proposal they appeared to be as well satisfied as if I had visited him on shore, and Coleman, with *Tennavee*, immediately departed to communicate this plan to the chief; to whom also, the better to insure his confidence, I again sent a present of red cloth and other articles. These had the desired effect, and the messengers soon returned accompanying *Trytooboory*, who, without the least hesitation, desired he might be hoisted into the ship, which he entered, and was placed on the quarter-deck with the most implicit confidence.

Trytooboory appeared to be about thirty-three years of age, his countenance was fallen and reduced, his emaciated frame was in a most debilitated condition, and he was so totally deprived of the use of his legs, that he was under the necessity of being carried about like an infant; to these infirmities was added, a considerable degree of fever, probably increased by the hurry and fatigue of his visit.

The usual compliments, and mutual exchange of friendly assurances, having passed, I requested the favor of his company below; to this with much pleasure he assented, but no sooner were his intentions known to the natives in the canoes about the ship, than a general alarm took place, and he was earnestly recommended not to quit the deck; from a suspicion, as I imagined, amongst the crowd, that the works of death were not yet finally accomplished. *Trytooboory* however disregarded all remonstrances, and ordered the people who were carrying him in the chair, and who, in consequence of the alarm, had stopped, to proceed to the cabin, where he found a comfortable resting place, and appeared to be perfectly at home. He then informed me, that he had not been ill above sixteen or eighteen days; and as Mr. Menzies had now prepared him some medicines, I gave him hopes that his health would soon be reinstated.[1]

Notwithstanding his indisposition, his conversation was cheerful and pleasing; and I had the happiness of hearing him confirm every part of the evidence that he had been given against the three unfortunate wretches who had suffered in the morning. He spoke of them all as being equally guilty,

---

[1] He 'appeared very weak and emaciated from a pulmonary complaint that now produced hectic symptoms, for which I gave him some medicines, accompanied with some general directions how to manage his complaint.' – Menzies, 22 March.

and of having always borne extremely bad characters; and said there were many others of the same description at Woahoo, but hoped the example of the morning would be the means of frightening them into a more discreet mode of behaviour.

The proposed peace with Owhyhee was next adverted to. He highly applauded the measure, and said, if such a business could be effected, it would be of the utmost importance to them; as the chiefs and people would then return to their habitations; by this means the country would be better governed, the lands better cultivated, and, by the production of a greater abundance from the soil, they could be enabled to procure a more ample supply of European commodities. The same want of confidence however that the contending parties entertained, was evident in the opinions of this chief; and although the negociation at Mowee had put on a favorable appearance, I began to fear this unfortunate prevailing sentiment would be fatal to the establishment of a general and permanent peace. He likewise took an opportunity to apologize, and to express his concern, that the reduced state of the country precluded his making me any suitable return for the obligations I had conferred upon him. In reply, I made him a similar answer to that given his father at Mowee; adding, that on a future visit he might probably have more to spare, and I less to bestow.

The fame of our fire-works still attended us, and *Trytooboory* was very solicitous to be indulged with a sight of their effect. Considering that the present moment afforded no ill-timed opportunity to impress the minds of these people more deeply with our superiority, his curiosity was gratified in the evening, by the display of a small assortment, from the after part of the ship. These were beheld by the surrounding natives with more than the usual mixture of the passions already described; for, on the present occasion, they were regarded with a degree of awful surprize, that I had not before observed. This exhibition being finished, *Trytooboory* was conveyed into his canoe, in the same manner as he had entered the ship. Before his departure I complimented him with some additional articles, and with these, as well as his reception and entertainment, he seemed highly delighted.

With a pleasant breeze from the westward, on Sunday morning the 24th, we plied to the windward, along the south side of Woahoo, until the afternoon, when we anchored abreast of the westernmost opening or lagoon, mentioned in our former visit to this island, called by the natives *O-poo-ro-ah*,[1] and which had since been reported to us, by the natives, as capable of admitting vessels by warping into it. About half a mile from the reef that binds these shores, we found the soundings irregular from 5 to 15 fathoms, rocky bottom; but where the ship rode, the bottom was tolerably even, and composed of sand and coral; the depth of water, about half a league from the reef, was 25 fathoms. The evening was too fast approaching to investigate the truth of the report given by the natives. This was deferred until day-light the next

[1] Now Pearl Harbor.

morning, when Mr. Whidbey, with two armed boats, accompanied by *Tomohomoho*, was dispatched for that purpose.

The part of the island opposite to us was low, or rather only moderately elevated, forming a level country between the mountains that compose the east and west ends of the island. This tract of land was of some extent, but did not seem to be populous, nor to possess any great degree of natural fertility; although we were told that, at a little distance from the sea, the soil is rich, and all the necessaries of life are abundantly produced.

Whilst we remained in this situation, a few only of the natives paid us their respects; their canoes were small and indifferent, and their visit was that of curiosity only, as they were furnished with little for barter.

Mr. Whidbey returned in the forenoon. He found the opening in the reef, about four hundred yards wide, to be occupied by a sandy bar about two hundred yards across, on which there was not more than nine or ten feet water; but on each side of it the water suddenly increased in depth to five and soon to ten fathoms. These soundings were regular on each side of the bar; on the inside the bottom is a stiff mud, or clay; this, with the same soundings, continued to the entrance of a small harbour about half a mile within the bar, formed by two low sandy points, about the same distance asunder. From each of these sandy points extended a shallow flat, near a cable's length on either side, contracting the width of the deep-water channel to not more than the fourth of a mile; in this is ten fathoms water; but the entrance is again further contracted by a sunken rock, stretching nearly into mid-channel from the northern shore, with which it is connected; on this was found only two feet water, although the depth is ten fathoms within a few yards of it. From the entrance, this little harbour, about a quarter of a mile wide, took a north-westerly direction for about a mile; the depth from 10 to 15 fathoms, muddy bottom; it then seemed to spread out, and to terminate in two bays, about a mile further to the northward, forming a very snug and convenient little port. Unfortunately, the bar without renders it fit only for the reception of very small craft.[1]

Mr. Whidbey, under this impression, lost no time in any further exami- nation, but returned to the ship; and as I was now very anxious to proceed on our voyage, no delay for matters of little importance could be admitted. Mr. Whidbey observed, that the soil in the neighbourhood of the harbour appeared of a loose sandy nature; the country low for some distance, and, from the number of houses within the harbour, it should seem to be very populous: but the very few inhabitants who made their appearance was an indication of the contrary. At the time the bar was sounded, it was low water, and Mr. Whidbey being unacquainted with the rise and fall, was not able to say what depth there might be on the bar at high tide.

The other opening to the eastward, called by the natives *Honoonoono*,[2]

---

[1] The vast U.S. Navy Pearl Harbor base has since been constructed here.
[2] Honolulu Harbor.

Tomohomoho represented as being much more shallow, and a smaller place; this induced me to pass it without examination: but to shew how liable we are to be mistaken in such inquiries amongst the natives, I was afterwards informed, by Mr. Brown of the Butterworth, that although it is smaller, and of less depth of water, yet it admits of a passage from sea five fathoms deep between the reefs; and opens beyond them into a small but commodious bason, with regular soundings from seven to three fathoms, clear and good bottom, where a few vessels may ride with the greatest safety; but the only means of getting in or out is by warping.

About noon, with a light breeze from the S.S.W., we weighed, and stood to windward; and in the afternoon, our very attentive and useful friend *Tomohomoho*, having executed all his commissions, and rendered us every service and assistance in his power, bad us farewel. On this occasion I presented him with such an assortment of articles as afforded him the highest satisfaction. Of these he was richly deserving, from the uniformity and integrity of conduct that he had supported from the first to the last moment of his being with us.

We found the western side of Woahoo lie in a direction from its S.W point N. 25 W., 6 leagues to the west point of the island, which forms also the S.W. point of Whymea bay.[1] The S.W. side of the island is principally composed of steep craggy mountains, some descending abruptly into the sea, others terminating at a small distance from it, whence a low border of land extends to the sea-shore, formed by sandy beaches, chiefly bounded by rocks, over which the surf breaks with great violence.

From these shores we were visited by some of the natives, in the most wretched canoes I had ever yet seen amongst the South-Sea islanders; they corresponded however with the appearance of the country, which from the commencement of the high land to the westward of Opooroah, was composed of one barren rocky waste, nearly destitute of verdure, cultivation, or inhabitants, with little variation all the way to the west point of the island. Not far from the S.W. point is a small grove of shabby cocoa-nut trees, and along those shores are a few straggling fishermen's huts. Nearly in the middle of this side of the island is the only village[2] we had seen westward from Opooroah. In its neighbourhood the bases of the mountains retire further from the sea-shore, and a narrow valley, presenting a fertile cultivated aspect, seemed to separate, and wind some distance through the hills. The shore here forms a small sandy bay. On its southern side, between the two high rocky precipices, in a grove of cocoa-nut and other trees, is situated the village, and in the centre of the bay, about a mile to the north of the village, is a high rock, remarkable for its projecting from a sandy beach. At a distance it appears to be detached from the land.[3] Between this and the high rocky point to the south of the

---

[1] Kaena Point. Vancouver evidently considered that Waimea Bay extended all the way W to this point.

[2] Waianae.   [3] Lahilahi Point.

village, is a small bank of soundings, that stretches some distance into the sea. On the south side of this bank the soundings were irregular, from 25 to eight fathoms, rocky bottom; but, to the north of it, near the rock, no ground could be reached with 90 and 100 fathoms of line, though not more than the fourth of a mile from the shore; this we found to be the case also a little to the southward of the bank. In both these places we were for some time very aukwardly situated, without wind, yet with a swell and current that set us so fast towards the land, that I was under some apprehension for the safety of the ship, as the united force of the current and swell prevented any effect from the assistance of the boats; from this dilemma however we were happily relieved, by a breeze springing up, that enabled us to increase our distance from the land.

The few inhabitants who visited us from the village, earnestly intreated our anchoring, and told us, that if we would stay until the morning, their chief would be on board with a number of hogs, and a great quantity of vegetables; but that he could not visit us then because the day was *taboo poory*. The face of the country did not however promise an abundant supply; the situation was exposed, and the extent of anchorage was not only very limited, but bad; under these circumstances, having, by eleven at night, got clear of the shores, I deemed it most prudent to make the best of our way, with a light S.E. breeze, towards Attowai.

We had not reached more than half way between the two islands, by noon the next day, Tuesday the 20th; when the observed latitude was 21° 19', longitude 201° 18'. In this situation Woahoo extended, by compass, from S. 88 E. to S. 64 E., and Attowai from N. 70 W. to N. 87 W. The weather was now calm, and continued so all the afternoon; this gave to some of the islanders, who were passing from Attowai to Mowee, an opportunity to visit the ship. The foremost of these, undertaking so distant a voyage in a single canoe, much attracted our attention; on her coming alongside, she proved to be without exception the finest canoe we had seen amongst these islands. This vessel was sixty-one feet and a half long, exceeding, by four feet and a half, the largest canoes of Owhyhee;[1] its depth and width were in their proportion of building, and the whole of the workmanship was finished in a very masterly manner.

The size of this canoe was not its only curiosity, the wood of which it was

[1] Ten months later Bell saw a larger canoe on the island of Hawaii: 'Here we saw some of the very large War Canoes measuring upwards of Sixty feet in length of one Tree, but at Tayamodu's [Keeaumoku's], when we returned we were shewn one of his large War Canoes, reckoned among the finest though not the longest, in the Island. It was like all the large Canoes – double neatly and handsomely finished; and did infinite credit to the workmen – each Separate Canoe measured about Sixty five feet in length all one solid piece, form'd out of a Tree. It had eight beams or thwart pieces (which by securing the two Canoes to their ends, denominate a double Canoe). It was intended to carry fifty Paddlers, (twenty-five on each Side) and I should imagine between 30 and forty men on the platform that is always fixed fore and aft, on the Beams.' 27 January 1794.

formed was an infinitely greater, being made out of an exceedingly fine pine-tree. As this species of timber is not the produce of any of these islands, and as the natives informed us it was drifted by the ocean, it is probably the growth of some of the northern parts of America.

This, it seems, was left on the east end of Attowai, in a perfectly sound state, without a shake or a bruise. It remained there unwrought for some time, in the hope of a companion arriving in the same manner. In this case, the natives would have been enabled to have formed the grandest double canoe these islands could boast of; but their patience having been exhausted, they converted the tree into this canoe; which, by the lightness of its timber, and the large outrigger it is capable of supporting, is rendered very lively in the sea, and well adapted to the service it generally performs, – that of communicating intelligence to *Taio*, whilst he is absent from the government of his own dominions.

The circumstance of fir timber being drifted on the northern sides of these islands is by no means uncommon, especially at Attowai, where there then was a double canoe, of a middling size, made from two small pine-trees, that were driven on shore nearly at the same spot. Some logs of timber, with three or four trees of the pine tribe, were then lying on the island, that had at different times been lodged by the sea, but were too much decayed and worm-eaten to be usefully appropriated.

As this kind of timber is the known produce of all the northern part of the west side of America, little doubt can remain of these trees having come from that continent, or its contiguous islands; since it is more than probable, that if any intervening land did exist between the Sandwich islands, and the countries on every side of them, and particularly in the direction of the prevailing winds, such would have been discovered before now. And hence we may conclude, that trees do perform very distant voyages, and sometimes arrive in a sound state at the end of their journey. This instance alone will be sufficient to develope the mystery attending the means by which the inhabitants of Easter island procure their canoes, since the distance of that island from South America, is not so far by 80 leagues as Attowai is from the shores of North America.

The object of this canoe expedition, we learned, was to inform *Taio* of some commotions that had arisen against the government of *Enemo* the regent. But these having been timely opposed, they had subsided, without any loss on the part of *Enemo*, or his adherents; whilst on the side of the conspirators, two chiefs and five men had been killed, and some others wounded, who had made their escape to the woods.

The leg bones of the two unfortunate chiefs were in the canoe, and had some of the sinews and flesh still adhering to them; in this state they were to be presented to *Taio*, as trophies of victory over the rebels. This large single canoe was charged with the official dispatch and important part of the business, whilst the others were employed in conducting a certain number of the ringleaders as prisoners to *Taio*, for his examination, and sentence on their conduct. Amongst these were several of his nearest relations; one in particular was his half-sister, who had also been his wife or mistress, and had borne him some children.[1]

The charge of this embassy was intrusted to a young chief, about twenty-two years of age, named *Oeashew*.[2] Our meeting him must be considered as rather a singular circumstance, as the business that had carried *Poorey*[3] to Mowee, (a chief we had taken on board at Woahoo, and was on his return home to Attowai) had been some matters of importance relative to the government of that island; in consequence of which *Titeeree* and *Taio* had appointed this young man chief of the district of Whymea, one of the most important trusts on the island; where his presence at this time was considered as highly necessary. *Poorey* requested I would permit *Oeashew* to return in the ship to Attowai, which being granted, the latter instructed another chief with the purport of his commission. This occupied them in very secret conversation for about half an hour; when, the charge being properly and completely transferred, the canoes pushed off, and made the best of their way towards Woahoo, where they expected to arrive early the next morning, having quitted Attowai at sun-set the preceding evening.

During the night the wind was light from the northward, but in the morning of Wednesday the 27th, it freshened to a pleasant, though unfavorable breeze, that prevented our weathering the north-east point of Attowai, as I had intended, for the purpose of examining its northern shores. The water being smooth, and the wind steady in force and direction, I was in hopes we should have been able to beat round it, until we had approached the shores; when it became evident we were in a strong current setting to leeward.

I however did not wish to abandon hastily the project I had in view, and therefore, about nine o'clock, we tacked about two miles from the shore, then extending, by compass, from N. 8 W. to S. 20 W.; these extremities, which lie from each other N. 14 E. and S. 14 W., are each formed by low land, are about nine miles asunder, and constitute what may be deemed the east side of the island. The former in a rounding point projects into the ocean, from a very remarkable forked hill,[4] that is, in a great measure, detached from the rest of the connected mountains of the island. The latter extends from a range of low hills that stretch along the coast, at a small distance within the beach. Beyond these hills, towards the foot of the mountains that are at some distance from the shore, the country presented a most delightful, and even enchanting,

---

[1] 'the mother of a favourite young son named *Tapo* who I know was formerly a great favourite of his.' – Menzies, 26 March.

[2] More correctly Oneashew, chief of Waimea, Kauai.

[3] Pule, chief of the district of Waimea, Kauai.

[4] Presumably what is now named Hole-in-the-Mountain. The tradition is that the spear of a chief who was participating in a spear-throwing contest pierced the mountain and fell on the beach.

appearance; not only from the richness of its verdure, and the high state of cultivation in the low regions, but from the romantic air that the mountains assumed, in various shapes and proportions, clothed with a forest of luxuriant foliage, whose different shades added great richness and beauty to the landscape.

About a league to the south of the southern extremity, lies the south-east point of the island,[1] formed by a bold, bluff, barren, high, rocky headland, falling perpendicularly into the sea. Between this and the low point is a small cove,[2] accessible for boats only, where, near a rivulet that flows into it, is a village of the natives. This part seemed to be very well watered, as three other rapid small streams were observed to flow into the sea within the limits above mentioned. This portion of Attowai, the most fertile and pleasant district of the island, is the principal residence of the king, or, in his absence, of the superior chief, who generally takes up his abode in an extensive village, about a league to the southward of the north-east point of the island. Here *Enemo* the regent, with the young prince *Tamooerrie*,[3] were now living; who sent Williams (the Welshman mentioned in our former visit) to acquaint me, that, in the course of the forenoon, they would visit the ship, if we were near enough the shore for them to embark. I understood from Williams, that we had gained so much on the esteem and regard of *Enemo*, the young prince, the principal chiefs, and others, on our last visit, that, for a great length of time, the hogs, and every other production of the major part of the island, had been *tabooed*, in order that on our arrival our wants might be amply supplied. Of these kind intentions we were made acquainted before our departure from Owhyhee; but I knew too well the little regard that the whole of the great South-Sea nation of islanders bear to truth, to rely implicitly on such tales; and it was very fortunate that I did not, and that I had availed myself of the bounty of *Tamaahmaah*, and the rest of the Owhyhean friends: for I was given to understand, that, in consequence of our having exceeded the period of our promised return, the pressing demands of the trading vessels, and the extravagant prices paid by their commanders, in fire-arms, ammunition, and other commodities, for such things as their necessities or fancies prompted them to purchase, the regent had been prevailed upon to suspend the interdiction, under the persuasion that we should not return, and that most of the supplies had been disposed of. Some few hogs, I found, might probably be procured from the north side, and I was happy to discover, that the few supplies we were likely to obtain, were in the route I wished to pursue; but I was again mortified, on hearing that the current sat, almost without intermission, from the N.W. along the north side of the island; and following the direction of the shores, on the southern and western side of the island; caused a stream almost always round it; so that the easiest mode of arriving at the north-east point, now scarcely more than two leagues distant, was to

---

[1] Kawai Point, which the *U.S. Coast Pilot* 7 describes as being 'a bold rocky headland, 525 feet high, very irregular and jagged in appearance'.

[2] Nawiliwili Bay.   [3] Kaumualii.

sail to leeward round its west extremity, and then to turn up along its northern side, which Williams informed me afforded no shelter, nor convenient anchorage, for shipping. Several vessels, he said, since he had been at Attowai, had fallen, as we had done, to leeward of the north-east point, and all their attempts to beat round it proved ineffectual; one vessel only having succeeded after a a week's trial, and which then passed the point merely by an accidental spirt of wind from the southward.

Williams confirmed also the account of the insurrection that we had heard of the preceding day. He stated, that the disaffection had been produced by the conduct of the regent *Enemo*,[1] (or, as he is frequently called, *Ataia*); that no harm was meditated against *Taio*, or his son *Tamooerrie*; but, on the contrary, it was the general wish of the people, that the young prince would either direct the government himself, or that *Taio* would appoint some other person to officiate in his absence, until his son should be considered equal to the talk. The principal dislike to the regent, arose from his having put several people to death, and confiscated the property of others, for having been suspected of witchcraft,[2] a notion that universally prevails, and is confided in by the generality of the people belonging to the Sandwich islands. It seemed, by his account, to have been a fortunate circumstance, that the insurrection was discovered in its infancy, and that he and Rowbottom, with five other English or American sailors (who since our last visit had deserted from different trading vessels) had sided with the governor, as, on their instantly attacking the leaders of the rebellion it was easily quelled. This circumstance was afterwards mentioned by the natives, who spoke in the highest terms of their courage, and propriety of conduct.

We again stood in shore, and about noon were honoured with the presence of *Enemo*.

On this occasion, I expected much satisfaction in the renewal of our former acquaintance; but instead of deriving any pleasure in our meeting, I experienced sensations of a very opposite nature the instant he entered the ship. His limbs no longer able to support his aged and venerable person, seemed not only deserted by their former muscular strength, but their substance was also entirely wasted away, and the skin, now inclosing the bones only, hung loose and uncontracted from the joints, whilst a dry white scurf, or rather scales which overspread the whole surface of his body from head to foot, tended greatly to increase the miserable and deplorable appearance of his condition; and I was not a little shocked and surprised that one so wretchedly infirm, should have taken the painful trouble of this visit. The compliment

---

[1] Spelled Enemoh elsewhere. Inamoo may be a more correct spelling. A year later Vancouver noted that he had changed his name to Wakea.

[2] Menzies states that the trouble had arisen because he had 'exercised his present delegated authority with the imperious sway of a despotic Governor by frequent private assassinations for the most frivolous reasons, even among the Chiefs, sparing neither rank nor sex in the accomplishment of his Views...' – 29 March.

was a very flattering one, and I did not fail to receive it as it was intended, by acknowledging myself considerably obliged.

Notwithstanding his corporeal infirmities, and the decline of his life, he still supported a degree of cheerful spirits, said he was very happy to see us, and much concerned that we had not arrived on an earlier day, according to our promise, when he should have had an abundant quantity of refreshments for our use, and lamented that those supplies were now greatly exhausted. I acknowledged that it was our misfortune, not his fault, that we had not arrived at the time appointed; thanked him for the interest he had preserved, and the attention he had shewn to our welfare during our absence; and rewarded his friendship by presents similar to those I had made the principal chiefs of the other islands. With these he was highly-gratified, especially with the scarlet cloak, and a complete set of armourer's tools. These are in high estimation, as these people are fond of forming the iron for their several purposes after their own fashion.

Enemo remained on board most of the afternoon, made many sensible and judicious inquiries, and soon took an occasion to express, in the warmest manner, his satisfaction at the measures I had taken for the purpose of establishing a general peace. This he had learned from *Poorey*, who had visited *Enemo* on shore early in the morning. The old regent, with great understanding, adverted to its necessity for the mutual good happiness, and prosperity of all parties; and observed, that to him it would be particularly grateful, as it would relieve him from much care and anxiety, by the return of his relations, friends, and countrymen. He then desired to know, whether on my return to England I would take him thither, as his principal wish in this life was to see that country, and to have the gratification of speaking to His Majesty King George; after this, he said, he should die in peace, without having another wish to indulge. On this subject he seemed so earnest, that I thought proper, by a promise in the affirmative, to favor his fond hopes.

The ship being near the shore, about four in the afternoon the good old regent took his leave, after acquainting me, that as the next day was *taboo-poory*, neither himself nor the prince could leave the shore; but that he would direct a chief to bring off such hogs and vegetables as could be collected by the morning; and that if we would remain off this part of the island until the day following, he would either bring himself, or send off, such further supplies as could be procured in the neighbourhood. Thus we parted from this friendly old chief, with little expectation of ever seeing him again.

Soon after the departure of *Enemo*, *Tamooerrie*, attended by *Poorey*, came on board. The young prince appeared to be in high spirits, and was totally divested of those fears which he had entertained on his former visit. He seemed to be made very happy by our return; but, as his guardian had done, upbraided us for not having come before, when the several productions of his country were in the greatest abundance, and had been reserved for our use and service. The approach of night, and the distance we were to leeward of his habitation, conspired to shorten his visit. I made him some presents suitable to his rank and condition, after which, with the chiefs who were on board, he reluctantly took leave, desiring we would remain in the neighbourhood two or three days, that we might receive such articles of refreshment as could be obtained. This, I said, would depend upon circumstances; and on the departure of the canoes we made all sail to windward, with a pleasant steady breeze at N.N.E.; notwithstanding which, the next morning, Thursday the 14th,[1] we had not advanced more than a mile to windward of our situation the preceding evening.

Being near the shore in the forenoon, and seeing some canoes making towards the ship, we tacked and brought to, to give them an opportunity of coming alongside. These presently were proved to contain our friends *Poorey*, *Too*, and some other chiefs, who had brought us eight middling sized hogs, and some vegetables. This was but a scanty supply; and as the apologies we received, proved we had little probability of procuring more, and as little chance of beating round this part of the island in any tolerable time, I declined persisting, and bore up for Whymea bay. There I intended to complete our water; and then, without further delay, to direct our course to the northward; having still remaining of our Owhyhean stock, a number of hogs, exclusive of six hogsheads and ten barrels that had been salted and headed down, and every man in the ship having been daily served with as much pork as he liked.

These refreshments, with those we had before obtained from our Spanish friends in New Albion, had so perfectly re-established the health and strength of every individual on board, that I hoped we should be able to encounter the difficulties I had reason to apprehend in our next campaign, with all the firmness and alacrity that such services demand.

Poorey and the rest of the chiefs accompanied us, in order that they might afford us their good offices at Whymea; where, owing to light baffling winds in its neighbourhood, we were prevented anchoring until eleven at night; when we took our former station, conceiving it to be the best in the bay, in 33 fathoms water, dark sandy bottom, about half a league from the shore.

The next morning, Friday 29th, as the few natives who had visited us brought little for sale, *Poorey* and the rest of his friends betook themselves to the shore, for the purpose of collecting in the neighbourhood such hogs and vegetables as could be procured. The launch was hoisted out, and sent with a guard of marines under the orders of Lieutenant Swaine, for a supply of water.

I was engaged on shore most of the day, in regulating a comfortable establishment that I had procured from the chiefs, for our two female passengers, the one named *Raheina*, the other *Tymarow*, whom we had met with, as already stated, at Nootka, in October, 1792, and had brought from thence, to restore them to this their native country; from whence thay had

---

[1] 28 March, not 14 March. The mistake is in both editions.

been forcibly taken, and had endured an uncomfortable absence of upwards of a year. This office of humanity, to which their behaviour and amiable disposition so justly intitled them, I was fortunate enough to accomplish to their satisfaction; and I had the pleasure of finding that they both acknowledged this, and the civil and attentive treatment they had each received from every person on board the Discovery and Chatham, with expressions of gratitude, and the most affectionate regard.

Amongst the various reports industriously circulated at Nootka by the citizens of the United States of America, to the prejudice and dishonor of the British subjects trading on the coast of North West America, it had been positively asserted, that some of the latter had brought the natives of the Sandwich islands from thence to the coast of America, and had there sold them to the natives of those shores for furs. These two young women were particularly instanced, as having been so brought and disposed of by Mr. Baker, commanding the Jenny, of Bristol; and the story was told with such plausibility, that I believe it had acquired some degree of credit with Senr Quadra, and most of the Spanish officers who heard it. The arrival of the Jenny, however, in the port of Nootka, gave a flat contradiction to these scandalous reports, and proved them to be equally malicious and untrue; as the two girls were found still remaining on board the Jenny, without having entertained any idea that they were intended to have been sold; nor did they mention having received any ill usage from Mr. Baker, but on the contrary, that they had been treated with every kindness and attention whilst under his protection.

Although I had not any personal knowledge of Mr. Baker previous to his entering Nootka, yet I should conceive him totally incapable of such an act of barbarity and injustice; and if there were the least sincerity in the solicitude he expressed to me for the future happiness and welfare of these young women, it is impossible he could ever have meditated such a design. I do not, however, mean to vindicate the propriety of Mr. Baker's conduct, in bringing these girls from their native country; for I am decidedly of opinion it was highly improper; and if the young women are to be credited, their seduction and detention on board Mr. Baker's vessel were inexcusable. They report, that they went on board with several others of their countrywomen, who were permitted to return again to the shore; but that *they* were confined down in the cabin until the vessel had sailed, and was at some distance from Onehow. On the other hand, Mr. Baker states, that he put to sea without any knowledge of their being on board his vessel. But be that as it may, we found them thus situated at Nootka; and the future objects of Mr. Baker's voyage leading him wide of the Sandwich islands, he requested, as I then noticed, that I would allow them to take their passage thither on board the Discovery. To this I assented, and on our sailing from Nootka, they were sent on board and taken under my protection.

The names of these unfortunate females we first understood were *Taheeopiah* and *Tymarow*, both of the island of Onehow. The former, about fifteen years of age, was there of some consequence; the latter, about four or five years older, was related to the former, but was not of equal rank in the island.

Taheeopiah, for some reason I never could understand, altered her name to that of *Raheina*, a short time after she came on board, and continued to be so called.

After leaving Nootka, our visit to the Spanish settlements, especially during the first part of our residence there, afforded them some recompence for the long and tedious voyage they had been compelled to undertake from their native country.

The sight of horses, cattle, and other animals, with a variety of objects to which they were intire strangers, produced in them the highest entertainment; and without the least hesitation or alarm, they were placed on horseback on their first landing, and, with a man to lead the animal, they rode without fear, and were by that means enabled to partake of all the civilities and diversions which our Spanish friends so obligingly offered and provided. On all these occasions they were treated with the greatest kindness and attention by the ladies and gentlemen; at which they were not less delighted, than they were surprized at the social manner in which both sexes live, according to the custom of most civilized nations; differing so very materially from that of their own.

These pleasures, however they enjoyed but a short time; for soon after our arrival at Monterrey, they were both taken extremely ill; and notwithstanding that every means in our power was resorted to for the re-establishment of their health, they did not perfectly recover until after our arrival at Owhyhee.

They seemed much pleased with the European fashions, and in conforming to this new system of manners, they conducted themselves in company with a degree of propriety beyond all expectation. Their European dress contributed most probably to this effect, and produced, particularly in *Raheina*, a degree of personal delicacy that was conspicuous on many occasions. This dress was a riding habit, as being best calculated for their situation, and indeed the best in our power to procure. Its skirt, or lower part, was soon found to be intended as much for concealment, as for warmth; and in the course of a very short time, she became so perfectly familiar to its use in this respect, that in going up and down the ladders that communicate with the different parts of the ship, she would take as much care not to expose her ancles, as if she had been educated by the most rigid governess; and as this was particularly observable in the conduct of *Raheina*, it is probable her youth rendered her more susceptible of fresh notions, and of receiving new ideas and impressions from the surrounding objects, than the more matured age of her friend *Tymarow*.

The elegance of *Raheina's* figure, the regularity and softness of her features, and the delicacy which she naturally possessed, gave her a superiority in point of personal accomplishments over the generality of her sex amongst the Sandwich islanders; in addition to which, her sensibility and turn of mind, her sweetness of temper and complacency of manners, were beyond any thing that could have been expected from her birth, or native education; so that if it were fair to judge of the dispositions of a whole nation from the qualities of these two young women, it would seem that they are endued with much affection and tenderness. At least, such was their deportment towards us; by which they gained the regard and good wishes of, I believe, every one on board, whilst I became in no small degree solicitous for their future happiness and prosperity.

Onehow being the place of their birth and former residence, I had promised to set them on shore on that island; but on our arrival at Owhyhee, I had understood that the inhabitants of Onehow had almost intirely abandoned it, in consequence of the excessive drought that had prevailed during the last summer; which had nearly caused the total destruction of all its vegetable productions. Finding on my arrival at Attowai this information to have been well grounded, I came to a determination to leave our female friends at this island.

Being well aware that the mode of living they had lately been constrained to adopt, and that their having eaten at mine and other tables in the company of men, was an offence of so heinous a nature against their laws as to subject them both to the punishment of death, I took much pains to point out to *Titeeree* and *Taio* their innocence in this respect; and obtained from them both the strongest assurances, that they should not be liable to the least injury on that account, but that on their landing they should be immediately taken care of and protected.

These intreaties I enforced with *Enemo*, in the presence of *Raheina* and *Tymarow*, when he was on board; and had the satisfaction of receiving from him similar assurances of his protection, not only of their persons, but their property; and that whatever articles we might think proper to give them, should be secured to them, and no one should be permitted to wrest or extort any thing from them. These assurances being given not only by *Enemo*, but by the rest of the chiefs then present,[1] I thought by the purchase of a house and a small portion of land, to add to their future respectability and comfort. This *Enemo* would not permit me to do, but instantly directed *Oeashew* to allot to each of them an estate in his newly acquired district of Whymea; to which *Oeashew* with much apparent pleasure consented.

The better to make sure of this donation, and to secure the permanent

---

[1] Menzies noted that their possessions 'consisted mostly of a number of small articles, such as Knives Scissars looking Glasses Beads Buttons Ear rings Needles Tapes Nails Axes Fish hooks pieces of iron files rasps & a variety of other tools besides a great quantity of different Cloths & ornamental articles from Owhyhee & the other Islands.' Some of these had been given to them by Puget before the *Chatham* parted company with the *Discovery*. Menzies had little expectation that they would be able to retain these possessions for long: 'The Chiefs however wishd to know if they [the girls] were to be allowd to make presents to whomsoever they liked themselves, this certainly could not with propriety be prevented, & we had no doubt but their whole property would soon be disposed of in this way, as they were constantly surrounded by a number of begging friends & relations or such as pretended to be so, who were likely to strip them of every thing.' – 29 March.

possession of it to these young women, I desired that the houses and land might be given to me, that the property should be considered as vested in me, and that no person whatever should have any right in it, but by my permission; and that I would allow *Raheina* and *Tymarow* to live upon the estates.

Matters having been in this manner arranged, *Oeashew* had gone on shore in the morning to fix upon the lands that were to be thus disposed of; and about three in the afternoon he returned, saying that he had fixed upon two very eligible situations adjoining to each other, which if I approved should be mine; if not, I was at liberty to make choice of any other part of the district I might think more proper. In consequence of this offer, I attended him on shore, accompanied by some of the officers and our two females, who had received such an assortment of articles from us, as were deemed sufficient to make them respectable, without exciting the envy of the chiefs or their neighbours.

We found the situation proposed by *Oeashew* to be a very large portion of the fertile valley, noticed on our former visit on the western side of the river, commencing at the sea beach, and extending along the banks of the river to a certain established landmark, including a very considerable extent of the inland mountainous country. The contiguity of these estates to the commerce of all the Europeans who visit this island, and the territory which it comprehended, was in value so far above our most sanguine expectations, that I was led to suspect the sincerity of the intended donation. But to this we became reconciled, from the protestations of the chief himself, as also from the universal declaration of many of the natives who had accompanied us, and who asserted that *Oeashew* really intended thus to dispose of the land in question; to which he added the most solemn assurances that he would protect them in the possession of it; together with their canoes, and all the articles they had brought with them from the ship; which declarations seemed perfectly to satisfy the young women, that they would be put into possession of these estates; and that their persons and property would be protected according to the assurances we had now received.

A long established line of division, formed by trees and a common road, separated the two estates. The lower one nearest the sea, which was the most extensive, was allotted to *Raheina*, the other to *Tymarow*; each of which they respectively took possession of, and in the warmest and most grateful terms acknowledged the obligations they were under, for this last mark of our attention to their future happiness; and for the friendship and kindness they had experienced during their residence amongst us. They attended us to the beach, where they took an affectionate leave, and we embarked for the ship, leaving them to meditate on their new situation, and the various turns of fortune that had conspired to place them in such comfortable circumstances.

On my arrival on board, I found our friends who had been employed in procuring us supplies had returned with little success. Seventeen middling sized hogs, a few potatoes, and some taro, without any yams, was the whole amount of their collection. Our stock of water was completely replenished; and being satisfied from the report of the chiefs that no additional quantity of provisions was to be had at this island, I informed them that we should depart the first favorable opportunity. They enquired if I intended to visit the north side, as *Poorey* and *Too* would in that case continue on board for the purpose of assisting us in procuring some yams, which they said were more plentiful there than on the south side of the island; but as nothing less than a very tempting opportunity would have induced me to go thither, I declined giving them further trouble, and having presented them with such articles as their services and the occasion demanded, they took their leave, with expressions of the highest satisfaction, promising to pay every attention, and afford all possible assistance and protection, to their countrywomen whom we had just landed, and in whose future happiness and welfare they knew we had great interest.

A light breeze of wind springing up from the land, about ten at night we put to sea and stood to the westward, to take the advantage of the south-westerly winds, which we were led to believe prevailed generalliy at this season of the year.

On Saturday morning the 30th, Attowai bore by compass from N. 20 E. to S. 77 E.; Onehow,[1] S. 64 W. to S. 85 W.; and Oreehooa,[2] west. But, instead of the promised south-west wind, we were met by a fresh trade wind from the north-east. As this circumstance precluded our making a speedy survey of the north side of the island, I gave up that object for the present.

A report having prevailed that Captain Cook had erroneously separated Oreehooa from Onehow, it being asserted that the inhabitants walked from one place to the other; and that Captain King had been misinformed as to the number of inhabitants being four thousand. As these facts could be easily ascertained, we steered over for Orrehooa, and passed within a quarter or half a mile of its shores. It was soon proved that Oreehooa is positively separated from Onehow by a channel about a mile in breadth; and though the depth of the sea appeared by its colour to be irregular, it was manifestly far too deep for people to walk across from one island to the other. As this channel lies immediately open, and is exposed to the whole force and influence of the trade wind, and the swell of the sea consequent upon it, (neither of which were very moderate at the time of our examination,) it is natural to infer, that if the channel did admit of foot passengers crossing it, the causeway would have been visible above the surface of the water; or, from the violence with which the sea broke on the contiguous shores, that it certainly would have broken over a space so shallow, as to allow people to pass and repass on foot; but the sea did not break in any part of the channel, which, on the contrary, seemed to be nearly of a sufficient depth to admit of a passage for the Discovery.[3] With respect to the population, Captain King

---

[1] Niihau.
[2] Lehua Island, a small island off the N end of Niihau.
[3] A channel between the islands has a minimum depth of 9 fathoms.

must doubtless have been led into an error.[1] The island of Orrehooa is of very small extent, and wholly composed of one rugged, naked, barren rock, to all appearance destitute of soil, and presenting no indication of its being, or having ever been the residence of human creatures.

Having completely satisfied our minds in these respects, we hauled our wind to the north-west, and with all sails set, we bade adieu to the Sandwich islands for the present, and made the best of our way towards Nootka.

[1] See Cook, *Journals*, III, pp. 619, 120n. Bligh reduced the estimate from 4000 to 200.

BOOK THE FOURTH.

SECOND VISIT TO THE NORTH; SURVEY OF THE AMERICAN
COAST FROM FITZHUGH'S SOUND TO CAPE DECISION;
AND FROM MONTERREY TO THE SOUTHERN EXTENT OF
OUR INTENDED INVESTIGATION.

CHAPTER I.

*Passage towards the Coast of America—Anchor in Trinidad Bay—Description of
the Bay, its Inhabitants, &c. &c.—Arrival at Nootka—Quit Nootka, and proceed
to the Northward—Join the Chatham in Fitzhugh's Sound.*

WE took our departure from the Sandwich islands on Saturday the 30th of
March, with the trade wind blowing principally from the N.N.E. and N.E.
accompanied by very pleasant weather; and in one week afterwards,[1] Saturday
the 6th of April, we reached the variable winds, having a light breeze from
the southward, with which we steered N. by E.; our observed latitude at this
time was 30° 35′, longitude by Kendall's chronometer, 197° 26′, Arnold's No.
14, 196° 57½′, No. 176, 197° 42′, and Earnshaw's, 196° 37½′. The variation
of the compass was 13° 46′, eastwardly.

Since our leaving the islands, I observed a very extraordinary rise and fall
of the mercury in the barometer. Early in the morning it would be three or
four tenths of an inch higher than at noon; its mean height at that time of
the day being 30. 38, varying only from 30. 43, to 30. 34; whereas in the
morning it would stand at 30. 70; it did not regularly descend, but fluctuated
until it settled as above stated. This day, however, it gradually fell from 30. 40,
its point at the preceding noon, to 30. 27, without any fluctuation whatever.
As there was no sensible alteration in the state of the atmosphere, nor any

---

[1] Menzies mentions an event that Vancouver ignores: 'The first of April being the
[second] anniversary of our leaving England, the Captain & Officers [of the *Discovery*] dind
together in the Cabin in the best Cheer the country afforded, which was Turtle, & the
people were indulgd with a double allowance of Grog to commemorate the day.'

visible indication of a change in the weather, I was at a loss to account for this deviation; since the instrument did not appear to have received any injury.

Some few small albatrosses and petrels had lately been seen about the ship; and in the morning of Sunday the 7th, the wind shifted suddenly to the north-west, attended with squalls and rain, which produced a considerable alteration in our climate. The thermometer now fell from 73 at noon in the former day, to 59 this day at twelve o'clock.[1]

Our pork and other refreshments, procured at the Sandwich islands, being all expended, the regular provisions were now served, with portable soup five times a week in the peas for dinner, and three times a week in the wheat for breakfast, with a due proportion of sour krout. On our former passage to the northward, I had been less prodigal of these healthy articles, under the fear that some accident had befallen the expected store ship; but, as our stock was now replenished, I ordered a double quantity to be regularly served, that we might preserve the excellent state of health we had all acquired by the refreshments we had procured in New Albion, and at the Sandwich islands. The general state of health on board both vessels, on our return to the southward last autumn, clearly convinced me, that too much nourishing and wholesome food cannot be given to people employed on such arduous services, as those in which we were engaged.

A small flock of curlews, or some such coasting birds, with several others of the petrel tribe, were about the ship: on Monday the 8th we also saw several whales, and passed through a large quantity of the medusa villilia. Our observed latitude was 33° 4′, longitude by Kendall's chronometer, 201° 4¾′; by Arnold's No. 14, 200° 37½′; Arnold's No. 176, 201° 26′; and Earnshaw's, 200° 18′. The wind, though generally moderate, was very variable, as well in force as in direction. The weather gloomy, with some rain; the air sharp and unpleasant. We however made a tolerably good progress, and on Saturday the 13th, at noon, had reached the latitude of 35° 27′, longitude by Kendall's chronometer, 209° 22½′; Arnold's No. 14, 208° 57′; Arnold's No. 176, 210° 1′; and Earnshaw's, 208° 45¼′; in this situation we were visited by some flocks of coasting birds, with albatrosses, and some variety of the petrel tribe. The sea was covered with abundance of the medusa villilia, but we had not lately seen many whales. In the course of the night we passed over a part of that space, where Mr. Meares states that Mr. Douglas, of the Iphigenia, in two different passages, found the compass so affected, by flying about four or five points in a moment, as to make it impossible to steer the ship by it.[2]

---

[1] The *Chatham*, which had sailed earlier, had also encountered 'a material Alteration in the Weather insomuch so that we were obliged to put on our warmest Cloathing. The Live Stock suffered mostly by the Cold which not only destroyed the major part of the Sandwich Island Poultry but also three or four large Hogs.' – Puget, 23 March. Later they 'felt the Cold exceedingly, which proved fatal to the three remaining Monterey Sheep & the Major part of our Live Stock.' – 6 April.

[2] 'It may be proper, however, to mention, that in the beginning of April [1789], for two or three days together, it became impossible to steer the ship, the compasses flying

We however met with no phænomenon of that nature, either now, or at any former period of our voyage, unless when the violence of the wind and sea produced such an agitation, as to render it utterly impossible that any machine of that sort could remain steady.

The wind remaining in the north-west quarter, and the sky obscured in one continual dense haze, or dark heavy gloom, occasioned the weather to be damp, chilly, and unpleasant. The thermometer fluctuated between 52 and 55; the barometer, though not altogether regular, was more uniform than it had lately been, being on an average about 30. 30. Tuesday 16th, on winding up Earnshaw's watch, it stopped; but on applying a little gentle horizontal motion, it went again, after stopping about two minutes and a half; I was much concerned at this unexpected circumstance, having hitherto found this excellent piece of workmanship to be highly intitled to our praise.

Though we were now in a much more western situation, we were advanced as far to the north as we were on the 16th of April, 1792; and having no object to lead us to the coast between this parallel and our appointed rendezvous at Nootka, then lying from us N. 47 E. at the distance of 312 leagues, we had reason to expect we should be at that port as soon as could be necessary for resuming the examination of the continent to the northward from Fitzhugh's sound, whence we had taken our departure in the month of last August. The observed latitude wass 38° 58′, longitude according to Kendall's chronometer, 217° 40½′, Arnold's No. 14, 217° 19½′, Arnold's No. 176, 218° 31½′. Many of the medusa villilia were still about the ship; a heavy swell rolled from the north-westward; some few oceanic birds were seen, but not any whales.

After the weather had been calm, or nearly so, during the greater part of Wednesday the 17th, and Thursday the 18th, the wind fixed in the northern board, and varied little between N.N.E. and N. by W. This obliged us to stand to the eastward, and I was not without hope, that in case it should continue so until we made the coast of New Albion, we should there have more favorable opportunities of advancing to the northward. This opinion was founded on the experience we derived the last spring, when close in with its shores.

A continuation of the same gloomy unpleasant weather still attended us, with an increase of wind that sometimes obliged us to take in the third reefs in our topsails. The cross-jack yard having been carried away, it was replaced on Monday the 22nd by a spare maintop-sail yard. At this time we were rendered very uncomfortable by the increasing from two or three inches to upwards of a foot per hour of a leak that had been discovered a few days after we had left the Sandwich islands, and had been suspected to have arisen

about each way four or five points in a moment. – Captain Douglas remarks, that he experienced the same phaenomenon last year about the same latitude. The latitude at this time was from 36° 19′ to 36° 10′ North, and the longitude from 208° 15′ to 210° 13′.' – Meares, *Voyages*, p. 360.

from some defect in the bows; the water in this quantity had not only found its way into the well, but had also filled the coal hole up to the deck, which could scarcely be kept under by constant baling, and from thence had reached the magazine, where I was apprehensive some of the powder might receive material damage. At noon our observed latitude was 38° 54'; longitude by Kendall's chronometer, 228° 21'; Arnold's No. 14, 228° 8'; and No. 176, 229° 25'.

The jib-boom and foretop-gallant-mast were, the next morning, Tuesday the 23rd, carried away, and at day-light the foretop-mast cross-tree was also found broken; these were immediately replaced; and the same unfavourable winds and unpleasant weather still continued; which, however, brought us, on the evening of Friday the 26th, within sight of cape Mendocino,[1] bearing by compass N.E. by N. seven or eight leagues distant. The leak in the ship's bows, though daily increasing when the wind blew strong, we had every reason to believe was above water, as in light winds no ill effects were produced from it, and therefore no material consequences were apprehended.

It may not be improper to notice, that we found the medusa villilia, though not without some intervals of clear spaces, existing on the surface of the ocean from the place where they were first observed on the 8th of this month, to within about 40 leagues of our then situation. At eight in the evening we tacked and stood off the land. The wind at N.W. by N. increased very much; but as the sea was smooth, I was flattered with the hope of making some progress by turning to windward along the shore, and tacking occasionally as advantages were presented. The observed latitude at noon the next day, Saturday the 27th, was 39° 54', so that we had gained only four leagues to the north-ward in 24 hours.

The land was not in sight, nor could we obtain any observations from the chronometers. On winding them up, it appeared that Earnshaw's had intirely stopped about eight hours after it was wound up the preceding day. I repeated my efforts to put it again in motion, but did not succeed; and as its cases were secured by a screw, to which there was no corresponding lever in the box that contained, it, I concluded that in the event of any accident, it was Mr. Earnshaw's wish that no attempt should be made to remedy it; it was therefore left for the examination and repair of its ingenious maker. I had for some time suspected something was wrong in this excellent little watch. On its first coming on board it beat much louder than any of the others, and so continued until we quitted the Sandwich islands, when it gradually decreased in its tone until it became weaker than any of them; from whence I was led to conjecture, that probably too much oil had been originally applied, which was now congealed, and clogged the works.

---

[1] Menzies states that they made the coast 'very unexpectedly, as our old time keeper placed us near a degree & a half to the westward of our real situation agreeable to our former Settlement of this part of the Coast which we in great measure attribute to the change in temperature of the weather since her rate was taken at Karakakooa in Owhyhee.' – 26 April. By 'our old time keeper' Menzies meant the Kendall chronometer.

We continued to ply with adverse winds to little effect. On Monday the 29th, we had only reached the latitude of 40° 16′. The weather was serene and pleasant, and although the thermometer stood at 55°, the air was sharp. The promontories of cape Mendocino bore by compass, at four in the afternoon, from E. to N. 25 E.; this, agreeably to the situation assigned to those points on our former visits, placed the ship in latitude 40° 22′, and in longitude 235° 42′. Our observations placed the ship at this time in latitude 40° 21½′, longitude by Kendall's chronometer, 234° 20′ 45″, Arnold's No. 14, 234° 14′ 45″, and by his No. 176, 236° 4′; hence, according to their rates as settled at Karakakooa, Kendall's appeared to be 1° 21′ 15″, and Arnold's No. 14, to be 1° 27′ 15″, to the westward of the truth; and No. 176, 22′ to the eastward of the truth. The variation of the compass was 16° 20′, eastwardly. Such had been the very gloomy and unpleasant weather during the whole of this passage as to preclude our making any lunar observations that might have tended either to correct, or substantiate the errors of the chronometers. In the evening the sky was again overcast, the weather unpleasant, and the wind mostly at N.N.W. attended by some fogs, continued the two following days.

On Thursday the 2d of May, in the morning, the weather was for some time calm, and there were other indications of an alteration in the wind; though the heavy swell that continued from the northward, and the sharpness of the air, were unfavorable to such wishes. At noon we had reached the latitude only of 41° 2′. The land was in sight, but was so covered with haze, that its parts could not be distinctly discerned. The northerly wind soon returned; with this we stood for the land, and fetched it a few miles to the southward of Rocky point; just at the spot discovered by the Spaniards in Senʳ Quadra's expedition to this coast in the year 1775, which they named Porto de la Trinidad.[1] According to the description of this place in the Annual Register for the year 1781, translated from the journal of Don Francisco Maurelli, who was one of the pilots on that expedition, and given to the public by the Hon. Daines Barrington,[2] it appeared to be an eligible place for shipping; but as we had passed it before unnoticed as a port, I was desirous of being better acquainted with it on the present occasion. Our tardy passage had greatly exhausted our wood and water, which was a further inducement for stopping, especially as there was not the most distant prospect of any favorable alteration in the wind.[3]

[1] Now Trinidad Harbor. Discovered 10 June 1775 by Bruno de Hezeta, in the *Santiago*, who commanded the expedition. Quadra was Captain of the *Sonora*, which accompanied the *Sanitago*.

[2] Francisco Antonio Mourelle. His 'Journal of a Voyage in 1775' was published by Daines Barrington in his *Miscellanies* (London, 1781).

[3] There was scant hope that Vancouver would cease to be plagued by head winds from the N. Winds and currents in the North Pacific move in a vast circle, with the prevailing winds on the west coast of the United States from the north or northwest. This movement was noted by the Comte de Fleurieu (1728–1810) and has been dubbed Fleurieu's Whirlpool. Copies of pilot charts illustrating the residual winds in the four seasons are

About six in the evening we anchored in eight fathoms water, dark sandy bottom, in Porto de la Trinidad. Our station here was in a small open bay or cove; very much exposed, and bounded by detached rocks lying at a little distance from the shore. When moored, the bearings from the ship were a high, steep, rounding, rocky head land, projecting a small distance from the general line of the shore into the ocean,[1] forming by that means the bay. This was the northernmost land in sight, and bore by compass N. 75 W. distant about three quarters of a mile; a high round barren rock,[2] made white by the dung of sea fowl, between which and the above head land we had entered the bay; S. 50 W. at the like distance; the high distant land of Cape Mendocino, the southernmost land in sight, south; a rugged rocky point forming the southeast point of the bay, S. 62 E. distant one mile and a half; and the nearest shore north-east, about half a mile from us.

We had not been long anchored before we were visited by two of the natives in a canoe; they approached us with confidence, and seemed to be friendly disposed. In exchange for a few arrows, and other trivial articles, they received some iron, with this they returned highly pleased to the shore; and after dark, another party followed their example.[3] These came with a large fire in their canoe; two of them ventured on board; but could not be tempted to descend below the deck, by any presents which were offered to them for that purpose; these, however, consisted of articles for the possession of which they appeared to manifest so earnest a desire, that they easily obtained them without violence to their inclinations, and departed, seemingly much satisfied with their visit.

The next morning, Friday the 3rd, I went on shore with a guard of marines, and a working party, in search of wood and water; these were found conveniently situated a little to the southward of a small Indian village. The landing was tolerably good, being within several rocks, which lie a little way from the shore, and greatly protect the beach from the violence of the surf, caused by the north-west swell, that breaks with great force on all parts of this coast.

reproduced in R. P. Bishop, 'Drake's Course in the North Pacific', *British Columbia Historical Quarterly*, III (1939), p. 164. Sailing ships leaving California for the Strait of Juan de Fuca now stand well out to sea, in order to be carried along by the northbound winds and currents on the western side of the whirlpool.

[1] Trinidad Head, which rises 380 feet.   [2] Pilot Rock.

[3] These were Yurok Indians, a small tribe who lived in the lower valley of the Klamath River and on the sea coast N and S of its mouth. Menzies describes their approach: 'the whole Crew consisting of four men stood up & gave us a song accompanied by a dance, if bending their bodies forwards & moving them to & fro with the most ludicrous gestures without changing their situation in the Canoe could be called such. They kept beating time with their paddles on the sides of the Canoe seemingly in perfect unison with their song which was a kind of solemn air not destitute of harmony & ended in a loud shriek in which they all joind rising up their heads at the same time, one of them also broke off at intervals during the Song with a kind of shrill noise in imitation of some wild Animal.' – 2 May.

Most of the inhabitants of the village were absent in their canoes, trading alongside the ship, leaving a few old women only to attend us; these, after setting our people to work, I accompanied to their habitations, which consisted of five houses built of plank, rudely wrought like those of Nootka, neither wind nor water tight; but not exactly in that fashion; every one of these houses being detached at a small distance from each other, and in no regular order; nor are there roofs horizontal like those at Nootka, but rise with a small degree of elevation to a ridge in the middle, and of course are better calculated for carrying off the rain. The upright boards forming the sides and ends of the house are not joined close enough to exclude the weather, the vacancies are filled up with fern leaves and small branches of pine trees. The entrance is a round hole in one corner of the house close to the ground, where with difficulty a grown person can find admittance; I found this so unpleasant in two instances, that I declined satisfying my curiosity any further than could be done by removing the materials that filled up the interstices. Four of these houses seemed to have been recently built, and were on a level with the ground. These appeared to be calculated for two families of six or seven persons each; the other, which was smaller and nearly half under ground, I supposed to be the residence of one family, making the village according to this estimate to contain about sixty persons. To the matrons of these rude habitations, I distributed some nails, beads, and other trivial matters, who in return, insisted on my accepting some muscles of a very large size, which they candidly acknowledged were the only things they had to offer. After revisiting our party at work, who were proceeding with much dispatch, I left them under the care of Mr. Swaine and returned on board, where I found our few Indian visitors trading in a very honest and civil manner. Their merchandize consisted of bows, arrows, some very inferior sea otter skins, with a scanty supply of sardinias, small herrings, and some flat fish. Their numbers during the forenoon seemed to multiply from all quarters, particularly from the southward, from whence they arrived both by land and in their canoes. These people seemed to have assembled in consequence of signals that had been made the preceding evening, soon after the last party returned to the shore. A fire had been then made, and was answered by another to the southward on a high rock in the bay; the same signal was repeated in the morning, and again answered to the southward.

Whilst we were thus engaged in supplying our wants, Mr. Whidbey was employed in sounding and taking a sketch of the bay.[1]

The weather was cloudy and rainy during a few hours in the middle of the day, and contrary to expectation the night brought with it no land wind; but as the rest of the twenty-four hours was perfectly calm, we had hopes that a favourable change was at hand. We were however again disappointed,

---

[1] Whidbey's sketch appears as an inset on Vancouver's chart of the N.W. Coast from lat. 38° 15' N to 45° 46' N.

as towards noon on Saturday the 4th, the wind returned to us from its former quarter.

Few of the natives visited the ship, though the party on shore had the company of more than a hundred. The number of the inhabitants belonging to the village seemed to be about sixty; the others, who came from the southward, were all armed with bows and arrows. These they at first kept in constant readiness for action, and would not dispose of them, nor even allow of their being examined by our people. They seated themselves together, at a distance from our nearer neighbours, which indicated them to be under a different authority; at length however they became more docile and familiar, and offered for sale some of their bows, arrows, and sea otter skins. The bow and arrow were the only weapon these people appeared to possess. Their arrows were made very neatly, pointed with bone, agate, or common flint; we saw neither copper nor iron appropriated to that purpose; and they had knives also made of the same materials.

In the afternoon we had taken on board about twenty-two tons of water, and as much wood as we thought requisite. With a light northerly breeze we unmoored, but in weighing our small bower, the cable, that was afterwards found to be excessively rotten, broke near the clench of the anchor; this obliged us to let go the best bower, until we should recover the other; and by the time this service was performed it was again calm, and we were under the necessity of remaining in this uncomfortable exposed situation another night, and until eight o'clock in the morning of Sunday the 5th; when, although the same adverse winds still prevailed from the N.W. by N., we stood to sea, without the least regret at quitting a station that I considered as a very unprotected and unsafe roadstead for shipping.

How far the place we had quitted is deserving the denomination of a port, I shall not take upon me exactly to determine; but in the language of mariners it can in no respect be considered as a safe retreat for ships; not even the station occupied by the Spaniards, which I conceived to be close up in the N.N.W. part of the bay, between the main and a detached rock lying from the head land, that forms the north-west point of the bay, N. 72 E. about half a mile distant. There, two or three vessels moored head and stern may lie in six and seven fathoms water, sandy bottom. The point above-mentioned will then bear by compass S.W.; and the rocks lying off the south-east point of the bay, S. 50 E. Between these points of the compass, it is still exposed to the whole fury and violence of those winds, which, on our return to the southward the preceding autumn, blew incessantly in storms; and when we approached the shores, were always observed to take the direction of the particular part of the coast we were near. Under these circumstances, even that anchorage, though the most sheltered one the place affords, will be found to be greatly exposed to the violence of these southern blasts, which not only prevail during the most part of the winter seasons, but continued to blow very hard in the course of the preceding summer. Should a vessel part cables, or be driven from this anchorage, she must instantly be thrown on the rocks that lie close under her stern, where little else than inevitable destruction is to be expected. The points of Trinidad bay lie from each other S. 52 E. and N. 52 W. about two miles asunder. From this line of direction, the rocks that line the shore are no where more than half a mile distant. The round barren rocky islet lies, from the north-west point of the bay, S. by W., distant three quarters of a mile; this is steep to, and has eight or nine fathoms water all round it, and admits of a clear channel from nine to six fathoms deep, close to the above point; from thence to Rocky point, the shores of the coast are bounded by innumerable rocky islets, and several sunken rocks lying a little without those that appear above water; but I know of no danger but what is sufficiently conspicuous. The soundings of the bay are regular from nine to five fathoms, the bottom clear and sandy; but as our anchors were weighed with great ease, and came up quite clean, we had reason to consider it to to be not very good holding ground.

The latitude of the ship's station when at anchor, observed on two days by different persons and different sextants, was, by the mean result of five meridional altitudes of the sun, 41° 3';[1] this is 4' to the south of the latitude assigned by Maurelli to the *port* of Trinidad, and the same distance south of the situation I had in my former visits given to this *nook*; not regarding it as deserving either the name of a bay, or a cove. The latter position was however calculated, after eight hours run, by the log, subsequent to the observation for the latitude at noon. But as I consider the observations made upon the spot, to be infinitely less liable to error, I have adopted those so obtained; and as Rocky point lies only five miles to the north of our anchorage, I have been induced to correct its latitude in my chart from 41° 13', to 41° 8',[2] but not having obtained any authority for altering, or correcting the longitude of the coast, it will remain the same as determined on our last visit; which places Trinidad bay in longtitude 236° 6',[3] from whence it will appear that our chronometers had acquired an error, similar to that in our former run from the Sandwich islands to this coast. By five sets of altitudes of the sun, taken on different days for this purpose, though not agreeing remarkably well, the mean result was fully sufficient to shew, that according to the rate as settled at Owhyhee, the longitude by Kendall's chronometer was 234° 43'; by Arnold's No. 14, 234° 39'; and by his No. 176, 236° 37'. The cloudy weather having precluded any observations being made for ascertaining the variation, I have considered it to remain as we found it in this neighbourhood the preceding year; that is 16° eastwardly. The tides appeared to rise and fall about five feet, but they were so very irregular, that no positive information could be gained of their motion. The first morning that I went on shore it was nearly low water, about six o'clock; and when the working party landed the next

[1] The correct position.
[2] Again the correct position.
[3] The long. of Trinidad Head light is 124° 09' W (235° 51' E).

morning about five o'clock, the tide was higher than it had been the whole of the preceding day. This was owing probably to the very heavy north-west swell that rolled into the bay; and as no stream nor current was observed, it would appear that the tides had but little influence on this part of the coast. Further nautical information may be derived on reference to the sketch of the place.

In an excursion made by Mr. Menzies to the hill composing the projecting head land, that forms the north-west side of the bay, he found, agreeably with Sen[r] Maurelli's description, the cross which the Spaniards had erected on their taking possession of the port;[1] and though it was in a certain state of decay, it admitted of his copying the following inscription:

CAROLUS III. DEI. G. HYSPANIARUM. REX.

The identity of porto de la Trinidada therefore cannot be doubted; and this affords me an opportunity of remarking, that as our attention whilst employed in exploring these shores, had been constantly directed to the discovery of openings in the coast, and secure retreats for shippings, it is by no means improbable that very many other *such ports* as that of Trinidada may be found to exist, and intirely to have eluded the vigiliance of our examination.

We had little opportunity of becoming acquainted with the country, as our travels were confined to the vicinity of the water side. About the out-skirts of the woods, the soil, though somewhat sandy, appeared to be a tolerably good mould lying on a stratum of clay, frequently interrupted by protruding rocks. The grounds bordering on the seashore were interspersed with several rocky patches of different extent; these did not produce any trees, but were covered with fern, grass, and other herbage. Beyond this margin the woods formed one uninterrupted wilderness to the summit of the mountains, producing a variety of stately pine trees; amongst these was observed, for the first time in the course of the voyage, the black spruce, which with the maple, alder, yew, and a variety of shrubs and plants, common to the southern parts of New Georgia, seemed principally to compose the forest. Of the land animals we could form no opinion but from their skins, worn as garments by the inhabitants; these seemed to be like those found in the more northern part of the continent. And as to the productions of the sea, we knew no more of them than what have already been enumerated. Our stay was too short to enable us to obtain any other knowledge of the inhabitants than their external character. Their persons were in general but indifferently, though stoutly made, of a lower stature than any tribe of Indians we had before seen. They wore their hair chiefly long, kept very clean, neatly combed and tied; but the paint they use for ornament, disfigures their persons, and renders their skins infinitely less clean than those of the Indians who visited us the former year,

---

[1] Hezeta took formal possession on 11 June 1775. Menzies makes no mention of this shore excursion in his journal.

to the southward of cape Orford; to whom in most respects these bear a very strong resemblance, as well in their persons, as in their friendly and courteous behaviour. Their canoes also were of the same singular construction, observed only among these people, and a few of those who visited us off cape Orford, and at Restoration point. Like the other tribes on this side of America, they sang songs on approaching the ship, by no means unpleasant to the ear. Their cloathing was chiefly made of the skins of land animals, with a few indifferent small skins of the sea otter. All these they readily disposed of for iron, which was in their estimation the most valuable commodity we had to offer. The men seemed very careless and indifferent in their dress; their garment was thrown loosely over them, and was little calculated either for warmth or decency; for the former, they provided whilst afloat, by burning a large fire in their canoes; of the latter they were completely regardless. The women attended more particularly to these points; some were covered from head to foot with a garment of thin tanned hides; others with a similar though less robe of the like materials; under this they wore an apron, or rather petticoat, made of warmer skins not tanned of the smaller animals, reaching from the waist below the knees.

Amongst these people, as with the generality of Indians I had met with, some mutilation, or disfiguring of their persons, is practised, either as being ornamental, or of religious institution, or possibly to answer some purpose of which we remain ignorant. At Trinidad the custom was particularly singular, and must be attended with much pain in the first instance, and great inconvenience ever after. All the teeth of both sexes were, by some process, ground uniformly down, horizontally, to the gums; the women especially, carrying the fashion to an extreme, had their teeth reduced even below this level; and ornamented their lower lip with three perpendicular columns of punctuation, one from each corner of the mouth, and one in the middle, occupying three fifths of the lip and chin. Had it not been for these frightful customs, I was informed that amongst those who visited our party on shore the last day, there were, amongst the younger females, some who might have been considered as having pretentions to beauty. The men had also some punctuations about them, and scars on their arms and bodies, from accident, or by design, like the people who had visited us to the southward of Cape Orford; but as their language was wholly unintelligible to us, without the least affinity to the more northern dialects, our curiosity could only be indulged in those few respects that inspection gratified.

At noon the coast was in sight, extending from S. 10 E. to N. 20 E.; Rocky point bore by compass N: 40 E., and the bay of Trinidad N. 62 E.; our observed latitude 41° 1′. The adverse wind, having continued since we had made the land, gave us hopes that, by keeping near the shore, we might now and then acquire a favourable breeze; in these conjectures however we were totally mistaken, having anchored three successive nights within half a mile of the coast, and found not the least advantage from land winds during the night. This determined me to stand out into the ocean, hoping the winds there would be more suitable to our northern destination.

In the afternoon, a range of very high inland mountains were observed, in a parallel direction to the coast, behind Rocky point; rearing their summits above the mountains that compose that shore, and which concealed them on our former passage, when we were nearer in with the land. As we proceeded to the westward the wind gradually came to about N.N.E., the weather gloomy and unpleasant, attended with sleet and rain; the thermometer varying from 51° to 53°. The leak in the bows increased so much, as to keep us constantly pumping and bailing.[1]

On Friday the 10th we had reached the latitude of 45°, longitude 226°. The wind at N.N.E. was moderate, the sea smooth; and having at length discovered the leak to have been occasioned by the caulking being washed out of the rabbitting of the stem that assisted in securing the wooden ends of the starboard side, we brought to, to apply some temporary remedy; which being accomplished, and finding the winds no less adverse to our proceeding, although we were upwards of 140 leagues from the land, we again directed our course to the eastward, with a continuation of nearly the same unpleasant winds and weather, until Tuesday the 14th, in latitude 45° 5'; and, what I considered to be the true longitude, 231°. After a calm during the last twenty-four hours, we had a light air from the southward, attended by a cloudy sky, and a much milder atmosphere. The thermometer rose to 60°, the barometer that had lately acquired its usual regularity stood at 29° 95', and the variation of the compass was 16° 42', eastwardly.

The wind continued in the southern quarter, blowing light airs, or gentle breezes; this day Wednesday the 15th, the atmosphere assumed a degree of serenity, and with the mildness of the air indicated the approach of a summer season; but in the evening the sky was again overcast; and in the night we had much rain, with a heavy swell from the south-east, which was also attended by very variable weather until Friday the 17th, in latitude 47° 53', longitude 233° 17'. At this time the wind became fixed in the north-west, and blowing a moderate breeze we stood with it to the N.N.E., and at day-light on the following morning, Saturday the 18th, saw the coast of the island of Quadra and Vancouver, bearing by compass from N.W. to E.N.E.; the nearest shore N.N.E. about four or five leagues distant. We stood for the land until seven o'clock, when being within a league of ponta de Ferron,[2] we tacked. The east

---

[1] 'This and the following day...the Leak seemd to encrease, as we found it sometimes making 18 inches of water an hour & so choakd up the coal hole notwithstanding the people were kept constantly employd in scooping it out, that we were at last obligd to scuttle the main deck over it & get a pump down into it. We hove to, & every means was tryd to stop the Leak such as lightening the Ship forwards etc in order to lessen the fatiguing exercise of the Men at the Pumps.' – Menzies, 9 May.

[2] The Punta de Ferron (so spelled on Baker's MS chart); now Portland Point, at the N end of Wickaninnish Bay. Wagner contends that the Spanish name was Punta de Terron, and that Vancouver misread the initial letter on Eliza's map, but the spelling there is clearly Ferron.

point of the entrance of Nitinat[1] bore by compass N. 80 E. and the east point of Clayoquot, N. 51 W.; the air was very sharp, and the atmosphere being clear and serene, afforded a tolerable view of the country that composes this part of the island.

On the sea shore the land may be considered rather as low, forming alternately rocky cliffs, and sandy beaches, with many detached rocks lying at a little distance from the shore, that seemed to be well wooded with pine trees. The surface of this low country is very uneven, and at a small distance from the sea meets a compact body of rugged dreary mountains; whose summits were covered with snow, which extended on many, though not on all of them, a considerable way down, and impressed us with no great opinion of their fertility.

About noon we again stood in shore; the coast then bore by compass from N.W. to E. by N., ponta de Ferron bore N. 52 E., and the east point of Clayoquot N. 10 W. The latitude of these points, as laid down from Spanish authority, agreed very well with our observations of 48° 48';[2] but differed about 5' to the eastward of the longitude shewn by the nearest of our chronometers.

This was Mr. Arnold's No. 176, allowing the assigned correction when off cape Mendocino and in Trinidad bay.

In the evening we fetched well up along shore of the isle de Ferron;[3] off which, beside many small islands, there are several sunken rocks lying about a mile within them, where the surf broke with great violence. The wind continuing in the western quarter, we stood off shore during the night, and at noon the next day, Sunday the 19th, the observed latitude was 49° 7'; longitude by Kendall's chronometer, allowing the above rate, 233° 8'; Arnold's No. 14, 233° 23'; and by No. 176, 233° 41'. At this time point Breakers[4] just shewing itself above the horizon, bore by compass N. 32 W., and according to its position ascertained on our former visit, it placed the ship in longitude 233° 39'. The nearest shore, which I took to be point St. Rafael of the Spaniards,[5] N. by E. four or five leagues distant. The easternmost land in sight, point de Ferron, E. ½ N. and the westernmost extreme N.W. With a moderate breeze from the west we stood for the land, and fetched about five miles to the south-eastward of point Breakers, into the entrance of an

---

[1] Barkley Sound. The reading should be S. 80 E., not N. 80 E.

[2] The lat. of Portland Point is 49° 04' N.

[3] Isla de Feran, and so named on Vancouver's chart. An island in the entrance to Clayoquot Sound, renamed Vargas Island (a name still retained) by Galiano, probably in 1792. Here again Wagner contends that Vancouver misread the initial letter and that the earlier Spanish name was Teran.

[4] Estevan Point.

[5] Defects in the Spanish charts, to which Vancouver refers, but which both Baker's MS chart and the engraved chart follow closely, make identification of the various points referred to in this and the succeeding paragraph difficult. The Puerto de San Rafael was in the present Sydney Inlet, and Vancouver places the Punta de San Rafael in the vicinity of Sharp Point, on the W side of the entrance to this inlet. The present Rafael Point is farther S, on Flores Island.

opening that had the appearance of admitting us a considerable way up, though in the Spanish chart this inlet is not noticed,[1] the first opening to the eastward of point Breakers being at point de Rafael, four leagues from this point.[2]

About six in the evening we suddenly reached soundings, at the depth of nine fathoms, hard bottom; the further examination being no object of my present pursuit, after heaving a few casts with the lead without finding any alteration, we tacked. In this situation, a point which lies about S. 33 E., two miles and a half from point Breakers, being the westernmost land then in sight, bore by compass N. 75 W., about two miles and a half from us;[3] a point, off which lie some rocks, forming the nearest shore on the western side, N.N.W., one mile and a half;[4] a point on the eastern side formed by a sandy beach, N.N.E., distant about a league;[5] the upper part of the inlet to the northward, where it seemed to take a winding direction towards the north-east, about four or five miles from us, and point de Ferron, S. 75 E. In this neighbourhood there is a much greater extent of low country than about Nootka or Clayoquot. It produced forest trees of many sorts and of considerable size; and on examination there might probably be found a more eligible situation for an establishment, than at either of those places. The wind being still adverse to our proceeding northward, we stood to the south-west during the night. The next day at noon, Monday the 20th, our observed latitude was 49° 18';[6] the westernmost land in sight bore by compass N. 50 W.; Woody point,[7] N. 42 W.; point Breakers, N. 27 E. being the nearest shore, at the distance of about three leagues; the west point of the opening we were in the preceding night, N. 41 E.; and point de Ferron, S. 84 E. At this time a schooner was seen to windward. The air was very keen, the thermometer being at 52°, and the clearness of the atmosphere gave us an opportunity of beholding the rugged craggy mountains that compose this country, whose summits were encumbered with infinitely more snow than had been seen on any of my former visits to these shores.

The wind just permitted us to fetch Nootka. About four in the afternoon we saw another sail to windward, apparently a brig; and as there was a chance of its being the Chatham, the private signal was made, but was not acknowledged. At five o'clock we reached Friendly cove, and anchored in eight fathoms water.[8] An officer was immediately dispatched on shore, to acquaint

[1] Hesquiat Harbour. In spite of having sighted it, both Baker and Vancouver, like the Spaniards, omitted it from their charts.

[2] Sydney Inlet.

[3] Presumably Matlahaw Point, the SE point of the Hesquiat Peninsula.

[4] A point N of Matlahaw Point would appear to fit this description.

[5] Hesquiat Point.

[6] Misprinted 48° 19' in the second edition. The figure shown is confirmed in the logs of both Baker and Swaine.

[7] Cape Cook.

[8] 'We found here the Princessa Spanish Frigate in the same situation in which we left her about seven months before together with two American Traders, one of them the Brig

Sen[r] Fidalgo[1] of our arrival, and that I would salute the fort, if he would make an equal return; this was accordingly done with eleven guns.

A Spanish officer, who visited us prior to our anchoring, delivered me a letter, journal, and other papers, left by Mr. Puget. By these documents I became informed, that the Chatham had arrived in this port on the 15th of April, and had departed thence on the 18th of May, agreeably to the instructions I had given Mr. Puget, in the event of my not arriving here by about the middle of May;[2] in order that no time might be lost in prosecuting the survey of this coast.

His examination of the north side of Morotoi, had determined that it did not afford any safe or convenient anchorage for shipping, and that it presented a similar dreary, and barren aspect, to that on the south side of the island. Few occurrences had taken place on board the Chatham, between the Sandwich islands and Nootka, worthy particular notice, excepting that the winds had been very favorable, contrary to those which we had contended with; that she arrived within sight of the coast of this island on the 7th of April, when the high land over Woody point was seen bearing by compass N.E. by N.; and that Mr. Puget had directed his course from thence towards Nootka. But meeting a strong S.E. gale on the 9th, attended by all the circumstances that indicate an approaching storm, he put into Porto Bueno Esperanza,[3] to wait more favourable weather; and although several attempts were made to gain Nootka from that port, none succeeded until the 14th, when it was accomplished with the expence of a bower anchor, owing to the breaking of the cable on the sea coast.[4]

Hancock belonging to Boston commanded by Mr. Crowel [Samuel Crowell] who had been on the Coast last year, the other a Brigantine [the *Amelia*, a brig of 150 tons]...There was also a small American Schooner in the Cove [the *Resolution*, 90 tons] which had been built at the Marquases by the ship Jefferson who left Boston about 18 months before...' – Menzies, 20 May.

[1] Salvador Fidalgo, who had been in command at Nootka during the winter of 1792-3.

[2] Puget opened his sealed orders on 16 May and found himself 'under Orders to proceed without a moments Loss of time to Detention Cove [in Burke Channel], a Place known to Mr. Johnstone...' – Puget, 16 May.

[3] Esperanza Inlet; but, as will appear, the *Chatham* had actually entered Nuchatlitz Inlet, to the S, under the impression that it was Esperanza Inlet.

[4] Puget's log shows that, contrary to the impression given by Vancouver, the *Chatham* had had a dangerous and frightening experience well 'worthy particular notice' after she entered Nuchatlitz Inlet. Hecate Channel, an arm of Esperanza Inlet, leads to Tahsis Inlet, which in turn runs S to Nootka Sound, thus providing an inland sheltered route to Friendly Cove. Nuchatlitz Inlet consists of the inlet proper and an Inner Basin, connected with the inlet by a narrow passage through which the tides run with great strength. When a combination of wind and tide made it impracticable to get out to sea, believing that he was in Esperanza Inlet, Puget 'determined to try the Inland passage...for this purpose we weighed at five [on 9 April] & stood up the Inlet.' A boat had been sent ahead to sound: 'At 7 we came in Sight of an Indian Village close to a Small Opening which apparently trended East & as this is nearly the Direction & Situation of a Branch laid down by the Spaniards I was in hopes it would have proved the proper Channel, & as it was Calm with a Moderate Stream I ventured to keep on towards it. Before the Boat ahead could make

Mr. Puget had on his arrival at Nootka lightened the Chatham, and laid her on shore on the beach; and found that most part of her false keel had been knocked off, the lower part of the gripe considerably damaged, and most of the copper rubbed off from the starboard bilge. The highest of the spring tides being insufficient on its falling to answer all purposes, the Chatham was obliged to be hove down, both sides had consequently been examined, and she had undergone as thorough a repair as circumstances would admit, and which had become essentially necessary.[1] In the execution of this business Mr. Puget stated, that His Majesty's service had been greatly forwarded by the polite attention of Sen[r.] Fidalgo, who afforded Mr. Puget every assistance in his power. This was of material importance at this juncture, as several of the Chatham's people were indisposed with large tumours, that prevented their

the signal for Danger, a most rapid Fall hurried [her] through the opening & I had the mortification to perceive the Chatham under the Influence of the same Stream, nor could all our Efforts check her to either Shore. I was therefore obliged to make the best of our Situation, an anchor could not possibly hold her, so that the only alternative left, was to put her before the Stream & run through the Passage, which was afterwards found to be but One Hundred Feet across, & what added more to my Apprehensions for the safety of the Vessel, were the Repeated Clamours of the Indians to warn of Danger but we were too far to secede & in a few moments the Fall hurried us through the Narrows with amazing Rapidity & in going through the Main Yard tore away the Branches of one of the Trees that overlooked the Rocks on its Starboard Side. This I certainly reckon a most providential Escape for had we been in any other Situation but end on we must have gone over, as in all probability she would have hung in the passage.' – 9 April. How to get out of the Inner Basin now became the pressing problem. Twice frustrated in attempts to get back through the narrows, Puget was successful in a third attempt on 11 April. Bad weather then prevented him from sailing for Nootka until the 15th. All agreed that their misadventures had been due to 'the shameful inaccuracy of the Spanish Chart, which had alone been all along our guide, this Chart had been very recently made & was given to us by Mr. Quadra.' – Bell, April.

[1] Puget gives some details of the repairs made: 'though the Copper was off in many Places we had the Satisfaction to find the Planking as perfect as possible. We had received 8 Sheets of Copper & the same quantity of Nails from the Discovery for the Repairs which were found very insufficient to answer the purpose, we were therefore obliged to use some supplied by Government as Trade, & save all the Nails that had not been broken by the Rocks, this Copper I have not the Smallest Doubt will fully answer as well as the Ships, as it is nearly as thick as that commonly used for Sheathing.' – 23 April. Repairs were also made to the rudder, and Puget seized the opportunity to move the main mast: 'Previous to our Arrival in this Port I had determined to move the Step of the Main Mast the first Opportunity further forward. There were two essential Reasons for making the Alteration, the first by giving the Mast more Inclination Aft, it added to the Support & consequently would allow more Room for the Staysails to act. Secondly it might alter the Rate of Sailing. In going large, the Main Mast being upright without the least Rake, the Stays were always so much Slackened with the pressure of Sail we were continually obliged to carry, to keep up with the Discovery, that it has frequently caused the Greatest Astonishment how the Mast Stood with so little After Support when going against a Head Sea.' – 21 April. The first real test of the new rig did not come until June: 'At 8 am had a Strong Breeze from the SSW & with pleasure we perceived on a trial with the Discovery the alterations of the Main Mast had had some Effect on her Sailing, as we now kept up with her.' – Puget, 11 June 1793.

attending to any duty. These complaints however, though affecting most of the crew, were not of long duration.[1] By the 15th of May the Chatham was in readiness to proceed to sea, but adverse winds prevented her so doing until the 18th, when she quitted Nootka.

The vessel we had seen in the offing anchored here soon after us, and proved to be His Catholic Majesty's snow St. Carlos, from St. Blas, commanded by Sen[r] Don Ramon Saavedra,[2] ensign in the Spanish navy.

The next day, Tuesday the 21st, we were employed in various necessary services; and about noon I was favoured with the company of Sen[r] Fidalgo, who received from us the usual marks of ceremony and respect. This gentleman informed me, that the officer commanding the St. Carlos was to supersede him in the government of this port, and that he should immediately return to St. Blas; and offered to take charge of, and forward any dispatches, I might wish to send through that channel to Europe. This opportunity I gladly embraced, and intrusted to his care a letter for the Lords of the Admiralty, containing a brief abstract of our transactions since the commencement of the year 1793;[3] as also a reply to some very friendly and polite letters I had received by the St. Carlos, from his excellency the count de Revilla Gigedo, the vice-roy of New Spain, residing at Mexico; and from Sen[r] Quadra,[4] at St. Blas; informing me of the welfare of Mr. Broughton, and the means that each of these gentlemen had used to render his arrival in Europe as speedy as possible.

In one of his excellency's letters, I received the most flattering assurances of every support and assistance that the kingdoms of New Spain were capable of bestowing. These were extremely acceptable, as we had still a considerable extent of the coast of New Albion to examine; and we were made very happy by learning, that the friendly and hospitable treatment we had already received from the Spaniards, was likely to be thus continued.

The very unpleasant weather that attended us soon after our last departure hence, led me to inquire of Sen[r] Fidalgo, how the winter had passed at Nootka. From whom I understood that their situation here had been very irksome,

---

[1] Bell commented on the health problem: 'for all the time we lay here, we had seldom less than ten & a dozen patients in the Surgeons list.' – May. There was no improvement, even after the *Chatham* had been at Nootka for a fortnight: 'The Sick List still kept up its Numbers, nor did the plenty of Refreshments appear to make any Alteration in their Disorders. The Eruptions continued breaking out with as much Virulence as ever nor could all our Endeavours make the Spruce [beer] even palatable.' – Puget, 29 April. A week later the health of the crew began at last to improve.

[2] Saavedra had come to take over command of Nootka from Fidalgo.

[3] Vancouver's letter to the Admiralty, dated 22 May 1793, is in P.R.O., Adm. 1/2629, ff. 53–5. It is printed in the appendix.

[4] Bell notes that the 'Letters from our good friend Sr. Quadra' were 'accompanied by some presents of different very acceptable articles to Capt[n] Vancouver & his Officers, – so that here is an instance that this good man's kindness was not confined to us when only before his Eyes, he always said he ever should remember us, and I believe he was in earnest.' – May.

having been almost constantly confined to the house by incessant rain; that on the 17th of February a very severe shock of an earthquake had been felt, and on the 1st of April a most violent storm from the south-east.

Notwithstanding the badness of the season, he had found means to erect a small fort on Hog island, that mounted eleven nine pounders, and added greatly to the respectability of the establishment. He very justly considered employment as essentially necessary to the preservation of his people's health,[1] which began to decline towards the spring, and a man and a boy of puny constitutions had fallen victims to scorbutic disorders; the rest had for some time past been perfectly recovered, owing principally to the wild vegetables procured from the woods.

In the confidence that our arrival here must have been before the end of April, I had intended to have made the necessary observations for ascertaining the rate and error of our chronometers at this place, whilst the Chatham should undergo the repair she so evidently required. But in consequence of our long and tedious passage from the Sandwich islands, I was now determined to proceed immediately to the northward, in order to join the Chatham, and whilst our boats should be employed in examining those regions we had left unexplored the former year, to make the necessary observations for ascertaining the rate of the chronometers, and for carrying into execution our future investigations.

On our arrival here we had been visited by *Maquinna, Clewpenaloo, Annapee*, and other chiefs.[2] When we were last here I had understood, that

---

[1] Vancouver here tends to dismiss the building of these new fortifications as a make-work programme; others held different opinions. Menzies commented: 'These preparations did not indicate any inclination in the Spaniards to relinquish their claim to this port, on the contrary it would seem that they only prolonged the Negotiation to gain time for preparation, in expectation perhaps of a more favorable opportunity for vindicating what they conceived to be their right by prior discovery.' – 20 May. Puget also commented: 'The Guns are planted to annoy Vessels on their Entrance into the Cove, four appear directed to the Southward four to the Eastward & the other three command the Northern Side of the Cove. The Princesa was moored close to the Larger Island, where she could bring her Guns to bear on the Entrance & prevent any attack from the Western low Land. When it was the general opinion that the Cove was to have been delivered into the Hands of the English,the former Battery was dismantled by Mr. Quadra & the Guns sent away in the Aransasu & As we were given to understand publicly at Monterey that the Spaniards had orders to warn the Americans from the Coast I concluded this new Fort was built to enforce those Orders.' – 17 April. Bell was not impressed by the new fort: 'this cou'd only annoy Vessels of small force, and may have been probably thrown up in consequence of the order to warn foreigners [except the English] coming on this Coast...' – May.

[2] The spelling of Indian names varies in the different logs and journals, as each writer endeavoured to record the names as he heard them. Menzies' notes read: 'Our old friend *Hoopannanoo* was the first Chief that came on board to us...We were afterwards visited by *Harrape* & his Son, the latter could speak & understand English better than any other Native in the Sound...We also had a visit from Maquinna & his brother Waghelaropulth & several other of our old acquaintances who came to express their joy at our return & renew their friendship.' – 20 May.

Maquinna's eldest child, being a daughter named *Ahpienis*,[1] had in the course of the last summer been proclaimed as the successor to the dominions and authority of *Maquinna* after his death; and had about that time been betrothed to the eldest son of *Wicananish*, the chief of a very considerable district in the neighbourhood of Clayoquot and Nittinat.

This chief with his son, attended by a considerable retinue, came in form to *Maquinna's* residence,[2] now situated without the sound on the sea shore, about a league to the westward of this cove[3] where, after presenting an assortment of certain valuable articles, he had demanded *Maquinna's* daughter; the considerations on this dower caused great consultation and many debates. At some of these a few of the officers of the Discovery were present, who understood, that the compliment was deemed inadequate to the occasion; but on the forenoon of Thursday the 23d, I was informed, that matters between the two fathers were finally adjusted to the satisfaction of both parties, and that *Wicananish*, with his suite, had returned to Clayoquot; but that *Ahpienis* was still to reside some time longer at Nootka. Her youth, most likely, as she did not then exceed ten or twelve years of age, was the reason for postponing the nuptials.[4]

Wicananish did not favour us with his company, but sent his brother *Tahtoochseeatticus*,[5] to congratulate us on our arrival. This chief came with some little apprehension about the manner in which he would be received, in consequence of the dispute with Mr. Brown of the Butterworth;[6] his fears were however soon dispelled, on receiving some copper and blue cloth, which were esteemed presents suitable to his rank and condition. By him I also sent similar presents to *Wicananish*; which he promised faithfully to deliver, and

[1] Menzies spells the name Apinnas; Warren Cook's version is A-pã-nas.
[2] Wickaninnish 'was a robust good looking man advanced a little beyond the prime of life; His brothers & the other Chiefs that accompanied him on this occasion were a set of the most athletic men & of the most comely appearance I had ever seen any where on this Coast, few of them were under six feet high & in general well proportioned, except their limbs, which their habitual posture from infancy of lowering down on their heels in sitting has somewhat distorted, a custom very common with most Savages.' – 21 May. Menzies estimated that Wickaninnish's followers were about a thousand in number and he describes their arrival and the negotiations with Maquinna at some length.
[3] 'the Village of *Caaglee* about three Miles from the Cove where Maquinna & his Tribe generally reside during the summer months for the conveniency of fishing in the Bay, ever since they were deprivd of the place which the Spaniards at present occupy [at Friendly Cove].' – Menzies, 21 May.
[4] The intended bridegroom was 'a youth of about 14 years of age with fine open features.' – Menzies, 21 May.
[5] An alternative spelling is Tootoocheetticus (Hoskins' narrative in Howay, *Voyages of the 'Columbia'*, p. 184).
[6] In the first days of August 1792, in a clash with the natives, one of the *Butterworth's* seamen had been killed and two others severely injured. Brown contended that the Indians made an unprovoked attack, but other accounts suggest that it was caused by an attempt to rob the Indians of their furs. See F. W. Howay, 'The Voyage of the Hope', *Washington Historical Quarterly*, XI (1920), 25.

added, that his brother would no longer entertain any doubts of our sincerity, and would be made extremely happy by the proofs I had transmitted of my friendship and good wishes.

Having a light breeze at S.S.W. though it was still attended with hazy, rainy, unpleasant weather, we weighed, worked out of the Sound, and saluted the fort as on our arrival.[1]

During our short stay in Friendly cove, we were not so fortunate as to procure any observations for ascertaining the rate of our chronometers; we had however taken four sets of the sun's altitude on the 20th, as we sailed into the port. These shewed the longitude of Nootka, agreeably to their rates of gaining as ascertained at Karakakooa bay to be, by Kendall's chronometer, 231° 42′; by Arnold's No. 14, 231° 52′ 22″; and by his No. 176, 234° 10′ 45″;[2] Hence Kendall's erred, according to our settlement of this place the preceding year, 1° 49′ 30″ to the westward; Arnold's No. 14, 1° 36′ 8″ to the westward also; and Arnold's No. 176, 39′ 14″, eastwardly. Considering this error in Kendall's chronometer to have taken place since our departure from Whymea bay, in Attowai, where it had agreed within two miles of all our former calculations, it will be found to have been gaining since that time, instead of 8″ 52‴, as established at Karakakooa bay, 16″ 55‴ per day, and to be fast of mean time at Greenwich on the 20th of May, at noon, 2^h 1′ 2″. The other two instruments erred very materially between Karakakooa and Whymea, the same way that their errors were now found to be; therefore I have supposed those errors to have commenced on our departure from Karakakooa bay, and by so doing, Arnold's No. 14 will be found to be gaining at the rate of 20″ 32‴ per day, and fast of mean time at Greenwich on the 20th of May, at noon, 1^h 56′ 26″; and No. 176, to be gaining 41″ 36‴ per day, and fast of mean time at Greenwich on the 20th of May, at noon, 4^h 36′ 55″; instead of the rates settled on shore at the observatory on Owhyhee. As this estimated corrected rate was found to agree much nearer with the longitude of Trinidad bay, according to its position as determined by us the preceding year, I shall continue to allow the above rate and error, until I shall have authority sufficient to alter my opinion of its correctness.

As we proceeded towards the ocean the wind gradually veered to the south-east, with which we steered along the coast to the north-westward, passing the entrance of Buena Esperanza, which had a very different appearance to us, from that exhibited in the Spanish chart. The same was

---

[1] Menzies and Bell note what had become of the two small ships that were under construction when the *Discovery* left Nootka in October 1792. When the *Three Brothers* and the *Prince William Henry* sailed from Nootka they left 'Artificers who in their absence set up two small Vessels of about fifteen Tons burthen each, one of these was yet unfinished & was on shore on the Stocks.' – Menzies, 22 May. Bell commented: 'they discovered too late that these Vessels were of no use of them, and Mr. Fidalgo had a Letter for Captn. Vancouver which we understood was from Mr. Ewing [Ewen] of the Pr. Wm. Henry, wishing him to buy one of them.' – May.

[2] The position of Friendly Cove is long. 126° 27′ W (233° 33′ E).

noticed by Mr. Puget; but we had no opportunity of fixing more than its exterior points, nor was any correction made in consequence of the Chatham's visit. At eight in the evening we were within about three leagues of Woody point, bearing by compass N. 66 W. As the general appearance indicated very unpleasant weather, and as I was desirous of obtaining, if possible, a more competent knowledge of the space between cape Scott and the entrance into Fitzhugh's sound, than we were able to obtain by our inconclusive observations on our former visit; the third reefs were taken in the topsails, and we hauled to the wind off shore, until the weather should be more favorable to this inquiry. During the night the gale increased with hard squalls and a heavy rain. The topsails were close reefed, and the top-gallant yards got down. At eight the next morning, Friday the 24th, we again stood in for the land, and at eleven it was seen at no great distance; but we were not able to direct our course along shore until the afternoon. About eight the following morning we were abreast of cape Scott, which terminates in a low hummock, joined to the main land by a narrow isthmus, and forms, with the islands that lie from it N. 80 W. a clear navigable channel about three miles wide. There are a few breakers at a small distance from the cape, in a direction from it S. 27 E. about seven miles. About seven miles to the south-eastward of this cape on the exterior coast, we passed an opening with two small islets lying off its north point of entrance.[1] This appeared clear, and promised to afford very good shelter. From cape Scott, forming the west point of the island of Quadra and Vancouver; the coast on the interior side takes a direction N. 62 E. about eleven miles to the west point of entrance between that island, and those of Galiano and Valdes.[2]

The weather becoming serene and pleasant in the forenoon, afforded me an opportunity of correcting in some measure our former erroneous delineation of the space between cape Scott, and the southern entrance into Fitzhugh's sound, comprehending the positions of the several islands, islets, rocks, and breakers, in the entrance of, and about Queen Charlotte's sound. On comparing this view with our former chart, it appeared that land had been placed where in reality it had no existence, and *vice versa*, owing to the deceptions of the foggy weather that prevailed whilst we were in this neighbourhood in August 1792. It is therefore requisite to repeat, that the coast, islands, islets, rocks, &c. &c. between Deep-water bluff[3] and Smith's inlet, both on the continental, and opposite side of Queen Charlotte's sound; excepting the western extremities, that on this occasion were in some degree corrected; and are to be considered as likely to have been erroneously described, as well in respect to their positive, as relative positions; the former occasioned by our not being able to procure any celestial observations; the latter by the thick foggy weather, that continually produced deceptions, and

---

[1] Sea Otter Cove.

[2] Now Nigei and Hope islands respectively.

[3] Deep Sea Bluff, on the N side of the entrance to Tribune Channel.

left us no rule on our former visit, for estimating the distance between one indistinct object and another.

As I would by all means with to guard against too great reliance being placed on this particular part of our survey, I must beg leave to state, that I consider myself answerable only for the certainty of the connection of the continental shores between the stations before mentioned, those having been traced in such a manner, as to ascertain that fact beyond all possible dispute.

At noon the observed latitude was 51° 9′, the true longitude 231° 58′. In this situation the islands of Galiano and Valdes bore by compass S. 68 E.; the south point of Calvert's island, N. 6 W.; a low point on the same island, N. 30 W.; and cape Scott, S. 8 W.; distant 23 miles. This placed cape Scott in latitude 50° 48′:[1] two miles further north than the latitude I had before assigned to it, owing to our imperfect observations at that time; but I found no reason to make any alteration in its longitude. The nearest shore to us bore by compass N. 48 E., distant two or three leagues. This was the most westerly projecting part of the continent in this neighbourhood; from whence the shores of the main land take a N.N.E. and south-eastwardly direction, and make it a conspicuous cape, terminating in rugged, rocky, low hummocks, that produce some dwarf pine, and other small trees and shrubs. This cape, from the dangerous navigation of its vicinity, I distinguished by the name of CAPE CAUTION; it is in latitude 51° 12′, longitude 232° 9′.[2] Cape Caution, though not named, was noticed on our former visit, and erroneously placed, from the causes before stated, in latitude 51° 18′, longitude 232° 8′. An error also at that time took place, in the situation of the south point of entrance into Smith's inlet,[3] now found to be in latitude 51° 18′, longitude 232° 11½′. The south point of Calvert's island, being in latitude 51° 27′, longitude 232° 5′,[4] was found to be correctly placed. The variation of the compass allowed in this situation was 18° eastwardly.

Soon after noon, some very dangerous breakers were discovered, over which the sea, at long intervals of time, broke with great violence. These had escaped our attention the last year, although we must have passed very near them; they consist of three distinct patches, and seemed to occupy nearly the space of a league. Their eastern part lies from cape Caution, N. 72 W., distant about five miles;[5] but the rocks that lie off the shore to the northward of the cape, reduce the width of the channel between them and the breakers to about a league, through which we passed without noticing any other obstruction that was not sufficiently conspicuous to be avoided.

With a gentle breeze from the E.N.W. we stood up Fitzhugh's sound in the evening with all the sail we could spread. This by four the next morning,

---

[1] This was very close to the correct position, which is lat. 50° 47′ N.

[2] The correct position is lat. 51° 10′ N, long. 127° 47′ W (232° 13′ E).

[3] Presumably meaning Macnicol Point, in lat. 51° 15′ N, long. 127° 46′ W (232° 14′ E).

[4] Cape Calvert, in lat. 51° 25′ N, long. 127° 54′ W (232° 06′ E).

[5] Probably the Paddle and Dugout Rocks.

Sunday the 26th, brought us opposite to the arm leading to point Menzies,[1] whose extent was left undetermined, and where in a cove on the south shore, about eight miles within its entrance, I expected to join the Chatham; but the wind being unfavorable, and the ebb tide setting out, we made little progress until six o'clock, when we worked up the arm with the flood tide, and a light easterly breeze, attended with much rain, and thick misty weather.

The Chatham was seen at eleven, and about noon we anchored within about half a mile of her in 60 fathoms water, gravelly bottom.[2]

Mr. Puget informed me, that he had arrived here on the 24th, and that nothing material had occurred since he had left Nootka;[3] and I had the happiness to understand that himself, officers, and crew, were in a perfect state of health.

[1] Burke Channel.

[2] The rendezvous with the *Chatham* had been fixed for Detention Cove, the name given to the cove about a mile and a half E of Hvidsten Point. Owing to wind and tidal conditions it was not possible for the *Chatham* to reach this cove, and she anchored instead in a second cove about a mile and a half W of Hvidsten Point, where the *Discovery* found her. Puget was content to remain there because 'the Discovery could not possibly pass without our seeing her.' – 24 May. Bell states that 'this place afterwards obtained the name of Port Chatham'. – 24 May. Heddington refers to it as Chatham Bay. – 11 June. Neither name has survived.

[3] Both Puget and Manby give detailed accounts of the *Chatham's* stay at Nootka. One unexpected incident described by Manby involved humming birds: 'An Indian in one of the Canoes had with him a live Humming bird, of very beautiful plumage...tied by the Leg with a single human hair. On seeing it, all on board became anxious to become the purchaser of this little curiosity, which enabled the owner to sell his little prisoner for something considerable. The Indians along side, eyed with peculiar attention, the avidity all on board express'd for this Bird, which apparently produced the greatest surprize. In an instant every Canoe left the Ship, and paddled with all their strength to the Shore...however, in two hours, the little Fleet of Canoes again made towards us, paddling with all their might, on gaining us, the object of their flight and return, evidently bespoke the pursuit of the whole, as every Man, Woman and Child, had three or four Live humming birds, to dispose of, which in a few Minutes so overstocked the Market, that a brass button was willingly received for two. – Letters, 13 April.

CHAPTER II.

Anchor in Restoration cove—Account of two Boat Expeditions—Astronomical and Nautical Observations—Proceed to the Northward—Visited by many of the Natives—Their Character—Account of the Boats Excursion—Seaman poisoned by Muscles.

As many necessary repairs in and about the Discovery demanded our immediate attention, and that no time might be lost, on Sunday the 26th of May, I determined, that whilst those on board were employed on the requisite duties, two boat parties should be dispatched to prosecute the examination of the broken region before us. Recollecting there was a large cove to the northward that I had noticed on our former visit,[1] and supposing it more likely to answer all our purposes than the station we had taken, I sat out after dinner to take a view of it, and finding it a very eligible place, I returned in the evening, and with the flood tide the following morning, we stood towards this bay or cove, bearing by compass N. 28 E. distant five miles.

The flood tide assisted our progress but a little way up the arm, after which we had to contend with those counter currents that have been before stated as not only rendering the vessel nearly stationary, but totally ungovernable. It was not until two in the afternoon of Monday the 27th, that we anchored in 12 fathoms water, and with a hawser moored the ship to the trees on the shore; this was a fine sandy beach, through which flowed an excellent stream of water into the cove, close to the station we had taken. Near this stream, by the felling of a few trees, a very good situation was obtained for the observatory and tents. The seine was hauled with tolerable success, so that we had a prospect of much convenience, and of acquiring some refreshment from the sea. These were advantages beyond our expectations in this desolate region, where the rain had been almost incessantly pouring down in torrents ever since our arrival on it.

On Tuesday the 28th, our several repairs were begun. The leak in the bows of the ship claimed our first attention; by ripping the copper off down to the water's edge this seemed likely to be got at, and to be completely stopped. The after part of the ship required caulking, the launch stood in need of repair, the sails in use wanted mending, the powder airing, and several spars were required to replace those we had carried away since our last departure from

---

[1] Restoration Cove, now Restoration Bay.

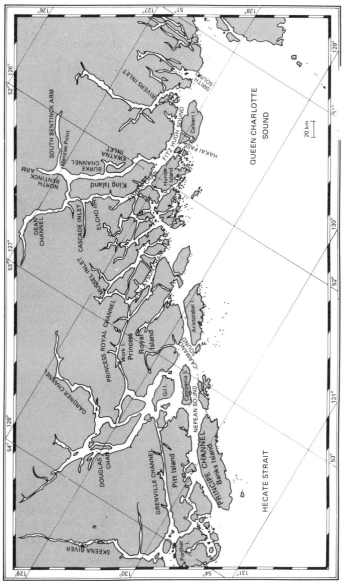

Figure 5. Queen Charlotte Sound to Skeena River. *Base map by Michael E. Leek.*

this coast; but the rainy weather still continuing, we proceeded very slowly in these several services.

On Wednesday the 29th, Mr. Johnstone was dispatched in the Chatham's cutter, attended by our small one, to finish the examination of this inlet, which he was prevented doing last year by the badness of the weather. The next morning, Thursday[1] the 30th, accompanied by Lieutenant Swaine in the cutter, I sat out in the yawl to examine the main arm of this inlet, that appeared to take its direction northerly to the west of, or without, the arm in which the ships were at anchor. This, after the Right Honourable Edmund Burke, I named BURKE'S CHANNEL.[2]

On this occasion I deemed it expedient, that those employed on boat service should be supplied with an additional quantity of wheat and portable soup, sufficient to afford them two hot meals every day during their absence; and, in consequence of their being much exposed to the prevailing inclement weather, an additional quantity of spirits, to be used at the discretion of the officer commanding each party; a practice that was found necessary to be continued throughout the season.[3]

About nine in the forenoon we arrived in what appeared to be the main branch of the inlet, leading to the north from Fitzhugh's sound. After a much-respected friend, I named this FISHER'S CHANNEL.[4] Some detached rocks were passed, that lie N. 14 W. about a league from the north-west point of entrance into Burke's channel, which obtained the name of POINT WALKER; it is situated in latitude 51° 56½', longitude 232° 9';[5] its opposite point of entrance, named POINT EDMUND,[6] lies from it S. 60 E. near two miles. Off

[1] Misprinted Tuesday in the second edition.

[2] Burke's Canal in the first edition; now officially Burke Channel.

[3] Menzies noted other improvements: 'our Boats & people were much better fitted out for withstanding the inclemency of the weather than they were on the preceeding season, as it was the study of both Commanders & Officers during their visit to the southern regions to render them as commodious & comfortable as possible. The Stern Sheets of each Boat were coverd with a canopy & surrounded with Curtains of painted Canvas so fitted that they could be put up or taken down at pleasure for the conveniency of the Officers in the day time or for those who slept on board in charge of them at night. Besides this a large awning spread over the whole Boat that equally screend the people & their provision & clothing from getting wet in rainy weather which was too apt to relax their strength in their constant & fatiguing exercise on the oars. Each Boat had likewise a small Tent furnishd with a thick painted floor cloth sufficient to shelter the whole Boats Crew comfortably at night or in bad weather. And all their provisions & spare clothes were snugly packd up in painted Canvas bags secure from any harm. They were also well armed & the arms & ammunition perfectly securd & in good order. Thus equippd they were enabled to with stand the changes of the Weather & guard themselves from any attack of the Natives.' – 29 May.

[4] Here and in subsequent references Fisher's Canal in the first edition; now Fisher Channel. Walbran states that it was named in honour of the Rev. John Fisher, vicar of Stowey, Wiltshire, later Bishop of Exeter and of Salisbury.

[5] Named after William Walker, surgeon of the Chatham; now Walker Point. Its position is lat. 51° 55' N, long. 127° 54' W (232° 06' E).

[6] Named after Edmund Burke (already commemorated in Burke Channel).

point Edmund lie several rocky islets; with one on the opposite shore, a little within point Walker; but the channel is fair to navigate.

We had a fresh southerly gale in our favor, but the cloudiness of the weather prevented my obtaining an observation for the latitude. For this purpose, though we did not succeed, we landed on some rocks near the western shore; here we were visited by a few of the natives, who were at first somewhat shy, but the distribution of a few trinkets amongst them soon gained their confidence and friendship. These people appeared to be a different race from those we had seen to the southward, used a different language, and were totally unacquainted with that spoken by the inhabitants of Nootka.[1] The stature of the few here seen, (not exceeding twenty) was much more stout and robust than that of the Indians further south. The prominence of their countenances, and the regularity of their features, resembled the northern Europeans; their faces were generally broad, with high cheek bones; and had it not been for the filth, oil, and paint, with which, from their earliest infancy, they are besmeared from head to foot, there is great reason to believe that their colour would have differed but little from such of the labouring Europeans as are constantly exposed to the inclemency and alterations of the weather. From these rocks we steered over to the opposite shore, the channel being from a mile to half a league wide. The eastern, almost a compact shore, lies in a north direction, to the south point of a small opening, in latitude 52° 6½'; this extended E. by N. four miles,[2] and terminated as is usual with the generality of these branches. Its north point of entrance lies from its south point N. 14 E. distant two miles. Before its entrance are two small islands,[3] and towards its northern shore are some rocks. This opening formed a good harbour, and was by me named PORT JOHN.[4] From the north point the eastern coast still continued nearly in its former direction for two miles and an half, and then took a more eastwardly bend. The country we had passed along, since we had entered Fisher's channel, might, on the western side, be considered of a moderate height; its surface, composed principally of rocks, was uneven, and full of chasms, where a soil, formed by the decay of vegetables, produced some different sorts of pine trees of slender growth, the maple, birch, small-fruited crab, and a variety of shrubs, and berry bushes. The eastern shore rose more abruptly, and was bounded behind by very lofty rugged mountains, covered with snow.

As we proceeded along the eastern shore, we passed, and left for future examination an opening on the opposite shore, that took a N.N.W. direction,[5]

[1] These were Bella Bella Indians, one of a group of Kwakiutl tribes known as the Heiltsuk. The Bella Bella villages were chiefly in the region of Milbanke Sound, but some were as far N as Tolmie Channel, and others to the S in Fisher Channel, Johnson Channel, and the lower reaches of Dean Channel, which Vancouver was about to explore.

[2] Evans Inlet, in lat. 52° 06' N.

[3] Luke Island and Matthew Island.

[4] Named after the Rev. John Fisher (already commemorated in Fisher Channel).

[5] Johnson Channel.

and was of such considerable extent, as to make me doubtful whether it might not be the main branch of the inlet. Agreeably, however, to my former practice, we kept the starboard shore on board, as the most positive means of ascertaining the continental boundary; and as we advanced, the land to the north-east of the above opening, forming the north-west side of the channel, rose to an equal if not a superior height to that on the south-east side.

The evening was very rough, rainy, and unpleasant, and what contributed to render our situation more uncomfortable, was the steep precipices that constituted the shores, not admitting us to land until near midnight; when with difficulty we found room for erecting our tents that had been constructed on a small scale for the convenience of this service.

During the night we had a very heavy fall of rain, and at day-light on Friday the 31st, our lodging was discovered to have been in a morass, and most of our things were very wet. In this very unpleasant abode we were detained by the weather until eight o'clock, when, although the rain continued, the haze cleared sufficiently to allow of our proceeding northward to a point on the opposite shore, situated in latitude 52° 14½′, longitude 232° 12½′; where the channel divided into two branches, one leading to the N.N.E. the other N. 63 E.[1] The latter, for the reasons before given, became the object of our pursuit. From Mr. Johnstone's sketch the preceding year, and from the direction this branch was now seen to take, we had some reason to suppose the eastern land was an island. Towards noon the weather enabled me to get an indifferent observation for the latitude, which shewed 52° 19′. The inlet now extending to the north-eastward was generally about a mile wide, the shores steep, rocky, and compact, if a small opening, or sheltered bay, on the south-west shore be excepted.[2] In the afternoon two openings on the north-west shore were passed.[3] The northernmost of these had the appearance of being extensive. At its south point of entrance, in latitude 52° 23½′, longitude 232° 28½′,[4] we met with a small party of the natives, whose appearance and conduct much resembled those we had met the day before. They strongly solicited us to visit their houses; but as their signs gave us reason to believe their habitations were behind us, though at no great distance, I declined their civil intreaties, and prosecuted our survey until seven in the evening, when we arrived at a point, from whence this inlet again divides into two arms, one taking a northerly, the other a south-easterly direction.[5] From this point, named by me POINT EDWARD, situated in latitude 52° 25½′, longitude 232° 37½′,[6] and forming the northern extremity of the eastern shore, we directed our route to the south-east, in order to take up our lodging for the

---

[1] Cousins Inlet to the N.N.E., and the much larger Dean Channel. They come together in about lat. 52° 15′ N, long. 127° 45′ W (232° 15′ E).   [2] Jenny Inlet.

[3] Elcho Harbour and the much larger Cascade Inlet.

[4] Cape McKay. Its position in lat. 52° 24′ N, long. 127° 25′ W (232° 35′ E). The Indians were Bella Bellas.

[5] The continuation of Dean Channel to the N, and Labouchere Channel to the SE.

[6] Edward Point, in lat. 52° 26′ N, long. 127° 16′ W (232° 44′ E).

night, having little doubt of finding that channel to be the same that Mr. Johnstone had the last year left unexplored, extending to the northward.

About four in the morning of Saturday the 1st of June, the weather being mild, though cloudy, we again prosecuted our researches to the south-east, and about seven came to a point that left no doubt as to our situation, and that the starboard shore which we had thus far pursued, was one side of an extensive island, which I distinguished by the name of KING'S ISLAND, after the family of my late highly-esteemed and much-lamented friend, Captain James King of the navy.[1] Point Menzies was seen from this station lying S. 83 E. about three leagues distant, and the north-east point of Burke's channel on the opposite shore S. 78 E. two miles and an half distant. The continuation of the inlet to the eastward was evidently the same that had undergone the examination of Mr. Johnstone, and determined to a certainty that we had the continent again in view.

At this point I left in a conspicuous place a note, desiring Mr. Johnstone would return to the vessels by the way he had come; having before received directions, in case of his finally exploring the arm before us leading to the eastward, to endeavour to return to the vessels by the route we had pursued; this had now become unnecessary; and as the inlet at point Menzies had again divided itself into two branches, one extending in a south-easterly, and the other in a north-easterly direction,[2] I had acquainted Mr. Johnstone, that I should prosecute the examination of the north-eastern branch, whilst he was employed in the other, if I met with no indications of his having preceded me. After quitting this point, we landed to breakfast on the before mentioned point of the continental shore, and there found, either left by accident or design, one of our kegs, which proved that Mr. Johnstone had reached that spot before us. In its bung-hole I left a note similar to the former.

The weather was now serene and pleasant. With a gentle south-west breeze, after breakfast, we continued to examine the north-east branch, and at noon I observed the latitude in its entrance to be 52° 19′ 30″; whence point Menzies will be found to lie in 52° 18′ 33″;[3] being 4′ further north than the latitude assigned to that point on our former visit; but its longitude did not appear to require any correction.

On the north point of entrance into this branch I left a third note for Mr. Johnstone, lest he should not at this time have finished his south-eastern survey, and should hereafter pursue the examination of this arm, directing him as before to return home, as the whole extent within the limits of his intended excursion would now fall under my own investigation.

[1] King joined Cook's third expedition as second lieutenant of the *Resolution*. Owing to the deaths of Captain Cook and Captain Clerke he returned as captain of the *Discovery*. He wrote the third and last volume of the official account of the expedition, which was published in June 1784. King died of consumption only four months later at the early age of 34.

[2] South Bentinck Arm and North Bentinck Arm.

[3] 52° 18′ 30″ in the first edition, which is very close to the true position.

From hence we directed our course over to the eastern shore, where, observing a fire on the beach amongst the drift wood, we landed, and not only found evident signs of Mr. Johnstone's party having recently quitted the beach, but on a tree was written with a burnt stick, '*Gone by.*' Any further attempts here on our part became therefore useless. That branch extended to the south-east, and from the light colour of the water we had passed through this morning, there was no doubt it had terminated in the usual way. In our progress to this station, we had passed five openings on the larboard or continental shore. Our attention was now directed to these objects, and having dined, we returned by the same way we had come, and rested for the night near our lodging of the preceding evening.

The appearance of the country we had passed by, varied in no respect from what has already been frequently described, excepting that the maple, birch, crab, and other small trees, seemed to be more numerous, and of a larger size. Two or three whales, one near point Menzies, several seals, and some sea otters had been seen; these were remarkably shy, as were two black bears that were observed on the shores.

The tide in this neighbourhood appeared to rise and fall about ten feet; and it is high water 10^h 20' after the moon passes the meridian; but neither the ebb nor the flood appeared to occasion any general, or even visible, stream.

Early the next morning, Sunday the 2d, with rainy unpleasant weather, we again proceeded, keeping the starboard or continental shore on board, to the fifth unexamined opening, lying from point Edward on King's island nearly north,[1] about six miles; in general a mile, but sometimes a league wide. We passed an islet and some rocks,[2] lying on the eastern or starboard shore, where we breakfasted, and afterwards continued our researches until about two o'clock, when we stopped to dine in a bay on the western shore, into which flowed the most considerable rivulet I had yet seen in this country.[3] The tide was then at the lowest, yet it admitted our boats into its entrance, which is about thirty yards wide, and four feet deep, and discharged a rapid stream of fresh water, until prevented by the flood tide. The spring tides appeared to rise about seven feet. High water 11^h 10' after the moon passes the meridian. This brook soon decreased in dimensions within the entrance, and shortly lost itself in a valley bounded at no great distance by high perpendicular mountains. Three Indians appeared on the opposite side of the brook. I endeavoured by signs and offers of trinkets to prevail on their crossing over to us, but without success; at length they gave us to understand by signs, that if we would go back to our party, who were at no great distance, they would follow in their canoe. They paddled after us a few yards, but again returned to the shore, on which one of them landed, and the other two again came forward. The man who had landed hastened back along the banks of the brook with visible marks of fear, as we conjectured, towards their habitations. His apprehensions

---

[1] The continuation of Dean Channel.   [2] Nascall Islands and the Nascall Rocks.
[3] Skowquiltz Bay and the Skowquiltz River.

operated on the other two, who also retired up the brook in their canoe. As we were preparing to depart about three o'clock, this canoe, attended by another containing six or seven Indians, came down the rivulet; but notwithstanding every means was used to invite them, they would not venture nearer us than their companions had done before. I left some iron, knives, and trinkets near our fire, whither I had little doubt their curiosity would soon be directed.[1]

From hence we proceeded about nine miles up the arm, still extending to the north-east, and preserving the same width. We passed a small island lying near the western shore,[2] here we took up our abode for the night, and the next morning, Monday the 3d, again proceeded. The water was nearly fresh at low tide, but was not of a very light colour. Having gone about a league we arrived at a point on the western shore, from whence the arm took a direction N.N.W. for about three leagues, and then, as was most commonly the case, it terminated in low marshy land. On a small spot of low projecting land from the eastern shore, three or four natives were observed, who would not venture near us; and at a little distance from the shore, the trees appeared to have been cleared away for some extent, and a square, spacious platform was erected, lying horizontally, and supported by several upright spars of considerable thickness, and apparently not less than twenty-five or thirty feet high from the ground. A fire was burning on it at one end, but there was no appearance of any thing like a house, though we concluded that such was the use to which it was appropriated.[3] After breakfast we returned by the same route we had arrived, and stopped at the point above mentioned to observe its latitude, which I found to be 52° 43½', and its longitude 232° 55'. To this point I gave the name of POINT RAPHOE, and to the channel we had thus explored, DEAN'S CHANNEL.[4] Quitting this point, we dined on our return at the same brook where we had stopped the preceding day; the Indians had taken the trinkets we had left for them, and although they were heard in the woods they did not make their appearance. From thence we proceeded towards the next unexplored inlet,[5] until near dark, when we halted again

---

[1] These were Bella Coola Indians, an isolated Salishan tribe living along North and South Bentinck Arms, the Bella Coola River (which empties into North Bentinck Arm), the upper reaches of Dean Channel, and the valleys of the Dean and Kimsquit rivers, which flow into the head of the channel. This was Vancouver's first contact with them; Johnstone and Menzies had met some of them in 1792.

[2] Vancouver overestimated distances as he travelled up the channel. The island (Ironbound Island) is about six miles, not nine miles from Skowquiltz Bay.

[3] Presumably part of Kimsquit, a Bella Coola village on the E shore of Dean Channel, at the mouth of the Dean River. The 'small spot of low projecting land' evidently masked the mouth of the river, as it escaped Vancouver's notice.

[4] These two names were related in origin. Dean Channel (Dean's Canal in the first edition) was named after the Rev. James King, father of Vancouver's friend, Captain James King. He was Dean of Raphoe, in county Donegal, Ireland. The position of Raphoe Point is lat. 52° 43' N, long. 126° 58' W (233° 02' E).

[5] Cascade Inlet.

for the night, and on the following morning, Tuesday the 4th, reached its entrance about half a mile wide, lying in a N. 50 W. direction. The weather was rough, chilly, and unpleasant, attended with much rain until near noon. At this time we had reached within a mile of the head of the arm, where the observed latitude was 52° 32′, longitude 232° 17′;[1] this terminated like the others, and we returned by the same route we had come.

The width of this channel did not any where exceed three quarters of a mile; its shores were bounded by precipices much more perpendicular than any we had yet seen during this excursion; and from the summits of the mountains that overlooked it, particularly on its north-eastern shore, there fell several large cascades. These were extremely grand, and by much the largest and most tremendous of any we had ever beheld. The impetuosity with which these waters descended, produced a strong current of air that reached nearly to the opposite side of the channel, though it was perfectly calm in every other direction. At first I considered these cascades to have been solely occasioned by the melting of the snow on the mountains that surrounded us; but, on comparing them with several smaller falls of water, which, by their colour, by the soil brought down with them, and other circumstances, were evidently produced from that temporary cause; the larger torrents appeared to owe their origin to a more general and permanent source. This arm I distinguished by the name of CASCADE CHANNEL.[2] Near its south point of entrance, we again met the friendly Indians who had so civilly invited us to their habitations; their intreaties were repeated, with which we complied, and we found their village to consist of seven houses, situated in a small rocky cove close round the point. On approaching near to their dwellings, they desired we would not land there, but on the opposite side of the cove; which we did, and by that means ingratiated ourselves in their favor, and secured their confidence. We were visited by about forty of the male inhabitants, but the women and young children who appeared to equal that number, remained in their houses. The construction of these was very curious; the back parts appeared to be supported by the projection of a very high, and nearly perpendicular, rocky cliff, and the front and sides by slender poles, about fifteen or eighteen feet high. I was much inclined to be better acquainted with these curious mansions; but the repugnance shewn by their owners to our entering them, induced me to decline the attempt, lest it might give them serious offence, and disturb the harmony that had taken place between us.[3] Not one of them had a weapon of any kind, and they all conducted themselves in the most civil and orderly manner. Some medals and a few trinkets were given them, and in return we received a very indifferent sea otter skin, and some pieces of halibut. In this

---

[1] The correct position would be approximately lat. 52° 35′ 30″ N, long. 127° 37′ W (232° 23′ E).

[2] Cascade Canal in the first edition; now Cascade Inlet.

[3] This was a Bella Bella village. The Bella Coola Indians also constructed elevated houses, one of which was visited and described by Johnstone, as noted in the entry in Vancouver's narrative dated June 9. The village was in McKay Bay.

traffic they proved themselves to be keen traders, but acted with the strictest honesty.

Our visit here detained us about half an hour, after which we proceeded to the third unexplored opening.[1] This was about S. 52 W., and about a league distant from the south point of Cascade channel; here we rested, and in the morning of Wednesday the 5th, found it terminate about two miles in a westerly direction. From thence we proceeded to the next arm,[2] this was the first we had noticed to the eastward of that, of which on the 30th of May I had entertained doubts of its being the main branch of the inlet.

We were now favored with pleasant weather, and a gentle gale from the N.E. and S.E. This, by noon, brought us within about a mile of this arm's termination, which, from its entrance in a N.N.E. direction, is about five miles; here I observed the latitude to be 52° 19′, the longitude 232° 13½′.[3] This branch finished in a similar manner with the many others, though its shores were not so steep, nor did they afford such falls of water as were seen in Cascade channel. From hence we continued along the continental shore until the evening, when we reached the doubtful opening, and found its entrance to be in latitude 52° 12′, longitude 232° 7′;[4] it is about three quarters of a mile wide, and has a small islet[5] and several rocks extending from its north-east point. Between these rocks and the western shore there appeared to be a fair navigable channel.

About a mile up this opening on the starboard, or continental shore, we

---

[1] Elcho Harbour, which Vancouver explored on 5 June. One of the interesting 'near misses' of history occurred here. Six weeks and five days after Vancouver's visit, Alexander Mackenzie, having completed the first crossing of North America N of Mexico, 'mixed up some vermilion in melted grease, and inscribed, in large characters, on the South-East face of the rock on which we had slept last night, this brief memorial – "Alexander Mackenzie, from Canada, by land, the twenty-second of July, one thousand seven hundred and ninety-three."' The rock was a little to the N of the entrance to Elcho Harbour; the area around it now forms Sir Alexander Mackenzie Park. Mackenzie found the Indians in the vicinity anything but friendly: 'One of them in particular made me understand, with an air of insolence, that a large canoe had lately been in this bay, with people in it like me, and that one of them, whom he called *Macubah*, had fired on him and his friends, and that *Bensins* had struck him on the back, with the flat part of his sword. He also mentioned another name, the articulation of which I could not determine. At the same time he illustrated these circumstances by the assistance of my gun and sword; and I do not doubt but he well deserved the treatment which he described.' Other Indians told Mackenzie 'that *Macubah* had been there, and left his ship behind a point of land in the channel, South-West of us; from whence he had come to their village in boats, which these people represented by imitating our manner of rowing.' – W. Kaye Lamb (ed.) *The Journals and Letters of Sir Alexander Mackenzie* (Cambridge, 1970), pp. 375–6. 'Macubah' was clearly a reference to Vancouver, but the account is badly garbled. It has been suggested that by 'Bensins' the Indians meant Menzies, but Menzies was not a member of Vancouver's boat expedition. Nor is there any record of any clash with the Indians of the kind reported to Mackenzie.

[2] Cousins Inlet. The town of Ocean Falls is at the head of this inlet.

[3] The position would be approximately lat. 52° 21′ N, long. 127° 43′ W (232° 17′ E).

[4] The 'doubtful opening' was Johnson Channel. The position given for its entrance is very close to the correct reading.   [5] Dean Island.

remained during the night on an insulated rock, that had formerly been appropriated to the residence of the natives. It forms the north point of entrance into a cove,[1] where a sunken rock lies, not visible until half tide; within this rock is a clear sandy bottom, that might be found convenient for the purpose of laying small vessels aground to clean or repair, as we estimated the tide, though not near the height of the springs, to rise fourteen or fifteen feet, and to be high water at the time the moon passes the meridian. We were detained at this station by thick, foggy, and rainy weather, attended with a strong south-east gale, until ten o'clock in the forenoon of Thursday the 6th, when the fog in some measure clearing away, we proceeded in our researches up this arm. It lies in a general direction of N. 20 W., for about three leagues; the eastern or continental shore is steep and compact; but, on the western shore, we passed, five or six miles within the entrance, five rocky islets[2] producing some trees, and admitting a passage for boats between them and the shore; and on the same side, about seven miles within the entrance, is a larger islet,[3] having between it and the shore a rock; on which was an Indian village that contained many houses, and seemed to be very populous.[4] We were no sooner discovered, than several large canoes were employed in transporting a number of the inhabitants to the shore on the western side, who instantly ran to the woods and hid themselves. Our route however, lying wide of either their village or their retirement, we did not increase their apprehensions by approaching nearer to them, but continued our survey up the arm that still took a northerly direction, leaving on the western shore a spacious opening extending to the westward,[5] and passing a small island covered with pine trees, that lies nearly in mid-channel of the arm we were pursuing.[6]

Having reached, about two in the afternoon, a point on the eastern shore, about ten miles from the entrance, we stopped to dine, and were here visited by some of the Indians from the village in two canoes. These were totally unarmed, and at first acted with a considerable degree of caution. A few trivial presents however soon dissipated their fears, and they became equally civil with those we had before seen, from whom they did not appear to differ, excepting in their being less cleanly; or more properly speaking, in being more bedaubed with oil and paints. They remained with us until our dinner was over, sold us two or three otter skins, the only commodity they brought for barter, and when we proceeded they returned home.

From this point we found the arm take first a direction N. 40 E. near a league, and then N. 30 W. about five miles further; it was in general from half to three quarters of a mile wide, and terminated as usual in low swampy

[1] The cove behind Stokes Island. A narrow channel, dry at low tide, which Vancouver does not mention, runs on to Fisher Channel, thus creating the island.

[2] The McCroskie Islands.

[3] Beaumont Island.

[4] Vancouver later describes this village.   [5] Return Channel.

[6] Nicholson Island, in the middle of the entrance to Roscoe Inlet, which Vancouver considered to be the continuation of Johnson Channel.

land, in latitude 52° 28½′, longitude 232° 4′.[1] From hence we returned and halted for the night, about two miles from its head on the western shore.

The next morning, Friday the 7th, we proceeded to the branch leading to the westward, that we had passed the preceding day;[2] and about eight o'clock reached a small island lying near the northern shore, about two miles to the westward of its entrance, situated in latitude 52° 19¾′, longitude 232° 1′.[3] Here we stopped to breakfast, and were again visited by our friends from the village on the rock, whose behaviour was similar to what we had before experienced.

The weather became serene and pleasant, with a gentle breeze from the south-west. We now quitted the high steep snowy mountains, composing the shores we had lately traversed; for the sides of the opening before us, comparatively speaking, might be considered as land of moderate height. Its surface covered with wood was very uneven, and being very similar to the general appearance of the land near the sea coast, gave us reason to believe this channel would lead towards the ocean.

The continental shore had been accurately traced to our present station, and the communication of this channel with the ocean became an object I much wished to ascertain, before the vessels should be removed further into this interior and intricate navigation; well knowing the tardy and disagreeable progress in so doing. To effect this purpose in the best manner I was able, I continued to trace the channel leading westward, passing by on the starboard or continental shore, an opening that appeared to terminate in a spacious bay, at the distance of about two miles.[4] Another opening was seen immediately to the westward of this bay, that appeared of considerable extent, leading to the N.N.W.[5] and had two small islands nearly in the centre of its entrance; but, as we had now been nine days from the ship, our stock of provisions was too much reduced to admit of our undertaking further examinations, especially as every foot we advanced we had additional reasons for supposing we should find a channel in this neighbourhood that would lead to the ocean. From the last opening the coast trended S. 40 W.; in which direction I well knew we could not long continue, without meeting the sea; and having proceeded thus nearly a league, I stopped about noon at a point on the north-west shore to observe the latitude, which was 52° 17′,[6] longitude 231° 54′; and whilst I was so employed, Mr. Swaine was sent forward with directions, on his discovering a clear channel to sea, to return. As I was preparing to follow him, the cutter was seen coming back; Mr. Swaine reported, that from a point lying S. 48 W. a mile and a half from our then

[1] Vancouver evidently did not go sufficiently far to see Roscoe Narrows, where Roscoe Inlet swings to the NE and on various courses extends eastward for another 10 miles. He considered that it ended in the present Boukind Bay, N of the Narrows. The head of the bay is in lat. 52° 27′ 30″ N, long. 127° 56′ W (232° 04′ E).

[2] Return Channel.

[3] Rochester Island, in lat. 52° 19′ N, long. 127° 59′ W (232° 01′ E).

[4] Briggs Inlet (formerly Sisters Inlet).

[5] Bullock Channel.   [6] Probably McArthur Point, in lat. 52° 18′ N.

station, he had seen the ocean in a direction S. 70 W.; the furthest land being about three or four leagues distant.

Being now satisfied that all the land forming the sea coast, from the south entrance into Fitzhugh's sound, to the place from whence we now looked into the ocean, consisted of two extensive islands, that were again probably much subdivided; I considered the object of our errand accomplished, and we sat off on our return towards the station of the vessels, from whence we were 45 miles distant. In the evening we passed close to the rock on which the village last mentioned is situated; it appeared to be about half a mile in circuit, and was intirely occupied by the habitations of the natives. These appeared to be well constructed; the boards forming the sides of the houses were well fitted, and the roofs rose from each side with sufficient inclination to throw off the rain. The gable ends were decorated with curious painting, and near one or two of the most conspicuous mansions were carved figures in large logs of timber, representing a gigantic human form, with strange and uncommonly distorted features.[1] Some of our former visitors again came off, and conducted themselves as before with great civility; but these as well as those on shore, had great objections to our landing at their village; the latter making signs to us to keep off, and the former giving us to understand, that our company was not desired at their habitations. Their numbers, I should imagine, amounted at least to three hundred. After gratifying our friends with some presents, they returned to their rock, and we continued our route homewards.

About noon of Saturday the 8th, in a bay opposite an opening on the western shore, that had the appearance of communicating with the ocean,[2] we fell in with about forty men, women, and children of the same tribe of Indians we had met on the first day. These received us with the same kind of caution we had before experienced, and desired we would land at a rock a little distant from the party. On complying with their wishes, we were visited by most of the men and boys, who, after receiving some presents, gave us fully to understand, that the women would have had no objection to our company;[3] but having still a long pull against wind and tide before we could reach the ships, I declined their civil solicitations.

[1] Bell gives the following description: The village 'was situated on a bare Rock about fifty yards from the main Land and was not more I suppose (the Rock) than three or four Hundred Yards in circumference. This Rock was covered with Houses built close to each other, and indeed I believe connecting one with another, for it had more the appearance of one large House than many different ones, they were most curiously painted in all Colours, with the most extravagant grotesque figures of Men, Beasts and Fishes, the floors of these houses were raised about two Yards from the Rock by Strong Pillars, or rather compleat Trunks of Stout Pine Trees, and on the fronts of them had Stages or a kind of Balconey projecting from before their doors to which they ascended by a Ladder. From appearances I should suppose its Inhabitants might amount to about a hundred & fifty at least.' – 13 June.

[2] Lagoon Bay, opposite the entrance to Lama Passage, which does lead to the ocean through Hunter Channel to the SW, or Seaforth Channel to the N.

[3] Hewett comments: 'this I deny', but it is not a matter about which Vancouver would be likely to exaggerate.

The whole of this party were employed in gathering cockles, and in preparing a sort of paste from the inner bark of a particular kind of pine tree, intended we supposed as a substitute for bread; this they washed in the sea water, beat it very hard on the rocks, and then made it up into balls. It had a sweetish taste, was very tender, and if we may judge from their actions, it seemed by them to be considered as good food.

This, as well as the cockles, they offered in abundance, in return for nails and trinkets, but we accepted only a few of the latter.

About ten at night we arrived on board, where I found all well, and most of our material work executed. Mr. Baker informed me, that the weather had been very unpleasant during my absence, and according to his account infinitely worse than what we had experienced; this had greatly protracted the necessary duties of the ship, and prevented due observations being made for ascertaining our situation, and the rate of the chronometers; I was apprehensive, that the few that had been obtained were all that on the present occasion were likely to be procured.

The next morning, Sunday the 9th, Mr. Johnstone informed me, that on the forenoon of the 30th of May he reached point Menzies, from whence he found an arm lying in a direction with little variation S. 33 E.[1] By noon they had advanced about five miles from point Menzies, where the latitude was observed to be 52° 15', and about four miles further passed an island on the eastern shore.[2] The weather being pleasant, great progress was made until the evening, when they reached its termination in latitude 52° 1', longitude 233° 18'.[3] Its width in general a little exceeded a mile, and the surrounding country exactly resembled that which we had found contiguous to the branches of the sea that have been so repeatedly described. Here the party halted for the night, and at day-light the next morning returned. On the eastern side of this channel, near the head of a small rivulet, they had noticed on the preceding evening a house of a very singular construction, but perceived no signs of its being inhabited. As they now advanced some smoke was observed, and three Indians approached them with much caution, and shewing great disapprobation at their landing; on receiving some nails and trinkets they however became reconciled, and attended Mr. Johnstone with some of the gentlemen of his party to their habitations. These were found to be of a different construction from any they had before seen; they were erected on a platform similar to that seen in my late excursion, and mentioned as being raised and supported near thirty feet from the ground by perpendicular spars of a very large size; the whole occupying a space of about thirty-five yards by fifteen, was covered in by a roof of boards lying nearly horizontal, and parallel to the platform; it seemed to be divided into three different houses, or rather apartments, each having a separate access formed by a long tree in an inclined position from the platform to the ground, with notches cut in it

---

[1] South Bentinck Arm.   [2] Bensins Island.

[3] Johnstone assumed that the Arm ended at Taleomey Narrows, but it actually runs on for about three miles beyond that point.

by way of steps, about a foot and a half asunder. Up one of these ladders Mr. Johnstone, with one of his party only, was suffered to ascend, and by removing a broad board placed as a kind of door on the platform where the ladder rested, they entered on a small area before the door of the house or apartment to which the ladder belonged. Here they found four of the natives posted, each bearing a rude weapon made of iron, not unlike a dagger. They only permitted Mr. Johnstone to look about him, and seemed much averse to his entering the house, which he prudently did not insist upon; but so far as he was able to observe within doors, their internal arrangements differed little or nothing from the domestic œconomy of the Indians already seen on the shores of North West America. The number of inhabitants seen at this curious place did not exceed a dozen or fourteen, but amongst them were neither women nor children. Mr. Johnstone discovered from this that their landing had excited no small degree of alarm; which greatly subsided on their departure. Three very small canoes only were seen, and these seemed, from their construction, capable of performing no other service than that of fishing in the small streams that are frequently met with at the head of these channels. At the mouth of the creek were a great number of wicker fish pots, which induced the party to ask for something to eat, but instead of fish, the natives brought them a kind of paste or bread, supposed to be made from the inner rind of the pine.[1] Their language was quite new to our party, and they appeared to be totally unacquainted with that of Nootka.[2]

From this curious place of residence Mr. Johnstone came back along the eastern shore, and about five miles from the termination of the channel he observed the latitude to be 52° 4'. About seven the next morning (1st of June) the arm leading to the north-eastward was entered;[3] this was found about one mile and a quarter wide, lying in a direction of N. 62 E. from its north point of entrance; and, at the distance of eleven miles, it terminated in the usual way; in latitude 52° 26', longitude 233° 16'.[4] Here was another habitation of the same sort.[5] Having now completed the examination of this branch, the party returned along its northern shores, and at the point of

[1] 'there is a piece of this type of bread in the Cook collection in the British Museum...which is described as "bread of the pine bark." The bark is probably not pine but spruce. Such cakes were widely used on the Northwest Coast and also were found inland. The shredded bark was pounded together with mashed berries and salmon eggs or herring eggs. It was formed in oblongs and laid out to dry.' – Gunther, *Indian Life on the Northwest Coast* (Chicago, 1972), pp. 111–12.

[2] As already noted, these were Bella Coola Indians. Their language was a dialect of interior Salish.

[3] North Bentinck Arm. The town of Bella Coola is at the head of the arm, at the mouth of the Bella Coola River.

[4] The correct position is lat. 52° 23' N, long. 126° 46' W (233° 14' E).

[5] This was part of the Bella Coola village at the mouth of the Bella Coola River, which would be visited by Alexander Mackenzie a few weeks later. Mackenzie first saw 'elevated houses' on 18 July 1793 at a village some distance up the Bella Coola River. It 'consisted of four elevated houses, and seven built on the ground.... The former are constructed by fixing a certain number of posts in the earth, on some of which are laid, and to others

entrance Mr. Johnstone found my directions to return to the vessels, which they reached in the forenoon of the next day. In their way they saw several bears; two young cubs were killed, and proved excellent eating.

I now directed Mr. Johnstone to proceed immediately and examine the arm leading to the north north-westward, which I had passed on the forenoon of the 7th;[1] to follow it as far as it might lead, or his provisions allow, and to return to its entrance, where he would find the vessels at anchor near the two small islands; but in the event of his business being finished before the ships should arrive, he was to leave a note on the northernmost of the islands, mentioning his arrival and departure, and proceed to the survey of the coast further to the westward, and to gain every information with respect to the channel we had discovered leading to sea. With these directions, and a week's provisions, attended by Mr. Barrie[2] in the Discovery's small cutter, he departed in the forenoon.

I had intended to proceed with the ships the next morning, but on visiting the observatory, I found another day's corresponding altitudes would be very desirable; for which purpose I determined to remain a day longer. The magazine also, being yet damp, would be benefited by further airing with fires. The powder which had been all aired, and found in better condition than was expected, remained on shore until the next morning. Monday the 10th, when the weather being rainy and unpleasant, without the least prospect of any alteration, the observatory with every thing else was taken from the shore; and in the afternoon we weighed and towed out of the cove, which I distinguished by the name of RESTORATION COVE, having there passed and celebrated the anniversary of that happy event.[3]

During my absence some excellent spruce was brewed from the pine trees found here, and a sufficient supply of fish for the use of all hands was every day procured. The gentlemen on board did not long remain without being visited by the natives, who seemed to be of three different tribes, each having distinct chiefs, named *Keyut, Comockshulah, Whacosh*;[4] they seemed all on very

---

are fastened, the supporters of the floor, at about twelve feet above the surface of the ground: their length is from an hundred to an hundred and twenty feet, and they are about forty feet in breadth. Along the centre are built three, four, or five hearths, for the two-fold purpose of giving warmth, and dressing their fish.' The next day he reached the village at the mouth of the river, ' consisting of six very large houses, erected on pallisades, rising twenty-five feet from the ground, which differed in no one circumstance from those already described, but the height of their elevation.' – W. Kaye Lamb (ed.), *The Journals and Letters of Sir Alexander Mackenzie* (Cambridge, Hakluyt Society, 1970), pp. 366, 372.

[1] Bullock Channel.

[2] Robert Barrie, midshipman.

[3] May 29, the anniversary of the restoration of Charles II in 1660.

[4] Gunther adopts Vancouver's spelling of the names; Menzies' versions are Cait, Coomoghshalla and Wacash. Coomoghshalla (Comochshulah) he described as 'a good looking young man of about 18 years of age with mild open features & a pleasing affable behaviour. He was decently dressed in a garment of red Cloth bordered round with white leather curiously ornamented with rude paintings.' Wacash was 'a good looking Man of a middling stature, in the prime of life, with a mild open countenance'. – June 1 and 8.

friendly and amicable terms with each other, and conducted themselves with the greatest good order on board. Their language, it seems, much resembled that of the people on Queen Charlotte's islands, through which some on board were able to make themselves understood. From *Whacosh* they had learned, that he had fallen in with our boats at some distance; this had been really the case, as he was one of those who had visited me from the large village on the detached rock. They brought for barter the skins of the sea otter and other animals, some of which were purchased with copper and iron.[1]

This uninteresting region afforded nothing further worthy of notice, excepting the soundings, the dimensions of the cove, and the very few astronomical and nautical observations, that, under the unfavorable circumstances of the weather, could be procured.

The breadth of the cove at the entrance, in a north and south direction, is about a mile and a quarter, and its depth, from the centre of the entrance in a north-east direction, is three quarters of a mile. The soundings, though deep, are regular, from sixty fathoms at the entrance, to five and ten fathoms close to the shore. The land on the opposite side of the arm is about two miles and a half distant.

[1] The skins 'were eagerly bought up by our people for Copper Cloths Iron Ear Shells & other articles; but Lieut. Baker who was commanding officer [of the *Discovery*] observing that some Copper had been given away to these Natives...which appeard to be Ship's Stores, he ordered that no further trafic whatever should be carried on until this business should be cleard up before the Captain on his return, which was complied with'. – Menzies, May 31. Trade was also brisk in the *Chatham*, as Puget notes, adding a condemnation of the traffic in arms that echoed Vancouver's denunciation of the similar traffic in Hawaii. The Indians approached the *Chatham* in a small canoe: 'We were much astonished at the Quantity of excellent Skins this little Canoe contained & which they were happy to part with for Blue Cloth Copper & the former they held in high Estimation & was immediately on the Exchange converted into a Garment; But still Musquets Powder &c was their first demand, but finding a Reluctance or rather positive refusal to part with those Articles on any Consideration, they shortly after gladly seized that Opportunity of disposing of their Articles for what was at first offered. This Circumstance Though exceeding trivial will certainly contradict the many Assertions that have been industriously circulated by the different Traders, in a Manner to exculpate the Infamous Custom of supplying the Indians with Fire Arms & this Conduct has been defended as compulsatory – the Natives refusing to have any Intercourse unless Musquets &c were the Stipulated Article of Commerce. If this had been the Case how did Mr. Portlock and Dixon get their Cargo & among these identical Tribes....I am certain if the Traders had formed a Combination early among themselves not to purchase any Furs in exchange for Musquets &c that the Indians would now have been equally as happy to sell their Skins for Cloth Copper &c as they were on Capt Cook's first Visit in the Resolution.' – May 31. Bell makes a comment that shows that the crews of both ships took it for granted that they would be permitted to trade for furs: 'The Articles most in demand were Copper and Blue Cloth, Copper Tea and Cooking Kettles, Bright large Metal Buttons and Ear Shells, – of this last article of Merchandise there was a good Store on board both the Vessels for the people having been apprized of their Value gathered them at Monterrey where they grow on the Rocky Shore in great numbers, for four of these Shells each a considerable number of excellent Skins were purchased.' – May.

The astronomical observations made at this station were,
Fourteen sets of lunar distances taken by Mr.
   Whidbey, on the 3d and 5th of June, gave a mean
   result of   232° 8′ 45″
Fourteen sets taken by Mr. Orchard, ditto   232 15 51
The mean of twenty-eight sets as above   232 12 18
The latitude by six meridional altitudes of the sun   52   0 58[1]
By single altitudes on the 31st of May, Kendall's
   chronometer shewed the longitude to be by the
   Karakakooa rate   230 11 15
Arnold's No. 14, by the same rate   230 35
   Ditto, No. 176, ditto   233   2 45
   Ditto, No. 82, on board the Chatham, ditto   234   5 45[2]
Having corresponding altitudes on the 3d and 5th
   of June, that interval was considered too short;
   a single altitude taken on the 7th, and another on
   the 10th, were therefore made use of, for
   ascertaining the rates of the chronometers. From
   this authority, and considering the longitude of
   this place as fixed by our last year's observations
   in 232° 20′ to be correct,[3] it appeared that
   Kendall's chronometer was fast of mean time at
   Greenwich, on the 10th of June, at noon   2^h 8′ 15″ 46‴
And gaining per day at the rate of   23 15
Arnold's No. 14, fast of mean time at Greenwich   1 57 29 46
And gaining per day at the rate of   20 32
Arnold's No. 176, ditto, ditto   4 50   46
And gaining per day at the rate of   42 58
Arnold's No. 82, ditto, ditto   6   4 19 46
And gaining per day at the rate of   29 41

But, as I considered this authority insufficient for establishing the several
rates of the instruments, the longitude of the different stations hereafter
mentioned will be deduced from such observations as we were able to obtain,
when an opportunity offered for getting the observatory again on shore.

The variation by two compasses taken on shore, differing in six sets from
17° 49′ to 20° 28′, gave a mean result of 19° 15′, eastwardly.

The tide was found to rise and fall fourteen feet, the night tides were in
general one foot higher than in the day time, the flood came from the south,
and it was high water at the time the moon passed the meridian.

---

[1] Puget gives the lat. of the observatory as 52° 00′ 57″ N.

[2] Puget's figure for long. is 234° 05′ 15″ E. Both the lat. and long. are given in a note
following the entry in his log. for June 11.

[3] The correct reading was probably 127° 37′ 30″ W (232° 22′ 30″ E).

The winds were light and variable, attended with rainy unpleasant weather; we continued under sail all night, and with the assistance of the ebb tide in the morning of Tuesday the 11th, reached Fisher's channel. A moderate breeze springing up from the S.S.W. we directed our course to the northward, and by noon arrived in the arm of the inlet that had been discovered by the boats to lead into the sea.[1] Our observed latitude at this time being 52° 12', agreed very nearly with our former observations. The favorable breeze soon left us, and at three o'clock we anchored within a cable's length of the western shore in fifty-eight fathoms water, about a league to the southward of the Indian village on the detached rock. Though it was not in sight from the ship, yet our arrival was not long unknown to its inhabitants, several of whom came off, and brought in their canoes sea otter and other skins to exchange for iron and copper; the articles principally in request amongst them. All their dealings were carried on with confidence, and the strictest honesty.

A small stream of tide making in our favor, we weighed, and although we had the assistance of all our boats a-head until near midnight, we did not advance above a mile before we were obliged to anchor again near the western shore in fifty-three fathoms water. In this situation we remained until eight in the morning of Wednesday the 12th, when we proceeded; but so slowly, that at noon the village bore west of us at the distance of about half a mile,[2] and the rendezvous appointed with Mr. Johnstone nearly in the same direction about a league further. This we reached by six in the evening, and anchored in twenty-two fathoms water, steadying the ship by a hawser to a tree, on the northernmost island;[3] where I found a note from Mr. Johnstone, stating that he had quitted that station at three o'clock on Monday afternoon, and had proceeded in the examination of the arm before us leading to the north north-westward.[4] We were therefore to wait his return here.

The next morning, Thursday the 13th, we tried the seine, but it was not attended with the least success. A great number of muscles however were procured, and converted into good palatable dishes. Our Indian friends, though

[1] Johnson Channel.

[2] Menzies seized the opportunity to visit a deserted village on the E shore. This consisted of five large houses, the largest of which 'coverd a space of 12 or 14 yards long by about 8 yards wide, four posts were stuck in the ground & arangd equidistant at each end, these supported four beams that reachd one end to the other; the outer posts & beams were rather slender for the size of the house, but the inner posts were very bulky & supported beams of immense size & weight, so much so that we were astonished how the Natives could manage to raise them to their present evaluation, or what mechanical powers in their state of ignorance they could make use of to effect that purpose... The large posts were carvd on the inside into the shape of huge human figures, & though the Carving was but rudely done, yet the representations were on the whole not destitute of proportion and expression, the necks were short & the hands in all of them pressd against the fore part of the thighs by which the bodies seemd to bend forward under the immense weight which they supported; These monstrous figures were fantastically ornamented with Carvings of smaller human faces in different parts, particularly in the places of the eyes of each figure...' – 12 June.

[3] The small island at the entrance of Bullock Channel.

[4] Bullock Channel, of which no complete survey has yet been made.

not far from us, were out of sight, and did not make their appearance; this might be partly owing to the dark, gloomy, rainy weather, that continued all Friday the 14th, but which did not then prevent our receiving the compliments of some, amongst whom was *Whacosh*, with two other chiefs of consequence, one named *Amzeet*, the other *Nestaw Daws*. The latter I had seen on our boat excursion, amongst the first natives who came from the village; from whence, exclusive of the chiefs, we were now visited by many of the inhabitants, who brought the skins of the sea otter and other animals for barter, but we could not obtain any supply of fish. The same uncomfortable weather, with little or no intermission, continued until towards noon of Sunday the 16th, when the rain ceased, but the weather continued unpleasant, dark, and gloomy.

Most of our Indian friends were about us, and besides the chiefs before mentioned came a chief I had not before seen, whose name was *Moclah*. The whole party, consisting of an hundred and upwards, conducted themselves with great good order. One or two trivial thefts were attempted, but these being instantly detected, and great displeasure shewn on the occasion, nothing of the sort happened afterwards. Amongst the skins brought for sale, was that of the animal from whence the wool is procured, with which the woollen garments, worn by the inhabitants of North West America, are made. These appeared evidently too large to belong to any animal of the canine race, as we had before supposed. They were, exclusively of the head or tail, fifty inches long; and thirty-six inches broad, exclusively of the legs. The wool seemed to be afforded but in a small proportion to the size of the skin. It is principally produced on the back and towards the shoulders, where a kind of crest is formed by long bristly hairs, that protrude themselves through the wool, and the same sort of hair forms an outer covering to the whole animal, and intirely hides the wool, which is short, and of a very fine quality. All the skins of this description that were brought to us were entirely white, or rather of a cream colour; the pelt was thick, and appeared of a strong texture, but the skins were too much mutilated to discover the kind of animal to which they had belonged.[1]

In the afternoon we had the honor of a female party on board. Those of

[1] These were skins of the mountain goat. Gunther comments: 'This is the only time in all the accounts used in this study [of Indian life] where the matter of blankets and their weaving has appeared frequently, that the wool has been identified with an animal. That none of the explorers ever saw a mountain goat is not surprising. They stay in the high mountains and wander from one meadow to another as they graze....The mountains are very high in the Bella Coola valley, and the people were the best mountain-goat hunters among the Northwest Coast tribes.' – *Indian Life on the Northwest Coast*, p. 110. Menzies made a shrewd guess about the identity of the animal: 'from the small strait horns which were producd for Sale at the same time & which they assured us belongd to the same Animal, we were led to suppose it to be of the Goat kind, but in all probability a new Animal as yet undescribed.' When he asked if he could see one 'they gave me to understand that they could not be got, as they were at this time of the year high up in the Mountains, but in the winter time that they came low down near the water side, & it was then they had an opportunity of killing them.' – 16 June.

the women who appeared of the most consequence, had adopted a very singular mode of adorning their persons. And although some sort of distortion or mutilation was a prevailing fashion with the generality of the Indian tribes we had seen, yet the peculiarity of that we now beheld, was of all others the most particular, and the effect of its appearance the most extraordinary.[1] A horizontal incision is made, about three tenths of an inch below the upper part of the under lip, extending from one corner of the mouth to the other intirely through the flesh; this orifice is then by degrees stretched sufficiently to admit an ornament made of wood, which is confined close to the gums of the lower jaws, and whole external surface projects horizontally.

These wooden ornaments are oval, and resemble a small oval platter or dish made concave on both sides; they are of various sizes, but the smallest I was able to procure was about two inches and a half; the largest was three inches and four tenths in length, and an inch and a half broad; the others decreased in breadth in proportion to their length. They are about four tenths of an inch in thickness, and have a groove along the middle of the outside edge, for the purpose of receiving the divided lip. These hideous appendages are made of fir, and neatly polished, but present a most unnatural appearance, and are a species of deformity, and an instance of human absurdity, that would scarcely be credited without ocular proof.[2]

It appeared very singular, that in the regions of New Georgia, where the principal part of the people's clothing is made of wool, we never saw the animal nor the skin from which the raw material was procured. And though I had every reason to believe, that those animals are by no means scarce in this neighbourhood, yet we did not observe one person amongst our present visitors in a woollen garment. The clothing of the natives here was either skins of the sea otter, or garments made from the pine bark; some of these latter have the fur of the sea otter, very neatly wrought into them, and have a border to the sides and bottom, decorated with various colours. In this only

[1] In the first edition the latter part of this sentence reads: 'was of all others the most extraordinary, and the effect of its appearance the most undescribable.'

[2] The labret was first described by the Franciscan friars (Crespi and Pena) who accompanied Pérez on his voyage north in 1774. Dixon describes it in his *Voyages*, p. 172. Vancouver had now met the Heiltsuk Indians, a branch of the Kwakiutl, amongst whom the wearing of the labret was customary. Puget described it as 'that Horrid Custom'. 'We had an Opportunity of seeing a Young Girl, who had with some Difficulty been prevailed on to sell the ornament from her Lip take it out & anxious about the Article offered in exchange for it, rather neglected to conceal the Place therefore we had a perfect view of her Face, it appeared to me like two complete Mouths & in that Situation it was abolutely more disgusting than when adorned with the ornament.' – 16 June. Bell commented: 'As may readily be supposed, this beauteous ornament affects their Speech – or rather their articulation in a very great degree, and it is droll to observe this enormous Trencher wagging up and down at every word the wearer says, and this it does with a most extravagant motion very often, for the Women in this part of the world, like many other parts, wear the Breeches, and are not only great Scolds, but great Orators, and the vehemence and violence with which they speak, gives ample play to the Trencher.' – June.

they use woollen yarn, very fine, well spun, and dyed for the purpose; particularly with a very lively and beautiful yellow.

We at first considered the inhabitants of this region to be a much finer race of men than those further south; the difference however appeared less conspicuous, when they were seen in greater numbers, probably owing to our having become more familiar with their persons, and to their having performed a long journey to visit us, in extremely rough rainy weather. Their dispositions, as far as our short acquaintance will authorize an opinion, appeared to be civil, good-humoured, and friendly. The vivacity of their countenances indicated a lively genius, and from their repeated bursts of laughter, it would appear that they were great humourists, for their mirth was not confined to their own party, or wholly resulting from thence, but was frequently at our expence; so perfectly were they at ease in our society.

The chiefs generally approached us with the ceremony of first rowing round the vessels, and departed in the same manner, singing a song that was by no means unpleasing; this was sometimes continued until they had retired a considerable distance. They seemed a happy cheerful people, and to live in the strictest harmony and good fellowship with each other. They were well versed in commerce; of this we had manifest proof in their disposal of the skins of the sea otter, and other animals; about one hundred and eighty of the former I believe were purchased by different persons on board, in the course of their several visits.[1] This number seemed nearly to have exhausted their stock, as most of the chiefs took their leave, as if they had no intention of returning, and in the same friendly and cheerful manner as before related.

The bay immediately to the eastward of this opening, which I had not very minutely examined, had been found by a shooting party not to be closed, as I had imagined, but to communicate, by a channel about a cable's length in width, with a narrow arm, about a fourth of a mile wide, extending in another direction;[2] this, on Monday morning the 17th, I sent Mr. Swaine to

---

[1] Vancouver participated in the trading, as Menzies records: 'Capt. Vancouver had a hide of thick buff leather which he got last year in New Georgia & which he this day disposd of for 5 Sea Otter Skins besides some other Furs of less value, so that this kind of leather is by far the best trade that can be brought to this part of the Coast.' – June 16. Puget notes that this was 'A Hide of Moose Deer which had been purchased from the natives of Columbia River when the Chatham was surveying that Place.' – June 17. Menzies adds: 'Of these dressed Hides the Natives here make their War dresses, by doubling it up into a kind of loose mantle which they slip over head to defend their bodies from Arrows & other missile weapons for which they are well adapted, as we have seen some of them even resist the force of a pistol ball at a few yards distance.' – June 16.

[2] Briggs Inlet. The *Chatham* had lost her small boat before she arrived at Nootka, and Puget 'was under the necessity of procuring a Canoe from the Natives, My Friend Chipannanulth furnished me with one, in exchange for two Sheets of Copper & of equal Burthen to our own Launch.' – Puget, April 26. On June 15 Menzies and others 'took the Chatham Canoe & went to explore the Bay running off to the Northward...& in the bottom of which to our great surprise we found an opening going off in such a manner that it did not appear till we were close upon it, but it was of sufficient extent to lead us to suspect that it might penetrate some way into the country in a northerly direction; This

explore, who found it terminate about three leagues from the entrance of the bay, in latitude 52° 29′, longitude 232° 2′.

This day in the afternoon, and for a few minutes about one o'clock the day before, the sun made its appearance, and enabled me to procure some observations for the longitude by the chronometers, but not for the latitude; I had however, whilst on the survey in the boats not more than two leagues to the westward of this station, an excellent observation for this purpose; and from hence I judged, that by placing our anchorage in latitude 52° 20½′, longitude 231° 58½′, it will be found nearly correct.[1]

In the evening the Chatham's cutter, and the Discovery's small cutter returned, after having had a very disagreeable, fatiguing, and laborious excursion; rendered very distressing by the melancholy loss of John Carter, one of our seamen, who had unfortunately been poisoned by eating muscles. Two or three others of the party narrowly excaped the same fate.

The first day after their departure from the vessels, they met with some of the natives who had some halibut recently caught, and although very high prices were offered, the Indians could not be induced to part with any of these fish; this was singular, and indicated a very scanty supply of this species of food. As they passed the village on the rock,[2] the inhabitants appeared to regard them with great attention and friendship. Their chief *Whacosh* being down on the rocks, some presents were sent to him, and he seemed to receive them with great pleasure. When the party left this station, they found the opening, though not more than a quarter of a mile wide in some places, to be a clear and navigable channel, lying in a direction N. 18 W. for about eight miles, where it united with a more extensive one about half a league wide,[3] which took a direction N. 15 E. and S. 15 W. This[4] appeared the most extensive, but their object was the pursuit of the other. On its eastern side were found two large bays, or rather basons. In the southernmost of these are some rocky islets. The next morning brought no alteration in the weather, which continued extremely bad and rainy; yet they proceeded again, and were joined by half a dozen of the natives in two small canoes, of whom they purchased a small fish, being all they had to dispose of. The wind blew very strong in squalls from the south-east, attended with constant rain. At five in the afternoon they reached the head of the arm, where it terminated in latitude 52° 36½′, longitude 232°.[5] The evening being fair, some progress was made

we reported to Capt. Vancouver on our return on board.' – Menzies, June 15. Briggs Inlet has not yet been surveyed in detail.

[1] The position of the island near which the ships were anchored is lat. 52° 19′ 20″ N, long. 128° 02′ 30″ W (231° 57′ 30″ E).

[2] Why boats setting out to explore Bullock Channel should pass the village on the rock in Johnson Channel is not clear. It seems probable that Vancouver misread a source when preparing his narrative. [3] Spiller Channel, formerly Ellerslie Channel.

[4] Meaning the part of the channel to the SW.

[5] At the head of Spiller Inlet, a continuation of Spiller Channel. The channel has not been surveyed, and it is not described in the official sailing directions.

in their way back by the same route they had advanced; and having stopped
for the night, the above channel was pursued in its southern direction in the
morning of the 12th. This continued nearly straight, making the land that
forms the west side of this opening an island.[1] On its western shore they found
a considerable village, from whence several of the natives visited them in their
canoes. These were mostly small, containing only four or five persons in each;
excepting one, in which there were thirty-two men. They conducted
themselves in a very proper manner, and in a friendly way invited our party
to their habitations; a civility that it was thought most proper to decline.
Having passed to the northward of some detached rocks, and rocky islets, they
reached the south-west point of the channel, situated in latitude 52° 15′,
longitude 231° 45′.[2] This communicated with another channel about two
miles wide, that took an east and west direction; the former towards the station
of the ships, the latter towards the ocean, being the same that had been
discovered on my examination.[3] From thence they pursued the continental
coast about a league, lying in a direction from this point N. 72 W.; its shores
are low and rocky, with several detached islets and rocks lying near them.
From this situation they had an unlimited view of the ocean, between south
and S.W. by W. The wind blowing strong from this quarter, produced a very
heavy surf on the shores, which prevented their making any further progress
to the westward; and being then a-breast of a small opening extending to the
northward, interspersed with rocks and breakers,[4] Mr. Johnstone entered it
contrary to his inclinations, as it was by no means eligible for the navigation
of shipping, but the wind and sea totally preventing their making any progress
further westward, he was compelled to take shelter there from the inclemency
of the weather; and during the night it blew a strong gale of wind, attended
by torrents of rain. The return of day (the 13th) presented no alternative, but
that of remaining inactive, or of pursuing the small branch leading to the
northward. This soon communicated with a more extensive channel.[5] The
length of the narrow passage is about half a league, the width fifty yards, and
the shoalest water five fathoms. The larger channel had communication with
the sea by falling into an opening about a league in a south-west direction,
and thence continued nearly north about three miles. In this line they pursued
the examination of the continent, through another very narrow channel that
suddenly widened to three quarters of a mile, and a little further increased
in width to two miles, extending, though somewhat irregularly, N. 15 E.[6]

[1] Vancouver means the *east* side, which is Yeo Island. The west side is the Don Peninsula,
part of the mainland, as Johnstone knew.
[2] Presumably the point near the Bullen Rock. Its position would be about lat. 52° 15′
30″ N, long. 128° 17′ 30″ W (231° 42′ 39″ E).
[3] Seaforth Channel, into which Return Channel runs.
[4] Reid Passage, between Cecilia (formerly Mary) Island and the mainland.
[5] The entrance to Mathieson Channel, to the W of Cecilia Island.
[6] The boats had gone through Lady Trutch Passage, between Lake Island and the
mainland, and were now back in Mathieson Channel.

about twenty-eight miles, to an arm leading to the eastward, whose northern point of entrance is in latitude 52° 46½′, longitude 231° 51′.[1] This arm was not reached before noon on the 14th, when it was found to extend from the above point about four miles and a half, in nearly an east direction; about two miles from whence, further to the north-east, it terminated. In general it was about half a mile wide. On the northern shore of this arm, some Indians visited them without the least hesitation, attended them up the arm, and gave our party to understand that it was closed; which afterwards proved so.[2] In returning they passed near the village of these good people, who having remained with them most of the afternoon, took their leave, after conducting themselves in a very orderly and friendly manner. Mr. Johnstone describes their habitation as consisting of only one large dwelling made with broad planks; the roof covered with the same materials, and nearly flat. It was built on the top of a precipice against the side of the steep rocky cliff, by which means the access to it was rendered difficult; the party did not land, but they estimated the number of its inhabitants to be about seventy or eighty. They were not visited by any of the women; but those who were seen in passing wore the hideous lip ornaments above described. Towards the evening the weather cleared up, and the night was tolerably fair.

In the morning of the 15th, the examination of the continental shore was continued, and from the above north point of this arm the channel was found to extend in a direction N. 24 W. about five miles, where the larboard or western shore formed a sharp point,[3] from whence another branch took a direction S. 55 W.,[4] and united with that which they had navigated for about four miles and a half north; then took a direction N. 70 E., four miles further, where it terminated in latitude 52° 56½′, longitude 231° 54′, forming some little bays on the southern side.[5] In one of these they stopped to breakfast, where finding some muscles, a few of the people ate of them roasted; as had been their usual practice when any of these fish were met with; about nine o'clock they proceeded in very rainy unpleasant weather down the south-westerly channel, and about one landed for the purpose of dining. Mr. Johnstone was now informed by Mr. Barrie, that soon after they had quitted the cove, where they had breakfasted, several of the crew who had eaten of the muscles were seized with a numbness about their faces and extremities; their whole bodies were very shortly affected in the same manner, attended with sickness and giddiness. Mr. Barrie had, when in England, experienced a similar disaster, from the same cause, and was himself indisposed on the present occasion.

[1] Kynock Inlet. The position given is very near the correct reading.
[2] Menzies adds an interesting detail, which he must have learned from Johnstone: 'These Indians by joining the tips of the fingers of both hands together, endeavourd to make them comprehend that the Arm soon closed, which they found to be the case.' – June 17.
[3] Mathieson Point.
[4] Sheep Passage.
[5] Beyond Mathieson Narrows, which end at Mathieson Point, the continuation of Mathieson Channel becomes Mussel Inlet.

Recollecting that he had received great relief by violent perspiration, he took an oar, and earnestly advised those who were unwell, viz. John Carter, John McAlpin, and John Thomas, to use their utmost exertions in pulling, in order to throw themselves into a profuse perspiration; this Mr. Barrie effected in himself, and found considerable relief; but the instant the boat landed, and their exertions at the oar ceased, the three seamen were obliged to be carried on shore. One man only in the Chatham's boat was indisposed in a similar way. Mr. Johnstone entertained no doubt of the cause from which this evil had arisen, and having no medical assistance within his reach, ordered warm water to be immediately got ready, in the hope, that by copiously drinking, the offending matter might have been removed. Carter attracted nearly the whole of their attention, in devising every means to afford him relief, by rubbing his temples and body, and applying warm cloths to his stomach; but all their efforts at length proved ineffectual, and being unable to swallow the warm water, the poor fellow expired about half an hour after he was landed. His death was so tranquil, that it was some little time before they could be perfectly certain of his dissolution. There was no doubt that this was occasioned by a poison contained in the muscles he had eaten about eight o'clock in the morning; at nine he first found himself unwell, and died at half past one; he pulled his oar until the boat landed, but when he arose to go on shore he fell down, and never more got up, but by the assistance of his companions. From his first being taken his pulse was regular, though it gradually grew fainter and weaker until he expired, when his lips turned black, and his hands, face, and neck were much swelled. Such was the foolish obstinacy of the others who were affected, that it was not until this poor unfortunate fellow resigned his life, that they could be prevailed upon to drink the hot water; his fate however induced them to follow the advice of their officers, and the desired effect being produced, they all obtained great relief; and though they were not immediately restored to their former state of health, yet, in all probability, it preserved their lives. From Mr. Barrie's account it appeared, that the evil had arisen, not from the number of muscles eaten, but from the deleterious quality of some particular ones; and these he conceived were those gathered on the sand, and not those taken from the rocks. Mr. Barrie had eaten as many as any of the party, and was the least affected by them.

This very unexpected and unfortunate circumstance detained the boats about three hours; when, having taken the corpse on board, and refreshed the three men, who still remained incapable of assisting themselves, with some warm tea, and having covered them up warm in the boat, they continued their route, in very rainy, unpleasant weather, down the south-west channel,[1] until they stopped in a bay for the night, where they buried the dead body. To this bay I gave the name of CARTER'S BAY, after this poor unfortunate fellow; it is situated in latitude 52° 48′, longitude 231° 42′:[2] and to distinguish

---

[1] Sheep Passage.
[2] Now Carter Bay, in lat. 52° 50′ N, long. 128° 24′ W (231° 36′ E).

the fatal spot where the muscles were eaten, I have called it POISON COVE,[1] and the branch leading to it MUSCLE CHANNEL.[2]

In the morning of the 16th, having advanced a small distance from Carter's bay, they found the arm divide into two branches; one taking a southerly direction,[3] about two miles wide, had the appearance of communicating with the ocean, the other took a north-westerly direction[4] along the shores of the continent; and, from the appearance of the neighbouring mountains, it seemed likely to prove extensive. But, from the reduced state of the party, Mr. Johnstone, very judiciously, did not think it adviseable to undertake its examination, but pursued that leading to the southward; convinced that this, if found to communicate with the channel they had been in leading to the sea, would be by far the most eligible route for the vessels or boats to pursue, in carrying into execution the further survey of the continental shore.

This branch soon took a south direction, the shores on both sides were much broken, and each had the appearance of composing an archipelago of islands. The wind being against them their progress was slow; however before dark they gained a very satisfactory view of the ocean, being now further advanced to the westward, in the same channel from whence it had been before observed.[5] The next morning they passed the narrow channel they had been obliged to enter on the 12th, and arrived on board, as before stated. The very unfavorable weather, during their absence, had not afforded them one fair day, or an opportunity of ascertaining the latitude, either by meridional or double altitude.

McAlpin and Thomas, by this time, as well as the man belonging to the Chatham, were a little recovered; they were excessively weak, and still complained of numbness and dizziness, as also of a violent pain in their bowels. They were instantly taken under the surgeon's care, and treated with every attention and assistance which the nature of their situation required.[6]

[1] The cove extends SE from the head of Mussel Inlet.

[2] Muscle Canal in the first edition; now Mussel Inlet. Vancouver used the Old English spelling throughout.

[3] Finlayson Channel.

[4] Hiekish Narrows, leading to Princess Royal Channel.

[5] Seaforth Channel is meant. Johnstone was in Milbanke Sound, which lies in part between the S end of Finlayson Channel and the W end of Seaforth Channel, and thus connects the two.

[6] Menzies notes that the men 'both recovered in the course of 5 or 6 days & were discharged to their duty.' The order to stop eating mussels was most unwelcome, as 'they were at this time our greatest resource of refreshment, for we scarcely procurd a mess of Fish from the Natives all the time we staid here'. – June 17. Mussels in the area are still suspect; the 1974 edition of the official *Sailing Directions* refers to a caution 'with respect to eating shellfish when in Sheep Passage, Mussel Inlet and adjacent waters.'

CHAPTER III.

The Vessels proceed—Pass through Milbank's Sound, and along the continental Shore—Arrive in a small Cove—Two boat Parties dispatched on the Survey— One Returns—Account of their Discoveries—The Vessels again proceed— Tedious Navigation—The other boat Party returns—Their Report.

No time was to be lost in proceeding to the station where Mr. Johnstone had quitted the examination of the continental shore. For this purpose, about nine in the morning of Tuesday the 18th, it being calm, all our boats were employed in towing us round the west point of this opening, which, though not more than a mile from our anchorage, was not effected until one o'clock in the afternoon. By eleven at night we had advanced only two leagues further to the south-west, where we anchored. Our situation was nearly a mile to the north-east of the south point of the island, forming the west side of the opening we had quitted,[1] and from which Mr. Swaine had seen the ocean. This channel is a more northerly one than that by which Mr. Johnstone had returned.[2]

On the next morning. Wednesday the 19th, either a brig or a schooner was seen standing towards the sea, in a passage to the southward of our then station, but was soon out of sight, owing to the many intervening islands between us and the ocean. In our way thither were some islands and rocks; Mr. Johnstone had passed to the south of these, but as our nearest way was to the north of them, I went with the boats to take a short survey of the channel before us, and obtained some necessary angles for fixing its several parts, leaving directions for the vessels to follow in my absence. Although I saw many rocks and breakers in this channel, they were all sufficiently conspicuous to be avoided in fair weather, so that I had no hesitation in proceeding with the vessels, although the channel was extremely intricate; and having got a good observation for the latitude at noon, I returned on board. On my arrival I found, that in near four hours the Discovery had gained only half a mile, and was beginning to lose even that advantage. This compelled us to anchor between the above south point of the island, and a small round island, at a

---

[1] The 'south point of the island' was the S point of Yeo Island; Vancouver probably had the point adjacent to Holt Rock in mind.

[2] Johnstone evidently returned by a route S of Dearth Island; Vancouver intended to pass N of it.

little distance from the east point of which lie an islet and a sunken rock.[1]
The depth of water was 35 fathoms, soft bottom. The south point of the island,
situated in latitude 52° 17½′, longitude 231° 53′,[2] bore by compass N.W. a
fourth of a mile distant; the passage leading out to sea,[3] S. 53 W., and the
small round island, S.S.E., at the distance of a cable and an half. The weather
was clear and pleasant, but as we had a fresh breeze from S.W., we remained
at anchor until eleven at night; when the wind ceasing, and the ebb tide making
in our favor, with the assistance of our boats we made some progress towards
the north-west extreme of a cluster of islands, lying off the north-west point
of a spacious sound, extending to the S.E.E.[4] amongst the islands that lie before
the continent. This extremity is not more than two miles S. 68 W. from our
last anchorage;[5] yet it was not until after day-light on the morning of
Thursday the 20th, that we passed between it and a cluster of low barren rocks,
that lie from it S. 74 W. at the distance of a mile.

About half a league within these rocks, in a westerly direction, nearly
reaching to the continental shore, are two rocky islets covered with wood;[6]
about them are some sunken rocks, and another cluster of low barren rocks,
between the rocky islets and the rocks first mentioned; in whose neighbourhood
are several sunken rocks, so that the safest passage is that we had passed
through, in which there are some detached rocks near the shores of the cluster
of small islands; these however extend but a little distance; and in all other
respects, so far as appeared to us, the passage was tolerably free from danger.
Having got through this passage, we were favored with a light north-easterly
breeze, with which we stood to the westward in a channel about two miles
wide, that led into the arm by which Mr. Johnstone had returned from Carter's
bay.[7] The southern side of this channel being entirely covered with trees,
presented, from the lowness of the shores, a prospect very grateful to the eye,
and the several bays formed by the projecting parts of the sandy beaches that
chiefly compose the shore, indicated a pleasant communication with the land;
but the coast on the opposite side was formed by a rude, confused mass of
low rugged cliffs, and bounded by innumerable rocky islets and rocks, as well
beneath as above the surface of the water.

Having passed between this rugged north-eastern shore and some rocks that
lie about half a league to the westward of it, we were so far advanced as to

[1] Law Island.
[2] The position of the point nearest to Holt Rock is approximately lat. 52° 16′ 30″ N,
long. 128° 09′ 30″ W (231° 50′ 30″ E).
[3] Seaforth Channel.
[4] Dearth Island and the other islands adjacent to it. The 'spacious sound' was Seaforth
Channel, which extends to the SE.
[5] Three miles would be nearer the correct distance.
[6] Foote Island and Locke Island.
[7] Seaforth Channel leads to Milbanke Sound, in which Vancouver would sail N to the
entrance of Finlayson Channel, down which Johnstone had come on his return from Carter
Bay.

gain a distant view of this inlet in most directions, particularly in that towards
the ocean; and on comparing it with some printed sketches on board, no doubt
remained of its being the same that had been discovered by Mr. Duncan, and
named Milbank's sound.[1] The delineation of the shores by Mr. Duncan, bore
a strong resemblance to those before us, although we materially disagreed with
him in the latitude; there could, however, be no doubt as to the identity of
the place,[2] and I have therefore continued the name given to it by Mr. Duncan.

The north-east wind was succeeded by a calm; during this interval, the swell
and tide sat us towards the eastern shore near some of its sunken rocks, where
the soundings were very irregular, from sixty to thirty-five fathoms, rocky
bottom. We were, however, soon relieved from this unpleasant situation, by
a fine breeze springing up from the south-west; when our course was directed
up the arm leading from Milbank's sound to Carter's bay.[3] The wind blowing
a gentle gale, attended with serene and cheerful weather, gave the country
as we passed a very pleasant appearance. The land constituting the shores of
the external or sea-coast was low, or rather moderately elevated, rising in a
pleasing diversity of hills intirely covered with wood; and had we not been
well acquainted with the rocky foundation from which such forests are
produced, we might have been led to suppose that the soil before us was in
the highest degree luxuriant.

Some observations were procured for ascertaining our situation. These, with
those made the preceding day, were very satisfactory, and corrected Mr.
Johnstone's survey during his late expedition, when he was prevented making
any celestial observations by the inclemency of the weather. At noon the
observed latitude was 52° 24', longitude 231° 37'.[4] The north-west point of
entrance into Milbank's sound now bore by compass S. 16 W. and the
south-east point, named after the third lieutenant of the Discovery, CAPE
SWAINE,[5] S. 13 E.; in this direction was a small island[6] about two miles and
a half from us; and from that island S. 14 W. at the distance of about half
a league, lies a very dangerous sunken rock.[7] We passed to the westward of

---

[1] Vancouver undoubtedly had a copy of the engraving of Charles Duncan's chart of
'Milbank's Sound' published by Dalrymple on 24 December 1789. Duncan visited the
sound in July 1788.

[2] Vancouver evidently did not notice that the lat. given by Dixon (52° 14' N) was the
'Lat. of the Cove' in which he had anchored, not that of Milbanke Sound. His chart shows
that the cove was some distance to the SE, in an inlet running southward from Seaforth
Channel. In spite of its shallowness, Cavin Cove, near the N end of Campbell Island, in
lat. 52° 11' N, seems to be the most likely identification.

[3] Finlayson Channel.

[4] The ships were nearing the entrance to Finlayson Channel. The long. given was at
least 5 miles too far to the E, as it would have placed the ships in the middle of Dowager
Island.

[5] The name has been retained.

[6] Dallas Island.

[7] Now Vancouver Rock. The name was adopted in 1866 by Capt. Daniel Pender of
the chartered survey ship Beaver because the rock is mentioned in Vancouver's Voyage.

these, but the Chatham went between them and the eastern shore, which still continued broken and rocky, forming a passage[1] with the above sunken rock and breakers about half a mile wide, where the soundings were found to be very irregular. On the western shore an opening was seen extending N. 88 W. having the appearance of leading to sea,[2] with two very large low flat rocks lying before it; the nearest shore was on that side, and bore W.N.W. at the distance of a mile.

Cape Swaine was found by our observations to be in latitude 52° 13′, longitude 231° 40′;[3] and the north-west point of entrance into Milbank's sound, which I called POINT DAY, off which lie several barren rocky islets, in latitude 52° 14½′, longitude 231° 27′;[4] being in point of latitude 15′ to the south of the situation assigned to it by Mr. Duncan, and who considers its longitude to be 50′ to the westward of our calculations. As the day advanced the south-westwardly breeze freshened with pleasant weather. The Chatham was directed to lead, and by four in the afternoon, having reached the extent of Mr. Johnstone's researches, we directed our route up a channel about half a mile wide, leading to the north-westward, whose entrance from Milbank's sound is situated in latitude 52° 47′,[5] and longitude 231° 37′. As we advanced in a direction from its entrance N. 55 W. the channel narrowed to about a fourth of a mile, and having proceeded about four miles, the Chatham suddenly found only six fathoms water, on a shoal stretching from the starboard or continental shore into mid-channel; this we passed on the opposite side in 18 and 20 fathoms water. Beyond this, which is the narrowest part of the channel, formed by a high round projecting part of the south-west shore, appearing like an island; the arm widened to near half a league, and an extensive opening, taking a southerly direction, indicated a communication with the ocean.[6]

The wind continuing favorable, and the weather pleasant, we made a tolerably good progress along the continental shore[7] until about nine in the evening, when we anchored in 58 fathoms water, within about half a cable's length of the south point of an opening leading to the eastward,[8] where the tides were very strong and irregular. The region we had been navigating since noon, had gradually increased in its elevation, and we were again encompassed

[1] Merilia Passage.

[2] Higgins Passage, formerly Schooner Passage.

[3] Its position is lat. 52° 14′ N, long. 128° 26′ W (231° 34′ E).

[4] Day Point, in lat. 52° 16′ N, long. 128° 40′ W (231° 20′ E).

[5] Hiekish Narrows, leading to Princess Royal Channel. Vancouver evidently considered that the narrows began at or near Adze Point, whereas Finlayson Head, farther N in lat. 52° 49′, is now taken as marking the entrance.

[6] Tolmie Channel. Beyond this point Vancouver was sailing up Graham Reach, the S part of Princess Royal Channel.

[7] Neither Vancouver's text nor his chart takes any notice of Green Inlet, which branches off to the E about two miles N of the junction with Tolmie Channel.

[8] Khutze Inlet.

by high, steep, rocky, snow-capped mountains, forming various chasms, and producing a forest of pine trees nearly to their very summits.

As I intended to prosecute our examination thus along the starboard shore, until I should find sufficient employment for two parties to take different directions in the boats, we proceeded the next morning, Friday the 21st, but it being calm, with the utmost efforts of our boats a-head we gained only half a league by noon. Soon after this time, the wind, though variable, assisted us, and we advanced about two leagues. Another opening was passed on the starboard shore;[1] and about seven in the evening we arrived in a situation N. 32 W. from our last anchorage, where the main branch of the inlet appeared to take two directions, one to the northwest, the other to the westward, with an island lying at their junction;[2] the two branches being divided by a high ridge of steep mountains. Off the extremity of the starboard shore, in the above line of direction, was a small islet,[3] and south of it a little sandy bay, where we anchored, and steadied the ship with a hawser to the shore.

The following morning, Saturday the 22d, Mr. Whidbey, with the large cutter, attended by Mr. Humphrys in the launch, provided with supplies for a week, were dispatched to the openings we had left unexplored behind. And Mr. Johnstone, in the Discovery's small cutter, attended by Mr. Barrie in the Chatham's launch, were sent to examine the branch leading to the westward and larboard shore, so long as their week's supplies would hold out, or until the branch should be found to communicate with the sea,[4] or bring the party back to the ship's station; in which case a report was to be made on board, prior to undertaking the survey of the north-west branch, as I intended that service for Mr. Whidbey's execution after he should have examined the openings to the southward, in the event of his returning before Mr. Johnstone.

The poison which our people had received by eating the muscles, appeared by no means of so malignant a nature as to have remained unsubdued, could proper remedies have been timely applied. The means used for their recovery on their arrival on board was first an emetic; this operated very well; at bed time anodynes procured them good rest; these were followed the next day by cathartics, which had a powerful effect, gave great relief, and produced considerable abatement in the unpleasant symptoms; and with the assistance of diaphoretic medicines, and a strict attention to the complaints in their bowels, so entirely removed the malady, that one of the men was able this day to take his station in the boat, but the others not being quite so much recovered, were excused from duty some days longer.

[1] Aaltanhash Inlet.
[2] Klekane Inlet to the NW and the main channel to the W. Work Island lies at the junction of the two.
[3] Klekane Island.
[4] 'As we were now so far inland with the Vessels it was likewise of some consequence to us to determine whether we should be able to get to the Sea further to the Northward or be obliged to return back again the way we came.' – Menzies, 21 June.

The melancholy event that attended the discovery of the poisonous quality in the muscles, though it may probably be the means of preserving many lives in future, was to us, independently of the loss we had sustained, attended with circumstances additionally mortifying. Wherever we had found these fish, they were sure to afford us a pleasant and palatable fresh meal. Prudence however now directed that we should abstain from them; which, to persons in our situation, especially when detached from the ships, and frequently on a very scanty allowance, was the privation of no small comfort.

The weather enabled me to obtain some good observations, and in the evening Mr. Whidbey returned, having found the southern opening to extend N. 85 E. about five miles,[1] and the other N. 72 E. about three miles,[2] where each terminated as usual. This ascertained and traced the continental shore completely up to this station. At four o'clock next morning, Sunday 23d, Mr. Whidbey with his party was again dispatched to the north-west branch.[3] This he had examined by eleven in the forenoon. He reported, that it extended N. 28 W. for five miles, and that it there terminated. He had also traced the continental shore into the branch of the inlet, under the examination of Mr. Johnstone; but as the tenor of Mr. Johnstone's orders might induce him to pass some openings on the starboard shore, the provisions of Mr. Whidbey's party were recruited to a supply for a week, and he was again dispatched to continue his researches along the continental shore; on which occasion Mr. Menzies, in pursuit of botanical information, accompanied Mr. Whidbey.[4]

This forenoon some additional observations were obtained for the longitude; in the evening, the sky was again overcast, and the wind that had blown fresh from the S.E. during the day, now increased to a strong gale, attended with small rain.

The wind abated next morning, Monday the 24th, but the rain that had been very heavy during the night, still continued. The wind from the S.E. again freshened in the evening, and blew hard in squalls, with torrents of rain. During the night, the tide rose three feet perpendicularly higher than it had been observed usually to flow, and floated away some of our water casks, that had been left to all appearance in perfect security. Our seine hooks and lines having been repeatedly tried without successs, rendered our situation here very

[1] Khutze Inlet.
[2] Aaltanhash Inlet.   [3] Klekane Inlet.
[4] While Johnstone and Whidbey were away exploring, Puget seized the opportunity to make an alteration in the *Chatham*: 'I had intended to board up the Vessel, this Season, from the Gunwale to the Rough tree Rail, as at Sea the People were continually wet from Sprays on the Passage from the Sandwich Islands to the Coast. I therefore here began to put the Plan into Execution, merely as an Experiment for though no doubt it would greatly add to our Comforts yet it was not certain that the Vessel by the Addition of so much top Weight would hold so good a Wind, however if we on trial found it any impediment to her Sailing, it would easily be removed, without the least Expence to Government. – June 24. 'Rough-tree' is defined in the OED as 'A mast, yard, or boom, serving as a rail or fence above the ship's side, from the quarter-deck to the forecastle.' Puget seems to have made no comment on the ship's behaviour after the alteration.

unprofitable, neither the sea nor the shores afforded us the smallest refreshment, nor the least relaxation; and the weather being extremely unpleasant, without any prospect of a change, necessarily increased the labour, and retarded the progress of our boats in the examination of this inhospitable region; whose solitary and desolate appearance, though daily more familiarized to our view, did not become less irksome to our feelings.[1]

The weather continued to be variable and unsettled until the morning of Thursday the 27th, when, it becoming fair and pleasant, some observations were procured for ascertaining the latitude, longitude, and variation.

About noon on the following day, Mr. Johnstone returned, and communicated the following particulars of his excursion.

The western branch he found to extend N. 55 W. about 12 miles, where it united with two extensive arms, one leading nearly north, the other about west.[2] The western one continued near two leagues, where it united with two other branches more extensive than the former; one taking a southerly, the other a north-westerly direction.[3] The first of these was pursued, and having by noon of the 23rd advanced about two leagues, the latitude was observed on the larboard side to be 53° 11′, longitude 231° 3′; the variation of the compass 21° 40′, east; and high water 20′ after the moon passed the meridian. From hence, in a south direction, this southern branch reached about two leagues further, where it took a sharp turn to the W.S.W. about four miles, and there communicated with a still more extensive opening, stretching to the S.W. and N.W.[4] The land on the western side appeared to form a large island, on which rose a conspicuous ridge of mountains, with a remarkable peak nearly in their centre, considerably above the rest;[5] their summits were naked rocks, without the least appearance of verdure; the land to the southward was much lower, seemed greatly broken, and probably afforded several passages to sea. The wind blew strong from the south-east, attended with much rain. In the morning of the 24th, the wind abated, but the rain continued. The opening leading to the westward[6] was pursued, until the party was overtaken by a strong gale from the S.E. attended with very heavy rain and thick misty weather. This obliged them to seek shelter round a low point of land on the western shore, forming the north point of the apparent

---

[1] 'This Place appears to be the most Miserable Station we have been obliged to Stop at during the Summers Season.' – Puget, June 22. Bell notes that on the 25th a canoe with only two Indians in it approached the *Chatham*: 'they brought nothing to sell but a Beaver, and a Young Seal which had both been fresh kill'd. These were purchased of them and, (as we were by no means well stocked with Fresh Provisions,) Cooked, – the Seal was tolerably good, but the Beaver was indeed execrable.' On the 29th he wrote: 'We now quitted this place which from its inhospitable qualities obtained the name of Starve-Gut Cove'.

[2] Ursula Channel to the N; McKay Reach to the W.

[3] Whale Channel to the S; Wright Sound to the NW.

[4] Campania Sound to the SW and Squally Channel to the NW.

[5] Campania Island; the peak would be Mount Pender, 2415 ft.

[6] Otter Channel, at the N end of Campania Island.

large island, in a small cove;[1] which, though screening them from the violence
of the wind and sea, admitted of very indifferent communication with the
shore, being chiefly composed of steep rocky precipices. The wet and
comfortless situation of the party, however, made it indispensibly necessary
that some place should be sought where the advantage of a fire might be had;
and having ascended the top of a bare rock, some distance above high water
mark, it was fixed upon for their night's abode, where they remained in the
most uncomfortable manner, until by the unusual flow of the tide, produced
by the increased violence of the storm, they were dislodged from this resting
place, and obliged to retire to such shelter as the less inhospitable woods
afforded. Here their hours passed with the most anxious concern till the return
of day, lest their boats should have been driven out of the cove; happily this
did not prove to be the case; but a continuation of the same inclement weather
detained them until the 26th, when, it becoming rather more moderate, they
had for the first time a tolerably distinct view of their situation. This was in
a spacious channel about two miles in width, stretching in a westerly
direction,[2] which they followed about a league, when it opened to their view
another still more extensive, taking a north-west and south-east course,[3] and
bounded by land near two leagues distant; this Mr. Johnstone concluded to
be Banks's island, so named by some of the traders;[4] and under that impression
a passage to the ocean was deemed certain of being found by that route, for
which reason, after Mr. Johnstone had observed the latitude on the south-west
point of the westerly channel, off which lie an islet and some rocks about a
mile from the shore, to be in 53° 10', and its longitude 230° 41',[5] he
commenced his return to the ship.

Mr. Johnstone had little doubt that the land, forming the west side of the
channel that led him to the southward as he proceeded to his last station, and
the east side of that which led him to the north-westward, was an island; and
if his conjectures were right, a more direct passage to the vessels would
necessarily be found, by which they might proceed to sea.[6] These ideas proved
in the sequel to be correct, and the island was found to be five leagues long
in a north and south direction, and five miles in breadth; of a moderate though
uneven height, composed chiefly of rock materials, covered with pine trees
of inferior growth, and having to the north and north-west of it much broken
and divided land. About noon on the 26th the weather again became rainy
and boisterous; this continued until noon the next day, when they arrived
at the north point of the above island, and observed its latitude to be 53° 18',

---

[1] The cove must have been near Fanny Point, the NE point of Campania Island.
[2] Otter Channel.
[3] Nepean Sound.
[4] Banks Island. Both the island and Nepean Sound were named by Duncan in 1788.
[5] The lat. is near the mark but the long. would be about 129° 33' W (230° 27' E).
[6] Johnstone had sailed around Gil Island, which lies between Whale Channel and
Squally Channel. He hoped the ships could follow a much shorter route, across the N end
of the island.

longitude 230° 53½'.[1] From hence, with fair pleasant weather, they made the best of their way towards the ships, where they arrived as before stated. The country that had fallen under their observation, differed little from the general character of the surrounding region. That on the sea coast was somewhat less mountainous, chiefly covered with wood, and less encumbered with snow than the barren rugged summits of the mountains of the interior country.

Those parts that had lately occupied Mr. Johnstone's attention, appeared to be the same that had been visited by Mr. Duncan, and called Nepean's sound; Sen[r] Caamano had also resorted thither the preceding year, and had named the island which Mr. Johnstone circumnavigated, Isle de Gil.[2] These names I accordingly adopted.

As this report rendered our stay here no longer necessary, I determined to proceed immediately to the western arm,[3] where, on the continental shore, Mr. Johnstone had observed a bay that appeared likely to afford good anchorage, and which was so situated that Mr. Whidbey on his return must necessarily perceive the ships; in the event, however, of his passing that station in the night, or in thick weather, I left a letter, sealed up, in a bottle, in a situation that had been agreed upon between us before his departure, containing such information and directions as should be necessary for his government.

By the time our brewing utensils and other matters were brought from the shore, the wind blew a strong gale from the S.E. attended with heavy squalls and thick rainy weather. This continued until the morning of Saturday the 29th; when, about ten in the forenoon, with the assistance of the tide we towed out of the cove, and, a light breeze springing up from the eastward, we sailed up the western arm. Whilst we remained at anchor, only two small canoes, with three persons in each, had visited us; one on the preceding Sunday, bringing nothing to dispose of, the other just before our departure, which brought three sea-otter skins and a few salmon, that were exchanged principally with iron.

In this dreary and uninteresting place nothing further attracted our attention. The astronomical and nautical observations made there were very satisfactory, and by the former the cove was found to be situated in latitude 53° 10', longitude 231° 26'.[4] The variation of the compass, by sixteen sets of azimuths taken on shore, shewing from 19° to 24°, gave a mean result of 21° 37' eastwardly; and, independently of the influence that the stormy weather seemed to have upon the tide, at the springs, the day tide rose fifteen feet three inches, the night tide about six inches higher, and was high water 10[h] 15' after the moon passed the meridian.

[1] Presumably Turtle Point is meant. It position is lat. 53° 19' 30" N, long. 129° 16' 30" W (230° 43' 30" E).
[2] Actually named 'Gil y Lemos' by Caamaño, after the Viceroy of Peru.
[3] Fraser Reach of Princess Royal Channel.
[4] The lat. is correct; the correct long. is 128° 37' W (231° 23' E).

By seven in the evening we had advanced from the anchorage we had quitted only five miles up the western arm; it was about a mile in width, and the steepness of its rocky sides afforded little prospect of obtaining any anchorage on which we could depend for the night. We had repeatedly traversed from shore to shore without finding bottom with 165 and 185 fathoms of line, though within half the ship's length of the rocks. The tide now making against us, we were constrained to rest our sides against the rocks, and by hawsers fastened to the trees to prevent our being driven back. Our present resting place was perfectly safe, but this is not the case against every part of these rocky precipices, as they are frequently found to jet out a few yards, at or a little beneath low water mark; and if a vessel should ground on any of those projecting parts about high water, she would, on the falling tide, if heeling from the shore, be in a very dangerous situation.

The weather was foggy for some hours the next morning, Sunday the 30th, and was afterwards succeeded by a calm; this, in addition to an unfavourable tide, detained us against the rocks until about noon, when a breeze from the westward enabled us to make sail, though with little effect. In the afternoon the breeze again died away; but with the assistance of our boats, and an eddy tide within about fifty yards of the rocks, we advanced by slow degrees to the westward, and found soundings from forty-five to sixty fathoms, hard rocky bottom, about half a cable's length from the shore; but at a greater distance no ground could be gained. In this tedious navigation, sometimes brushing our sides against the rocks, at others just keeping clear of the trees that overhung them, we had advanced at midnight about four miles; and having at that time, bottom at the depth of forty-five fathoms, about forty yards from the shore, we let go the anchor; but such was the projecting declivity of the rocks on which the anchor at first rested, that it almost instantly slipped off into sixty fathoms. By this time however a hawser was made fast to the trees, and being hauled tight, it prevented the anchor slipping lower down, and just answered the purpose of keeping us from the projecting rocks of the shore.[1]

About eight in the morning of Monday the 1st of July, with the tide then seemingly in our favor, and a moderate westerly breeze, we made some progress, and by two in the afternoon we arrived at the place where I purposed to wait Mr. Whidbey's return. It was a commodious cove;[2] the south point of it was formed by a rocky clump covered with trees, which became an island

[1] A further note on the difficulties of navigation: 'The Sets of the Tide here were remarkable, which on [one] Side of the Inlet was carrying the Discovery rapidly to the SE & our Vessel [the *Chatham*] on the other Side to the NW & in Ten Minutes both Vessels would be nearly on board each other in Mid Channel, nor could we get Soundings on either Shore with fifty fathoms of Line, though sometimes these streams would notwithstanding all our Efforts carry us so Close to the Rocks, that the Jib Boom touched the Branches of the Trees & sometimes in those Situations we should be flying past the Shore at the Rate of 3 knots to the NW & then as rapidly back to the SE.' – Puget, 30 June.

[2] Angler Cove.

at high water. There a note was found from Mr. Whidbey, stating that he had quitted this station at seven in the evening on the same day he had left the ship; a distance that had taken us now three days to gain. We anchored in forty-six fathoms, sandy bottom, and moored with a hawser to the rocky clump, which was our nearest shore, at the distance of a cable and an half. This little bay is formed by a stony beach, through which a considerable run of water falls into the sea; this flattered us with the hope of taking a few fish, but the seine was worked to no other purpose than that of tearing it to pieces; nor were we more successful with our hooks and lines. The shores however afforded us some raspberries, with black and red berries, and the labradore tea; these were all gathered at some little distance in the woods.

On Tuesday the 2d at noon, I observed the latitude to be 53° 18', longitude 231° 14'.[1] The cutter and launch were then seen approaching the ships, by the channel Mr. Johnstone had pursued towards the ocean; and on their arrival on board, Mr. Whidbey communicated to me the following account of his expedition.

From this station he continued on the eastern shore, which took nearly a north direction.[2] A small inlet[3] was examined extending easterly about half a league, whose north point of entrance lies north from this place, about a league distant; there the party rested for the night in a very uncomfortable situation, owing to the extremely bad weather, and the rugged rocky shore, that scarcely afforded them a sufficient horizontal space to land and remain upon. The next morning (June 24th) as they were preparing to proceed, a smoke was discovered issuing from amongst the stones on the shore, that, at low tide, formed a kind of beach. On examination, a run of hot water was found passing amongst the stones, which at high tide must be at least six feet beneath the surface of the sea. They were not able to discover its source, and having no thermometer, its degree of heat could not be ascertained. Some of the seamen attempted to wash their hands in it, but found the heat inconvenient. It has a saltish taste, and Mr. Whidbey was of opinion, that the rapidity with which it flowed could scarcely permit of its receiving this savour from the sea water. Its colour and taste were thought to resemble much the waters at Cheltenham.

From hence Mr. Whidbey continued his route along the continental shore. This took a north-westerly direction to a point in latitude 53° 32', longitude 231° 5';[4] in their way to this station, about two leagues to the south-east of it, a small branch was examined.[5] It was about a mile in width; its first direction was N. 30 E. for about a league, and then S. 68 E. about two miles further, where it terminated in a round bason, having near its centre a small

---

[1] The correct position is lat. 53° 19' N, long. 128° 53' W (231° 07' E).
[2] Whidbey was exploring Ursula Channel.
[3] Goat Harbour.
[4] Moody Point, in lat. 53° 32' 30" N, long. 128° 59' W (231° 01' E).
[1] Bishop Bay, also referred to as Bishop Cove.

island on the southern shore. Both sides were composed of perpendicular cliffs covered with pine trees. The breadth of the channel they had thus pursued was in general about half a league, until they approached this point, where it decreased to about half that width. The western shore was found to be nearly straight and compact, until the party were abreast of this point; there it formed a deep bay,[1] whose shores appeared to be a little broken at the bottom. From this point the inlet taking an easterly direction widened to about half a league, and the continental shore first took a direction N. 75 E. about four miles, where it left but a narrow neck of land between it and the north side of the above-mentioned small branch. From thence it extended N. 50 E. about four miles further, to a point where the width of the inlet increased to about three miles and an half, and it divided into two branches; the principal one, or continuation of the former branch, stretched about N. by W.; the other S.E by E., about a mile wide.[2] This station they gained about breakfast time on the 25th, after passing a very uncomfortable night in consequence of the tide having flowed into their tents at the bottom, whilst a heavy torrent of rain was falling over their heads.

This point was named by Mr. Whidbey POINT STANIFORTH, and is situated in latitude 53° 34′, longitude 231° 17′.[3] The shores they had passed were in part composed of lofty steep mountains, that rose nearly perpendicularly from the sea, and were covered from the water side to their summits with pines and forest trees. The other parts, equally well wooded, were less elevated, and terminated in sandy beaches with projecting points, forming several small bays and coves; and before they reached that part of the inlet which took an easterly direction, Mr. Whidbey observed more drift wood than he had seen on any other part of the coast. After breakfast the party entered the south-easterly branch,[4] and found its shores composed of mountains that were barren towards their summits, but well wooded near the water side. As they advanced, its width increased to about half a league; and in a direction S. 60 E. three miles and an half from point Staniforth, an island lies nearly in mid-channel,[5] where they stopped to dine. At the entrance into this arm a tide was found in their favor, and not being more than half flood by the shore, Mr. Whidbey was flattered with the prospect of carrying the flood tide some distance; it however shortly turned, with a breeze, down the arm, and they were six hours advancing about four miles. They quitted their dinner station, leaving unexamined a small arm extending from the southern shore,[6] and

[1] Whidbey had followed Ursula Channel, which meets Verney Passage at Moody Point. The 'deep bay' was part of Verney Passage, which Whidbey (who considered it to be the continuation of Ursula Channel) followed eastward to its junction with Gardner Canal.

[2] This was the junction of Verney Passage and Gardner Canal, which unite to form Devastation Channel, leading to the N. The 'branch' to the S was Gardner Canal.

[3] The lat. is correct; the correct long. is 128° 49′ W (231° 11′ E). Why Whidbey chose this name is not known.

[4] Gardner Canal.

[5] Rix Island, formerly Channel Island.   [6] Triumph Bay.

pursued the main branch, taking a direction from the islands S. 55 E. This was traced along the southern shore ten miles, until they arrived at a place that had the appearance of being a small bay;[1] here they stopped for the night, after having advanced through a very desolate country, whose inhospitable shores were formed by such steep barren rocky precipices, as rendered the landing very difficult. A very few trees were thinly dispersed, of a slender dwarf kind, produced upon the naked rock.

The cutter having been very leaky during the afternoon, was instantly cleared and hauled up, when one of her planks under the larboard bow was discovered to have been stove in by some means, of which no one could form any conjecture. A piece of lead was nailed over the injured part, and the boat was again made tight.

At day-light on the 26th, their situation was discovered, instead of being in a small bay as had been supposed, to be a little way within the entrance of a small rivulet,[2] about a cable's length wide, admitting, for about a fourth part of that extent, a passage of five fathoms water. It took a winding course to the S.W. between two mountains; the tide of flood ran strongly up, and the ebb returned with such impetuosity, that the boats could not make the least way against the current.

As many sunken rocks were lying across its entrance, Mr. Whidbey did not think it an object worth the risk of any further examination; and for that reason he proceeded immediately up the arm, taking an irregular direction, first about N. 50 E., for eight miles, and then about S. 55 E., twenty-two miles; where, as usual, it terminated in shoal water, before a border of low land, through which flowed several small streams or rivulets of fresh water. The latitude appeared to be 53° 20′, longitude 232° 17′;[3] it was high water by the shore 36′ after the moon passed the meridian, and the rise and fall of the tide was about fourteen feet.

On the morning of the 27th they returned down this arm, which, after Sir Alan Gardner, I called GARDNER'S CHANNEL.[4] On this occasion Mr. Whidbey observed, that the face of the country through which they had passed from the little rapid rivulet, was almost an intirely barren waste, nearly destitute of wood and verdure, and presenting to the eye one rude mass of almost naked rocks, rising into rugged mountains, more lofty than any he

[1] The mouth of Kiltuish Inlet.

[2] Kiltuish Inlet, about six miles in length, is narrow and shallow, and would have the appearance of a river. Menzies, who was with Whidbey, records that the inlet was named Bear River: 'On our landing we saw two very large Bears but they made off on seeing us into the woods before we could have a shot at them, on which this place obtained the name *Bear rivulet*.' – 25 June. The small Kiltuish River runs into the inlet.

[3] The correct position would be about lat. 53° 15′ N, long. 127° 53′ W (232° 07′ E).

[4] Gardner's Canal in the first edition; Gardner Canal is now the official name. Named by Vancouver after his friend and patron, Admiral Sir Alan Gardner. The Canal is divided into five reaches; the first has been named Alan Reach, after Sir Alan, and Whidbey and midshipman Barrie are commemorated in Barrie Reach and Whidbey Reach.

had before seen, whose towering summits seeming to overhang their bases, gave them a tremendous appearance. The whole was covered with perpetual ice and snow, that reached in the gullies formed between the mountains, close down to the high-water mark; and many water-falls of various dimensions were seen to descend in every direction.

By the morning of the 28th, they had reached the small arm on the southern shore, that had been passed unexamined on the afternoon of the 25th.[1] This they now found extending S. 35 E. nine miles from point Staniforth, where it terminated as usual. From thence the party proceeded about seven miles up what appeared to be the main branch of the inlet,[2] where they rested for the night, on the eastern shore, opposite to an island lying nearly in mid-channel.[3] This station lies from point Staniforth N. 10 W. eight miles. The shores of the continent, from the south-eastern arm, were nearly straight and compact. Here they were visited by eight Indians in two canoes, the first that they had seen during this expedition. The natives behaved in a very civil and friendly manner, and presented the party with two fine salmon, each weighing about 70 pounds; these were the finest and largest that had been seen during our voyage, and the Indians, after being recompensed with a small piece of iron, departed very well pleased with the exchange.[4]

The weather was calm, with heavy rain in the morning of the 29th, and so it continued all the day; notwithstanding this Mr. Whidbey resumed his examination in the afternoon, along the eastern or continental shore. From their place of rest it took a north direction for nine miles, to a projecting point that obtained the name of POINT HOPKINS,[5] forming within those limits a deep bend, in which were many sandy bays. The shores here were moderately elevated and well covered with wood. Two openings to the south of this point were passed on the opposite shore.[6] From hence the main inlet appeared to divide into two branches, one taking a north-easterly, the other a north-westerly direction.[7] The former, as being a continuation of the continent, was first attended to, and was found to extend N. 37 E. seven miles to the south point of a small branch about half a mile wide.[8] The eastern shore here formed a large sandy bay, and to the westward some rocky islets, and an island about four miles long were passed.[9] Here they were met by the same Indians who had furnished them with the two salmon, and who attended the party up the above-mentioned small branch. This, from its south point of entrance, took a direction S. 78 E. seven miles, where it terminated as usual by shoal water

---

[1] Triumph Bay.

[2] Devastation Channel. The name does not commemorate any catastrophe; it recalls H.M. paddle sloop *Devastation*, which served on the Pacific Station, 1862–5.

[3] Dorothy Island.

[4] These would be Heiltsuk Indians, who inhabited both Gardner Canal and Douglas Channel, which Whidbey would soon be exploring.

[5] The derivation of the name is not known.

[6] Sue Channel and Loretta Channel.   [7] Amos Passage and Kitimat Arm.

[8] Kildala Arm.   [9] Coste Island.

in latitude 53° 54¼', longitude 231° 30'.[1] They stopped here to dine, and were visited by ten canoes, containing about sixty Indians; the largest of these, in which was the chief and his family, had its head and stern curiously decorated with carved work, and rude and uncouth figures in painting, resembling those with which they adorn their houses. The skins of the sea otter and some land animals they readily disposed of, for copper, blue cloth, and blankets, but the former seemed highest in their estimation. They all behaved very civilly and honestly, and were very compliant in doing whatever they were desired. Mr. Whidbey permitted the chief to sit with him at dinner; which he considered as a great indulgence, and conducted himself very well. He drank some grog, and appeared to be very fond of bread and sugar; he preferred the latter, and seemed greatly astonished at the taste of it; he gave some to several of his attendants, who seemed to be equally surprized. After dinner Mr. Whidbey returned down this branch, accompanied by the the chief and his whole party, who every now and then sung songs, by no means unmelodious or unpleasing. The party reached the entrance in the evening, where they stopped for the night in a small cove within a bay. On making signs to the Indians that they were going to rest, all these immediately retired to another cove, at a little distance, where they remained perfectly quiet; and at four the next morning (the 30th) they accompanied them again in their researches up the main branch of the inlet.[2] From hence it was about two miles wide, and took nearly a north direction nine miles, to the latitude of 54° 4', longitude 231° 19', where it was terminated by a border of low land;[3] whence extended a shallow flat from side to side, through which a small rivulet discharged itself at its eastern corner, navigable for canoes only.[4] This termination differed in some respect from many of the others; its shores were not very abrupt, but were bounded on each side by a range of lofty mountains, which, however, were not (as had been constantly the case) connected at the head of the arm, but continued seemingly in a direction parallel to each other. The valley between them, which was three or four miles wide, formed nearly a plain, and was covered with tall forest trees, mostly of the pine tribe. This plain was supposed by Mr. Whidbey to extend some leagues, to where the distant mountains appeared to connect the two ranges. Our party made a late breakfast near the entrance of the rivulet, where they found the remains of an Indian village. On their moving from thence, their Indian attendants took their leave, went up the rivulet in their canoes, and were seen no more. Contrary winds, though the weather was now pleasant, retarded their progress so much, that by nine at

[1] The correct position in lat. 53° 50' N, long. 128° 30' W (231° 30' E).

[2] Kitimat Arm.

[3] The correct position is about lat. 54° 00' N, long., 128° 40' W (231° 20' E). The town of Kitimat and a huge aluminum smelter have been built on the E side of the head of the arm.

[4] The Kitimat River, which empties into the arm, is something more than a rivulet. Ready as usual to criticize Vancouver, Hewett noted that he once used the word to describe 'a very large river ½ mile wide, 5 to 8 fms. deep'.

night they had not reached more than eleven miles in a direction S. 20 W. from the head of the inlet. Here they stopped for the night on the western shore, close to a very large water-fall, about ten feet above high water mark, that had its source in a lake of fresh water which appeared to be deep, lying in a north-west direction.[1]

About three in the morning of the first of July the party proceeded down the western shore, and soon arrived at the western division of the main inlet, mentioned on the 29th of June to have been seen from point Hopkins.[2] This, which took a direction S. 35 W., was about a mile wide; its western shore being still a continuation of the continent, its eastern having the appearance of being an island, or a group of islands; so that little doubt was entertained of finding a passage by that route, instead of returning by the way they had come. For this reason Mr. Whidbey did not hesitate to proceed down the arm, and having advanced about five miles along the continental shore, he came to a point in latitude 53° 50′, longitude 231° 8½′, which he named POINT ASHTON.[3] Here another branch extended from that they were pursuing to the northward, and, at a little distance, appeared again to divide into two arms, to the north and the north-west.[4]

By this time their provisions were nearly exhausted; and as there was no certainty of gaining a passage to the ship by this route, Mr. Whidbey deemed it most prudent to quit the further examination of the continental shore, and to make the best of his way towards the vessels. At point Ashton they breakfasted, and by the shore found it high water there 13′ after the moon passed the meridian. From this point in a southerly direction were several rocky islets, and two small islands. After breakfast they made considerable progress, and found the arm take a direction S. 30 W., 14 miles to a point on the east shore. About half way from point Ashton, they passed on that shore by an opening, stretching to the north-east, and communicating most probably with one of those they has passed on the opposite side of the land, extending to the westward.[5] From this last station the channel ran nearly south,[6] and by ten in the forenoon of the 2d of July, their former opinion was confirmed, by their arriving at the south-west extremity of the land, which in their way up to point Hopkins, had formed their western, and on their return from point

[1] Jesse Falls, the outlet of Jesse Lake.
[2] Douglas Channel. No clear reference to the channel had been made on the 29th.
[3] The correct position is lat. 53° 46′ N, long. 128° 57′ W (231° 03′ E). The origin of the name is not known.
[4] Gilttoyees Inlet, from which Miskatla Inlet branches off to the NE.
[5] Sue Channel, between Maitland Island and Hawkesbury Island. As Whidbey surmised, he had passed its E Entrance when going up Devastation Channel.
[6] Menzies now found himself on familiar ground: 'Here I came upon known ground having penetrated thus far in open boats from Banks's Isles into the interior Country in my former visit to this part of the Coast, for near the bending of the Channel we passed an opening on the western shore [presumably Kiskosh Inlet] which I knew to be a large rivulet I formerly examined a considerable way up to a Village where there were then about 300 Inhabitants.' – 1 July.

Ashton, their eastern shore. This, which I called POINT CUMMING, is situated in latitude 53° 18½', longitude 2300° 58',[1] from hence the islet, on which Mr. Whidbey had left a note the 23d of June, was seen lying nearly east, at the distance of about nine miles. Thus his conjectures were proved to have been well founded, and that the intervening land composed an extensive island about thirty-three miles in length, and from three to eleven miles in breadth.

This island, after that noble and indefatigable promoter of the British commerce, Lord Hawkesbury,* I named HAWKESBURY'S ISLAND.[2] From point Cumming the party returned to the ships as already related.

* Now Lord Liverpool.

[1] The SW point of Gribbell Island; the lat. is correct, but the long. is 129° 07' W (230° 53' E).

[2] Sir Charles Jenkinson, bart., was created Baron Hawkesbury in 1786 and Earl of Liverpool in 1796. Meares dedicated his *Voyages* to him in 1790; he was then President of the Board of Trade. Walbran notes that 'Hawkesbury island was long supposed to be one large island; it is now known to be divided into four islands, Gribbell, Hawkesbury, Maitland and Loretta.' But Hawkesbury Island is much the largest of the four.

CHAPTER IV.

Mr. Whidbey again dispatched with two Boats—Anchor near the Isle de Gil—Account of Mr. Whidbey's Excursion—Quit Fisherman's Cove—Pass between Banks's Island and Pitt's Archipelago into the Ocean—Enter Chatham's Sound—Meet three English Vessels—Arrive in Observatory Inlet—Anchor in Salmon Bay—Boats again dispatched on the Survey.

OUR distance from the place where Mr. Whidbey had quitted the examination of the continental shore being at least 15 leagues, and the probability there was, that the branches he had left unexamined, on the western shore, were only small arms, induced me not to proceed in the vessels so far in such a tedious and disagreeable navigation, but to take a situation somewhere in the neighbourhood of the north-west part of Mr. Johnstone's researches; where the vessels would be conveniently stationed for proceeding in the inland navigation, should this be found advisable, or for pursuing the route Mr. Johnstone had explored leading towards the ocean.

With a favorable breeze we steered to the westward, but we had no sooner entered the channel by which the boats had returned,[1] which was about half a league in width, and communicated with Nepean's sound,[2] than the favorable breeze died away, and it was succeeded by light baffling winds in the contrary direction. As we at first advanced in this channel, soundings were gained from 40 to 45 fathoms, at the distance of near two cables' length on each side; but, the ebb tide being in our favor, and we being also in hopes of finding soundings as we proceeded, I was not induced to anchor until the flood should return; at which time, the wind intirely dying away, and we being in the middle of the channel, it was not until midnight, though with the assistance of all our boats a-head towing, that we arrived in 60 fathoms water, about half a cable's length from the southern shore, and four miles and an half from our late anchorage. The bottom did not appear by the lead to be rocky. The anchor, however, in the morning of Wednesday the 3d, slipped off the bank, and the ship was adrift; it was immediately hove up, and with

---

[1] McKay Reach.

[2] Vancouver's chart shows that he considered that Nepean Sound extended eastward from Principe Channel through Otter Channel, across the N end of Squally Passage and through Cridge Passage. The name is now confined to the waters at the junction of Principe Passage, Otter Channel, Estevan Sound and Otter Passage.

light variable winds attended with much rain, we attempted to advance until two in the afternoon; when finding we lost ground, we came to an anchor on the southern shore, about half a mile to the eastward of the place we had left in the morning, in 40 fathoms water; but before a hawser could be made fast to the shore, the anchor again slipped into 60 fathoms; this precaution however prevented our being again adrift, or the anchor from slipping into deeper water.

Such being the unavoidable and tedious delays attendant on moving the vessels, I dispatched Mr. Whidbey in the large cutter, attended by Mr. Barrie in the small one,[1] to prosecute the inland navigation; appointing a rendezvous not likely to be mistaken, whither we should proceed by such advances as were in our power. But, in case this service should be early completed, and he himself returned before the arrival of the vessels at the appointed place, which was that where Mr. Johnstone's investigation was intended to commence, he was then to proceed in that route, leaving, in a situation easily to be discovered, due information of his proceedings; by which means any further examination in that quarter would become intirely unnecessary. With these directions, and ten days' provisions, he departed about noon.

We remained in this situation until about half past ten in the forenoon of Thursday the 4th, when a moderate breeze springing up from the south-westward, we made sail to windward. Our progress was so slow, that at seven in the evening we had only reached point Cumming; and we had no sooner rounded this point, than the wind, that had been against us the whole day, and would now have been favorable, instantly shifted to the very point for which, on entering Nepean's sound, we had wanted to steer, in order to reach our rendezvous now at the distance of about four miles.[2] This disappointment compelled us, at ten o'clock, to anchor, and make fast to the trees, two miles to the northward of the above point, in fifty fathoms water; the bottom sand and stones, about half a cable's length from the eastern shore. In the morning, the appointed rendezvous for meeting Mr. Whidbey's party not having been visited by any of our boats, I ordered the master of the Chatham[3] to go thither, and to ascertain the best anchorage for the vessels. About ten o'clock a light breeze from the N.W. springing up, we made sail to windward in order to follow him.

On heaving up the best bower anchor, to our great surprize and mortification, we found it broken. The palm, with half the arm of the anchor, was broken off.[4] It had evidently struck slantingly against a rock, as the mark

[1] Puget also accompanied Whidbey. The rendezvous was at the S end of Promise Island, at the W side of the entrance to Douglas Channel.

[2] The rendezvous was at the S end of Promise Island, at the W side of the entrance to Douglas Channel

[3] Thomas Manby.

[4] The palm is the inner surface of the fluke of an anchor, the flukes being 'the broad triangular plates…on each arm of the anchor which enter the ground and hold the ship.' – OED.

of the rock still remained on the broken part of the anchor; and as there was not the least strain in weighing it, there is little doubt that its own weight broke it in the act of falling. The anchor appeared to have been composed of vary bad materials, and to have been very ill wrought; it had broken quite short off, and had it not been for the shape of the bars, that remained in its inside in their original state, the texture of the metal would rather have induced the belief of its being cast, than wrought, iron.

Such were the anchors with which we were supplied for executing this tedious, arduous, and hazardous service. Happily, neither on this, nor on the former similar occasion, about this time in the preceding year, were we exposed to any immediate danger, otherwise the chances of our escaping would have been much against us. A loss of confidence in the stability of these our last resources, must always be attended with the most painful reflections that can occur in a maritime life. From our unfortunate experience, little dependence could be placed in future on the services of our anchors, should we be driven to the cruel necessity of resorting to them as a last resource.

On Mr. Manby's return, he reported, that although the neighbourhood of the spot he had been sent to examine afforded anchorage, yet it was very much exposed, and the soundings gained were off a small sandy beach, that extended but a little way in any direction. On more minutely noticing the western shore of this inlet, being the east side of the isle de Gil, I saw a situation that promised to answer our present purpose, having now to break out the main hold for another anchor. I sent a boat to sound it, and on receiving a favorable report, about three o'clock we anchored in forty fathoms; stones, shells, and sandy bottom; mooring with a hawser to the shore. The bay[1] is situated on the north-east part of the island, about two miles from its northern extremity. Its outer points bearing by compass from N.W. to S.E. by E., our distance about a cable's length from the shore.

My intentions now were, that the Chatham should proceed to, and remain at, the rendezvous, for the information of the boats; and that the Discovery should continue at this more eligible station for the service we had to perform. But on observing the Chatham haul her wind, instead of anchoring at the place appointed, I concluded the anchorage was not found very desirable; the signal was therefore made for them to join us, which was accordingly done about five in the evening. We immediately sat about replacing the anchors; this was accomplished, and the hold re-stowed by noon the next day, Saturday the 6th.

The Chatham's launch requiring some repairs, detained Mr. Johnstone and his party until four o'clock on Sunday morning, when, with supplies for a week, he departed, in order to resume his examination of the coast towards the ocean; with directions to call at the place appointed for Mr. Whidbey's rendezvous, bearing by compass N. 27 W. distant three miles, and there to leave information of his departure, and of the station the vessels had taken.

[1] The cove, unnamed on the chart, adjacent to Juan Point, Gil Island.

About nine Mr. Johnstone returned, having found a note from Mr. Whidbey, which stated, that the openings he had pursued to the northward in the inland navigation, had been all found to terminate in the usual way; that he had quitted the rendezvous the preceding day at noon, whither he had then traced the continental shore, and had departed with the view of continuing its further examination up an arm leading to the north-west. Mr. Johnstone left the directions according to his orders, and returned on board, as this intelligence of Mr. Whidbey's proceedings had rendered his expedition unnecessary. On his arrival he pointed out a situation round the north point of this island, which appeared to him more eligible for waiting the return of the boats than the station we had taken; but as this afforded an abundance of berries and of the labradore tea, I was induced to remain here another day, that our people might have the advantage of a ramble into the woods, and of partaking of these excellent refreshments.

As the wind blew from the northward directly into the bay, attended with thick misty weather, we remained quiet until Tuesday the 9th, when we proceeded to the station pointed out by Mr. Johnstone. On anchoring, the best bower was in thirty-three, the small bower in forty-three fathoms, about a quarter of a mile from the shore; the bottom dark sand and mud. Our situation was directly to the south-westward of the north point of the isle de Gil,[1] whose shores bore by compass from S. by E. to N.E. by E.; the nearest opposite shore west, about half a league distant; the arm under Mr. Whidbey's examination north-west, distant two miles; and the appointed rendezvous distant about a league.

The next morning, Wednesday the 10th, the seine was hauled, and a good meal of fish procured for all hands; an abundance of berries were produced on the adjacent shores and a sufficient quantity of fish caught to supply our wants during our stay, which continued without any particular occurrence until Sunday the 14th. About seven in the morning the boats returned, after having pursued the examination of the continental shore, through an arm[2] whose entrance, two miles from this station, was in a direction N. 30 W.; in which its boundaries were traced to the latitude of 54° 24′, longitude 229° 42′, and considered to be there the eastern part of Chatham's sound, so named by some former visitors.[3] From thence the continental shore, which took a northerly direction, appeared to be compact, and formed the eastern side of a very spacious and extensive opening, lying in the same direction with the continent from two to three leagues in width, and nearly unlimited in its northern direction. The continental shore was composed of a range of lofty mountains covered with snow; but the western side of the sound was divided

---

[1] The small bay to which Vancouver later gave the name Fisherman Cove, which it still retains. It is adjacent to Turtle Point, the N extremity of Gil Island.

[2] Grenville Channel.

[3] Probably named by Duncan in 1788, in honour of the 2nd Earl of Chatham, who became First Lord of the Admiralty the same year.

into large and small islands, through which Mr. Whidbey saw two channels communicating with the ocean. By one of these he intended to have returned, but the strong southerly winds that prevailed induced him to return by the inland navigation. The following is an account of this excursion.

By noon of the 4th the party reached point Ashton,[1] where Mr. Whidbey on his former expedition had quitted the examination of the continental shore. Having dined they proceeded round this point along the continent, up the northern branch then left unexplored,[2] and found it, as it had appeared to be, divided into two small arms, the first scarcely half a mile wide,[3] taking a direction N. 18 E., about four miles, where it terminated in low land, rising gradually to a moderate height within the country. The east side of the arm bore a similar appearance, indented with several sandy bays; but the western side was high, steep, and rocky. The other branch of this opening, extending from point Ashton N. 10 W., was about the same width; with an island situated nearly in its middle, and some sunken rocks on its eastern shore. This branch terminated by low swampy land, surrounded on every side by high mountains, with deep gullies between them where the snow had lodged, and in some places remained frozen, though not more than twenty feet above the level of the sea. Each side of the arm was well wooded, but composed of steep rocky shores. Having thus satisfied themselves the party returned, and rested for the night in a small cove on the continental shore, three miles to the southward of point Ashton.[4] From hence the continental shore first took a direction S. 31 W. fifteen miles; here it formed a small cove, in which is a fresh water brook;[5] from thence it extended nearly south, twelve miles; and having examined in their way a small bay about a mile wide, and half a league deep,[6] they entered a narrow opening that first took nearly a south-west direction about a league,[7] and then S. 15 E., about three miles and a half further; where it again communicated with the main channel, making the eastern shore a small island about a league and a half long,[8] whose south end was the appointed rendezvous. In this neighbourhood Mr. Whidbey expected to have found the vessels; but being disappointed, he left the note as before mentioned, and prosecuted the examination of the continent up the arm already pointed out,[9] which they entered about noon. During their morning's excursion they were visited by seven canoes, in which were about thirty of the natives, most of whom Mr. Whidbey described to be little old

[1] At the N end of Douglas Channel.
[2] Gilttoyees Inlet, about seven miles in length.
[3] Miskatla Inlet.
[4] Drumlummon Bay, connected by a very narrow entrance with Foch Lagoon, which was not explored. Puget thought that this was the point at which Caamaño ended his explorations, and refers to the bay as Spanish Bay. – 5 July.
[5] Kitkiata Inlet, into which flows the Quaal River. The distance from Drumlummon Bay is about 11 miles, not 15 miles.
[6] Hartley Bay.   [7] Stewart Narrows.
[8] Promise Island.   [9] Grenville Channel.

men; there were few young men amongst them, and no women nor children. They brought a very inferior assortment of sea otter skins to dispose of, and their general appearance indicated them to be a very poor tribe; they stayed with our party about an hour, and conducted themselves in a very orderly manner.

At the south-east point of entrance into this arm, which lies west about two miles from the rendezvous point, and for two miles within, the sea abounded with sea otters. These, in the most sportive manner, played about the boats, rearing themselves half way out of the water, and holding up their young ones in their fore paws, as if to view the boats as they passed.[1] The arm at this place was not more than half a mile wide, with straight and compact shores on each side; they found its direction N. 40 W., until they had advanced about twenty-four miles from the entrance, when they arrived at a small harbour, or rather cove, on the eastern shore,[2] where they passed a very rainy and uncomfortable night.

At day-light, in the morning of the 7th, some rocks were found near the head of this cove, which was bounded by a sandy beach, having a lagoon of water behind it.[3] Off its north-west point was an island,[4] from whence the arm was found to continue the same width and direction about four miles further. It then stretched N. 27 W. about eight miles to the south point of an opening on the western or continental shore,[5] about a mile wide; its opposite point of entrance lying north. At this point the width of the main arm increased to half a league. Off the south point lie many rocks, both above and beneath the surface of the water. The shores, along which they had thus navigated from the entrance of the arm, were mountainous on the east or continental side, but, on the opposite side, low and rocky; both produced pine-trees, and were interspersed with bare and naked patches. From this point the opening was found to take a course first S. 37 E. for four miles, where it ended in a sandy bay, in which were some sunken rocks; from thence it extended N. 9 W., six miles,[6] where it finally terminated in the usual manner, with some rocky islets, and sunken rocks, about half way up. Immediately

---

[1] Menzies describes the scene: 'We met in mid-channel with a vast crowd of Sea Otters consisting of several hundreds basking on the surface of the water with their young & moving with the Tide, the report of a musket suddenly alarmed them & they instantly divd with the greatest precipitation leaving several of their young on the surface who were not old enough to dive of themselves, but the Dams no sooner missed them than they returned & carried them all off excepting one which we got into the Boat; the noise of it brought the Dam after us & she made frequent attempts to rescue it by approaching near the boat at the hazard of her own life, which shews the great affection of these Animals for their Young.' – 10 July. Menzies had been most anxious to capture a sea otter, as he had not seen a whole animal out of the water.

[2] Puget's log shows that the distance from the entrance was 14 miles, not 24, as Vancouver states. The 'cove' was Lowe Inlet.

[3] Nettle Basin. [4] Tom Island.

[5] Klewnuggit Inlet. The E shore, not the W shore, was the continental shore.

[6] East Inlet.

within its north point of entrance lies a small island, behind which is a deep sandy cove.[1] From this northern point the eastern shore took a direction N. 45 W., three miles and an half, to a small cove,[2] where they rested for the night, which as well as the day, was very rainy and unpleasant.

Although the rain still continued, the party again proceeded at four the next morning along the continental shore,[3] N. 31 W. ten miles to the south point of a bay, about a mile wide, and two miles deep, in the north-east direction, with many inlets and several sunken rocks about it.[4] Here they were detained by thick foggy weather until near noon, when it cleared up, and permitted Mr. Whidbey to observe the latitude of the above point to be 53° 53', its longitude 230° 12½'.[5] Having examined the bay, they proceeded, and found the east shore to take a rounding direction westerly[6] to a cove, lying from the above bay N. 23 W. distant about nine miles.[7] Here they rested for the night, which, like the former, was very wet and uncomfortable.

In their way hither the continental shore was found to be lined with innumerable rocky islets and rocks, above and below the surface of the sea; nor was the middle of the channel free from these obstructions, where was also a cluster of islands; and behind them an extensive opening on the opposite shore ran to the S.S.W.[8] appearing to divide the land. To the north-west of that opening the south-west shore still continued N. 35 W. from whence the main arm increased its width to near half a league, and formed a channel leading to the north-westward, with land lying between it and the continental shore.[9] This last now took a direction N. 5 W. and formed a channel with the eastern shore of the above intermediate land, from two to three miles wide.[10] The south point of this land bore from hence N. 69 W. distant three miles. In the morning of the 9th, they bent their way up this channel, passing along the continent, and found the shores composed of steep rocky cliffs, difficult to land upon, though but moderately elevated; their lower parts being well wooded, but towards their summits rugged and barren; here also they met with immense numbers of sea otters playing about the boats, which were frequently fired at, but without effect.

Soon after they had left the cove, they found themselves opposed by a very rapid stream, against which the boats could scarcely make any way; it was remarked, that no part of this stream seemed to enter the passage which the boats had pursued, but was wholly directed towards the above S.S.W. opening, that appeared to divide the south-western shore, and left little doubt

---

[1] Harriot Island. [2] Kxngeal Inlet.

[3] Whidbey and Puget did not notice the entrance to Baker Inlet, which is not surprising, as it is only about 200 feet wide. The inlet is about four miles in length.

[4] Kumealon Inlet.

[5] McMurray Point, in lat. 53° 51' N, long. 130° 00' W (230° 00' E).

[6] Northerly, not westerly.

[7] Fleming Bay. [8] Ogden Channel.

[9] Arthur Passage. The land between was Kennedy Island.

[10] Telegraph Passage.

of that passage communicating with the ocean, as the current was evidently the ebb tides.

Having advanced seven miles along the main land in the above direction, they arrived at a point from which the intermediate land before-mentioned was clearly perceived to be a high island, about seven miles long; its north point[1] lying N. 77 W. at the distance of three miles and a half. This formed the south-west point of a passage[2] communicating with a very extensive sound,[3] in which were several islands; between these the open sea was supposed to be seen, as the horizon appeared unbounded beyond those islands. From this point also, the east point of that passage bore N. 64 W. $1\frac{1}{2}$ miles distant. This proved to be the south point of a high island,[4] where the party met with a flood tide, and found the continental shore continue in the same direction about a league, when they suddenly came into four feet water; and found themselves at the entrance of a branch leading to the north-east, about two miles wide.[5] To gain a greater depth of water, they hauled over to its northern shore, passing many dead trees that were lodged on the bank, where no more than three to six feet water were found, until within half a mile of the northern shore, when the water suddenly deepened to seven fathoms. This bank joins on to the south point of entrance into this branch, to which I gave the name of POINT LAMBERT, after commissioner Lambert of the navy; it is situated in latitude 54″ $10\frac{1}{2}$′.[6] From it the shoal forms a rounding spit, and terminates on the southern shore, about two miles within the point. They now proceeded in the direction of the branch N. 30 E.[7] with soundings from ten to seven fathoms, for about seven miles, when they came abreast of some islands on the northern shore, lying before the entrance of a narrow opening which took a south-east direction.[8] Having passed this, they continued in mid-channel about two miles further, when they came into two fathoms water. Here Mr. Whidbey remained till high water, which was 1^{h} 45′ after the moon passed the meridian, and then dispatched Mr. Barrie to the northern shore, whilst he sounded the southern side, towards the above islands, where he found no more than three fathoms water.

At one of these islands, which, from the quantity of excellent raspberries it produced, obtained the name of RASPBERRY ISLAND, Mr. Barrie joined the party, and reported, that the shoal extended within a cable's length of the north shore, where it formed a narrow channel with the main land seven fathoms deep. Under these circumstances Mr. Whidbey determined to stay at the island

---

[1] Georgy Point.
[2] Marcus Passage, between Kennedy Island and Smith Island.
[3] Chatham Sound.
[4] Parry Point, the S extremity of De Horsey Island.
[5] The mouth of the Skeena River.
[6] On the mainland about opposite the N end of Kennedy Island. Named after Captain Robert Lambert. Its position is lat. 54° 05′ N, long. 130° 05′ W (229° 55′ E).
[7] The estuary of the Skeena River.
[8] The Raspberry Islands. The 'narrow opening' was the Ecstall River.

until low water, that a better judgment might be formed of their actual situation, since, from the rapidity and regularity of the tides, he began to suspect it to be a river.[1]

In the evening Mr. Barrie was sent to the opening extending to the south-east, and Mr. Whidbey went to the above seven fathom channel; but found that it was too narrow to be navigated, and that it was interspersed with sand banks and sunken rocks. On his return to Raspberry island, he was met by Mr. Barrie, who made a similar report of the opening he had been sent to explore. Mr. Whidbey, however, wishing to be more fully satisfied, went himself on the morning of the 10th to the south-east opening, and found its entrance obstructed with innumerable sunken rocks, and the tide rushing down it in violent overfalls. He retired to Raspberry island for the purpose of returning to take a second view there at low water; as the night tides in this country rise in general much higher, and fall much lower than those that flow in the day. This proved to be so much the case in this instance, that they were enabled to see, at low tide, the whole space of the branch above them from side to side intirely dry, up to its very head, which was about four miles from the island they were then upon, encumbered with sunken rocks, and innumerable large round stones scattered in all directions. From its head there appeared in this point of view three small rivulets, that flowed over this shallow space, very dangerous for boats on account of the rapidity of the tide, and of the rocks and stones that could scarcely be avoided. Mr. Whidbey prudently declined wasting any more time in its further examination,[2] and taking the advantage of the ebb tide that commenced at three in the afternoon, he returned, and directed his course towards the entrance into the extensive sound he had seen on the 9th. During their late researches in this branch, which I have called PORT ESSINGTON, after Captain Essington of the navy,[3] the flood tide was observed to run up at the rate of four, and the ebb tide down at the rate of five knots per hour; the tides regular nearly six hours each way, and the water perfectly fresh at low tide, though brackish at high water. Many sea otters were seen playing about, and diverting themselves amongst the rocks at all times of tide. The surrounding country was in general moderately

---

[1] The Skeena River.

[2] Puget defends this decision: 'Some Objection may arise from our Cursory Examination of the River in not Strictly sounding out all its Shores, yet when it is considered that no Break appeared in the Mountains & the Difficult & Intricate Navigation of the Channel leaves no doubt in my Mind that its Source is derivd from the Snow, which hurls down with its Rapidity the Trees and large Stones which are every where strewed among the Shoals – But at all Events the Channel could not be termed Navigable therefore we had no Business to pursue [it] but this would not have prevented its further Examination had it not absolutely been attended with very great Danger to the Boats.' – 14 July. Earlier Puget had remarked that 'it appeared wonderful how the Boats could have gone clear of the Sunken Rocks.' – 10 July.

[3] Captain William Essington. Here, as on his chart, Vancouver ignores the Skeena River; he was naming its estuary. The name is now confined to the settlement near the mouth of the Ecstall River.

elevated, particularly its north-west side, where, in several places, low land seemed to stretch to some distance; but to the northward and eastward, the view was bounded by lofty barren mountains, wrapped in perpetual frost and snow.

About five in the evening, they reached the north point of the island[1] forming the south side of the passage into the large sound,[2] nearly four leagues from Raspberry island. This passage, which is two miles long, and about a mile wide from island to island, was mostly occupied by shoals and overfalls, from three feet to three fathoms, contracting it to a very narrow channel close on the southern side, where the depth was fifteen and sixteen fathoms all the way through into the sound. From hence a view was gained of the spacious opening before them, from six to seven miles wide, whose width seemed to increase further to the N.W. interspersed, in most directions, with small islands, rocky islets, rocks and shoals. One extensive dry sand-bank, in particular, was seen lying from this point, N. 53 W. a league distant. The south-western shore of the extensive arm they had passed through from Nepean's sound, still continued its last-mentioned course, and formed the south-west side of the spacious sound, that has been mentioned already to have been discovered before, and named after the Earl of Chatham. From this point they steered towards some islands that lie to the south-west of the above sand-bank. The soundings were irregular, from ten to three, and sometimes only two, fathoms water. At one of these islands, lying from the point they had left, N. 65 W. at the distance of four or five miles, the party rested for the night.

The next morning (July 11) as Mr. Whidbey was taking his bearings, he found the compass vary 13° from his former observations. He altered its situation, then placed it on a tree, yet the same difference appeared; from whence he was led to suspect, that some mistake had been made on the preceding day; but, on revising his former angles, he was convinced that the deviation had commenced in this, and not at any former station; proving that the component parts of this island are strongly impregnated with a magnetic quality, a circumstance that had occurred in other instances during our former investigation, but more particularly in New Georgia than in these northern regions.

From this island they steered over towards the larboard side of the sound, and soon passed the northern extremity of the land, mentioned before as forming its south-west side; the extreme point of which terminates the N. 35 W. direction of that shore, and forms a very conspicuous point, surrounded on all sides with many rocks and islets. To this point I gave the name of POINT HUNT; it is situated in latitude 54° 10½′, longitude 229° 48′.[3] From hence the shores of that land took an irregular direction S. 50 W. for

[1] Kennedy Island.
[2] Marcus Passage.
[3] Now Hunt Point, the N extremity of Porcher Island. The derivation of the name is not known. Its position is lat. 54° 06′ N, long. 130° 25′ W (229° 35′ E).

seven miles, to a point which I called POINT PEARCE;[1] the intermediate space is bounded by innumerable rocks and other impediments, forming at first a wide channel, with the land to the north-west of it, but decreasing at this point to about a mile. Its nearest opposite side bore N. 72 W.; to the westward of this point the channel again expanded, and the larboard shore fell back considerably, forming a deep bay,[2] in which were several small openings running to the south-eastward. In a direction W. by S. about three miles from point Pearce, Mr. Whidbey landed on the south point of a small island, lying before the northern shore of this channel,[3] where he observed the latitude to be 54° 5', longitude 229° 34½', and from whence he had a clear and distinct view of the ocean. The western point of the northern shore lying N. 58 W. and the western point of the southern or larboard shore S. 78 W. This latter, forming a very conspicuous projecting land, I named, after Mr. Ibbetson of the Admiralty, CAPE IBBETSON; it is situated in latitude 54° 4', longitude 229° 30',[4] having between it and the westernmost land, on the northern shore, a cluster of rocky islets; exclusively of which, the channel out to sea appeared to be without interruption, though, about the northern shore, there were several rocks and islets.

By this unequivocal view of the ocean, it was positively ascertained, that the land forming the south-west side of the extensive channel they had pursued, from Nepean's sound to point Hunt, and from thence to cape Ibbetson, constituted either an archipelago of islands, or one island upwards of twenty leagues in length; but as I considered the former most likely to be the case, I named it after the Right Hon. William Pitt, PITT'S ARCHIPELAGO.[5] Mr. Whidbey much wished to have returned to the ships along its southern side; but, as a strong S.E. wind prevailed, attended with a good deal of sea, against which they were not likely to make much progress in the open ocean, and their stock of provisions being reduced to a very low state, Mr. Whidbey abandoned that project in order to return by the way he came; but first went back into Chatham sound for the purpose of acquiring some farther information respecting it.

On repassing the channel just mentioned as being a mile in width,[6] Mr. Whidbey noticed to the north-east of it, on the shores of Pitt's archipelago, two sandy bays, that appeared likely to afford good anchorage; but having

[1] Now Pearce Point, on the W side of the entrance to Refuge Bay, Porcher Island. The origin of the name is not known.

[2] The broader part of Edye Passage, W of Pearce Point.

[3] Arthur Island, which is about two miles in length. The size of an island that Vancouver described as 'small' varies considerably.

[4] Now Ibbetson Point, the N extremity of William Island. Its position is lat. 54° 03' N, long. 130° 42' W (229° 18' E). The 'southern or larboard shore' actually consisted of William, Henry and Porcher islands, but the channels between them would not be clearly visible from Whidbey's position on Arthur Island.

[5] The name is now confined to Pitt Island, 57 miles in length, which forms the W side of Grenville Channel.   [6] Edye Passage.

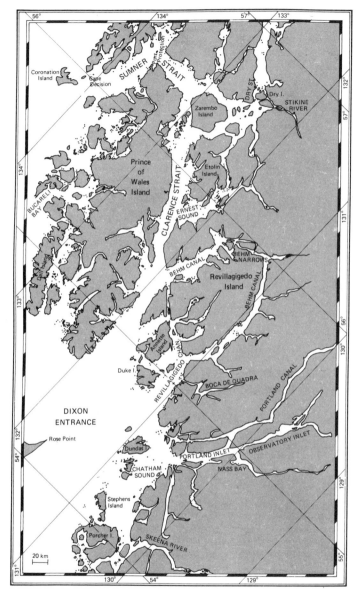

Figure 6. Skeena River to Cape Decision. *Base map by Michael E. Leek.*

other objects in view, he did not enter them, but proceeded up the sound, where the afternoon was employed in fixing the situation of the several islands, rocks, &c. which it contained. From one of the former, lying from point Hunt N. 43 W. at the distance of eight miles, a distant view was again obtained of the ocean, making the western shore of the sound, from the passage they had left leading to sea, an island about four leagues long. To this, after Sir Philip Stephens of the Admiralty, I gave the name of STEPHENS'S ISLAND.[1] Its north point lies, from this island, N. 85 W. distant five miles; and the opposite side of this channel leading out to sea, N. 45 W. From hence they visited another cluster of islands, where the party rested for the night, and which terminated the northern extent of their excursion.

Returning on the morning of the 12th, Mr. Whidbey passed close by point Hunt, and pursued the channel observed to stretch to the north-west, on the evening of the 8th;[2] where, towards its southern part, several sunken rocks were found in mid-channel, and in passing through the cluster of islands mentioned at the same time, they found them to be surrounded by rocks and shoal water. From hence they lost no time in making the best of their way to the ship, through the same channel by which they had advanced.

This channel, about 22 leagues long,[3] communicating between Chatham's and Nepean's sound, I named, after the Right Hon. Lord Grenville, GRENVILLE'S CHANNEL.[4]

The result of this expedition left no doubt as to the measures that were to be pursued. I therefore directed that the brewing utensils and other matters should be immediately removed from the shore, and the vessels unmoored; my intention being to proceed through the channel that Mr. Johnstone had found leading towards the ocean,[5] and from thence to continue to the north-westward, through the passage formed by Banks's island to the south-west, and Pitt's archipelago to the north-east. This channel had already been navigated by Senᵣ Caamano, who had named it Canal del Principe,[6] and in whose chart it is represented as fair and navigable.

Whilst our business with the shore was going forward, three canoes, in which were some of the natives, made their appearance; these, with one canoe seen some days before at a distance, in which were some people, were the

---

[1] Stephens Island, with which Whidbey lumped Prescott Island, which is separated from it by a narrow, crooked channel.

[2] Arthur Passage.

[3] A slight exaggeration; the distance is about 60 miles.

[4] Grenville's Canal in the first edition; now Grenville Channel.

[5] Otter Channel.

[6] Now Principe Channel. Menzies refers to it as 'Duncan's Channel so named from Mr. Duncan being the first Navigator who sailed through it in the sloop Princess Royal in the year 1788.' – July 18. It is named 'Duncan's Inlet' on Duncan's own 'Sketch of Port Stephens', published by Dalrymple in 1789, and as 'Duncan's Inlet or Strait' on the Arrowsmith map published in 1795; but Vancouver's preference for the Spanish name has prevailed.

only inhabitants we had noticed during our residence in Nepean's sound.[1] One only of these canoes ventured near us this morning; it contained four or five persons, who made their approach with the utmost diffidence and caution. They disposed of a few indifferent sea otter skins, and seemed, in a trifling degree, to differ in their persons from the people we had been accustomed to see; they were not taller, but they were stouter, their faces more round and flat, their hair coarse, straight, black, and cut short to their head; in this respect they differed from any of the tribes of North West America with whom we had met, who, though in various fashions, universally wore their hair long, which was in general of a soft nature, and chiefly of a light or dark brown colour, seldom approaching to black.

The wind being light and variable, kept us stationary until near noon, when, seeming to be settled in the north-east quarter, we quitted our anchorage. Although the shore here formed no very great indent, I distinguished it by the name of FISHERMAN'S COVE, from our success in procuring fish, which in these regions were a very scarce commodity. In this cove are two considerable runs of fresh water, and wood may be easily procured in abundance. The soundings are from 15 to 40 fathoms good holding ground, where a few vessels may ride with great safety and convenience.

Whilst we remained in Fisherman's cove, I procured observations sufficient to ascertain its situation, by which its latitude was found to be $53° 18\frac{1}{2}'$, its longitude deduced from six sets of the sun's altitude and the chronometers, $230° 53'$;[2] the variation, by three different compasses taken on shore, shewing from $20° 29'$ to $22° 18'$, gave the mean result of $21° 17'$ eastwardly. Fisherman's cove being situated at the extremity of an island, in the midst of this very broken region, it was impossible to ascertain with the least regularity any thing respecting the tides, as they were so much influenced by the winds and other latent causes.

It was seven in the evening before we had passed through the northern entrance into Nepean's sound, when the wind, which blew in very light airs, being favorable, our course was directed slowly up the Canal del Principe.

The next morning, Monday the 15th, a light breeze springing up, we stood to windward, and at noon Banks's island extended from S. 51 E. to N. 70 W., the latter being in a line with a part of the shores of Pitt's archipelago; so that, as yet, we had not the passage to sea open. At this time we were a-breast of a small opening about N.E. by N., at the distance of a mile, apparently the same that had been named by Mr. Duncan, Port Stephens; its entrance was obstructed by many rocky islets and rocks, and it presented no very tempting appearance as a port. The easternmost land in sight, on the northern

---

[1] Vancouver was entering the area, centring on the Skeena River, which was inhabited by the Tsimshian Indians. They may well have come from the Tsimshian village in Hartley Bay, on the W side of Douglas Channel, near its mouth.

[2] The position of Fisherman Cove is lat. 53° 19' 30" N, long. 129° 16' 30" W (230° 43' 30" E).

side of the channel, bore by compass S. 58 E., and the nearest shore of Banks's island S.W. by W., about a mile distant; here the observed latitude was 53° 26½′, longitude 230° 19′.[1]

In the afternoon, we passed the Port de Canaveral;[2] it seemed to be extensive, and to have an entrance, free from obstruction, about a league and a half wide. Its outer points lie N. 35 W. and S. 35 E. from each other; off the latter lies a small round island, in latitude 53° 29′, longitude 230° 16′.[3] As we made a tolerable progress in plying, we continued under sail until nine in the evening; when we anchored in 34 fathoms, within the length of three cables from the shores of Pitt's archipelago, which consisted here of a number of small islands and rocks, lying in front of land more compact, extending westward from the north point of Port del Canaveral, and bearing by compass from N. 73 W. to E. by S.; each extreme being about two miles distant. Here we had a view of the ocean between a projecting point on the shores of Pitt's archipelago, and the N.W. point of Bank's island; the former bearing by compass N. 80 W., the latter N. 86 W., and the nearest opposite shore on Bank's island S. by W., about two miles distant.

The wind prevented our sailing until 9 o'clock in the morning of Tuesday the 16th, when a patch of rocks was discovered that had not more than three fathoms water over them about half a cable's length from the ship's anchorage, bearing by compass W.N.W. By eight in the evening we had reached nearly the western extent of this channel, and finding soundings near the eastern shore in 35 fathoms water, we anchored for the night. In this situation, the N.E. point of the Canal de Principe bore by compass N. 66 W., about a league distant; its N.W. point S. 72 W.; this latter is the north point of Banks's island, and is situated in latitude 53° 39½, longitude 229° 47′.[4] The nearest shore E.N.E. about three cables' length distant.

This channel, from the north point of entrance into Nepean's sound, to the north of Banks's island, extends first in a direction N. 43 W., to the south point of Puerto del Canaveral, and from thence to its N.W. point N. 63 W., in all about fourteen leagues. The southern shore is nearly straight and compact, without soundings, the northern shore is much broken, bounded by many rocks and islets, and affording soundings in several places. On the south-west side the acclivity is the greatest, but both sides of the channel may be considered as elevated land, and are intirely covered with pine trees, which seemed to

___

[1] Vancouver's latitudes at this time were usually within a minute or two of correct, and the 'small opening' was probably the S entrance to Ala Passage, in lat. 53° 28′ N. It was certainly not the present Port Stephens, which is in lat. 53° 19′ 30″ N. Ala Passage here has the appearance of an inlet, and is the only opening on the E side of Principe Channel that bears the least resemblance to Duncan's sketch. Duncan gives the lat. as 53° 30′ N.

[2] Puerto de Canaveral, now Petrel Channel, extends from Principe Channel to Ogden Channel and separates Pitt Island from McCauley Island.

[3] Freberg Islet, in lat. 53° 30′ N, long. 131° 01′ W (229° 59′ E).

[4] Deadman Islet, close to the N extremity of Banks Island, is in lat. 53° 38′ N, long. 130° 28′ W (229° 32′ E).

be produced principally from a soil of decayed vegetables in the chasms of the rocks. The shores abounded with a great number of very shy sea otters.

Light variable winds, attended by dark gloomy weather, detained us at anchor until four on the morning of Thursday the 18th, when we weighed, in company with the Chatham. We had a moderate breeze from the westward, with cloudy weather, that soon turned to drizzling rain, approaching nearly to a fog; we continued, however, to turn towards the ocean, and by eight in the evening, gained a good offing between Queen Charlotte's islands and the north-west part of Pitt's archipelago, where we found a good space to work in, the wind blowing N.N.W. exactly in the direction we wanted to steer. Our soundings, during the night, were between 30 and 40 fathoms muddy bottom; but in the morning of Friday the 19th, we passed over a bank of sand and shells, on which there was only from twenty-three to twenty-five fathoms; but the depth suddenly increased on each side to thirty fathoms water, muddy bottom.

The wind was now at N.N.W., blowing a fresh gale, with hazy weather, the land of Queen Charlotte's island was in sight, but the haze prevented our distinguishing any of its conspicuous points. At noon, the north-west point of Banks's island bore by compass S. 83 E., the island of Bonilla[1] S. 55 E., and the northernmost land in sight, N. 55 E. The latitude observed was 53° 46′, longitude 229° 20′.

From this station we ran five miles W.S.W. in twenty-one fathoms water, sandy and shelly bottom; this I considered to be a continuation of the bank we had crossed in the morning. The wind still remaining unfavorable, we continued to ply all night with soundings from twenty-five to fifty-three fathoms; the bottom at the latter depth black sand and mud, at the former light brown sand and shells.

The next morning, Saturday the 20th, we had again an indistinct view of Queen Charlotte's islands; but the wind veering to the S.E., accompanied by thick misty weather, they were soon again obscured.

About noon, the wind freshened with all the appearance of an approaching gale, and rendered our situation by no means so pleasant as could have been wished. By the transient view we had had of the shores to the north of us, they appeared broken, and bounded with many rocky islets and rocks. We had now passed the north point of Stephens's island, which bore by compass S. 84 E., at the distance of two leagues, and were a-breast of the opening through which, from Chatham's sound, Mr. Whidbey had seen the ocean; but at too great a distance to discern the innumerable rocky islets and rocks that nearly occupied the whole passage leading out. These dangers, the gloominess of the weather, and the impending gale from the S.E., combined to give this unexplored channel an appearance so forlorn, as scarcely to admit the idea of its being navigable. I was still very unwilling to abandon the prospect we now had, of speedily arriving at the station to which our boats had already

[1] Bonilla Island, SW of the N end of Banks Island.

traced the boundaries of the continental shore; and for this reason I directed our course towards the intricate inhospitable labyrinth, lying between us and the point I was so anxious to gain; in the hope, that amongst the numerous islets and rocks, some place of secure anchorage might be found, until the weather should become more favorable to our views. As we advanced our prospects became less flattering. The lucid intervals of the mist only exhibited our situation to be more intricate and dangerous, by discovering rocks and breakers that had not been seen before. In this painful situation of care and apprehension, I experienced no small degree of relief, by unexpectedly discovering a whale-boat rowing towards the ship; we instantly brought to, and on the officer coming on board, I learned that he belonged to the Butterworth of London, then at anchor in a very commodious place, on the eastern side of the rocky group before us, whither he very civilly offered to conduct us. We made sail immediately for the channel we had before been steering for, which was the same as that by which the Butterworth had entered the sound, between the northernmost of the above group of islets, breakers, and rocks, and a ledge of sunken rocks to the north, on which the sea broke only at intervals. We reached our promised station about six in the evening, and anchored in company with the Chatham, in thirty-six fathoms water.[1] The Butterworth, Prince Lee Boo, and Jackall schooner, belonging to the same concern, we found riding here, under the orders of Mr. Brown, commander of the Butterworth, who saluted us with seven guns, which compliment was returned by five.

Soon after we had anchored, Mr. Brown visited the Discovery, and I believe I may venture to assert, that the satisfaction arising from meeting with our fellow countrymen in such distant regions of the globe, was very mutual on this occasion. Mr. Brown informed me, that he had spent some time in this immediate neighbourhood, and on coming out of a harbour that lies to the N.N.W. of this station, about three leagues distant, his ship had struck upon a rock that seemed to be a small pinnacle situated by itself, as no soundings were gained near it; the ship remained but a short time upon the rock before the rising of the sea disengaged her, though not without knocking off her rudder. This however was fortunately recovered, and its damages were nearly repaired.

Whilst the Butterworth had remained stationary, Mr. Brown had been employed in his small vessels in various directions, and to some extent, about this coast, particularly to the north-westward, in procuring of furs. He very obligingly communicated to me every information he had been able to obtain. The principal circumstance was that of his having sailed up a large opening, whose southern entrance was in latitude 54° 45'.

[1] Captain Walbran, who had an intimate knowledge of the coast, believed that the ships were in Qlawdzeet Anchorage, on the E side of the N extremity (Hooper Point) of Stephens Island, but Vancouver's chart indicates that they had taken shelter behind one of the small islands to the N – probably Rushton Island, the largest of the Tree Nob Group.

This is probably the same as that laid down in Senr Caamano's chart, named *Estrecho de Almirante Fuentes.*[1] Mr. Brown found it extend to the north-westward, with several arms branching from it in various directions to the latitude of 56° 20'; where, in a south-westerly direction, it again communicated with the North Pacific. He had understood, from the natives, that there was in this neighbourhood a very extensive inland navigation, communicating with a sea to the northward, that employed the inhabitants nearly three months in reaching its extent, where they traded for whale oil, sea otter skins, and other marine productions. This inland navigation Mr. Brown supposed to be in an extensive arm, lying from hence towards the N.N.E. about nine leagues distant;[2] the entrance of which he had visited, and found it spacious and large, but had not penetrated any distance into it. At its south-east point of entrance a small branch extended to the south-eastward,[3] up which he proceeded with his sloop and schooner about six miles, where they anchored before a village of the natives, whose improper conduct made it necessary to fire upon them from the vessels, which was attended with some slaughter.

As these openings were near the continent, some leagues to the northward of Mr. Whidbey's late excursion, they would, it was probable, fall under our future inspection; this made me particular in my inquiries respecting those shores, about which Mr. Brown stated that there were many lurking rocks; and as it was probable that there were others that had escaped his notice, he obligingly offered me one of his small vessels to precede us, and sound the channel, and begged I would retain her as long as I should find it expedient; which very kind offer I readily accepted.

The weather became more temperate the following morning, Sunday the 21st, yet the land was so obscured by the haze, that it was late in the forenoon before we could get any tolerable view of the surrounding shores; when, the north part of Stephens's island bore by compass S. 20 E. to S. 9 E., distant half a league;[4] the north extreme of the rocky group N. 58 W., distant three miles, part of the ledge of rocks forming the north side of the passage by which we had entered the sound, N. 31 W. to N. 20 W., distant four miles and an half. This passage, after the commander of the Butterworth, I named BROWN'S PASSAGE.[5] The westernmost part of the land, forming the north side of Brown's passage, bore N. 52 W. eight miles; the easternmost point of the same land being an island, N. 9 E. seven miles; and an intermediate point of the same shore N. 37 W., distant six miles; between this land and the above ledge of rocks are other rocks and two islets; the northernmost part of the east side

---

[1] The Estrecho del Almirante Fontes. Wagner refers to it as 'one of Jacinto Caamano's fancies'; its identity is uncertain. *Cartography of The Northwest Coast*, II, 455.
[2] Portland Inlet.   [3] Work Channel.
[4] This distance should probably be one league, not half a league; Rushton Island is three miles from Stephens Island. The other bearings and distances given, with one exception, support the surmise that Vancouver's ships anchored off Rushton Island.
[5] Now Brown Passage. Butterworth Rocks, Jackal Point and Prince Leboo Island (not named by Vancouver), all in this region, commemorate the visit of Brown's ships.

of the sound in sight N. 13 E.; a group of islands from N. 35 E. to N. 40 E.; a saddle island from N. 74 E. to N. 77 E.; another group from N. 80 E. to N. 84 E.; point Hunt, S. 75 E.; distant fourteen miles; and the station to which Mr. Whidbey had traced the continental boundary, being a small projecting point with an island to the south of it, N. 28 E. eleven miles distant.[1]

Having thus gained a very competent view of the surrounding region in all directions, Mr. Whidbey was dispatched in the large cutter, to recommence his examination of the continental shore towards the above N.N.E. opening. In this pursuit I purposed to follow him with the vessels. About eleven, in company with the Chatham, and the sloop Prince Lee Boo sounding a-head, we again departed; on this occasion the Butterworth saluted us as on our arrival, which was returned in the same manner.

The anchorage we had quitted, situated in latitude 54° 18′, longitude 229° 28′,[2] is on the eastern side of a range of innumerable rocky islets and rocks, extending from the north side of Stephens's island N. 30 W., about a league and a half, and occupying a space of about two miles in width. To the westward of this group, at the distance of two or three miles, lies a low detached rock with some breakers near it; there are other lurking rocks, lying about the same distance from the west side of Stephens's island.

As the day advanced the weather became serene and pleasant; and as the wind was favorable, we made a very good progress along the eastern shores of the sound. These were low, and somewhat indented with small bays, but were bounded by a reef of rocks at the distance of a quarter of a mile from the shore. The more interior country was composed of a lofty range of mountains covered with perpetual snow. These, as well as the islands of the sound, produced a great number of pine trees, though apparently of no great size. In the evening we passed two clusters of low rocks, with some breakers about them to the west of us, as also the north point of the island forming the west side of Chatham's sound to the northward of Brown's passage. This island, in a direction N. 20 W., is fifteen miles long, and five miles broad from east to west. To this island I gave the name of DUNDAS'S ISLAND, after the Right Honorable Henry Dundas.[3]

To the north of this island we had a distinct view of the ocean to the westward, through a spacious channel that appeared free from interruption; and by the sun-set we entered the arm, up which we expected to find this extensive inland navigation. To its south-east point of entrance I gave the name

---

[1] Ryan Point, with Tugwell Island S of it. The distance from Rushton Island is about 14 miles rather than the 11 miles Vancouver suggests. Though neither Puget in his log nor Vancouver in his narrative gives any details, it is evident that Whidbey's expedition had gone some distance N of the mouth of the Skeena River. Puget notes that they turned back 'having carried the Continent to 54° 27″ (his log, 12 July); there is a discrepancy in lat. as Ryan Point is at 54° 22′ N, but conditions for observations were not favourable.

[2] Rushton Island is in lat. 54° 16′ N, long. 130° 49′ W (229° 11′ E).

[3] Vancouver lumps together the four Dundas Islands – Dundas (much the largest), Baron, Dunira and Melville.

of POINT MASKELYNE, after the astronomer royal; it is situated in latitude 54° 42½',[1] and longitude 229° 45',[2] and off it lie two rocky islets, and to the south of it a small island close to the shore.

The apparent extent of this inlet did not answer my expectations, from the description that had been given of it. Its entrance is not more than two miles and a half across, and this, at the distance of a few miles, seemed to be materially contracted. If this be the same branch described by the natives, which is much to be questioned, especially as some of Mr. Brown's gentlemen considered the opening meant by those people to be further to the westward,[3] it is called by them *Ewen Nass*. The word *Ewen* we understood to signify great, or powerful; as, *Ewen Smoket*, a great chief; but the word *Nass* was completely unknown to Mr. Brown, and all of his party.[4]

The divided country we had now examined, from the forty-seventh degree of north latitude to this station, and the information derived from Mr. Brown, rendered it highly probable that the continental shore still continued to have extensive islands lying between it and the ocean, to a very considerable distance further north.

The length of time which, as Mr. Brown understood, occupied these people in making so distant a journey, may be accounted for by their tardy mode of travelling through each others dominions, or in passing through the various windings and crooked shallow channels, many of which, though sufficient for their canoes, were very probably unfit for the navigation of shipping. I have ever found it extremely hard, almost impossible, indeed, to make the inhabitants of these remote parts, and even the Sandwich islanders, with whose language we are much better acquainted, comprehend the kind of passage that is required for ships to pass through, or the kind of port or opening in the land that is capable of affording them safe and convenient shelter. In addition to which difficulty selfish or sinister views too frequently regulate them, in the information they communicate. Be this as it may, it was our business now to determine the question, and embracing the favorable opportunity of a fair wind, we steered up the inlet, and were joined by Mr. Whidbey in the cutter,

[1] Misprinted 24° 42½' in the second edition.

[2] Nevil Maskeleyne, Astonomer Royal from 1765 to his death in 1811. In 1766 he published the first number of that invaluable aid to seamen, the *Nautical Almanac*. Maskelyne Point, on Maskelyne Island, at the entrance to Portland Inlet, is in lat. 54° 39' N, long. 130° 27' W (229° 33' E).

[3] Clarence Strait, to the NW, was probably the waterway meant.

[4] Portland Inlet, into which the Nass River flows, was the dividing line between the territories occupied by the Tsimshian Indians to the S and the Tlingit to the N. Archdeacon Collison, who was well acquainted with the Indian languages, explained the name of the river in a letter to Walbran: 'The term Nass is from the Tlingit tongue, and when, as was probable, the Tlingits from Tongass, at the entrance of Observatory Inlet, met Captain Vancouver they gave him their name for the river, *i.e.*, Nass, which means literally "the stomach," from the fact that their food supplies of salmon, oolachan, &c., came from there; then, as now, a noted fishery.' – John T. Walbran, *British Columbia Coast Names* (Ottawa, 1909), p. 352.

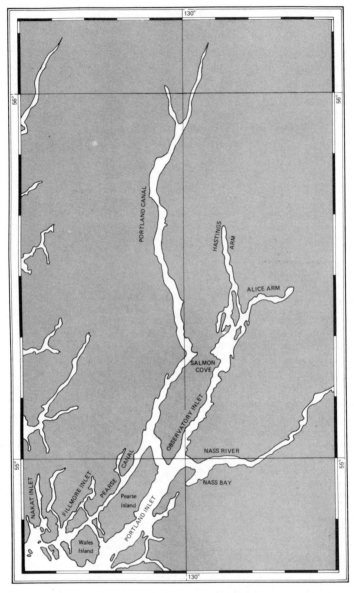

Figure 7. Portland Canal and Observatory Inlet. *Base map by Michael E. Leek.*

who had traced the continental shore to point Maskelyne; where, on its becoming broken, he had desisted from any further examination until a future opportunity.

From point Maskelyne, the two clusters of low rocks and breakers before noticed, lie, the northernmost S. 28 W. eight miles, and the southernmost S. 33 W. distant ten miles and a half; these, in the day time, and in clear weather, are easily avoided, as there are always some of them above the surface of the water; but in dark nights, or foggy weather, they must render the navigation of the sound very dangerous. After passing between the northern cluster of these rocks, and the continental shore, with which they form a channel about a mile in width, we had about that distance from the main land, soundings at the depth of 45, 55, 30, 19, 12, and 8 fathoms, soft bottom; the latter about half a mile from point Maskelyne. No bottom was however gained, after passing that point with 60 and 70 fathoms of line, until ten at night, when the Prince lee Boo having reached the contracted part of the inlet, made the signal for having soundings and anchorage. We arrived at this station about eleven, and anchored in 35 fathoms water, soft bottom, after passing two openings on the eastern shore,[1] besides that immediately round point Maskelyne, where Mr. Brown had had his dispute with the natives.[2]

We found our station the next morning, Monday the 22d, to be off the north-west part of an island, lying near the eastern shore,[3] and further up the inlet than those in the sloop had yet been; no information from them could therefore be any longer of use, though a continuation of their services would have been very acceptable. This made me regret, that we had not one or two vessels of thirty or forty tons burthen, calculated as well for rowing as for sailing, to assist us in this intricate investigation, by which means much dispatch would have been given to our survey, and our labours would have been carried on with much less danger and hardship than we had constantly endured.

I intended to proceed up this inlet, until I should see sufficient employment for two boat parties, which I was convinced the surrounding region would soon afford; and also to seek a convenient situation where the vessels might remain; and whilst this service was executing, to embrace the opportunity for making such astrononical observations as might be procured, and which were become necessary for correcting our survey, and ascertaining with precision the situation of the several parts of the broken region, through which we had passed in the vessels and in the boats from Restoration cove to this inlet. Pursuant to this determination we weighed about seven in the morning, and the Prince le Boo[4] returned to the Butterworth.

[1] Emma Passage and Steamer Passage.
[2] The entrance to Work Channel.
[3] Truro Island near the S end of the much larger Somerville Island.
[4] The name is spelled wrongly in both editions.

At our anchorage, lying from point Maskelyne N. 24 E., distant six miles, the width of the inlet was scarcely half a league. On the western shore a small opening appeared to branch off in different directions.[1] North of the island the breadth of the inlet increased again to about two or three miles, trending N. 39 E. In pursuing this line about four miles, we passed the south point of an opening on the eastern shore two miles wide, appearing to divide itself into several arms;[2] but the western shore seemed to be compact, from the opening opposite the anchorage, until we arrived abreast of an opening, about two miles wide at its entrance, on the western shore,[3] seemingly divided into two or three branches, taking a direction about N. 18 W. The observed latitude at this time was 54° 58′, longitude 230° 3′.[4] The branch of the inlet we were now navigating was not of greater width, nor did it appear likely to become more extensive, than that to the westward of us just discovered. This made it uncertain which to consider as the main branch. Four other openings had been passed on the eastern shore, whose extent had not yet been ascertained; and although I was much inclined to follow the north-westerly branch, yet I was apprehensive, that by so doing we might be led too far from the continent, and by that means cause additional labour and loss of time. Our route was, for this reason, continued to the N.N.E., and another division of the inlet stretching to the eastward[5] was soon discovered.

In the event of a convenient situation being found in this branch, I intended to stop the vessels there, and made the Chatham's signal, who had preceded us during the forenoon, to steer for the eastern opening, and shortened sail for the purpose of sending a boat before us to sound. Whilst we lay to wait the boat's return, a few of the natives visited the ship in five or six canoes; they brought little to dispose of, yet appeared to be anxious that we should remain in their neighbourhood. Several inquiries were made for *Ewen Nass*, but these people seemed to be totally ignorant of the phrase,[6] until it had been repeated several times, and we had pointed in various directions; upon which, some of them repeated the words, and imitated our motions, giving some amongst us reason to imagine, that they meant that *Ewen Nass* was up this identical branch of the inlet; though in all other respects we remained totally ignorant of their language.

The appearance and direction of this opening, however, by no means

---

[1] Wales Passage, opposite Truro Island.

[2] The broadening of Portland Inlet out of which branch Nasoga Gulf, Kwinamass Bay and the E portion of Steamer Passage.

[3] The entrance to the Portland Canal.

[4] The lat. is correct; the long. would be about 130° 06′ W (229° 54′ E).

[5] Nass Bay, the estuary of the Nass River. Here Portland Inlet ends and divides into Observatory Inlet, which the ships followed, and Portland Canal.

[6] Although Vancouver evidently happened to meet a number of Tlingit Indians as he was about to enter Portland Inlet, this inlet, Portland Canal and Observatory Inlet were all inhabited by Tsimshian Indians, unfamiliar with the term 'Nass', which, as already noted, was of Tlingit origin.

favored the opinion, that it was an extensive channel communicating with the ocean to the north. The water that flowed from it remained, without mixing, on the surface of the water of the inlet. The upper water was nearly fresh, of a lightish colour, interspersed with thick muddy sheets, indicating it to have flowed from a small river whose source was not very remote.[1]

At three o'clock the cutter returned, with a very unfavorable account of the place so far as their examination had gone; especially on the northern side of the opening, from whence a shallow flat extended some distance, on which there was not more than from one to three fathoms water. The latter depth suddenly increased to 30, and, at the distance of a cable's length from the edge of the bank, to 50 and 60 fathoms. This shallow flat made the communication with the shore very unpleasant, and appeared to be continued all round. To those in the cutter the opening seemed to be nothing more than a deep bay with very shallow water, excepting in its north-east part, where a branch from which the muddy water flowed, seemed to extend into the country. Across this branch they had also sounded, and found shallow water. As it did not, from this report, seem likely to answer our purpose, we proceeded round its north point of entrance, and again made sail up the inlet, which, beyond this bay, was in general about half a league wide. The shores on both sides were nearly straight and compact; in this pursuit our progress was greatly retarded by a counter tide, or under tow, and notwithstanding that we had a fresh gale from the south-east, the strength of this repelling current was such, that the wind had no influence whatever, though in other situations the vessel with such a gale would have gone five or six knots per hour. On this occasion the ship became totally unmanageable; the wind was sometimes a-head, at others a-stern, a-broadside, and in every other direction; and we were drifting from side to side in the most unpleasant situation imaginable for two hours and a half, when the force of the wind prevailing, we advanced slowly up the inlet until about eleven at night. The distance of its shores had now again increased, and the country became less elevated. A small cove was discovered on the eastern shore,[2] where we anchored in 30 fathoms water.

This place, however, not appearing likely to suit our purpose, Mr. Whidbey was dispatched early the next morning in quest of a more convenient situation, which the adjacent shores promised to afford, particularly in the northern quarter, where the land was moderately elevated, and seemed to be much broken. The interior country was, however, still composed of lofty, barren, and snowy mountains.

In the forenoon Mr. Whidbey returned, having examined two or three coves, of which the most eligible appeared to be one that we had passed in the dark the preceding evening on the western shore, nor more than a mile

---

[1] As noted in the next paragraph, the lower reaches of the Nass are filled with sand-flats and give the impression, especially at the low water season, that the river is much smaller than it is. It is not navigable, and the shallow channel shifts with each freshet.

[2] The ships evidently anchored in the bend of the inlet N of Dawkins Point.

from our actual station.[1] This afforded good anchorage, with every other convenience that we required. Having a moderate breeze from the southward, we lost no time in proceeding thither, where we anchored in 31 and 35 fathoms water, muddy and small-stony bottom. The points of the cove bore by compass N.N.E. and S. by E., the nearest shore W. by S., about a cable and a half distant, and the opposite shore of the inlet E.N.E., one mile distant.

On going on shore, we found a small canoe with three of the natives, who were employed in taking salmon, which were in great abundance, up a very fine run of fresh water that flowed into the cove.[2] Some of these fish were purchased with looking glasses and other trinkets. They were small, insipid, of a very inferior kind, and partaking in no degree of the flavor of European salmon.

In the afternoon, the tents, observatory, chronometers, and instruments, were sent on shore, under the directions of Mr. Whidbey; and Mr. Johnstone in the Chatham's cutter, accompanied by Mr. Barrie in the Discovery's small cutter, and supplied with ten days provisions, departed for the purpose of recommencing the survey of the continental shore, northward from point Maskelyne.

The account I had received of this famous inlet from Mr. Brown, inducing me to undertake the principal examination of it myself, the Discovery's yawl and launch were equipped with supplies for a fortnight, being as much as they could possibly stow; Lieutenant Swaine was directed to attend me in the latter, and Mr. Puget, with Mr. Menzies, accompanied me in the yawl. The appearance of the country, on the western side of this inlet, left me little doubt of its being the continent; and we departed in full expectation, that, during this excursion, we should finally determine the reality of the discoveries attributed to the labours of Admiral de Fonte.

With Mr. Whidbey I left the charge of the observatory, with orders to make all necessary observations for correcting the errors, and ascertaining the rate of the chronometers; and the more completely to effect the former, I desired that Mr. Baker, and some others of the gentlemen, would assist in making as many observations as the circumstances would admit of, for determining the true position of the station we had taken.

[1] Salmon Cove.
[2] Menzies commented: 'This being about the beginning of the Spawning season for Salmon on this Coast, a stream of fresh water that emptied into the bay swarm'd with them, though there was scarcely water sufficient to cover them, so that they could be caught with the hand in any quantity we chose; in shooting the Seine across the entrance of this Stream it surrounded such a prodigious quantity of these Salmon that it was impossible to haul them all on shore without endangering the Seine, they therefore took what quantity they pleas'd & sufferd the rest to escape.' – July 23. All accounts agree that the numbers taken were immense. 'P.M. hauled the seine and caught near 2000 salmon in one haul.' – Orchard, July 26. Heddington states that 'the Discovery at one haul of the Seine catch'd 3000'. – August 17.

CHAPTER V.

An extensive Boat Excursion—Party attacked by the Natives—Astronomical and Nautical Observations.

MATTERS being all adjusted and arranged, we departed at five o'clock on Wednesday morning the 24th, in thick, rainy, unfavorable weather, which continued until the forenoon, when it became fair and pleasant. Our course was first directed along the eastern shore, which, from our anchorage on the night of the 22d, took a direction N. 14 E. for six miles. We passed an island to the west of us, two miles long and half a mile broad,[1] lying nearly in the same direction, about three fourths of a mile from the eastern shore; and having reached this extent, we entered a narrow arm,[2] leaving to the west a coast apparently much broken, and divided by water.

As we rapidly advanced up this arm, with a southerly wind, and a flood tide in our favor, its width increased to about a mile, and taking a winding course to the E.N.E., it was terminated by a low border of land, in latitude 55° 26′, longitude 230° 36′.[3]

We stopped to dine about a mile short of the low border of land, which composed the head of the arm. Here we were visited by seven of the natives, who approached us in a canoe with much caution, and landed some of their party at a little distance, whilst the others advanced, seemingly with no small suspicion of our friendly intentions; this, however, was soon removed by the distribution of some trivial presents amongst them; and their reception being made known to their companions who had landed, these without the least hesitation joined our party also. They were well prepared with arms, consisting of long spears, bows and arrows, together with an iron dagger, that each man wore about his neck or wrist. The chief of this party was soon pointed out, who, by means of signs easily understood, desired to partake of our repast. He was given some bread and dried fish, and afterwards a glass of brandy, all which were much relished by himself, and two or three of his friends. These people differed very little from the generality of the circumjacent natives, and rather seemed to be an exception to the trivial differences pointed out in those

---

[1] Brooke Island.
[2] Alice Arm.
[3] The correct position would be approximately lat. 55° 28′ N, long. 129° 28′ W (230° 32′ E).

few inhabitants who visited us in Fishmonger's cove.[1] Their language appeared to be similar in some respects to that spoken at Queen Charlotte's islands, at least a few common-place expressions of that language were understood by these people. They made use of these, with many signs, to solicit us to visit their habitations, pointing out their situation to be on the low land, at the head of the arm; but as it was out of our route, we declined their invitations, and, with a favorable ebb tide, returned towards the entrance of the arm, being accompanied by these our new acquaintances, who were soon joined by another party from the village in a smaller canoe. On finding, however, that we did not return for the purpose of trading, they all retired to the village.[2]

About eight in the evening we reached the entrance of this arm, where we took up our abode for the night. The land of the shores which we had thus traced, was, comparatively speaking, low, yet the interior country rose suddenly, and terminated our view by a range of high barren mountains, mostly covered with snow. The soil of the lower parts near the shores, is chiefly composed of a light mossy substance, formed by the decay of trees and other vegetable productions, lying on an uneven rocky substance, which is the general foundation of this country, and of all the coast we had yet seen this season.

At four o'clock the next morning, Thursday the 25th, we proceeded again, with thick cloudy weather, attended with some flying showers of rain. Our course was directed up the branch that appeared to be the main arm of the inlet, through a narrow passage, occasioned by an island lying in mid-channel, about a league long,[3] and three quarters of a mile broad, and having near it some rocks and breakers, like that we passed the preceding day. From the west point of the arm we had quitted, that which we were now pursuing[4] extended N. 20 W. nearly straight, about ten miles; where, as usual, it was terminated by low swampy ground; and in latitude 55° 32′, longitude 230° 16′.[5] Our expectations of discovering the extensive inland navigation, distinguished by the name of *Ewen-Nass*, were here a little disappointed; still, however, we entertained hopes of succeeding, by the appearance of the low land on the western shore; and we returned in the afternoon to prosecute its examination. It was found to be a compact shore, much indented with small bays and coves, and abounding in some places with sunken rocks. In the south-westernmost of these coves,[6] which is the deepest, we halted for the night; and although a situation for our tents was fixed upon amongst the pine-trees, at least twenty feet above the surface of the water at our landing, and as we thought sufficiently without the reach of the tide, yet, about two

[1] Fisherman Cove is meant. [2] These were Tsimshian Indians.
[3] Larcom Island.
[4] Hastings Arm of Observatory Inlet.
[5] The correct position is lat. 55° 38′ N, long. 129° 48′ W (230° 12′ E).
[6] Granby Bay. Anyox, once an important mining and smelting centre, is at the entrance to this bay.

in the morning of Friday the 26th, it flowed into the tents, and we were obliged
to retire to our boats. At day-light we pursued the western shore of the inlet,
towards the ships, where we arrived about noon.

I now entertained no doubt of this being the continental shore; and it was
equally evident to me, that it extended itself far up that branch which we had
passed in the afternoon of the 22d, leading to the N.N.W. Having therefore
determined to prosecute my researches in that quarter, our stock of provisions
was recruited; and, after dining on board, we recommenced our examination
along the western shore of the inlet, and rested for the night in a small cove,
about twelve miles to the southward of the ships. The afternoon and night
were very rainy and unpleasant, but early the next morning, Saturday the 27th,
we set out, with fair weather, and having a rapid tide in our favor, soon reached
the east point of entrance into the N.N.W. branch; which, after Mr.
Ramsden, the optician, I called POINT RAMSDEN, lying in latitude 54° 59',
longitude 230° 2½'.[1] Off this point are some dangerous rocks, that are visible
only at low tide; from hence we directed our course N.W. three miles to a
low point on the larboard shore, where we found this arm to communicate
with another, leading in a S.W. and N.N.E. direction,[2] and being in general
about half a league in width. After breakfast, we pursued the latter direction,
and steered for the eastern or continental shore. This extends first from point
Ramsden N. 21 W. six miles, and takes a N.N.E. course.

As we advanced, we were joined by a party of fifteen natives in two canoes.
A smoke had before been observed amongst the trees on the eastern shore,
but we then saw no appearance of any habitations. These people approached
us without much hesitation, and in their countenances was expressed a degree
of savage ferocity infinitely surpassing any thing of the sort I had before
observed in the various tribes that had fallen under my notice. Many of those
we had before seen had their faces painted in various modes; but these had
contrived so to dispose of the red, white, and black, as to render the natural
ugliness of their countenances more horribly hideous. This frightful appearance
did not seem to be a new fashion among them, but to have been long adopted
by their naturally ferocious dispositions, and was correspondent to the stern
and savage deportment they took so much pains to exhibit. I offered them
such presents as we had been accustomed to make on similar occasions, but
they were rejected by some with disdain, whilst the few who deigned to accept
any thing, received our gifts with a stern and cool indifference. Amongst the
party was a woman who was additionally disfigured by one of those
extraordinary lip ornaments; this did not a little augment her froward,[3]

[1] Jesse Ramsden, F.R.S., a noted instrument maker. Some of the instruments in the
Discovery and *Chatham* had been supplied by him. He made great improvements in the
sextant which increased its accuracy. Ramsden Point is in lat. 54° 59' N, long. 130° 06' W
(229° 54' E).

[2] Pearse Canal to the SW; Portland Canal to the NNW. The international boundary
between British Columbia and Alaska runs through the middle of these two canals.

[3] Perverse or refractory (arch.). OED.

shrewish aspect. I offered her a looking glass, with some trinkets, but, at the instance of the most savage fellow of the party, she contemptuously rejected them. This Indian then arranged his spears, about six or eight in number, and placed them with their points just over the bow of the canoe, near where he sat; he also laid near him his bow with some arrows; then put on his war garment, and drew his dagger. Some in the other canoe made similar preparations, either to menace an attack, or, what seemed to us more likely, to convince us they were upon their guard against any violence we might be inclined to offer them.[1]

At this time we were considerably a-head of the other boat; and as it was necessary that we should shortly land on the point from whence the continent takes its N.N.E. direction, for the purpose of taking angles, we waited for the launch to come up; and during this interval, we used our endeavours to gain the confidence, and, if possible, to conciliate the good opinion of our visitors. But all was to no effect; they refused to accept any more presents, whilst those who had condescended to receive any, made signs that we should go to their place of abode, which we had by this time passed; and frequently made use of the words 'Winnee watter,' signifying to stop and trade,[2] producing at the same time some very indifferent sea otter skins. Recollecting the avidity with which all the inhabitants of these parts enter into commercial intercourse, I thought their uncourteous behaviour might have arisen from our backwardness in following the same pursuit; and hoped, by offering to trade with them, we should be able to obtain their friendship. But neither cloth, iron, copper, nor any thing we had, was in their opinions sufficient in quantity, or equal in quality, to the value of their skins; which were, without exception, the worst I had yet seen on the coast. On the launch coming up, we pulled towards the shore; they now seemed better pleased, and on landing they offered their skins again for sale, but it was not within our reach to purchase them. Whilst we remained together on shore, their behaviour was more civil, and we seemed to part on much better terms than we had met.

---

[1] Puget felt that the Indians had attack rather than defence in mind: 'Finding they were inclined to be troublesome, we got some of the Fire Arms ready the Hint was sufficient, for the Indians soon returned the War Garment & Dagger to their former Situation.' – July 27. Except for an occasional detail, Puget's account of this encounter parallels Vancouver's very closely.

[2] Gunther notes that this was 'the usual call of the Indians when they were asking for trade.' Menzies was interested in the relationships of the various Indian languages, and here put into practice his simple means of testing this: 'By prevailing on some of these Natives to repeat their numerals, we found they spoke a broken dialect of what we call the Woaganian language or that which is spoken along the Coast between Admiralty Bay & Queen Charlotte's Isles, of which we had a short vocabulary. On our reciting the numerals of Nepean's Sound & those of Queen Charlotte's Isles they perfectly understood both & pointed in the direction in which each were used.' – July 27. The Indians at Nepean Sound were Tsimshians; those on the Queen Charlotte Island were Haida. Although their aggressiveness suggests the Tlingit, who lived just to the N, these Indians were probably Tsimshians.

They remained at the point, and we proceeded up the arm. Their absence, however, was not of long duration, as they shortly followed us, waving their skins, and exposing them for sale; and it was not a little extraordinary, that they should now exchange their skins, and other articles of traffic, for the very identical commodities which they had before rejected with so much contempt.

It was not easy to account for the singular appearance and rude behaviour of this tribe, so very different from what we had hitherto experienced; some amongst us suggested, that these people might probably belong to that party on whom Mr. Brown had recently been obliged to fire in this neighbourhood, and at no great distance from our actual station; but it appeared to me far more likely, that their resentment had been excited by our perfect indifference to their commodities brought for sale, and our having declined their invitations to the place of their abode. This opinion was soon confirmed by their subsequent conduct; on being now offered blue cloth for their skins, they began a song, that continued until they came close to us, when I observed that their arms and war garments were all laid aside; and having disposed of such things as they had for sale, they began to betray a somewhat thievish disposition. I endeavoured to make them sensible of my disapprobation of this conduct, and made signs that they should depart, with which they reluctantly complied.

I did not observe that these people differed from the generality of the North West Americans, otherwise than in the ferocity of their countenances.[1] Their weapons seemed well adapted to their condition; their spears, about sixteen feet long, were pointed with iron, wrought in several simple forms, amongst which some were barbed. Their bows were well constructed, and their arrows, with which they were plentifully supplied, appeared but rude, and were pointed with bone or iron. Each man was provided with an iron dagger, suspended from his neck in a leather sheath, seemingly intended to be used when in close action. Their war garments were formed of two, three, or more folds, of the strongest hides of the land animals they are able to procure. In the centre was a hole sufficient to admit the head and left arm to pass through; the mode of wearing them being over the right shoulder, and under the left arm. The left side of the garment is sewed up, but the right side remains open; the body is however tolerably well protected, and both arms are left at liberty for action. As a further security on the part which covers the breast, they sometimes fix on the inside thin laths of wood; the whole is seemingly well contrived, and I doubt not answers the essential purpose of protection against their native weapons.

The weather though pleasant was unfortunately cloudy about noon, and

[1] 'These People appeared taller and more robust than any I have particularly noticed and the Natural Ferocity of their Countenances was if possible made more hideous, by a Mixture of Red and Black Paint laid on indiscriminately on every part of the Face.' 'Their only Ornaments was a Collar of Copper or Iron made of a large Kind of Wire & four parts twisted together.' – Puget, July 27.

prevented any observation being made for the latitude. The same unfavorable circumstance attended us during our excursion to the northward of the vessels. We continued to the N.N.E., without meeting any interruption or break in the shores until about eight in the evening, when we arrived at a point on the western shore, situated in latitude 55° 16', longitude 230° 8'. Near this point we rested for the night. From hence the arm took a direction N. 15 W., continuing in general about the same width. Between us and the opposite shore was a small island nearly in mid-channel.[1]

The weather being fair and pleasant, we started early the next morning, Sunday 28th, continuing our researches up this branch. At noon the observed latitude on the eastern shore was 55° 25', the longitude 230° 5'. From hence it took a more northerly direction, and then trended a little to the eastward of north, where, by ten in the forenoon of Monday the 29th, it was found to terminate in low marshy land, in latitude 55° 45', longitude 230° 6'.[2] The shores of this inlet were nearly straight, and in general little more than a mile asunder, composed mostly of high rocky cliffs, covered with pine trees to a considerable height; but the more interior country was a compact body of high barren mountains covered with snow. As we pursued this branch, salmon in great plenty were leaping in all directions. Seals and sea otter were also seen in great numbers, even where the water was nearly fresh, and which was the case upwards of twenty miles from its termination.

Mortified with having devoted so much time to so little purpose, we made the best of our way back. At noon I observed the latitude to be 55° 42'; from whence to our reaching the western shore, near where we had entered this branch, occupied our time until late in the evening of Tuesday the 30th, when we brought to in a small cove, behind an island about half a league from us, and not far from the place where we had met the ungracious natives on the preceding Saturday.

The night was mild and pleasant, but a thick fog in the morning of Wednesday the 31st, not only obscured the surrounding shores, but prevented our departure until eight o'clock; when, on its dispersing, we directed our examination along the western, or continental shore, to the S.S.W. in a continuation of the branch we had seen on the morning of the 27th.[3] The shores of both sides were straight, compact, of moderate height, and in general little more than a mile asunder. At noon the observed latitude on the western shore was 54° 55½', longitude 229° 47'; the inlet still continuing in the same direction. On the western shore, about half a league to the southward of this station, we entered a small opening not more than a cable's length in width, stretching to the northward;[4] up this we had made a little progress, when

[1] Hattie Island, in lat. 55° 17' N, long. 129° 58' W (230° 02' E).
[2] The correct position his lat. 55° 56' N, long. 130° 00' W (230° 00' E). The town of Stewart is at the head of the Canal, at the mouth of the Bear River.
[3] Pearse Canal.
[4] Hidden Inlet: 'we came to a small narrow opening out of which the Tide came so rapid that it baffled all our endeavours to enter it till the Tide slacken'd, & we then got

the launch, which had preceded us and had reached its extremity, was met on her return. Mr. Swaine informed me, that its termination was about a league from its entrance, and that its width was from a quarter to half a league.

We stopped for the purpose of dining, and were visited by a canoe, in which were three persons; they approached us with little hesitation, and seemed well pleased on receiving a few trivial presents. They earnestly solicited our return to the head of this little arm, where, it appeared, their chief resided, and who had abundance of furs to barter for our commodities; but as it was out of our way, we declined their proposal; at which they seemed hurt and disappointed, but retired in perfect good humour.

After dinner we attempted to return by the way we had come, but on approaching the entrance, the rapidity of the flood tide prevented our advancing against it until near high water, about six in the evening. Many of the small trees, at the place where we had dined, had been cut down with an axe, an implement not yet in use with these people, who, on all such occasions, prefer any kind of chisel. The trees appeared to have been felled, for the purpose of gaining convenient access to the run of water hard by; and this gave rise to an opinion, that our dining place had lately been the resort of other civilized people.

Having again reached the arm leading to the S.S.W., we proceeded in that direction, and passed two small rocky islets, about a mile to the south of the last mentioned small arm. Finding the main channel now regularly decreasing to half a mile in width, and having a strong southerly breeze, we did not proceed more than three miles, before we rested for the night. The narrowness of the channel, and the appearance of its termination before us, would have induced me to have relinquished all thoughts of finding a communication with the ocean by this route, had it not been for the indications presented by the shores on either side. These gradually decreasing in height, with a very uneven surface, were intirely covered with pine trees; and as such appearances had, in most instances, been found to attend the broken parts of the country immediately along the sea coast, I was encouraged to persevere in this pursuit.

We had not been long landed, before the natives, who had visited us at dinner time, made their appearance again, accompanied by a large canoe, in which was the chief of their party.

I directed them to land at a small distance from our boats, with which they readily complied. The chief received some presents, and in return, gave me two or three sea otters' tails. This intercourse seemed, by our signs, and such words as we had picked up, to be an assurance of a good understanding between us; and, on a promise of entering further into trade the next morning, they retired to a small cove about half a mile from us, with every appearance of being perfectly satisfied; but, about an hour afterwards, one of their canoes was seen paddling towards us. On this a pistol was fired in the air, which had

up a small Creek leading to the northward about four Miles'. – Menzies, August 1. The inlet can only be entered at slack water, as the tide rushes through the entrance at from 8 to 10 knots.

the good effect of shewing that we were upon our guard, and prevented their giving us any further disturbance.

As soon as it was day-light in the morning of Thursday the 1st of August, these people, accompanied by another canoe, were with us according to appointment the preceding evening. They offered for sale the skins of the sea otter, and a large black bear, that seemed to have been killed by a spear in the course of the night. I was not backward in complying with our part of the agreement; but, like those whom we had seen on Saturday, these rejected every article we had with us for the purpose of barter; and, excepting fire-arms and ammunition, which were not offered to them, we could not discover on what their inclinations were placed. They followed us however for two miles, persisting in desiring we would ' *Winnee watter*,' until, at length, finding no other articles were tendered them than those they had before declined, they retired, exclaiming ' *Pusee*' and ' *Peshack*;' which could not be misunderstood as terms of disapprobation.

This party, including one woman with a lip ornament, consisted of sixteen or eighteen persons, who, in character, much resembled (though I think they were not quite so ferocious) those we had seen the preceding Saturday. This woman, as well as the other we had seen on the 27th, steered the canoe. She appeared to be a most excessive scold, and to possess great authority.[1] She had much to say respecting the whole of their transactions, and exacted the most ready obedience to her commands, which were given in a very surly manner, particularly in one instance to a man in the bow of the canoe; who, in compliance to her directions, immediately made a different disposition of the spears. These had all lain on one side of him, just pointed over the bow of the canoe, with several things carelessly lying over them; but on his receiving her commands the outer ends were projected further, their inner ends cleared of the lumber that was over them, and the whole, amounting to about a dozen, were equally divided, and regularly laid on each side of him.

From the place at which we had slept, this channel took a direction S. 42 W., about a league and a half, to a point in latitude 54° 48′, longitude 229° 39½′,[2] from whence the continental shore takes a direction N. 25 W. about a league, through a narrow channel[3] not a fourth of a mile in breadth; having in it several islets and rocks. In order to make sure of keeping the continental shore on board, we pursued this, and left the south-westerly channel, whose width had increased to about a mile, and whose shores appeared to be much broken, as if admitting several passages to the sea. At the north end of this narrow channel we came to a larger one extending N. 35 E. and S. 35 W.[4] The former first attracted our notice; this by noon was found to end in latitude 54° 55½′,

[1] Again this suggests that these Indians were Tlingit, as they were accustomed to having a vixenish woman in stern of their canoes to urge on the warriors, if need be; but Vancouver was still in the area thought to have been inhabited by the Tsimshians.

[2] The correct position would be about lat. 54° 50′ N, long. 130° 29′ W (229° 31′ E).

[3] Edward Passage.   [4] Fillmore Inlet.

longitude 229° 40′; not in low marshy land, as had been generally the case in the interior parts of our survey, but by low though steep rocky shores, forming many little bays and coves, abounding with rocks and rocky islets. Here were seen an immense number of sea otters, and amongst them some few seals, but more of the former than I had yet noticed. Having dined we pursued the examination of the continent in a south-westerly direction, which brought us by the evening to its end in that direction, in latitude 54° 48½′, longitude 229° 31½′. From hence the channel extended to the S.S.E. and met that which we had quitted in the morning,[1] making the land which formed the western shore of the narrow channel, and that before us to the eastward, an island[2] about ten miles in circuit. The shores, that had been nearly straight and compact since we had quitted the rocky arm above-mentioned, became again indented with bays and coves, bounded by many rocks and rocky islets.

In examining these broken parts of the shore, the launch had preceded the yawl whilst I was taking the necessary angles. On our turning sharp round a point, I discovered her endeavouring as I supposed to pass a most tremendous fall of water; the evening at this time was nearly closing in, and being now about high tide, the fall appeared to be adverse to their proceeding; but finding they continued to advance, I hailed, and waved them to desist. On our meeting, I found they had possessed but sufficient strength and time to extricate themselves from a very alarming situation. The direction of the fall was in a contrary line to what they had expected, as the water was rushing with great impetuosity through a narrow rocky channel, and falling into a bason whose surface appeared to be greatly beneath the level of the channel we were navigating; on their perceiving this, their utmost exertions were required for a short time, to prevent the boat from being drawn within its vortical influence.[3] About a mile from the above point, nearly in a south direction, we brought to for the night.

In the morning of Friday the 2d we set out early, and passed through a labyrinth of small islets and rocks along the continental shore; this, taking now a winding course to the south-west and west, shewed the south-eastern side of the channel to be much broken, through which was a passage leading S.S.E. towards the ocean.[4] We passed this in the hope of finding a more northern and westerly communication; in which we were not disappointed, as the channel we were then pursuing was soon found to communicate also with the sea;[5] making the land to the south of us one or more islands. From the north-west point of this land, situated in latitude 54° 45½′, longitude 229° 28′,[6]

---

[1] Pearse Canal.

[2] Fillmore Island.

[3] Presumably this incident occurred off the narrow entrance to Willard Inlet, where (in the words of the *U.S. Coast Pilot 7*) 'the currents have great velocity, forming swirls that extend well out from the mouth.' Vancouver did not explore the inlet.

[4] Tongass Passage.   [5] Through Sitklan Passage.

[6] Vancouver was evidently on the NW point of Kanagunut Island, which is in lat. 54° 45′ N, long. 130° 44′ 30″ W (229° 15′ 30″ E).

the Pacific was evidently seen between N. 88 W. and S. 81 W. Off the point, at a little distance from the main land, was an island about half a mile from us;[1] the opposite, or continental shore, lying north-east, not quite half a mile distant. Between this and the westernmost land in sight the shores appeared to be much divided, with small rocky islets and breakers in most directions. Between these and the continental shore, our way was directed N. 26 W.; at the distance of two miles was passed a large deserted village, on the north point of a small cove; which point may also be considered as the south-east point of entrance into a narrow arm, taking nearly a north direction;[2] half a league to the northward of this point the eastern shore formed three small bays or coves, with four or five islets before them.[3] On the point which divides the two southernmost of these coves, I observed the latitude to be 54° 49', the longitude 229° 29'; from whence the inlet took a direction about N. 8 W.; the shores became nearly straight and compact, and were in general about half a mile asunder. The surrounding land being of moderate height, and of that uneven surface generally exhibited by the insular countries lying on the sea coast, afforded reasonable grounds to believe the western shore to be an island; in which case we should have been enabled to trace the continental boundaries a considerable distance to the north. About six in the evening our hopes vanished, by our arriving at the head of the arm, where it terminated in a small fresh water brook, flowing from low marshy ground, in latitude 54° 56', longitude 229° 28'.[4] Before it were several rocks and some rocky islets.

This disappointment occasioned us no small degree of motification, since we had already been absent from the ship a whole week, with the finest weather the season had yet afforded; and though our utmost exertions had been called forth in tracing the continent through this labyrinth of rocks, we had not advanced more than thirteen leagues in a right line from the ships to the entrance of this inlet, and that in a south-west direction; very different from the course we could have wished to have pursued. It was also now evident that we had the exterior coast to contend with, and from the length of time we had been indulged with fine weather, we could not reasonably expect it continuing much longer; indeed, the appearance of the evening indicated an unfavorable alteration, which made me apprehensive, that probably the finest part of the season had been devoted, in our late pursuit, to a very perplexing object of no great value or consideration.

On the low land forming the upper extremity of this arm, we saw some animals like wolves, but the shallowness of the water prevented our approaching near enough to fire at them with any probability of success. From hence we returned by the western shore, passing three or four rocky islets, and rested for the night about a league to the N.N.W. of our station at noon. During the night there fell a great quantity of rain, but towards the morning

[1] Tongass Island. [2] Nakat Inlet.
[3] The three arms of Nakat Harbour.
[4] The correct position would be about lat. 54° 54' N, long. 130° 45' W (229° 15' E).

of Saturday the 3d it in some measure abated, though the weather still continued very gloomy and hazy; we had however no time to spare, and it becoming necessary that we should proceed as far as circumstances would admit, we started early, and kept along the continental shore, which was much indented with small bays, and bounded by innumerable rocks. We passed to the south of us a cluster of rocks and islands, extending nearly in a south-west and north-east direction about half a league. The outermost lies nearly south-east, about two miles and a half, from the point seen the former morning, and stated to be the north point of the passage leading towards the ocean. We arrived at this point by noon, but the weather then becoming thick and hazy, attended by heavy rain, and a strong gale from the south-west, obliged us to make for the first place of safety we could reach. Close round to the north-west of the above point, which, after the Right Honorable Charles James Fox, I called CAPE FOX, in latitude 54° 45½′ longitude 229° 22′,[1] we retired to a very unsheltered cove, where we remained some hours, though by no means pleasantly circumstanced. The weather in the afternoon for a short time bore a more favorable aspect, and tempted us again to proceed along the exterior coast, which now took nearly a west direction; but we had scarcely advanced beyond the rocks that encumber the shore, when the gale from the southward increased, attended with a very heavy swell, and thick misty weather. This obliged us again to seek some place of security, which we very fortunately found about half a league to the westward of cape Fox, in a very commodious well sheltered little cove; which protected us during the night from an excessively heavy rain, and a very hard gale of wind from the south-east, which brought from the ocean so heavy a sea upon these shores, as to invade even our snug retreat.

About eight o'clock the next morning, Saturday the 4th, the weather again moderated, and the wind favoring our pursuit, we again proceeded, although it continued to rain and was otherways very unpleasant. We resumed our examination along the coast, taking a rounding direction from the cove N.W. by W. four miles and then N. 15 W. near seven miles further, to a projecting point on the shore that obtained the name of FOGGY POINT, situated in latitude 54° 54½′, longitude 229° 11′.[2]

The weather continued very unfavorable to our researches; it permitted us to distinguish the rocky shores along which we passed only from point to point; landing was not only difficult but very dangerous, and could only be effected in the chasms of the rocks, near to the several points on which it was indispensibly necessary to land, for the purpose of ascertaining the positive direction of the coast; which, by the time we had reached Foggy point, not being visible at the distance of fifty yards, we stopped to dine, having in the course of the morning been again excluded from the ocean. And though the thickness of the weather had prevented our seeing by what means this had

[1] The correct position is lat. 54° 46·2′ N, long. 130° 50′ W (229° 10′ E).
[2] Its position is lat. 54° 55′ N, long. 130° 58′ 30″ W (229° 01′ 30″ E).

taken place, it was manifest, that either land or shoals now intervened, as we had intirely lost the oceanic swell, that a few miles to the south had rolled in, and broke with great violence from the shores.

By the time we had dined the fog sufficiently cleared away, to admit of our gaining a tolerably distinct view of our situation. It was on the south point of a bay,[1] in which were many small islands and rocks. The opposite side of the opening in which we had advanced during the fog, was also indistinctly seen to the westward and north-west, composed of a country moderately elevated, covered with trees, and which seemed much divided by water. After taking the necessary angles, we proceeded along the continent round the shores of the above bay; and in its northern corner, our time was again unprofitably spent in examining a narrow opening about two miles in extent to the north-east.[2] From thence, through a labyrinth of rocks and shoals, we steered over to the north-westernmost and largest of those islands lying from Foggy point, N. 20 W. near a league,[3] where we took up our abode for the night. The wind blew strong attended with heavy rain, which towards day-light the next morning, Monday the 5th, abated, and we again proceeded along the continental shore. This, from the narrow N.E. opening, took first a N.W. course for two miles and a half, and then N. by E., about the same distance, to a point in latitude 55° 1', longitude 229° 8½',[4] forming the S.E. point of an inlet[5] (its opposite point of entrance[6] lying a quarter of a mile distant N. 25 W.) apparently of some extent, to the north-eastward; but its entrance, and its exterior shores to the north and south, were rendered almost inaccessible by islets and rocks. It was, however, indispensably necessary, that we should visit such branches of the sea, as the boundaries of the continental shore could only be established by the strictest examination of every arm, inlet, creek, or corner.

Having breakfasted, we proceeded along the starboard or continental shore. This took a direction first N. 50 E., to a point about seven miles from the entrance; within which distance we observed the latitude on the opposite, or N.W. shore, to be 55° 4½'. From this point, the shores became less elevated than those we had passed from the entrance of the inlet; particularly that on the starboard side, which took a S.S.E. direction, and had now increased to two miles in width. Having advanced about four miles in this line, a small branch was seen in the former direction, about half a mile wide, having a small island in its entrance;[7] about two miles from whence it terminated in low marshy land; situated, according to my survey, not more than four miles distant, and in a direction N.N.W. from the head of the arm we had quitted

---

[1] Foggy Bay.   [2] Very Inlet.
[3] The largest of the De Long Islands.
[4] Kah Shakes Point (named after a Tlingit chief) is in lat. 55° 04' 50" N, long. 130° 59' 20" W (229° 00' 40" E).
[5] The Boca de Quadra. Vancouver adopted the name (still in use) on Caamaño's map, where it appears as Bocas de Quadra.   [6] Quadra Point.
[7] Vixen Bay, with Gannet Island at its entrance.

on the evening of the 2d,[1] making the shores of the main land along which we had navigated since that time a peninsula, fifteen leagues round, united by this narrow isthmus. Such was the slow and irksome process by which our researches were carried into execution, on account of the extremely divided state of this extraordinary inhospitable region.

From the entrance of this small branch, the starboard shore of the inlet takes a direction N. 60 E. for a league, to another branch of the same extent and direction,[2] passing a small round island in mid-channel,[3] another in the entrance of the little arm,[4] and a third a little way within it.[5] From hence, the width of the inlet became contracted to three quarters of a mile, taking a course N. 5 E. two miles, to a third small branch about a mile further,[6] where we rested for the night; and in the morning of Tuesday the 6th found it extend N. 73 E. for two miles. Here it terminated in low land at the head; but the sides were so steep and rocky, that it was with some difficulty we could find a sufficient space for making a fire to dress our provisions. From hence we pursued the main branch of the inlet, about three quarters of a mile wide, which took nearly a direction N. 25 E., 4½ leagues; where it finally terminated in latitude 55° 17′, longitude 229° 36½′.[7]

The sides of this channel are nearly straight, firm, and compact, composed of high steep rocky cliffs, covered with wood as high as the thick rainy weather permitted us to see. At its head was a small border of low land, through which flowed two small rivulets.[8] On the larboard shore, about eight miles within the entrance, we had passed two openings; these, on our return, were found to be very inconsiderable; the easternmost, which was the largest,[9] did not extend more than two miles north from the shores of the main inlet, where it terminated in latitude 55° 9′, longitude 229° 19′; the other, not more than a mile in length,[10] and in a parallel direction, ended S.W. by S., about a mile from the head of the former.

The weather continued very rainy and unpleasant until two in the afternoon of the following day, Wednesday the 7th; at which time we had reached a small islet,[11] lying N. 70 E. one mile and three quarters from the point where we had breakfasted on the morning of the 5th; at this islet we stopped to dine. The atmosphere soon after became clear, and gave us a most distinct and

[1] Nakat Inlet.   [2] Mink Bay.
[3] Kite Island.
[4] Cygnet Island.   [5] Grouse Rock.
[6] Marten Arm, actually about six miles in length, as it extends beyond a bend that Vancouver seems to have assumed was its termination.
[7] The inlet ends about lat. 55° 20′ N, long. 130° 29′ W (229° 31′ E).
[8] The party dined at the head of the inlet 'at the Side of a Fresh Water Rivulet, in which were an immeasureable Quantity of Salmon [in poor condition]...Here we likewise found a Great Growth of Wild Celery Black and Red Berries Wild Mint & a few Gooseberry Bushes.' – Puget, 6 August. The area is now known as a waterfowl nesting area.
[9] Badger Bay.
[10] Weasel Cove.
[11] Later named Slate Islet by Vancouver.

satisfactory view of the surrounding region, and proved our situation to be in a spacious branch of the ocean, extending in two or three different directions.

Since we had left cape Fox, we had conceived ourselves to be in the southern entrance of the Canal de Revilla Gigedo,[1] as represented in Senr Caamano's chart. Although this gave but a faint idea of the shores we were tracing, it had sufficient resemblance, in the general outline, to leave no doubt of our being in the precise situation intended in that representation; and hence it appeared, that the inlet which had occupied our time the two preceding days, was called Bocas de Quadra. The south point of its entrance in the chart is, however, placed in 55° 11', which is 10° further north than it appeared to be by our observations.

An extensive opening, dividing the western land between N. 60 W., and N. 46 W., was evidently a continuation of the Canal de Revilla Gigedo, and its southern side, the Island de Gravina.[2] The width of this channel at Foggy point is about four miles, and abreast of this land not quite a league; though, in the Spanish chart, it is laid down at the width of eight or nine miles, from the entrance to this station. The land in the Canal de Revilla Gigedo was too distant to admit of our ascertaining the situation of any of its particular points, excepting that above mentioned, lying N. 46½ W., five miles from this island; it is very conspicuous, and forms the west part of an extensive branch, taking apparently a northern course along the shores of the continent. To this point I gave the name of POINT ALAVA, in compliment to the Spanish governor at Nootka.[3]

The opposite, or western shore, particularly to the south of the Canal de Revilla Gigedo, seemed to be much broken. The shores in most directions were low, or of a moderate height; but the more interior country was composed of mountains covered with snow, not only in the eastern quarter, but to the northward and westward.

The islet on which we had dined, seemed to be formed of different materials from those we had been accustomed to visit; it being one intire quarry of slate. In walking round and across it, through the trees, we found no other sort of stone. Slate had been frequently seen forming a kind of beach, or in thin strata, lying between the rocks; but, till now, we had never met with this substance in such a prodigious mass. This islet, which obtained the name of SLATE ISLET,[4] we quitted, leaving the Canal de Revilla Gigedo to the westward of us, and directing our inquiries along the continental shore, to a point that lies from Slate islet N. 10 W. four miles. This, after one of the

---

[1] Now Revillagigedo Channel.

[2] It was Annette Island that Vancouver was seeing at this time. On Caamano's chart Annette Island and Gravina Island to the NW were shown as one. Vancouver would learn later that they were separate islands.

[3] Brigadier General José Manual de Alava, Commandant of San Blas and commissioner for Nootka.

[4] Now grouped with three other islands as the Slate Islands.

SALMON COVE OBSERVATORY INLET

Plate 39. 'Salmon Cove, Observatory Inlet.'

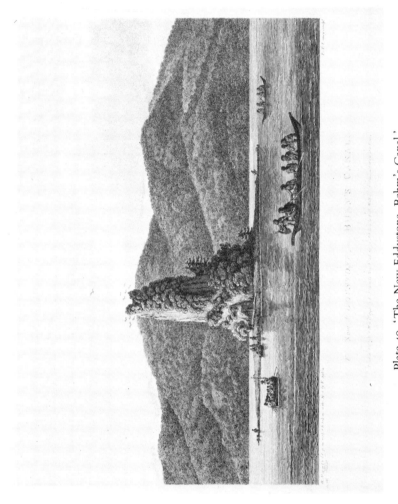

Plate 40. 'The New Eddystone, Behm's Canal.'

gentlemen of the Discovery, I named POINT SYKES.[1] From thence, the
continental shore, which is a little indented and has a few small islets and rocks
lying near it, takes a direction about N. 37 E. to a point, which, after Captain*
Nelson of the navy, I named POINT NELSON, situated in latitude 55° 15',
longitude 229° 17½',[2] and which we reached the next morning. Thursday the
8th, by half past six. The inlet up which we had thus navigated,[3] was from
two to four miles wide. From this point it seemed to be divided into three
branches; one leading to the north-west;[4] another to the north,[5] in the centre
of which, four or five leagues distant, was a rock much resembling a vessel
under sail, lying N. 7 W., and seemingly detached from the shores; and the
third took an easterly direction[6] along the continuation of the continent. The
last occupied our attention, and employed the whole day, which was very
rainy and unpleasant. It was found to be about three quarters of a mile wide,
irregularly extending N. 80 E. for two leagues, and then towards the north-east
for four miles further, where it terminated in the usual manner, in latitude
in 55° 18½', longitude 229° 29½';[7] having a bay or cove on its eastern shore,[8]
which, in an E.S.E. direction, approached within about two miles of the
northern part of Bocas de Quadra.

The surrounding country consisted of a huge mass of steep, barren, rocky
mountains, destitute of soil; whose summits were perpetually covered with
snow. Excepting at the head of the arm where the land was low, these
mountains rose in nearly perpendicular cliffs from the water's edge, producing
only a few scattered dwarf trees.

Not far from the spot on which we had dined, and near the ruins of a few
temporary huts of the natives, we found a box about three feet square, and
a foot and a half deep, in which were the remains of a human skeleton, which
appeared, from the confused situation of the bones, either to have been cut
to pieces, or thrust with great violence into this small space. One or two other
coffins, similar to this, had been seen in the excursions of the boats this season;
but as we had met with so few of this description, I was inclined to suppose
that this mode of depositing their dead is practised only in respect to certain
persons of their society, since, if it had been the general usage, we should in
all probability have more frequently noticed them.

* Now Lord Nelson.

[1] John Sykes, at this time master's mate in the *Discovery*. He had joined the ship as a
midshipman at the age of 19. He was an artist of considerable ability and many of the plates
in the *Voyage* were engraved from his drawings. His father, James Sykes, was Vancouver's
Navy Agent (i.e. business agent) in London.

[2] The correct position is lat. 55° 18' 05" N, long. 130° 55' 30" W (229° 04' 30" E).

[3] The Behm Canal, the entrance to which is between Point Alava and Point Sykes.

[4] Princess Bay.

[5] Behm Canal proper.

[6] Smeaton Bay.

[7] Wilson Arm of Smeaton Bay extends to about lat. 55° 23' N, long. 130° 37' W
(229° 23' E).

[8] Bakewell Arm of Smeaton Bay.

By the evening we reached the main inlet again, where, on a point which I named POINT TROLLOP, in a direction from point Nelson N. 20 W. distant a league and a half,[1] we rested for the night, and the next morning started at an early hour.

Having advanced about a mile among the continental shore, we again quitted the main branch of the inlet, and entered a very narrow channel,[2] in some places navigable only for boats and canoes. This extended, with little deviation, N. 7 W. seven miles, when it again communicated with the branch of the inlet, making the western shore two long narrow islands.[3] The southern-most is about half a league long. A small round island lies off the north-west point of the most northern,[4] from whence we again saw the remarkable rock resembling a ship under sail, before mentioned, lying N. 22 W. near a league distant, having between it and the continental shore several rocks and islets. Its situation and elevation, if accessible, promised to afford us an excellent view of the inlet; and its singular pyramidical appearance from this point of view invited our curiosity. We reached this rock about seven, and found the main inlet, (whose sides were compact for four or five leagues, excepting in the appearance of an opening lying N. 37 E. about a league from us)[5] to take nearly a north direction, maintaining a width from two to three miles. On the base of this singular rock, which, from its resemblance to the Light House rock off Plymouth, I called the NEW EDDYSTONE,[6] we stopped to breakfast, and whilst we were thus engaged, three small canoes, with about a dozen of the natives, landed and approached us unarmed, and with the utmost good humour accepted such presents as were offered to them,[7] making signs, in return, that they had brought nothing to dispose of, but inviting us, in the most pressing manner, to their habitations; where, they gave us to understand, they had fish skins, and other things in great abundance, to barter for our commodities; amongst which blue cloth seemed to be the most esteemed. They pointed out the situation of their residence to be on the eastern shore; but as that was behind us, and as we had no time for unnecessary delays, their civil intreaties were declined, and we departed from the new Eddystone, which is certainly a very remarkable rock. Its circumference at its base is about fifty yards, standing perpendicularly on a surface of fine, dark coloured sand. It is intirely detached, at the distance of two miles from the eastern, and one from the western shore of the inlet, in latitude 55° 29', longitude 229° 15'.

[1] Probably named for Captain Henry (later Admiral Sir Henry) Trollop, a native of Norwich. Point Nelson and Point Trollop are respectively the S and N points of entrance to Smeaton Bay.

[2] Shoalwater Pass.

[3] There is only one 'long narrow' island – Winstanley Island, with the much smaller Candle Island off its S end.

[4] Entrance Island.   [5] Rudyerd Bay.

[6] Now New Eddystone Rock.

[7] These were Tlingit Indians. Vancouver would soon meet a much larger and much less friendly group of them.

Its surface is uneven, and its diameter regularly decreases to a few feet at its apex, which is nearly flat, and seemed to be in every direction perpendicular to the centre of its base; its height, by a rude measurement, was found to be upwards of two hundred and fifty feet.[1] The fissures and small chasms in its sides, quite up to its summit, afforded nourishment to some small pine trees and various shrubs. The south and eastern part of its base is an intire bed of sand; to the north, about two hundred yards from it, extended a ledge of rocks, that stretched a small distance, and was visible only at low tide, beyond which the bottom was unfathomable with our lines.

The natives attended us for a short time, but finding that our course was not directed towards their habitations, they retired; after having given us to understand by signs, that at night we should find the inlet closed on all sides, that we should sleep at its termination, and requested that on our return we would visit their habitations.

We soon arrived at the point that had in appearance formed an opening in the eastern shore, and found that our conjectures had been well founded; it being the south point of a branch,[2] in general about three quarters of a mile wide, irregularly extending N. 53 E. two leagues, with a cove on the southern shore,[3] and forming at the above extent two other coves; one in a direction S. 24 E. two miles and a half long, the other north, two miles long, terminating in latitude 55° 37½', longitude 229° 29'. The examination of this insignificant branch, winding between an immense body of high, barren, snowy mountains, occupied the remainder of the day. About ten at night we reached the main inlet, and took up our abode until the next morning, Saturday the 10th, at a point on the continental shore.

The weather being again fair and pleasant, we early directed our way along the continental shore, which was nearly straight and compact, and trending about N. 5 W. About our time of breakfast, we arrived at the south point of another of those arms,[4] about half a mile wide, which had hitherto employed the major part of our time to so little purpose.

Our situation at this juncture required some attention. The time was expired for which our provisions had been supplied, and we were now one hundred and twenty miles from the ships by the nearest route we could pursue. It was extremely mortifying to reflect, that after all our exertions, no one point had been gained to facilitate the progress of the vessels; as the way by which we had advanced thus far was infinitely too intricate for them; and if the want of provisions should now oblige us to return before we could determine the extent of this spacious inlet, which still continued to be between

---

[1] *U.S. Coast Pilot 7* gives its height as 234 feet. Its position is lat. 55° 30·2′ N, long. 130° 56·2′ W (229° 03·8′ E). Menzies noted that the Indians 'called the pinnacle by the name of *Shekil*.' – 9 August. Sykes drew the sketch from which the engraving in the *Voyage* was prepared.
[2] Rudyerd Bay.
[3] Punchbowl Cove.   [4] Walker Cove.

two and three miles wide, our labours would become ineffectual, because it would be necessary that the same space should be traversed again, to accomplish what we might be compelled to leave unfinished.

Under these considerations, and well knowing from experience that all the small branches leading to the eastward either terminate at the foot of the lofty range of rugged mountains, or else form into islands parts of the shores of these inlets; I determined to decline their further examination, and to proceed in the main channel to ascertain the truth of the information derived from the natives, or to discover some eligible passage, by which the vessels might advance towards the extent of our present researches. Our prospect of succeeding in this particular was not very flattering. We lost no time, however, in making the best of our way; and from the entrance of this arm, which is situated in latitude 55° 41', longitude 229° 16',[1] as we advanced up the main inlet, the general opinion seemed to support the account of the natives; and that the evening would certainly bring us to its final termination. The water was of a very light colour, not very salt, and the interior country of the western shore rose to rugged mountains, little inferior in height to those on the eastern side; which we knew to be a continuation of the continent, now taking a direction N. 35 W. In the forenoon we passed a small cluster of rocks and islets a mile in extent, lying in the line of the eastern shore,[2] at the distance of about half a mile from it. The latitude at noon I observed to be 55° 44'; and soon afterwards we passed a small opening, that appeared to form a bay half a mile wide, and about a mile deep, in a north-east direction.[3] As we pursued our route in the afternoon, the shores, which were no where more than two miles asunder, took a more westerly direction, affording some small bays and coves.

The weather being calm and pleasant, we made a tolerable progress until late in the evening, when we arrived at a point in latitude 55° 56', longitude 228° 54½';[4] and although the night was too far advanced to see distinctly about us, yet we had no doubt of our having reached the confluence of this inlet with two other branches, lying nearly at right angles to it.[5] A fresh breeze blew up the branch leading to the south-west till after dark; this I considered as the sea breeze, indicating our vicinity to the exterior coast; or possibly, our approach to wider channels leading more immediately towards the ocean. The whiteness and freshness of the water, with other circumstances common to our general observation, presented themselves however in opposition to this opinion; and gave us some reason to believe that we should be obliged to return by the same track we had come. Such was the uncertainty with which,

[1] Its position is lat. 55° 43' N, long. 130° 54' W (229° 06' E).

[2] The Channel Islands.

[3] The bay at the mouth of the Chickamin River, which is larger than this description suggests, but is largely occupied by flats.

[4] Point Fitzgibbon, in lat. 55° 59' N, long. 131° 13' W (228° 47' E).

[5] Burroughs Bay to the NW and Behm Narrows, a continuation of Behm Canal, to the SW.

in general, all our conjectures were attended, from the various appearances that occurred in exploring this country.

I felt much regret that I had left unexamined the small branch we had seen in the morning, and the bay we had passed in the course of the afternoon; as these researches would have completely ascertained the continental shore to this point, which I distinguished by the name of POINT FITZGIBBON.[1] I determined, however, to pursue the branch that now appeared to the north-east, and seemed of some extent; as, should this be found to terminate, there would be little reason to suppose, even if we had been able to examine them, that the others would have led to any thing of importance.

The next morning, Sunday the 11th, we accordingly proceeded; the north-east branch was found in general to be about a mile wide; and keeping on its southern shore, which is much indented with small bays; at half past six we arrived at its termination in latitude 56° 1½′, longitude 229° 1′, by low land; through which two or three small rivulets appeared to flow over a bank of mud,[2] stretching from the head of the arm, and reaching from side to side, on which was lodged a considerable quantity of drift wood. The water was perfectly fresh, extremely muddy, and the whole surface was strewed over with salmon, either dead, or in the last stages of their existence. Many had life sufficient to give them motion, though wanting vital powers to keep them beneath the surface of the water. In the course of this excursion great numbers of these fish had been seen, not only in all the arms, but in almost every run of fresh water, particularly near the terminations of the several inlets, where they were innumerable, though most of them were in a sickly condition. We had no difficulty to take as many of the best as we were inclined to make use of; they however had little of the colour, and nothing of the flavor of salmon, and were very insipid and indifferent food. They were all small, of one sort, and were called by us *hunch-backed* salmon; from an excresence that rose along the upper part of the backs of the male fish, where the back fins are inserted. This protuberance is much thinner than the body of the fish, which below it takes nearly a cylindrical form. These were the worst eating fish; the females were not so deformed, though the mouths of both were made in a kind of hook, resembling the upper mandible of a hawk.[3] The sickly condition of these fish appeared to be consequent on the season of their spawning, and may possibly be occasioned by their exertions, in forcing their way up the runs of fresh water, against the impetuosity of the torrents that rush into the sea; by which means they had evidently received many bruises and other injuries. If any just conclusion is to be drawn from the appearance

[1] Walbran surmises that this point was named in honour of John Fitzgibbon, Earl of Clare.

[2] The Unuk River and the Klahini River. The mud banks at their mouths meet in about lat. 56° 03′ N, long. 131° 06′ E (228° 54′ E).

[3] These were pink salmon, the smallest of the Pacific salmon, averaging 3 to 5 pounds in weight. The males develop the hooked jaws and back humps that Vancouver describes, and for that reason are often called humpbacks.

of the immense numbers found dead, not only in the water, but lodged on the shores below high water mark, it should seem that their death takes place immediately after spawning.[1]

Having traced the north-east extent of this branch, and finding it only to form a deep bay (which obtained the name of BURROUGH'S BAY,)[2] we returned along the northern shore, which took a direction somewhat irregularly S. 53 W. down the south-westerly branch, to a point on which I observed the latitude to be 55° 54', longitude 228° 46'. At this station, which I call POINT LEES,[3] the width of the south-west channel was decreased to less than a mile, and from hence its north-east point of entrance, which I named POINT WHALEY,[4] lies N. 68 E. distant four miles.

As we advanced, the colour of the water gradually, though slowly, turned dark; and the wind blowing fresh from the south-west, still cherished the hope that the land, forming the western side of the extensive northern arm we had navigated from point Alava to point Whaley, and southern sides of this south-westerly branch, would be found to compose an extensive island,[5] and that we should obtain a passage to the ships by the route we were then pursuing.

On this point was found the remains of a deserted village, the largest of any I had yet seen for some time, and so constructed as to contain, by our estimation, at least three or four hundred people, who appeared to have quitted it not many months before.[6] Shortly after noon, we reached a narrow opening on the northern shore leading to the northward;[7] this was passed by unexamined, and we stopped to dine about a mile to the south-west of it; and in a direction S. 63 W. distant about a league from the deserted village. We soon proceeded again, and by eight in the evening arrived at a point on the southern shore in latitude 55° 50', longitude 228° 30'.[8]

The doubts we had entertained respecting our situation were now in a great measure satisfied, for the water had again nearly resumed its oceanic taste and colour; and the channel which from hence turned sharp to the south, seemed to widen in that direction. A point on the northern shore lying N. 49 E. about a mile distant,[9] formed the south-east point of a small opening, that appeared to branch off in two directions; one leading to the north,[10] the other to the

[1] Vancouver's surmise was correct; the Pacific salmon die after spawning time. Their 'sickly condition' was thus not due to disease, but the natural end of their life cycle.

[2] The derivation of the name is not known.

[3] Its position is lat. 55° 57' 40" N, long. 131° 23' 25" W (228° 36' 35" E).

[4] The origin of the names Point Whaley and Point Lees is not known.

[5] Vancouver's hopes were fulfilled; he was circumnavigating Revillagigedo Island.

[6] Menzies commented: 'the whole place was so filled with rubbish & filth & the stench issuing from it so intolerable that we could not stay long to examine it, & as it did not seem to be deserted many months, it is probable that this circumstance alone may have obligd the inhabitants to change their situation.' – 11 August.

[7] Anchor Pass.

[8] Evidently Curlew Point, in lat. 55° 55' N, long. 131° 35' W (228° 25' E).

[9] Snipe Point.   [10] Bailey Bay.

E.N.E.; the latter having the appearance of communicating with that seen in the afternoon, making the land on which we had dined in that case an island.[1] About nine o'clock we took up our abode for the night, and on the following morning, Monday the 12th, proceeded to the southward, with little doubt of finding by that course our way back to the station of the vessels; from whence we were now at least one hundred and forty miles distant. The weather being calm and hazy, prevented our seeing distinctly the surrounding regions, yet we were able to discern two openings on the western shore, leading towards the north-west. The southernmost of these seemed spacious, and about two miles in width.[2] South of this opening the western shore appeared to be nearly compact, with one or two small bays only, and a few detached islets lying at a distance from it; whilst the eastern shore, along which we passed, was considerably broken. Its several inlets however were disregarded,[3] as we had barely time to obtain at the different stations the necessary angles for fixing the general outline of the shores of this channel, whose width as we advanced appeared to increase from one to nearly two leagures.[4]

As our route was directed to one of these necessary stations, some of the natives were observed in their canoes near the shore; four of these canoes appearing to be large and well manned, went towards the launch, then some distance astern of us; and by their singing, which we heard, appeared to be very peaceably inclined. We were also visited by a small canoe containing only two of the natives, who approached us without hesitation, and with the greatest good humour accepted such trifling presents as were offered to them, and made known our friendly behaviour to some of their associates who were still on the shore. These, apparently at the instance of the other two, came off in two small canoes, that just reached us as we were putting on shore for the purpose of taking the requisite angles. Their behaviour was civil and inoffensive, and they seemed equally well satisfied with the presents that were distributed amongst them. They offered their skins and other commodities to barter, which were accordingly exchanged; and thus, without the least apprehension on our parts of any evil design in these people, who like most of the natives we had lately seen were well armed, I landed, leaving Mr. Puget in the yawl, using his endeavours to entertain our new visitors. In a little time they became extremely clamorous, and were hallowing to the large canoes that were near the launch. On my return into the boat, Mr. Puget informed me that the natives had betrayed a very thievish disposition, and that he had great reason to suspect they were inclined to be turbulent. I immediately ordered the boat from off the shore, hoping by that means to get quit of them,

[1] Bell Arm, which, as Vancouver surmised, meets Anchor Pass and completes the waterway around Bell Island.

[2] Yes Bay and the much larger Spacious Bay.

[3] As these inlets were not on the continental shore, Vancouver was not greatly interested in them.

[4] Vancouver was now descending the W arm of Behm Canal, a huge U-shaped waterway whose two arms are connected by Behm Narrows.

but in this attempt they were excessively troublesome; the number of their canoes was by this time four or five, in these they laid fast hold by the boat's quarters, calling out '*Winnee watter*'; though at our solicitations they frequently quitted their hold, but which they almost instantly again resumed; we had however put off from the rocks, and had partly got the use of our oars, without being obliged to resort to any hostile measures, when the largest of the canoes, under the steerage of an old woman, with a remarkably large lip ornament, laid us on board across the bow; this vixen instantly snatched up the lead line that was lying there, and lashed her canoe with it to the boat; whilst a young man, appearing to be the chief of the party, seated himself in the bow of the yawl, and put on a mask resembling a wolf's face, compounded with the human countenance. About this time the Indian who had first visited us, watching his opportunity, stole a musket out of the boat. Our situation was now become very critical and alarming; we had discovered too late the treacherous designs of these people, and to add to our embarrassment, the launch was yet too far distant to afford us any immediate succour. The only chance we had for our preservation, was, if possible, to ward off the blow by a kind of parley, until our friends might come up, who were hastening with their utmost exertions to our assistance. With these ideas, I went forward with a musket in my hand in order to speak to the chief; on which the surrounding Indians, about fifty in number, seized their daggers, brandished their spears, and pointed them towards us in all directions. I was not yet without hopes of effecting an amicable separation, without being under the necessity of resorting to extremities. The chief instantly quitted the boat at my request, and gave me to understand by signs, that if I would lay down my musket, his people would lay down their arms; on my disposing of my gun, the conditions were complied with on all sides, and tranquillity appeared likely to be restored; not do I believe that any thing further would have happened, had they not been instigated by the vociferous efforts of their female conductress; who seemed to put forth all the powers of her turbulent tongue to excite, or rather to compel the men, to act with hostility towards us. Her language appeared to have the most effect upon those who were towards the stern of our boat, and who were likewise greatly encouraged by a very ferocious looking old man in the middling sized canoe. This old fellow, assisted, by his companions, seized hold of our oars on the starboard side, and prevented their being used. Observing this, and that the spears were again brandishing in that quarter, I again made signs for peace, and went immediately aft; where I found Mr. Puget using his utmost endeavours to accomplish the same desirable object, which seemed once more likely to take place by their laying down their arms a second time.

This posture of affairs continued however but for a few moments. I had scarcely turned round, before I saw the spears, in the canoe which contained the chief and the old woman, all in motion; but on my stepping forward they were again dropped. Whilst I was thus engaged, the Indians near the stern of the boat became very troublesome; and, as I was passing back along the boat, a general commotion seemed to have taken place; some spears were thrust, one or two of which passed very near me, and the Indians, in all directions, began to seize all the moveables in our boat that they could possibly reach, and to commit other acts of violence. Our destruction now seemed almost inevitable; as I could hardly flatter myself that the force we had to oppose against the number that surrounded us, and, as it were, held us so completely within their power, would have been sufficient to make them retire.

By this time, however, which was about ten minutes from my return to the boat, the launch had arrived within pistol-shot; and being now thoroughly satisfied that our forbearance had given them confidence, and that our desire for peace had rather stimulated them to acts of temerity than dissuaded them from their hostile intentions; and seeing no alternative left for our preservation against numbers so superior, but by making use of the coercive means we had in our power, I gave directions to fire; this instantly taking effect from both boats, was, to my great astonishment, attended with the desired effect, and we had the happiness of finding ourselves immediately relieved from a situation of the most imminent danger.

Those in the small canoes jumped into the sea, whilst those in the large ones, by getting all on one side, raised the opposite sides of their canoes, so that they were protected from the fire of the yawl, though they were in some measure exposed to that of the launch; and in this manner they scrambled sideways to the shore.

The only arms they had left us in the yawl, besides those in the arm chest, were a blunderbuss, a musket, a fowling-piece loaded with small shot, and a brace of pocket pistols; the rest of the arms that had usually been kept at hand, consisting of three muskets and a fowling-piece, having been stolen, in the affray, together with two cartridge-boxes, some books, and other articles of little value.[1] The arm chest, however, afforded a sufficient supply for our future defence, and were immediately got in readiness for our protection; whilst the chastisement I intended to bestow on these treacherous people, by destroying their canoes, should be carried into execution. But, as we were pulling towards the shore for this purpose, I understood that two of our boat's crew were very badly wounded, which circumstance had escaped my notice, by their having continued to exert themselves in their respective stations; and

---

[1] Puget described the theft of the firearms: 'Nearly at that time a Musquet was Stolen from the Rods of the Canopy, to which four were suspended with their Cartridge Boxes & though this fellow might have been Shot, yet it was thought most prudent not immediately to notice the Robbery.' The ease with which this first theft had been committed having encouraged others 'two other Musquets and a fowling Piece of Captn. Vancouvers were Stolen with their Cartridge Boxes from the Rods of the Canopy.' – 12 August.

this very unpleasant intelligence immediately induced me to decline the punishment I had meditated to inflict for the unprovoked aggression of the natives.

The Indians, on reaching the shore, ascended the high rocky cliffs of which it is composed, from whence they endeavoured to annoy those in the launch by stones, some of which fell into her at the distance of thirty or forty yards from the shore, and from whence also they fired a musket. The arms they had stolen from our boat were all loaded; beside these, they had fire arms of their own, but I had reason to believe they were not charged at the time of their attack upon us, as one of the most savage-looking fellows amongst them, just as I gave orders to fire, snapped his piece at me; but it missed fire, and he immediately laid it down, and took up his spear with all imaginable composure.

The launch was now ordered to join us, and an equal distribution of the remaining arms and ammunition was made in both boats. Being now fully prepared to repel any further attack, we rested on our oars about a quarter of a mile from the precipice the Indians had gained, until Mr. Menzies had dressed the wounded men. Robert Betton,[1] in the act of removing the arm chest, was first wounded in the breast, but by his seizing the spear, he in a great measure parried the blow, and destroyed its force; but on its being instantly repeated, he received a very deep wound in the upper part of his thigh, which was little short of being mortal. George Bridgeman[2] was also badly wounded lower down in the thigh, by a spear that passed quite through, from one side to the other. I had the satisfaction however to learn from Mr. Menzies, after he had dressed the wounds, that he considered neither of them likely to be attended with any present danger, nor with consequences that would be inconvenient hereafter.

Betton and Bridgeman had both received their wounds as I was returning the second time to the stern of the boat, and just before I was compelled to give the order to fire; the former as above stated, and the latter in preventing those in the large canoe, lying across our boat's bows, from unshipping one of the wall-pieces. Their wounds being dressed, and births as convenient as circumstances would admit, one in each boat, being made for our unfortunate ship-mates, we departed, giving the point on which we had landed the name

[1] Sailmaker's mate at this time; he had joined the *Discovery* at Deptford as an AB, aged 25.

[2] In a highly critical note Hewett relates that 'in the Capts boat they [ha]d been so careless [as] not to have any [of] their Muskets ready [alt]ho Geo. Bridgeman [a s]eaman who had been [in] this Country before [tol]d Capt. V. he was [cer]tain the Indians [int]ended to attack & [wa]s by C: V. desired [to] hold his Tongue [and m]ind his own business [to si]t still and let [th]e arms remain [in the] Chest till he [g]ave orders for their [be]ing taken out (here behold the little God Almighty) at this [in]stant an Indian seized by the mussle the Capts. fowling piece the [on]ly Firearm out except a brace of pocket pistols and struggled [wi]th V. for it.'

of ESCAPE POINT, situated in latitude 55° 37′, longitude 228° 30′;[1] and to a small opening about a league to the northward of this point, the name of TRAITOR'S COVE;[2] these treacherous people having from thence made their first appearance.

From Lieutenant Swaine and Mr. Menzies I learned, that when these audacious people first approached them in the launch, they behaved with the greatest friendliness and good humour, offering their skins for sale, two of which were thrown into the launch; and in return they accepted any thing that was given them with apparent satisfaction. In consequence of the friendly intercourse that had taken place, and the avidity of the Indians in their commercial pursuits, they pressed on the boat to take hold of her, but on this being objected to, and the canoes obliged to keep at a respectable distance, some little discontent was observed to shew itself amongst them. This was attributed to their great eagerness for trading, until the canoe conducted by the old virago, who was the only female of the party, finding the launch would not comply with their solicitations to stop and trade, paddled across the bow of the boat with the intention of stopping her progress. On this occasion a musket was presented, with menaces that had the desired effect of making her drop a-stern; much against the will of the old shrew, whose designs were evidently not of the most friendly nature.

It was now deemed expedient to be vigilantly upon their guard, to have all their arms at hand, and to charge such as were unloaded; which was done in the most private way, lest any alarm should be given to the Indians, who were kept by signs at a proper distance, and only one canoe at a time allowed to come near enough to receive the presents that were offered; these were accepted with great civility, and the general tenor of their conduct betokened a friendly disposition. In this humour, to all appearance, they paddled hastily towards the yawl, seemingly in consequence of the invitation of their comrades, who were by this time assembled about our boat. Notwithstanding they were observed by the gentlemen in the launch to use uncommon exertions for the purpose of reaching the yawl, yet their efforts were at first attributed to diversion, or eagerness to arrive at a better market; until they observed their spears to be in motion, when they lost no time in coming to our relief.

The conduct of these people, so unlike that of any of the natives we had hitherto met with, inclines the mind to advert to some cause that could have produced a deportment so opposite to that which we had in general experienced. I was apprehensive at first, that during my absence from the boat some offence, however inadvertently, had been given; but on inquiry, nothing of the sort appeared to have happened; on the contrary, to the moment of

---

[1] Its position is lat. 55° 39′ N, long. 131° 43′ W (228° 17′ E).

[2] Now spelled Traitors Cove. Manby refers to the cove as Skirmish Bay and to Escape Point as Cape Skirmish. – 21 and 23 August.

my return from the shore, the Indians had spared no pains to impress us with the most favorable idea of their good intentions, by frequently uttering the word ' *Wacon*,' signifying in their language, *friendship*. Their attack upon us should therefore appear, either to have been planned on their first seeing us, or determined upon in consequence of our temporizing conduct, which it is easy to imagine they would interpret into fear of their superior numbers. Whether their motives were rather to take revenge on us for injuries they have sustained from other civilized visitors; or whether they conceived the valuable articles we possessed, were easily to be obtained by these means, is difficult to be determined.

It was manifestly evident that they had been acquainted with civilized commercial people, by the muskets and other European commodities in their possession; and when we considered the particular behaviour of the first man who visited us, we had reason to suspect that they had been ill-treated in their traffic with white men. This Indian, by means of signs and words too expressive to be mistaken, gave us clearly to understand, that they had reason to complain of one or more muskets that they had purchased, which burst into pieces on being fired: a fraud which I know has been practised too frequently, not only on this coast, but at the Sandwich, and other islands in the Pacific Ocean. These defects have not arisen from ignorance or mis-management on the part of the Indians, but from the baseness of the metal and imperfect workmanship of the firearms. Of this dishonesty the chiefs of the Sandwich islands most loudly complain; and with great justice contend, that the produce of their country, being bartered for such articles, of the very best quality, whatever was received by them in exchange, ought to have been so likewise.

And I am extremely concerned to be compelled to state here, that many of the traders from the civilized world have not only pursued a line of conduct, diametrically opposite to the true principles of justice in their commercial dealings, but have fomented discords, and stirred up contentions, between the different tribes, in order to increase the demand for these destructive engines. They have been likewise eager to instruct the natives in the use of European arms of all descriptions; and have shewn by their own example, that they consider gain as the only object of pursuit; and whether this be acquired by fair and honorable means, or otherwise, so long as the advantage is secured, the manner how it is obtained seems to have been, with too many of them, but a very secondary consideration.

Under a conviction that repeated acts of such injustice had taken place, it was not unreasonable to suppose, that these people, who had experienced the like frauds, should be of opinion that our muskets, and the other arms that we carried for our protection, were of a superior quality to those they had procured from the traders. This, indeed, was proved by their praising ours and comparing them with those in their possession; and they might possibly from thence have been tempted to trespass on the laws of honesty, in order to acquire by force those really valuable commodities, which, by fair commercial dealings on their part, they could only procure in a defective state. It may also not be impossible, that they reconciled amongst themselves any acts of violence, which should become necessary in order to the attainment of them, as not being less offensive to justice, than the impositions that had been practised upon them by a people who, from every appearance, they might naturally conclude were of the same country and connections with us; and that they might thus consider themselves justified in using every artifice of retaliation, to effect their purpose.

I cannot however avoid observing, that through our want of caution they had, in this instance, sufficient address to succeed by their friendly professions, in nearly assembling all their force round us, though in the more early part of our voyage, we should have regarded their conduct with much suspicion; particularly their vociferous hallooing to each other, the haste with which the party came to us from the launch, their throwing overboard their dogs, and other hostile preparations that did not escape our notice, and would formerly have been deemed sufficient indications to have awakened our suspicions, and to have put us completely upon our guard against any unfriendly design they might have had in contemplation. But, having been so long accustomed to a series of tranquil intercourse with the several different tribes of Indians we had met with, our apprehensions of any molestation from them were totally done away; and that attentive wariness which had been the first object of my concern on coming amongst these rude nations, had latterly been much neglected. For although we had now more arms than we were provided with during the preceding summer, namely, two wall-pieces cut short for the purpose of being more handy in the boats, each of which was loaded with a dozen pistol balls,[1] yet these as well as some of our muskets, had been so neglected by disuse, that they were unserviceable on this pressing emergency.

The good fortune we had experienced until now, had given me hopes, that an equal success would continue to the close of our researches; and that I should have the happiness of concluding our voyage, without being under the painful necessity of firing one shot in anger.

To what degree our firing did execution, was not ascertained. Some of the natives were seen to fall, as if killed or severely wounded,[2] and great

[1] Voyce and Stevenson's *Military Dictionary* (London, 1876) describes a wall-piece as being 'an enlarged flintlock or firearm mounted on a swivel or placed on the walls of a fort or other fortified place.'

[2] Estimates of the casualties varied: 'when we fired about Eight or Ten were killed but those wounded we could not ascertain, though it must have greatly exceeded that Number.' – Puget, August 12. Baker, who was not present, noted that 'six or seven Indians were supposed to be killed in the fray.' – August 16. Sherriff states that 'they suppose about 12 Natives were kill'd'. – August 16. Puget records that 'the Launch did great Execution with her Swivels' and in his opinion 'If the Indians had begun their attack when the Launch was astern, nothing could have saved us'. – August 12. Puget's long account gives few details not included in Vancouver's narrative.

lamentations were heard after they had gained their retreat in the woods, from whence they shewed no disposition to renew their attack.

Our route was now uninterruptedly directed across an extensive bay,[1] in which were several small openings, appearing to lead to the eastward and south-east. About three o'clock we reached a small island lying N. 9 W.[2] from Escape point, at the distance of five miles. Our progress hither had been slow, occasioned by a fresh south-west wind, which however was attended with pleasant weather. The width of the southerly channel we thus pursued, had diminished from being nearly two, to scarcely one league; this was occasioned by an island lying about a mile from the eastern shore, half a league broad, and a league long, in a direction N. 60 E. and S. 60 W. This island I named BETTON'S ISLAND,[3] after our wounded shipmate; on its north-west side are several dangerous rocks, lying half a mile from its shore, and between it and the eastern shore are several smaller islands. We traversed this eastern passage, and took up our night's abode near a conspicuous point on the eastern shore, which I named POINT HIGGINS, after his Excellency Senʳ Higgins de Vallenar, the president of Chili. It is situated in latitude 55° 27½′, longitude 228° 25′,[4] from whence a very remarkable projecting point on the opposite shore lies N. 78 W. distant four miles and a half;[5] and two small islands, with some trees upon them, S. 40 W. half a league distant.[6]

We started early the next morning. Tuesday the 13th, and were favoured with pleasant weather, though with an adverse southerly wind. Immediately to the south of point Higgins, we passed an opening about two miles wide,[7] and having advanced five miles in a direction S. 10 W. from that point, we reached another,[8] that proved our situation to be in the north-east part of the extensive opening laid down in Senʳ Caamano's chart, and distinguished by the name of *Estrecho del Almirante Fuentes, y Entrada de Nostra Senʳ del Carmin*: and although the chart in this, as well as in the former instance, did not bear any very strong resemblance to the regions before us, yet it was sufficient to prove the identity of the place.

Point Higgins evidently formed the north-west point of the northern

---

[1] Naha Bay.

[2] This bearing should read 'S. 9 W.' The island was Grant Island.

[3] Now Betton Island.

[4] Don Ambrosio O'Higgins de Vallenar, governor of Chili when Vancouver visited Valparaiso on his way home to England. In an acid comment on the margin of his copy of the *Voyage* Hewett points out that 'at this time Vancouver did not know him.' This is not a valid criticism; it simply indicates that a good many of the place names in Vancouver's text and on his charts were given some time after the features named had been surveyed. The point is in lat. 55° 27′ 28″ N, long. 131° 50′ W (228° 10′ E).

[5] Caamano Point, which Vancouver assumed to be the Cabo Caamaño on Caamaño's chart of 1792.

[6] Guard Island and Vallenar Rock.

[7] Tongass Narrows.

[8] Vallenar Point, from which Vancouver could see both the S and the N parts of Clarence Strait.

entrance into the Canal de Revilla Gigedo.[1] Its south point, which I called point Vallenar, is the north-west extremity of the island Gravina, lying from point Higgins S. 8 W. at the distance of two miles, and forming the opening above alluded to. From point Vallenar lies a ledge of rocks, parts of which are visible only at low tide; this ledge nearly joins on to the above two small islands. The remarkable projecting point, noticed the preceding evening on the western shore, is that which I considered to be cape Caamano, and is a point of separation, dividing this arm of the sea into two principal branches; one being that which we had navigated to this station; the other, extending towards the north-west,[2] seemed to be about four miles wide; and is I suppose the channel by which Mr. Brown of the Butterworth had found his way to the ocean, in the latitude of 56° 20'. The opposite shore of Estrecho de Fuentes, &c. that is, the supposed straits of de Fonte, to the southward of cap Caamano, was not more than seven or eight miles distant, but in the chart before alluded to, it is represented to be double that distance; and, on comparing the latitude of the points as therein expressed, with those resulting from my observations, they were found to differ also very materially.

We now entertained no doubt of finding a passage to the vessels by this route; though there was reason to expect we should have some extent of the exterior coast to encounter. The land to the north of the Canal de Revilla Gigedo was now proved to be, what had been before conjectured of it, an extensive island which we had nearly circumnavigated.

On this occasion I cannot avoid a repetition of my acknowledgments for the generous support we received from Sen[r] Quadra, acting under the orders of the Conde de Revilla Gigedo, viceroy of New Spain; as also for his Excellency's offers of whatever further assistance the countries under his authority might afford. In commemoration therefore of his excellency's very kind attention, I have not only adopted the name of the channel after that nobleman, but have further distinguished the land to the north of it by the name of the ISLAND OF REVILLA GIGEDO.[3]

Opposite to the eastern entrance into the channel is situated the Bocas de Quadra; and as I had always regretted that no opportunity was taken to commemorate the weighty obligations conferred by Major Behm on the officers and crews of the Resolution and Discovery, whilst at Kampschatka in the year 1779, by the introduction of that gentleman's name in the charts of that voyage; I embraced this occasion to name the channel that separates the island of Revilla Gigedo from the continent, BEHM'S CHANNEL.[4] These

[1] Tongass Narrows is in effect a continuation of Revillagigedo Channel.
[2] Clarence Strait.
[3] Now Revillagigedo Island.
[4] Behm's Canal in the first edition and now officially Behm Canal. Magnus von Behm was Governor of Kamchatka when Cook's ships called there in May and June of 1779. He was most hospitable and insisted upon supplying their needs without payment, accepting only a receipt in return. See Captain King's account in Cook, *Journals*, III, pp. 664–73.

tributes are of a very insignificant nature when compared with the merit to which they are offered, and are only to be regarded as memorials to bear testimony of the zeal for advancing of science in these noble and distinguished characters, displayed by their friendly and liberal support of those who have been engaged in the several laborious undertakings projected by His Britannic Majesty, for the attainment of a true and perfect geographical knowledge of the earth.

Quitting this station, we continued along the west side of the island of Gravina; where a few rocks extended from the projecting points of its shores; these are nearly straight and compact, stretching S. 13 E. to a point[1] where I observed the latitude to be 55° 10'; longitude 228° 28'. From this point, and for two leagues to the north of it, the width of the channel did not exceed a league and a half; but, as we advanced to the south, it again increased in its width to two and three leagues. The western shore appeared to be much broken, and the land to be more elevated than on the eastern side, which is of a moderate height, and is covered with wood.

From this station the eastern shore took a direction S. 30 E. for five miles, and then turned short to the eastward and north-east, appearing to divide the island of Gravina by a passage about two miles wide,[2] in which were seen innumerable rocks and rocky islets; but the haziness of the weather did not permit our acquiring any competent knowledge of them, or of the shores forming the passage.

I was much inclined to pursue our way home by this channel, as in all probability it would have materially shortened our journey, and made it less laborious, by following a more direct line, and in smooth water; but as the main branch still led to the south, it was evidently the most proper for the vessels to navigate, and I was for that reason extremely anxious that it should undergo our examination. We therefore passed by this opening, and continued our route until near ten o'clock, when we rested for the night in a small cove near a point, situated in latitude 55° 0' 30", longitude 228° 40'. This point I named POINT DAVISON, in compliment to Alexander Davison, Esq. the owner of our storeship.[3] Here, in consequence of a strong gale of wind from the south-west, attended with a heavy rain, we passed a very disagreeable night. By the dawn of day, Wednesday the 14th, the wind was less violent, and we departed from this unpleasant station; but the agitation of the sea much retarded out progress, until we passed a projecting point of land, which I distinguished by the name of POINT PERCY,[4] when we derived some tolerable assistance from our sails for the first time during this excursion.

[1] Dall Head.
[2] Nichols Passage, which divides Gravina and Annette islands.
[3] The storeship *Daedalus*. The position of Point Davison Light, at the SW tip of Annette Island is lat. 54° 59·7' N, long. 131° 36·8 W (228° 23·2' E).
[4] Percy is the family name of the Dukes of Northumberland, who were soon again commemorated in Cape Northumberland and Duke Island.

Point Percy is the western extremity of a long narrow cluster of low islands, lying S. 5 W. from point Davison,[1] distant four miles. This cluster of islands and rocks seems to extend about five miles in an E.N.E. direction, nearly uniting to the eastern shore, which is much broken both on the north and south of these islands, and appears to form another division of the island of Gravina.[2] From point Percy, the south point of this land, or isles of Gravina, which I named CAPE NORTHUMBERLAND,[3] in honour of that illustrious family, lies S. 65 E. at the distance of three leagues. Our course was directed thither through several clusters of dangerous rocks, lying in all directions a considerable distance from the shore, with very irregular soundings from four to thirty fathoms water; the weeds, however, which grow in their neighbourhood, are a sufficient warning in the *day time* to avoid those dangers.

About noon I landed on a small island lying to the south from cape Northumberland, where I observed the latitude to be 54° 51½', longitude 228° 55½';[4] from this island, which is tolerably high, I gained a very distinct view of the surrounding rocks and breakers in all directions; the outermost of these towards the north-west lies N. 57 W. three miles and a half distant, those towards the southwest S. 67 W. four miles and half; the southernmost, which were the furthest off, south six miles and a half; and the south-easternmost S. 50 E. five miles distant. The intermediate spaces were occupied by an immense number of rocks and breakers. From hence also the west point of entrance into this arm of the sea, called by Sen[r] Caamano cape de Chacon,[5] lies S. 67 W. eight of nine leagues, and cape Fox, E. by S. five leagues distant. About a mile to the north-eastward of us, on a high detached rock, were the remains of a large village, much more exposed to the inclemency of the weather than any residence of the natives I had before seen. Here was found a sepulchre of a peculiar character. It was a kind of vault, formed partly by the natural cavity of the rocks, and partly by the rude artists of the country. It was lined with boards, and contained some fragments of warlike implements, lying near a square box covered with mats and very curiously corded down. This we naturally conjectured contained the remains of some person of consequence, and it much excited the curiosity of some of our party; but as the further examination could not possibly have served any useful purpose, and might have given umbrage and pain to the friends of the deceased, should it be their custom to visit the repositories of their dead, I did not think it right that it should be disturbed. Not from motives of superstition as some were

[1] The Percy Islands.
[2] Nichols Passage divides Gravina Island and Annette Island, and, as Vancouver surmised, this second passage, Felice Strait, divided Annette Island from Duke Island.
[3] The S point of Duke Island.
[4] Not identified, but probably the islet now named Vancouver Island, less than a mile SW of Cape Northumberland. The position of the cape is lat. 54° 51' 30" N, long. 131° 20' 30" W (228° 39' 30" E).
[5] Now Cape Chacon, the S extremity of Prince of Wales Island, which forms the W side of Clarence Strait.

then pleased to suppose, but from a conviction, that it was highly proper to restrain our curiosity, when it tended to no good purpose whatever.[1]

Our course was directed from hence across the south-east entrance of the Canal de Revilla Gigedo, with a favorable gale, though we were not more fortunate in being able to see round us, than when we passed the same region on the 4th; for immediately after noon the weather became extremely thick and hazy, with intervals of fog; and, towards the evening, a very heavy swell rolled from the S.W. and broke upon the shores with great violence, and with every other appearance of an approaching storm. Before dark, however, we reached the cove that had afforded us shelter under similar circumstances on the evening of the 3d; here we rested for the night, which was more temperate than we had reason to expect, and early on the following morning, Thursday the 15th, we again bent our way towards the vessels.

In the forenoon we reached that arm of the sea, whose examination had occupied our time from the 27th of the preceding to the 2d of this month. The distance from its entrance to its source is about 70 miles; which, in honor of the noble family of Bentinck, I named PORTLAND'S CHANNEL.[1][2]

Our provisions being now so nearly exhausted, that we each dined this day on half a pint of peas, we were under the necessity of keeping on our oars, or under sail, all night; and about seven in the morning of Friday the 16th, we arrived on board, much to the satisfaction of all parties, as we had now been almost intirely confined to the boats for twenty-three days; in which time we had traversed upwards of 700 geographical miles, without having advanced our primary object of tracing the continental boundary, more than 20 leagues from the station of the vessels. Such were the perplexing, tedious, and laborious means by which alone we were enabled by degrees to trace the north-western limits of the American continent.

Our return was attended with much relief to the feelings of those on board, who had begun to suffer the greatest anxiety for our welfare; all of whom I had the satisfaction of finding perfectly well, and also that the several requisite services were completed, and that the weather had been sufficiently clear to admit of such astronomical observations being procured as were satisfactory for all our purposes.

By the timely assistance, and the great care that had been taken of the two wounded men, who were each valuable in their respective stations, they were both in a fair way of recovery; and as we had no object to detain us longer in this situation, I gave directions that every thing should be taken from the

[1] Vancouver's attitude had evidently met with some criticism. He had taken a similar stand in 1792, when surveying Puget Sound, where he was 'particularly solicitous to prevent any indignity which might be wantonly offered' to the Indian burials. [See p. 539, note 1.] Puget and Hewett both cited instances in which his wishes were then ignored.

[2] Portland's Canal in the first edition; Portland Canal on the engraved chart, and now officially so named. Bentinck is the family name of the Dukes of Portland.

shore, and the vessels got in readiness to proceed down the inlet in the morning.

Mr. Johnstone had returned on the 30th of July. I learned from him, that on his quitting the ship he had been greatly retarded in his progress southward, by strong breezes that prevailed from that quarter, and that it was not until five in the evening of the 24th, that he and his party reached the northernmost opening, or bay, that we had passed by in the ship.[1] They used their utmost endeavors to commence their survey on the continental shore at point Maskelyne; but the wind, attended with much sea, being adverse to this design, they entered this opening, in order to prosecute the further examination of it, until the weather might become more moderate. This engaged but little of their time, as it proved to be only a spacious bay, with a very shallow bank extending from its shores in all directions; along this they rowed with scarcely a sufficient depth of water for the boats, until they arrived at its north-east end, when the water suddenly deepended from five feet to two and five fathoms, and then as suddenly became shallow again. The bank, which was flat a long way from the shore quite round the bay, prevented their landing for the night, and obliged them to come to a grapnel and rest in the boats. The small opening in the shallow bank was the mouth of a little river, not exceeding in width, according to Mr. Johnstone's estimation, a ship's length; and from every appearance it seemed to be navigable only for canoes.[2] Through this narrow entrance both the flood and ebb tide rushed with great force, but more particularly the latter; and though it is not more than four

---

[1] Nass Bay.

[2] The 'little river' was the Nass River, and Vancouver, scornful of the supposed Rio de los Reys, dismissed it as a stream of no importance. Johnstone seems to have gone up the bay about four miles. Menzies, who copied Johnstone's account into his journal, added an interesting comment: 'From the shallowness of this river it was deemd unnecessary to pursue it further, & in this we have not the least doubt but Mr. Johnstone strictly complied with his general instruction, yet had he known at the time that this was the opening the Natives called Nass it is probable curiosity would have prompted him to trace it, to know how far their information concerning it was likely to be true, for though it might not appear an eligible navigation for large Vessels at its entrance, which is the case with many Rivers, yet it might issue from or communicate with some interior Lake extending to a considerable distance inland & thereby afford a sufficient scope for a Voyage of two or three Moons in Canoes as reported by the Natives; in this case to ascertain the direction & extent of such an opening would not merely be an object of curiosity, but might in the end turn out of the greatest utility to the commercial interest of our Colonies on the opposite side, by directing the adventurous & persevering views of the Canadian & Hudson's Bay Traders to a part of the Coast where their laudable endeavours would most likely succeed in penetrating across by an interior chain of Lakes & Rivers, & by that means might be enabled to draw yearly from this Coast the greatest part of its rich & valuable Furs, for which purpose the entrance of the present opening could not be better situated, as from all accounts this is the most abundant part of the Coast for Furs of superior quality. We cannot therefore help regretting that this River whatever it is, had not been pursued a little further, as the examination of it might in this respect prove of some consequence to future adventurers.' – August.

miles from the main arm, where the water is in all respects completely oceanic, that which was discharged here at the latter part of the ebb was perfectly fresh. The natives,[1] who had visited the ships when in its vicinity, now paid their respects to the boats, and by repeating their visit in the night, occasioned some little alarm to the party. They had soon, however, the satisfaction of being convinced, that these Indians had no inhospitable design; for, on their being made sensible that their attendance was unseasonable, they immediately retired, after throwing some fish into one of the boats. On the Indians first meeting our party in the evening, they had been desired to procure them some fish; this they promised to do, and it is therefore charitable to suppose, that this was the object of their late visit.

In the morning of the 25th, being assisted by a strong ebb tide, they quitted this small river, which, with the other in port Essington observed in Mr. Whidbey's late excursion, are the only two streams that had yet been discovered to the north of the river Columbia.[2] These are too insignificant to be dignified by the name of rivers, and in truth scarcely deserve the appellation of rivulets; but should it hereafter be thought expedient, in support of the late prevailing conceits, and to establish the pretended discoveries of De Font, De Fonta, or De Fuentes, that one of these brooks should be considered as the Rio de los Reys leading into lake Bell,[3] I must beg leave to premise, that neither of their entrances will be met with under the parallels of 43, 53, or 63 degrees of north latitude; these being the several different positions assigned to the entrance of this most famous Rio de los Reys, by speculative closet navigators.

Had any river or opening in the coast existed near either the 43d or 53d parallel of north latitude, the plausible system that has been erected would most likely have been deemed perfect; but, unfortunately for the great ingenuity of its *hypothetical projectors*, our *practical labours* have thus far made it totter; the position of the former stream, seen by Mr. Whidbey, falling into port Essington, being in latitude 54° 15′, that of the latter, in latitude 54° 59′; neither of which will correspond with any of the positions above mentioned.

The 25th was wholly employed by Mr. Johnstone's party in reaching point Maskelyne, where the next morning they re-commenced the survey of the continental shore from this point, pursuing it up a branch that took immediately a southeast direction from it,[4] until late in the afternoon, when it was found to terminate in latitude 54° 20′, longitude 230° 21′.[5] Its shores

[1] These were Tsimshian Indians, as were those that Brown had encountered in Work Channel.

[2] There is no sign of the Fraser on Vancouver's chart.

[3] De Fonte was alleged to have sailed up the coast 'to the river *los Reyes* in 53 Degrees of N. Latitude' and to have ascended the river for 20 leagues to Lake Belle.

[4] Work Channel.

[5] The position of the head of the channel is approximately lat. 54° 18′ 30″ N, long. 129° 59′ W (230° 01′ E). Beyond this point Davies Bay and the Davies Lagoon extend somewhat more than a mile to the NE. The channel is about 28 miles in length.

approach within about half a mile of the north-east part of port Essington. The south-west shores of this arm were nearly straight and compact, its general width from one and a half to two miles, excepting about six or seven miles within the entrance, where it was much narrower. From the head of this branch they returned along the north-east shore, and about dark entered a narrow opening, which, on the morning of the 27th, was found to stretch irregularly, first towards the north and N.W. near four miles, and then to the E.N.E. to latitude 54° 31½', longitude 230° 16'.[1] This branch, generally preserving the width of a mile, decreased at the end of its north-westerly course, by the projection of two points, to about 50 fathoms.[2] The point extending from the western shore is a remarkably steep, rocky precipice, and at high water becomes an island. This had formerly been appropriated to the residence of a very numerous tribe of Indians, whose habitations were now fallen into decay, but still retained the appearance of having been one of the most considerable and populous villages that Mr. Johnstone had yet seen. On their return its entrance was reached about noon; and the latitude observed there was 54° 24', longitude 230° 10'.[3]

As it was in this arm that Mr. Brown had found occasion to chastize the natives by cannonading their village, our party was much surprized that not a single inhabitant should have been seen, since those who had visited them on the 24th at night; this induced a more minute examination of the shores, and in the morning of the 28th, their attention was more particularly directed to those of that bay in which as they had understood the affray had happened. At the head of it was found a small projecting rock, on which were the remains of a few Indian habitations that appeared to have been very recently deserted. The holes where the shot had made their way through the houses, proved it to be the identical place described by Mr. Brown.[4]

As they kept along the east or continental shore, they arrived in the main inlet by a narrow channel about half a mile long,[5] and about two miles to the eastward of the place where they had entered it, making the intermediate land an island,[6] a league long, and half a league broad. Behind this island was

[1] Quottoon Inlet; its head is in lat. 54° 30' 30" N, long. 129° 59' W (230° 01' E).

[2] Quottoon Narrows; its width is less than two cables.

[3] Reservation Point, at the entrance to the inlet, is in lat. 54° 25' N, long. 130° 06' W (229° 54' E).

[4] Bell describes the precautions taken: 'we conceived it but prudent to be on our guard, as the Indians remarking an apparent small force might be tempted to revenge the death of their Countrymen upon us. We therefore after Breakfast got every thing ready in case of attack, the Arms were all overhauled and loaded afresh, and every man buckled on his Cartouch Box. A match was kept burning, and in this manner we proceeded up the Arm. The Arms and defensive Weapons belonging to our Cutter were a Swivel carrying a half pound Shot – fitted in a Stock in the Bow, two large Wall pieces and a Musquetoon likewise fitted in Stocks besides a Musket & Bayonet, Pistol, Cutlass & Tomehawk for each Man; the other Boat was armd in the same way except that she carried no Swivel.' – 27 July.

[5] Paradise Passage.   [6] Hogan Island.

a small arm extending to the south-east, about two miles, and then to the
north-east about twice that distance.[1] The following day another small arm
about three quarters of a mile wide was entered in latitude 54° 45', longitude
229° 50½';[2] which, after stretching four miles to the N.N.E. divided into two
branches, one taking a course of about a league N. by E. where it joined the
main inlet,[3] making the western land an island lying about N.N.E. and S.S.W.
five miles in length,[4] and half a league broad; the other extending irregularly
towards the S.E.[5] where, in latitude 54° 40½', longitude 230° 13', it terminated
in low marshy land, like the generality of the others which we had explored.

The survey of this arm occupied the party the whole of the 29th, and on
the 30th they entered the only opening remaining unexamined. Its S.W. point
of entrance, off which lie some rocky islets, is situated in latitude 54° 51½',
longitude 229° 57';[6] this is about a mile in width, and terminated at the
distance of about six miles from its entrance, in a direction N. 50 E.

Having thus accomplished the service they were sent to perform, Mr
Johnstone returned with his party towards the ships, where they arrived about
nine in the evening, after experiencing, during this excursion, nearly an
uninterrupted series of fair and pleasant weather.

Nothing of any note having occurred during my absence, I shall conclude
this chapter by the insertion of the astronomical and nautical observations made
at this place; and, in consequence of our having been so fortunate as to be
able to obtain those that were essential for correcting our former survey, and
for our future regulation in that respect, this branch obtained the name of
OBSERVATORY INLET; and the cove, where the vessels were stationed, that of
SALMON COVE, from the abundance of that kind of fish that were there taken.[7]

ASTRONOMICAL AND NAUTICAL OBSERVATIONS.

Longitude of the observatory, by Kendall's
chronometer, on the 24th of July, according to the
Restoration-bay rate,   230° 53' 15"
    Arnold's No. 14, by the same rate,   230   9 45
      Ditto   176,   ditto,   230   27 30
      Ditto   82,   ditto,   on   board   the
          Chatham,   230   10
                                         ——————————

---

[1] Union Inlet.

[2] Steamer Passage. The correct reading would be about lat. 54° 41' N, long. 130° 22' W
(229° 38' E).

[3] The continuation of Steamer Passage.

[4] Somerville Island.

[5] Khutzeymateen Inlet, 14 miles in length.

[6] Nasoga Gulf. Trefusis Point, the SW point of entrance is in lat. 54° 51' N, long.
130° 10' W (229° 50' E).

[7] Both names have been retained.

Longitude of the observatory, deduced from
lunar distances, taken by Mr. Whidbey,

9 sets on	27th July, ☉ east of ☾	229° 56′ 37″
15	28,	230 7 9
16	29,	230 9 25
12	30,	230 8 59
6	31,	230 4 47
12	11th, Aug. ☉ west of ☾	230 34 34
16	12,	230 36 16
12	15,	230 26 49

The mean of 98 sets, *collectively* taken,   230 15 32

Mr. Baker

12 sets on	28th July, ☉ east of ☾	230° 4′ 27″
16	29,	229 58 33
12	30,	230 10
12	11th Aug. ☉ west of ☾	230 34 36
12	12,	230 12 12
12	15,	230 25 2

The mean of 76 sets, *collectively* taken,   230 15 10

Mr. Orchard

9 sets on	27th July, ☉ east of ☾	230 7 5
12	28,	230 4 31
16	29,	229 55 25
10	30,	230 13 16
12	11th Aug. ☉ west of ☾	230 38 54
16	12,	230 5 28
8	15,	230 16 36

The mean of 83 sets, *collectively* taken,   230 21 20

Mr. Ballard

2 sets on	27th July, ☉ east of ☾	229 46 45
12	28,	230 7 48
16	29,	230 2 39
6	30,	230 15 7
12	11th Aug. ☉ west of ☾	230 34 23
12	12,	230 31 41
12	15,	230 17 48

The mean of 72 sets, *collectively* taken,   230 16 39

Mr. Pigot

6 sets on	30th July, ☉ east of ☽	230	13	12
6	31,	230	2	55
5	12th Aug. ☉ west of ☽	230	22	21

The mean of 17 sets, *collectively* taken,   230 12   8

The mean of the whole, amounting to 346 sets, each set, as usual, containing 6 observations, *collectively* taken,   230 16 30[1]

Latititude, by 12 meridional altitudes of the sun, and one meridional altitude of a star, differing from 55° 15 to 55° 16½′, gave a mean result of   55 15 34[2]

Allowing the true longitude of the observatory to be 230° 16′ 30″, and by ten days' corresponding altitudes, Kendall's chronometer was, at noon on the 15th of August, found to be fast of mean time at Greenwich, 2^h 32′ 15″ 42‴

And gaining, per day, on mean time, at the rate of   24 23
Arnold's No. 14, fast of mean time at Greenwich,   2 20 46 42
And gaining, per day, at the rate of   19 37
Arnold's No. 176, fast of mean time at Greenwich,   5 37 13 42
And gaining, per day, at the rate of   42 54
Arnold's No. 82, fast of mean time at Greenwich,   6 39 2 42
And gaining, per day,   32 25

The variation of the magnetic needle, by four compasses, on shore, in 40 sets of azimuths, differing from 22° 16′ to 28° 16′, gave a mean result of   25° 18′ eastwardly

The vertical inclination of the magnetic needle was,

Marked end North		
face East,	74	33
face West,	76	33
Marked end South		
face East,	75	53
face West,	76	47

Mean inclination of marine dipping needle   75 54½

The tide was observed to rise generally about 16 feet, and to be high water 1ʰ 8′ after the moon passed the meridian.

N.B. The longitude of the several stations between Restoration bay and Observatory inlet, are corrected by the observations made at the latter place.

[1] The correct location is long. 129° 51′ W (230° 09′ E).
[2] The correct lat. is 55° 16′ N.

CHAPTER VI.

Quit Observatory Inlet—Proceed to the North-west Description of Port Stewart—
Visited by the Natives—Account of two Boat Excursions

THE route by which the vessels had advanced to Salmon cove, being infinitely better for them to pursue towards cape Caamano, than the intricate channel through which I had passed in the boats, we weighed with the intention of directing our course thus about six in the morning of Saturday the 17th; but having a strong gale from the southward, we made little progress windward.

On heaving up the best bower anchor, we found the cable nearly divided, and although this cable had been very little used, it was intirely worn out; under this circumstance, I thought we were very fortunate in saving the anchor, which, had the cable broke, must have fallen to a fathomless depth.

By eight in the evening, we had advanced about seven miles from Salmon cove, where we anchored for the night, near some rocks on the western shore, in 85 fathoms water, and steadied with a hawser to the trees on the shore. At five the following morning, Sunday the 18th, we again made sail with the tide in our favor, but with a strong unfavorable gale from the southward, with squally and misty weather; and, notwithstanding the wind was very powerful, the ship was so much affected by counter currents, that both staying and wearing were attended with many disappointments, and accomplished with great difficulty. These very unpleasant interruptions constantly attended our navigating this broken region. The Chatham drew three feet less water only than the Discovery; and it is a circumstance worthy of remark, that she but seldom felt, and never in an equal degree, the influence of these contending streams, by which we had been so continually annoyed. These were sometimes indicated by ripplings on the surface of the water, but at others we felt their effect, though there were no visible signs of their existence.

As we passed the small rivulet that Mr. Johnstone had visited,[1] we again observed the sea to be covered, to the depth of two or three feet, by a very light coloured muddy water, under which it evidently retained its oceanic colour and qualities.

The Indians, inhabiting the neighbourhood, approached us without fear, and seemed very friendly disposed, but no one of them would accompany us to the opposite shore; where, about three in the afternoon, on the flood-tide making against us, we anchored in 45 fathoms water, and, as before, steadied

---

[1] The Nass River.

by a hawser to the trees. During the afternoon the wind blew strong from the southward, and our time was employed in replacing our disabled cable with a new one. A want of wind, and the flood-tide, prevented our weighing until nine the following morning, Monday the 19th, when, with the ebb tide, we again proceeded, but did not reach the entrance of Observatory inlet until two o'clock in the morning of Tuesday the 20th; a distance of not more than 13 leagues from Salmon cove.

The west point of Observatory inlet I distinguished by calling it POINT WALES, after my much-esteemed friend, Mr. Wales, of Christ's Hospital; to whose kind instruction, in the early part of my life, I am indebted for that information which has enabled me to traverse and delineate these lonely regions.[1]

Having again reached Chatham's sound, we lay to until day-light, when our course was directed along the northern shore, to the southward of the islets and rocks that lie off cape Fox, passing between two and three miles of the north side of Dundas's island, along which are a great number of rocks, W. by S. three miles from its north-west point, which is situated in latitude 54° 38′, and longitude 229° 20′,[2] lies a smaller island, surrounded by many rocks; it appeared to be about two leagues in circuit, and is called in Senr Caamano's chart, the Isle de Zayas.[3] A favorable breeze now attended us; and, by our observations, the latitude at noon was 54° 44′, longitude 228° 59′. In this situation, the north side of Dundas's island bore, by compass, from N. 80 E. to S. 82 E.; the island of Zayas, S. 55 E. to S. 73 E.; distant three or four leagues; the southernmost of the rocks, lying off cape Northumberland N. 89 W.,[4] three miles and a half; (this is a round lump of barren rock, very small, always above water, and which has some breakers lying at a little distance off its south-east side;) and the south-easternmost of those rocks N. 22 W. This last lies from the south rock N. 43 E., distant four miles and a half, and is a low, flat, double rock,[5] always above water, and has much broken ground in its neighbourhood.

In the afternoon we passed the south-westernmost of the above rocks. These latter are two small rocks, above water, with much broken ground to the north and north-east of them, and in a direct line towards the south-easternmost rocks; they bear by compass, from the south rock, N. 44 W., five miles and a half distant.[6] Between these and the eastern shore lie many dangerous rocks

[1] Wales Point, the W point of entrance to Portland Inlet, which Vancouver here lumps with Observatory Inlet. William Wales, a noted astronomer, was mathematical master at Christ's Hospital from 1775 to 1798. Previous to this, in 1772–75, he had been astronomer on Cook's second voyage in the *Resolution*, in which Vancouver was serving.

[2] Arniston Point, in lat. 54° 38′ N, long. 130° 54′ W (229° 06′ E). The name is related to that of Dundas Island; Henry Dundas, after whom the island was named, was the son of Robert Dundas, of Arniston, Scotland.   [3] Zayas Island.

[4] Barren Island.   [5] Yellow Rocks.

[6] Distance (about 6 miles) and bearing suggest that West Rock and the smaller rock S of it were meant.

and breakers; but as we passed the south rock, I did not observe any danger
to the north of it, between it and the other rocks; where the channel, to all
appearance, seemed to be as free from impediments, as that which we were
pursuing towards the western shore of Sen[r] Caamano's supposed straits of De
Font.[1] Having at this time a fresh gale from the S.W., with a very threatening
unpleasant appearance of weather, which however gave us no other annoyance
than a little rain, we were enabled to make great progress, and passed a small
opening that, for a short distance, took a south-westerly direction. Its entrance
is situated in latitude 54° 58$\frac{1}{2}$′, longitude 228° 22′;[2] from whence, about a
league N. by W., an extensive sound was passed, taking a south-westerly
direction, and appearing to be divided into several branches, with some islands
lying before its entrance. From this sound, which I have distinguished as
MOIRA'S SOUND,[3] after the noble Earl of that title, the western shore takes
a direction nearly north, and forms some bays; the largest of these, situated
in latitude 55° 8′, has, in and before it, several small islets; the outermost
is by far the largest; and as it, in many points of view, resembled a wedge,
it obtained the name of WEDGE ISLAND;[4] from its south point lies a ledge of
dangerous rocks, on which the sea broke with great violence.

The land in the neighbourhood of Moira's sound is high, and rather steep
to the sea: but as we advanced beyond Wedge island, the straight and compact
shores were more moderately elevated, and the interior country was composed
of lofty, though uneven mountains, producing an almost impenetrable forest
of pine trees, from the water side nearly to their summits; but by no means
so high as those we had been accustomed to see in the more inland countries.
About eight in the evening, still continuing along the western shore, we
arrived off a projecting point, situated in latitude 55° 16$\frac{1}{2}$′, longitude 228° 18′,[5]
where, gaining soundings at the depth of 47 fathoms, we anchored for the
night about a quarter of a mile from the shore.

The winds were light and variable the next morning, Wednesday the 21st,
but having a flood tide in our favor we again proceeded, and soon afterwards
we passed the entrance of another sound, which in extending to the southward
divided into several branches; this I called CHOLMONDELEY'S SOUND.[6] A small
island lies to the north-west of its entrance,[7] the east point of which lies
N. 75 W., two miles and a half from the point, under which we had last
anchored. Noon brought us by our observations to the latitude of 55° 22′,
longitude 228° 21′. In this situation we had a more distinct view of the two
great branches of this arm of the sea, than we had as yet obtained. That leading
to the north-east,[8] being the same we had passed through in the boats, we

---

[1] Clarence Strait.

[2] Ingraham Bay. The entrance is in lat. 54° 58′ 30″ N, long. 131° 58′ 30″ W
(228° 01′ 30″ E).

[3] Now Moira Sound.　　　　　　　　　　[4] The name has been retained.

[5] Chasina Point, in lat. 56° 16′ 50″ N, long. 132° 01′ 30″ W (227° 58′ 30″ E).

[6] Named after the Earl of Cholmondeley.

[7] Skin Island.　　　　　　　　　　　[8] Behm Canal.

were in some measure acquainted with, but the other stretching to the north-west[1] appeared of greater extent, and seemed to be the main branch of the inlet.

On reference to Sen[r] Caamano's chart, a very distant land on its north-eastern shore appeared to be that to which he had given his own name. We were now much higher up the inlet than that gentleman had been, and as the land in that neighbourhood did not appear to form any conspicuous point, and as I wished to commemorate his researches, I gave his name to the point that divided the two branches, calling it CAPE CAAMANO, which, in our then situation, bore by compass N. 50 W. four or five miles distant, and is situated in latitude 55° 29', longitude 228° 17'.[2] The north-easternmost land before mentioned in the north-west branch, bore by compass N. 64 W., its remotest part on the opposite shore, N. 80 W., and its south point of entrance S. 74 W. To the southward of this point another opening[3] of much apparent consequence extended in a parallel direction, and the shores in its neighbourhood seemed to be greatly divided.

The weather being calm, a good opportunity was afforded to a party of the natives from the western shore to pay us a visit. They approached us with little hesitation, and one amongst their number, who bore the character of an inferior chief, requested our permission to be admitted on board. On this being granted, he gave us to understand that he was acquainted with most of the traders on the coast, and said that he belonged to a powerful chief whose name was O-non-nis-toy, the U-en-Smoket, of U-en-Stikin,[4] and pointed out his residence to be up the north-west branch. He desired we would fire a gun, on the report of which this great chief would visit us, with an abundance of salmon and sea otter skins to barter for our commodities. His request being complied with, he desired to know if I intended to go up the north-west branch, and on being answered in the affirmative he appeared to be much pleased; but on being told that we should first visit that to the north-east, the intelligence seemed not only to produce in him a great disappointment, but to incur his disapprobation. He endeavoured to make us understand, that in those regions we should neither meet with chiefs, skins, nor any thing worth our research; and that the people who resided in that quarter were great thieves, and very bad men.

Not being more than a dozen miles at this time from Escape point, the greatest attention was paid to the countenances and deportment of these strangers, using our endeavours to recognize in them any of the treacherous

---

[1] Clarence Strait.

[2] Now Caamano Point, in lat. 55° 29·9' N, long. 131° 58·9' W (228° 1·1' E). Although Caamaño did not sail this far N himself, he placed the name Punta Caamaño on his map in this vicinity.

[3] Kasaan Bay.

[4] Gunther gives the name of the chief as Ononnistoy and notes: 'The word *smoket* which Vancouver and Roquefoil used for "chief" is not known in the Tlingit language. *U-en* might be identified with *tlen* meaning "big".' – *Indian Life on the Northwest Coast*, p. 166n.

tribe by whom we had so recently been attacked; but as we did not discover a face that we had ever seen before, we were led to believe there might be some truth in the character now given of those resident upon the north-east branch.[1] I had, however, long been convinced, that, consistently with prudence, little reliance ought to be placed in such representations; for had our reception by those people been the very opposite to what we had experienced, this man's report would most probably have been the same, as he was not of their society. All the tribes of Indians we had lately met, had used every endeavour and artifice to tempt us to their habitations, but their motives for such pressing solicitations we were not able to discover.

About two o'clock a breeze sprang up from the south west, with which our course was so directed as to pass to the north-east of cape Caamano, along the western shore of the north-eastern branch; which when our visitors perceived, they declined attending us any further; and as the chief on his coming on board had given me the skin of a sea otter recently killed, I made him an ample return, and added a piece of blue cloth, which I desired he would present in my name to his chief *Ononnistoy*. This he undertook to perform with much apparent pleasure, and on my promising to visit their neighbourhood, he took leave of us, seemingly well satisfied with his reception.

On this occasion I was much disposed to proceed up the north-west branch, until we should meet a convenient stopping place for the vessels; but as there was yet a probability that the unexplored openings on the western shore might communicate with that branch, or possibly with the ocean further to the north, I was induced to seek an anchorage nearly midway between the points in question. For this purpose the Chatham was sent a-head, and in the evening she made the signal for having discovered an eligible port on the western shore, in which she shortly anchored; but the wind failing us, we were compelled to anchor at eight in the evening on the outside in 54 fathoms water, and steadied as before with a hawser to the trees; having in our way, about two leagues to the north of cape Caamano, passed a tolerably deep bay,[2] with some islands in it, which I did not consider sufficiently centrical for our purpose.

Thursday the 22d. The port[3] was found to be formed by a small, though very convenient bay, with several islets lying before it, which secured it from the wind in all directions; and being situated and circumstanced much to my wishes, we ran in and moored in sixteen fathoms water, sandy bottom, about a cable's length from the western shore. The south point of the port bore by compass S. 60 E., the bottom N. 52 W., and the north point N. 3 W.; the intermediate space, between the north and the south point of the port, was chiefly occupied by islets and rocks, admitting of channels in various directions. The southernmost of these islets, having a safe passage all round it, bore by compass N. 48 E.

Great plenty of excellent water was found close at hand. The shores

[1] Behm Canal.
[2] Helm Bay.   [3] Port Stewart.

continuing still of a moderate height, and being covered with pine trees, berry bushes, and other shrubs, rendered this as eligible a situation as we were likely to obtain.

The boats were immediately prepared for two long excursions; Mr. Whidbey in the Discovery's large cutter, accompanied by Lieutenant Baker in the launch, with supplies for a fortnight, were to proceed and finish the survey of those branches, which I had been obliged to decline towards the conclusion of my last excursion; and afterwards, to continue their researches along the continental shore, so long as their provisions might last, or till it led them back to the station of the vessels.

To Mr. Johnstone, with the two cutters, as usual, the other expedition was entrusted with provisions for ten days. He was to return to cape Caamano, for the purpose of examining the starboard shore of the north-west branch, until he should find it communicate with the ocean. With these directions both parties proceeded early in the morning of Friday the 23d.

The situation of this port was nearly opposite to, and about four miles distant from, Traitor's cove; but as we now saw no smoke or other sign of inhabitants, I concluded that the inhospitable natives had abandoned that station.

In the forenoon, the Indians who had attended us on the 21st visited us again, though without any addition to their party. The man, to whose care I had consigned the present for his chief, told me, that in a day or two *Ononnistoy* would pay us a visit. He said the chief was at some distance, and that it would require time to prepare for his journey; in the mean while he solicited a further present for him, as a testimony of our friendly intentions. With no small difficulty he made me understand that molasses would be very acceptable to *Ononnistoy*, with some bread to eat with it. Accordingly, these, with such other articles as I considered the occasion demanded, were entrusted to his care, and he departed the next morning.

The weather, since the evening of the 21st, had been very rainy, attended with strong winds and squalls from the S.E., which continued until the morning of Sunday the 25th; when the sky being serene and clear, I was enabled to procure some good observations for ascertaining the situation of this place, and found them to agree very nearly with my calculation in our late boat excursion. The southernmost island noticed off this port having then been a particularly marked point.

About midnight we were disturbed by the singing of a party of the natives, as they entered the harbour; from whose noise we were at first led to suppose them a very numerous tribe, but, on a nearer approach, it proved to be only one canoe containing seventeen persons; who, after paddling round the vessels with their usual formalities, landed not far from the ship, where they remained singing until day-break. It appeared that much time had been bestowed on the decoration of their persons; their faces were painted after various fancies, and their hair was powdered with very delicate white down of young sea fowls. With the same ceremony they again approached the ship, and then came along side with the greatest confidence.

The chief of the party, named *Kanaut*, requested permission to come on board, which being immediately granted, he presented me with a sea otter skin, and on my making him a proper acknowledgment, he desired that a traffic with his people and ours might be entered into; in the conduct of which they proved themselves to be keen traders, though, in their praise it must be acknowledged, they observed the strictest honesty and propriety in the whole of their dealings, which were accompanied by a cheerful, sociable, and friendly disposition. These good folks continued in our neighbourhood until Wednesday the 28th; when, having disposed of such articles as they were inclined to part with, they took a most friendly leave, seemingly much pleased with their visit,[1] and speaking in the highest terms of *Ononnistoy*; who they acknowledged as their chief, and the head of a very numerous tribe.

In the afternoon Mr. Whidbey and his party returned, after having traced the boundaries of the continental shore, from the place where I had quitted it to this station. The several arms that I had left unexamined were found to be of little extent.

The party did not pursue the exact route by which I had proceeded to the first of these arms, but by mistake entered the fourth opening,[2] which I had passed by on the evening of the 11th, and found that it communicated with the third opening, making the intermediate land, as I then suspected it to be, an island, which, after one of the gentlemen of the Chatham, obtained the name of BELL'S ISLAND;[3] it was about two leagues long, lying in a north-east and south-west direction. This led to the examination of the third opening, which, in latitude 55° 57', longitude 228° 42', was found to terminate in the usual manner; and from its head, nearly in a south direction four miles, it communicated with the channel I had pursued; having in that route passed the fifth opening, and another leading to the north behind Bell's island.[4] The shores of this channel, in some places not more than a quarter of a mile apart, were high, steep, and rocky, yet covered with pine trees.

[1] 'One of these Natives was during this time very anxious in his solicitations to go with us to England & Capt. Vancouver seemed inclined to indulge him as it was his own voluntary request, but on the 28th punishments were inflicted on board the Discovery of a very unpleasant nature, on seeing which all the Natives left the Bay & he that was before so solicitous to go with us now went away without taking leave of us & never afterwards returnd to the Vessels.' – Menzies, 28 August. Many punishments are recorded in the various logs, but no mention is made of those inflicted on 28 August.

[2] In the next few pages Vancouver refers to seven openings, numbered as follows: (1) Walker Cove, (2) Chichamin River, (3) Anchor Pass, (4) Bell Arm, (5) Bailey Bay, (6) Yes Bay, and (7) Spacious Bay.

[3] Whidbey had gone up Bell Arm, travelled S through Anchor pass, and later returned by way of Behm Narrows, thus circumnavigating Bell Island. Edward Bell, a native of Dublin, was clerk of the *Chatham*. There seems to be no doubt that he was the author of the excellent anonymous journal that is usually ascribed to him.

[4] Short Bay.

Rainy unpleasant weather, attended with adverse winds, rendered their progress so slow, that it was seven in the morning of the 25th before they reached the first unexamined opening, which after the surgeon of the Chatham I called WALKER'S COVE;[1] this was found to take a direction N. 60 E. about two leagues, where it terminated in low marshy land, extending a small distance from the high steep rocky barren precipices of the surrounding shores. On returning, they passed between some small rocky islets, lying off its northern point of entrance; on these were produced some groveling pine trees, and about their shores were a great number of sea otters. The next object of their pursuit was what I had considered as a bay, lying from Walker's cove N. 27 W., distant about five miles.[2] This was found to be about one mile and a half deep, and a mile wide; the shores, for the most part, were moderately elevated, covered with wood, and terminated at the bottom by a sandy beach; from hence in their way to point Fitz-Gibbon three other small bays or coves were examined.[3]

Although I was perfectly satisfied with my own examination of Burrough's bay, yet from the muddy appearance and freshness of its water, I was induced to direct this further examination, which however discovered no new circumstance, excepting the addition of a *third small brook* flowing in from its north-west side.

These researches were accomplished on the 26th; on their way that morning the party had stopped to breakfast at point Fitz-Gibbon, where they had met some Indians, who were extremely circumspect and cautious in their behaviour.

One man by himself invited them at first to the shore, whence, on seeing the boat stop, he retired; and presently four canoes, containing about ten of the natives, made their appearance from a small cove, a little to the southward of the point; one of these only advanced within musket shot of the party, singing songs, and making speeches, but they could not be prevailed upon to approach nearer, though every sign of friendship that could be thought of was made use of for this purpose; and when the boats were preparing for their departure, these good folks retired into the cove from whence they had first appeared. As the boats proceeded the canoes were soon again observed to follow, having now increased their party to fifteen or twenty persons. They still continued to observe the same distant deportment, and on seeing the boats return they crossed over, and landed on a point before the boats on the northern shore. Notwithstanding that looking glasses, and some other trifling presents, were fastened to pieces of wood, and dropped a-stern for them whilst they continued to follow the boats, and that these were all carefully picked

---

[1] Whidbey was back in the reach of Behm Canal S of Point Fitzgibbon. William Walker was surgeon of the *Chatham*.

[2] The bay at the mouth of the Chickamin River.

[3] Two of these would be Saks Cove and Fitzgibbon Cove, the latter near Point Fitzgibbon. Presumably the third was Portage Cove, opposite the Chickamin River.

up by them, they could not be induced to lessen the respectful distance they had at first observed.

When the boats came near to the point on which these people had landed, all of them excepting three who remained behind, seemingly for the purpose of guarding their arms, and one old man, who was seated on the rocks at some distance, advanced unarmed to the water side, each bearing a green bough, and singing and dancing in a most savage and uncouth manner. The boats remained stationary whilst these rude performances were exhibiting; after which one of the natives made signs that two persons should land from the boats, and immediately they laid down on the rocks a long twist of white wool, which was considered as an additional token of peace; it was, however, deemed most prudent to decline their invitations, and having thrown them a few trivial articles more, the boats pursued the survey of the continental shore, and the canoes returned to the place from whence they had departed.

The behaviour of these people was so totally unlike the conduct of any we had yet met with, as to induce an opinion in Mr. Whidbey and his party, that these Indians were a part of that tribe who had attacked the yawl, and that the very extraordinary exhibition they had made, was a supplication for mercy and forgiveness.[1] Some of the gentlemen then present having accompanied me in my last boat excursion, were perfectly satisfied that some of these Indians were amongst the number of those treacherous people.

About seven in the morning of the 27th, they entered the small arm above-mentioned to the westward of the third unexplored opening. This was found to be about half a mile wide, stretching in a northerly direction about a league, and there terminating in latitude 55° 57', longitude 228° 36',[2] by a sandy beach, over which several streams of fresh water rushed with great impetuosity. The land composing the upper part of this small arm was of a moderate height, and thickly wooded. Here they met another small party of the natives, consisting of seven men only, who seemed to be prepared to oppose their landing. Their canoes were lodged close to them, near a miserable small hut. After they had put on their war garments, they advanced to meet the boat; one of them was armed with a musket, and another with a pistol; these they cocked, whilst the other five, each provided with a bow, and plenty of arrows, had them in readiness for immediate service. Beside these, an elderly person made his appearance at a little distance; he was without any weapon, or his war garment, and whilst he made long speeches, he held in one hand

---

[1] These were Tlingit Indians. Bell was convinced that 'for all their seeming humility, and Sorrow' they were motivated not by contrition but by fear – 'fear that we were come to take further revenge for their treacherous conduct'; they feared the destruction of their village 'where besides their families, they most probably had all their property.' – August. Puget differed: 'Fear was on this Occasion out of the Question, for they could have retreated to the Woods and not have ventured near the Boats, but here we find them Sensible of their Error boldly come forward & acknowledge the offence and Outrage they have committed.' – 27 August.

[2] Short Bay; its head is in about lat. 56' N, long. 131° 31' W (228° 29' E).

the skin of a bird, and with the other plucked out the young feathers and down, which at the conclusion of certain sentences in his speech, he blew into the air. These actions being considered by Mr. Whidbey and his party as overtures of peace, they threw some spoons, and other trivial articles to the orator, and gave him to understand that they wanted something to eat. This had the desired effect; for this pacific individual ordered those who were armed to retire, and some salmon was soon brought. He now directed the boats to come to the rocks, where he delivered them the fish, and he received in return such articles as appeared to be highly acceptable, still continuing to blow the down into the air, as he plucked it from the bird's skin.

This custom I had before noticed with the inhabitants of this coast, but had never so good an opportunity of seeing it practised, nor have I a clear idea to what particular end it is directed; but as it had generally been accompanied by pacific measures, it is fair to presume that it is intended to display an hospitable disposition.[1]

To have landed amongst these people, who appeared to be so watchful and to keep themselves so readily on their defence, could have answered no good purpose; nor would it have been prudent, for the sake of a more minute, though perhaps not less equivocal, inquiry into these mysterious ceremonies, to have attempted a further acquaintance, at the risk of any misunderstanding. For these reasons, therefore, they were left in quiet possession of their dreary rocks; every inch of which they seemed disposed to have disputed, had our people persisted contrary to their inclinations; particularly as it is by no means improbable, that this party had either been concerned in the attack upon the yawl, or that they had received intelligence of that affray from some of their neighbours.

In the forenoon the fifth opening[2] was examined. Its entrance is situated S. 56 W., about a league from that which they had just quitted. It was found to be not more than half a mile wide, extending in a northerly direction about a league, and then terminating, in like manner with the various other branches before described.

The sixth unexplored opening[3] employed the afternoon. This was found to be in general somewhat less than a mile in width; in it were several sunken rocks. It extended from its entrance N. 50 W., about four miles, and there terminated as above, in latitude 55° 51′, longitude 228° 19′. In a bay on the north-east shore, the remains of an Indian village, that had been formerly of considerable extent, was observed; but it was intirely over-run with weeds,

---

[1] Down and feathers, usually white, were used in this and kindred ways over much of the Northwest Coast. On 30 March 1778, the day Cook's ships entered Nootka Sound, King noted in his journal that the hair of the first natives who approached was clotted with dirt, '& to make themselves either fine, or frightful, many put on their hair the down of young birds.' – Cook, *Journals*, III, 1393. One Indian that particularly attracted his attention was 'holding a rattle in each hand, which at intervals he laid down, taking handfulls of red Ocre & birds feathers & strewing them on the Sea.' – Ibid, III, 1394.

[2] Bailey Bay.   [3] Yes Bay.

shrubs, and small trees; amongst which the small fruited crab was in the greatest abundance, and its fruit was larger and better tasted than any before found.

The weather during the greater part of this excursion having been rainy and very unpleasant, and still continuing so, the party were detained in this arm until the forenoon of the 28th, when they proceeded to the last opening I had left unexamined;[1] and which, I had imagined, would be found either to have communication with the great north-west branch, or to extend far to the northward; but it was now proved that I had been mistaken in both these conjectures, as the opening formed only a spacious bay. Its entrance was nearly a league wide, lying N. 8 W. and S. 8 E.; its northernmost point is situated in latitude 55° 48', longitude 228° 25', from whence the north side of the bay takes nearly a west direction about a league and a half, forming in that space three or four coves, and rounding somewhat irregularly to its southern point of entrance; within which is an island[2] about a league in circuit, not admitting of any navigable channel between it and the south side of the bay. The shores bounding this bay are very moderately elevated, thickly wooded, and terminating in a sandy beach nearly all round. The interior country was not very high, particularly in the western quarter, where a very low woodland country extended nearly as far as the eye could reach. This low land, at the distance I had passed in the boats, had put on an appearance that induced me to believe it to be much broken and divided.

The examination of this bay concluded the service the party had been sent to perform, and they returned on board, keeping along the continental shore as before stated.

A short interval of fair weather, with which we had but seldom been indulged, enabled me in the forenoon of Friday the 30th to make some further celestial observations; and in the afternoon we were visited by a party of the natives consisting of twenty-five persons, who came in three canoes from the southward. These were all intire strangers to us, and were conducted by two chiefs, neither of whom was the famous *Ononnistoy*. They approached us with the same formalities as those observed by our former visitors, and if any just conclusions were to be drawn from their deportment on coming on board, we had reason to think them people of some importance; and I was consequently induced to compliment them with presents suitable to their apparent rank. These they accepted with indifference, and appeared to be more engaged in common conversation with each other, than in noticing us or any of the surrounding objects. Early in the evening they retired to the shore, where they formed a temporary habitation; and the next morning, Saturday the 31st, we were again favoured with their company. They now appeared to be more sociably inclined, and each presented me, in return for the civilities they received the preceding evening, a sea otter skin, and desired that a commercial intercourse might be established between us, as they had brought many things

---

[1] Spacious Bay.   [2] Square Island.

for barter, amongst which was an abundance of the finest fresh salmon we had seen in the course of the season. Of these a number sufficient for every one in both vessels were immediately purchased.[1]

The chiefs remained on board the greater part of the forenoon, and became very sociable. One of them had a very open cheerful countenance, and was the finest figure of a man, and the stoutest made Indian, I had yet seen on this coast. He had many scars about him, which indicated his having been a great warrior. Bread and molasses were the greatest treat we could give these people: the chiefs ate heartily of it, and distributed some amongst their particular friends in the canoes alongside. In return for this delicious repast, they took much pains to recommend to us some of their whale oil, which stunk most intolerably. This was brought into the cabin in a bladder, out of which a spoonful was very carefully poured by the chief, who extolled its superior qualities, and gave us to understand that, as a delicacy, it was quite equal to our treacle; and it was not without much difficulty, that I was able to excuse myself from partaking of their nauseous meal, which they seemed to relish in the highest degree; and finished it with a large glass of rum, a luxury to which they seemed by no means strangers.

In the afternoon, as these new friends of ours were visiting the Chatham, they were suddenly surprized by the arrival of a large canoe full of men singing a song, and keeping time by the regularity of their paddling. Their course, directed towards the Discovery, seemed not to correspond with the wishes of the former party, who immediately equipped themselves in their war garments, and their spears, which had lain in the bottom of their canoes, were now got to hand, and couched in an inclined position, with their points towards the new comers. Thus prepared they advanced slowly to meet them, making most violent and passionate speeches, which were answered in a similar tone of voice by some persons who stood up in the large canoe. They continued to paddle with much regularity towards each other; yet those who had now entered the harbour, did not appear to be so hostilely inclined as those who had already occupied the port; as the lances of the former, though in readiness for action, were not disposed in a way so menacing. On a nearer approach they rested on their paddles, and entered into a parley; and we could then observe, that all those who stood up in the large canoe were armed with pistols or blunderbusses, very bright, and in good order.[2] Their conversation seeming to have ended in a pacific way, the opposing party returned with

[1] The Indians 'every day supplied us with excellent Salmon which they sold for common Pewter Spoons; these Salmon were by no means like those got at Observatory Inlet, but proper large Red Salmon, they Speared them at the head of the Harbour where they were in great numbers...' – Bell, 30 August.

[2] 'Those Fire Arms the Indians got from Mr. Magee who commanded an American Ship called the Margaret & it is principally from these Americans that the Indians are so well furnished with such excellent weapons, which I sincerely hope, if ever they are used in an hostile Manner, it may be against those people who supplied the Indians with them.' – Puget, 1 September.

the new comers, who, on passing by the Chatham, laid down their arms; but just as they came alongside the Discovery, one of the chiefs who had been on board, drew, with much haste, from within the breast of his war garment, a large iron dagger, and appeared to be extremely irritated by something that had been said by those in the large canoe, who again with great coolness took up their pistols and blunderbusses; but on an explanation appearing to be made, their arms were again returned to their proper places; their pistols and ammunition were carefully wrapped up, and a perfect reconciliation seemed to have taken place on both sides.[1]

The chief of the large canoe requested permission to be admitted into the ship, which being assented to, he came on board accompanied by a man, who, though not assuming the character of a chief, appeared to be a person of no small consequence, as the chief seemed to appeal to him on all occasions, and his countenance bespoke much penetration.

After a few words and signs had passed in assurance of peace, and of a good understanding between us, this minister, for in that capacity this man seemed to act, gave us to understand, that the chief who now visited us, was the great *Ononnistoy*, and his intelligence was almost immediately confirmed by *Kanaut* (the messenger before mentioned) who arrived in a small canoe, and was received by the tribe in other canoes with similar ceremonies, but in a manner not quite so fierce and hostile.

Ononnistoy did not observe the distant formalities shewn by the chiefs of the other party, but accepted with great cheerfulness such presents as I considered it proper to make on this occasion. These seemed to afford him much satisfaction, and to gain the approbation and applause of all his party. The chiefs of the other tribe came on board at the same time; to these also some articles were given, which they now received with much pleasure, and appeared to be in very good humour, not only with us, but with *Ononnistoy* and all his attendants.

Towards the close of the day this great chief, with two or three of his suite, lamented that they had no habitation on shore, and requested for that reason permission to sleep on board. This was granted, and when it was dark some fire-works were exhibited for their amusement; but, excepting the water rockets, they were viewed with little attention.

From our previous acquaintance with *Kanaut*, I was not at a loss to know in what manner to provide some refreshment for *Ononnistoy*; bread and molasses, with rum and wine, were set before him, to which was added some

---

[1] This was Vancouver's only contact with the famous Haida Indians. Most of them lived on the Queen Charlotte Islands, but some had migrated to Prince of Wales Island, and eventually occupied its southern half. They were known there as the Kaigani Indians. The first party of natives to visit Port Stewart were Tlingit, many of whom the expedition had met already. The later arrivals were Kaigani. Both the Tlingit and the Kaigani were aggressive and warlike, and it is surprising that no clash occurred. They may well have been acquainted previously, as some of the Kaigani villages, on the W side of Clarence Strait, were only 20 miles or so from Port Stewart.

of their own dried fish; on which he and his whole party seemed to regale very heartily, and then retired to rest with as much composure, I believe, as if they had been in their own habitations.

Early the next morning, Sunday, September the 1st, *Ononnistoy* with his friends joined the party on shore, where they were very busily employed in adorning their persons in the manner already described; which being accomplished by breakfast time, he, attended by all the other chiefs, came off in his large canoe, and, according to their custom, sang while they paddled round the vessels. This ceremony being ended, they came alongside the Discovery, and exhibited a kind of entertainment that I had not before witnessed. It consisted of singing, and of a display of the most rude and extravagant gestures that can be imagined. The principal parts were performed by the chiefs, each in succession becoming the leader or hero of the song; at the several pauses of which, I was presented by the exhibiting chief with a sea otter skin; and the Indian spectators seemed to regret the performance was at an end, from which they had apparently derived great amusement.

There were five chiefs belonging to the associated parties; these, after they had played their parts, desired to be admitted on board. *Ononnistoy* gave us to understand, that as peace and goodwill were now completely established,[1] he wished that trading might be allowed; this taking place accordingly, several sea otter skins of a middling quality, a great number of salmon, and various trivial articles, were purchased. Fire-arms and ammunition were at first demanded in exchange, but on finding that these were positively and uniformly with-held, they very soon became reconciled to the refusal, and entered into a brisk traffic for blue cloth, files, and tin kettles, which they preferred next to fire-arms, in exchange for their sea otter skins;[2] but their fish and other less valuable articles, were readily parted with, for pewter spoons, looking glasses, beads, and other trinkets. The party of Indians thus assembled amounted to about sixty persons, who conducted themselves with strict honesty and much propriety.

Amongst these visitors was one whose character we could not define. This was a young man, who seemed to differ very materially from the rest in his general deportment. He was dressed in a blue jacket and trowsers, and seemed to be perfectly at his ease, particularly with respect to the pockets, which,

---

[1] The number of armed Indians about the ship caused much anxiety in the small *Chatham*: 'notwithstanding their friendly appearance we continued on our Guard – as in the Chatham with the Boats Crews [away on survey] & Liberty Men [on shore] we had scarcely Eight left on board all together & the largest of the Canoes was for some time under our Bows, with near Twenty Indians in all armed...' – Puget, 1 September.

[2] The vagaries of Indian taste became apparent: 'for a yard of Cloth and one or two Such pieces of Iron [two feet long], the best Skin might be purchased; how different the demand here in articles of Traffic to what it was a Couple of degrees to the Southward of this, and Copper that there was their Gold, wou'd not here be accepted of in a present. Kettles of any kind however but particularly of Iron, was a good article of Trade.' – Bell, 30 August.

to persons unacquainted with their use, generally produce embarrassment; he was very fond of segars, which he smoked in the Spanish fashion, discharging the fumes through his nostrils, and also of snuff; and we had great reason to believe that he had made free with a snuff-box that was in the cabin, and which was the only thing missed during the visit of these people. All our different kinds of provisions were perfectly familiar to this young man, who ate and drank of every thing that was given to him for this purpose, without the least hesitation, and with the greatest glee and appetite. His person had nothing of the European character in it, but from attentively observing his countenance, we were inclined to suppose him a native of New Spain, who might possibly have deserted from some of the Spanish vessels employed in the examination of this coast. He was more intelligent than any of the Indians we had found on these shores, particularly in respect of the different channels leading through this divided country. From his information we clearly understood, that the opening to the north-west of cape Caamano would be found to have some branches on its northern shore terminating at some distance in land; and although it was a great distance from hence, yet that that branch led to the ocean. His fondness for tobacco favored the conjecture of his not being a native of these shores, as he was the first who had sought after this luxury. Under the idea of his having deserted from the Spaniards, we interrogated him in their language, but to no effect; and if we were right in this conjecture, he conducted himself in a manner so as to evade our questions, and to avoid detection; for he did not betray the least knowledge of the Spanish tongue. This, however, he might have artfully concealed, lest he should have been taken from this present way of life, which he undoubtedly preferred, as he declined my offer of taking him with me on board the Discovery.

Monday the 2d. The period for Mr. Johnstone's return began now to draw near, and that we might on his arrival be immediately ready to follow up his researches, the brewing utensils and all other matters were taken from the shore, the ship was warped out of the port, and anchored near its southern point of entrance, in 25 fathoms water, soft bottom.

This port I named after Mr. John Stewart, one of the mates, PORT STEWART, in compliment of that gentleman's having made a very good survey of it; its south point of entrance is situated in latitude 55° 38′ 15″, longitude 228° 24′,[1] with 28° 30′ eastwardly variation. It is formed, as before stated, by a bay in the land, having several islets and rocks lying before it; within these, from the south point of its entrance, it takes a course N. 27 W. about half a league in length, and three quarters of a mile in breadth. In this space it affords good and secure anchorage, from four to eighteen fathoms water, good holding ground. The communication with the shore is easy, and wood

---

[1] Stewart was at this time master's mate of the Discovery. His chart of Port Stewart was published as an inset on Vancouver's chart of the Northwest Coast from lat. 51° 45′ to lat. 57° 30′ N. There is a copy in Stewart's own log. The SE point of entrance is Point Francis, in lat. 55° 40·2′ N, long. 131° 49′ W (228° 11′ E).

and water may be conveniently procured in the greatest abundance. Towards its head are two very snug coves or basons, one of which is a continuation of the port, the other formed by an indent in the land; the soundings are from six to nine fathoms, having a navigable though narrow channel into them. It has been stated, that the islets lying before this harbour admit of passages in several directions; these, however, are not very safe, in consequence of several rocks between and about their shores, visible only at low tide. The best passage into port Stewart, through which we warped, is between the southernmost islet and the main land; this is perfectly free from any obstruction, with soundings from four fathoms at the sides to eleven fathoms in the middle. These are the most material circumstances respecting this harbour, which, from its interior situation, and want of inhabitants, does not seem likely to be much frequented; but should further information be required, reference may be had to the chart, which I believe will be found liable to little if any error.

The Indians having observed our motions, inquired if it were not our intention to visit their place of abode; and as I thought it was probable their residence might lie in our route, I replied in the affirmative: this appeared to give them great pleasure; and having disposed of most of their saleable cargo, they took their leave, and returned to the southward.

The morning of Wednesday the 4th brought no intelligence of our boats, and having understood from *Ononnistoy* and his party, that there were many inhabitants in the region they were directed to explore, who, like them, were well provided with fire-arms, I began to be very solicitous for their return. About noon, however, my anxiety was relieved, by the safe return of Mr. Johnstone and all his party. He had not actually discovered a passage to the ocean by the way he had pursued, but had brought back such evidences as left little doubt that the channel he had navigated would ultimately be found to communicate with it.

The day on which they quitted the vessels was employed in reaching cape Caamano, which they effected by about dark, having been greatly impeded by a strong southerly gale, attended with a heavy sea, and a great fall of rain. In addition to these delays, they were further retarded by carrying away one of the boat's masts, and getting most of their things wet. Their time was occupied until eight the next morning (25th August), in putting these matters to rights, when they proceeded in the examination of this channel, keeping the starboard or continental shore on board. This, from cape Caamano, was found to take first a direction N. 55 W. near two leagues, then N. 23 E. to a point which, after one of the gentlemen of the Chatham, who generally attended Mr. Johnstone, I named POINT LE MESURIER,[1] and is situated in latitude 55° 46′, longitude 227° 58′. The opposite shore, which from the haziness of the weather was but indistinctly seen, seemed to take a more

---

[1] William LeMesurier was master's mate of the *Chatham*. The point is in lat. 55° 45·9′ N, long. 132° 16·9′ W (227° 43·1′ E).

westwardly direction, increasing the width of the channel; which from cape Caamano, S. 58 W. to its opposite point of entrance, named by me POINT GRINDALL,[1] (after Captain Grindall, of the navy) is only from four or five miles across; though at this station it was seven miles to the opposite shore. This point[2] projects from the main land to the westward, with some rocks and breakers extending about a mile from it. Four or five miles to the south-east of it is a small bay, with some islets and rocks lying off it; half way between it and cape Caamano our party passed a small island lying near the same shore,[3] admitting of a passage between it and the main land.

From hence another branch of this inlet, which I called after his Royal Highness Prince Ernest, PRINCE ERNEST'S SOUND, presented itself, leading to the north-eastward,[4] and is nearly as spacious as that they were pursuing; its opposite point of entrance, which I called POINT ONSLOW,[5] lies from point Le Mesurier, N. 30 W. five miles and a half distant. This, because it led along the continental shore, became the object of their immediate attention, and was the occasion of their quitting at that time the other channel.

As they advanced in this pursuit, they found the general direction of the continental shore, from point Le Mesurier, N. 29 E. for about four leagues, indented with several bays of different capacity, and along it were some scattered rocks and rocky islets. At this station, the opposite side of Prince Ernest's sound approaches within two miles of the continent, and from its entrance at point Onslow it appeared to be much broken, with several islets about its shores. Here the shores of the main land inclined a little more to the eastward. In the above direction, about a league and a half from thence, is situated the south point of an island, in front of a bay on the continental shore,[6] in which are some islets and rocks. This island extends N. 25 W. five miles, and is about half a league in breadth; its western side is much broken, and about its shores are several islets; notwithstanding these it admits of a tolerably good channel between it and the shore of the continent, which from the north point of the above bay takes a direction N. 13 W. two leagues and a half, to a point which I named POINT WARDE, situated by observation in latitude 56° 9', longitude 228° 10½'.[7] The western shore was seen to be very irregular in its direction, and much broken by water, especially in that part opposite to the island, where the sound was nearly six miles across; but here, its shores, which were in general moderately elevated, and were covered with the usual productions, approached within a mile of each other.

From point Warde the continental shore took a sharp turn N. 60 E. four miles, to a point where this arm divided into two branches. That which took

---

[1] The SE point of Kasaan Peninsula. The island off Grindall Point is now Grindall Island, and the passage between the point and the island is Grindall Passage.

[2] Lemesurier Point is meant.

[3] Ship Island.　　　　　　　　　　　　　　　[4] Now Ernest Sound.

[5] Onslow Point. Wagner suggests that it was named after George, 1st Earl of Onslow.

[6] Deer Island.

[7] The correct position is lat. 56° 10·5' N, long. 131° 58·1' W (228° 01·9' E).

an easterly direction claimed their first attention, and was found to extend about three leagues; and then winding to the N.E. by N. two miles further, terminated in the usual way, in latitude 56° 14½', longitude 228° 37'. Their examination of this branch, which I named BRADFIELD CHANNEL,[1] occupied their time until noon of the 26th; the progress of the party having been much impeded by adverse winds, and very unpleasant weather.

On setting out in the morning, one canoe with three Indians, (the first inhabitants seen during this excursion) accompanied them some distance; but on finding our party was bound up Bradfield channel, the natives made signs that it was closed, and that they would wait the return of the boats in a certain situation where, without any increase of numbers, they were found in the evening.

In the morning of the 27th they continued their researches in rainy unpleasant weather up the other branch.[2] This was not more than three quarters of a mile wide, with a small island[3] and two islets in its entrance; it extended nearly in a N.N.W. direction, three leagues, to a point where the latitude was observed to be 56° 20', the longitude 228° 11';[4] here this branch was again divided, one division stretching about N. 10 E., the other taking a westerly direction. The former,[5] about half a mile wide, terminated as usual at the distance of about a league from its entrance, near which, and likewise before the entrance of the westerly branch, lie several rocks and small islets. Here their Indian attendants, after receiving some trivial presents, took their leave. This westerly branch was not more than a quarter of a mile in width, and extended irregularly to the north-west and south-west, forming a passage about a league long to a point I called POINT MADAN;[6] where it communicated with a more spacious channel, that took two directions, one to the S.S.W.[7] through a broken insulated region; the other, stretching to the N. 28 W., was nearly two miles in width.[8]

Notwithstanding that the weather during the following day was extremely inclement, the party continued their examination, and found the land that formed their western shore to terminate in its northern direction about sixteen

[1] Officially the Bradfield Canal, the name as given in the first edition. Johnstone evidently considered that the canal ended about 12 miles from Point Warde, where it is almost closed at Duck Point. The position of the point is lat. 56° 11' N, long. 131° 36' 40" W (228° 23' 20" E).

[2] Blake Channel.   [3] Blake Island.

[4] This must have been close to Neptune Island, which is in lat. 56° 20' 50" N, long. 132° 00' 15" W (227° 59' 45" E).

[5] Berg Bay.

[6] The E part of Eastern Passage, extending from Blake Channel to The Narrows, where the passage is only 250 yards wide. This description and Vancouver's chart indicate that he placed Point Madan at The Narrows and not at its present location, farther W. Wagner hazards the guess that the point was named after Bishop Spencer Madan.

[7] W of The Narrows, Eastern Passage widens suddenly, with the bay here referred to on the S.

[8] The broad W part of Eastern Passage.

miles from point Madan, by a very conspicuous point, in latitude 56° 34′, longitude 227° 48′. To this point I gave the name of POINT HIGHFIELD;[1] and although through the badness of the weather a distinct view of their situation was not obtained, yet it was manifest that they had now arrived at the confluence of three extensive branches. The most spacious stretched to the westward;[2] that which they had navigated was the least, and the line of the continental shore appeared still to continue in the above direction up the third branch, whose east point of entrance I distinguished by the name of POINT ROTHSAY. Towards this point their course was directed, but they were soon stopped by shallow water, which obliged them to quit the shores of the continent,[3] and to proceed along the edge of the shoal in nearly a west direction; and having traced it about a league, in six to nine feet water, it was found to be connected with the north-east side of an island, lying from point Highfield N. 63 W., distant four miles.[4] To the south of the shoal and in its immediate vicinity, were four small islands, and two or three islets,[5] one of the former was upon the shoal, and the others at the distance of a league and an half, extended to the south and south-west of it. Besides these, three small islands were lying to the north of the shoal, and the land in that neighbourhood had the appearance of dividing the third branch into two or three arms, the easternmost[6] of which being the object of their pursuit, they were in expectation of finding a passage towards it to the westward of this island,[7] which in a direction N.N.E. and S.S.W. is about two miles in length, and one mile in breadth. They were however disappointed, as they found the shoal to extend from the north-west part of this island, and to unite with the land, forming the western point of entrance into the third branch, which I called POINT BLAQUIERE, in latitude 56° 39′, longitude 227° 40′.[8] This land being thus connected by this shoal to the opposite shore near point Rothsay,

[1] Its position is lat. 56° 29′ 15″ N, long. 132° 23′ 15″ W (227° 36′ 45″ E).

[2] Sumner Strait. Johnstone had not yet seen Zimovia Strait and Stikine Strait, both of which join Sumner Strait W of Point Highfield. He had come to a veritable meeting of the waters.

[3] This 'third branch' was part of the wide and very shallow estuary of the Stikine River. Johnstone's efforts to explore it are outlined in the rest of this paragraph.

[4] Kadin Island. The distance is only about three miles.

[5] Vancouver's references to the islands Johnstone encountered after he passed Point Highfield are confusing, and Johnstone's own account, which Puget copied into his log, does not help to identify them. The 'four small islands' were probably Rynda Island ('upon the shoal'), Sokolof Island and Vank Island (all as large or larger than Kadin Island) and the much smaller Greys Island. Liesnoi Island and Fivemile Island were probably two of the islets.

[6] The shallow estuary of the southern mouth of the Stikine River to the E and Dry Strait (so called because it is mostly bare at low water) to the W. They are separated by Dry Island and Farm Island, and Johnstone seems to have thought that the bay at the mouth of the narrow waterway that separates them might be the entrance to a third 'arm'.

[7] Kadin Island is meant.

[8] Blaquiere Point, the E point of Mitkof Island. Its position is lat. 56° 35′ N, long. 132° 32′ 30″ W (227° 27′ 30″ E).

was considered to be a continuation of the continent.[1] The depth of water along the edge of the shoal was from two immediately to ten fathoms at high water; many unsuccessful attempts were made at this time to pass it, but the depth decreased too fast to venture further, and as the tide fell, patches of dry sand became visible in all directions.

This investigation employed most part of the day, during which they were accompanied by nine of the natives, in three small canoes; who behaved with great civility, and departed in the evening.

The next morning, the 29th, the party quitted this shallow navigation, and continued along what was then considered to be the continent; which was now found to take first a direction S. 48 W. for two leagues and an half, to a point named by me POINT HOWE.[2] These shores were indented in small bays, with some islets lying at a little distance from the land. From this point, the nearest part of the opposite or southern shore of this western branch, which shore seemed to lie nearly in an east and west direction from point Highfield, bore south about a league distant; and to the westward of a point on this shore, which I called POINT CRAIG, lying from point Howe S. 55 E, distant two leagues, the shore appeared to be firm and compact; but to the eastward of point Craig it seemed to be much broken, and divided by water.[3] From hence the supposed continental shore took a rounding westerly direction, to a point in latitude 56° 36', longitude 227° 18'; this was called by me POINT ALEXANDER,[4] forming the east point of an opening about a mile wide,[5] with a rock nearly in the centre of its entrance; this opening took a direction N. 7 W. about two leagues; both shores were nearly straight and compact, and were about half a mile asunder as far as to this extent; but here they became much broken, and the supposed continental shore, extending N. 20 E., formed a narrow arm about a league and a half long, which was terminated in latitude 56° 47', longitude 227° 21', by shoal water,[6] at the edge of a low plain producing very long grass, behind which rose lofty barren mountains, covered with snow.

From hence the party returned along the same shore, passing between it

[1] A mistaken assumption that was to involve the expedition in considerable unnecessary exploration. Blaquiere Point is the W point of entrance to Dry Strait (Vancouver's 'third branch') which connects Sumner Strait with Frederick Sound, to the N. The Continental shore thus runs on northward, instead of swinging to the W, as Johnstone thought.

[2] Johnstone was proceeding along the N side of Sumner Strait. Presumably Point Howe was named after Admiral Lord Howe, who had already been commemorated in the naming of Howe Sound.

[3] From Craig Point the shore turns SE to South Craig Point, and the entrance to Stikine Strait, which runs S to Clarence Strait. Farther E, beyond Woronkofski Island, is the entrance to Zimovia Strait, which runs S to Ernest Sound.

[4] Its position is lat. 56° 30·6 N, long. 132° 56·9' W (227° 03·1' E).

[5] The entrance to Wrangell Narrows.

[6] Johnstone evidently considered that Wrangell Narrows ended in the vicinity of Spruce Point, about 9½ miles from Point Alexander. It is now navigable for ships of some size to its junction with Frederick Sound, a total distance of about 21 miles.

and the broken western land, through a narrow channel only three fathoms deep, which led to a point to which I gave the name of POINT HOOD,★ in latitude 56° 44′, longitude 227° 11′, Here it communicated with a more spacious branch about two miles wide, leading southward into the above-mentioned westerly branch, making the western shore of the small opening they had passed through to this station, an island about two leagues long, and two miles wide;[1] the broken land being a group of islets lying between its north side and the supposed continent. From hence, the opposite direction of this branch, which after Admiral Duncan I distinguished by the name of DUNCAN'S CHANNEL, stretched irregularly about N. 40 W., where it ultimately terminated in a shallow bay, bounded to the north by a low sandy flat, in latitude 56° 58′, longitude 226° 52′,[2] having in it several islets and shallow bays, the latter principally on the south-west shore, along which they returned. By noon of the 31st they reached a point, from whence the continuation of the great western branch was directed to the south-west. This appeared to increase greatly in width; it contained some islands and islets, particularly along its northern shore, which from this point took a direction S. 20 W., four miles, to a point which after Captain William Mitchell of the navy, I named POINT MITCHELL, in latitude 56° 29′, longitude 237° 3′.[3] The weather which, with little intermission, had been extremely bad and unfavorable to their pursuits, still continued so, and prevented their obtaining any satisfactory view of their surrounding regions. No doubt however could exist of their having now arrived in a very spacious arm of the sea, which was divided into three very large branches. That extending to the eastward[4] they had already navigated, but that which appeared to be the main branch, being nearly three leagues wide, stretched to the westward and S.W.;[5] the third, taking a S.S.E. direction, seemed also of importance,[6] and had the appearance of being connected with the main channel of the branch stretching to the north-west from cape Caamano.[7]

As far as any conclusions could be drawn from the view now before them, it seemed to be pretty clear, that the south-westerly channel communicated with the ocean; but as such communication might be through various intricate

---

★ After Admiral, now Lord Bridport. [Alexander Hood, brother of Admiral Viscount Hood.]

[1] Woewodski Island.

[2] Duncan's Canal in the first edition and now officially Duncan Canal. Named after Admiral Adam Duncan. The point to which Johnstone assigned this position cannot be identified. The most northerly of the several arms into which Duncan Canal divides extends to lat. 56° 53′ N.

[3] 237° 3′ is a misprint for 227° 3′ in both editions. Mitchell Point is in lat. 56° 27′ N, long. 133° 12′ W (226° 48′ E).

[4] The part of Sumner Strait from Mitchell Point eastward to the islands off the mouth of the Stikine River.

[5] The W part of Sumner Strait, which runs to the W and then to the SW.

[6] Snow Passage, which runs SE to the head of Clarence Strait.

[7] Clarence Strait.

channels, it appeared to be an object of too extensive a nature to enter upon, at a time when their provisions were much reduced, and at the close of their expedition. The winding rocky channels also, through which they had passed in reaching this station, were by no means proper for the vessels to pursue; for these weighty reasons Mr. Johnstone declined prosecuting his researches any further, and considered it most prudent to find, if possible, a more direct and less intricate passage for the vessels to this station.

For this purpose the next morning (1st September) the party steered for the S.S.E. branch before mentioned, and found its north-east point of entrance, which I called Point Macnamara, after Captain Macnamara of the navy, situated in latitude 56° 21½′, longitude 227° 14½′;[1] from whence its western point of entrance, which I named after Admiral Colpoys,[2] bore west a league and a half, and the nearest opposite shore south-west, about three miles distant. Their course was directed along the eastern shore which from point Macnamara took a direction S. 41 E. Nearly in this line, at the distance of four miles, the width of the channel decreased to about three quarters of a mile, by means of an island that I named Bushy Island[3] lying in the channel, about two miles long; having from its shores on both sides some detached rocks, but admitting between it and the eastern shore a channel free to navigate. From the north-west side of this island lies also a chain of small islets, extending northward to the entrance of this opening. A very strong southerly wind so much retarded their progress, that it was night before they reached the south part of this narrow passage; here they rested until the morning, and found a very rapid flood tide setting from the westward, which confirmed the opinion of the south-westerly branch having communication with the ocean. They found the eastern shore still continue its former direction to a point named by me Point Nesbitt, in latitude 56° 15′, longitude 227° 26′;[4] from whence the branch they were pursuing communicated with a wide opening leading towards the north-east,[5] which most probably divided the intermediate land, between them and the channels they had examined leading to the northward from Prince Ernest's sound. This opening is about two leagues across, in a direction S. 43 E. to its south point of entrance, which I called Point Harrington,[6] from whence the eastern shore extends S. 8 E., about ten miles, to a projecting point which I named Point Stanhope, where at noon Mr. Johnstone observed the latitude to be 56° 2′, longitude 227° 38′;[7] and from the view they now obtained of this branch, they entertained no doubt

[1] Macnamara Point, in lat. 56° 19′ 50″ N, long. 133° 03′ 45″ W (226° 56′ 15″ E). It is on the E side of the N entrance to Snow Passage.

[2] Point Colpoys, on the W side of the entrance to Snow Passage.

[3] Vancouver's chart, though not his description, suggests that Johnstone thought that the present Bushy Island and Shrubby Island, S of it, were one island.

[4] In lat. 56° 14′ N, long. 132° 52′ W (227° 08′ E). The name was wrongly spelled Nesbit in the second edition. The individual commemorated has not been identified.

[5] Stikine Strait.   [6] The derivation of the name is not known.

[7] In lat. 56° 00′ N, long. 132° 36′ 10″ W (227° 23′ 50″ E). Probably named after the Stanhope family, which was related to William Pitt by marriage.

of its being a continuation of that seen extending to the north-westward from cape Caamano; the shores of which appeared much broken, and had some rocky islets lying near them. Their passage to the vessels by this route was now well ascertained, and a fresh favorable gale so accelerated their progress, that by midnight they reached point Onslow, making the land which they had gone round since the 24th of August an island, or a group of islands,[1] which in honour of his Royal Highness the Duke of York, I called DUKE OF YORK'S ISLANDS.[2] In the course of the day they had passed three deserted villages, two of which occupied a considerable space, but discovered no signs of these, nor any other part of the shores they had lately traversed, being then inhabited. Here they rested for a few hours, and the next morning proving tolerably fair, the party were early in motion. In consequence of a strong adverse southerly wind, it was near sun-set before they reached cape Caamano; near which they were surprized by the sudden appearance of twenty canoes from behind a small low projecting point of land that seemed to contain not less than 250 Indians; a very formidable party, especially as experience had taught us, that the inhabitants of these regions never went from place to place without being well armed.

Our party immediately put themselves on the defensive, and made signs to the Indians to keep off; to this they paid no attention, and Mr. Johnstone seeing that they still advanced directly towards the boats, ordered a musket to be fired over them; but this having no effect, a swivel loaded with grape shot, was fired, sufficiently a-head of them to avoid doing any harm, but near enough to shew its effect. They now made a temporary halt but soon pushed forward again; a musket was then fired over the main body of the canoes, on which they stopped until the boats rowed past them, when they paddled over to the opposite shore. So large a body of the natives coming so unawares upon our boats was the occasion of much alarm, particularly as in passing close along the shores no signs had been observed of their being inhabited.

Being unacquainted with the cause of their assembling, and their numbers being so great, Mr. Johnstone very prudently declined any nearer acquaintance, lest their intentions should have been hostilely directed, which there was too great reason to apprehend; as no such party had visited the ship at any one time, or had been seen in such numbers together. As they were informed of the absence of our boats, it is not very improbable that the whole force of the neighbourhood might have been collected on this occasion, to intercept our party on their return; yet, on the other hand, their having been so easily deterred from any molestation which they might have intended, though superior in numbers, makes it equally probable that the meeting was purely accidental on the part of the natives. A light breeze springing up, favorable to the boats, they kept under sail all night, and arrived on board as before related.

[1] A group of islands, much the largest being Etolin, Wrangell and Zarembo islands.

[2] Duke of York Island on the chart; the outline is incomplete. The name is no longer used for the group; the islands are named individually.

CHAPTER VII.

Leave Port Stewart, and proceed to the North-westward—Visited by the Natives—Port Protection—Account of Boat Excursions—Proceed to the Southward—Description of Port Protection—Departure thence—Passage along the western side of Queen Charlotte's Islands to Nootka—Quit Nootka.

CALM weather prevented our moving until the morning of Thursday the 5th, when by the assistance of all our boats, we directed our course towards cape Caamano; intending to proceed with the vessels by the channel through which Mr. Johnstone had returned to the branch which he considered as communicating with the ocean; and to prosecute our further inquiries from some convenient station in that neighbourhood.

On the approach of evening I endeavoured to find anchorage near the continental shore, but without success; this rendered our situation very unpleasant, as we were reduced to the necessity either of returning to the place from whence we had come, or of keeping under sail all night, to which the gloomy and threatening appearance of the weather gave little encouragement. As the day closed in the wind increased to a strong gale from the south-east, attended with dark, misty, rainy weather, that occasioned us a very irksome uncomfortable night, being compelled to turn to windward towards cape Caamano, through a channel not a league in width, whose shores on either side were bounded by many lurking and dangerous rocks; these, however, we very providentially escaped, and, by four in the morning of Friday the 6th, reached a more spacious and navigable opening at the junction of two branches.[1] Here the hawser by which the launch was towed broke, and had this accident happened before, in the dark of the night, whilst we were turning through the narrow channel, it would, in all probability have been attended with her total loss; which, next to that of one of the vessels, would have been the severest we could possibly have sustained. Having now plenty of sea room, on the dawning of the day we brought to, and the boat was soon recovered. By this time the strength of the south-east gale had so increased as to oblige us to close-reef the topsails, and get down the top-gallant yards.

Under the unfavorable circumstances of such weather, in this intricate navigation, where anchorage is so precarious and difficult to be found, and where innumerable steep lurking rocks as well beneath as rising to different heights above the surface of the sea, were constantly presenting themselves, it

---

[1] Behm Canal and Clarence Strait.

must ever be regarded as a very happy circumstance that we had to leeward of us the great north-west branch, of which some information had been gained by Mr. Johnstone having passed through it; and, as far as he had been able to observe, he had considered it free from danger. The gale being attended with thick misty weather, rendered it however most prudent to lie to, until about ten in the forenoon; when, the wind abating, and the weather in a great measure clearing up, we bore away along the north-east shore of the north-west branch,[1] and at noon observed the latitude to be 55° 44′, longitude 227° 54′. The south-west shore of the branch, in this situation, bore by compass from S. 64 W. to S. 42 E., and the north-east shore N. 40 W. to S. 50 E.; the nearest part of the former shore S.W.; distant four miles, and that of the latter, being point Le Mesurier N.E. by N., three miles. The wind continuing to be favorable, we made a great progress until near dark, when we anchored for the night in seven fathoms water, on the north side of a small island, close under the shores of the Duke of York's islands, in latitude 56° 7½′, longitude 227° 34½′,[2] having some rocky islets between it and the above shores. This situation is tolerably well sheltered from the southerly and south-east winds, but the soundings are irregular, and the bottom in some places is rocky.

The night was squally with much rain, but the next morning, Saturday the 7th, the weather was more favorable, and about four o'clock we directed our course towards point Nesbitt, passing a cluster of low rocks nearly in mid-channel, and also a ledge, extending southward from that point about two miles; these are very dangerous, as most of them seemed as if they were only visible at low tide. We were well advanced by noon in the passage between the Duke of York's islands and Bushy islands,[3] having abreast of point Nesbitt soundings from 20 to 12 fathoms. By an indifferent observation the latitude was found to be 56° 16′,[4] the longitude 227° 20′. The wind having veered to the north, we were under the necessity of turning through this passage, and in so doing the soundings were found to be irregular, from 10 to 30 fathoms; and the bottom in some places rocky. The ebb tide, which commenced about noon, was favorable to our pursuit, as it sat to the north and north-west, so that about three in the afternoon we reached the spacious branch leading to the south and south-westward;[5] towards this quarter our route was now directed. The clearness of the weather gave us a very perfect view of the adjacent shores bounding the horizon in every direction. To the westward, the distant land was moderately elevated, and appeared to be similar to that we had generally found along the sea coast; of an uneven surface, and very much divided by water. These circumstances, together with the ebb tide

[1] Clarence Strait.

[2] Probably Marsh Island, in lat. 56° 07′ N, on the W side of Etolin Island, which Vancouver included in his Duke of York's Islands.

[3] It is surprising that Vancouver makes no mention of having passed the broad entrance to Stikine Strait, which divides Etolin and Zarembo islands.

[4] The lat. of Point Nesbitt is 56° 14′ N.   [5] Sumner Strait.

1053

setting strong to the westward, left little doubt of our finding a passage to the ocean by that route, though not without the prospect of its being dangerous and intricate; for beside the broken appearance of the distant land, this spacious branch seemed to be spotted with several islets and rocks, just even with the surface of the water; but more particularly so between us and the northern shore. Our soundings were very irregular, shoaling suddenly from 45 to 7, 11, and 9 fathoms; then deepening to 50 fathoms, and then no bottom with 110 fathoms of line, as quick as the lead could be thrown. This we experienced three distinct times in the course of the afternoon, which was for the most part calm, consequently our motion was slow, and was governed in a great degree by the tides or currents; these making greatly against us, about eight in the evening, with the assistance of our boats, we gained soundings and anchored in 47 fathoms water, near the southern shore; which by compass extended from S. 70 W., to N. 70 E., the latter, being point Colpoys, was about four miles from us; a rock above water, about the size of the launch, lying in mid-channel, N. 8 E. and the nearest shore south-east, about a quarter of a mile distant.

A few Indians had visited us in the course of the day, and by this time their number had considerably increased in six or seven canoes; who, after they had performed their ceremonies, indicative of friendship, similar to those I have before had occasion to notice, conducted themselves very orderly, and when they were made to understand that it was time for rest, the whole party immediately retired to the shore, where they remained, though not very silently, until the following morning, Sunday the 8th, when they repeated their visit with many songs, accompanied by a large augmentation to their party. This addition was principally of women, who, without the assistance of a single man, conducted two or three middling sized canoes, and used their paddles with great dexterity. They were by no means disinclined to entertain us with their vocal abilities; most of the full grown women wore very large lip ornaments, and as we were now visited by all ages, an opportunity was afforded of seeing the progress of this horrid piece of deformity in its several stages. In their early infancy, a small incision is made in the centre of the under lip, and a piece of brass or copper wire is placed in, and left in the wound. This corrodes the lacerated parts, and by consuming the flesh gradually increases the orifice, until it is sufficiently large to admit the wooden appendage. The effecting of this, if we may be allowed to judge by the appearance of the young girls who were undergoing this cruel treatment, was attended with the most excruciating pain; and which they seemed to endure for a great length of time. These women appeared to possess in general a degree of liveliness, and a cheerful disposition, very different from any we had before seen with this hideous mark of distinction; and could this tribe be prevailed upon to dispense with this barbarous custom, there would have been some amongst them whose features would have intitled them to be considered as comely.

The want of wind which detained us at anchor, gave us an opportunity of purchasing from these people a large supply of very good salmon, and a few sea otter skins; in return for which they received spoons, blue cloth, and tin kettles, with trinkets of different descriptions.[1] In all the commercial transactions the women took a very principal part, and proved themselves by no means unequal to the task. Nor did it appear, that either in these or in any other respect they were inferior to the men; on the contrary, it should rather seem that they are looked up to as the superior sex, for they appeared in general to keep the men in awe, and under subjection. The knowledge we obtained of their manners and customs, in our short acquaintance, was however too superficial to establish this or any other fact, that did not admit of ocular demonstration. Amongst the party there did not appear to be any chief, or other person of importance,[2] unless such authority was vested in some of the females. They all conducted themselves with great honesty, and seemed to have the utmost confidence that we should govern our conduct towards them by the same principles.

A light breeze of wind springing up from the S.E., we got under sail, and our Indian friends took their leave. We now directed our course towards the northern, or what had been supposed to be the continental, shore, to the westward of point Mitchell, intending, as on former occasions, to survey as far as we possibly could in the vessels, before the boats again were dispatched; but, on a nearer approach to this shore, it proved to be so incumbered with rocks and rocky islets, that it became necessary to alter our intended mode of proceeding; and as the weather began to wear a very threatening appearance, we crossed over to the southern shore, in order to gain shelter in the first place of security that could be found there, making the Chatham's signal to lead in that pursuit; which, from the increase of the S.E. wind, attended by dark, gloomy weather, soon became an object of the most anxious concern.

In the afternoon, the wind, which blew in heavy squalls, shifted to the S.W., and obliged us to ply in that direction in quest of anchorage; but we could reach no bottom, even when we tacked close in with the shore. We were

[1] The conduct of the Indians who approached the *Chatham* was quite different: 'In the Afternoon we were visited by a Number of Natives in about a Dozen large Canoes, but [they] excluded all Idea of Trade by the extravagance of their Demands, they had brought a large Quantity of Salmon in its highest perfection but requesting Spoons in exchange, we had the Mortification to see all go from alongside except two or three. The People were daring and Insolent & apparently perfectly Indifferent whether the[y] disposed of their Articles or not; they had plenty of Skins; but required Musquets or Powder for them.' – Puget, 8 September. Referring to the salmon, Bell remarks that 'they wou'd not part with them for any thing but Pewter Spoons, none of which we had out of the hold.' – September.

[2] Menzies' account differs: 'The Chief of this Tribe whose name was *Whoagua* came on board, he was a very stout man & seemingly of a mild disposition, he was dressed in a long Cloak made of Martin Skins, on which he placd a great value, as he would not part with it for considerable offers; the rest of the Natives were mostly cloathed in woollen dresses of European Manufactory, some in Jackets & Trowsers, others in square pieces thrown over their shoulders.' – 8 September. Bell notes that one of the Indians who came to the *Chatham* 'seemed ready dressed to play the Ghost in Hamlet, having on a compleat suit of Stage Armour.' – September.

however extremely fortunate in finding before night an excellent port, round the point considered at our preceding anchorage as the extreme of the southern shore; which, after the first lieutenant of the Discovery, received the name of POINT BAKER. This the Chatham entered, making the necessary signals for us to follow; but just as we reached its entrance the wind fell calm, and the tide, to our great mortification, sat us out. In this very anxious situation (for appearances too strongly indicated the approach of much boisterous weather) we did not remain long; for a light breeze from the N.W. springing up, and blowing directly into the port, conducted us to a safe and secure situation, where, about seven in the evening, we anchored in 16 fathoms water.

We had scarcely furled the sails, when the wind shifting to the S.E., the threatened storm from that quarter began to blow, and continued with increasing violence during the whole night; we had, however, very providentially reached an anchorage that completely sheltered us from its fury, and most probably from imminent danger, if not from total destruction. Grateful for such an asylum, I named it PORT PROTECTION.[1] Had we not been so happy as to have gained this place of safety, we must have passed a most perilous night, the preceding day having shewn us that the neighbouring shores on the outside of this harbour, afforded no bank of soundings on which our anchors would have lodged, nor would the low sail to which we must have been reduced, have kept us to windward of the dangers we must necessarily have encountered; these, together with the darkness of the night, and the irregularity of the tides, would have rendered it almost impossible for us to have avoided the land not quite two leagues to leeward of us, or the innumerable rocks lying before it, on which the sea, brought by the wind up a channel leading from the south, that we had now opened, broke with great violence. Thankful, in the highest degree, for so providential and secure a retreat from the stormy season which now appeared to have commenced, I determined to remain here, whilst the boats should prosecute the examination of the broken region before us.

After breakfast on Monday morning the 9th, though the S.E. gale continued to blow very strong, yet as the weather was clear, accompanied by Mr. Whidbey and Mr. Johnstone, I rowed out to point Baker, for the purpose of acquiring some information respecting the shores in its vicinity, with which the thickness of the weather, on the preceding day, had prevented our becoming acquainted.

From this station the inlet evidently appeared to be divided into three branches; the first was that by which we had arrived; the second took a northerly direction, through a very broken country;[2] and the third evidently communicated with the ocean, in a S.S.W. direction.[3]

---

[1] Both this name and that of Point Baker have been retained.

[2] The bay at the S end of Keku Strait.

[3] The S part of Sumner Strait, which is roughly L-shaped; at Point Baker it changes from an east-west direction to north-south.

As the continental boundary had already been considered as traced to point
Mitchell by Mr. Johnstone, I directed him to recommence his examination
at that place, which lay from this station E.N.E. seven or eight leagues distant;
and to follow that shore up the above mentioned northern branch. Should
it not be found to communicate with the ocean, he was in that case to continue
his researches to a certain point on the opposite shore, lying N. 30 W. from
hence, at the distance of eight or nine miles; where I intended that Mr.
Whidbey should commence his survey of the western shore southward from
that point, until he should arrive in the ocean, either by the channel that
appeared to communicate with it, or by any other in a more northerly or
westerly direction.

Matters having been thus arranged, we returned on board; and the next
morning Mr. Whidbey in the cutter, accompanied by Lieutenant Swaine in
the launch, with a fortnight's provisions, and Mr. Johnstone, attended by Mr.
Barrie in our small cutter, set out to execute their respective commissions.

Mr. Johnstone's excursion was of short duration, for on Wednesday the 11th,
in the afternoon, he returned, having continued his examination of the
supposed continental shore from the place where he had quitted it on his last
expedition, and found it to take an irregular direction from thence to a point
which, after Mr. Barrie who accompanied him, I named POINT BARRIE;[1] being
the east point of the opening before mentioned leading to the northward. In
that space innumerable rocks were found; and nearly in the middle, between
the two points, a large bay was seen, about four miles wide at the entrance,
and of about the same extent to its bottom; in which were two or three rocky
islets, with many rocks. The opening leading to the north seemed to be also
a large open bay, bounded with such an infinite number of rocky islets and
rocks above and beneath the surface of the water, that the navigation was very
intricate and dangerous even for the boats. Under these circumstances, Mr.
Johnstone considered it most prudent to keep without the rocks which
extended along that shore, until he was abreast of the station that was to
conclude his researches; and which, proving to be an island, acquired the name
of CONCLUSION ISLAND,[2] where Mr. Whidbey had already commenced his
survey. From hence Mr. Johnstone returned on board, without meeting with
any particular occurrence, or seeing any of the inhabitants; five of whom,
however, had visited us in the course of the day, but had not brought any
thing to dispose of.

In the evening we had a fresh gale from the N.W. but in the night the

[1] Robert Barrie, a midshipman in the *Discovery*.
[2] Keku Strait (in the words of *U.S. Coast Pilot 8*) 'consists of three parts: a large bay
at the southern and northern ends, and a narrow intricate passage, about 18 miles long,
known as Rocky Pass, which connects the two bays.' Johnstone had made a somewhat
cursory examination of the southern bay, which might be considered an arm of Sumner
Strait, and had not noticed the entrance to Rocky Pass. The bad weather he encountered
and the multitude of reefs and shallows that are found in the bay make this quite
understandable. The northern bay is an arm of Frederick Sound.

wind veered to the S.E. and again blew very hard, attended by heavy squalls and much rain. This boisterous unpleasant weather continued until Sunday the 15th, when it became more moderate, and enabled me to employ a boat in making a survey of this port.[1]

The two following days the wind was moderate, but very variable between the north and western quarters, attended by dark heavy gloomy weather; this on the night of Tuesday the 17th, brought on a very violent gale from the S.E. attended with heavy squalls and torrents of rain. The same weather continued until the forenoon of Friday the 20th, when both wind and weather became more temperate; yet I was very anxious for the safety of our friends in the boats, lest they should have been overtaken by any of these storms in an exposed and dangerous situation. In the afternoon, however, we were agreeably relieved from our unpleasant state of solicitude, by their arrival on board, all well, though very much fatigued with the inclement weather they had encountered during almost the whole of their excursion.

On leaving the vessels, their route was directed towards Conclusion island, passing in their way thither a smaller island, that lies nearly in the same direction from point Baker,[2] distant about four miles. This island is low, and is about a mile long, in a north and south direction, with a ledge of very dangerous rocks extending from its south point. From the north point of Conclusion island, which is about three miles and a half long, in a direction N. 40 W. and S. 40 E. and has some rocks lying off its shores, they steered N. 13 W, two miles; to a point forming the north point of a bay in latitude 56° 31', longitude 226° 21',[3] where they commenced their examination; and in pursuing a southerly course, the launch struck on a sunken rock, and knocked off her rudder with part of her sternpost. This accident obliged them afterwards to steer with an oar, which was not only very unpleasant, but likewise much retarded their progress. Off the south point of this bay, which in the south direction is four miles across, are a great many scattered rocks and islets, stretching nearly to the south-west point of Conclusion island, as also along the shore of the main land; which from that point takes a direction S. 20 E. about a league to the north point of the bay;[4] off which, in the same line, at the distance of about a mile, is a small island about half a league long,[5] with two smaller ones lying off its south point. This bay was found to be about two miles across, in a direction S.W. by W. and extending from its entrance to the W.N.W. two miles and a half; containing many rocks, whose tops were upon a level with the surface of the water. From hence the coast takes an irregular direction about S. 10 E. along which the party rowed,

[1] The survey was published as an inset on Vancouver's chart of the Northwest Coast from lat. 57° 07½' N to 59° 59' N.

[2] Strait Island.

[3] The N point to No Name Bay. The lat. is correct but the long. is 133° 53' W (226° 07' E).

[4] Meaning 'to the north point of *another* bay', Alvin Bay.

[5] Sumner Island.

passing some bays and islets until they reached a point in latitude 56° 17', longitude 226° 23',[1] which formed the north-east point of entrance into an opening leading to the north-west; this they entered on the morning of the 11th, and found that it formed an extremely good harbour, which I called PORT BEAUCLERC;[2] its access and egress are free from every obstruction, but such as are sufficiently evident to be avoided. From its north-east point of entrance the shores first extended N. 40 W. four miles and a half, then S. 11 W. nearly the same distance; where they took a north-easterly direction, two miles towards its west point of entrance, which lies west, two miles from the opposite point. Nearly in the middle is a small island,[3] and sundry rocky islets, with regular soundings from 13 to 20 fathoms; and an islet with some rocks before its entrance,[4] lying from the north-east point of entrance S. 35 E. at the distance of one mile. These admit a good channel on every side. The surrounding shores are in general moderately elevated, well covered with wood; and water is very easily to be procured, as the communication with the land is sufficiently commodious.

From point Beauclerc the party advanced about a league S. 30 E. to a point that I named POINT AMELIUS,[5] which forms the north-east point of a bay,[6] from whence they gained a clear and distinct view of the passage leading into the ocean.[7] It appeared to be about six or seven miles wide, taking nearly a south direction, with a high island, which, after Captain Sir John Borlase Warren, I called WARREN'S ISLAND, lying in about the middle of the entrance; each shore is bounded by innumerable rocky islets and rocks, but the middle of the passage seemed free from danger. The bay was found to fall back about a league to the westward; here the shores took a more southerly direction, and islets, rocks and breakers extended from them about a league. Some smart showers of rain fell in the fore part of the day, and as they pursued their inquiries through this labyrinth of dangers, in the afternoon, a strong gale from the ocean brought with it so heavy a sea that they were constrained to seek for shelter, and were very fortunate in finding a secure retreat in a cove that effectually protected them against a very strong easterly gale of wind, that blew during the night with great violence. In the following morning it moderated, and the party prepared to depart; but the weather at that instant becoming very thick and rainy, attended by an increasing gale from the S.E. it was deemed most prudent to remain in this snug cove, until the weather should be more favorable for carrying their designs into execution. This did not take place until the morning of the 15th; in which interval the launch was hauled on shore, and such temporary repairs were given to her, as were

[1] The lat. is correct but the long. would be about 133° 52' W (226° 08' E).
[2] Wagner states that the inlet was named for 'Amelius Beauclerc who served under Commander Gardner afterward admiral in the West Indies where no doubt Vancouver knew him.'　　　　　[3] Edwards Island.
[4] Beauclerc Island.　　　　　[5] After Amelius Beauclerc.
[6] The bight W of Point Amelius.　　　　　[7] The S part of Sumner Strait.

likely to answer their present purpose. This storm blew without intermission from between the east and south, and with such fury that it was scarcely possible to look against the wind; nor could the party when on shore stand exposed to it, without holding by the rocks, trees, or some other security.

From this cove they found the coast take a south direction nearly three miles, to a low rocky point, called by me POINT ST ALBAN'S, in latitude 56° 7', longitude 226° 18'.[1] The violence of the surf, which still continued to break upon the coast in consequence of the recent tempestuous weather, not only prevented their landing on this point, but rendered their navigating this rocky region perilous in the highest degree. Mr. Whidbey therefore determined to get at the outside of the rocks that extend about a league from the land, which with much difficulty and danger at length was effected, and they then proceeded round to point St Alban's, which forms the east point of an opening leading to the northward. This was entered, but the rocks still kept the party off from the main land, which first took a direction from point St Alban's, N. 50 W. about a league and a half, where the rocks extending along the eastern shore terminated; and from thence that shore became straight and compact, taking a direction N. 11 W. to the latitude of 56° 20', longitude 226° 9'; where also the northern extent of this opening finally ended.[2] Here they rested for the night.

The sides of this channel, which, after Admiral Affleck, I named AFFLECK'S CHANNEL,[3] were mountainous, but were not so steep as the shores of the more interior country. Its termination was formed by low flat land, covered with trees, that seemed to extend without interruption as far as could be discerned in a N.N.W. direction; through which flat country several small streams of fresh water flowed into the channel.

The next morning they returned nearly in a south direction along the western shore, and found the width of the channel to increase from half a mile near the head, to two miles at the distance of about eight miles from it, where the western shore still continuing its southern course, is indented with three large bays; the north point of the northernmost, which is the largest, being distant from the south point of the southernmost, nine miles.[4] These bays were examined, and were found to retire from the line of their entrances (being all nearly in the same direction) about a league; the northernmost and southernmost have several rocks and islets about them, and the neighbouring country is moderately elevated, of uneven surface, and is covered with dwarf, pine, and other trees.

---

[1] Now Point St. Albans in lat. 56° 05' N, long. 133° 59' 30" W (226° 00' 30" E).

[2] The correct reading would be about lat. 56° 19' N, long. 134° 04' W (225° 56' E).

[3] Affleck's Canal in the first edition and now officially Affleck Canal. As in most instances, 'channel' has been substituted for 'canal' in the sentences that follow.

[4] This description and Vancouver's chart are alike highly inaccurate. Kell Bay, middle bay of the three, is much the largest, and the chart exaggerates the size of the other two – Bear Harbor to the N and Port McArthur to the S.

The day had been foggy and very unpleasant, which obliged them to rest from their labours early in the evening, near to the south point of the southernmost bay, which lies from point St Alban's S. 72 W. distant five miles and a half; where they passed a very rainy and uncomfortable night.

Although the rain had ceased on the next morning, yet the weather continued very hazy and unfavorable; the party, however, embarked, and after proceeding about four miles along the continental shore, in a southerly direction, the fog obscured every object from their view; but as they continued their route towards the southernmost part of the main land they had before seen, they found themselves on a sudden within the influence of a very heavy long rolling swell, coming from the westward, and indicating their being arrived in, or very near to, the ocean.

Being anxious to acquire every possible information of the region before them, and of the cause of this sudden alteration, they remained stationary from eight in the morning until two in the afternoon, without the least appearance of the fog clearing away; on which they retired to a cove about a mile north of the point, which was sheltered by some islets and rocks lying before it. Here the fog prevented their departure until seven o'clock in the morning of the 18th, when the weather in some measure clearing up, they returned to the point, where they landed with some difficulty, and found it to be a very conspicuous promontory, extending in a south direction to the ocean.[1] From this promontory, the most northern extremity of the sea coast was seen to lie N. 58 W. and the most southern S. 54 W. the former about seven leagues distant, and the latter, which is the western extremity of an island of some extent,[2] about eight miles. From the north-east point of this island, which lies from the promontory S. 10 E. distant four miles, is a range of rocky islets extending to the north, within half a league from the main land, that obscured the channel before noticed as leading to the sea.

The intermediate space between these islets and the promontory, appeared to form a passage free from interruption; but the more spacious channel to the eastward of the range, seemed to be far the most eligible for vessels bound to the south or eastward. Those going to the northwest may possibly find no inconvenience in navigating this passage; in which case a very great circuit will be avoided, and they will much sooner arrive in a clear ocean; as no rocks or breakers were seen near its shores, that were not to be easily avoided; and the only interruption to the view towards the sea was a group of small islands, lying to the W.S.W. that were supposed to be those called the Hazy isles, by some of the traders.[3]

The party having now accomplished the principal object of their expedition, it remained at Mr. Whidbey's option to prosecute his researches further along

---

[1] Later named Cape Decision by Vancouver.

[2] Later named Coronation Island by Vancouver.

[3] Now the Hazy Islands. Wagner ascribes the name to George Dixon, who passed them in June 1787. The Quadra expedition of 1775 had named them Las Hermanas.

the exterior coast, or to desist from the pursuit. The frequent and long delays that had attended them thus far, left little probability of their now making any great progress along an open coast; especially as the very unsettled state of the weather was by no means favorable to the undertaking. Mr. Whidbey therefore very prudently declined the prosecution of his examination, and made the best of his way back towards the ships, stopping for the night in a cove a little to the south of that in which they had taken shelter during the storm, and which had the appearance of being sufficiently screened by rocks and islets to afford them protection; in this opinion, however, they were mistaken, for during the night so heavy a swell rolled from the southward, as to call forth their utmost exertions to prevent the boats from being dashed to pieces against the rocks. Here the party was detained until ten in the forenoon of the following day, before they could embark the tents and other matters that had been landed; and after this was accomplished, it was with no little difficulty that they extricated themselves from the surrounding rocks and breakers, when they returned to port Protection as already stated.

The communication of this intelligence, the boisterous state of the weather, the advanced season of the year, and the approach of long and dreary nights, left me in no doubt concerning the measures that ought to be now adopted; especially as the tracing of the continental boundary would now be exposed to the numerous inconveniences attendant on an open unexplored sea coast; and if, after our utmost endeavors, it should not be effected with that accuracy that had hitherto been observed, our anxious labours and exertions would be rendered very incomplete.

Notwithstanding that I was by no means satisfied with the progress we had made in our survey during the summer, yet as we had an extensive space to examine, that would occupy a great length of time, to the southward of Monterrey,[1] I was induced to yield to the measures which prudence dictated, and to decline entering on any new northern inquiries. It was now also become highly expedient that the vessels should retire to some milder region, where refreshments might be obtained; and where such relaxation and ease as now became necessary might be given to those under my command, whose zeal and laborious exertions, during the summer, had justly intitled them to my best thanks and highest commendation.

My mind was by no means satisfied with the small extent, in a direct line, which had been examined during the late summer; yet I derived great consolation in the reflection that, in all probability, we had overcome the most arduous part of our task, and that our future researches would be attended with less disappointment and fatigue. And further, that should the information we had thus obtained reach Europe, there would no longer remain a doubt

[1] Vancouver had been instructed to survey the coast as far south as lat. 30° N, or to the vicinity of Baja Point, in Lower California.

as to the extent or the fallacy of the pretended discoveries said to have been made by De Fuca, and De Fonte, De Fonta, or Fuentes.[1]

The very intricate passages by which our late researches were carried into effect, I have taken much pains to describe; yet it may not be amiss to endeavour, by assigning names to some particular places, and by a more concise account, to render so unentertaining a narrative at least more comprehensible.

It is in the first place necessary to premise, that our researches were not carried on in a continued or direct line, but through part of a very extensive, and hitherto unexplored region, in various directions, bounded to the eastward by the continent, and to the westward by the ocean; our navigation in the vessels on some occasions leading between islands, and on others along the continental shore.

That part of the archipelago, comprehended between the Chatham's and Fitzhugh's sounds, lies immediately behind, or to the eastward of, Queen Charlotte's islands, admitting of a spacious navigable channel, between the western shore of the archipelago and the eastern shore of those islands. This region, as I have already had occasion to observe, had been visited before our arrival in it by several traders, particularly by a Mr. Duncan,[2] but from whom no certain information could be obtained whether it was a part of the continent, or whether it was wholly composed of islands; this gentleman, however, was right in conjecturing the latter, and he named those parts between Nepean's and Fitzhugh's sounds,[3] PRINCESS ROYAL'S ISLANDS,[4] which name I have continued.

The continent adjacent to those islands, from point Staniforth at the entrance of Gardner's channel, to Desolation sound, the northern extent of New Georgia, I have distinguished by the name of NEW HANOVER,[5] after His Majesty's hereditary German dominions. To the northward from Nepean's sound, along the continental shore, is a continuation of this archipelago,

[1] Puget agreed. After reviewing at some length the de Fonte story, as told by Dalrymple, he noted that the only rivers found in the region (the Skeena and the Nass) were 'by no means navigable' and concluded: 'whatever Absurdities appear in that Account still are the public indebted to the Indefatigable Exertion of Mr. Dalrymple in bringing forward, those former Voyages to the World. But I am well persuaded that there does not at present Exist any River, that at all answers to that described as de Fonte's between the Boundaries of our Examination – or perhaps since that Distant period they have filled up with the falls from the Mountains.' – 19 September.

[2] Charles Duncan, commander of the *Princess Royal*, which traded on the Northwest Coast in 1787 and 1788.

[3] This should read Milbanke Sound, not Fitz Hugh Sound.

[4] The name now applies only to Princess Royal Island, by far the largest of the group, in which Vancouver included Gil Island and Campania Island.

[5] One of the four regional names that Vancouver applied to the lands between 45° N (which he assumed to be the N limit of New Albion) and Cross Sound. The others were New Georgia, New Cornwall and (in 1794) New Norfolk. None of these names ever entered into general use.

separated from the continent by Grenville's channel and Chatham's sound, nearly in a straight line; and north-westward from Chatham's sound, is a further and more extensive continuation of the same group of islands, separated from the continental shore by various channels; the most spacious of which is that by which the vessels arrived at this station, and which, in honor of His Royal Highness Prince William Henry, I have called THE DUKE OF CLARENCE'S STRAIT;[1] it is bounded on the eastern side by the Duke of York's islands, part of the continent about cape Caamano, and the isles de Gravina. It western shore is an extensive tract of land, which (though not visibly so to us) I have reason to believe is much broken, and divided by water, forming as it were a distinct body in the great archipelago. This I have honored with the name of THE PRINCE OF WALES'S ARCHIPELAGO;[2] and the adjacent continent, to the northward from Gardner's channel, to point Rothsay, the extent of our survey to the north this season, I have distinguished with that of NEW CORNWALL.

The shoal extending from point Blaquiere to point Rothsay[3] having been found by Mr Johnstone to be impassable by our boats, the land to the westward of the former point was considered as forming a part of the continent; as also that to the westward of Conclusion island, although it had not been positively so determined from point Barrie, owing to the rocks and other dangerous impediments which prevented Mr. Johnstone from keeping sufficiently near to the main land for ascertaining that fact: should, however, this conjecture be hereafter proved to have been ill-founded, and the land in question be found insular,* the channel or channels by which it may be divided or separated from the continent, are certainly not navigable for shipping; hence I have considered the continental shore to have been traced to the conspicuous promontory at which Mr Whidbey's last excursion terminated, and that its shores were there washed by the uninterrupted waters of the North Pacific. Under the impression of all the land north-eastward from that promontory to point Rothsay, being a continuation of the continental shores of New Cornwall, New Hanover, New Georgia, and New Albion, the extent of the discoveries of De Fuca, De Fonte, and other pretenders to a prior knowlege of these regions, must necessarily be decided, even admitting that such assumptions were true; hence I have distinguished this promontory, situated in latitude 56° 2', and longitude 226° 8', by the name of CAPE DECISION.[4] This cape forms (if the expression be correct) the north-west continental point, and cape Flattery in New Georgia, situated in latitude 48° 23', longitude 235° 38',[5] the south-east point of this very extensive archipelago.

* This was the following year proved to be the fact.

[1] Now Clarence Strait.

[2] As with Princess Royal Island, this name is now confined to Prince of Wales Island. Those adjacent to it are named separately.

[3] Across the S mouth of the Stikine River.

[4] Its position is lat. 56° 00' N, long. 134° 08·1' W (225° 51·9' E).

[5] Cape Flattery is in lat. 48° 22' N, long. 124° 44' W (235° 16' E).

These promontories, as it were, unfold the extremities of this broken region, which, from the former, extends to the north-eastward and south-eastward; and from the latter, to the south-eastward, north-eastward, and north-westward. The western side of the intermediate space of this extensive group of islands, between these two promontories, excepting that part opposite to Queen Charlotte's islands, forms the external or sea coast, and previous to this survey was generally laid down as the continental shore. This, at length, was found to compose the exterior coast at cape Decision, and flattered our hopes that our examination in the ensuing season would be carried into execution with less difficulty and fatigue than had hitherto attended our researches.

Conscious, however, that these additional observations may not be sufficiently explanatory, I beg leave to refer my readers to the charts for the further elucidation of our survey.

The reasons already assigned for declining the further prosecution of our inquiries along the continent, to the northward of cape Decision, induced me to lose no time in repairing to the southward; purposing in that route, should circumstances so permit, to fix the outline of the external coast, particularly the western side of Queen Charlotte's islands, which had been reported to have been very erroneously delineated in the charts already published.

Every thing was in readiness for our proceeding to sea on Friday the 20th; but contrary winds detained us until the morning of Saturday the 21st, when, with a light variable breeze, and the assistance of our boats, we were at noon about half a league to the westward of port Protection; a haven that had afforded us an asylum when we little expected it, amidst impending dangers.

Port Protection will be most readily found, by attending to the following directions. It is situated at the north-west extremity of the Prince of Wales's archipelago;[1] its southern extreme composes the base of a very remarkable, barren, peaked mountain, which I have called MOUNT CALDER, after Captain Calder of the navy;[2] this is conspicuous in many points of view, not from its superior elevation, when compared to the mountains I have had occasion to notice on the continent, but from its height above the rest of the country in its immediate vicinity, and from its being visible in various directions at a great distance. Point Baker, on an islet close to the shore, forms its north-east point of entrance, from whence the opposite point lies S. 27 W., at the distance of three quarters of a mile; the channel is good, and free to enter, yet there is one lurking rock, visible only at low tide, lying in a direction from point Baker S. 13 E., about three cables length distant; the weeds that it produces however makes it sufficiently evident to be avoided, even at high water, as it admits of a clear passage all round it, with soundings close to it from eight to twelve fathoms. About a mile to the north of point Baker is situated also

---

[1] The NW extremity of Prince of Wales Island.

[2] 3360 feet in height. Presumably the mountain referred to by Manby and others as Protection Peak. Named for Captain (later Admiral) Robert Calder.

a bank, on which the soundings are very irregular, from fifteen to thirty-two fathoms; this, with the meeting of the tides round the Prince of Wales's archipelago, causes an agitation or kind of race in the water, especially with the flood tide, that might appear dangerous to strangers; we, however, after many trials, found no where less than fifteen fathoms upon it, and no bottom could be gained with sixty and seventy fathoms of line, between it and the shore.

This harbour takes a general direction from its entrance S. 36 E., for about two miles and a quarter; its width from five to three cables length across its navigable extent; beyond which it terminates in small shallow coves. The soundings are rather irregular, from thirty to fifty fathoms; and where we anchored near a projecting rocky point, which at high water became an islet, the bottom, although the lead generally brought up mud, was hard, and probably rocky, as our cables received some damage; and just in that neighbourhood the depth was more irregular than in any other part of the harbour. From thence point Baker lies N. 25 W., the rock in the channel N. 33 W., the south point of the port N. 82 W., and the projecting rocky point, or islet at high water, east, at the distance of a cable's length. Our situation was somewhat exposed to the north and north-west winds, which might have been avoided by taking a station higher up in the harbour, or in a snug cove to the south-east of the rocky point or islet. The shores are in most places steep and rocky, and are covered with an impenetrable forest of pine and other trees. They afford several streams of fresh water, and with our hooks and lines a few halibut were caught, but the seine was worked to no effect. We sometimes deprived the gulls and crows of a kind of caplin,[1] which were left in some number by the high tides, on the beaches, and amongst the rocks; these proved to be the most delicate eating, to which our sportsmen added some ducks, geese, and other aquatic birds; of the latter we had also procured some in port Stewart; so that with different sorts of berries which the shores produced, the tables of the officers were by no means ill supplied. The wild fowl were not obtained in such numbers as to serve the ship's company, but of the fish and fruit they always had a due proportion. The irregularity of the tides prevented me from ascertaining any thing satisfactory concerning their motion, owing probably to the insular situation of the port, and the boisterous weather that had constantly prevailed. Our observations, however, served to shew that the flood-tide came from the south, and that it is high water 7^h 40′ after the moon passes the meridian. I procured only one day's observation for the latitude, for fixing the true position of this port, but it was one upon which I could much depend. That was by no means the case with the observations I made for ascertaining the longitude by the chronometers, which, since our departure from port Stewart, seemed to have gone very irregularly; the longitude therefore of this place, as likewise of the

---

[1] The oolichan or candlefish, found along the coast from northern California to Alaska. The Indians valued it because of its oiliness.

several points and stations, from hence southward to Nootka, is deduced from subsequent observations made at that port, by which the longitude of the entrance into port Protection appeared to be 226° 35′, its latitude 56° 20′;[1] and the variation, by two compasses, differing from 28° 37′ to 22° 42′, shewed the mean result to be 26° 27′ eastwardly.

Although we had passed thus far through Clarence's straits without ‏interruption, it is nevertheless a navigation that ought to be prosecuted with much circumspection; particularly from the anchorage which we quitted on the 7th, to port Protection, and from thence to sea, by the route we were now pursuing through the main channel, to the eastward of cape Decision.

Little progress was made on Saturday night, owing to the light variable winds. Several signals were made to denote our situation to the Chatham, and though soundings were frequently sought, no bottom could be gained with 160 fathoms of line. On Sunday the 22d, with the approach of day a gentle breeze sprang up from the northward, but was unfortunately attended with a very thick fog. We had however procured a tolerably good view of our situation before its commencement; and Mr. Whidbey having paid particular attention to the course we had to pursue, we made sail accordingly.

About eight o'clock we were within hearing of a very heavy surf to the westward, and shortly after, by a partial dispersion of the fog, our situation was shewn to be, as we expected, abreast of point St. Alban's, and about two miles from the nearest of those dangerous rocks that surround it. The fog gradually cleared away, and towards noon the weather became pleasant, with a favorable breeze from the north-west; this made me regret the obscurity of the morning, which had prevented our delineating the eastern shore with more exactness than had been effected by the very distant view of it obtained in the boats.

Our course had been directed between Warren's island and the islands lying to the southward of cape Decision. The southernmost of these is the largest, being about seven leagues in circuit; this I called CORONATION ISLAND, the day of our passing it having been the anniversity of that happy event.[2] At noon, it bore by compass from S. 40 W., distant four miles, to S. 23 W.; cape Decision S. 87 W., nearly two leagues; mount Calder N. 13 E.; a conspicuous point on the eastern shore, forming the south-east point of entrance into this strait, N. 76 E., distant two leagues; to which, after Captain Pole of the navy, I gave the name of CAPE POLE;[3] the east point of Warren's island S. 87 E.

---

[1] The position of the entrance is lat. 56° 20′ N, long. 133° 38′ W (226° 22′ E).

[2] The coronation of George III, 22 September 1761. Johnstone and Menzies had been shipmates in the *Prince of Wales* which was hereabouted in 1788. Referring to Cape Decision, Menzies noted: 'on the outside of it is a round Island of a moderate height [Coronation Island] with some small ones intervening which Mr. Johnstone in his Chart of this part of the Coast in a former Voyage named Charles's Isles...' – 22 September. The chart by Johnstone referred to does not seem to have survived.

[3] The W point of Kosciusko Island, which Vancouver assumed was part of Prince of Wales Island, as he had no knowledge of the narrow passage that separates the two.

about two leagues distant; its north-west point, named by me POINT BORLASE, S. 63 E., distant one league; and its south-west point S. 51 E., five miles distant. In this situation our observed latitude was 56°, longitude 226° 17′.[1]

Soon after mid-day our favorable breeze gradually decreased, so that it was past sun-set before we reached the ocean.

We had now become pretty well acquainted with this entrance into the strait, formed on the west by cape Decision, and on the east side by cape Pole; these lie from each other S. 72 E., and N. 72 W., eleven miles asunder; having to the southward of this line the island above mentioned, by which are formed three passages into the strait. That between cape Decision and the islands to the south of it, has been already described; that which we pursued beween Coronation and Warren's islands is by far the most spacious and fair to navigate, for in that between cape Pole and Warren's island some lurking rocks were observed.

To the southward of this island are three clusters of very dangerous rocks, the first lying from its north-west point S. 15 E., at the distance of three miles and a half; the second south, distant six miles; and a small islet lying from them south-east, at the distance of about half a league. The third cluster lies off the south-east point of the island, which, from its north-west point, lies S. 55 E., four miles, from whence those rocks lie in a direction S. 30 E., about four miles distant. Nearly in mid-channel between the islands, bottom could not be gained with 120 fathoms of line. We saw nothing of the land to north-west of cape Decision,[2] but that to the south-east and south of cape Pole seemed to be much divided by water.

Having once more the satisfaction of being in an open sea, our course was directed to the south-east, but our sails were scarcely trimmed to the favorable breeze that prevailed, when it suddenly shifted to the S.E., and blew a fresh gale, with which we stood to the southward. The sky soon became overcast, and towards the morning of the 23d the wind had so much increased, attended by an heavy sea, that we pitched away our sprit-sail-yard, and were obliged to get down our top-gallant-yards. About this time the Chatham made signal for having sprung a lower yard.

In the forenoon the south-east gale moderated, and died away in the evening to a calm, which afforded us an opportunity of learning that the Chatham's main boom had been carried away, an accident that we had immediately in our power to repair.[3] The calm was shortly succeeded by a fresh gale from the westward, with which we directed our course for the north-west point of Queen Charlotte's islands; these were in sight about ten the next morning,

[1] Named, like the island, for Sir John Borlase Warren. Its position is lat. 55° 55′ 10″ N, long. 133° 56′ 28″ W (226° 03′ 32″ E).

[2] A surprising remark, as Menzies states that he saw Cape Ommaney to the NW.

[3] 'The Discovery's Boat came on board [the Chatham] with one of their Yard Arm Pieces, ready fitted to repair the Defect in the Main.... The Carpenters were employed fixing the Yard Arm Piece to the Boom which made it as compleat as before.' – Puget, 25 September.

bearing E.N.E. ½ E.; and at noon, being within about three leagues of the shore, we sailed along it to the south-eastward; our observed latitude 54° 14′, longitude 226° 42′, and the variation of the compass 24° 33′ eastwardly.

In this situation the north-west point of this land, which it seems is an island, named by Senr Caamano Isle de Langara,[1] bore by compass N. 37 E. to N. 48 E, and the southernmost land in sight S. 42 E.: by our observations the north-west point of this island is situated in latitude 54° 20′, longitude 226° 59½′; and by Mr. Dixon's chart it is placed in latitude 54° 24′, longitude 226° 36′; which is no very material disagreement.

From this point, which I have called POINT NORTH,[2] we found the general trending of these shores first take a direction N. 14 W., twenty-two miles to a projecting land, appearing like two islands; the west extremity of which I named POINT FREDERICK;[3] and then S. 17 E. twenty-six miles to a high steep cliffy hill, called by Mr. Dixon Hippa island;[4] this ended in a low projecting point to the north-eastward, off which lie some breakers, though at no great distance. The coast to the N.N.E. and S.E. of Hippa island appeared to be much broken, particularly to the south-eastward; where a very extensive sound takes an easterly direction, named by Mr. Dixon Rennell's sound; its entrance by our observations is in latitude 53° 28′, longitude 227° 21′.[5] Having reached this extent about dark, we hauled our wind, and plied under an easy sail to preserve our station until the next morning. At the dawn of the following day, Wednesday the 25th, we continued along the coast, composed of steep mountainous precipices, divided from each other by the water; these seemed to have gradually increased in height from point North, from whence along the shores to this extent, were some scattered islets and rocks at a small distance from the land. Our progress was slow, the wind being light, accompanied with pleasant weather. At noon, in the observed latitude of 53° 2′, longitude 227° 22′, Hippa island by compass bore N. 42 W.; and a conspicuous projecting point, nearly the southernmost land in sight, which I named CAPE HENRY, S. 82 E.; these forming the outline of the coast, lie from

---

[1] North Island on Dixon's chart, and so named by him; named Isla de Langara by Caamaño in 1792. Vancouver adopted the latter name. Now Langara Island.

[2] Named Punta Santa Margarita by Pérez in 1774; known for many years as Cape North, but now named Langara Point. Its position is lat. 54° 15′ N, long. 133° 05′ W (226° 55′ E).

[3] Point Frederick does not appear in the British Columbia gazetteer but the feature Vancouver named was the W extremity of the present Frederick Island.

[4] Named in July 1787 by Dixon, who spelled the name *Hippah* in his text (*Voyage*, p. 205) but *Hippa* on his chart and in the caption to the engraving of the island opp. p. 205. He so named it because the natives 'lived in a very large hut, built on a small island, and well fortified after the manner of an hippah' – the fortified dwellings of the natives in New Zealand. Joseph Ingraham gave the name Frederick Island to Hippa Island in 1791, after his nephew, Frederick. Vancouver may have been aware of this, and have preserved the name Frederick by moving it N to Frederick Point.

[5] Kunakun Point, the N point of entrance to Rennell Sound is in lat. 53° 28′ N, long. 132° 54′ W (227° 06′ E). Kindakun Point, the S point of entrance, is in lat. 53° 19′ N.

each other S. 32 E. and N. 32 W., 15½ leagues apart. This cape, situated in latitude 52° 53', longitude 227° 45½', forms the south point of a deep bay or sound, its shores apparently much broken; to this I gave the name of ENGLEFIELD BAY, in honour of my much esteemed friend Sir Henry Englefield.[1] Its north point of entrance lying from cape Henry N. 27 W., at the distance of seven leagues, I called POINT BUCK, which also forms the south point of entrance into a sound falling deep back to the eastward, named by me CARTWRIGHT'S SOUND.[2] Its north point of entrance, which likewise after my very particular friend and physician I named POINT HUNTER,[3] lies from point Buck, N. 25 W., distant ten miles; and a little within this line of direction is an island near the northern shore.[4]

From cape Henry, which we passed in the afternoon, at the distance of four or five miles, the shores, so far as we had reached by sun-set, seemed to be compact and to take a more easterly direction. The southernmost land in sight bore by compass S. 72 E., and nearest shore N.N.E., five miles, and the northernmost land in sight N. 33 W. During the night the wind was light and variable, by which means our distance from the coast was increased greatly beyond what I had intended. At day-light on Thursday the 26th the land, near the south extremity of Queen Charlotte's islands, which is named by Mr. Dixon cape St. James, was seen bearing by compass S. 87 E. the northernmost land in sight N. 68 W. and the nearest shore N. 11 W., four or five leagues distant.

With a favorable though light breeze, our course was directed along the shore, but at too great a distance to admit of our making any particular or exact delineation of it; nor is the sketch we were enabled to obtain of these islands to be considered as correct, or to be depended upon,[5] because their numerous divisions would have demanded a survey that would have occupied infinitely more time than we had now to bestow. Our examination was wholly confined to the general direction of the shores, and to ascertain the position of their conspicuous projecting points. Towards cape St. James the land was

[1] Englefield was a noted antiquary and scientific writer of the day. Cape Henry is in lat. 52° 56' N, long. 132° 22' W (227° 38' E).

[2] This sentence is confused and misleading. Cartwright Sound is N of Englefield Bay. The N point of entrance to the latter is now named Annesley Point, and the name Buck Point has migrated northward to the S point of entrance to Buck Channel. Even so it is still some miles S of Tcenakun Point, the S point of entrance to Cartwright Sound. Wagner points out that the Buck family was prominent in Norwich, in Vancouver's native county of Norfolk, and that John Cartwright served in the Royal Navy and was later a noted political reformer.

[3] From 1781 to 1783 Dr. John Hunter was superintendent of military hospitals in Jamaica; no doubt Vancouver knew him there, as he was serving on the West Indies Station at the time in H.M.S. Fame. The S limit of Cartwright Sound is now taken to be Tcenakun Point, N of Buck Point. This point is the S point of entrance to Skidegate Channel, then undiscovered, which divides Graham Island and Moresby Island; but the entrance is narrow and Vancouver had no reason to suspect its existence.

[4] Marble Island.

[5] The chart is part of the larger chart of the Northwest Coast from lat. 51° 45' N to 57° 30' N.

very moderately elevated, but, like that on the northern parts of the islands, it rose gradually to rugged and uneven mountains, which occupied the centre of the country, descending towards its extremities to a less height, and is of a more uniform appearance.

The wind blew a gentle breeze from the W.N.W. attended with clear and pleasant weather. At noon our observed latitude was 52° 3½′, longitude 228° 29′. In this situation cape St. James bore by compass N. 76 E., the nearest shore N. 53 E., distant five or six leagues; and the northernmost land in sight N. 42 W.; these, with other angles taken in the course of the day, shewed cape St. James, according to our observations, to be in latitude 51° 58′ longitude 229° 6½′,[1] although by Mr. Dixon's chart it is placed in latitude 51° 48′, longitude 230°. These islands are also described by him to occupy an extent of 2° 36′ in latitude, and 3° 24′ in longitude; whereas by our estimation they include only 2° 22′ of latitude, and 2° 7′ of longitude. This difference appears to have originated in fixing the position of Rennell's sound, and to have increased uniformly to cape St. James.

From cape St. James some rocks and rocky islets extend between the directions of S. 22 E. and S. 35 E., at the distance of about a league; though Mr. Gray, in the Columbia, struck and received some material damage upon a sunken rock, which he represented as lying at a much greater distance, though nearly in the same line of direction.

The prevailing breeze favouring our wishes, the Chatham's signal was made to lead during the night; in which so little progress was made, that on the following morning, Friday the 27th, the land about cape St. James was still in sight. At noon the observed latitude was 51° 15′, longitude 229° 40′. The winds were still favorable, though very gentle, attended with delightfully pleasant weather, making a very material alteration for the better in our climate. This agreeable change, however, from our last year's experience, we had no great expectation would long continue. The whales, seals, and sea otters, seemed to be aware of this, as great numbers of these animals had been sporting about us for the two or three previous days, enjoying the sun-shine, and probably taking their leave of the summer season.

In the evening of Saturday the 28th we gained sight of the westernmost of Scot's islands, bearing by compass E. ½ N. The night was nearly calm, and the next morning the favorable breeze was succeeded by light airs from the eastward. At noon the westernmost of Scot's islands bore by compass N. 44 E., and the easternmost N. 61 E. The observed latitude 50° 45′, the longitude being at that time 230° 29′; this longitude was deduced from the above latitude, the bearings of these islands, and their position as fixed by our observations made the preceding year; which I considered to be as accurately ascertained as any station on this coast. This circumstance now afforded me an excellent opportunity of discovering the several errors of our chronometers, which were by these means proved beyond all doubt to be going very

---

[1] Its position is lat. 51° 56′ N, long. 131° 01′ W (228° 59′ E).

incorrectly. The longitude shewn at noon by Kendall was 230° 56', by Arnold's No. 14, 230° 20' 38", and by Arnold's No. 176, 231° 12' 37". These being deduced from very excellent observations made both before and after noon, shewed Kendall's to be 27' 15", and Arnold's No. 176 to be 43' 37" to the east, and No. 14, to be 8' 22" to the west of the truth.

From hence our course was directed in the best manner we were able towards Nootka, then lying S. 58 E., at the distance of 45 leagues. Such however was the tardiness of our progress from adverse winds, calms, squally, thick, rainy, or foggy weather; that it was not until about noon of Saturday the 5th of October that we reached that port.[1]

The usual ceremonies of salutes, and other formalities having passed, accompanied by Mr. Puget I waited on Senr Saavadra, the commandant of the port;[2] who informed me, that he had not received any intelligence, either from Europe or from New Spain, since our departure from hence in the spring; and that neither the Dædalus, nor any other ship with stores addressed to me, had been there. The Dædalus I had some expectation of meeting here, in the event of her having made a good passage to port Jackson, and not having been there detained.

The only vessel we found at Nootka, was the San Carlos laid up for the winter; but Senr Saavadra gave me to understand, that in the course of the summer the port had been visited by a French ship called La Flavia, having on board a very valuable cargo of European commodities, which was carried to Kamschatka, there to be disposed of to the Russians for furs, with which a cargo of tea was to have been purchased in China; but that their expedition hitherto had not answered their expectations.

Senr Saavadra further stated, that whilst the vessel remained at Nootka the crew had been very mutinous; and so unruly, that the commandant had been on the point of employing force to compel them to due obedience of their commander's orders, to which at length they seemed to be tolerably well

---

[1] It had been a trying voyage for the *Chatham*, as excerpts from Puget's log will demonstrate: 'we have had incessant Rain & the Weather so thick in general that the Discovery was frequently not visible, though within hale.... We have had no Observations now these four Days past.' – 2 October. 'During the Night the Fore top Gallant Yard was carried away & both Top Gallant Sails Split, this was occasioned by the continual Pressure of Sail we were obliged to carry to keep Station with the Discovery.' – 3 October. Later 'we experienced so great a motion, that those on Deck could Scarely stand, occasioned by a heavy Swell from the East crossed by that from the SW. At Midnight in wearing with the Discovery we had the Misfortune again to carry away the Main Boom four feet from the Jaws by both Main Sheets giving way to a Sudden Roll & though it went with amazing Rapidity from Rigging to Rigging, yet fortunately no Person was hurt.' – 4 October.

[2] Ramón Saavedra, who had succeeded Fidalgo. The latter had assured Puget that the *Discovery* and *Chatham* could expect 'abundance of Greens Sallad &c.' when they returned to Nootka, but they found only 'a very Small allotment of Vegetables were preserved for our Use.' – a great disappointment after their arduous service on the coast. Puget had 'not the Smallest Doubt' that if Fidalgo had remained in command 'we Should have been better Supplied.' – 6 October.

reconciled, and departed for China less disorderly inclined.[1] Some few American vessels had also arrived in our absence, but in a most deplorable condition, totally in want of provisions, naval stores, and even such articles of merchandize as were necessary for trading with the natives.

A strong gale of wind from the S. E. the next morning, Sunday the 6th, obliged us to strike the top-gallant-masts. The carpenters were employed on shore in cutting down a new main boom, a gaff spritsail-yard, and other spars that were wanted; whilst the rest of the respective crews were engaged in the several other duties that now required attention. These fully occupied our time until Tuesday morning the 8th, when, having requested the favor of Senr Saavadra to take charge of a letter containing instructions for the guidance of the commander of the Dædalus, or of any other vessel that might arrive at Nootka with dispatches for me, or with stores for our service; we sailed from that port with a light northerly wind, paying and receiving from the fort the usual compliments.[2]

On the preceding day I procured some excellent observations, both before and after noon, for ascertaining the error of our chronometers at this place. The mean result of which shewed that Kendall's was 34' 50"; Arnold's No. 176, 47' 21" to the east; and that No. 14, was 18', 20" to the west of the truth. These observations, with those made when off Scot's islands, completely manifested the increase of error in that lapse of time, by which means a new rate of going was pretty well ascertained; and which having been adopted in calculating and correcting the longitude assigned to the several stations between port Stewart and Nootka as before mentioned, I trust will be found liable to little objection.

The error and rate of the chronometers as resulting from the before mentioned observations, shewed Kendall's at noon on the 7th, to be fast of

---

[1] *La Flavie*, of 600 tons, much the largest trading ship to visit the Northwest Coast at this time. The failure of her voyage was due to a mutiny that brought echoes of the French Revolution to the Pacific. Saavedra described her as having been 'fitted out for a Commercial Expedition and employed by the [French] Government to look after Monsieur de Peyrouse [La Pérouse]. The People had mutinied on board La Flavie to the Northward in the Harbour of St. Peter and Paul at Kamschatka; but were brought by the Exertion of her Officers to a proper Sense of their Duty. They attempted a Second Insurrection at Nootka & even when Mr. Saavedra was on board. The Officers again quelled it & the Ringleader secured; but so determined were they to pursue such Measures in which they had twice proved unsuccessful, that no one could be persuaded to inflict any Corporal Punishment on the Offender, & after that the French Officers were under the Necessity of inforcing the Necessary discipline with Fire Arms, but fortunately were not drove to the Necessity of using them.... However with the Assistance of Mr. Saavedra the Ringleaders were punished, though the whole threatened loudly to lay such Ill Usage before the National Assembly.' – Puget, 6 October.

[2] Saavedra was a good host. When the ships were about to sail he 'gave a grand Entertainment to the Captains and Officers of the two Vessels, he return'd Captn. Vancouver's Salute on his landing, and after dinner the health of the two Kings was drank with Twenty one Guns.' – Bell, 8 October.

mean time at Greenwich,   2^h 51′ 4″   ‴

And to be gaining per day at the rate of   22   23

Arnold's No. 176, ditto, ditto,   6   11   14

And to be gaining per day at the rate of   40″ 45‴

Arnold's No. 14, ditto, ditto   2   38   59

And to be gaining per day at the rate of   21   37

    These rates will regulate our further observations, until we may have an opportunity of ascertaining the errors more correctly.

CHAPTER VIII.

Passage to the Southward—The Chatham sent to Port Bodega—Arrival of the Discovery at Port Francisco—Chatham arrives there—Account of her Proceedings—Proceed to Monterrey—Joined by the Dædalus—Conduct of the Governor—Proceed to the Southward—Anchor at S^(ta) Barbara—Visit Bueno Ventura—Proceed along the Coast to the Southward—Arrive at St. Diego and the adjacent Islands—Astronomical and Nautical Observations.

On leaving the port of Nootka, our progress was so much impeded by the want of wind, and by the influence of those very extraordinary counter tides or currents already noticed, that by six in the evening of Tuesday October 8th we were not more than two leagues to the southward of point Breakers,[1] about which time a strange vessel was seen from the mast head to windward; but as the night was approaching, and as I wished to avoid any delay, we took no other notice of her,[2] but continued our course to the S.E. agreeably to my former determination of recommencing our researches on the southern parts of New Albion, and of procuring such of the necessary refreshments as those countries afford, and which we now very preceptibly began to require.

As I had little doubt that the store ship would join us before we should have quitted those shores, and as St. Diego appeared to me to be the most likely harbour to answer several purposes, I intended to unload her there, and to give our vessels such necessary repair and requipment as each might demand.

With variable winds from the N.W. and S.E. we made the best of our way. These winds, particularly the former, though blowing a moderate breeze, were frequently attended with very foggy weather; we however made so good a progress, that by the afternoon of Monday the 14th, we passed cape Orford; to the southward of which, as we proceeded along the coast, we observed on the eminences and hills that form the shores, at certain distances, large fires burning throughout the whole night; a circumstance that had not before occurred to my observation on this coast.

Being anxious to obtain some certain information respecting the port of Bodega,[3] of which the inclemency of the weather the preceding season had disappointed me, I directed Mr. Puget, on Tuesday the 15th, to make the best of his way thither, whilst I proceeded to St. Francisco, in the hope of meeting

---

[1] Estevan Point.　　　　[2] The vessel was the storeship *Daedalus*, as will appear.
[3] Now Bodega Bay.

Senr Quadra there, or at Monterrey, with sufficient credentials for settling the business depending about Nootka; which, it was not improbable, might render our return thither immediately necessary. Mr. Puget having received his directions, and having appointed St. Francisco as a rendezvous where he would either meet or hear from me, he immediately departed for the port of Bodega; and as there was not the least probability of Mr. Menzies being able to visit that part of the coast by any other opportunity, he accompanied Mr. Puget in pursuit of botanical information.

In the evening cape Mendocino was seen bearing S.E. at the distance of seven or eight leagues. During the night, and all the next day, Wednesday the 16th, the wind was light and very baffling, attended with a thick fog, or hazy weather, that continued until the morning of Thursday the 17th, when, with a fine breeze from the N.N.W. we steered along the coast to the southeast of cape Mendocino. At noon the observed latitude was 39° 18'; the coast then in sight extending by compass from N. to E.S.E. the nearest shore N.E. distant about a league.

In the afternoon we passed point Barro de Arena,[1] and to the north-west of it some breakers were now seen, about two miles from the shore, that had not been noticed on our former visit.

The Chatham, though at some distance before us, was yet in sight, and kept close to the land; but we directed our course for point de los Reys.[2] Light baffling winds, attended by fogs or thick weather, prevented our reaching that distance until noon of Saturday the 19th; when we passed that promontory with a pleasant breeze from the N.N.W. which, by seven in the evening, brought us to an anchor in port St. Francisco, near our former berth off the Presidio.

We were soon hailed from the shore, upon which a boat was dispatched thither, and immediately returned with our civil and attentive friend Senr Sal; who, in addition to the offers of his services and hospitality, gratified us by communicating the interesting intelligence of the state of Europe, up to so late a date as the preceding February; which, as may be naturally expected, had long been an object of our most anxious curiosity. After supper Senr Sal retired to the shore, and the next morning I received from him two letters;[3] the one requesting, in an official form, that I would acquaint him in writing of our arrival in port St. Francisco, of the supplies we should want, and of the time I intended to remain in that port, in order that he might immediately communicate the same to the governor of the province; the other stating that, under the superior orders by which alone his conduct could be governed, he was obliged to make known to me, that no individual could be permitted to come on shore, but for the purposes of producing wood and water,

---

[1] So named on Vancouver's chart; now Point Arena.

[2] Now Point Reyes.

[3] For copies of Vancouver's correspondence with Sal in San Francisco see P.R.O., Adm. 1/2629, ff. 68–75v.

excepting myself and one officer, or midshipman, who might pass to the Presidio, where I should be received and attended as on our former visit.

These restrictions were of a nature so unexpected, ungracious, and degrading, that I could not but consider them as little short of a dismission from St. Francisco,[1] and I was left in the greatest perplexity to account for a reception so totally different from what we had experienced on a former occasion, and so contrary to what I had been taught to expect, by the letters with which I had been honored from the viceroy of New Spain, in return to my letter of thanks for the great civilities that had been conferred upon us.

I was given to understand, that a captain in the Spanish infantry, named Arrillaga,[2] had arrived at Monterrey some time in the course of the preceding

[1] Bell and others were critical of Vancouver's mild reaction to the restrictions imposed: 'Captain Vancouver when he received the Letter, expostulated with Seignr. Sall on these Strange restrictions, and asked him to permit two of his Officers to attend him on shore, which was granted. But here surely Captn. V. condescended to act below his dignity and consequence as Commander of a British Man of War. Surely he ought to have treated these narrow illiberal restrictions as they deserved and so far from even going on Shore at all himself he should have formerly demanded what refreshments he wanted in the name of the King of Great Britain, watered his Ships and proceeded to Monterrey, where (if he did at all mean to demand an explanation) he might see, and expostulate with the very Officer from whom these orders sprung. But Cap. V. treated the matter too lightly, he even permitted the limits of the ground he was to walk over to be pointed out to him, and a guard accompanied him to prevent their being encroached upon.' – Bell, October. Menzies noted that when Vancouver 'went on shore attended by his limited retinue to pay his respects to the Commandant of the Presidio...he solicited leave for three more of his Officers to be permitted on shore to take a short ride with him, which was allowed & they were suffered to ride about two Miles beyond the Garrison attended by a soldier, but were positively refusd leave to go as far as the Mission.' When Vancouver entertained Sal and his wife at Dinner, Sal proposed to bring his guards with him, but 'Vancouver informed him that no foreign Guards whatever could be admitted on board an English Ship of War, but if he was desirous of being attended by these Men, they might go on board as Visitors & being military men would be allowed to wear their side arms, to which he acceded & made them leave their Muskets on the beach till they landed again.' – Menzies, 21 October. These restrictions were regretted at the Mission: 'The two principal fathers of the Missions of San Francisco & Sta Clara came on board...to pay their respects & condole with us on our restraints...[they assured us] that their good wishes towards us still remained unalterable, which they were anxious to testify by sending us whatever they could spare that was likely to be most acceptable...' – Menzies, 22 October. A supply of vegetables was received the next day. 'Capt. Vancouver made up an handsome Assortment of Carpenters Tools of all Sorts & some unwrought Iron as a present to the Mission...' – Puget, 23 October. Sal also received 'a Ton of Iron besides an assortment of such Tools & Utensils of our Manufactory as they had made choice of from the trading articles we had found.' – Menzies, 23 October. These items may have been given in part payment for supplies received, for, as Menzies notes, 'this year he [Vancouver] had to pay for every thing, although formerly they would not take even a receipt or the least acknowledgement for any thing we had from the settlement.' – 23 October.

[2] José Joaquín Arrillaga, who had been lieutenant-governor of the Californias from 1783 to 1792, with headquarters at Loreto, in Baja California, had become acting governor of Alta California.

spring; and being the senior officer, had taken upon himself the jurisdiction of the province, with sentiments apparently not the most favorable toward foreign visitors.[1]

In support of this opinion, and in justice to our worthy friend Senr Sal, it is necessary to remark, that it evidently appeared to be with the utmost repugnance that he was compelled to deliver, in compliance with the orders of his senior officer, these injunctions. In reply to which, I stated briefly to Senr Sal, that I had put into port St. Francisco to recruit our wood and water, to procure such refreshments as the country might afford, and to wait the arrival of our consort the Chatham; with which vessel this port had been appointed our next rendezvous previous to our parting company. That as soon as we should have obtained our necessary supplies, which would not occupy more than two or three days, we should depart; and that he might be assured the restrictions contained in his other letter, respecting our communication with the shore, should be duly observed.

This port, however, was the rendezvous of the Chatham; and as I had not been denied the privilege of procuring some fresh beef, I determined to remain until she should arrive. This took place, however, much earlier than I could have expected from the nature of the service on which she had been dispatched, as we had the pleasure of seeing her at St. Francisco the next day, Monday the 21st.

Our water had been procured, when we were here before, just behind the beach, in a low space covered with spiry grass, which was at that time flooded by the rain; this being now quite dry, we were obliged to resort to a small stream of most excellent water; but as this was surrounded by a loose morass, through which we were obliged to pass, the accomplishment of this object was rendered so tedious, as to detain us here until the evening of Wednesday the 23d, when we prepared for our departure; and at four the next morning, Thursday the 24th, having the ebb tide, and a fresh breeze from the N.W. we turned out of the port. The wind in the offing was very light and baffling, but we directed our course with it in the best manner we were able towards Monterrey; where I expected to find the deserters of the Chatham, and where, by explaining the peculiar nature of our situation to Senr Arrillaga, the acting commandant of the province, I was in hopes of meeting a reception worthy of our situation, notwithstanding his former restrictive orders.

It appeared by Mr. Puget's journal, that from light variable winds, calms and fogs, he did not reach the entrance into port Bodega until the morning

[1] The Spaniards were becoming suspicious of British intentions on the Northwest Coast; some weeks before Vancouver arrived 'Arrillaga had received orders...to be on guard in case any British vessels arrived.' These orders he had relayed to presidio commandants in the Californias on 23 September. Warren Cook, *Flood Tide of Empire*, p. 407n. Guards were to be posted to see that men on shore for wooding, watering and other duties 'did not infringe on the Rules and Regulations of the Port. I will not pretend to doubt the right of placing the Guard. *Delicacy might have pointed out* a different line of Conduct, but Distrust appeared to reign predominant in every thing respecting us.' – Puget, 21 October.

of the 20th, when he stood in between its north point, and the flat rock lying off it, noticed on the 13th of February,[1] 1792; and anchored in six fathoms water, the flat rock bearing by compass S.W. and an opening in the land supposed to be the mouth of the harbour, W.N.W.[2] Here Mr. Puget remarks, that in gaining this station it was again his misfortune to be incommoded by a thick fog; but as such impediments had already detained him far beyond his expectations, he had embraced the opportunity of the first clear interval to bear away for this narrow passage, and found the depth of water from ten to four fathoms; the flat rock was found to lie from the north point of the port S. 63 E. distant a quarter of a mile. About a mile from the flat rock a reef of rocks extends S. 13 W.; off its north point is a shoal two or three ship's lengths in extent; this ought not to be nearer approached than the soundings of four fathoms will admit, and is discoverable by the weeds it produces. The best passage through this narrow channel to the anchorage which the Chatham occupied, is found by keeping the northern or continental shore on board; at which station Mr. Puget inserts the following account of his transactions.[3]

'Immediately after the vessel was secured, Mr. Johnstone was sent, accompanied by Mr. Menzies, to examine port Bodega, which they accomplished by noon, having rounded out the sandy bay to the northward in nine and twelve fathoms water.[4] The entrance of the harbour is obstructed by a shoal of sand, on which the greatest depth is nine feet at the last quarter's flood. Mr. Johnstone went through this passage close to the high land, and at the back of the low spit before us, he found an extensive lagoon, which also had the same soundings as in the entrance. On landing they were joined by some Indians,[5] who had previously made a large fire on the north corner of the bay. These people, in their manners and conduct, were perfectly inoffensive; their numbers did not exceed thirty, of all ages and of both sexes; some few had bows and arrows, which they disposed of to our party for beads and trinkets; the language they spoke was a mixture of Spanish and their own provincial dialect, and from this we may infer, that they were either subordinate to the Spaniards, or that they had a constant connection with the settlement at St. Francisco.

'On the bluff of the entrance is fixed, in a conspicuous place, a pole, having a stave lashed across its upper end, which was conjectured to be the Spanish token of possession; indeed by the Indians our party learned, if they were rightly understood, that some of that nation were actually there, at the extremity or north-west end of the lagoon.

[1] Between Bodega Head and Bodega Rock. The date should be 13 November 1792.
[2] The entrance to Bodega Harbor, the N part of Bodega Bay.
[3] The account follows Puget's log very closely but there are minor variations in wording. It will be noted that the narrative begins in the third person but later changes to the first person of the original.
[4] 'in 9 and 10 feet of water' in Puget's log.
[5] These would be Coast Miwok Indians.

'Mr. Johnstone observed the men to be in general naked, but the women, wore skins of animals about their shoulders and waists, and were as much tatooed, or punctured, as any of the females of the Sandwich islands; the hair of both sexes was black, which they wore clubbed behind.

'The soil is sandy, and in general covered with bushes and different sorts of verdure; the country, inland, is of a moderate height; but as their examination was confined to the beach and its environs, they remained ignorant of the vegetable productions the more inland parts afforded.

'Great numbers of the feathered tribe were seen, white and brown pelicans, gulls, plover, and a variety of aquatic fowl; on the shores they observed eagles, hawks, the red-breasted lark, crows and ravens. No quadrupeds were seen, they only distinguished the track, and saw the dung, of what was considered to be black cattle.

'Having completed their examination of this part of the bay, and seeing no likelihood of a favorable change in the weather, we weighed at two in the afternoon, it being my intention immediately to proceed to the examination of the next opening; but the wind coming to the S.W. with a very threatening appearance from that quarter, when we were off it, deterred me from pursuing my first plan.

'This opening is formed by two apparently low points, from which extends a vast deal of broken water; but whether there was a passage between them we could not determine. I should be inclined to think there is not; for which reason I did not think it prudent to stand too far in, as, from the direction of the wind, we should not have been able to have hauled out clear of the land; had we met with shoal water, our depth in that situation being seven fathoms, having from our anchorage to abreast of this opening had from that depth to thirteen fathoms, irregular hard bottom, but not rocky; and as this part of the coast does not afford any known safe shelter, from whence we could have dispatched the boats, and left the vessel in perfect security; I judged it best, from such circumstances, and the continual thickness and bad appearance of the weather, to give up the examination until a more favorable opportunity should offer, and make the best of my way to join the Discovery at St. Francisco.'

I was much disappointed that these untoward circumstances had prevented Mr. Puget from completing his survey of port Bodega; and I should certainly have given directions for a second attempt, had it not been for the reception we had met with at St. Francisco; which had probably arisen either from the jealousy or too general instructions of the acting governor of the province; whose displeasure, under our present circumstances, I did not think it prudent to excite, especially as I had understood that the Spaniards had it in contemplation to make an establishment at port Bodega, in which case a second visit might have been productive of offence.

In proceeding towards Monterrey we made so little progress, that we were still at no great distance from St. Francisco the next morning, Friday the 25th;

when a vessel was descried to the N.N.W. and on standing towards her, she proved to be the Dædalus.

About noon, Lieutenant Hanson came on board, and informed me that he had pursued the route I had directed towards New South Wales. That he had taken from New Zealand two of the natives, in order that they might instruct the inhabitants of port Jackson in the use and management of the flax plant.[1] That he had arrived at the settlement on the 20th of April, 1793, and was in readiness to depart on the 20th of June, but that he did not receive orders from Major Grose[2] until the end of that month; when he put to sea, and passed to the westward of the Society islands, in sight of the island of Scilly,[3] the only land seen between port Jackson and Owhyhee, which was in sight on the 1st of September; and that, after procuring some refreshments amongst those islands, he took his departure on the 8th of that month for Nootka, which land was made the evening we left that port; the Dædalus being the vessel we then saw to the westward. She anchored in Friendly cove the next morning; and having obtained a supply of wood, water, and other necessaries, Mr. Hanson sailed from thence on the 13th of October, agreeably to the directions I had there left for his future proceedings.

Mr. Hanson brought a supply of provisions, and such parts of the stores which I had demanded, as could be procured. From him I learned that Major Grose was very solicitous that I should again attempt the introduction of the cattle of this country into New South Wales; notwithstanding, that out of the number I had before sent thither in the Dædalus, one cow, three ewes, and a ram only, had survived the voyage. The failure of the rest had been attributed to their being too old,[4] and it was therefore hoped that an

---

[1] Flax with very long fibres had been found on Norfolk Island, and it was hoped to develop an industry that would be valuable to the infant colony in New South Wales. The natives were in effect kidnapped: 'A Canoe came off; two Indians were Enticed on board, the Dædalus having a fresh Breeze made Sail & the Canoe unable to hold on went astern leaving these two poor Natives on board.' – Puget, 19 November. The men kidnapped were an unfortunate choice: 'One was a priest and the other a warrior, and on Norfolk Island they proved themselves inexperienced in the art of dressing and weaving flax. They explained that in New Zealand the women worked the flax. Even so, before they were repatriated, they taught the convicts to improve the quality and output of the cloth.' – Geoffrey Blainey, *The Tyranny of Distance* (Melbourne, 1966), p. 35.

[2] Major Francis Grose, who had arrived at Sydney in February 1792 to serve as lieutenant-governor of New South Wales. Governor Arthur Phillip left in December and Grose took over. He remained in New South Wales until December 1794.

[3] One of the Leeward group of the Society Islands.

[4] Puget gives a different cause for the loss: 'She Sailed from Monterey in December last having on board 21 head of Cattle and 26 Sheep...But the Difficulty of procuring proper and sufficient provender was against the Probability of their reaching New South Wales. The Carpenters from both Vessels had been employed erecting Stalls in her Lower Deck which certainly were rather too confined...A Mortality took place shortly after leaving the port, it was occasioned principally from the Sores on their Hips and Sides by continual Rubbing in the Motion of the Ship against the Stalls, which generally terminated in mortification.' – Puget, note following the log entry for 8 November.

assortment of young ones would be more successful. With respect to the swine, Mr. Hanson's endeavours had been attended with greater success, as he had carried from Otaheite, and had landed at Port Jackson, seventy of those animals, which, from the excellency of the breed, must necessarily prove a most valuable acquisition.

The wind continued variable between the south and east, blowing a moderate breeze, and sometimes accompanied with foggy weather; in which, on the evening and night of Monday the 28th, although many guns were fired to denote our situation, we parted company with the Chatham; but the Dædalus kept her station near us. This unpleasant weather continued with little alteration, attended generally by adverse winds, until the morning of Friday the 1st of November, when, with a breeze at W.S.W. and thick hazy weather, we reached Monterrey, where we anchored with the Daedalus about eleven in the forenoon, and moored nearly in our former station. Here we found our consort, which, notwithstanding the disadvantages of the weather, had reached this place on the 30th of the preceding month.

Whilst we were employed in securing the ship, I sent an officer to acquaint the governor of our arrival, and of the object of my visit, and also with an offer on my part to salute the garrison, if an equal compliment would be returned.

This being assented to, I waited on Senr Arrillaga, the commandant, and was received with the ceremony usual on such occasions; as soon as this was ended I was preparing to state my reasons for having entered the ports under his government, when he stopped me from proceeding further, and begged that the subject might be referred to a written correspondence, by which mode he conceived matters would be more fully explained. I then made inquiries after the deserters from the Chatham, and was given to understand by Senr Arrillaga, that a few days after our departure from hence, in the month of January, they had made their appearance; on which they were taken into custody, and sent prisoners to St. Blas, in order to be removed from thence to Nootka. The armourer, sent on board the Chatham from the mission of St. Carlos, I had promised to return thither, either on receiving the deserters at Nootka, or in the event of their not being taken at the conclusion of the season; he was therefore discharged from the Chatham, and sent on shore.

In the afternoon, on a signal being made from the shore for one of our boats, a Spanish officer was brought off, who delivered to me two letters from Senr Arrillaga. One stating that he was without orders for the reception of foreign vessels into the ports under his jurisdiction, excepting in cases where the rights of hospitality demanded his assistance; and requesting that I would communicate to him the objects that had brought me hither, by which his future determinations would be governed. The other contained expressions desirous of preserving the subsisting harmony; but at the same time stated, that without departing from the *spirit* of the orders by which his conduct was to be regulated, he could not permit any persons to come on shore, excepting the commander of foreign vessels, with one or two officers; or the individuals employed in procuring wood and water, which service was to be performed with all possible speed; and that the rest of our wants would be supplied with the greatest dispatch on my giving him previous notice.

The tenor of these letters being very different from what my conversation with Senʳ Arrillaga had given me reason to expect, when I visited him at the Presidio; I was reduced to the necessity of sending him the next day, Saturday the 2d, a full explanation of the objects of our voyage, and of the motives that had induced me to enter the ports under his jurisdiction. In this I stated, that I had been intrusted by his Britannic Majesty with a voyage of discovery, and for the exploring of various countries in the Pacific Ocean; of which the north-west coast of America was one of the principal objects. That previously to my departure from England, I had been given to understand, not only that I should be hospitably received on this coast by the subjects of the Spanish crown, but that such information of the progress of my voyage as I might wish to communicate to the Court of Great Britain, would be forwarded by way of St. Blas by the officers of his Catholic Majesty residing in these ports; and that I was instructed to make a free and unreserved communication of all discoveries made in the course of my researches, to any Spanish officer or officers whom I might chance to meet, engaged in similar pursuits with myself; and that I now purposed to transmit to Senʳ Quadra a copy of my charts and surveys, that had been made since our departure from this port the preceding year. That the voyage in which we were engaged, was for the general use and benefit of mankind, and that under these circumstances, we ought rather to be considered as labouring for the good of the world in general, than for the advantage of any particular sovereign, and that the court of Spain would be more early informed of, and as much benefited by my labours, as the kingdom of Great Britain. That in consequence of these instructions, I had exchanged some charts with Senʳ Quadra, and others were ready for his reception. That I had not only been treated on my former visit here with the greatest friendship, and unbounded hospitality; but had received from his Excellency, the viceroy of Mexico, the strongest assurances, that these attentions had been shewn in compliance with the desire of his Catholic Majesty, and of the orders he had issued for that purpose; and that I had inclosed his Excellency's letters for his perusal, to certify him, that I did not intend any deception. That our examination and survey would still require another year to complete it; and that I had made choice of this port, or St. Diego, for the purpose of refitting our vessels, unloading the store-ship, and making such astronomical observations as were become necessary for prosecuting our researches with correctness. The manner in which these services would require to be performed on shore I particularly pointed out, and hoped that the officers and people would be permitted the same recreation on foot and on horseback, with which they had been indulged on our former visit, under such limitations and restrictions as he might think proper to prescribe.[1]

On Monday the 4th I received from Sen[r] Arrillaga a reply to my letter, in which he was pleased to compliment me upon my ingenuousness; and thanked me for having given him the perusal of the viceroy's letters. In vindication of himself he said, that there was no royal order for the reception of our vessels, like that produced by M. de la Pérouse. That he did not comprehend that his excellency expected that we should repair a second time to the ports under his jurisdiction; and that even Senr Quadra before his departure had given the commander of the garrison to understand, by a letter of which Senr Arrillaga sent me a copy, that the attentions we had received on the former occasion were for that time only; and were not to be considered as necessary to be shewn us in future.[2] Notwithstanding however all these objections, being desirous of contributing to the public undertaking in which we were engaged, he requested I would inform him of the precise number of days in which the store-ship could be unloaded; he offered to give me the key of the warehouse at the landing place, for the reception of her cargo, near which we might erect the observatory; and allowed the gentlemen and officers to recreate themselves within sight of the Spanish officer, who should be stationed for the protection of the cargo and observatory; which latter was only to be erected in the day time, as he could not permit any of our people to be on shore between sun-set and sun-rise; and lastly, he had no objection to our recruiting our wood and water, provided all those employed on that service should retire on board at night, and that I would engage that the greatest dispatch should take place in these and all our other transactions.

The situation pointed out by him, where we might be allowed to lodge such of the provisions and stores as required to be landed, was not only inconvenient on account of the surf which generally ran very high in its vicinity, but the place proposed for their reception, was in the midst of the common slaughtering of all their cattle, the neighbourhood of which, to a considerable distance in all directions, was rendered extremely offensive and unwholesome, by the offal having never been cleared away, but left from time to time in a continual state of putrefaction.[3] In addition to which, the stores

---

[1] This summary follows closely the text of Vancouver's letter (Adm. 1/2629, ff. 70v–74), which is printed in the appendix.

[2] Quadra's brief letter, addressed to Arguello, was written at Monterey on 12 January 1793, just before he and Vancouver sailed. The somewhat ambiguous text read (in translation): 'By the convention with the Court of London, all foreign Vessels are prohibited the entrance into our establishments, (except they execute it in case of an accident,) without the order of His Majesty, or permission of His Excellency; as has been verified this time with Commodore Vancouver. They are to be assisted with the necessaries which hospitality demands, without being permitted to delay; which I notice to you for your intelligence and government.' – Adm. 1/2629, f. 75; for the original Spanish see f. 78.

[3] The treatment of the animals to be slaughtered as well as the condition of the area disgusted Puget: 'Received Fresh Beef from the Presidio – but by no means good Meat.

thus deposited were to be left every night under the care of the governor's troops, without any check on the fidelity of those people, which I had some reason to believe would be very necessary. In the centre of this intolerable nuisance we had also leave to erect the observatory, and to attend to our astronomical pursuits, but *in the day time* only; and in its vicinity, and within sight of it and the Presidio, we might be allowed to recreate ourselves on shore.

On due consideration of all these circumstances, I declined any further correspondence with, or accepting the incommodious assistance proffered by Senr Arrillaga; and determined, after finishing our investigation of these shores, to retire to the Sandwich islands, where I had little doubt that the uneducated inhabitants of Owhyhee, or its neighbouring isles, would cheerfully afford us that accommodation which had been unkindly denied us at St. Francisco and Monterrey.[1]

The observations made on shore by Mr. Whidbey, with the artificial horizon for ascertaining the longitude by the chronometers, allowing the presumed rate and error as settled off Scot's islands, and in Nootka sound, shewed by six sets of observations made on two different days at St. Francisco, that Kendall's chronometer was 11′ 10″; Arnold's No. 14, 16′ 48″; and No. 176, 6′ 18″; to the westward of the truth, and by four sets of observations made on two different days at this place, Kendall's chronometer was found to be 4′ 33″, and Arnold's No. 14, 14′ 13″ to the westward; and No. 176, 15′ 47″ to the eastward of the truth. Hence it appeared that Arnold's No. 14, was going with greater regularity than any of the others.

As our situation afforded no better means of ascertaining a point of so interesting a nature, the above rate and error was of necessity adopted; subject however to correction by subsequent observations, which was accordingly done, and the longitude so corrected is affixed to all our future situations, as also to the position of the coast and adjacent islands, until our departure from New Albion.

In the forenoon of Tuesday the 5th we unmoored, and about ten at night, with a light southerly breeze, we weighed and sailed out of the bay; but the wind continuing light and variable, we made little progress until the forenoon of Wednesday the 6th, when, with the regular northerly breeze, we hauled in close to point Pinos, and there recommenced our survey of this coast south-eastward from Monterrey.

Point Pinos, as already described to form the south-east point of Monterrey

---

It is always Spoilt by the Manner in which it is brought down by the Soldiers, who always take care to make the Animals undergo some Baiting, till they are nearly mad & indeed it appears to afford the *whole Presidio* an Infinity of Amusement.' – 31 October.

[1] Vancouver was at last reacting in a manner that Bell and others doubtless approved. His report to London read in part: 'the whole tenor of his [Arrillaga's] letter, though in some measure offering to alleviate our necessities, was in such a sneering, forbidding and ungracious stile, I considered it far too degrading and humiliating to the character and situation in which I am placed to accept such offers, but under circumstances of the greatest distress and necessity which fortunately not being our situation...we sailed out of Monterrey Bay...' – Vancouver to Stephens, 6 December 1793. Adm. 1/2629, f. 86v–87.

bay, is a low projecting point of land, covered with trees, chiefly the stone-pine. From hence the exterior coast takes a direction S. 28 W., about four miles to the north point of the bay of Carmelo,[1] which is a small open and exposed situation, containing some detached rocks; and having a rocky bottom is a very improper place for anchorage. Into this bay flows the river Carmelo, passing the mission of St. Carlos, and at a little distance from the sea, it is said to abound with a variety of excellent fish.

In a direction about E. by S. from St. Carlos, at the distance of about 15 leagues, is the mission of St. Antonio, established in the year 1792.[2]

From the north point of the bay of Carmelo, the coast takes a direction S. by E. four leagues, to a small, high, rocky lump of land, lying about half a mile from the shore, which is nearly barren; indeed, the trees from point Pinos extend a little way only to the southward of the bay of Carmelo, where the mountains rise rather abruptly from the sea; and the naked shores, excepting one or two sandy beaches, are intirely composed of steep rocky cliffs.

Southward from the detached lump of land, the coast, which takes a direction S. 40 E., is nearly straight and compact; the mountains form one uninterrupted, though rather uneven, ridge, with chasms and gullies on their sides; the whole to all appearance nearly destitute of vegetation.

In the evening we hauled our wind, and plied in order to retain our situation, for the purpose of prosecuting our researches in the morning of Thursday the 7th, when, notwithstanding that the wind was favorable to this design, yet the fog prevented my putting it into execution, and we were obliged to stand to windward all that day under an easy sail. Unpleasant weather like this had attended many of our favorable N.W. winds since our departure from port Protection, and in a manner I had not been accustomed to notice. The fog did not in general rise more than ten or twelve degrees above the horizon; above which the atmosphere was clear and pleasant, admitting us frequently to see not only the summits, but also some distance down the sides of the mountains that compose the coast. These now appeared in a double ridge; the interior ones produced forest trees, that shewed their tops above the summits of those that seemed to rise abruptly from the sea shore, the lower parts of which continued to be totally obscured by the density of the fog, until the morning of Friday the 8th, when it in some measure dispersed, and permitted us to see that part of the coast from whence we had stood to sea on the evening of the 6th, and enabled us to ascertain, that, southward from that station, the coast still continued in a direction S. 40 E., and was equally compact. The same wind, with a continuance of thick hazy weather, scarcely allowed us to see from point to point as we sailed along the coast, and prevented our delineating its position with that degree of accuracy and precision I could have wished; though it did not preclude our

[1] Now Carmel Bay.
[2] The date is given later as 1772; both are incorrect. This Mission of San Antonio de Padua was founded in July 1771.

ascertaining the continuation and connexion of the continental shore, which, as we advanced, became less abrupt; and the country, composed of vallies and mountains that gradually descended towards the sea shore, which consisted of alternate rocks and sandy beaches, put on a more agreeable appearance, as vegetation again seemed to exist: some dwarf trees were produced, and the surface was interspersed with a few dull verdant spots.

About nine o'clock we passed a low projecting point, off which lie, at a small distance, two or three rugged detached rocks; the outermost is situated in latitude 35′ 42″, longitude 239′ 6″;[1] from whence the line of the coast, for a short distance, inclines a few degrees more to the eastward; the mountains fall further back from the water-side, and the intermediate country appeared to be a plain, or to rise with a very gradual ascent, for the space of about four leagues along the coast. This land was tolerably well wooded, even close down to the shore; and by the assistance of our glasses some of the trees were seen to be very large, with spreading branches; and being for the greater part distributed in detached clumps, produced a very pleasing effect, and a prospect more fertile than we had lately been accustomed to behold. This difference in the appearance of the country was not confined to inanimate nature, for its inhabitants seemed to benefit by its superior productions, as we soon discovered a canoe approaching us, of a construction I little expected to have met with.[2] Instead of its being composed of straw like those we had seen on our first visit to port St. Francisco, it was neatly formed of wood, much after the Nootka fashion, and was navigated with great adroitness by four of the natives of the country. Their paddles were about ten feet long, with a blade at each end; these they handled with much dexterity, either intirely on one side, or alternately on each side of their canoe. Their exertions to reach us were very great, but as we were favored with a fresh gale, with all sails set, they were not able to come up with us; and I regretted that I could not afford some leisure for a better acquaintance with these people, who seemed, by the ingenuity displayed in their canoe, to differ very materially from those insensible beings we had met in the neighbourhood of St. Francisco and Monterrey.

Our progress by noon brought us to the latitude of 35° 33′, longitude 239° 15½′; in this situation the northernmost part of the coast in sight bore by compass N.W. by W.; a point forming the north point of the bay S. 75 E.; a high conical hill, flat at the top, appearing to be an island in the bay, S. 67 E.; the south point of the bay S. 46 E.; and the nearest shore N. 26 E., two miles distant. At the north point of this bay, which is situated in latitude 35° 31′,

[1] Point Piedras Blancas, off which are two large white rocks. The position of the light on the point is lat. 35° 39·9′ N, long. 121° 17·1′ W (238° 42·9′ E).

[2] Vancouver was entering the coastal area inhabited by the Chumash Indians, who built their canoes of lashed planks. For drawings illustrating the various types of canoe used by the California Indians and a map showing their geographical distribution, see R. F. Heizer and M. A. Whipple (comps. and eds.) *The California Indians: A Source Book* (2nd ed. Berkeley and Los Angeles, 1971), pp. 10–11.

longitude, 239° 22',[1] the woodland country ceases to exist, and the shores acquire a quick ascent, with a very uneven surface, particularly in the neighbourhood of the bay. Some detached rocks are about its southern point, which lies from the northern S. 25 E., distant thirteen miles, and is formed by steep cliffs, falling perpendicularly into the ocean. From the line of the two outer points the shores of the bay fell back about five miles; they appeared to be much exposed; and, unless the conical rock is connected with the shores, they did not seem to form any projecting point, but were composed of a sandy beach, that stretched from a margin of low land, extending from the rugged mountains that form the more interior country; from whence four small streams were seen from the 28' mast head to flow into the bay.

This bay was the first indent in the shores to the southward of Carmelo Bay, and, according to the Spanish charts, is called Los Esteros;[2] the north point above mentioned is called Ponto del Esteros, which is placed in Senr Quadra's chart only two miles further south than the situation of it by our observations;[3] but in the printed chart it is placed ten miles further south, and is represented in a different point of view from that in which it had appeared to us.

To the southward of Ponto del Esteros, the whole exterior country had a steril, dreary, unpleasant aspect; yet I had understood that the Spaniards had some establishments, in fertile and pleasant situations, not far from the shores of this neighbourhood. Near the northern parts of the bay was the mission of St. Luis, formed in the year 1772,[4] and about 25 leagues to the northeast of it was another named St. Antonio, established the same year. The precise situation of these missions may be liable to error, as the information respecting them was principally obtained from cursory conversation.

The south point of Esteros forms the north-west extreme of a conspicuous promontory;[5] this takes a rounding direction about S. 36 E., eight miles, where the coast retires again to the eastward, and forms the northern side of an extensive open bay. This promontory is named in the printed chart The Mountain del Buchon,[6] off which, at the distance of about eight leagues, I understood an island had lately been discovered, but we saw nothing of it. Our view however was very confined, occasioned by a very thick haze, sometimes approaching to a fog, which totally prevented our seeing any object

[1] Point Estero, in lat. 35° 28' N, long. 121° 00' W (239° 00' E).

[2] Now Estero Bay.

[3] More correctly, Punta del Esteros. This name (for the present Point Estero) appears on Vancouver's chart, but it is not shown on Quadra's maps of 1791 and 1792.

[4] The Mission of San Luis Obispo de Tolosa, founded in September 1772.

[5] Point Buchon.

[6] Wagner explains the name. 'When the Portolá expedition [of 1769] ascended Price Cañon just north of Pismo they came to a native settlement the chief of which had a large goiter [buchon]. Although Fr. Crespí named the place "San Ladislao" the soldiers nicknamed it "Buchon". The name is perpetuated in Pt. Buchon and the mountains back of it' in which Mount Buchon is prominent. – Cartography of the Northwest Coast (Berkeley, 1937), II, 378.

further than from two to four leagues in any direction; insomuch that we stood into this bay to the southward of Mount del Buchon, without knowing it to be such, until the south point discovered itself through the haze, at the distance of about three leagues.

This not being named in the Spanish charts, I have, after our friend the commandant at St. Francisco, called it POINT SAL;[1] and being in the line of the two points of this bay, they were found to lie from each other S. 40½ E., and N 40½ W., twenty miles asunder, the nearest part of the bay bearing by compass N.E., was five or six miles distant. As the day was fast declining, we hauled our wind to preserve our situation during the night, with so strong a gale from the N.W. as obliged us to close-reef our topsails. In the morning, the weather being more moderate and the atmosphere more clear, we steered for Point Sal, and had a good opportunity of seeing the northern shores of the bay which like those of Esteros, seemed compact, without any projecting points that would afford shelter or security for shipping.

The interior country consisted of lofty barren mountains, in double and treble ridges, at some distance from the shore; the intermediate land descended gradually from their base, interspersed with eminences and vallies, and terminated on the coast in sandy beaches, or low white cliffs, Point Sal, which is a high steep rocky cliff, projecting from the low shore, with a country of similar appearance to the south of it, is situated in latitude 34° 57', longitude 239° 43½',[2] from whence the coast takes a direction S. 4 E. nineteen miles, to another high steep rocky point projecting in the like manner, and rising very abruptly in rugged craggy cliffs. This I called POINT ARGUELLO;[3] near it are two or three detached rocks lying close to the shore; the coast between these two points falls a little back to the eastward. The intermediate shores and interior country continued to bear the same appearance; the whole was destitute of wood, and nearly so of other vegetable productions, excepting near a rivulet that we passed about nine in the forenoon, situated from point Arguello N. 12 E., at the distance of about six miles. This appeared to be the largest flow of water into the ocean we had yet seen, excepting that of Columbia river; but the breakers that extended across its entrance, seemed to preclude the possibility of its being navigable even for boats. In the Spanish charts it is called Rio de St. Balardo.[4]

About eleven o'clock we passed point Arguello, from whence the coast takes a direction S. 51 E., ten miles to a point of but little elevated, or rather low, land; this, according to the Spanish charts, is called Point Conception,[5] forming the north-west point of entrance into the channel of Sᵗᵃ Barbara. Being now favored with a fresh N.W. gale, though attended with hazy weather, we

[1] The name has been retained.

[2] Its position is lat. 34° 54' N, long. 120° 40' W (239° 20' E).

[3] The name has been retained. Menzies refers to it by its earlier Spanish name, Punta Pedernales, given by the Portola expedition.

[4] The Rio de San Verardo, so named by Portola in 1769. Now the Santa Inez River.

[5] Named Punta de la Limpia Concepcíon on a plan by Palacios dated 1603.

were by noon abreast of this point; the observed latitude was 34° 30′, longitude 239° 52′; in this situation the easternmost part of the coast in sight bore by compass E.N.E.; point Conception being the nearest shore, N. 32 E., two or three miles distant; the northernmost part of the coast in sight, N. 48 W.; the westernmost, or first island, forming the channel of Sta Barbara,[1] called in one of the Spanish charts St. Miguel, in the other St. Bernardo, (the former of which I have adopted) bore from S. 25 E. to S. 32 E.; the next called in one of those charts Sta Rosa, in the other St. Miguel, (the former of which I have continued) bore from S. 42 E. to S. 54 E.; and a high hill on the third island, called in the Spanish charts Sta Cruz, bore S. 70 E.[2]

Point Conception is rendered very remarkable, by its differing very much in form from the points we had lately seen along the coast. It appeared to stretch out into the ocean from an extensive tract of low land, and to terminate like a wedge, with its large end falling perpendicularly into the sea, which broke against it with great violence. By our observations it appeared to be in latitude 34° 32′, longitude 239° 54′;[3] the former corresponding with both the Spanish charts within two or three miles, being there placed so much further to the southward.

Immediately to the eastward of Point Conception (the coast from thence taking an eastern direction) we passed a small Indian village, the first we had observed along the shores of these southern parts of New Albion.[4] The inhabitants made a fire the instant we came within their view, but no one ventured to pay us a visit. The prevailing strong gale at the time of our passing probably prevented their embarking.

It is not unlikely that this village was attached to the mission of Sta Rosa, which I had been informed was established in the vicinity of this point in the year 1788,[5] and had the reputation of being situated in a very fertile country. Another report had stated this mission to be near the banks of the Rio St. Balardo; and, as it is not improbable that the stream may take a southern course from its entrance, both informations may be correct.

The coast continued in this easterly direction about twenty-three miles from point Conception, to a point where it took a southerly turn, from whence the country gradually rose to mountains of different heights. In the vicinity

[1] Canal in the first edition and on Vancouver's chart; now the Santa Barbara Channel.

[2] Wagner discusses at some length the numerous names that have been attached to the three islands on the S side of Santa Barbara Channel. (*Cartography*, pp. 411–12.) Vancouver had fairly recent Spanish charts, some of which named them (west to east) San Bernardo, San Miguel and Santa Cruz; on others they appeared as San Miguel, Santa Rosa and Santa Cruz. Vancouver adopted the latter names, which have survived.

[3] Point Conception light is in lat. 34° 26·9′ N, long. 120° 28·2′ W (239° 31·8′ E).

[4] The Chumash Indians lived along the coast from Point Estero southward to Point Conception, and thence eastward along the shore of Santa Barbara Channel. They also occupied the three Channel Islands to which Vancouver referred in the preceding paragraph.

[5] The Mission La Purisima Concepcíon was founded in December 1787 on the Santa Rosa River.

of the shores, which are composed of low cliffs or sandy beaches, were produced some stunted trees and groveling shrubs; and notwithstanding the dreary appearance of the coast as we passed along, it seemed to be well inhabited, as several villages were seen at no great distance from each other in the small bays or coves that form the coast.

By four in the afternoon we had sailed beyond the influence of our favorable N.W. gale, which still continued to blow a little way astern of us, whilst we were perplexed with light variable winds from every quarter. With these however, we endeavoured to approach the shores of the main land, in order to anchor for the night. About sun-set we were visited by some of the inhabitants in a canoe from one of the villages. Their visit seemed to be dictated by curiosity alone, which being satisfied, as they were about to depart, I gave them some iron and beads, with which they appeared to be highly delighted, and returned to the shore.

By seven in the evening it was nearly calm, and having at that time soundings at the depth of 37 fathoms, muddy bottom, we anchored in company with the Chatham and Dædalus.

The surface of the sea, which was perfectly smooth and tranquil, was covered with a thick slimy substance, which, when separated, or disturbed by any little agitation, became very luminous, whilst the light breeze that came principally from the shore, brought with it a very strong smell of burning tar, or of some such resinous substance. The next morning, Sunday the 10th, the sea had the appearance of dissolved tar floating upon its surface, which covered the ocean in all directions within the limits of our view and indicated that in this neighbourhood it was not subject to much agitation.

From this anchorage, situated in latitude 34° 24', longitude 240° 32', the coast as before mentioned takes a southerly turn, S. 48 E. about two leagues to a point bearing by compass N. 81 E. half a league distant from our station; the centre of the island of St. Miguel bore from S. 27 W. distant 11 leagues; Sta Rosa from S. 11 W. to S. 5 E.; the former 25, the latter 26 miles distant; the island of Sta Cruz from S. 81 E. to S. 55 E.; and the main land in sight from S. 82 W.' to S. 87 E.

The want of wind detaining us in this situation, afforded an opportunity to several of the natives from the different villages, which were numerous in this neighbourhood, to pay us a visit. They all came in canoes made of wood, and decorated with shells like that seen on the 8th.[1] They brought with them some fish, and a few of their ornaments; these they disposed of in the most cheerful manner, principally for spoons, beads, and scissars. They seemed to

---

[1] Menzies gives an excellent description of their lashed-plank canoes: 'The make & formation of their Canoe shewd no small degree of ingenuity as it is regularly built of different pieces of boards of various sizes & figures & neatly fastened together with Thongs & Sinews & glewd so close as to be quite water tight & preserves its shape as well as if it had been made in one piece, without any other Timber to strengthen it but one small thort in the middle, from thence it rises gradually & tapers to both extemities.' – November 17. The canoes were 'from 12 to 18 feet in length & in the middle about 4 feet wide.'

possess great sensibility, and much vivacity, yet they conducted themselves with the most perfect decorum and good order; very unlike that inanimate stupidity that marked the character of most of the Indians we had seen under the Spanish jurisdiction at St. Francisco and Monterrey. These people either did not understand the Spanish language, or spoke it in such a manner as to be unintelligible to us; for as we were totally unacquainted with their native dialect, we endeavoured, but to no effect, by means of Spanish, to gain from them some information.

On a light breeze springing up from the westward, at about eight o'clock, we directed our course along shore to the eastward; our progress was very slow, owing to light winds, though the weather was very pleasant. About two in the afternoon we passed a small bay, which appeared likely to have afforded good anchorage, had it not been for a bed of sea-weed that extended across its entrance, and indicated a shallow rocky bottom.

Within this bay a very large Indian village was pleasantly situated, from whence we were visited by some of its inhabitants; amongst whom was a very shrewd intelligent fellow, who informed us, in the Spanish language, that there was a mission and a Presidio not much further to the eastward. About five in the evening this establishment was discovered in a small bay, which bore the appearance of a far more civilized place than any other of the Spanish settlements. The buildings appeared to be regular and well constructed, the walls clean and white, and the roofs of the houses were covered with a bright red tile. The Presidio was nearest to the sea shore, and just shewed itself above a grove of small trees, producing with the rest of the buildings a very picturesque effect.[1]

As I purposed to anchor somewhere for the night, and as this bay seemed likely not only to answer that purpose, but another equally essential, that of procuring some refreshments, we hauled in, and anchored in six fathoms water, sandy bottom; the southern land in sight, called by the Spaniards Conversion point,[2] bore by compass S. 70 E.; a low cliffy point in the bay N. 42 E.; the Presidio N. 32 W.; the nearest shore N.N.W. distant half a mile; the north-west point of the bay S. 64 W.; the north-west extreme of the island of Sta Rosa S. 34 W. distant thirty-two miles; its western extreme was shut in with the west point of Sta Cruz, which bore from S. 22 W. to S. 28 E. seventeen or eighteen miles; the nearest part of that island S. 20 E. distant thirteen miles; and the southeasternmost of the islands in sight S. 28 E.; appearing from our anchorage like a single rock, but consisting of three small islands.

[1] 'The Presidio forms a large square space surrounded by a range of Barracks & Store houses which are occupied by the Commandant two Serjeants & between 60 & 70 Soldiers with their families, who are securely walled in in the same manner as we have already describd at Monterrey.' – Menzies, November 17.

[2] Vancouver means the present Point Hueneme, but the Spanish name was actually applied to what is now Point Mugu.

Having thus anchored before the Spanish establishment, I immediately sent Lieutenant Swaine to inform the commanding officer at the Presidio of our arrival, and as I intended to depart in the morning, to request that the Indians, who had shewn a great desire to trade with us, might be permitted to bring us, in the course of the night, such articles of refreshment as they had to dispose of; which, as we understood, consisted of an abundance of hogs, vegetables, fowls, and some excellent dried fish.

Mr. Swaine returned after meeting with a most polite and friendly reception from the commandant Sen[r] Don Felipe Goycochea,[1] who with the greatest hospitality informed Mr. Swaine, that every refreshment the country could afford was perfectly at our command; and desired that I might be made acquainted, that he hoped I would remain a few days to partake of those advantages, and to allow him the pleasure of administering to our wants and necessities.

On his learning from Mr. Swaine which way we were bound, he observed that wood and water would not only be found very scarce, but that a supply could not be depended upon at St. Diego, or any other port to the southward; and if it were necessary that we should replenish our stock of those articles, it would be well to embrace the opportunity which our present situation afforded for so doing.

The general deportment of this officer was evidently the effect of a noble and generous mind; and as this place, which was distinguished by the name of S[ta] Barbara,[2] was under the same jurisdiction as St Francisco and Monterrey, our very friendly reception here rendered the unkind treatment we had received on our late visits at the two other establishments the more paradoxical, and was perhaps only to be referred to the different dispositions of the persons in power.

The intelligence communicated to me by Mr. Swaine, and the polite and liberal conduct we had reason to expect from the commandant, induced me to think of accepting the advantages he had so obligingly offered.

The next morning, accompanied by Lieutenants Puget and Hanson, I paid my respects on shore to Sen[r] Don Felipe Goychochea, the commandant of the establishment of S[ta] Barbara, and Lieutenant in the Spanish infantry. He received us with the greatest politeness and cordiality, and renewed, with great earnestness, the offers he had made to Mr. Swaine the preceding evening. He was pleased to say, that he should derive the greatest satisfaction in rendering us every service compatible with the orders under which he acted. These orders only required, that those who were employed for the service of the vessels on shore, or engaged in taking their recreation in the neighbouring country,

---

[1] Felipe de Goycoechea, officer commanding the small garrison guarding the Santa Barbara Mission.

[2] Named after Santa Barbara Channel, which had been named by Vizcaino in 1602. The presidio was founded in 1782 and the mission followed in December 1786.

should return on board every night. This stipulation I assured him should be punctually attended to, as well as every other regulation that his prudence might suggest.

We were likewise introduced to Friar Miguel Miguel,[1] one of the reverend fathers of the mission of S[ta] Barbara, who, in the name of himself, and his companion the Rev. Father Estevan Tapis,[2] expressed the greatest anxiety for our welfare; and repeating the civilities of the commandant, offered whatever services or assistance the mission could afford.

Accompanied by these gentlemen we went from the Presidio, in order to ascertain the spot from whence we were to obtain our wood and water. As the former was to be procured from the holly-leaved oak that grew at some distance from the water-side, our reverend father offered us the waggons of the mission, and some Indians to carry the wood, when cut, down to the beach. The cart of the Presidio was directed by the commandant to be at our orders for that or any other service. The water, which was not of the best quality, was in wells close to the sea shore. We were in no imminent want of these necessaries; yet, from the experience of our late retarded progress from light baffling winds, in consequence of the coast taking so easterly a direction, and obstructing the general course of the north-west winds that prevail most part of the year, it was highly probable we might find the same sort of weather further south, as we must necessarily keep near the shore, for the purpose of examining the coast, which I now found would occupy more time than I had supposed. This circumstance, in addition to the information we had received, that the further we advanced the worse we should fare in respect of these essential articles; I thought it prudent, notwithstanding the business appeared likely to be somewhat tedious, to give orders for its being immediately carried into execution; convinced that we should greatly benefit in point of health whilst these services were going forward, by the excellent refreshments the country promised to supply.

The commandant had ordered us to be furnished with fresh meat in such quantities as I might think proper to demand; vegetables and fowls were principally purchased from private individuals, whilst our reverend fathers at the mission, and the commandant, shared the productions of their gardens with us; which, like those of the more northern establishments, were but of small extent.[3]

---

[1] Father José de Miguel.

[2] He and Father Miguel were the two priests in charge of the Santa Barbara Mission. Father Tapis was later president of the California missions.

[3] Menzies gives details of the supplies that were available: 'We had here excellent refreshments of every kind, far preferable to what we got at any other Settlement in California, Beef, Mutton, Poultry & a variety of fish & Vegetables were in great abundance & procurd at an easy rate, Black Cattle were about five dollars a head & the reason of their being a little dearer than to the Northward was that the Settlement was not yet so plentifully stockd with them, Sheep were about two dollars each & far preferable in point

Since the recreation that had been denied us at Monterrey was here granted without limitation, I felt myself bound to adopt such measures as were most likely to prevent any abuse of the indulgence, or any just cause of complaint. For when I reflected on the unrestrained manner in which most of the officers and gentlemen had rambled about the country, during our former visit at Monterrey, I was not without my suspicions that the unpleasant restrictions imposed upon us on our late return to that port, had been occasioned by our having made too free with the liberty then granted. To prevent the chance of any such offence taking place here, I issued positive injunctions that no individual under my command should extend his excursions beyond the view from the Presidio, or the buildings of the mission, which, being situated in an open country of no very uneven surface, admitted of sufficient space for all the exercise on foot or horseback that health or amusement might require.

Notwithstanding the water on the beach was the same as that with which all the Spanish vessels that had visited this roadstead had been supplied, and although much pains had been taken to clean out the wells, yet they were very dirty and brackish; and as they afforded a very scanty supply, we were induced to make search for better water.

At the distance of only a few yards further than where the wells had been made, a most excellent spring of very fine water was discovered, amongst some bushes, in a kind of morass; and though it flowed but slowly, yet it answered all our purposes, and was obtained with more ease than the water from the wells. This spring was totally unknown to the resident Spaniards, and equally so, I presume, to those employed in their shipping; or they would not so long have been content with the dirty brackish water procured from the wells. At the Presidio is a large well of excellent water, from which also, by the assistance of the cart, a portion of our stock was obtained.

Our business being thus in a train for easy execution, the agreeable society of our Spanish friends, the refreshments we procured, and the daily recreation

of goodness to those we got at the northern settlements but both Cattle & Sheep could be procurd much cheaper in the way of barter from the Soldiers, for instance an Ox could be got for three Axes & a Sheep for small culinary utensils or trading articles of little value, & as for Poultry I dare say there were near 30 dozen of good fowls procurd by the three Vessels during our stay from among the soldiers families for Beads & small trinkets: Maize Wheat Pease Beans & other Vegetables were got from the Commandant & the fathers, & a plentiful supply of fish of different kinds were procurd for Beads daily from the Indians. We killd & carried away with us between the three Vessels 18 head of Cattle & about two dozen Sheep & yet when the whole came to be settled for the Commandant positively refus'd to make any charge whatever....How different the conduct of this generous Spaniard to that of the Governor General at Monterrey.' – 17 November. Bell noted that when the Commandant became aware that the ships were short of candles and soap, he gave them a supply of both; indeed, Bell adds, 'such was the disposition of this good old Gentleman, that we were afraid at last of admiring or praising any thing that deserved either, in his possession, for in that case he was Sure to force our acceptance of it.' – November.

which the country afforded, rendered our situation at Sta Barbara extremely pleasant.[1]

We here procured some stout knees from the holly-leaved oak, for the security of the Discovery's head and bumkins;[2] this, and our other occupations, fully engaged our time until the evening of Sunday the 17th, when preparations were made for sailing on the day following.

The pleasing society of our good friends at the mission and Presidio was this day augmented by the arrival of Friar Vincente Sta Maria, one of the Rev. Fathers of the mission of Buena Ventura;[3] situated about seven leagues from hence on the sea coast to the south-eastward.

The motives that induced this respectable priest to favor us with his company, evidently manifested his christian-like benevolence. Having crossed the ocean more than once himself, he was well aware how valuable the fresh productions of the shores were to persons in our situation; under this impression he had brought with him, for our service, half a score sheep, and twenty mules laden with the various roots and vegetables from the garden of his mission. This excellently-good man earnestly intreated that I would accompany him by land back to Buena Ventura; saying, that I should be better able on the spot to point out to him, and to his colleague the Rev. Friar Father Francisco Dume,[4] such of the productions of the country as would be most acceptable, and contribute most to our further comfort and welfare. Of this journey I should have been very happy to have been able to have availed myself, had the existing circumstances not obliged me to decline the pleasure I should thereby have received.

Our new benevolent friend, accompanied by the commandant and Father Miguel, honored us with their company to dine on board, where, in the course of conversation, I was informed that the mission of Buena Ventura was situated near a small bay of easy access; and as Friar Vincente seemed much pleased

[1] Menzies noted some of the hospitality offered. On the 12th, on his return from a botanizing expedition, he 'found that different parties had been this day on shore, some shooting others riding & enjoying the bent of their inclinations in various amusements without the least check or restraint.' On the 14th the Commandant 'provided an elegant entertainment for all the English Officers that could be spared from the duty of the Vessels' and on the 15th 'a large party of the English Officers' went to the mission 'where an elegant & sumptuous dinner was provided for us by the venerable Fathers who received their guests with a hearty welcome.' Only the botanizing was disappointing: 'the day was very favorable for my pursuit, but the season of the year & the arid state of the Country was much against it, for though I was surrounded by new & rare objects in almost every step of my journey, yet finding very few of them either in flower or seed, I was able to receive but little pleasure or advantage from my excursion.'

[2] Timbers having a natural bend, resembling a knee in shape, much sought after for use in building or repairing the hull or fittings of a wooden ship.

[3] He had served at the mission since 1782, the year it was founded. His first name was Vicente, not Vincente, as Vancouver spells it throughout.

[4] Father Francisco Dumetz, who had come to California in 1771. Vancouver shortened the name to Dume, and later named Point Dume in his honour.

with his visit on board, I requested he would favor me with his company in the Discovery to his residence. This offer he cheerfuly accepted, and in doing so I had only reason to regret the short time I was to be indulged with the society of a gentleman, whose observations through life, and general knowledge of mankind, rendered him a most pleasing and instructive companion.

In the evening our friends returned on shore, and I took that opportunity of soliciting their acceptance of a few useful articles which they had no other opportunity of obtaining; though I must confess they were a very incompetent return for their friendly, generous, and attentive services; and I trust they will accept this public acknowledgment as the only means within my reach to shew the grateful sense I shall ever entertain of the obligations they so liberally and unexpectedly bestowed.

We were attended at breakfast the next morning, Monday the 18th, with our friends from the shore; and the want of wind detained us at anchor until near noon; when we took leave of our Sta Barbara friends, and, accompanied by Father Vincente, we directed our course towards Buena Ventura.

Whilst we remained at Sta Barbara, Mr. Whidbey, whose time was principally devoted to the several duties on shore, embraced that opportunity of making some necessary astronomical observations with the artificial horizon; the only means we had of ascertaining the latitude, variation, and the longitude by the chronometers. The mean results shewed the latitude, by four meridional altitudes of the sun, to be 34° 24'; the variation, by six sets of azimuths, differing from 11° 14' to 9°, to be 10° 15' eastwardly; and the longitude, by eight sets of altitudes of the sun between the 11th and 15th, allowing the error and rate as calculated at Monterrey, was shewn by Kendall's chronometer to be 240° 45' 40"; Arnold's No. 14, 240° 44' 16"; No. 176, 240° 56' 45"; and the true longitude deduced from subsequent observations, 240° 43'. As I continued to allow the same rate, the situation of the coast has been laid down by No. 14; and I should hope, by the regularity with which it had lately gone, with some degree of precision. The tide, though shewing here no visible stream, regularly ebbed and flowed every six hours; the rise and fall, as nearly as could be estimated seemed to be about three or four feet; and it is high water about eight hours after the moon passes the meridian.

To sail into the bay, or more properly speaking the roadstead, of Sta Barbara, requires but few directions, as it is open and without any kind of interruption whatever; the soundings on approaching it are regular, from 15 to 3 fathoms; the former from half a league to two miles, the latter within a cable and half of the shore. Weeds were seen growing about the roadstead in many places; but, so far as we examined, which was only in the vicinity of our anchorage, they did not appear to indicate shallower water, or a bottom of a different nature. The shores of the roadstead are for the most part low, and terminate in sandy beaches, to which however its western point is rather an exception, being a steep cliff moderately elevated; to this point I gave the name of POINT FELIPE, after the commandant of Sta Barbara.[1]

The interior country a few miles only from the water side, is composed of rugged barren mountains, which I was informed rise in five distinct ridges, behind and above each other, a great distance inland towards the E.N.E.; which space is not at present occupied either by the Spaniards, or the native Indians.

After we had passed Point Conception, the wind continued to blow in very faint breezes, and our progress was slow along the coast, which rose about two or three leagues to the south-eastward of Sta Barbara with a steep ascent in rocky cliffs, that mostly composed its shores.

At eight in the evening we anchored in fifteen fathoms water, about a league to the westward of Buena Ventura. Our reverend friend expressed great satisfaction at the mode of his return to the mission; and said, that his voyage hither would probably lay the foundation for removing the absurd and deep-rooted prejudice that had ever existed amongst the several tribes of Indians in his neighbourhood who from their earliest infancy had invariably regarded all strangers as their enemies. This sentiment had totally prevented any amicable intercourse, or communication between their different societies, although living within a small distance of each other. And it seemed to have been a matter of no small difficulty on the part of the missionaries, to persuade the native inhabitants of the channel of Sta Barbara, who had been informed of our intention to visit the coast, that we were their friends, and should treat them with kindness and civility; having probably been taught at some earlier period, to consider the English under a very different character. Proofs were not wanting that such notions still continued to exist, for notwithstanding that four or five favorite Indian servants, who attended on father Vincente, had witnessed the cordial reception and friendly intercourse that subsisted between us, yet on his giving them directions to return home with his horses and mules by themselves, as he should go thither in the ship, they instantly, and with one voice, prayed for the sake of God that he would not persist in his determination; being thoroughly convinced that if he did they should never see him more: nor was it in the power of language, either by arguments or assurances, to remove these ill founded impressions. To the last moment they remained with him on the beach, supplicating in the most earnest manner that he would give his attention to their advice; and frequently repeating, that though they had hitherto confided in every thing he had told them, yet in this instance they were sure they should be deceived. The Rev. Father, though gratified by their affectionate anxiety, smiled at their groundless apprehensions for his safety, gave each of them his blessing, and again directed them to follow his orders and return home to Buena Ventura.

We found our situation on the succeeding morning, Tuesday the 19th, to be within about two miles of the shore, its nearest part bearing by compass N. by E., the landing-place near the mission of Buena Ventura, S. 68 E., three

[1] Now Santa Barbara Point.

miles distant; Point Conversion[1] S. 62 E.; a group of three islands, called by the natives Enneeapah,[2] (the westernmost being the largest and highest island) from S. 10 E. to S. 1 E.; the island of Sta Cruz, from S. 23 W., to S. 48 W.; and point Felipe, N. 68 W.

The coast immediately opposite, and to the northward of us, chiefly consisted of high steep cliffs, indented with some small sandy coves. The general face of the country was mountainous, rugged, barren and dreary; but towards the mission, a margin of low land extended from the base of the mountains, some of which were of great height, and at a remote distance from the ocean; and being relieved by a few trees in the neighbourhood of the establishment, gave this part of the country a less unpleasing appearance.

Having taken an early breakfast, I attended Father Vincente to the shore, where a large assortment of refreshments was in readiness for embarkation. The violence of the surf prevented our landing, nor was it without the greatest caution and circumspection that the Indians, though very dexterous in the management of their canoes, could venture off to us. From these people I understood, that this inconvenience was unusual, and that about noon, or towards the evening, it would probably subside, so as to permit our landing. We therefore determined to wait, and in the mean time the canoes brought off some of the good things which our reverend friend had ordered to be provided, consisting of sheep, fowls, roots, and other vegetables in such abundance, that it required four boats to convey them to the ships.

In this situation we waited at a grapnel until the afternoon; when finding the surf not sufficiently abated to admit of our landing in perfect safety, and my reverend friend not having sufficient courage to venture on shore in any of the canoes, after several had been filled and overset, we returned on board; not a little mortified at the disappointment, which seemed to damp the spirits and lively conversation of our worthy guest. When about half way to the ship, the uneasiness of Father Vincente was greatly increased by his recollecting, that he had intrusted both his bible and prayer book to the care of a faithful servant, with the strongest injunctions to deposit them securely on shore; this service had been punctually performed; for on our return, these spiritual comforts, with which he had too hastily parted, had been forgotten to be recalled. The omission produced no small addition to the dejection of spirits that had already taken place, and which became almost insupportable by an untoward accident, that for a moment presented a situation of danger, until it was discovered to proceed from the plug having unfortunately worked out of the boat's bottom, by which means a great quantity of water was received, and kept increasing until the cause was found out and removed; when

---

[1] Vancouver evidently thought that this name applied to the present Point Hueneme, but Wagner was convinced that Point Mugu, 8 miles SE of Point Hueneme, was the feature named Point Conversion by the Vizcaino expedition of 1603. *Cartography of the Northwest Coast*, II, 444.

[2] Enecapah on Vancouver's chart; now the Anacapa Islands.

the effect instantly ceased, and the boat was soon relieved. Yet this accident, amidst other misfortunes and disappointments, appeared to the good priest a matter of the most serious concern, and might perhaps be a little aggravated by some smiles at his distress, which it was impossible to suppress.

Our excellent friend was now so much disconcerted, and his spirits so depressed, that I found it as difficult to convince him that we should arrive safe at the ship, as he had before found it to persuade his trusty servants of his security in embarking with us at Sta Barbara; and I verily believe that at this moment he heartily repented that he had not yielded to their advice.

We were however soon alongside, and our friend was by no means reluctant to leave the boat; when on board the ship he soon recovered from his former apprehensions of danger, yet the absence of his books was still a matter of regret and vexation that he could not overcome; and unfortunately it was out of our power to afford him any consolation, as those we had on board were in a language he did not understand. His servants being aware of the uneasiness which the want of these religious comforts would occasion their master, came on board in the evening with the bible and prayer-book, without either of them having been wetted by the waters of the ocean, to preserve them against which had been an object of much care and attention. The very great comfort this circumstance imparted was too evident in the countenance of our worthy friend to pass unnoticed. He immediately retired, and after having been closeted about three quarters of an hour, he returned to supper, and was as cheerful, and in the same high spirits, as before these uncomfortable events had happened. I then took an opportunity of apologizing for our smiles in the boat, and I believe we obtained perfect forgiveness, as he laughed heartily at the adventures of the day, and the evening passed in the most cheerful manner.

Such are the happy effects resulting from a religious education, and such the consolations that are derived by the habitual exercise of the principles it inculcates.

Whilst deprived of those comforts to which in the hour of peril or misfortune he had been taught to resort, I am convinced the mind of our friend was far from being in an enviable state; but when the opportunity was afforded him of conscientiously discharging the sacred duties which he felt it incumbent upon him to perform, I believe there were few in the world with whom he would have wished to have changed conditions.

The next morning, Wednesday the 20th, we had an early visit from some of the Indians, who came to inform Father Vincente that the surf was intirely abated, and that he might land in the most perfect security. His anxiety to get on shore induced me to lose no time in making another attempt, leaving directions, in the event of our being able to land, for the vessels to proceed along the coast as soon as the sea breeze should set in, where I would join them off the mission.

When we reached the shore the surf still ran very high, but with the assistance of our light small boat we landed with great ease, perfectly dry, and much to the satisfaction of our worthy companion; of whose bounty there was yet remaining near the beach a large quantity of roots, vegetables, and other useful articles, with five head of cattle, in readiness to be sent on board. One of these being a very fine young bull was taken on board alive, for the purpose of being carried if possible to Owhyhee. The others were killed, and produced us an ample supply; had they not been sufficient, a greater number were at hand, and equally at our disposal.

Our hospitable friend now conducted us towards the establishment, which was situated about three quarters of a mile from the waterside; from whence we had not advanced many paces before the road became crowded with Indians of both sexes, and of all ages, running towards us. This assemblage I at first attributed to curiosity, and the desire of seeing strangers, but I was soon agreeably undeceived, and convinced that it was not to welcome us, but the return of their pastor and benefactor. Although it was yet very early in the morning, the happy tidings had reached the mission; from whence these children of nature had issued, each pressing through the crowd, unmindful of the feeble or the young, to kiss the hand of their paternal guardian, and to receive his benediction. His blessings being dispensed, the little multitude dispersed in various directions.

With us, as strangers, their curiosity was very soon satisfied, a few only accompanying us to the mission. These made many inquiries of Father Vincente how he had fared, and how he had been treated on board the ship; to all which his answers were returned in such pleasing terms of kind familiarity, as apparently afforded them great satisfaction, whilst it produced in them much surprize. This conversation we were only able to understand through his interpretation, as it was held in the Indian language, which Father Vincente spoke very fluently.

On our entering the mission we were received by Father Francisco Dume, and entertained in a manner that proved the great respectability of the Franciscan order, at least of that part of their numerous community with whom we had become acquainted.

The morning, which was most delightfully pleasant, was employed in viewing the buildings of the mission, the arrangement of the gardens, and cultivated land in its immediate vicinage. These all appeared to be in a very superior stile to any of the new settlements I had yet seen, and would have tempted me to have made a more minute inquiry, had not my anxious desire for proceeding onward prohibited the delay it would necessarily have occasioned.

The day passed most agreebly in the society of our ecclesiastical friends; and the pleasure of it was greatly heightened by the arrival of a mail from Europe in its way to Monterrey. By this conveyance our reverend friends had intelligence from the old world, that could not fail of being very interesting to persons in our situation. Thus we concluded a very pleasant day, and in the evening returned to the vessels, which had been prevented moving by the calmness of the weather.

On attempting to weigh with a gentle breeze of wind from the westward on the morning of Thursday the 21st, the tenacity of the bottom proved too strong for our cable, and it parted near the clench. This accident kept us employed the whole of the day; and after breaking all the best hawsers we had then remaining, the anchor was at length recovered by sweeping it with the stream cable late in the evening. This unlooked-for detention was highly mortifying, as the westerly breeze blew a cheerful gale from day-light until dark, for the first time since we had entered the channel of Sta Barbara.

With light baffling winds from the north-east quarter, and some slight showers of rain, we directed our course on the morning of Friday the 22d to the south-eastward, gratefully thankful for the hospitable reception and benevolent donations of our religious friends at Buena Ventura.

The anchorage we had just quitted, was according to our observations by two meridional altitudes of the sun, in latitude 34° 16'; and the longitude by six sets of altitudes, on two different days, was 241° 2'.[1] In consequence of the general serenity of the weather almost throughout the year, according to the information I obtained, the roadstead may be considered as a tolerably good one, and anchorage may be had nearer the shore in the vicinity of the mission; but neither situations are so commodius as at Sta Barbara, being much more exposed to the south-east winds and oceanic swell, which frequently render the communication with the shore very unpleasant.

At noon our observed latitude was 34° 10', longitude 241° 4'. In this situation the isles of Enneeapah bore by compass from N. 4 E. to S. 20 W.; the island of Sta Cruz, from S. 36 W. to S. 61 W.; the westernmost part of the main land in sight, W.N.W., the nearest shore N.E. by N., four or five miles distant, point Conversion, N. 84 E., and the southernmost land in sight, S. 85 E.

Point Conversion was passed in the afternoon, and found to be situated in latitude 34° 9', longitude 241° 9'.[2] The shores from Buena Ventura, which as far as this point continued low and flat, produced some small trees and shrubs; but from hence they again assumed a steep and rugged form.

From our anchorage this morning, as we advanced towards the shore to the south-east of the mission, our depth of water regularly decreased to eight fathoms, within two miles of the shore of the main land; but by noon it had increased to 14, and by five in the afternoon to 46 fathoms. At this time the westernmost part of the main land in sight bore by compass N. 55 W.; Point Conversion, N. 45 W.; the easternmost part of the main land in sight N. 65 E.; and the isles of Enneeapah from S. 63 W. to west. On passing these isles we were nearer to them than to any other of the islands in the channel

---

[1] The anchorage was off Ventura, site of the mission; its position is lat. 34° 17' N, long. 119° 20' W (240° 40' E).

[2] Point Mugu. Its position is lat. 34° 05' N, long. about 119° 05' W (240° 55' E).

Sta Barbara; the whole of which wore the same barren appearance, and were now seen as we passed to be composed of rugged rocks, nearly destitute of wood and verdure. The westernmost, already stated to be the largest, is about a league in length from north to south, and about two miles in breadth; its centre is situated in latitude 34° 1½′, longitude 240° 56½′. The easternmost of these isles, about two miles in circuit, lies from the above N. 80 E., at the distance of about a league, and the south-east point of the island of Sta Cruz lies from the same station S. 80 W., distant four miles and an half.

The night was nearly calm as was the succeeding day, Saturday the 23d, so that in twenty-four hours we had not advanced more than about sixteen miles along the coast, nor was our progress much accelerated afterwards; for by noon of Sunday the 24th, we had only reached the latitude of 33° 54′, longitude 241° 42′. In this situation Point Conversion was still in sight, bearing by compass N. 71 E.; here the coast took a direction S. 67 E., sixteen miles to the north point of a deep bay, off which lie two or three small rocks; this point, which I called POINT DUME,[1] bore N. 59 W.; the south point of the same bay, being the easternmost part of the main land in sight S. 67 E.; this being a very conspicuous promontory, I named after Father Vincente;[2] the island Sta Catalina, (so called by the Spaniards) the easternmost of the group, forming the channel of Sta Barbara, from S. 40 E. to S. 19 E.; a small island, called by the Spaniards Sta Barbara, S. 25 W., distant 12 leagues; and the isles of Enneeapah west, at the same distance. Our situation was before an extensive bay, at the distance of about three leagues from its nearest shores. These appeared to be compact, and the whole bay to be open and exposed; but our distance from its termination, or bottom, which was nearly four leagues, was too great to ascertain any thing respecting it with certainty; and the light prevailing wind, blowing directly on the shore, would not admit of a more minute survey without much retarding our progress along the coast, which had already occupied more time than I wished, or could well spare for its examination; and which on our departure from Monterrey I had expected would ere now have been drawing nearly to a conclusion.

The north-west side of this bay was observed to be composed chiefly of steep barren cliffs; the north and eastern shores terminated in low sandy beaches, rising with a gradual ascent until they reached the base of a mountainous country, which had the appearance of being rugged and barren, not only at some distance behind the centre of the bay, but extending towards the sea coast, and forming its extreme points, viz. point Vincente and point Dume; which lie from each other S. 51 E., and N. 51 W., 26 miles asunder.

According to the Spanish charts, I at first supposed this bay to be that which is there called the bay of St. Pedro; but I was afterwards informed that conjecture was ill founded.[3] I had also been given to understand that a very

---

[1] Although wrongly spelled Dume instead of Dumetz, Vancouver's name has been retained.   [2] Now correctly spelled Point Vicente.
[3] The bay was Santa Monica Bay, between Point Dume and Point Vicente.

advantageous settlement is established on a fertile spot somewhere in this neighbourhood within sight of the ocean, though at the distance of some miles from the coast, called Pueblo de los Angelos, 'the country town of the Angels,' formed in the year 1781. This establishment was looked for in all directions, but nothing was perceived that indicated either habitations or inhabitants.[1]

In the evening we passed point Vincente, composed of steep barren cliffs, and forming the north-west extremity of a conspicuous promontory that takes a direction of S. 70 E., near ten miles, to a point in latitude 33° 42½', longitude 242° 3'. This point, which after the father president of the Franciscan order I called POINT FERMIN,[2] is the west point of the bay, from whence its western shores take a northerly direction, and constitute a projecting promontory between two bays, the shores of which terminate on all sides in steep cliffs of a light yellowish colour. These extend along the northwestern shore of the supposed bay of St. Pedro about a league, where they seemed to end, having a small island lying off their northern extremity, beyond which the bay appeared to retire to the north-westward, probably affording anchorage and shelter; but near Point Fermin soundings could not be gained with 90 or 100 fathoms of line, or I would have stopped to have given this bay a more minute examination.

At day-light in the morning of Monday 25th, we found ourselves driven much further from the land than I had expected, and intirely past the bay of the south-eastward; the northern and eastern sides of it were now seen to be composed of a low country, terminating in alternate low white cliffs and sandy beaches. On this low extensive tract some small trees and shrubs were produced, but the interior country, which still consisted of rugged lofty mountains, presented a dreary and steril appearance.

At noon the latitude was 33° 36', longitude 242° 11'. In this situation the easternmost land in sight bore by compass S. 83 E.; the south-east point of the island Sta Catalina S. 13 W., distant 17½ miles; its north point S. 48 W., distant 14 miles; and its north-west point S. 62 W., 23 miles; point Vincente N. 67 W., and point Fermin N. 59 W. In the latitude of this point we differed some miles from that assigned to it by the Spaniards; Senr Quadra's chart placing it in latitude 33° 50', and the printed chart in latitude 33° 54'.

This situation would equally well correspond with the description of the bay of St. Pedro, as that we had been off the preceding day; yet, from the shape, appearance, and other circumstances attending the bay now before us, I had reason to conclude this to be the bay of St. Pedro.[3]

Towards its south-east part is a small bay or cove, and a low point of land

[1] 'El Pueblo de Nuestra Señora de Los Angeles de Porciuncula, as it was called, was founded on Sept. 4, 1781, by 44 colonists from Sinaloa and Sonora. It consisted of a few adobe houses and a chapel built around a plaza. It was about 20 miles inland, too far to be visible.' – Marguerite Eyer Wilbur (ed.), *Vancouver in California* (Los Angeles, 1953), p. 176n. From this small beginning the vast city of Los Angeles has grown.

[2] Honoring Father Fermin de Lasuen.

[3] Bay of St. Pedro on Vancouver's chart; now San Pedro Bay.

forming its east point, called by me POINT LASUEN,[1] bore by compass at noon, N. 40 E., distant seven miles. In the neighbourhood of that station I had been informed was the mission of St. Gabriel, founded in the year 1773;[2] this establishment is said to be in sight also of the sea, but we were not able to discern it, or the Pueblo de los Angelos; yet had great reason to believe that their respective situations corresponded with the intelligence I had received.

The wind continuing light and variable, rendered our progress still excessively slow; by the evening, however, I considered that we had reached the south-east extremity of the channel of Sᵗᵃ Barbara, having sight of the island of St. Clement, (so called by the Spaniards)[3] and which we found to lie S. 18 W., distant about five or six leagues from the south-east point of the island of Sᵗᵃ Catalina.

Thus finished our tedious examination of the continental shore of this channel; and although we were able nearly to ascertain the positive, as well as relative, situation of the different islands forming its south-west side, yet we passed at too great a distance for the delineation of those shores with that degree of accuracy, that may be depended upon with confidence.

There are some rocks and shoals introduced in the Spanish charts which we saw nothing of; and, excepting the very light and baffling winds that prevailed, there were neither currents nor any other obstruction, so far as our examination went, to interrupt its navigation; which, to those who may have occasion *only to pass through it*, will be found neither difficult nor unpleasant.

Early the next morning, Tuesday 26th, we were favored with a light breeze from the westward; with this we steered along the land, and by 9 in the forenoon, being within about 2 miles of the shore, our attention was suddenly called to a Spanish establishment erected close to the water-side, in a small sandy cove, near the centre of which was a little detached rock, and another lying off its north point. The former is represented in the Spanish charts as a small island lying nearly three miles from the shore, yet we passed it within half that distance, and could scarcely discern that it was detached. Its appearance, and situation relative to the mission of St. Juan Capistrano, corresponding with the description I had received of that settlement, made me conclude it to be the same, and that it is the last establishment between Sᵗᵃ Barbara and the Presidio of St. Diego.

This mission is very pleasantly situated in a grove of trees, whose luxuriant and diversified foliage, when contrasted with the adjacent shores, gave it a most romantic appearance; having the ocean in front, and being bounded on its other sides by rugged dreary mountains, where the vegetation was not sufficient to hide the naked rocks, of which the country in this point of view seemed to be principally composed.

[1] Again honoring Father Fermin de Lasuen.
[2] Founded in 1771, not 1773.
[3] San Clemente Island, named by Vizcaino in 1602.

The buildings of the mission were of brick and of stone, and in their vicinity the soil appeared to be of uncommon and striking fertility. It was founded in the year 1776, and is in latitude 33° 29′, longitude 242° 35′. The landing on the beach in the cove seemed to be good; and had it not been for the very favorable gale with which we were now indulged, I should have been tempted to have passed a few hours at this very enchanting place.

The observed latitude, at noon, was 33° 23′, longitude 242° 41′. The easternmost land in sight bore by compass S. 70 E.; the nearest shore N. 12 E., distant three miles; the mission of St. Juan Capistrano N. 40 W.; and the westernmost land in sight N. 49 W. From the cove of this mission the coast takes first a direction S. 45 E., 7 leagues, and then S. 16 E., 26 miles, to a point in latitude 32° 51′, longitude 242° 59′, forming the north point of the bay in which is situated Puerto Falso;[1] the shores between this point and the above cove are in general straight, and intirely compact. The face of the country here assumed a more uniform appearance, and rose from the sea coast, which chiefly consisted of sandy beaches or low cliffs, with a gradual ascent. It was broken into some chasms and vallies, where a few small trees and shrubs in two or three places were seen to vegetate.

We plied as usual during the night with a light breeze from the E.S.E., having in and about the bay soundings from 65 to 23 fathoms, mud and sandy bottom. The land wind blew a moderate breeze on the morning of Wednesday the 27th, with which we stood to the southward along shore; but the weather was so excessively hazy as to prevent our seeing about us until after eight o'clock, when we discovered ourselves to be near the south-west point of entrance into port St. Diego, called by the Spaniards Ponta de la Loma,[2] bearing by compass S. 57 E. distant three or four miles; the northernmost of some small islands, named by the Spaniards the Coronados,[3] S. 15 E. and the Lagoon, that is to say, Puerto Falso, N.N.E. four miles distant. Point Loma is the southern extremity of a remarkable range of elevated land, that commences from the south side of Puerto Falso, and at a distance has the appearance of being insular, which effect is produced by the low country that connects it with the other mountains. The top of this tract of land seems to terminate in a ridge, so perfect and uniformly sharp, as apparently to render walking very inconvenient. The fact, however, is not so; but when viewed from sea, it has that singular appearance. It descends in very steep rocky cliffs to the water side, from whence a bed of growing weeds extends into the ocean, half a league, or two miles.[4]

[1] Now False Bay.
[2] More correctly, Punta de la Loma; now Point Loma.
[3] Still named Los Coronados.
[4] These were kelp beds, upon which Menzies commented: 'On the outside of this reef we went over beds of this plant [which he identified as *Fucus pyriferus Lin.*] growing in 30 fathoms of water & as the stems had at this time a considerable slanting direction, occasioned by the influence of the tide or current & eight or ten fathoms of the tops lay trailing on the surface, I am confident that many of these plants could not be far short of

The land wind died away as noon approached, and was succeeded by a gentle breeze from the N.W. with which we steered towards point Loma, through a continuation of the bed of weeds, extending in a south-westerly direction from that point, whence lie some breakers at the distance of a mile. Our soundings on first entering the weeds were 20 fathoms; this depth gradually, though not very regularly, decreased to six fathoms as we passed within about a mile of the southern part of the breakers; then deepened again to nine fathoms, and so continued until we entered the channel leading into port St. Diego, across which is a bar. This we passed in three fathoms and a half water, and, favored with the assistance of the flood tide, we turned into the port; where, about two in the afternoon, we anchored in ten fathoms water, fine sandy bottom, at the usual place of anchorage in the harbour. Point de la Loma, in a line with the south-easternmost of the Coronados, bore by compass S. 8 E.; ponta de Guiranos,[1] a low spit of land, projecting from the high steep cliffs within the former, and which, properly speaking, constitutes the west point of entrance into the port, S. 18 E.; the east point of entrance, which is also very low, but not a spit of land, bore S. 36 E.; the former distant about a mile, the latter about three fourths of that distance. The Presidio of St. Diego[2] bore N. 21 E. distant three miles and a half, and the nearest shore north-west, within a quarter of a mile of our anchorage.

Having taken this station without having seen, or been visited by, any of His Catholic Majesty's subjects, I dispatched Lieutenant Swaine immediately up the harbour to the Presidio, in order to inform the commanding officer of our arrival; and to inquire if any dispatches for me had been entrusted to his care, or if he knew of any that had passed this station on their way to Monterrey; as St. Diego is invariably the stopping place of the post passing from New Spain to their northern establishments on this coast. Mr Swaine was likewise directed to inquire, whether the officer so commanding would do me the favor of forwarding such dispatches as I might find necessary to transmit to England.

During the absence of Mr. Swaine I received a very polite letter from Sen[r] Antonio Grajero, a lieutenant in the Spanish cavalry, and commandant of this port and establishment,[3] requesting to be informed of the business that had brought our little squadron within the limits of his command.

Mr. Swaine returned soon afterwards, and acquainted me that he had been received with marks of great politeness and hospitality by the commanding officer, who informed him, that he had neither seen nor heard of any letters or other dispatches addressed to me; but that he would with great pleasure

fifty fathoms in length & yet its stem is not much thicker than a man's finger.' – 27 November.

[1] La Punta de los Guijarros (cobblestones); now Ballast Point.

[2] The presidio and a mission were both founded in July 1769. This was the first Spanish colony in what is now the State of California.

[3] Grajero had taken command as recently as October 1793. 'A heavy drinker, he was removed from office six years later.' – Wilbur, *Vancouver in California*, p. 185n.

take charge of, and forward to Europe, any thing of that nature which I might have occasion to transmit. He very obligingly assured Mr. Swaine, that such refreshments as the country afforded were perfectly at our command, and that it would be his study to shew us every civility within the line prescribed by the orders under which he acted; but was sorry to observe, that these would reduce his power of rendering us service, much within the limits of his inclination.

So polite and friendly a reception could not fail being extremely acceptable, and after making a satisfactory reply to the letter I had received from Senr Grajero, I intimated my intention of paying him my respects on the following morning.

This visit accordingly took place, accompanied by Lieutenants Puget and Hanson. On landing we found horses in waiting for us, on which we rode up to the Presidio, where we were received with that politeness and hospitality we had reason to expect from the liberal behaviour of the commandant on the preceding evening. His friendly offers were immediately renewed, and were accompanied by similar assurances of assistance from Senr Don José Zuniga, the former commandant, who had recently been promoted to the rank of captain of infantry, and appointed to the charge of an important post on the opposite side of the gulph of California, for which place he was then preparing to depart.[1]

These gentlemen informed us, that having been given to understand it was my intention to visit this port they had long expected us, and that about four days before, on being informed of the probability of our arrival, they had, to their great mortification, received at the same time from Senr Arrillaga such a list of restrictions as would inevitably deprive both parties of that satisfaction that could not otherways have failed to render our stay here very pleasant. These orders prohibited our transacting any business on shore, excepting that of procuring wood and water; particularly directed that the shore-ship should not be unladen at St. Diego; and expressed, that when the above supplies were furnished, which was to be done with all possible expedition, it was expected that we should immediately depart.[2] We were also prohibited from taking on board any live cattle or sheep, with many other severe and inhospitable injunctions.[3]

[1] Zuniga's new post was at Tucson, in what is now Arizona.

[2] Menzies states that Grajero told Vancouver and his party 'that Sr. Quadra when he knew of his [Grajero's] appointment to this settlement had particularly desird him to supply our wants & entertain us to the utmost of his power & that he would disburse whatever expenses were incurrd, an instance of our worthy friends munificence that deserves to be recorded as it in a particular manner points out the goodness of his heart & shews the kind attention & particular interest he took in our welfare.' – 28 November.

[3] In spite of this prohibition, Vancouver 'was fortunate enough here to purchase of a private Soldier a fine Milch Cow with two Bull Calves, for the purpose of taking to the Sandwich Islands.' – Bell, December. Menzies notes that 'As we were so unsuccessful in carrying Bulls last year that none of them hardly survivd the Voyage to the Islands, these two were chosen very young & by the care & attention of the sailors who made pets of

Notwithstanding these very ungenerous directions, our friends here desired that I would not abstain from demanding such refreshments as the country afforded; as their services should be at our command in every respect, and on all occasions, where they could possibly exert themselves, and appear to keep within the limits of the orders by which, although contrary to their own inclinations, they were now compelled to govern their conduct.[1]

The charts of our summer's survey we had no opportunity of copying whilst at sea, with a sufficient degree of accuracy; this business, therefore, fully occupied our time until Friday the 6th of December, without any circumstance occurring in this interval worthy of recording. When these were completed, I confided them, together with due information of the progress of our voyage up to this period to the care of Senr Don Antonio Grajero, contained in two packets addressed to the Secretary of the Admiralty,[2] as also a packet for Senr Quadra, at St. Blas, containing, agreeably to my promise, a copy of our discoveries during the last season, for the service and information of His Catholic Majesty. These the commandant very obligingly took care of, and gave me every assurance that they should be forwarded with the greatest punctuality and dispatch.

The wind coming from the south prevented our sailing on Saturday the 7th, as I intended; but I did not regret the detention, as it afforded us the pleasure of a visit from our very highly esteemed and venerable friend the Father president of the missionaries of the Franciscan order in this country,[3] who was then on a visitation to the several missions between St. Francisco and this port, where he had arrived the preceding evening from St. Juan Capistrano. He expressed much concern that our departure was so near at hand, since the great fertility of St. Juan's would have enabled him to add abundantly to our stock of refreshments. Although I was not less thankful for these offices of kindness than convinced of the sincerity with which they were made, yet I was under the necessity of declining them, having now determined to embrace the earliest opportunity of proceeding on our survey.

I had great difficulty to prevail on the father president to desist from sending

them, they soon became very fine animals, & we conceive that taking them on board in a young state, by which they soon become inurd to the Vessel is the most likely way to succeed in transporting these Animals to distant regions.' – 8 December.

[1] Just before the ships sailed 'Captain Zuniga & the Commandant came down in the forenoon of the 5th [December] & visited the Daedalus, they afterwards din'd on board the Discovery with Capt. Vancouver & a large party of Officers, they were both remarkably pleasant & intelligent men & seemd very partial to our little convivial parties. They often regretted with much sincerity the ridiculous & unmerited restrictions we lay under, which dampd all their proferrd friendship & hospitality towards us, & which they were confident was contrary to the wishes of the Viceroy & the Spanish Court...' – Menzies, 5 Devember.

[2] Vancouver to Stephens, 6 December 1793, in which Vancouver summarizes his activities during the surveying season and describes his difficulties with Arrillaga. The original is in Adm. 1/2629, ff. 82–89v. The chart that accompanied this letter has disappeared.   [3] Father Fermin de Lasuen.

to St. Juan's for the supplies he had proposed, as in all probability we should have sailed before they could have arrived from thence.

The enjoyment of the society of this worthy character was of short duration; it however afforded me the satisfaction of personally acknowledging the obligations we were under for the friendly services that had been conferred upon us, by the missionaries under his immediate direction and government; being perfectly assured, that however well disposed the several individuals might have been to have shewn us the kind attention we had received, the cordial interest with which the father president had, on all occasions, so warmly espoused our interests, must have been of no small importance to our comfort. This consideration, in addition to the esteem I had conceived for his character, induced me to solicit his acceptance of a handsome barrelled organ, which, notwithstanding the vicissitudes of climate, was still in complete order and repair. This was received with great pleasure, and abundant thanks, and was to be appropriated to the use and ornament of the new church at the presidency of the missions at St. Carlos.[1]

A continuation of southerly winds caused us to be detained, contrary to my expectations, until Monday the 9th, when we quitted the port of St. Diego. I felt myself greatly indebted for the hospitable attentions shewn us by our friends at the mission, as well as by those of the Presidio of St. Diego, for which, after making the most grateful acknowledgements I could express, I requested they would accept a few useful and necessary articles that they were not likely to procure through any other channel; and I had the gratification of seeing they were thankfully received.

Although we did not make any survey of the port of St. Diego, it may not be improper to state a few particulars relative to it, that came under our observation during the time we were there stationary. The mission of St. Diego is not within sight of the sea, nor of the port;[2] it is situated in a valley within the view of, and about two miles distant from, the Presidio to the north-east; which was the only building seen from our anchorage.

The sharp ridge of land, mentioned on the 27th of the preceding month, is connected with the other mountains by an isthmus, or tract of very low land, which in the rainy season is flooded, and at high spring tides makes the sharp land, forming the west and north-west side of the port, an island. The Presidio is on the continental side of this low sandy isthmus. The peninsula

---

[1] 'Captain Vancouver presented the Padri Presidenti at parting with a small Organ he had in the Cabin, set to a miscellaneous collection of about thirty different tunes to the music of which he seemed very partial in his different visits on board last year. This present he said he would carry with him to the seat of Government at Monterrey & there deposit it in the Church where it would be carefully preservd as a memento of our visit to this Country.' – Menzies, December 7. The organ is now in the museum of the San Juan Bautista Mission, in San Benito county, California. – M. B. McGuire, *The Vancouver Story* (New York, 1977), p. 179n.

[2] The mission, named for San Diego de Alcalá, was founded in 1769 and moved to another site farther inland in 1775.

bears a very different appearance when seen from the port, from that before described as observed from the ocean. It descends with an uneven surface, and some bushes grow on it, but no trees of a large size.

From the Presidio, south-eastward, the eastern side of the port is bounded by high land as far as its head, from whence a narrow tract of low land projects, covered with bushes, and forming the inner or upper harbour of the port; its north-west extremity was the eastern shore under which we anchored, and to which station we had been principally directed by a plan of the port published by Mr. Dalrymple in the year 1782.[1] This plan in point of correctness is justly intitled to much praise, but was yet capable, as far as came under my observation, of the following little improvements. The scale representing five nautical miles should only subtend three miles and a half; the shoals of Barros de Zooniga,[2] though well placed, instead of being two distinct shoals, ought to have been one intire shoal, stretching something further to the N.W. and S.E. than is therein represented; and the soundings between Barros de Zooniga and the land of ponta de la Loma (which is omitted) and are in no part, from the south extremity of the former directly across to the latter, more than four fathoms at high water, and from a narrow bar from the shore to the shoal, gradually deepening as well on the inside as on the outside of the bar, with a regular increase in mid-channel, from five close to the shore, to ten fathoms between the two low points that form the entrance of the port. This channel between the point de la Loma and the shoal is the only navigable passage for shipping; that to the north-eastward of the shoal does not anywhere exceed half a mile in width, which, with its shallow depth of water, renders it ineligible excepting for boats, or vessels of very small draught. The port however affords excellent anchorage, and is capable of containing a great number of vessels; but the difficulty, nay almost impossibility, of procuring wood and water under its present circumstances, reduces its value as a port of accommodation.[3]

At the distance of about eight leagues, somewhere about N. 55 W. or N. 60 W., from point de la Loma, by a very uncertain estimation, is situated an island called St John's;[4] between which and the coast we passed without seeing it, nor did we observe it whilst we remained at anchor; excepting on one very clear evening, when it was seen from the Presidio, at a time when I was unprovided with a compass, or any other means of ascertaining its direction, and was therefore only able to guess at its situation. It appeared to be low and flat, is but seldom seen from the Presidio of St. Diego, and was

[1] This plan, based on a Spanish manuscript communicated to Dalrymple by John Henry Cox, was dated 1782, but it was not published until 1789.

[2] Zuniga is the correct spelling; now Zuniga Shoal.

[3] A revised version of the Dalrymple plan, incorporating the changes here outlined, appears as an inset on Vancouver's chart of the Northwest Coast from lat. 30° N to lat. 38° 30′ N.

[4] Shown on Vancouver's chart, but with the warning 'Situation doubtful'. It may have been the SE corner of San Clemente Island.

undiscovered until seen by Martinez a few years before in one of his excursions along this coast.

The Coronados already mentioned consist of two islets and three rocks, situated in a south direction, four or five leagues from point de la Loma, occupying the space of five miles, and lying N. 35 W. and S. 35 E. from each other. The southernmost, which, in point of magnitude, is equal to all the rest collectively taken, is about a mile broad and two miles long, and is a good mark to point out the port of St. Diego, which however is otherwise sufficiently conspicuous not easily to be mistaken.

I shall conclude our transactions at St. Diego, by stating such astronomical and nautical observations as were made there, with those that had been made previously to our arrival and after our departure from that port, for the purpose of ascertaining the rates and correcting the errors of our chronometers; which, notwithstanding the restrictive orders that had been received at St. Diego, I had been enabled to accomplish to the utmost of my desires and expectations.

Astronomical and Nautical Observations.

On the 28th of November Kendall's chronometer, according to the last rate, shewed the longitude to be	243°	22′	15″
Arnold's No. 14, ditto ditto	243	7	15
Ditto 176, ditto ditto	244	5	30
Longitude, by 45 sets of lunar distances, taken before our arrival and reduced to St. Diego by Arnold's No. 14	243	23	52
Longitude, by 59 sets of ditto, taken in the harbour	243	8	13
Longitude, by 102 sets of ditto, taken after our departure, and reduced back to St. Diego by Arnold's No. 14,	242	58	28
The mean of the whole, collective taken	243	6	45
Out of the above 206 sets, 38 were made by myself; mean	243°	11′	10″
Thirty by Mr. Baker, ditto	242	53	8
Seventy-one by Mr. Whidbey, ditto	243	7	52
Sixty-seven by Mr. Orchard, ditto	243	6	8
Latitude of port St. Diego, by 11 meridional altitudes of the sun (viz.) 5 with the artificial horizon, and 6 with the natural, reduced to the place of observation	34	42	30

Allowing the true longitude of port St. Diego to be
243° 6′ 45″,[1] Kendall's chronometer was, on the
9th of December, at noon, fast of mean time at

Greenwich	3ʰ	13′	5″
And gaining per day		20	
Arnold's No. 14, ditto ditto	3	1	39
And gaining per day		21	38‴
Idem No. 176, ditto ditto	6	49	26
And gaining per day		36	27

Variation, by 2 compasses and 6 sets of observations,
 differing from 8° 28′ to 14° 54′, the mean   11 easterly

The vertical inclination of the magnetic needle,

Marked end, North Face East,			59°	23′
Ditto	ditto	West,	59	38
Ditto	South Face East,		58	32
Ditto	ditto	West,	59	45

Mean inclination of the marine dipping needle,   59   13

The tides were found to run in general about two knots, though faster at
spring tides, six hours each way. High water nine hours after the moon passes
the meridian.

The situations of the different parts of the coast, from Monterrey, are
corrected, and laid down, from the result of the above observations. The rates
and errors of the chronometers having been ascertained by observations made
with the artificial horizon at St. Diego.

[1] The position of Point Loma light, at the entrance to San Diego Bay, is lat. 32° 39·9′ N,
long. 117° 14·5′ W (242° 45·5′ E). The large error in lat. is unusual.

CHAPTER IX.

Proceed to the Southward—Description of the Coast—Some account of Port Bodega—Brief Account of the Spanish Settlements in New Albion.

HAVING quitted St. Diego, we were soon assisted by a pleasant breeze from the N.W. with which our course was directed along the coast, passing by the narrow tract of land that forms the inner harbour of that port, and divides it from an open bay on the external coast, between point de la Loma, and a high bluff point lying from it 55 E., about twelve miles distant. We passed between this bluff point and the Coronados, the latter lying about seven miles from the former, from whence the continent took a direction S. 18 E., six leagues. The shores are composed of steep rocky cliffs, which in general rise, though not very abruptly, to a very hilly country, remarkable for three conspicuous mountains, intirely detached from each other; rising in quick ascent at a little distance from the shore, on nearly a plain and even surface. The northernmost of these presented the appearance of a table, in all directions from the ocean.[1] The middle one terminated in a sharp peak, and the southernmost in an irregular form. The centre one of these remarkable mountains lies from port St. Diego S. 35 E., distant nine leagues, and at a distance may serve to point out that port. Not far from these eminences is situated, as I was informed, the mission of St. Miguel, established in the year 1787;[2] but it was not seen, owing probably to the approach of night. This was passed as usual in standing to and fro, though unattended with that serenity that we had lately been accustomed to; for the wind at N.E. and east blew a strong gale, attended by very heavy squalls, that made it difficult to preserve our station near the coast; which on the following morning, Tuesday the 10th, was about two leagues from us, consisting of high steep rocky cliffs rising abruptly from the sea, and composing a craggy mountainous country. The direction of the shores was S. 32 E. towards a conspicuous bay;[3] this we were prevented from entering by the wind blowing nearly in a direction from it, and which by eight in the morning obliged us to close-reef the fore and

[1] Table Mountain (2244 ft.), actually the middle one of the three; the others, farther inland, are Dos Picos (3291 ft.) and Cone Mountain (3782 ft.). Vancouver had now passed the present boundary between the United States and Mexico.

[2] The Mission San Miguel Arcángel, founded, as Vancouver states, in 1787.

[3] The Bahia de Todos los Santos. Bay of Todas Santos on Vancouver's chart.

main-topsails, and hand the mizen-topsail; the two topsails in the course of the next hour were both split and torn to pieces, but by the time they were replaced the gale had greatly abated; yet it continued adverse to our entering the bay. This I much regretted, as I wished to have given it a more minute examination, because it had every appearance of affording shelter, and towards its upper part of proving a good harbour.

During the forenoon immense columns of smoke were seen to arise from the shore in different parts, but principally from the southeast or upper part of the bay, which towards noon obscured its shores in that direction. These clouds of smoke, containing ashes and dust, soon enveloped the whole coast to that degree, that the only visible part was the south point of the above-mentioned bay, bearing by compass N. 42 E., about four miles from us; the observed latitude at this time was 31° 40', longitude 243° 31½'. The easterly wind still prevailing, brought with it from the shore vast volumes of this noxious matter, not only very uncomfortable to our feelings, but adverse to our pursuit, as it intirely hid from our view every object at the distance of an hundred yards. On this account I shortened sail, in order to wait a more favorable opportunity for continuing our examination.

This bay, being the first opening on the coast to the south of St. Diego, is undoubtedly that distinguished by the Spaniards by the name of Todos Santos; though we found a manifest difference in its position from that assigned to it in the Spanish charts. That of Sen[r] Quadra places its south point, called by me POINT GRAJERO,[1] in latitude 32° 17', the printed chart in 32° 25'; both charts correctly notice the rocky islets and rocks, that extend from it N. 50 W., about a league distant, give to point Grajero a sharp turn to the south-east, and in other respects represent the bay much as it appeared to us; the former more particularly so; yet by our observations, which were extremely good and to be confided in, point Grajero was found to be situated in latitude 31° 43', longitude 243° 34'.[2] I was informed, that in the neighbourhood of this bay the mission of St. Thomas, established in the year 1790, is situated.[3] This had also escaped our notice, in consequence most likely of the density of the atmosphere, which obscured these regions until four o'clock in the afternoon, when the easterly wind died away, and was succeeded by a light breeze from the southward, which dispersed the smoke, and discovered to us that we were some miles to the south of the bay. The night was spent as usual, and the next morning, Wednesday the 10th, we passed a cluster of detached rocks lying about half a league from a small projecting point, that forms a bay or cove on either side of it; but these being still obscured with the smoke, their extent could not be ascertained. These rocks lie from point Grajero, S. 12 E., distant about three leagues. At noon the observed latitude was 31° 27', the longitude 243° 41'. At this time the cluster

[1] Now Cabo Punta Banda.
[2] Its location is lat. 31° 45' N, long. 116° 45' W (243° 15' E).
[3] The Santo Thomás de Aquín mission at San Solano, founded in April 1791.

of rocks bore by compass N. 34 W., the nearest shore N. 36 E., distant about three miles; the southernmost land in sight S. 66 E., and point Grajero, N. 27 W., at the distance of sixteen miles.

Two opinions had arisen as to the cause of the very disagreeable clouds of smoke, ashes, and dust, in which we had been involved the preceeding day. Volcanic eruptions was naturally the first conjecture; but after some little time, the opinion changed to the fire being superficial in different parts of the country; and which, by the prevalence and strength of the north-east and easterly wind, spread to a very great extent. The latter opinion this morning evidently appeared to be correct. Large columns of smoke were still seen rising from the vallies behind the hills, and extending to the northward along the coast; this seemed the line of direction which the fire took, excluding the country from our view to the north of Todos Santos. To the south of us the shores exhibited manifest proofs of its fatal effects, for burnt tufts of grass, weeds, and shrubs, being the only vegetable productions, were distinguished over the whole face of the country, as far as with the assistance of our glasses we were enabled to discern; and in many places, at a great distance, the rising columns of smoke shewed that the fire was not yet extinguished. Under these circumstances, it cannot be matter of surprize that the country should present a desolate and melancholy appearance. The smaller portions of smoke which rose in various places directed our glasses in quest of inhabitants, but neither these nor any habitations, were seen within the limits of our examination.

Light winds and long nights rendered our progress so slow, that by the evening our researches had not extended more than eight leagues along the coast from Todos Santos, where we gained soundings in 30 fathoms water, about two miles from the shore; this from point Grajero takes a direction S. 35 E., and excepting the coves before mentioned, is nearly straight and perfectly compact. In this situation we noticed a conspicuous projecting point of land, very moderately elevated, stretching to the south-westward into the ocean, terminating in low steep cliffs, and rising with a very gradual ascent to the interior country, which is mountainous. Somewhere in the vicinage of this point, as I was informed, either the mission of Sta Vincenta, or that of St. Thomas, had been settled in the year 1778,[1] but we saw no appearance of any buildings, nor of land under cultivation.

During the first part of the night, which passed as before, the wind blew strong from the E.N.E.; this, though not so violent as we had experienced before from that quarter, nor attended with any smoke, was nevertheless very uncomfortable, by causing a dry parching heat, not only on the hands and face exposed to its immediate influence, but also, though in a less degree, over the whole body. This E.N.E. breeze died away about midnight, and was succeeded by light airs from the S.E.; against these we plied, and by our observation at noon on the following day, Thursday the 12th, we had reached

---

[1] The San Vicente Ferrer mission, founded in October 1780.

the latitude of 31°, longitude 243° 51'. In this situation the southernmost land in sight bore by compass S. 72 E., the projecting point, N. 81 E., and the northernmost land in sight, N. 21 W.; the above projecting point is situated in latitude 30° 57', longitude 244° 1', and notwithstanding it is very remarkable, from its shape and appearance, as likewise by its forming a bay on its north-west, and another on its south-east side, it is not taken any notice of in the Spanish charts; I have therefore called it CAPE COLNETT, after Captain Colnett of the navy.[1]

This promontory bore a very singular character as we passed; the cliffs already described as composing it are, about the middle between their summit and the water side, divided horizontally nearly into two equal parts, and formed of different materials; the lower part seemed to consist of sand or clay of a very smooth surface and light colour; the upper part was evidently of a rocky substance, with a very uneven surface, and of a dark colour; this seemed to be again divided into narrow columns by vertical strata. These apparent divisions, as well horizontally as vertically, existed with great uniformity all round the promontory.

Early in the afternoon we discovered to the south-eastward something like a cluster of islands, and observed, that the bay on the south-east side of cape Colnett extended to the north-east; which although of no great extent, appeared likely to afford tolerably good shelter. The wind continued in the southern quarter until the evening, when it was succeeded by light easterly breezes from the land, which continued until near noon the next day, Friday the 13th: we however made some progress, passing before an extensive bay, formed by cape Colnett, and a point of land off which these islands appeared to lie.[2] Our distance of eight or nine miles from these shores when off the bay, was much greater than I could have wished, and was occasioned by the direction of the wind, which had prevented our approaching as I had intended, with the hope of obtaining a view of the mission of El Rosario founded in the year 1776,[3] not far from the sea shore, and somewhere in this neighbourhood.

I was very anxious to become acquainted with this settlement, as there seemed to be a great probability of our being able to land near it, and to have acquired from the Rev. Fathers some substantial information respecting the Dominican missionaries, whose establishments commence southward from St. Diego, and continue all the way to cape St. Lucas;[4] and as we had not hitherto had any intercourse with this religious order, an interview with them would have been esteemed a very desirable consideration.

---

[1] Cabo Colonet, on Mexican maps. The lat. is correct.

[2] The Bahia San Román, which appears on Vancouver's chart as the Bay de Los Virgenes, a name that dates back to the Vizcaino expedition of 1602.

[3] Nuestra Señora del Santísimo Rosario, the first Dominican mission in Lower California, was founded in 1774.

[4] The Cabo San Lucas, the S point of the Lower California peninsula.

We were visited by one of the natives in a straw canoe like those seen at St. Francisco, who pointed to the appearance of a cove in the extensive bay before mentioned, and said that a mission was situated there; though we could not discern it with our glasses. Some other questions were put to this man, but on finding we were not Spaniards, he became very reserved, and, after receiving some beads, returned towards the shore, directing his course to the place where he had given us to understand the mission was situated. But having now passed it, and it being also to windward of us, to have returned thither would have occasioned a delay that I could not afford; and on that account I declined the attempt, in full expectation of being able to land at the mission of St. Domingo formed in the year 1774,[1] and said to be near the coast also, at the distance of 14 or 16 leagues southward from El Rosario.

Our course was now directed to the westward of all the apparent islands; the latitude at noon was 30° 35', longitude 244° 9½'; in this situation the northernmost land in sight bore by compass N. 28 W.; cape Colnett N. 26 W.; the south point of the extensive bay named by me POINT ZUNIGA, after the former commandant at St. Diego, on which stands a remarkable hummock[2] in latitude 30° 30½', longitude 244° 16½', and which had been considered to be the northern-most of the above mentioned islands, S. 66 E.; and the outermost of those islands, from S 56 E. to S. 47 E. This last was soon discovered to be the only detached land of the whole group, and according to the Spanish charts is called Isle de Cenizas;[3] it is about four miles in circuit, of a triangular form; its western side is formed by high steep cliffs, but its north-east and south-east sides terminate in low sandy land, extending towards the continent, with a detached rock lying off it. This, together with the colour of the water between it and the main land, were not favorable indications of that passage, which is about half a league wide, being navigable for shipping.

The continental shore southward from point Zuniga, which had been taken for islands, consisted of five remarkable hummocks, nearly of equal height and size, moderately elevated, with two smaller ones close to the water tide; the whole rising from a tract of very low and nearly level land, forming a very projecting promontory; this, like many other places, not having been distinguished by any name in the Spanish charts, I have called POINT FIVE HUMMOCKS;[4] and it is as conspicuous and remarkable as any projecting land the coast of these regions affords. The shores from point Zuniga take a direction S. 22 E. about eight miles, where, from the southern-most of these hills, point Five Hummocks terminates in a low point of land, forming the west point of a bay or inlet, that on our first approach had the appearance of being extensive; before, however, we could obtain a complete view of it, the day closed in, when the wind ceasing, and having regular soundings from

[1] The Santo Domingo mission was founded in August 1775.
[2] Wagner concluded that this was what is now known as Southwest Hill.
[3] Now the Isla San Martin.   [4] Now the Cabo San Quintin.

25 to 14 fathoms, we anchored for the night, in order to obtain some further information of it the next morning, Saturday the 14th. Day-light, however, presented nothing very remarkable, or worthy of the least delay; the whole was an open and exposed bay, formed by the sea coast retiring a little to the north and eastward of point Five Hummocks, off which at a little distance are some rocks and breakers. The north-west part of the bay[1] had an appearance of affording tolerable shelter from the west and south-west winds, provided a sufficient depth of water should be found to admit of anchoring near the shore, which, from the view we had thus procured, seemed to be very doubtful.

At noon we had advanced but a little distance from our anchorage, when the observed latitude was 30° 19', longitude 244° 24'. The southernmost land in sight now bore by compass S. 29 E.; point Five Hummocks, N. 43 W.; the island of Cenizas, N. 47 W.; and a point having behind it a remarkable mount of white barren sand, forming the south-east point of the bay just mentioned,[2] N. 67 E. at the distance of six miles. The wind chiefly from the southern quarter, was light and variable, so that we made no great progress along the coast; yet we advanced sufficiently to ascertain, that the southernmost land seen at noon was situated in latitude 29° 54', longitude 244° 33';[3] that the coast between us and that station, which by the evening was four or five leagues distant, was composed of nearly a straight shore, formed by steep perpendicular cliffs moderately elevated; and that the interior country was less mountainous than that which we had been accustomed to see further to the northward.

Having at length reached the 30th degree of north latitude, which was the southern limit of our intended survey of the western coast of North America,[4] and having now accomplished the laborious task of its examination from hence northward to the 56th degree of north latitude, it becomes requisite to state some of my observations made on the Spanish charts of that coast, to which I have latterly had frequent occasion to refer.

On comparing them with the shores, especially to the southward of Todos Santos, little resemblance can be found; whilst the situation of the several prominent parts and important stations are rendered doubtful by the very great disagreement in point of latitude. Between Todos Santos, and the bay off which we anchored the preceding evening, (which bay according to Sen[r] Quadra's chart is the bay of St. Francisco)[5] there are in those charts two spacious bays, whereas we found only one, in which we supposed the mission of El Rosario to be situated; this I considered as the bay de las Virgenes.[6] We

---

[1] Bahia San Quintin.   [2] Punta Baja, in lat. 29° 56' N.
[3] Its position is lat. 29° 56' N, long. approximately 115° 48' W (244° 12' E).
[4] Bell remarks that 'Point St. Felix terminated this Year's Survey.' – December. Wagner notes that Punta San Felix is shown on Quadra's 1791 map as at lat. 30° 15' and he identifies it with the present Cabo San Quintin, which is in lat. 30° 22' N, but it seems likely that Bell meant Punta Baja.
[5] The present Bahia San Quintin.   [6] The Bahia San Román.

did not see the isle de Sta Marios,[1] nor the isles de St. Geronimo,[2] nor the shoal that is laid down in the printed chart to the westward of the island of Cenizas. Hence it might appear, on reference to Senr Quadra's chart, that we had been mistaken in respect to the identical part of the coast we were now abreast of; that the land we had taken for the island of Cenizas, was the island of Marios, and that what we supposed to have been the bay of St. Francisco, was that of de las Virgenes. But in this case the isles of St. Geronimo, the island of Cenizas, and the bay of St. Francisco, would still be somewhere to the southward, and consequently their latitude would be yet more irreconcileable; for in Senr Quadra's chart the island of Cenizas is placed 40', and in the printed charts 52' further *north* than its real situation was found to be; and it is also represented to be of much greater extent than we found it to occupy. The west point of the bay of St. Francisco, (that is, point Five Hummocks) which was found by us to be in latitude 30° 23', longitude 244° 20', is placed by Senr Quadra's chart in latitude 31° 6', and in the other in 31° 22'.[3] Should these places, therefore, be really so much further to the south, they are necessarily beyond the limit of our survey, and the error in latitude must have increased beyond all calculation or probability.

For these reasons I have adopted my first ideas as to the names of the places in question, on a presumption that the apparent difference between ours and the Spanish surveys, must wholly be attributed to the inaccuracy of their charts; an opinion I feel myself authorized to entertain, since Senr Quadra warned me against the incorrectness of the manuscript chart, as he did not know on what authority the coast southward of Monterrey had been laid down; and consequently could not be answerable for its accuracy, further than of its being a true copy from one which was regarded by the Spaniards as the best chart of those regions.

As we drew near the southern limits of our researches along this coast, I was in anxious expectation of seeing the mission of St. Domingo, which had been stated to be situated in this neighbourhood, and which is the southernmost Spanish settlement on, what I have considered as, the coast of New Albion, as discovered and named by Sir Francis Drake; or, as the Spaniards frequently call the same country, New California.

The exterior shores of that part of the continent to the south of the limits before mentioned, being those of the peninsula bearing that name, I would gladly have undertaken the task of examining further, for the purpose of correcting any other such geographical errors, notwithstanding the very extraordinary slow and tedious progress that had attended our late endeavours; had we not been so much pressed for time, in consequence of the very importunate manner in which Major Grose had requested the return of the Dædalus to New South Wales.

Exploring these shores any further would however have exceeded the strict

---

[1] Not identified.
[2] Isla San Jeronimo, in lat. 29° 48' N.
[3] Cabo San Quintin (Point Five Hummocks) is in lat. 30° 22' N.

letter of my instructions, and might possibly have excited additional jealousy in the breast of the Spanish acting governor. Under these considerations I was compelled, though with infinite reluctance, to abandon this interesting pursuit, and to determine on making the best of our way to the Sandwich islands, where I could firmly rely on the sincerity of *Tamaahamaah*, and the professions of the rest of our *rude uncivilized* friends in those islands, for a hearty welcome, a kind reception, and every service and accommodation in their humble power to afford; without any of the inhospitable restrictions we must have been under from the then *civilized* governor at Monterrey.

But as the completion of our survey demanded that the relative situation of the island of Guadaloupe with these shores should be ascertained according to our own observations, our course was directed thither.

The island of Guadaloupe is generally made by the Spaniards when bound to the southward from Monterrey, or from their other northern establishments; in which route they pass to the westward out of sight of those islands that form the channel of Sta Barbara, for the advantage of continuing in the strength of the north-west winds; and thus they reach the island of Guadaloupe, from whence they shape a course for cape San Lucas.

As a considerable part of the commission entrusted to my charge and execution had now been accomplished, and thus far drawn towards a conclusion; and as the nature of new countries, and the progress of new colonial establishments, must ever be regarded as interesting subjects of inquiry; I shall now endeavour to recite such circumstances as had fallen within the sphere of my observations, and such miscellaneous information as I was able to procure with respect to the Spanish settlements on these shores, but which would have interrupted the foregoing narrative, confined chiefly to the occurrences which were inseparable from our nautical or geographical pursuits.

On this occasion, however, it may not be unfit to premise, that the communication we had with the shores of New Albion, and our intercourse with the resident Spanish inhabitants, were too limited, and of too short duration to permit of my obtaining any other information than such as arose in common conversation from the impressions of surrounding objects. In addition to which, the situation in which I stood was of a very delicate nature, and demanded the most cautious attention on my part, lest any thing should occur, either by too great curiosity to be instructed in the knowledge of their internal government, or in the number, strength, and situation of their several establishments along the coast, that might prevent our obtaining the essential refreshments we required; or become the cause of any national disagreement. Under these circumstances, it was absolutely requisite that all my inquiries should be conducted with the greatest circumspection; and hence the knowledge obtained must necessarily be of a very limited nature, and rendered additionally incorrect, by my labouring under the mortifying disadvantage of understanding but little of the Spanish language.

The profound secrecy which the Spanish nation has so strictly observed with regard to their territories and settlements in this hemisphere, naturally excites, in the strongest manner, a curiosity and a desire of being informed of the state, condition, and progress of the several establishments provided in these distant regions, for the purpose of converting its native inhabitants to christianity and civilization.

The mission of St. Domingo has already been stated to be the southernmost of the Spanish settlements in New Albion; and it is also to be understood as the most southern of those that are considered as *new establishments*, from having been formed subsequent to the year 1769, when the expeditions by sea and land were undertaken to settle Monterrey and St. Diego.[1] At this period their north-westernmost possession on this coast was Velicata, and S[ta] Maria[2] on the coast of the peninsula, in the gulph of California. Until that time these two missions had formed a kind of north-western barrier, or frontier, to the Spanish Mexican colonies. But, the rapid strides that Russia was then making in subjecting to its government the countries bordering on the north-western part of the North Pacific Ocean awakened the apprehensions and roused the jealousy of the Spanish court; and in consequence of the alarm thus given, those expeditions were undertaken. Since that time all the new establishments have been formed, and the mission of Velicata removed some leagues to the north-westward, nearer the exterior coast of California.

The new settlements are divided into four different counties, or rather are placed under four distinct jurisdictions, of which Monterrey is the principal; and the established residence as well of the governor, who is captain general of the province, as of the father president of the Franciscan order of missionaries. In each of the divisions is fixed one military post only, called the Presidio, governed by a lieutenant, who has under him an ensign, with serjeants, corporals, &c. And although the jurisdiction of the governor extends over the whole province, yet the respective commanders at the several Presidios are invested with great authority in the ordinary matters relative to their civil or military jurisdiction; but they seem to have very little influence or concern in any thing that appertains to the missions or ecclesiastical government, which appear to be wholly under the authority and management of the Rev. Fathers.

The most northern Presidio is that of St. Francisco, which has under its authority, or more properly speaking under its protection, the missions of St. Francisco and S[ta] Clara, the pueblo of St. Joseph, about 3 or 4 miles from S[ta] Clara, and the establishment which I understood had been formed during the preceding summer in the southern opening of port Bodega; to this opening

[1] Alarmed by Russian activities in the Alaskan islands, which they feared would spread to the coast of the continent, the Spaniards had determined to establish a chain of garrisons and missions in what is now California. San Diego was the first of these.

[2] The missions of San Fernando de Velicatá and Santa Maria de Los Angeles had been established in 1769 and 1767 respectively.

they have given the name of PORT JUAN FRANCISCO.[1] Of this port I saw a plan, of which I afterward procured a copy; by which it appeared capable of admitting vessels of small burthen only. The channel, which is not half a mile wide, is round its west point of entrance, and has across it a bar, on which at high water there is not more than three fathoms for some distance; after which it extends to two miles in width, and continues so, in a direction about south-east, for six miles. The soundings increase in mid-channel to six and seven fathoms, and decrease regularly towards the shore. Its head or upper part is bounded by shoal water, which extends some distance into the harbour. I could not discover in what part of the port the settlement is formed; though I was perfectly satisfied, that it had been undertaken by a Spanish officer named Sen[r] Don Juan Matoota,[2] and carried into effect by two expeditions from the port of St. Francisco; and although I was unable to ascertain the force employed on this occasion I had every reason to believe it was very inconsiderable.[3]

The next in succession southward is that of Monterrey, the capital of the province; under which the mission of S[ta] Cruz, near point Anno Nuevo,[4] is the most northern, and was established in the year 1789 or 1790; but was not at this time completed. In its immediate vicinity, I was given to understand a pueblo of the same name was formed in the year 1791;[5] and about nine leagues to the E.S.E. of it is the mission of la Soledad.[6] South and eastward from Monterrey are the missions of St. Carlos, St. Antonio, St. Luis and S[ta] Rosa la Purissima; the latter is situated near the entrance of the channel of S[ta] Barbara, and these constitute the division of Monterrey.

The next and smallest division is that of S[ta] Barbara. Although this Presidio and mission were not erected until the year 1786, the Spaniards had, prior to that time, resided in the neighbourhood for four or five years in small huts and tents; but they only date the establishment from the completion of the buildings, which, I believe, has been uniformly the case with the others; yet I was not informed, that in any other instance they had remained so long exposed to the inconveniences and dangers necessarily attendant on such a defenceless state, in the event of any misunderstanding taking place with the natives. Besides the mission of S[ta] Barbara, the Presidio has under its ordinary authority that of Buena Ventura, founded in the year 1784,[7] and the Pueblo

---

[1] Now Bodega Bay; named for Juan Francisco Bodega y Quadra. The Spaniards feared that the British intended to occupy the bay, and planned a settlement there to forestall them. (No doubt due to a typesetter's mistake the name is printed in the type Vancouver reserved for features named by himself or members of his expedition.)

[2] Juan Batuista Matute.

[3] An expedition under Matute in the *Sutil* had arrived at Bodega Bay late in May 1793, but it failed to found a settlement. A much more elaborate expedition planned for later in the year never materialized.

[4] Point Ano Neuvo, 18 miles N of Point Santa Cruz, the N point of Monterey Bay.

[5] Misprinted 1971 in the second edition.

[6] Founded in October 1791.   [7] Founded in 1782, not 1784.

de los Angelos, formed in 1781[1]; which latter, I was told, was subject also to the control of the Presidio at St. Diego, the fourth and southernmost of these new settlements. This presides over the mission of St. Diego, founded with the Presidio in the year 1770,[2] over St. Juan Capistrano, St. Gabriel, and St. Miguel. The last is not of the Franciscan order, but forms the northernmost of the Dominican missions. The religious of this order extend their missions southward; not only along the exterior coast, but also over the whole of the peninsula; and are under the regulations of the Presidio at Loretto,[3] which is the only military establishment to the south of St. Diego, on the peninsula of California.

The climate of the country comprehended between the bay and port of St. Francisco, the former under the 38th, and the latter under the 30th degree of north latitude, is, by our own experience, as well as by the information we obtained, subject to much drought. The rainy season is from the month of December to March, the autumn in general being very dry; and although in the early part of our visit the preceding year we had some rain, yet we experienced an almost uninterrupted series of fine weather, with a clear atmosphere, very unlike that which had attended us there in last November; when, notwithstanding that on many occasions no clouds were to be seen, yet the density of the atmosphere in consequence of an almost continual dry haze or fog, sometimes partial, and at others general, was such, that distant objects were not discernible, and those in our immediate neighbourhood were frequently obscured. The inconvenience, however, was not felt in the same degree by those whose occupations confined them to the shore.

On quitting Monterrey the preceding year, I had made some remarks on the heat and cold at that time, but I had no opportunity of making any fresh experiments for this purpose on our late visit. Our climate at sea was much more uniform; the mean height of the mercury in the thermometer was about 62°, without varying more than 5° in elevation or depression; though, in a few instances, for an hour or two in the day, the heat was oppressive, and some of the nights were extremely cold. The mercury in the barometer was also very uniform, not descending lower than 29$^{IN.}$ 90$^{10THS.}$ or rising above 30$^{IN.}$ 23$^{10THS.}$; nor did the shores indicate their being subject to frequent storms, or hard gales of wind; though it is imagined that the wind sometimes blows very strong from the S.E., west, and N.W., at the distance of a few leagues from the coast, from the heavy billows that roll in those directions, and break with great fury on the shore. The surf that prevented our landing at Buena Ventura, was attributed by the Spanish residents to the distant operation of a strong southerly gale, as the swell came from that quarter. The N.W. winds, however, are by far the most general, and occasion great difficulty in passing along these shores to the northward. The practice of the Spaniards is to stand a great distance into the ocean, until they reach far to

---

[1] Founded in 1780.　　　　　　　　　　[2] Founded in 1769.
[3] The presidio and mission of Nuestra Soñora de Loreto were founded in 1697.

the northward of the parallel of the port whither they are bound, and then steer for the land; but from our observations, during the time we were navigating these shores, such a precaution did not appear by any means necessary, at least at that season of the year; and as this coast had now been explored and the direction of its shores and conspicuous places ascertained, so far as our survey had extended, I was convinced that vessels, with the winds we had from the bay of St. Francisco to point Conception, or indeed further to the northward, would make as good a passage with the assistance of the land winds, which in general blow from the east and south-east to the north-westward, as they could make with the sea breeze to the south-eastward, since the land wind prevails during a larger proportion of the twenty-four hours than the sea breeze, and frequently blows stronger; besides which, most sailing vessels would gain some advantage in the day time, by turning to windward with the sea breeze, which generally blows steadily and moderately, over a sea that is smooth and tranquil.

The absence of rain, in the dry season, is in some measure compensated by the dews. These frequently fall very heavily, and tend to preserve the productions of nature from being intirely destroyed, though not in sufficient quantity to keep in constant action the springs of vegetation. Hence the dreary aspect of the country in most situations, which is further increased by the general scarcity of running water, as the whole country affords but a few small streams.

This very material disadvantage, so repeatedly stated already, we now found to continue to the most southern extent of our researches; the country, however, did not seem wholly destitute of this valuable article, though it did not frequently discover itself on its surface; and I entertain little doubt, that by digging wells to a proper depth, a sufficient and excellent supply for all domestic purposes would be obtained in most places. At least, the recourse that had been had to expedients of this nature, as well by ourselves as at some of the missions and Presidios justified me in this opinion; but the Spaniards, contented with the brackish pools of water, already formed to their hand, for the supply of their shipping, are too inactive to search for better, or to draw into one stream the several small branches that exist on the surface for a small extent, and then are lost, either by exhalation from the sun, or the absorption of the thirsty soil.

The climate seems to be as healthy at St. Diego, and in the channel of Sta Barbara, as at Monterrey; the salubrity of which was mentioned on our former visit. The soil of the country, at least that small portion of it that fell under my immediate inspection, at and to the northward of St. Diego along the sea coast, appeared of a light and sandy nature, varying in point of fertility; yet none seemed to be naturally steril, although it presented that outward appearance; and I am persuaded there are few spots that, with the assistance of manual labour, would not be made productive.

I had every reason to believe, that beyond the lofty mountains that range along and chiefly compose the shores of the continent under our present consideration, the surface would be found capable of receiving great improvement. This was remarked in our journey from the sea coast to the mission of Sta Clara. At St. Diego the soil rapidly loses its fertility; and I was informed, that from thence immediately southward to cape St. Lucas, the whole of the peninsula is composed of a soil so extremely unproductive and barren, that good mould had been sent thither from other places, to certain situations where it was deemed proper to plant missions, and deposited there for the purpose of raising the grain and vegetables necessary for the establishments.

I shall now proceed to consider more fully the appropriation of this country by its new masters the Spaniards, who, though possessing the very extensive and fertile tract of land lying to the northwest from St. Diego, have not turned it to any profitable advantage, notwithstanding that the soil, as stated on former occasions, may be considered to be rich and luxuriant, at least in the parts selected by the Spaniards for their settlements. That much skill or investigation was not required in making their choice, was evident from the difference in the natural productions observed in my journey to Sta Clara; when I became convinced, by the inquiries I had then an opportunity of making, that the soil of the missions of St. Antonio, La Soledad, and St. Luís, was equally fertile, especially that of the two former, which are said to be watered by several streams, and which yielded grain, fruits, and roots of the best quality, and in the greatest abundance. These were obtained with little trouble in clearing the ground, as spaces of great extent were found nearly free from trees or shrubs, and equally rich in soil with those parts that produced their lofty timbers and luxuriant forests. This fertility of soil seems to exist with little variation through the plains and vallies of the interior country, extending in some places to the water's edge on the sea coast. Such, however, is not the situation of Sta Barbara; the country about it to the northwest is chiefly composed of barren rocky cliffs, and towards the south-east is a low swampy salt marsh. The former, terminating very abruptly at no great distance from the water side, form between their base and the sea beach a plain, composed of a clayey and sandy soil; where, close about the foot of the cliffs, and protected by them from the sea winds, grow the holly-leaved oak trees, from which we obtained our supply of wood; and a few acres of land in that neighbourhood were inclosed, and in an indifferent state of cultivation. On the salt marshes that extend some distance further from the water side to the foot of the mountains, a few dwarf trees and grovelling shrubs were produced, but no part of it was under cultivation; and as the whole of the interior country in all directions seemed to be composed of high barren naked mountains destitute of soil, it is not likely that it should be very abundant in its vegetable productions. Sufficient, however, is afforded for the use of the mission; and was it well supplied with water, it is supposed capable of being rendered very fruitful even under these disadvantages. The sheep and poultry here far exceeded those of every other establishment that we had visited, not only in point of size, but in the flavor and delicacy of the meat. To these was added from the sea a daily and abundant supply of most excellent fish, procured throughout the year by the natives, who are very expert in that, as well as in many other useful and necessary occupations.

The Presidio is principally supplied with grain and pulse from the pueblo de los Angelos, and the mission of Buena Ventura, which, though situated close to the water-side, has the reputation of being amongst the most fertile of the establishments in this country. Its buildings were some time ago burnt down by accident; this circumstance, though attended with some temporary inconvenience, was the means of affording them an opportunity of replacing them on the same spot with more advantage, both in respect of their external appearance, and internal accommodation. These buildings surpassed all the others I had seen, being something larger, and more uniform; and the apartments were infinitely more commodious, and were kept extremely clean and neat. Both here and at Sta Barbara, very great advantages are derived from having near each of these establishments a great abundance of very good lime-stone, excellent earth for bricks and tiles, and flag-stones for paving. These valuable materials give the buildings at these places a manifest superiority over those that are erected with substances less fit for the purpose; but, to balance this advantage, it appeared that their labours in husbandry, especially in raising European grains and pulse, were not rewarded by that abundant return which we had found at Sta Clara. The average produce of their seed does not yield more than twenty-three for one in wheat, barley, and oats; the quality of which is not by any means equal to the same sort of corn grown in the more northern settlements. This inferiority is attributed more to the want of rain than to the comparative difference of the soil; since, although the soil and climate of the latter appeared to be more suitable to the agriculture of the open fields, yet the garden of Buena Ventura far exceeded any thing of that description I had before met with in these regions, both in respect of the quality, quantity, and variety of its excellent productions, not only indigenous to the country, but appertaining to the temperate as well as torrid zone; not one species having yet been shown, or planted, that had not flourished, and yielded its fruit in abundance, and of excellent quality. These have principally consisted of apples, pears, plumbs, figs, oranges, grapes, peaches, and pomgranates, together with the plantain, banana, cocoa nut, sugar cane, indigo, and a great variety of the necessary and useful kitchen herbs, plants and roots. All these were flourishing in the greatest health and perfection, though separated from the sea-side only by two or three fields of corn, that were cultivated within a few yards of the surf. The grounds, however, on which they were produced, were supplied, at the expence of some labour, with a few small streams, which, as occasion required, were conducted to the crops that stood most in need of water. Here also grew great quantities of the Indian fig, or prickly pear; but whether cultivated for its fruit only, or for the cochineal, I was not able to make myself thoroughly acquainted.

The mission is not conspicuous from situation, nor does it command an extensive prospect; in these respects that of Sta Barbara has some advantage; its Presidio likewise excels all the others in neatness, cleanliness, and other smaller, though essential comforts; it is placed on an elevated part of the plain, and is raised some feet from the ground by a basement story, which adds much to its pleasantness.

The Presidio of St. Diego seemed to be the least of the Spanish establishments with which we were acquainted. It is irregularly built, on very uneven ground, which makes it liable to some inconveniences, without the obvious appearance of any object for selecting such a spot. The situation of it is dreary and lonesome, in the midst of a barren uncultivated country, producing so little herbage, that, excepting in the spring months, their cattle are sent to the distance of twenty or thirty miles for pasturage. During that season, and as long as the rainy weather may continue, a sufficient number are then brought nearer for the use of the Presidio and mission; and such as have not been wanted are again sent back to the interior country when the dry weather commences; which, although more productive in point of grass, is not very prolific in grain, pulse, fruits, roots, or other culinary vegetables. I understood that they are frequently obliged to resort for a supply of these articles to the mission of St. Juan Capistrano, which abounded in vegetables and animal productions, consisting of great herds of cattle, flocks of sleep, and goats; and I was assured it was one of the most fertile establishments in the country.

The pueblos differ materially from either the missions or the Presidios, and may be better expressed by the name of villages, being unsupported by any other protection, than that of the persons who are resident in them. These are principally old Spanish, or creole, Soldiers; who, having served their respective turns of duty in the missions or in the Presidios, become entitled to exemption from any further military services, and have permission either to return to their native country, or to pass the remainder of their lives in these villages. Most of these soldiers are married, and have families;[1] and when the retirement of the pueblos is preferred, grants of land, with some necessary articles, are given them to commence their new occupation of husbandry, as a reward for their former services, and as an incitement to a life of industry; which, with the assistance of a few of the friendly and well disposed natives, they carry into effect with great advantage to their families. Fertile spots are always chosen for planting these colonies; by cultivating which, they are soon enabled to raise corn and cattle sufficient, not only for their own support, but

---

[1] 'The greatest part of the Troops at these settlements are married; this Ceremony takes place generally at an early age, particularly on the woman's Side who frequently marry at 12 & thirteen years old, their wives are pretty clean, and for Soldiers' wives remarkably dressy, and they are such good subjects of His Catholic Majesty's that all the houses swarm with children.' – Bell, November. Bell's remark about dress is borne out by a drawing by Suria, an artist with Malaspina, depicting a Monterey soldier's wife.

for the supply of the wants of the missions and Presidios in their neighbourhood. Being trained to arms, they early instruct the rising generation, and bring them up to the obedience of military authority; under the laws of which they themselves continue to be governed. There is no superior person or officer residing amongst them for the purpose of officiating as governor, or as chief magistrate; but the pueblos are occasionally visited by the ensign of the Presidio, within whose particular jurisdiction they are situated. This officer is authorized to take cognizance of, and in a certain degree to redress, such grievances or complaints as may be brought before him; or to represent them, together with any crimes or misdemeanors to his commanding officer; and also to report such improvements, regulations, or other matters arising in these little societies, as may either demand his permission or assent; from whose decisions there is no appeal, but to the governor of the province; whose powers, I understood, were very extensive, though I remained ignorant concerning the particular nature of his jurisdiction.

The pueblos generally consist of about thirty or forty old soldiers with their families, who may be considered as a sort of militia of the country, and as assisting in the increase of its population, which, as far as it respects the Spaniards, is yet in a humble state.

The mode originally adopted, and since constantly pursued, in settling this country, is by no means calculated to produce any great increase of white inhabitants. The Spaniards in their missions and Presidios, being the two principal distinctions of Spanish inhabitants, lead a confined, and in most respects a very indolent, life; the religious part of the society within a cloister, the military in barracks. The last mentioned order do nothing, in the strictest sense of the expression; for they neither till, sow, nor reap, but wholly depend upon the labour of the inhabitants of the missions and pueblos for their subsistence, and the common necessaries of life. To reconcile this inactivity whilst they remain on duty in the Presidio, with the meritorious exertions that the same description of people are seen to make in the pueblos, is certainly a very difficult task; and the contradiction would have remained very prejudicial to their character, had I not been informed, that to support the consequence of the soldier in the eyes of the natives, and to insure him their respect, it had been deemed highly improper that he should be subjected to any laborious employment. This circumstance alone is sufficient to account for the habitual indolence and want of industry in the military part of these societies.[1]

---

[1] Bell had commented upon the indolence of the soldiers while at Monterey: 'Except the Governor's we saw no Garden belonging to any one else here. It could not fail striking every one of us with astonishment to see how little had been done by the Spaniards in the space of upwards of 16 years, and in a Country as fine as any in the world; that except at the Missions, there was not a Soldier who had in that time, eaten any thing of his own production and were contented to live in the Hovels that they raised (one would imagine only for their temporary residence) when they first established the place, and why? – merely because they are too lazy and Indolent; they have Cattle, Sheep, Goats, Poultry &C., but

The introduction of Christianity amongst the natives, the cultivation of their minds, and making them disciples of the Romish church, being wholly intrusted to the religious of the respective orders; none of those Indians are suffered to be employed in the Presidios but such as are particularly recommended; to whom the officers who give them employ are obliged to pay a certain daily sum of money, according to the service received; whilst, at the same time, the fathers have hundreds at their command, who when employed by them are rewarded with the produce resulting from the labours of such of their own soceity as are engaged in agriculture, in manufacturing their woollen garments, or in gardening.

These are the payments by which the wages of the carpenter, the smith, the mason, and other mechanics are satisfied; and as they have few persons of these trades amongst themselves, the whole of such business is performed by the Indians, under the immediate instruction and inspection of the Rev. Fathers, who by these means, alone have erected all their fabrics and edifices. At Sta Barbara a new church was building, and at Buena Ventura the whole was to be rebuilt, both of which when finished, might be justly taken for the workmanship of more experienced artists. These two missions form each an intire square; the buildings are more lofty and extensive, and the superior quality of the materials with which they are erected, gives them a decided superiority over all the others.

These benevolent fathers are the corporeal as well as spiritual physicians of all the Indian tribes in the neighbourhood of the missions; and they exercise the arts both of surgery and medicine with great success, especially the latter, for the credit of which they may be indebted to the unimpaired constitutions of their patients, and the natural healthiness of the climate. The scarcity of spirituous liquors, and the great regularity of the inhabitants in food and employment, induces a life of temperance; and consequently, the diseases to which they are liable are seldom of a malignant nature, and in most instances readily yield to the simplest means of cure.

The number of the natives, at this period, who were said to have embraced the Roman Catholic persuasion under the discipline of the Franciscan and Dominican orders of missionaries in New Albion, and throughout the peninsula of California, amounted to about twenty thousand,[1] and they were

these things I do not suppose they would even now have, was there any trouble attending the propagating of them.' – November.

[1] Commenting on the missions, Bell noted that 'The power they have obtained over the Indians is amazing, and is certainly very politic', but he was highly sceptical about the success of their religious activities: 'As to converting them to Christianity it is certainly at present all a farce; – The Roman Catholic Religion of all others, from the mummery, parade, pomp and shew belonging to its forms, is certainly the religion that would strike an Indian with astonishment, and attract his attention Soonest, but it does not follow that because they can Cross themselves, Gabble over their Ave Maria's, & Patre nosters, and mutter a parcel of Latin after the Padres, that they are converted to Christianity. – for I will venture to say there is not one among them who knows what he says, or why he

estimated at an eighth or tenth of the whole native population of those countries. Their progress towards civilization seems to have been remarkably slow; and it is not very likely to become more rapid, until the impolicy of excluding foreign visitors shall be laid aside, and an amicable commercial intercourse substituted in its room; by which system, new wants becoming necessary, new comforts would be introduced; this would stimulate them to industry, their lands would be examined and cultivated, and their stock of cattle would, by attention, soon increase so abundantly, as to enable them to dispose of the surplus produce of their farms to strangers, for such articles of convenience as would tend to facilitate their labours, and otherwise render their lives more comfortable. Provisions, timber, and sea otter skins, would be the first commodities for their exportation; and though the sea otter skins obtained in these parts, are certainly inferior to those procured further to the north, they could not fail of becoming a profitable article of traffic.

I did not find that New Albion had yet been supposed to contain any valuable minerals, nor is California considered much richer in that respect; though I understood, that about 14 leagues to the north-west of the Presidio of Loretto, which is situated in the 26th degree of north latitude on the shores of the peninsula in the gulf of California, the Spaniards had lately discovered two silver mines that were stated to be tolerably productive. The Presidio of Loretto is on a more extensive plan than any in New Albion; its inhabitants amount to about seventy Spaniards and several families of Indians, besides a mixed race exclusive of the garrison, which is composed of a company of sixty soldiers, with their officers.

The missionaries of the Franciscan Order, who extend their functions no further south than St. Diego, act in all cases under the particular direction of their college, a branch of which is established at Mexico;[1] with which a constant correspondence is kept up, and by which their conduct appears, on

says it' – Bell, at Monterey, November 1793. Puget, evidently less prejudiced against the Catholic Church, begins his account of the mission at Santa Barbara by acknowledging that the treatment of the Indians by the Franciscans was 'in General... Mild and benevolent to a Degree, they inform us that the Natives who belong to the Mission, which any can obtain by a voluntary Offer of his Services, are instructed in Agriculture and most of the Mechanical Arts, such as Carpentry Weaving &c and their Endeavours to render this large Body of Men usefull to themselves & others have so far succeeded, that in Eleven Years, their Mission can boast of some excellent Workmen and Five Hundred & thirty three Indians, who have by the persuasion of these Padres become Converts to the Christian Religion. I will allow that so many Converts in so short a Space of time carries with it some probability that no Little Merit is due to these Missionaries, & I am likewise inclined to believe that in some Cases Exemplary and good Conduct on their parts has actuated more in the Minds of the Natives than persuasion. But when once converted, their Ideas become as it were chained to the Ceremonial Part of the Catholic Religion, that they dare not commit any Offence for fear of incurring the Displeasure of the Priests, therefore these Forms are most punctiliously attended to in all the Missions & which is certainly the most binding Security that can be given for the good behaviour of the Converted Indians.' – November 14.

[1] The College of San Fernando, in Mexico City.

all occasions, to be regulated; and they seem, in most respects, nearly independent of military subjection.

From this brief sketch, some idea may probably be formed of the present state of the European settlements in this country, and the degree of importance they are of to the Spanish monarchy, which retains this extent of country under its authority by a force that, had we not been eye-witnesses of its insignificance in many instances, we should hardly have given credit to the possibility of so small a body of men keeping in awe, and under subjection, the natives of this country, without resorting to harsh or unjustifiable measures. The number of their forces, between port St. Francisco and St. Diego, including both establishments, and occupying an extent in one line of upwards of 420 nautical miles, does not amount to three hundred, officers included; and from St. Diego southward, to St. Loretto, not above one hundred more, exclusive of the garrison and settlers residing at that port. These are all that are employed for the protection of the missions. Those of the Dominican order, to the southward of St. Deigo,[1] are sixteen in number, each of which is guarded by five soldiers only. Of the Franciscan order, to the northward of St. Diego, there are thirteen; some guarded by five, whilst other have eight, ten, or twelve soldiers for their protection, in those situations where the Indians are more numerous, and likely to prove troublesome. This seems to be more apprehended at La Soledad and at St. Antonio than at any other of the establishments. The Presidio of St. Diego and Sta Barbara are each garrisoned by a company of sixty men; out of which number guards are afforded to the missions of the same names. The garrison of Monterrey, generally, I believe, consists of a company of sixty or eighty men, and that of St. Francisco thirty-six men only. These soldiers are all very expert horsemen, and, so far as their numbers extend, are well qualified to support themselves against any domestic insurrection; but are totally incapable of making any resistance against a foreign invasion.

The number of vessels that have lately visited the coast of North-West America in new commercial pursuits, have been instrumental in awakening the attention of the Spaniards, and they have recently made some efforts to shew an appearance of defence. On our last visit to St. Francisco, eleven dismounted brass cannon, nine pounders, with a large quantity of shot, of two different sizes, were lying on the beach. These, we understood, were to be placed on the south-east point of entrance into the port; which is a steep cliff, well situated to command the passage into the harbour, but is commanded in return by a hill at no great distance, to the south-eastward. Several Spaniards, with a numerous body of Indians, on our late visit on the top of the cliff, were employed in erecting what seemed to be intended for a platform, or a barbet battery, but it was not at that time in a sufficient state of forwardness for us to decide, whether it might not be designed for a more regular work.

[1] In 1773 the Dominicans had taken over control of the missions in Lower California from the Jesuits. The Franciscans were responsible for the missions from San Diego northward.

At Monterrey the cannon, which, on our former visit, were placed before the Presidio, were now removed to the hill, mentioned at that time as intended to be fortified for the purpose of commanding the anchorge. Here is now erected a sorry kind of barbet battery, consisting chiefly of a few logs of woods, irregularly placed; behind which those cannon, about eleven in number, are opposed to the anchorage, with very little protection in the front, and on their rear and flanks intirely open and exposed.

Sta Barbara is a post of no small consequence, and might be rendered very tenable, by fortifying a hill conspicuously situated for such a purpose on the north-west side of the roadstead; yet they have here only two brass nine-pounders, placed before the entrance into the Presidio, which is situated in the valley or plain beneath, at the distance of about a mile from this eminence. As this post is the key to all the communication between their northern and southern establishments, it was worthy of remark, that they had not attempted to provide an intercourse by some other road, through the mountains, which rise perpendicularly immediately behind the Presidio, and in their present rugged state are inaccessible, lest this station should ever fall into possession of an invading enemy.

With little difficulty St. Diego might also be rendered a place of considerable strength, by establishing a small force at the entrance of the port; where, at this time, there were neither works, guns, houses, or other habitations nearer than the Presidio, which is at the distance of at least five miles from the port, and where they have only three small pieces of brass cannon.

Such is the condition of this country as it respects its internal security, and external defence; but why such an extent of territory should have been thus subjugated, and after all the expence and labour that has been bestowed upon its colonization turned to no account whatever, is a mystery in the science of state policy not easily to be explained.

The natives are not, nor can they be, rendered tributary, because they possess no tribute to offer; nor do these territories, though greatly favored by nature, contain, or under the present arrangement seem intended in future to contain, large towns or cities, whose inhabitants could in any respect add to the affluence, grandeur, or dignity of the monarch who upholds them. If these establishments are intended as a barrier against foreign intruders, the object in view has been greatly mistaken, and the most ready means have been adopted to allure other powers, by the defenceless state of what the Spaniards consider as their fortresses and strongholds. Should the ambition of any civilized nation tempt it to seize on these unsupported posts, they could not make the least resistance, and must inevitably fall to a force barely sufficient for garrisoning and securing the country; especially that part which I have comprehended under the denomination of New Albion, whose southernmost limits lie under the 30th degree of north latitude. Here the coast, washed by the waters of the Pacific, is not more than 30 leagues (if so much) from the shores under the same parallel, nearly at the head of the gulf of California.

This pass, being once well secured by any power, determined to wrest New Albion from the Spanish monarchy, would inevitably prevent an army by land from coming to the support of the present possessors, or to the annoyance of an invading enemy; for two very obvious reasons. The first is, that the natives of the country about the river Colorado, a most daring and warlike people, have from time immemorial been the inveterate and avowed enemies of the Spaniards; who not many years since surprized and cut off a Presidio and mission, containing near an hundred Spaniards,[1] and still continue to act on all occasions with hostility. The other reason is, that to the westward of the territory of these people, from the banks of the Colorado, the mountainous, barren, and inhospitable state of the country renders it at present so totally impassable, that the Spaniards could never penetrate by land at the back of these their new establishments. These facts were established by many inquiries, and confirmed by the route which the Spaniards pursue for the purpose of avoiding such difficulties, when passing between their settlements in New Albion, and those north-eastward of the river Colorado, which are instances that frequently occur; and on these occasions they are obliged to go as far south as the Presidio of Loretto before they cross the gulf of California, and then proceed along its eastern shores, northward, to their destination, even though it should be to the city of Sta Fee, the capital of New Mexico.[2]

This city was founded in the beginning of the last century, about the time when the Count of Monterrey was viceroy of New Spain; it is garrisoned with five hundred men only, and it is said to be situated in the finest country that America affords, nearly under the meridian of Loretto and the parallel of port St. Francisco; between which port and Sta Fee, an extent of about 160 leagues, the Spaniards have endeavoured to effect a communication by land, though hitherto unsuccessfully; their labours having been constantly defeated by the obstruction of the lofty range of mountains existing between New Mexico and the sea coast. This project, however, is not intirely abandoned, though little hope was entertained of its accomplishment.

The Spaniards, in doing thus much, have only cleared the way for the ambitious enterprizes of those maritime powers, who, in the avidity of commercial pursuit, may seek to be benefited by the advantages which the fertile soil of New Albion seems calculated to afford. By the formation of such establishments, so wide from each other, and so unprotected in themselves, the original design of settling the country seems to have been completely set aside, and, instead of strengthening the barrier to their valuable possessions in New Spain, they have thrown irresistible temptations in the way of strangers to trespass over their boundary.

From their dominions in New Spain they have stocked this frontier country with such an abundance of cattle of all descriptions, that it is no longer in

[1] Two missions near the Colorado River were destroyed by the Pueblo Indians in 1781.
[2] Now the city of Santa Fe, capital of the State of New Mexico. It was founded about 1609. Always a seat of government, it is the oldest capital city in the United States.

their power, even were they so inclined, to effect their extermination. They have also pointed out many fertile spots, some of which are very extensive, where they have introduced the most valuable vegetable productions, not only necessary to the sustenance, but ministering to many of the luxuries, of civilized society; and they have, by their previous experiments, fully ascertained in what degree each is found to succeed. A certain proportion of the natives have, by the indefatigable labour of the missionaries, been weaned from their former uncivilized, savage way of life, and are become obedient to social forms, and practiced in many domestic occupations. All these circumstances are valuable considerations to new masters, from whose power, if properly employed, the Spaniards would have no alternative but that of submissively yielding.

That such an event should take place appears by no means to be very improbable, should the commerce of North-west America be further extended. The advantages that have already been derived, and are likely still to accrue, in the prosecution of a well-conducted trade, between this coast and China, India, Japan, and other places, may on some future day, under a judicious and well-regulated establishment, become an object of serious and important consideration, to any nation that shall be inclined to reap the advantages of such a commerce.

Russia at present seems principally to engross these benefits, in consequence of the unwise competition between private adventurers of other nations, not only on the coast of America, but also at Canton and in its neighbourhood; the only market to which, at present, such adventurers can carry the furs of North-west America.

The importance of such a trade, politically considered, or the value of it, when duly appreciated, to private adventures, I shall leave to the decision of those who are better informed on such subjects; because I had no opportunity of receiving satisfactory information upon matters of that intricate nature.

BOOK THE FIFTH.

THIRD VISIT TO THE SANDWICH ISLANDS—CONCLUSION OF THE SURVEY OF THE COAST OF NORTH-WEST AMERICA.

CHAPTER I.

Leave the Coast of New Albion—Arrive off the East Point of Owhyhee—Examine Whyeatea Bay—Visited by Tamaahmaah—Proceed to Karakakooa Bay—Transactions there—Departure of the Dædalus for New South Wales.

OUR progress from the coast of New Albion, still attended with light variable winds, was so slow, that at noon of Sunday the 15th of December, the shores were yet in sight, bearing from N. 17 E. to S. 69 E.; the former, being the nearest, was distant seven leagues; the observed latitude was 30° 14′, longitude 243° 57½′.

In the afternoon, the wind blew a moderate gale at W.N.W. which brought us by day-light the next morning, Monday the 16th, within sight of the island of Guadaloupe. This island is composed of high naked rocky mountains; is about thirteen miles long, nearly in a north and south direction, with two rocky islets; one lying W.S.W. at the distance of half a league; the other lying south, two miles from its south point, which is situated in latitude 28° 54′, longitude 241° 38′.[1] The wind at N.W. continued to blow a pleasant gale with fair weather until midnight; but at this time it veered round, and settled in the north-east trade wind. Our distance was now about 75 leagues from the coast, and it is probable the north-west winds do not extend far beyond that limit, as the wind that succeeded continued without calms, or other interruptions, between the N.E. and E.N.E. blowing a steady, gentle, and pleasant gale.

On Sunday the 22d, in latitude 23° 23′, longitude 234° 37′, the variation of the compass was 7° eastwardly; here we had thirty hours calm, after which we had a gentle breeze from the N.E.; this, as we proceeded, was attended

[1] The centre point of Guadalupe is in lat. 29° 00′ N, long. 118° 16′ W (241° 44′ E).

first by cloudy and gloomy weather, and afterwards with rain, and sudden gusts or flurries of wind. On Wednesday the 25th, a tropic bird was seen, and a common gull that appeared to be much fatigued, and inclined to alight on board.

This very unpleasant weather, similar to that which we had experienced in this neighbourhood about the conclusion of last January, still continued; and on Sunday the 29th, in latitude 19° 1′, longitude 231° 58′, the wind, after veering to the S.E. became light, and, like the weather, was very unsettled. We were now passing the spot assigned to los Majos isles, at the distance of a few miles only to the southward of our former track; but we perceived no one circumstance that indicated the vicinity of land.

On Tuesday the 31st, the wind seemed to be fixed in the northern quarter, but the atmosphere was still very unpleasant, and the gloomy weather was now accompanied by much rain.[1] On Friday the 3d of January, 1794, in latitude 18° 34′, longitude 213° 32′, a very heavy swell rolled from the N.W. and the wind in that direction was light, with alternate calms, attended by foggy or dark hazy weather, until Monday the 6th, when, in latitude 19° 19′, longitude 208° 48′, we had a few hours of fair and pleasant weather; this was again succeeded by the same gloomy atmosphere that we had experienced during the greater part of this passage, and the wind continued to be very variable between the N.W. and S.S.W. In the afternoon of the following day, Tuesday the 7th, the weather was more favorable, and the wind from the northward settled in the N.E.: to this we spread all our canvass in the expectation of seeing the island of Owhyhee at day-light the next morning. The wind however slackened during the night, and the weather being dark and gloomy, it was not until about nine o'clock in the forenoon of Wednesday the 8th, that Mowna-kaah[2] was discovered shewing his hoary head above the clouds, bearing by compass W. ½ S.; but the haze and mist with which the district of Aheedo[3] was inveloped, prevented our discerning the shores. The observed latitude at noon was 19° 52′; at this time the east end of Owhyhee bore by compass S. 52 W. at the distance of ten leagues, by which it appeared that Arnold's chronometer, No. 14, had erred in longitude since our departure from the coast of New Albion, 27′; his No. 176, 21′; Kendall's, 52′; and the dead reckoning, 3° 40′; all being to the eastward of the truth.[4] This error has however been corrected, in assigning the several situations during this passage.

We stood for the land until sun-set, when, being within two leagues of the shore, we employed the night in preserving our station off that part of

[1] 'The Air by the Rain is close and Extremely Sultry & the Vapours which exhale from the Quantity of Wet Cloathes in the Confined Situation below cause such an Intolerable Stench that we are under the Necessity of Keeping constant fires below to prevent any Disagreeable Consequences arising from the Damps.' – Puget, 30 December.

[2] Mauna Kea (13,793 ft.).

[3] Later spelled Aheedoo; Hilo is meant.

[4] Arnold's No. 82 in the *Chatham* 'performed wonderfully well by the Sn Diego Rate, it being only 8 Miles to the Eastward.' – Puget, 9 January 1794.

the coast, where we expected to find the harbour or bay of Whyeatea;[1] in quest of which I dispatched Mr. Whidbey in the cutter the next morning, Thursday the 9th, attended by a boat from the Chatham, and another from the Dædalus, all well armed. The appearance of the shores did not seem much in favor of our finding a more eligible situation here than at Karakakooa,[2] for accomplishing our several purposes; notwithstanding the representation that had been made to us of its being very commodious.

The boats had scarcely departed, when some of the natives came off in their canoes, but owing to a very heavy swell from the northward, they could bring us but few refreshments. As soon as they understood who we were, they told us that Tamaahmaah,[3] with several of the principal chiefs, were then on shore waiting in expectation of our arrival; and then immediately made the best of their way towards the shore, proclaiming our return to their country with shouts, apparently of great joy and gladness.

About ten in the forenoon we were honored with the presence of the king,[4] with his usual confidence and cheerful disposition. It was impossible to mistake the happiness he expressed on seeing us again, which seemed to be greatly increased by his meeting us at this, his most favorite part of the island; where he hoped we should be able to remain some time, to take the benefits arising from its fertility; which, from the appearance of the neighbouring shores, seemed to promise an abundant supply of the various refreshments these countries are known to produce.

Tamaahmaah had noticed the boats in their way to the shore, and trusted they would return with a favorable report; which he, as well as ourselves, anxiously waited for until five in the evening. Mr. Whidbey now informed me, that during the prevalence of the southerly winds, in the more advanced part of the spring season, Whyeatea might probably be found a tolerably secure and convenient place, as the land formed a deep bay, which was additionally sheltered by a reef lying off its south-east point, with soundings from twenty-five to six fathoms, clear sandy bottom; at least as far as his examination had extended. This had not been very minute, as the bay was intirely exposed to the northerly winds, which then blew very strong; and being attended with a heavy sea from that quarter, rendered any attempt to land from our boats impracticable. On this report I determined to proceed to Karakakooa, as that bay was indisputably at this time the most secure and convenient port for shipping of any in the Sandwich islands.

My intention was directly made known to Tamaahmaah, and I requested

[1] Hilo Bay is meant.   [2] Kealakekua Bay.
[3] Kamehameha.
[4] Menzies notes that Kamehameha came off in a double canoe 'distinguished with an English pendant displayed at the mast head.... We found that his Majesty was not a little proud in displaying his English pendant which he had from us last year at Karakakooa when he was told that it was only Vessels of War belonging to our King that had a right to wear such a mark of distinction in *Britannee*.' – 9 January. On shore 'His Majesty's House was easily distinguished by the English Colours that were flying before it.' Bell, January.

that he would give us the pleasure of his company thither; well knowing that his influence over the inferior chiefs and the people would be attended with the most desirable consequences, in preserving the harmony and good understanding that already so happily existed. He did not, however, seem much inclined to accept my invitation,[1] or to give me a positive answer; but requested, that the vessels might remain some days in this neighbourhood, to avail ourselves of the ample supply of refreshments that might be procured here, before we proceeded to any other part of the island; adding, that he would remain with us to see this business properly performed.

I was by no means disposed to accede to the wishes of the king, nor was I satisfied with the arrangement he had proposed.

The vessels having been driven far to leeward on the morning of Friday the 10th, and the wind then blowing strong from the northward, attended with a very heavy sea, I pointed out and explained to *Tamaahmaah* the great improbability of our being able to comply with his desires, and the necessity of our proceeding without delay to some place of secure anchorage, for the purpose of refitting; renewing at the same time, and in the strongest terms, my solicitations for his company. I did not fail to enforce how important his presence would necessarily be, not only to us for whom he had repeatedly expressed the greatest respect and friendship, but also to the welfare of his own subjects. He readily acknowledged the propriety of my observations, and how much he was inclined to adopt the measure I had proposed; but he now avowed that he could not accompany us, as the *taboo* appertaining to the festival of the new year demanded his continuance for a certain period, within the limits of the district in which these ceremonies had commenced. The time of interdiction was not yet expired, and it was not possible he could absent himself

---

[1] Bell explains Kamehameha's reluctance to leave. He alleged that 'the Country here was preferable to that about Karakakooa, that the Surf on the Beach was greater here, on which lay one of his greatest amusements and lastly, and a very weighty reason was, that all his Canoes, property, Fire Arms, Ammunition &c. was also here, which it was necessary to keep a very careful watch over.' When it was decided that Kamehameha was to leave in the *Discovery* 'His Brother Trimomohao [Crymamahoo?] was then dispatched on shore to announce the news and to Stay, and take charge of the Royal Treasure in his Brother's absence.' – January 1794. Kamehameha evidently enjoyed surf-boarding. The only specific reference to the sport is in Puget's account of a short excursion northward from Kealakekua Bay that he made in company with Keeaumoku, chief of Kona: 'From his village we walked through some pleasant cultivated Grounds to a Small Stony Beach where the natives were amusing themselves in the Surf on Swimming Boards. Nammahana, the wife of Tayomodu [Keeaumoku], who is reckoned one of the most expert at that Diversion immediately Stript naked and she certainly notwithstanding her Corpulency performed her part with wonderful Dexterity. The first Sea or Surf that brought her in towards the Beach was immensely high, on its Top she came, floating on a Broad Board till the Break[er] had nearly reached the Rocks, she then suddenly turned, went under that & the one following and so on till she had regained her Situation at the back of the whole. Then she waited for a large Swell and once more performed her part with great Expertness; Numbers of Men Women and Boys were in her Company and I was in Momentary Expectation of seeing some dashed to pieces.' – January 27.

without the particular sanction of the priests. To obtain this indulgence, he considered his presence to be indispensibly necessary on shore at the morai. Aware of the superior influence possessed by the priesthood, and of the strict adherence of all ranks to their superstitions, I suspected that if *Tamaahmaah* went on shore they would not allow him to return; for this reason I recommended, that one of the chiefs in his suite should repair thither, and make known the king's pleasure. But as this proposal did not seem to meet his ideas, or to be consonant to his wishes, I resolved not to detain him contrary to his own free will and inclination, or by any other means than those of persuasion. Yet as I considered his attendance to be an object of too much importance to be readily relinquished, I had recourse to a sort of artifice, that I had reason to believe would answer my purpose by its operation on his feelings. I desisted from all importunities, and attributed his declining my invitation to a coolness and a relaxation in the friendship he had formerly shewn and pretended to entertain; and I stated, that I had no doubt of soon finding amongst the other islands some chief, whose assistance, protection, and authority, would on all occasions be readily afforded.[1]

Tamaahmaah had always been accustomed to attend our meals, and breakfast in particular he was extremely fond of partaking with us; but under the reproach he had just received, of a want of friendship, no solicitation could prevail on him to accept of any thing at table; he sat in a silent thoughtful mood, his sensibility was probed to the quick, and his generous heart, which continued to entertain the warmest friendship and regard, not only for me but for every one in our little community, yielded to our wishes; though at the risk of incurring the displeasure of the priests by an unprecedented breach of their religious rites. At length he determined that his half brother *Crymamahoo*[2] should be sent to the priests, to communicate his intentions of accompanying us. On my saying that this resolution made me very happy, and met my hearty concurrence, he replied, that I had treated him unkindly in suspecting that his friendship was abated, for that it remained unshaken, as his future conduct would demonstrate; but that he considered himself to be the last person in his dominions who ought to violate the established laws, and the regulations of the country which he governed.

Our little difference being thus amicably adjusted, he ate a hearty breakfast; and having given his brother the necessary instructions for governing this part of the island during his absence, in which business they were occupied an hour, *Crymamahoo* was dismissed, and directed to return with all convenient speed to communicate the answer of the priests.

---

[1] Bell states that Vancouver, having failed to persuade Kamehameha to go with him, 'at last told him that if he would not accompany him round, he would instantly quit the Island, and proceed to Mowee, where all the presents intended for him should be given to Titeree [Kahekili]; this Stagger'd him, and he then consented to go, provided he could get the permission of his Tahouna or High Priest who was then on shore'. – January. Bell was on the *Chatham* and the discussions with Kamehameha took place on the *Discovery*, but the story may well be true.   [2] Kalaimamahu.

Thoroughly convinced of the purity of *Tamaahmaah*'s friendly intentions, I had receded from my former determination with respect to him, or any other of the chiefs, sleeping on board the ship. Our party now consisted of seven chiefs, three of whom were accompanied by their favorite females; but *Tahow-man-noo*,[1] the king's consort, was not of the number. As she had never failed in her attendance on him, the cause of her absence became a subject of inquiry, and I had the mortification of understanding that a separation had taken place, in consequence of its having been reported that too great an intimacy had subsisted between her and *Tianna*.[2]

I understood from the king's attendants, that the infidelity of the queen was by no means certain; and as I well knew the reciprocal affection of this royal pair, and as she was then residing with her father at, or in the neighbourhood of, Karakakooa, I thought it a charitable office to make a tender of my endeavours for the purpose of bring about a reconciliation. In reply to this obtrusion of my services, *Tamaahmaah* expressed his thanks; and assured me, that he should be always happy to receive any advice on state affairs, or any public matters, especially where peace or war might be concerned; but that such differences as might occur in, or respect, his domestic happiness, he considered to be totally out of my province. This rebuff I silently sustained; cherishing the hope that the period would arrive when I should be able to prevail on him to entertain a different opinion.

The wind from the northward, attended with a very heavy sea, reduced us to our close-reefed topsails, and as we stood in shore in the afternoon a very strong current evidently pressed us to leeward. The appearance of the weather indicating no favorable or early change, there was little probability of our soon seeing *Crymamahoo*, or any of the inhabitants of Aheedoo; this induced the king to call his whole retinue together, both male and female, in order to take their advice as to his proceeding, without first receiving the religious assent he had dispatched *Crymamahoo* to obtain. The result of their deliberations was, a unanimous opinion that the priests would, on a certainty, accede to his wishes. This had been undoubtedly the previous sentiment of the king, or he would not have instructed his brother, in the manner he had done, how to conduct himself during his absence.

Although I earnestly wished to avoid being the cause of endangering his popularity, yet I was so anxiously desirous of his company, that I did not hesitate a moment in giving my hearty concurrence to this determination, in order that we might make the best of our way to Karakakooa.

Our course was now directed round the east point of the island, along its south-east side; we made a tolerably good progress; and as we passed the district of Opoona,[3] on the morning of Saturday the 11th, the weather being very clear and pleasant, we had a most excellent view of Mowna Roa's snowy summit,[4] and the range of lower hills that extend towards the east end of Owhyhee. From the tops of these, about the middle of the descending ridge,

[1] Kaahumanu.
[2] Kaiana.
[3] The district of Puna.
[4] Mauna Loa.

several columns of smoke were seen to ascend, which *Tamaahmaah* and the rest of our friends said were occasioned by the subterraneous fires that frequently broke out in violent eruptions, causing amongst the natives such a multiplicity of superstitious notions as to give rise to a religious order of persons, who perform volcanic rites; consisting of various sacrifices of the different productions of the country, for the purpose of appeasing the wrath of the enraged demon.

On approaching the shores of the district of Kaoo,[1] we were met by several of the inhabitants bringing in their canoes some refreshments and other productions of the country. Those who first approached us seemed to be much surprized, and many of them were not a little alarmed at seeing their king on board; inquiring with great earnestness, whether his being there, and having broken the *taboo*, was by his own choice, or by compulsion. On being assured by all present that *Tamaahmaah* and the rest of the chiefs were under no restraint whatever, but were accompanying us by their own free will, they became perfectly satisfied; and appeared to be equally so on understanding, that it was the king's pleasure, that the hogs and vegetables they had brought off should be delivered on board, without their receiving any equivalent in return;[2] nor could we, without giving *Tamaahmaah* serious offence, have infringed this order, which seemed to be very cheerfully complied with on the part of his subjects; and, in the course of the forenoon, the vessels procured a sufficient supply for their present consumption. Whether the king accounted with these people afterwards for the value of their property thus disposed of, or not, I could not rightly understand; but from the great good humour with which they complied with the royal order, and from some conversation with one of the king's attendants, respecting the value of the refreshments so delivered, I had reason to believe that a compensation would be allowed to them.

Shortly after noon we were opposite the south point of the island;[3] and, as a report had been circulated that close round, on its western side, good anchorage and excellent shelter had been found, (though it had escaped the notice of Captain Cook) Mr. Whidbey was dispatched in the cutter, in order to ascertain the truth of this assertion, which was soon proved to be void of foundation; for although a strong westerly gale prevented Mr. Whidbey from making a very minute examination, yet he clearly discovered that the shores were nearly straight, and exposed to a most tremendous surf, that broke with such fury as to render landing, if not impossible, highly dangerous, even to those of the inhabitants who are most expert in the management of their canoes.

The wind continued to blow very strong between W. and N.W. until the

---

[1] Kau district.

[2] Bell (in the *Chatham*) notes that Kamehameha 'sent a Priest of some authority to stay on board with us as a kind of provider, being invested with full powers to Seize on every species of Provisions that came near the Vessel, for our use, and without giving any thing in return.' – January.   [3] Ka Lae (South Cape).

morning of Sunday the 12th; when it became variable, and allowed us to make but a very slow progress towards Karakakooa. *Tamaahmaah* being very anxious that we should gain the place of our destination, went on shore for the purpose of placing lights to conduct us in the evening to our former anchorage; where, about ten the following night, we anchored near an American brig, named the Lady Washington, commanded by Mr. John Kendrick.[1]

As we worked into the bay many of the inhabitants were assembled on the shores, who announced their congratulations by shouts of joy, as, on our different tacks, we approached the shores of the neighbouring villages. At this late hour many of our former friends, particularly of the fair sex, lost no time in testifying the sincerity of the public sentiment in our favour. Young and Davis we had likewise the pleasure of finding in the exercise of those judicious principles they had so wisely adopted, and which by their example and advice had so uniformly been carried into effect. The great propriety with which they had conducted themselves, had tended in a high degree to the comfort and happiness of these people, to the gratification of their own feelings, and to a pre-eminence in the good opinion of the king, that had intitled them to his warmest affections.[2] The same sort of esteem and regard, we understood, was shewn to them, if not by all, at least by the well-disposed inhabitants of the island.

The Discovery was secured nearly in her former station on the following morning; and the Chatham and Dædalus were disposed of in the most convenient manner for carrying into execution the respective services that each had to perform.

Mr. Kendrick had been here about six weeks, and it was with infinite pleasure we understood that during that time he had not only been liberally supplied by the inhabitants of the island with its several productions, but that the same orderly and civil behaviour had been observed towards him which we had experienced on our former visit; and which we had every reason to

[1] Kendrick had been trading on the Northwest Coast and had come to the islands to winter. He went back to the coast in 1794 and returned to the Hawaiian Islands late in the year. On December 3, while his ship was anchored in Honolulu Harbor, he was accidentally killed by a shot from the *Jackal*, which was saluting him. Kendrick was one of the American traders who supplied the Hawaiians with firearms. Bell notes that Kamehameha was providing Vancouver's ships most generously with provisions, although he had no arms to offer in return, 'though Mr. Kendrick was buying the chief part of his refreshment with Swivels, Muskets, and Gunpowder.' – January.

[2] Davis and Young had been aided considerably by the testimonial Vancouver had left in the island in 1793: 'The King had placed so much confidence in them, that while at Whyatea [Hilo], he entrusted them to sell his property to any Vessels that might appear off the Bay, and Captain Vancouver's letter...proved of such utility, and had procured them such treatment from all the Vessels that had touched there, as rendered their Situations extremely happy; they were now Men of property & Chiefs among the Islanders, they were now looked on as men of no small consequence otherwise, and as the Chiefs and others knew it was in the power of these two Englishmen, to do them either good or harm in the opinion of the Merchant Vessels they were careful to preserve a good understanding with them, and not put it in their power to Speak ill of them.' – Bell, January.

expect would be continued, from the assurances we received from the chiefs, and from the acclamations of the people, which had resounded from all quarters on our arrival.

Tamaahmaah understanding that it would be necessary that we should land parts of the cargoes of all the vessels, appointed proper places for their reception; and knowing we had no more men than we could constantly employ for the speedy accomplishment of this business, he undertook to be answerable for the safety and security of every thing we might have occasion to put on shore, without our having any guard there for its protection. He also gave orders that his people should fill our water casks; and as he considered that bartering with the several chiefs, and other individuals, for the valuable refreshments of the country, would not only be troublesome and unpleasant, but might give rise to disputes and misunderstandings between the parties; he desired we would daily, or as often as should suit our convenience, make our demands known to him, and he would take care that the three vessels were duly supplied with every necessary refreshment.

This considerate and very friendly arrangement I was happy to concur in, and at day-light on Wednesday morning the 15th, three large canoes, laden with forty very fine hogs, and thirty small ones, with a proportionate quantity of vegetables, were, by the directions of the king, distributed amongst our three vessels.[1]

On this occasion it was impossible to avoid making a comparison between our reception and treatment here, by these untaught children of nature, and the ceremonious conditional offers of accommodation we experienced at St. Francisco and Monterrey, from the educated civilized governor of New Albion and California.

After the large canoes had delivered their acceptable cargoes, they received and took to the shore the live cattle, which I had been more successful in bringing from New Albion than on the former occasion. These consisted of a young bull nearly full grown, two fine cows, and two very fine bull calves, all in high condition; as likewise five rams, and five ewe sheep. Two of each of these, with most of the black cattle, were given to the king; and as those I had brought last year had thrived exceedingly well; the sheep having bred, and one of the cows having brought forth a cow calf;[2] I had little doubt,

---

[1] When these supplies arrived 'the serving of any Sea Provisions' in the ships stopped, and the crews were 'allowed as usual as much as they chose to cram themselves with, of every species of refreshment the Island produced.' – Bell, January. Puget and Bell both mention that Kamehameha 'by way likewise of compliment changed his name for the time being to Towtapu' – a point not mentioned by Vancouver. – Puget, January 13; Bell, January.

[2] Menzies states that there were three rams and three ewes, and adds: 'I am confident that success in transporting these Animals to distant regions will always depend in a great measure on embarking them in a young state when they will become more readily reconcild to the Vessel & may easily be brought to feed on any kind of food that is offerd them, of which the following circumstance affords a curious instance: One of the Cows

by this second importation, of having at length effected the very desirable object of establishing in this island a breed of those valuable animals.

I learned from *Tamaahmaah* that he had issued the strictest orders so to regulate the conduct and behaviour of his people towards us, as he trusted would be the means of insuring a continuance of the harmony that had so happily subsisted on our former visits to his dominions; and he added, that he had many enemies, even amongst the chiefs of Owhyhee, who were not unlikely to use their endeavours for the purpose of frustrating his good intentions, and that it was very important that the designs of such ill-disposed persons should be watchfully guarded against. I thanked *Tamaahmaah* for his vigilant attention to preserve our tranquillity and comfort, and informed him, that I had also issued orders and directions similar to those given on my former visit.[1] These having the same tendency, and operating to the same end, with those enjoined by himself, would, I hoped, be effectual in affording us the recreation and enjoyment of the country, and in securing to us a continuation of the then subsisting friendly intercourse.

These necessary precautions being taken on both sides, we immediately began upon the various services that demanded our attention.[2] Those

we left here last year provd to be in calf & calf'd some time after our departure, the Natives were so elated at this unexpected circumstance & so anxious that the Sovereign who was at Aheedoos [Hilo] near the East end of the Island should see it, that they immediately bundled the young Calf upon a man's back & carried it from this side across the Island in a journey of several days, during which they fed it with fish & water, & with this unnatural food the Animal has been reard without the least aid from its mother & they assurd me that it was at this time very fat & doing well.' – January 14.

[1] 'The same unpleasant restrictions to the Young Gentlemen of both Ships from going ashore as was last year in force, was now observed, and written orders to that purpose were sent on board the Chatham. The Officers were allowed to go on Shore, but on no account to carry fire Arms, this was certainly very mortifying to many of the Gentlemen who were grown up, and who, were there Vancancies would be promoted at once to Lieutenants, and more particularly so, when the Warrant Officers some of whom were but recently before the Mast, were permitted to take their pleasure where they Chose ashore.' – Bell, January.

[2] Menzies states that Kamehameha 'appointed a Chief to remain on board each Vessel to take care of them & prevent any misunderstanding between us & the Natives' and Bell reports that, in addition, John Young was attached to the *Discovery* and Isaac Davis to the *Chatham*. – Menzies, January 15; Bell, January. Kamehameha 'particularly requested that we should not barter for provisions like other Vessels, but that he would himself undertake to be our purveyor & supply us with every refreshment we stood in need of.' – Menzies, January 15. Puget suspected that Kamehameha had an ulterior motive: 'I certainly join with others in Admiration of the King's Conduct in this Respect, but I differ in Opinion of the Motives from which it Springs. he sees with the utmost Jealousy any Attention paid to the other Chiefs & appears extremely anxious to prevent their Receiving any Benefit from our visit. Every Present made to them he regards as an Acquisition of Power for by distributing these things with Liberality among their Adherents, it fixes more firmly their Attachment, Therefore if His Majesty can under the Cloak of Princely Liberality monopolize the Articles of Traffic (for he is to have on our Departure as much as he wishes for), it will not only serve himself in particular, but be the means of giving him additional Consequence, by making that great Distribution.' – January 12.

appertaining to the reception of the provisions and stores from the Dædalus, were the primary objects of our consideration,[1] and by the orderly and docile behaviour of all classes of the inhabitants, this business was carried into execution with a degree of facility and confidence in our perfect security, equal to the accommodation that could possibly have been obtained in any port of Europe.

There were not at this time many of the principal chiefs in our neighbourhood. Our former friend *Kahowmotoo*[2] paid us an early visit, with a present of twenty large hogs, and a proportionable quantity of vegetables. He was not, however, in his usually cheerful good spritis, but was much depressed, in consequence of a violent indisposition under which his favourite son *Whokaa*[3] laboured from a wound he had received in the exercise of throwing the spear with a man of mean rank. After a long contention for superiority, their play, it seemed, terminated in earnest, and the young chief received his adversary's spear, which was barbed, in the throat. Much difficulty had attended its being taken out, which had occasioned a wound that had baffled all their art to cure, and had reduced him to the last stage of his existence. His antagonist was soon seized, and the next day his eyes were pulled out, and, after remaining in that deplorable state two days, he was executed, by being strangled with a rope.

As some of the gentlemen intended to accompany Mr. Menzies on an excursion into the interior part of the country, they were, agreeably to our plan of regulations, on Thursday the 16th, attended by a chief of the village of Kakooa[4] with several of the king's people, who had directions to supply all their wants, and to afford them every assistance and service that they might require.[5]

---

[1] Heddington notes that the *Chatham* this day 'held a Survey upon Boatswain's Stores & Slops' and that the items condemned included '30 Waistcoats, 17 Pr Breeches, 7 Jackets, 10 Pr Stockings, 5 Night Caps.' – January 15.

[2] Keeaumoku.

[3] Puget spells the name Wakeah; Bell's version is Watea.

[4] Now Napoopoo; on the W side of Kealakekua Bay.

[5] Menzies' purpose was to botanize and to try to climb Hualalai (8,269 ft.), a peak about 15 miles from Kealakekua Bay. The party included Swaine and two or three of the midshipmen, one of whom was Heddington, whose drawing of the crater of the volcano on Hualalai was engraved for Vancouver's *Voyage*. Oddly enough, there is no mention of the excursion in Heddington's log, which is devoted wholly to ship's business. Howell, a former Anglican clergyman who had come to Hawaii from China in the *Lady Washington* also went along. Kamehameha arranged for a large retinue of followers: some carried 'provisions for the journey, which consisted of live hogs. Poultry Taro Yams Coco nuts & dried fish in quantities that loaded upwards of 20 Men... There were others appointed to carry our luggage, one carried a kettle, another a Gridiron & a third from the nature of his office might be termd a Butler as he carried & took charge of our liquor case. Among other appointments we found that each of us had a man whose sole business was to carry the cloth & mats for sleeping on, spread the couch each night & roll it up again in the morning, in short there was no end to these various appointments...' – Menzies, 17 January.

The harmony that had attended the execution of all our employments had so facilitated the equipment of the vessels, that, by the following Tuesday, the 21st, the business in the Discovery's hold was in that state of forwardness as to permit our attending to other objects. The astronomical department claimed my first thoughts; and being of such material importance, I was anxious to lose no time in sending the tents, observatory, and instruments on shore, now that a party could be afforded for their protection. On this occasion I was surprized to find the king make some objections to their being erected in their former situation, near the morai, giving us as a reason, that he could not sanction our inhabiting the *tabooed* lands, without previously obtaining the permission of an old woman, who, we understand, was the daughter of the venerable *Kaoo*, and wife to the treacherous *Koah*.* Being totally unacquainted before that the women ever possessed the least authority over their consecrated places, or religious ceremonies, this circumstance much surprized me, especially as the king seemed to be apprehensive of receiving a refusal from this old lady; and which, after waiting on shore for some time, proved to be the case. *Tamaahmaah* observing my disappointment, intreated me to fix upon some other part of the bay; but as it was easily made obvious to his understanding that no other spot would be equally convenient, he instantly assembled some of the principal priests in the morai, and after having a serious conference with them, he acquainted me, that we were at liberty to occupy the consecrated ground as formerly, which we accordingly took possession of the next morning, Wednesday the 22d.

Mr. Whidbey, who had charge of the encampment, attended it on shore under a guard of six marines; these were sent, however, more for the sake of form than for necessity; as *Tamaahmaah* had appointed one of his half

* Vide Captain King's account of Cook's death. [King's comment is part of his account of his efforts to recover Cook's body. The natives seemed hostile and were evidently anticipating an attack, yet he courageously approached the shore 'in a small boat, alone, with a white flag in my hand, which, by a general cry of joy from the natives, I had the satisfaction to find was instantly understood.' King was not entirely reassured, 'But when I saw Koah, with a boldness and assurance altogether unaccountable, swimming off toward the boat, with a white flag in his hand, I thought it necessary to return this mark of confidence, and therefore received him into the boat, though armed; a circumstance which did not tend to lessen my suspicions. I must confess, I had long harboured an unfavourable opinion of this man. The priests had always told us, that he was of a malicious disposition, and no friend of ours; and the repeated detections of his fraud and treachery, had convinced us of the truth of their representations. Add to all this, the shocking transaction of the morning [the murder of Cook], in which he was seen acting a principal part, made me feel the utmost horror at finding myself so near him....I told him, that I had come to demand the body of Captain Cook; and to declare war against them, unless it was instantly restored. He assured me this should be done as soon as possible...' Meanwhile other boats had approached 'so near the shore, as to enter into conversation with a party of the natives, at some distance from us; by whom they were plainly given to understand, that the body had been cut to pieces, and carried up the country; but of this circumstance I was not informed, till our return to the ships.' – James Cook, *A Voyage to the Pacific Ocean* (London, 1784), III, 62–3.]

brothers *Trywhookee*, a chief of some consequence, together with several of the priests, to protect, and render the party on shore every service their situation might demand. To this spot, as on our former visit, none were admitted but those of the society of priests, the principal chiefs, and some few of their male attendants; no women, on any pretence whatever, being ever admitted within the sacred limits of the morai.

The unfortunate son of *Kahowmotoo* had been brought by his father from one of his principal places of residence, about six miles north of the bay where the unfortunate accident happened, to the village of Kowrowa,[1] in order to benefit by such medical or other assistance as we might be able to afford, but without effect; for in the afternoon he breathed his last.[2]

The periodical *taboo*, that ought to have commenced the following evening, Thursday the 23d, was, on this occasion, suspended, to manifest that they were offended with their deity for the death of this young chief; whose loss seemed to be greatly deplored by all the family, but most particularly so by *Kahowmotoo*; of whom I took a proper opportunity of inquiring when the corpse would be interred, and if there would be any objection to my attending the funeral solemnities. To this he made answer, that the burial would take place the following day, and that he would come on board at any convenient hour, and accompany me on shore for that purpose.

I remained perfectly satisfied with the promise made by *Kahowmotoo*; and was the next morning, Friday the 24th, greatly disappointed on his informing me, that *Kavaheero*,[3] the chief of the village at which his son had died, had, in the course of the night, unknown to him or any of his family, caused the body of the young chief to be interred in one of the sepulchral holes of the steep hill, forming the north side of the bay. This circumstance could not but be received as an additional proof of their aversion to our becoming acquainted with their religious rites, and their determination to prevent our attendance on any of their sacred formalities.

---

[1] Kaawaloa, on the N side of Kealakekua Bay, near which Cook was killed.

[2] Bell and his friend Garnier, a midshipman, visited Watea briefly just before he died: 'On landing...our Ears were now perfectly stunned with the dismal, mournful cries and howlings of the Mourners. The people, of whom there was an amazing concourse, I suppose not less than three thousand were collected on an open spot of ground, near the Water Side....It appear'd strange that they should make such an amazing noise whilst the Sick man was yet living as it is natural for us at those times to preserve the greatest Silence and Stillness, but it is their custom in all stages of sickness.' A short time later Watea died, and Bell found that 'The Grief of the men was much the same as before, but that of the Women and common people was raised to a most violent degree.' When Bell returned to the *Chatham* he found that a man had sought refuge there in the belief that he would otherwise be killed as a human sacrifice, following the death of Watea. Bell also heard that an old blind chief, devoted to Watea, had offered himself as a sacrifice, but that Kamahameha had decreed that no sacrifices were to take place. The human sacrifices were often voluntary; Davis told Bell that should Kamemeha die, 'he knew upwards of twenty men who would voluntarily die with him.' – January.

[3] Keaweaheulu.

The party accompanying Mr. Menzies returned with him on Saturday the 25th after having had a very pleasant excursion, though it had been somewhat fatiguing in consequence of the badness of the paths in the interior country, where in many places the ground broke in under their feet. Their object had been to gain the summit of Mowna Roa, which they had not been able to effect in the direction they had attempted it; but they had reached the top of another mountain, which though not so lofty as Mownarowna, or Mowna-kaah, is yet very conspicuous, and is called by the natives Worroray.[1] This mountain rises from the western extremity of the island, and on its summit was a volcanic crater that readily accounted for the formation of that part of the country over which they had found it so dangerous to travel. The good offices of their Indian guide and servants received a liberal reward, to which they were highly intitled by their friendly and orderly behaviour.

The whole of the retinue that had attended *Tamaahmaah* from Aheedoo, with the addition of some new visitors, lived intirely on board the ship, and felt themselves not only perfectly at home, but very advantageously situated, in being enabled to purchase such commodities of their own produce or manufacture which were brought to us for sale, as attracted their attention, with the presents which they received from time to time. Notwithstanding this indulgence, which I thought could not have failed to keep them honest, such is their irresistible propensity to thieving, that five of my table knives were missing. The whole party stoutly denied having any knowledge of the theft; but as it was evident the knives were stolen by some of them, I ordered them all, except the king, instantly to quit the ship, and gave positive directions that no one of them should be re-admitted. Besides this, I deemed it expedient to make a point with *Tamaahmaah* that the knives should be restored. He saw the propriety of my insisting on this demand, and before noon three of the knives were returned.

The *taboo*, which had been postponed in consequence of *Whokaa*'s death, was observed this evening, though not without holding out a sentiment of resentment to their deity for having suffered him to die; for instead of its continuing the usual time of two nights and one whole day, this was only to be in force from sun-set to the rising of the sun the following morning, Sunday the 26th, which the king having observed, returned to us as soon as the ceremonies were finished.

Being very much displeased with the ungrateful behaviour of his attendants, I demanded of *Tamaahmaah*, in a serious tone, the two knives that had not yet been restored. I expatiated on the disgrace that attached to every individual of the whole party, and the consequence of the example to all the subordinate

---

[1] Hualalai. Vancouver was in error; Menzies' purpose was to climb Hualalai; the attempt to reach Mauna Loa was an afterthought. As is not unusual, it was found to be farther away than it appeared to be. Menzies describes the expedition at some length in his journal, and his narrative was published many years later in the *Magazine of Natural History*, I (1828), pp. 201–8; II (1829), pp. 435–42.

classes of his people. He appeared to be much chagrined, and to suffer a high degree of mortification at the very unhandsome manner in which I had been treated; this was still further increased, by one of his most particular favorites having been charged, and on just grounds, as one of the delinquents.

About noon he went on shore, in a very sullen humour, and did not return until I had sent for him in the evening, which summons he very readily obeyed; and soon another knife was returned, which he declared was the only one he had been able to find, and that if any more were yet missing, they must have been lost by some other means. The truth, as we afterwards understood, was, that the knife had been given, by the purloiner, to a person of much consequence, over whom *Tamaahmaah* did not wish to enforce his authority.

These knives had not been stolen, as might be naturally imagined, for their value as iron instruments, but for the sake of their ivory handles. These were intended to have been converted into certain neck ornaments, that are considered as sacred and invaluable. The bones of some fish are, with great labour, appropriated to this purpose; but the colour and texture of the ivory surpassing, in so eminent a degree, the other ordinary material, the temptation was too great to be resisted.

Under the particular circumstances, which we understood attended the missing knife, I readily put up with its loss; because, in so doing, I was relieved of the inconvenience which a number of noisy and troublesome visitors had occasioned. These, however, paid dearly for their dishonesty, in being abridged of the great source of wealth which they had enjoyed on board, and which had enabled them to procure many valuable commodities of their own country, at the expence of asking only for such of our European articles as the seller demanded.

Our business in the hold being finished on Monday the 27th, the seamen were employed in a thorough examination of all the rigging; and although this was the first time, with respect to the lower rigging, that an examination had taken place since the ship was commissioned, we had the satisfaction of finding it in much better condition than, from the trials it had endured, we could reasonably have expected.

Since the death of *Whokaa*, *Kahowmotoo* had not paid the least attention to the Owhyhean *taboos*; but as similar interdictions were to take place on Tuesday the 28th, on the island of Mowee, these he punctually observed; and on the following day *Tamaahmaah* also was again thus religiously engaged; but as there were no prayers on this day, the people at large seemed to be under little restriction.

On Thursday the 30th, we were favored with the company of *Terree-my-tee*, *Crymamahoo*, *Tianna*,[1] and some other chiefs, from the distant parts of the island.

Their arrival had been in consequence of a summons from the king, who

---

[1] Keliimaikai, Kalaimamahu and Kaiana.

had called the grand council of the island, on the subject of its cession to the crown of Great Britain, which was unanimously desired. This important business, however, for which their attendance had been demanded, appeared to be of secondary consideration to all of them; and the happiness they expressed on our return, together with their cordial behaviour, proved, beyond dispute, that our arrival at Owhyhee was the object most conducive to the pleasure of their journey. Even *Tianna* conducted himself with an unusual degree of good homour; but as neither he, nor his brother *Nomatahah*,[1] from their turbulent, treacherous, and ungrateful dispositions, were favorites amongst us, his humility, on this occasion, obtained him only the reputation of possessing a very superior degree of art and duplicity. But as the principal object I had in view was to preserve the good understanding that had been established between us, and, if possible, to secure it on a permanent basis, for the benefit of those who might succeed us at these islands, I waved all retrospective considerations, and treated *Tianna* with every mark of attention, to which his rank, as one of the six provincial chiefs, intitled him, and with which, on all occasions, he appeared to be highly gratified.

These chiefs brought intelligence, that a quantity of timber which had been sent for at my request, was on its way hither; it had been cut down under the directions of an Englishman, whose named was Boid, formerly the mate of the sloop Washington, but who had relinquished that way of life, and had entered into the service of *Tamaahmaah*. He appeared in the character of a shipwright, and had undertaken to build, with these materials, a vessel for the king, after the European fashion; but not having been regularly brought up to this business, both himself and his comrades, Young and Davis, were fearful of encountering too many difficulties; especially as they were all much at a loss in the first outset, that of laying down the keel, and properly setting up the frame; but could they be rightly assisted in these primary operations, Boid (who had the appearance of being very industrious and ingenious) seemed to entertain no doubt of accomplishing the rest of their undertaking.

This afforded me an opportunity of conferring on *Tamaahmaah* a favor that he valued far beyond every other obligation in my power to bestow, by permitting our carpenters to begin the vessel; from whose example, and the assistance of these three engineers, he was in hopes that his people would hereafter be able to build boats and small vessels for themselves.

An ambition so truly laudable, in one to whose hospitality and friendship we had been so highly indebted, and whose good offices were daily administering in some way or other to our comfort, it was a grateful task to cherish and promote; and as our carpenters had finished the re-equipment of the vessels, on Saturday, the 1st of February, they laid down the keel, and began to prepare the frame-work of his Owhyhean Majesty's first man of war. The length of its keel was thirty-six feet, the extreme breadth of the vessel nine feet and a quarter, and the depth of her hold about five feet; her name

[1] Namakeha.

was to be The Britannia, and was intended as a protection to the royal person of *Tamaahmaah*; and I believe few circumstances in his life ever afforded him more solid satisfaction.

It was not very likely that our stay would be so protracted, as to allow our artificers to finish the work they had begun, nor did the king seem to expect I should defer my departure hence for that purpose; but confided in the assertion of Boid, that, with the assistance we should afford him, he would be able to complete the vessel.[1]

In the evening a very strict *taboo* commenced; it was called *The taboo of the Hahcoo*, and appertains to the taking of two particular kinds of fish; one of which, amongst these islanders, bears that name; these are not lawful to be taken at the same time, for during these months that the one is permitted to be caught the other is prohibited. They are very punctual in the observance of this anniversary, which is, exclusively of their days, months, and year, an additional means of dividing their time, or, perhaps, properly speaking, their seasons. The continuance of this interdiction ought to have extended to ten days; but as it is the prerogative of the king to shorten its duration in any one particular district, he directed on our account that in the district of Akona[2] it should cease with the men on the morning of the 4th, and with the women on the day following.

Most of our essential business was nearly brought to a conclusion by Thursday the 6th, and our remaining here for the accomplishment of what yet remained to be done, was no longer an object of absolute necessity; yet I was induced to prolong our stay in this comfortable situation for two reasons; first, because the plan of operations I intended to pursue, in the prosecution of the remaining part of our survey on the coast of North-West America, did not require our repairing immediately to the northward; and secondly, because our former experience amongst the other islands had proved, that there was no prospect of obtaining that abundant supply of refreshments which

---

[1] James Boyd seems to have been a ship's carpenter. Menzies states that he 'had been Mate of an American trading Vessel, but from ill-usage said he had quitted her on the North West Coast & come to this Island in another Vessel a few Months before'. – January 9. He served Kamehameha for many years, repairing the various ships he acquired. Bell records that 'the Keel and most of the Timbers and Planks of this Boat were already cut out, and lying at Whyatea, where Boyd intended to have her set up,' but that when Vancouver offered assistance, Kamehameha 'instantly dispatched a Courier across the Country to Whyatea, ordering every thing belonging to the intended Boat to be brought hither in his largest Canoes with the utmost dispatch and with such punctuality were his orders obeyed that in three days after, three of the largest Canoes arrived with the greatest part of the materials that were ready cut; a large Canoe house was cleared for building her in, and the Carpenters from the Three Ships immediately set to work on her, hoping to finish her before we quitted the Bay.' He adds: 'By the Kings desire she was not to be decked but to be an open Boat, and to pull as many Oars as possible, as his greatest ambition seemed to be that of going off to Vessels that may touch at the Island, in a Boat after our manner.' – January. Menzies notes that 'she only wanted a little planking in the bottom' when the ships sailed. – February 24.

[2] The district of Kona, in which Kealakekua Bay is situated.

Owhyhee afforded, even at the expence of arms and ammunition; articles that humanity and policy had uniformly induced[1] me to with-hold, not only from these islanders, but from every tribe of Indians with whom we had any concern.

The completion of our survey of these islands required still the examination of the north sides of Mowee, Woahoo, and Attowai;[2] and reserving sufficient time for that purpose, I determined to spend here the rest I had to spare, before we should proceed to the American coast. This afforded an opportunity to Mr. Menzies and Mr. Baker, accompanied by some others of the gentlemen, to make another excursion into the country for the purpose of ascending Mowna Roa,[3] which now appeared to be a task that was likely to be accomplished: as we had understood from the natives, that the attempt would be less difficult from the south point of the island than from any other direction. For this purpose the party, furnished by *Tamaahmaah* with a large double canoe, and a sufficient number of people, under the orders of a steady careful chief, sat out, in the confidence of receiving every assistance and attention that could be necessary to render the expedition interesting and agreeable.

The Dædalus being, in all respects, ready to depart for port Jackson, Lieutenant Hanson, on Saturday the 8th received his orders from me for that purpose, together with a copy of our survey of the coast of New Albion, southward from Monterrey; and such dispatches for government as I thought proper to transmit by this conveyance, to the care of the commanding officer at that port.[4]

Some plants of the bread fruit were also put on board, in order that Mr. Hanson, in his way to New South Wales, should endeavour, in the event of his visiting Norfolk island, to introduce there that most valuable production of the vegetable kingdom.

[1] 'dictated' in the first edition.

[2] Maui, Oahu and Kauai.

[3] Mauna Loa. The party included George McKenzie and Thomas Heddington, midshipmen. Howell, the former clergyman, also joined the expedition.

[4] 'The Daedalus being now cleared of every thing she had for us, excepting some Iron, and a few bulky articles of Traffic that was of but little use, (the Ships having already taken upwards of a thousand Bars from her); She prepared for Sailing, whilst Captn. Vancouver's dispatches were getting ready. We had now on board the Chatham, fifteen months provisions of all species and the Discovery had 18 months Provisions. On the 8th every thing being ready, the Daedalus left the Bay to proceed to Botany Bay, and in her went two Young Gentlemen of the Discovery (the Honble. Mr. Thomas Pitt, and Mr. [Thomas] Clark), and one from us (Mr. [Augustus Boyd] Grant) to take their passage thither on the way to England.' – Bell, February. Vancouver's dispatch to the Admiralty, reporting on his voyage since the ships left San Diego, is in Adm. 1/2629, ff. 34–7, but the enclosures are missing. It was not received in London until November 1795 – after Vancouver himself had returned to England. A letter from Hanson to the Admiralty records the subsequent movements of the *Daedalus*. She sailed for England from Port Jackson on 16 December 1794, arrived at Rio de Janeiro on 3 March 1795, left Rio on 3 April, arrived at Cork in June and was to sail for Plymouth, convoyed by the frigate *Stag* on the 29th of the month. – Hanson to Evan Nepean, 28 June 1795. Adm 1/1913, Cap H 104.

CHAPTER II.

Sequel of Transactions at Karakakooa—Cession of the Island of Owhyhee—Astronomical and Nautical Observations.

Whilst the re-equipment of the vessels was going forward in this hospitable port, I had remained chiefly on board; but having now little to attend to there, on Sunday the 9th I took up my abode at the encampment, highly to the satisfaction of the king; who, for the purpose of obtaining such knowledge as might hereafter enable him to follow the example of our artificers, had paid the strictest attention to all their proceedings in the construction of the Britannia. This had latterly so much engaged him, that we had been favored with little of his company on board the vessels; yet I had the satisfaction of reflecting, that his having been occasionally with us, and constantly in our neighbourhood, had been the means of restraining the ill disposed, and of encouraging the very orderly and friendly behaviour that we had experienced from the inhabitants without the least interruption whatever. An uniform zeal directed the conduct of every Indian, in the performance of such offices of kindness as we appeared to stand in need of, or which they considered would be acceptable; these were executed with such promptitude and cheerfulness, as to indicate that they considered their labours amply repaid by our acceptance of their services; yet I trust they were better rewarded than if they had acted on more interested principles.

Our reception and entertainment here by these unlettered people, who in general have been distinguished by the appellation of savages, was such as, I believe, is seldom equalled by the most civilized nations of Europe, and made me no longer regret the inhospitality we had met with at St. Francisco and Monterrey. The temporary use that we wished to make of a few yards of the American shore, for our own convenience and for the promotion of science, was not here, as in New Albion, granted with restrictions that precluded our acceptance of the favor we solicited; on the contrary, immediately on our arrival an ample space, protected by the most sacred laws of the country, was appropriated to our service; whilst those of our small community whose inclinations led them into the interior parts of the island, either for recreation, or to examine its natural productions, found their desires met and encouraged by the kind assistance of *Tamaahmaah*, and their several pursuits rendered highly entertaining and agreeable, by the friendship and hospitality which was shewn them at every house in the course of their excursions.

A conduct so disinterestedly noble, and uniformly observed by so untutored a race, will not fail to excite a certain degree of regret, that the first social principles, teaching mutual support and universal benevolence, should so frequently, amongst civilized people, be sacrified to suspicion, jealousy, and distrust. These sentiments had undoubtedly very strongly operated against us on a recent occasion; but had the gentleman, to whose assistance we appealed, but rightly considered our peculiar situation, he must have been convinced there could not have existed a necessity for the unkind treatment he was pleased to offer to our little squadron; and he would have spared me at this moment the unwelcome task of making this comparison, by which the world will perceive what I must have felt upon that occasion.

A very strict *taboo* was on this day, Wednesday the 12th, to be enforced over all the island, and required that the respective chiefs should retire to their own estates, for the purpose of rigidly observing the attendant solemnities; which were to continue two nights and one day. In the event of the omens proving favorable, the chiefs would be permitted to eat of such pork as they might think proper to consecrate on this occasion; and high *poory*, that is, grand prayers would be performed; but should the omens be otherwise, the rites were instantly to be suspended.

I had frequently expressed to *Tamaahmaah* a desire of being present on some of these occasions; and he now informed me, that he had obtained for me the consent of the priests, provided I would, during the continuance of the interdiction, attend to all the restrictions which their religion demanded.

Having readily promised to comply with this condition, I was with some degree of formality visited by several of the principals of their religious order, one of whom was distinguished by the appellation of *Eakooa*,[1] *no Tamaahmaah*; meaning the god of *Tamaahmaah*. This priest had been one of our frequent attendants, notwithstanding which, he was, on this occasion, detected in stealing a knife; for which offence he was immediately dismissed from our party, and excluded from the precincts of our encampment.

The restraints imposed consisted chiefly in four particulars; first, a total seclusion from the company of the women; secondly, partaking of no food but such as was previously consecrated; thirdly, being confined to the land, and not being afloat or wet with sea water; and fourthly, not receiving, or even touching , the most trivial article from any one, who had not attended the ceremonies at the morai.

These restrictions were considered necessary to be observed by the whole of our party resident on shore; and about sun-set we attended the summons of the king at the morai, who was there officiating as high priest, attended by some of the principal residents of their religious orders, chanting an

[1] Aku, meaning god.

invocation to the setting sun. This was the commencement of these sacred rites; but as I propose to treat this subject more fully on a future occasion, I shall for the present postpone the detail of my observations, and briefly state, that their prayers seemed to have some regularity and form, and that they did not omit to pray for the welfare of His Britanic Majesty, and our safe and happy return to our native country. A certain degree of order was perceptible throughout these ceremonies, accompanied by many superstitious and mysterious formalities; amongst which, a very principal one was performed about the dawn of day. At this time the most profound silence was required of every creature within hearing of this sacred place. The king then repeated a prayer in a low tone of voice with the greatest solemnity, and in the middle of it took up a live pig tied by the legs, and with one effort dashed it to death against the ground; an operation which must be performed without the smallest interruption or cry from the victim, or without the prevailing silence being broken by any noise whatsoever, though of the most trivial kind. This part of the service is supposed to announce their being on terms of friendship with the gods, on which the further ceremonies were carried into execution. A number of hogs, plantations, and cocoa-nuts, were then consecrated for the principal chiefs and priests; the more common productions, such as fish, turtle, fowls, dogs, and the several esculent roots, that compose their food during the intervals between these more sacred *taboo*'s, were not now served up, but for the first time since our arrival, they fared sumptuously on those more delicious articles. The intermediate day, Thursday the 13th, and the second night, were passed in prayer, during which we found no difficulty in complying with the prescribed regulations; and soon after the sun rose on Friday the 14th, we were absolved from any further attention to their sacred injunctions.

Most of our Indian friends returned to our party the following day, Saturday the 15th; and as we all now fed alike on consecrated pork, they were enabled to be infinitely more sociable. Our mode of cookery was generally preferred, as far as related to the dressing of fish, flesh, or fowls; but with respect to roots and the bread fruit, they certainly preserved a superiority.

Tahowmotoo was amongst the most constant of our guests; but his daughter, the disgraced queen, seldom visited our side of the bay. I was however not ignorant of her anxious desire for a reconciliation with *Tamaahmaah*; nor was the same wish to be misunderstood in the conduct and behaviour of the king, in whose good opinion and confidence I had now acquired such a predominancy, that I became acquainted with his most secret inclinations and apprehensions.

His unshaken attachment and unaltered affection for *Tahowmannoo*, was confessed with a sort of internal self conviction of her innocence. He acknowledged with great candour, that his own conduct had not been exactly such as warranted his having insisted upon a separation from his queen; that although it could not authorize, it in some measure pleaded in excuse for, her infidelity; and, for his own, he alledged, that his high rank and supreme authority was a sort of licence for such indulgences.

An accommodation, which I considered to be mutually wished by both parties, was urged in the strongest terms by the queen's relations. To effect this desirable purpose, my interference was frequently solicited by them; and, as it concurred with my own inclination, I resolved on embracing the first favorable opportunity to use my best endeavours for bringing a reconciliation about. For although, on our former visit, *Tahowmannoo* had been regarded with the most favorable impressions, yet, whether from her distresses, or because she had really improved in her personal accomplishments, I will not take upon me to determine, but certain it is, that one, or both of these circumstances united, had so far prepossessed us all in her favor, and no one more so than myself, that it had been long the general wish to see her exalted again to her former dignities. This desire was probably not a little heightened by the regard we entertained for the happiness and repose of our noble and generous friend *Tamaahmaah*; who was likely to be materially affected not only in his domestic comforts, but in his political situation, by receiving again and reinstating his consort in her former rank and consequence.

I was convinced, beyond all doubt, that there were two or three of the most considerable chiefs of the island, whose ambitious views were inimical to the interests and authority of *Tamaahmaah*; and it was much to be apprehended, that if the earnest solicitations of the queen's father (whose condition and importance was next in consequence to that of the king) should continue to be rejected, there could be little doubt of his adding great strength and influence to the discontented and turbulent chiefs, which would operate highly to the prejudice, if not totally to the destruction, of *Tamaahmaah*'s regal power; especially as the adverse party seemed to form a constant opposition, consisting of a minority by no means to be despised by the executive power, and which appeared to be a principal constituent part of the Owhyhean politics.

For these substantial reasons, whenever he was disposed to listen to such discourse, I did not cease to urge the importance and necessity of his adopting measures so highly essential to his happiness as a man, and to his power, interest, and authority as the supreme chief of the island. All this he candidly acknowledged; but his pride threw impediments in the way of a reconciliation which were hard to be removed. He would not of himself become the immediate agent; and although he considered it important that the negociation should be conducted by some one of the principal chiefs in his fullest confidence, yet, to solicit their good offices after having rejected their former overtures with disdain, was equally hard to reconcile to his feelings. I stood nearly in the same situation with his favorite friends; but being thoroughly convinced of the sincerity of his wishes, I spared him the mortification of soliciting the offices he had rejected, by again proffering my services. To this he instantly consented, and observed that no proposal could have met his mind so completely; since, by effecting a reconciliation through my friendship, no umbrage could be taken at his having declined the several offers of his countrymen, by any of the individuals; whereas, had this object been accomplished by any one of the chiefs, it would probably have occasioned jealousy and discontent in the minds of the others.

All, however, was not yet complete; the apprehension that some concession might be suggested or expected on his part, preponderated against every other consideration; and he would on no account consent that it should appear that he had been privy to the business, or that it had been by his desire that a negociation had been undertaken for this happy purpose, but that the whole should have the appearance of being purely the result of accident.

To this end it was determined, that I should invite the queen, with several of her relations and friends, on board the Discovery, for the purpose of presenting them with some trivial matters, as tokens of my friendship and regard; and that, whilst thus employed, our conversation should be directed to ascertain, whether an accommodation was still an object desired. That on this appearing to be the general wish, *Tamaahmaah* would instantly repair on board in a hasty manner, as if he had something extraordinary to communicate; that I should appear to rejoice at this accidental meeting, and by instantly uniting their hands, bring the reconciliation to pass without the least discussion or explanation on either side. But from his extreme solicitude lest he should in any degree be suspected of being concerned in this previous arrangement, a difficulty arose how to make him acquainted with the result of the proposed conversation on board, which could not be permitted by a verbal message; at length, after some thought, he took up two pieces of paper, and of his own accord made certain marks with a pencil on each of them, and then delivered them to me. The difference of these marks he could well recollect; the one was to indicate, that the result of my inquiries was agreeable to his wishes, and the other that it was the contrary. In the event of my making use of the former, he proposed that it should not be sent on shore secretly, but in an open and declared manner, and by way of a joke, as a present to his Owhyhean majesty. The natural gaiety of disposition which generally prevails amongst these islanders, would render this supposed disappointment of the king a subject for mirth, would in some degree prepare the company for his visit, and completely do away every idea of its being the effect of a preconcerted measure.

This plan was accordingly carried into execution on the following Monday, the 17th. Whilst the queen and her party, totally ignorant of the contrivance, were receiving the compliments I had intended them, their good humour and pleasantry were infinitely heightened by the jest I proposed to pass upon the king, in sending him a piece of paper only, carefully wrapped up in some cloth of their own manufacture, accompanied by a message; importing, that as I was then in the act of distributing favours to my Owhyhean friends, I had not been unmindful of his majesty.

Tamaahmaah no sooner received the summons, than he hastened on board, and with his usual vivacity exclaimed before he made his appearance, that he was come to thank me for the present I had sent him, and for my goodness in not having forgotten him on this occasion. This was heard by every one in the cabin before he entered: and all seemed to enjoy the joke except the poor queen, who appeared to be much agitated at the idea of being again in his presence. The instant that he saw her his countenance expressed great surprize, he became immediately silent, and attempted to retire; but having posted myself for the especial purpose of preventing his departure, I caught his hand, and joining it with the queen's, their reconciliation was instantly completed. This was fully demonstrated, not only by the tears that involuntarily stole down the cheeks of both as they embraced each other, and mutually expressed the satisfaction they experienced; but by the behaviour of every individual present, whose feelings on the occasion were not to be repressed; whilst their sensibility testified the happiness which this apparently fortuitous event had produced.

A short pause produced by an event so unexpected, was succeeded by the sort of good humour that such a happy circumstance would naturally inspire; the conversation soon became general, cheerful, and lively, in which the artifice imagined to have been imposed upon the king bore no small share. A little refreshment from a few glasses of wine concluded the scene of this successful meeting.

After the queen had acknowledged in the most grateful terms the weighty obligations she felt for my services on this occasion, I was surprized by her saying, just as we were all preparing to go on shore, that she had still a very great favor to request; which was that I should obtain from *Tamaahmaah* a solemn promise, that on her return to his habitation he would not beat her. The great cordiality with which the reconciliation had taken place, and the happiness that each of them had continued to express in consequence of it, led me at first to consider this intreaty of the queen's as a matter of jest only; but in this I was mistaken, for notwithstanding that *Tamaahmaah* readily complied with my solicitation, and assured me nothing of the kind should take place, yet *Tahowmannoo* would not be satisfied without my accompanying them home to the royal residence, where I had the pleasure of seeing her restored to all her former honours and privileges, highly to the satisfaction of all the king's friends; but to the utter mortification of those, who, by their scandalous reports and misrepresentations, had been the cause of the unfortunate separation.

The domestic affairs of *Tamaahmaah* having thus taken so happy a turn, his mind was more at liberty for political considerations; and the cession of Owhyhee to His Britannic Majesty became now an object of his serious concern. On my former visit it had been frequently mentioned, but was at that time disapproved of by some of the leading chiefs, who contended, that they ought not voluntarily to surrender themselves, or acknowledge their subjection, to the government of a superior foreign power, without being completely convinced that such power would protect them against the ambitious views of remote or neighbouring enemies. During our absence this subject had been most seriously discussed by the chiefs in the island, and the result of their deliberations was, an unanimous opinion, that, in order to obtain the protection required, it was important that *Tamaahmaah* should make the surrender in question, formally to me, on the part of His Majesty; that he should acknowledge himself and people as subjects of the British crown; and that they should supplicate that power to guard them against any future molestation.

To this act they were greatly stimulated by the treatment they had received from various strangers, by whom they had been lately visited. Of some of these I was well persuaded they had had too just cause to complain; particularly in the fraudulent and deceitful manner in which the traffic with the natives had been conducted.

In many instances, no compensation whatever had been given by these *civilized* visitors, after having been fully supplied, on promise of making an ample return, with the several refreshments of the very best quality the country afforded. At other times they had imposed upon the inhabitants, by paying them in commodities of no service or value, though their defects could not be detected by the examination of the natives. This was more particularly the case in those articles which they were most eager to obtain, and most desirous to possess, namely, arms and ammunition; which chiefly composed the merchandize of the North-West American adventurers. Muskets and pistols were thus exchanged that burst on being discharged the first time, though with the proper loading. To augment the quantity of gunpowder which was sold, it was mixed with an equal, if not a larger, proportion of pounded sea or charcoal. Several of these fire-arms, and some of the powder, were produced for my inspection in this shameful state, and with the hope that I was able to afford them redress.

Many very bad accidents had happened by the bursting of these fire-arms; one instance in particular came within our knowledge a few days after our arrival. A very fine active young chief had lately purchased a musket, and on his trying its effect, with a common charge of powder, it burst; and he not only lost some of the joints of his fingers on the left hand, but his right arm below the elbow was otherways so dangerously wounded, that, had it not been for the timely assistance afforded him by some of our gentlemen of the faculty, his life would have been in imminent danger.

The putting fire-arms into the hands of uncivilized people, is at best very bad policy; but when they are given in an imperfect and insufficient condition for a valuable consideration, it is not only infamously fraudulent, but barbarous and inhuman. Notwithstanding which, should these inhabitants resort to measures of revenge for the injuries sustained, they would be immediately stigmatized with the epithets of savages and barbarians, by the very people who had been the original cause of the violence they might think themselves justified in committing.

Under a conviction of the importance of these islands to Great Britain, in the event of an extension of her commerce over the Pacific Ocean, and in return for the essential services we had derived from the excellent productions of the country, and the ready assistance of its inhabitants, I lost no opportunity for encouraging their friendly dispositions towards us; notwithstanding the disappointments they had met with from the traders, for whose conduct I could invent no apology; endeavouring to impress them with the idea, that, on submitting to the authority and protection of a superior power, they might reasonably expect they would in future be less liable to such abuses.

The long continued practice of all civilized natons, of claiming the sovereignty and territorial right of newly discovered countries, had heretofore been assumed in consequence only of priority of seeing, or of visiting such parts of the earth as were unknown before; but in the case of Nootka a material alteration had taken place, and great stress had been laid on the cession that *Maquinna* was stated to have made of the village and friendly cove to Senr Martinez. Notwithstanding that on the principles of the usage above stated, no dispute could have arisen as to the priority of claim that England had to the Sandwich islands; yet I considered, that the voluntary resignation of these territories, by the formal surrender of the king and the people to the power and authority of Great Britain, might probably be the means of establishing an incontrovertible right, and of preventing any altercation with other states hereafter.

Under these impressions, and on a due consideration of all circumstances, I felt it to be an incumbent duty to accept, for the crown of Great Britain, the proffered cession; and I had therefore stipulated that it should be made in the most unequivocal and public manner.

For this purpose all the principal chiefs had been summoned from the different parts of the island, and most of them had long since arrived in our neighbourhood. They had all become extremely well satisfied with the treatment they had received from us; and were highly sensible of the advantages they derived from our introducing amongst them only such things as were instrumental to their comfort, instead of warlike stores and implements, which only contributed to strengthen the animosities that existed between one island and another, and enabled the turbulent and ambitious chiefs to become formidable to the ruling power. They seemed in a great measure to comprehend the nature of our employment, and made very proper distinctions between our little squadron, and the trading vessels by which they had been so frequently visited; that these were engaged in pursuits for the private emolument of the individuals concerned, whilst those under my command acted under the authority of a benevolent monarch, whose chief object in sending us amongst them was to render them more peaceable in their intercourse with each other; to furnish them with such things as could contribute to make them a happier people; and to afford them an opportunity of becoming more respectable in the eyes of foreign visitors.

These ideas at the same time naturally suggested to them the belief, that it might be in my power to leave the Chatham at Owhyhee for their future protection; but on being informed that no such measure could possibly be adopted on the present occasion, they seemed content to wait with patience, in the expectation that such attention and regard might hereafter be shewn unto them; and in the full confidence, that according to my promise, I would represent their situation and conduct in the most faithful manner, and in the true point of view that every circumstance had appeared to us.

These people had already become acquainted with four commercial nations of the civilized world;[1] and had been given to understand, that several others similar in knowledge and in power existed in those distant regions from whence these had come. This information, as may reasonably be expected, suggested the apprehension, that the period was not very remote when they might be compelled to submit to the authority of some one of these superior powers; and under that impression, they did not hesistate to prefer the English, who had been their first and constant visitors.

The formal surrender of the island had been delayed in consequence of the absence of two principal chiefs. *Commanow*, the chief of Aheedoo,[2] was not able to quit the government and protection of the northern and eastern parts of the country, though it had been supposed he might have delegated his authority to some one of less importance than himself; but after some messages had passed between this chief and *Tamaahmaah*, it appeared that it had not been possible to dispense with his presence in those parts of the island.

The other absentee was *Tamaahmotoo*, chief of Koarra,[3] the person that had captured the Fair American schooner, and with whom I was not ambitious to have much acquaintance. Since that perfidious melancholy transaction, he had never ventured near any vessel that had visited these shores; this had been greatly to the prejudice of his interest, and had occasioned him inconceivable chagrin and mortification. Of this he repeatedly complained to *Tamaahmaah* on our former visit; and then, as now, solicited the king's good offices with me to obtain an interview, and permission for his people to resort to the vessels, for the sake of sharing in the superior advantages which our traffic afforded. But, to shew my utter abhorence of his treacherous character, and as a punishment for his unpardonable cruelty to Mr. Metcalf and his crew, I had hitherto indignantly refused every application that had been made in his favour. When, however, I came seriously to reflect on all the circumstances that had attended our reception and treatment at this island, on our former visit and on the present occasion; when I had reference to the situation and condition of those of our countrymen resident amongst them; and when I recollected that my own counsel and advice had always been directed so to operate on their hasty violent tempers, as to induce them to subdue their animosities, by exhorting them to a forgiveness of past injuries, and proving

---

[1] Presumably Great Britain, the United States, Spain and Portugal.
[2] Kamanawa, chief of Hilo district.
[3] Kameeiamoku, chief of Kohala district.

to them how much their real happiness depended upon a strict adherence to the rules of good fellowship towards each other, and the laws of hospitality towards all such strangers as might visit their shores, I was thoroughly convinced, that implacable resentment, or unrelenting anger, exhibited in my own practice, would ill accord with the precepts I had endeavoured to inculate for the regulation of theirs; and that the adoption of conciliatory measures, after having evinced, by a discrimination of characters, my aversion to wicked or unworthy persons, was most consistent with my duty as a man, and with the station I then filled.

In order, therefore, to establish more firmly, if possible, the friendship that had so mutually taken place, and so uninterruptedly subsisted, between us, I determined, by an act of oblivion in my own mind, to efface all former injuries and offences. To this end, and to shew that my conduct was governed by the principles I professed, at the request of *Tianna* and some other chiefs, I admitted the man amongst us, who was reputed to be the first person who had stabbed Captain Cook, and gave leave to *Pareea*★ to visit the vessels; who, during the late contests, had been reduced from his former rank and situation, and was at this time resident on an estate belonging to *Kahowmotoo* on the eastern part of the island, in a very low and abject condition.

Tamaahmotoo had already suffered very materially in his interest, and had sensibly felt the indignity offered to his pride, in being excluded from our society, debarred the gratification of his curiosity, and the high entertainment which his brethren had partaken at our tables, and in our company. I gave *Tamaahmaah* to understand, that these considerations, in conjunction with his repeated solicitations, had induced me no longer to regard *Tamaahmotoo* as undeserving forgiveness, and to allow of his paying us the compliments he had so repeatedly requested; provided that he would engage in the most solemn manner, that neither himself nor his people (for he generally moved with a numerous train of attendants) would behave in any manner so as to disturb the subsisting harmony of our present society, nor conduct themselves, in future, but with a due regard to honesty, and the principles of hospitality.

To these conditions I was given to understand, *Tamaahmotoo* would subscribe without a murmur; and, on their being imparted to him, I received in reply a most humble and submissive answer, that he would forfeit his own existence if any misdemeanor, either on the part of himself, or of any of his followers, should be committed. The district over which his authority regularly extended, was the next district immediately to the northward of us; but his apprehensions lest we should retaliate the injuries he had done to others,

★ Vide 3d Vol. Cook's Voyage, Chap. I. [Most accounts seem to agree that Cook was struck down by a chief, but his identity is by no means certain. Pareea (also spelled Parea and Palea) was prominent at the time of Cook's last visit, but there seems to be little evidence to connect him directly with the murder. Beaglehole points out that 'more than one man laid claim later to having struck the fatal blow.' Colnett met one such at Waimea Bay, Kauai, in 1788; another named Pihere was residing in Hawaii in 1792. See Cook, *Journals*, III, pp. 557 and 557n, 1192–3, 1198.]

had induced him to retire to the eastern parts of Amakooa,[1] as being the most remote from our station. His progress towards Karakakooa, since his visit had been permitted, had been very slow; and as he had advanced he had frequently sent forward messengers, to inquire if I still continued the same friendly disposition towards him; and to request that I would return a renewal of my promises, that he should be received in the same friendly manner as I had engaged myself he should to *Tamaahmaah*. Having no intention whatever to depart from this obligation, I felt no difficulty in repeating these assurances as often as they were demanded.[2]

My promises, however, were not sufficient to remove his suspicions, or to fix his confidence; but on his way he stopped at every morai, there made sacrifices, and consulted the priests as to what was portended in his visit by the omens on these occasions. At first they had been very unfavorable, but as he advanced the prognosticks had become more agreeable to his wishes; and at length, in the morning of Wednesday the 19th, he appeared in great pomp, attended by a numerous fleet of large canoes that could not contain less than a thousand persons, all paddling with some order into the bay, round its northern point of entrance.

Tamaahmaah was at this time with me, and gave me to understand that *Tamaahmotoo* generally went from place to place in the style and manner he now displayed, and that he was the proudest man in the whole island.

After the fleet had entered the bay, its course was slowly directed towards the vessels; but on a message being sent from me, desiring that *Tamaahmotoo* and his party would take up their residence at Kowrowa, he instantly retired with his fleet; and soon afterwards, accompanied by *Tamaahmaah*, and several of the principal chiefs, he visited the encampment. At this time I happened to be absent, but on my return I found him seated in our marquee, with several of our intimate friends, and some strangers, who were all in the greatest good humour imaginable, and exhibiting a degree of composure that the savage

---

[1] Hamakua district, on the N side of the island.

[2] Vancouver's decision to receive Kameeiamoku did not meet with universal approval. Bell, for one, was outraged: 'Here then is an instance of a Pirate, and a murderer, suffered to commit these acts with impunity . . . Surely Captain Vancouver's lenity has in this instance been carried to too great a length. Here was an opportunity of giving these people an idea, in what light we looked on such attrocious crimes – that rank or power (for this man was one of the Six great Chiefs of the Island) had no weight with us in administring justice, nor could it skreen him from the same disgraceful punishment that would have attended any common Malefactor.' Bell ends, however, by giving Vancouver the benefit of a doubt: 'But Captn. Vancouver very probably can produce better arguments *against* making an example of this man than I can find *for* it – so I drop the Subject.' – February. Menzies was equally critical: 'We cannot defend the policy of thus countenancing & soliciting either the acquaintance or friendship of such a notorious villain . . . On visiting the Discovery & Chatham, he made each of the Commanders a present of a rich feather Cloak, a suitable donation to such as could thus Cloak over his enormities. – He offerd one also to Mr. Kendrick Commander of the Lady Washington who with great propriety refusd to accept of it, & likewise refusd to admit him on board or even alongside of his Vessel . . .' – 21 February.

designing countenance of *Tamaahmotoo* could not even affect. Not the least difficulty could arise in distinguishing this chief from the rest of the company, as his appearance and deportment were a complete contrast to the surrounding group, and confirmed in our opinions the unworthiness of his character, and every report to his disadvantage that had been circulated by his countrymen.

Our first salutation being over, he caught the earliest opportunity to offer an apology for the offence that had so justly kept us strangers to each other.[1] He complained of having been very ill treated by the crews of some vessels that had visited Toeaigh bay,[2] and particularly of his having been beaten by Mr. Metcalf, commanding the Eleonora, at the time when his son, who afterwards had the command of the Fair American, was on board the former vessel; and alledged, that the indignities he then received had stimulated him to have recourse to the savage barbarity, before recited, towards the younger Mr. Metcalf and his people, by a sentiment of resentment and revenge; but that he entertained no such wicked designs against any one else; and that his future behaviour, and that of his dependants, would confirm the truth of the protestations he then made. After calling upon the several chiefs to vouch for the sincerity of his intentions, and making every concession that could be expected of him for his late unpardonable conduct, his apprehensions seemed to subside, as his friends appeared to give him credit for his assertions, and came forward as sureties for the propriety of his future behaviour.

This subject having been fully discussed, I shook *Tamaahmotoo* by the hand as a token of my forgiveness and reconciliation; and on confirming this friendly disposition towards him by presenting him with a few useful articles, approbation and applause were evidently marked in the countenance of every one present.

By the time this conciliatory interview was at an end, the dinner was announced; and as our consecrated pork was exhausted, *Tamaahmaah* had taken care to provide such a repast, consisting of dogs, fish, fowls, and vegetables, as was suitable to the keen appetites of our numerous guests. The day was devoted to mirth and festivity; and the king, *Terry-my-tee*, *Tahowmotoo*, *Tianna*, and indeed, all our old acquaintances, took their wine and grog with great cheerfulness, and in their jokes did not spare our new visitor *Tamaahmotoo*, for his awkwardness and ungraceful manners at table.

The glass went freely round after dinner; and as this ceremony was completely within the reach of *Tamaahmotoo*'s imitation, he was anxious to excel in this accomplishment, by drinking with less reserve than any one at table. I thought it proper to remind him, that as he was not in the habit of

---

[1] Bell was convinced that when Kameeiamoku came to meet Vancouver he was terrified: 'He entered the Marquee pale and trembling expecting momentary death, every conviction of his former barbarous conduct seem'd at that moment to have taken possession of him, he seem'd Struck with remorse & shame, and I may add terror too, for his own life, and his appearance and manner altogether displayed a great want of resolution and Fortitude.' – February. [2] Kawaihae Bay.

drinking spirituous liquors like *Tamaahmaah* and the other chiefs present, it was necessary he should be upon his guard, lest the wine and grog should disagree with him; but as his spirits became exhilarated he became less attentive to these admonitions, until the operation of the liquors obliged him to retire. In this state it is not possible to imagine a countenance more expressive of indignation or of savage barbarity and resentment; his eyes were fixed on me as he was carried out of the marquee, whilst his tongue, no longer confined within his lips, indistinctly uttered *attoou-anni*, signifying that I had poisoned him; and some present, even of our old acquaintance, seemed to be a little concerned for his safety. The king, however, laughed at their apprehension, and explained to them the cause of *Tamaahmotoo*'s indisposition, which, by the assistance of a little warm water, was almost instantly recovered, and he rejoined our party, to the great entertainment and diversion of his countrymen, who were still very pleasantly regaling themselves, and in the perfect enjoyment of each other's society.

In the front of the marquee, seated on the ground, were two or three of *Tamaahmotoo*'s most confidential friends and constant attendants. The behaviour of these people, on their master being taken from table, suddenly changed, from the most unreserved vivacity to a suspicious silence; their eyes sparkled, and their countenances were expressive of distrust and resentment; one of them in particular, who I had not observed before to be armed, had with him a dagger, made out of the broad part of an iron spit, which he handled with great agitation, and seemed to be more than half inclined to make use of it, to gratify the revenge that was struggling within his breast. This man contended, in a short conversation with *Tamaahmaah*, that *Tamaahmotoo* had been given a different bottle to drink out of from the rest of the company; but on the king and other persons drinking some wine from the same bottle, he became pacified; and the recovery of the intoxicated chief completely did away his suspicions of our having entertained towards his master any unfavorable intentions.

On this occasion, however, I could not avoid reflecting, how indispensably necessary it is, that the greatest circumspection and caution should be observed in our intercourse with such strangers, unaccustomed to our manners and way of life; because it may frequently happen, that the most disastrous and fatal consequences may arise from causes the least to be apprehended, and in themselves of the most innocent nature. Notwithstanding that in the instance before us nothing uncomfortable took place, yet I was firmly persuaded that we were greatly indebted for our tranquillity, on this occasion, to the great respect and esteem which our conduct towards these people had previously insured us; but had it unfortunately so happened, that *Tamaahmotoo* had died under the effects of the liquor to which his constitution was unused, and of which he had drank inordinately, our having poisoned him would have been generally received as a fact; whence the natives, naturally concluding that we had been guilty of the most unwarrantable treachery, they would have been pardonable in seeking revenge; and under such impressions ought rather to have been considered as intitled to our pity for being mistaken; than to our resentment for any acts of injury which the misunderstanding might have occasioned.

The convocation of the principal chiefs of the island by the royal mandate, failed not to assemble at the same time most of the persons of consequence of both sexes, who took up their residence in our immediate neighbourhood; which became so populous, that there was scarcely a place where a temporary habitation could be erected that remained unoccupied, especially in the vicinity of the two principal villages of Kakooa and Kowrowa. Their numbers amounted now to several thousands, whose cheerful good humour, eagerness to oblige, and orderly behaviour, could not be surpassed by the inhabitants of the most civilized country. The days passed pleasantly to those who devoted them to innocent amusements, and profitably to others who were engaged in bartering away the merchandize they had brought, to exchange for our more valuable commodities; whilst those of our society who extended their recreation on shore, beyond the limits of the bay, were received with the greatest hospitality, and entertained with the general amusements of the country; which rendered these excursions not less interesting than contributory to health.

The evenings were generally closed with singing and dancing, and the nights were as quiet as the most orderly towns in Europe; though it was a late hour most commonly before they retired to rest. The space between sun-set and that time was employed by some parties in social conversation, and by others at various games of chance; and I did not observe a single instance in which these were conducted, even by the losers, but with the greatest temper and good humour.

Desirous of being constantly upon the spot, lest any untoward circumstance should arise to interrupt the happiness we enjoyed, my excursions were confined to a small distance from our encampment. This however did not preclude my attending some of their evening amusements in our neighbourhood. At one of which, in particular, I was very well entertained.

This was a performance by a single young woman of the name of *Puckoo*, whose person and manners were both very agreeable. Her dress, notwithstanding the heat of the weather, consisted of an immense quantity of thin cloth, which was wound round her waist, and extended as low as her knees. This was plaited in such a manner as to give a pretty effect to the variegated pattern of the cloth; and was otherwise disposed with great taste. Her head and neck were decorated with wreaths of black, red, and yellow feathers; but excepting these she wore no dress from the waist upwards. Her ancles, and nearly half way up her legs, were decorated with several folds of cloth, widening upwards, so that the upper parts extended from the leg at least four inches all round; this was encompassed by a piece of net work, wrought very close, from the meshes of which were hung the small teeth of dogs, giving this part of her dress the appearance of an ornamented funnel. On her wrists she wore bracelets made of the tusks from the largest hogs. These were highly polished and fixed close together in a ring, the concave sides of the tusks being outwards; and their ends reduced to an uniform length, curving naturally each way from the centre, were by no means destitute of ornamental effect.

Thus equipped, her appearance on the stage, before she uttered a single word, excited considerable applause from the numerous spectators, who observed the greatest good order and decorum. In her performance, which was in the open air, she was accompanied by two men, who were seated on the ground in the character of musicians. Their instruments were both alike, and were made of the outsides or shells of large gourds, open at the top; the lower ends ground perfectly flat, and as thin as possible, without endangering their splitting. These were struck on the ground, covered with a small quantity of dried grass, and in the interval between each stroke, they beat with their hands and fingers on the sides of these instruments, to accompany their vocal exertions, which, with the various motions of their hands and body, and the vivacity of their countenances, plainly demonstrated the interest they had, not only in excelling in their own parts, but also in the applause which the lady acquired by her performance, advancing or retreating from the musicians a few short steps in various directions, as the nature of the subject, and the numerous gestures and motions of her person demanded. Her speech, or poem, was first began in a slow, and somewhat solemn manner, and gradually became energetic, probably as the subject matter became interesting; until at length, like a true actress, the liveliness of her imagination produced a vociferous oration, accompanied by violent emotions. These were received with shouts of great applause; and although we were not sufficiently acquainted with the language to comprehend the subject, yet we could not help being pleased in a high degree with the performance. The music and singing was by no means discordant or unpleasing; many of the actions seemed to be well adapted, and the attitudes exhibited both taste and elegance. The satisfaction we derived at this public entertainment, was greatly increased by the respectful reception we met from all parties, as well performers as spectators, who appeared to be infinitely more delighted by our plaudits, than by the liberal donations which we made on the occasion.

These amusements had hitherto been confined to such limited performances; but this afternoon was to be dedicated to one of a more splendid nature, in which some ladies of consequence, attendants on the court of *Tamaahmaah*, were to perform the principal parts. Great pains had been taken, and they had gone through many private rehearsals, in order that the exhibition that evening might be worthy of the public attention; on the conclusion of which I purposed by a display of fire-works, to make a return for the entertainment they had afforded us.

About four o'clock, we were informed it was time to attend the royal dames; their theatre, or rather place of exhibition, was about a mile to the southward of our tents, in a small square, surrounded by houses and sheltered by trees; a situation as well chosen for the performance, as for the accommodation of the spectators; who, on a moderate computation, could not be estimated at less than four thousand, of all ranks and descriptions of persons.

A difference in point of dress had been observed in the audience at the former entertainment, but on this occasion every one shone forth in the best apparel that could be procured; those who had been successful in their commercial transactions with us, did not fail to appear in the best attire they had procured; and such as were destitute of European articles, had exerted their genius to substitute the manufacture and productions of their own country in the most fashionable and advantageous manner. Feathered ruffs, and gartering tape in wreaths, adorned the ladies' heads, and were also worn as necklaces; red cloth, printed linen, or that of their own manufacture, constituted the lower garment, which extended from the waist to the knees. The men likewise had put on their best maros; so that the whole presented a very gay and lively spectacle.

On our arrival, some of our friends were pleased to be a little jocular with our appearance at so unfashionable an hour, having come much too early for the representation; but as we were admitted into the *green room* amongst the performers, our time was not unpleasantly engaged. The dress of the actresses was something like that worn by *Puckoo*, though made of superior materials, and disposed with more taste and elegance. A very considerable quantity of their finest cloth was prepared for the occasion; of this their lower garment was formed, which extended from their waist half way down their legs, and was so plaited as to appear very much like a hoop petticoat. This seemed the most difficult part of their dress to adjust, for *Tamaahmaah*, who was considered to be a profound critic, was frequently appealed to by the women, and his directions were implicitly followed in many little alterations. Instead of the ornaments of cloth and net-work decorated with dogs' teeth, these ladies had each a green wreath made of a kind of bind weed, twisted together in different parts like a rope, which was wound round from the ankle, nearly to the lower part of the petticoat. On their wrists they wore no bracelets nor other ornaments, but across their necks and shoulders were green sashes, very nicely made, with the broad leaves of the tee, a plant that produces a very luscious sweet root, the size of a yam.* This part of their dress was put on

* Vide Cook's last Voyage. [In the second edition 'tee' has been wrongly changed to 'tree', as John Vancouver evidently misunderstood the reference, which is to Ti or Ki. Bayly and Burney of Cook's expedition noted the plant, but they were interested in its roots rather than its broad leaves. Bayly wrote that the natives brought 'a Root that appears like a Rotten Root of a tree, & as large as a man's thigh. It is very much like brown sugar in tast but Rather Sweeter — The natives call it *Tee*.... The Natives eat it sometimes Raw & at other times Roasted. We made exceedingly good Beer, by boiling it in Water, then let it ferment, so as to purge itself'. Beaglehole adds that 'old Hawaiians cooked the swollen

the last by each of the actresses; and the party being now fully attired, the king and queen, who had been present the whole time of their dressing, were obliged to withdraw, greatly to the mortification of the latter, who would gladly have taken her part as a performer, in which she was reputed to excel very highly. But the royal pair were compelled to retire, even from the exhibition, as they are prohibited by law from attending such amusements, excepting on the festival of the new year. Indeed, the performance of this day was contrary to the established rules of the island, but being intended as a compliment to us, the innovation was admitted.

As their majesties withdrew, the ladies of rank, and the principal chiefs, began to make their appearance. The reception of the former by the multitude was marked by a degree of respect that I had not before seen amongst any inhabitants of the countries in the Pacific Ocean. The audience assembled at this time were standing in rows, from fifteen to twenty feet deep, so close as to touch each other; but these ladies no sooner approached their rear, in any accidental direction, than a passage was instantly made for them and their attendants to pass through in the most commodious manner to their respective stations, where they seated themselves on the ground, which was covered with mats, in the most advantageous situation for seeing and hearing the performers. Most of these ladies were of a corpulent form, which, assisted by their stately gait, the dignity with which they moved, and the number of their pages, who followed with fans to court the refreshing breeze, or with fly-flaps to disperse the offending insects, announced their consequence as the wives, daughters, sisters, or other near relations of the principal chiefs, who however experienced no such marks of respect or attention themselves; being obliged to make their way through the spectators in the best manner they were able.

The time devoted to the decoration of the actresses extended beyond the limits of the quiet patience of the audience, who exclaimed two or three times, from all quarters, 'Hoorah, hoorah, poaliealee,[1] signifying, that it would be dark and black night before the performance would begin. But the audience here, like similar ones in other countries, attending with a pre-disposition to be pleased, was in good humour, and was easily appeased, by the address of our faithful and devoted friend Trywhookee,[2] who was the conductor of the ceremonies, and sole manager on this occasion. He came forward, and apologized by a speech that produced a general laugh, and causing the music to begin, we heard no further murmurs.

The band consisted of five men, all standing up, each with a highly-polished wooden spear in the left, and a small piece of the same material, equally well finished, in the right hand; with this they beat on the spear, as an accompaniment to their voices in songs, that varied both as to time and

underground stem in the earth-oven, and chewed it like sugar cane. Their descendants mashed up the cooked root, and distilled an alcoholic liquor from it, which was probably more powerful than Bayly's beer.' – Journals, III, p. 573n.

[1] Hula hula pouliuli.   [2] Half brother of Kamehameha.

measure, especially the latter; yet their voices, and the sounds produced from their rude instruments, which differed according to the place on which the tapering spear was struck, appeared to accord very well. Having engaged us a short time in this vocal performance, the court ladies made their appearance, and were received with shouts of the greatest applause. The musicians retired a few paces, and the actresses took their station before them.

The heroine of the piece, which consisted of four parts or acts, had once shared the affections and embraces of *Tamaahmaah*, but was now married to an inferior chief, whose occupation in the household was that of the charge of the king's apparel. This lady was distinguished by a green wreath round the crown of the head; next to her was the captive daughter of *Titeeree*;[1] the third a younger sister to the queen, the wife of *Crymamahoo*,[2] who being of the most exalted rank stood in the middle. On each side of these were two of inferior quality, making in all seven actresses. They drew themselves up in a line fronting that side of the square that was occupied by the ladies of quality and the chiefs. These were completely detached from the populace, not by any partition, but, as it were, by the respectful consent of the lower orders of the assembly; not one of which trespassed or produced the least inconvenience.[3]

This representation, like that before attempted to be described, was a compound of speaking and singing; the subject of which was enforced by appropriate gestures and actions. The piece was in honor of a captive princess, whose name was *Crycowculleneaow*; and on her name being pronounced, every one present, men as well as women, who wore any ornaments above their waist, were obliged to take them off, though the captive lady was at least sixty miles distant. This mark of respect was unobserved by the actresses whilst engaged in the performance; but the instant any one sat down, or at the close of the act, they were also obliged to comply with this mysterious ceremony.

The variety of attitudes into which these women threw themselves, with the rapidity of their action, resembled no amusement in any other part of the world within my knowledge, by a comparison with which I might be enabled to convey some idea of the stage effect this produced, particularly in the three first parts, in which there appeared much correspondence and harmony between the tone of their voices, and the display of their limbs. One or two of the performers being not quite so perfect as the rest, afforded us an opportunity of exercising our judgment by comparison; and it must be confessed, that the ladies who most excelled, exhibited a degree of graceful action, for the attainment of which it is difficult to account.

In each of these first parts the songs, attitudes, and actions, appeared to me of greater variety than I had before noticed amongst the people of the great South Sea nation, on any former occasion. The whole, though I am unequal

---

[1] Kahekili, the chief who controlled Maui, Oahu and other islands to leeward of the island of Hawaii.

[2] Kalaimanahu.

[3] 'inaccommodation' in the first edition.

to its description, was supported with a wonderful degree of spirit and vivacity; so much indeed that some of their exertions were made with such a degree of agitating violence, as seemed to carry the performers beyond what their strength was able to sustain; and had the performance finished with the third act, we should have retired from their theatre with a much higher idea of the moral tendency of their drama, than was conveyed by the offensive, libidinous scene, exhibited by the ladies in the concluding part. The language of the song, no doubt, corresponded with the obscenity of their actions; which were carried to a degree of extravagance that was calculated to produce nothing but disgust even in the most licentious.

This *hooarah* occupied about an hour, and concluded with the descending sun, it being contrary to law that such representations should continue after that time of day. The spectators instantly retired in the most orderly manner, and dispersed in the greatest good humour; apparently highly delighted with the entertainment they had received. But as the gratification I had promised on this occasion required the absence of light, and could not be exhibited to advantage until a late hour, the multitude were permitted to re-assemble in our neighbourhood soon afterwards for this purpose.

Our exhibition commenced about seven in the evening, and as we still possessed a considerable variety of fire-works in a tolerably good state of preservation, an ample assortment was provided; and on being thrown off, they produced from the expecting multitude such acclamations of surprize and admiration from all quarters, as may be easily imagined to arise from the feelings of persons totally unacquainted with objects of such an extraordinary nature. *Tamaahmaah* fired the two first rockets; but there were only one or two of the chiefs who had courage sufficient to follow his example; and it was observed amongst those who were near us at the time, that in these apprehension was more predominant than pleasure. The whole concluded with some excellent Bengal lights, which illuminating the neighbourhood to a great distance, almost equal to the return of day, seemed to produce more general satisfaction than the preceding part of the exhibition; and on its being announced, that the light was shewn to conduct them safely to their respective habitations, the crowd retired; and in the space of half an hour the usual stillness of the night was so completely restored, that it would rather have been imagined there had not been a single stranger in our neighbourhood, than that thousands had so recently departed.

As the number of these strangers had increased, so a gradual augmentation of the king's nightly guard had taken place; but on this evening the guards were at least doubled, and in number amounted to about forty, armed with pallaloos[1] and iron daggers, and stationed in different places about the royal residence.

This having been the twelfth day's absence of Mr. Menzies and his party, and having far exceeded the limits of time that I expected their proposed

---

[1] palolu, a long war spear.

excursion could have required, I began to be anxious lest some accident or indisposition had detained them in the interior country (being perfectly satisfied that there was not the least danger to be apprehended from the natives) especially as I had received only one note from the party, and that on the commencement of their journey from the south point of the island; and although their excursion had not at that time been attended with the expedition I could have wished, yet I had reason before now to have expected their return.

The period of our departure being fast approaching, in order that we might be in readiness to sail on the arrival of the party, I directed that every thing should be prepared the next morning, Thursday the 20th, for embarking such matters as we had on shore. Most of the principal chiefs having, as usual, joined our party at breakfast, the highest satisfaction and admiration was expressed at the exhibition that closed the entertainments of the preceding day; whilst the preparations that were making for our departure occasioned a universal regret. It was well known that I had already exceeded the time of my intended stay, and that the hour would come when a separation must inevitably take place, and probably never to meet again. Such were the topics of our conversation round the breakfast table, when information was brought that a cartridge box, which the sentinel had suffered to lie carelessly about, had been stolen from on board the Chatham. On this unpleasant circumstance being first reported, *Tamaahmaah* seemed to be indifferent as to its recovery; alledging that the sentinel had been much in fault in not having taken proper care of his accoutrements. His reasoning was undoubtedly correct, and I would willingly have passed the transgression unnoticed, rather than have risked the chance of any interruption to our present harmony, had not the uniform negative that I had put upon every solicitation from these people, for arms or ammunition, and which was only to be supported by saying, that all such articles belonged to His Majesty King George, and that they were strictly *tabooed*, rendered it absolutely necessary that I should insist on the restitution of the thing stolen.

The conversation that this unlucky incident produced drew for a short time a veil of gloom over the cheerfulness which had generally prevailed; and although this was extremely unpleasant at so interesting a period, it was attended with the good effect of stimulating the king to send *Kahowmotoo* in quest of the cartridge box, who, in about half an hour brought it to us. It had been found in the house of *Cavaheeroo*, the chief of the district of Kaoo, and the principal person at the village Kowrowa; but of the thief, who was a woman, no tidings could be procured; as she had either made her escape, or was protected under the peculiar privileges with which that village is endowed, in giving protection to offenders of various descriptions, whilst they remain within its precincts.

The accoutrement, however, being restored, with its contents undiminished and in good order, all parties were instantly reconciled, and our society brought back to its former standard of harmony and good spirits; though it was apparent that the latter had received some little check, in consequence of the indications of the near approach of our departure, by the removal of our several matters from the shore to the vessels.

In the afternoon intelligence was brought that our travellers had reached the summit of Mowna Roa, and that they were on their way back; but, from the native who brought us this information, it appeared, that they would yet be some days before they arrived, as they intended to return by land, and the roads they had to pass were very indifferent.

Having resumed my residence on board the ship, I was on Friday the 21st complimented with a formal visit from all the great personages in the neighbourhood, except *Cavaheeroo*; who, having accepted the stolen cartridge box, I considered as an accessary in the theft, and on that account I would not permit him to enter the ship. This exception was no small mortification to his pride, nor disappointment to his interest, as none of his associates returned to the shore without a handsome token of my esteem. *Tamaahmotoo*, and his retinue, though less deserving of such marks of attention, and with little claim to any acknowledgment from me, were not omitted, but received . such presents as their respective conditions and the occasion seemed to demand. With this party had come a daughter of *Tamaahmaah*, about nine years of age. She had not visited us when we were here before, nor had we ever seen her until the arrival of *Tamaahmotoo*, to whose charge she had some time since been entrusted for the purpose of being educated and brought up agreeably to the custom of these islands. She bore a striking likeness to her father, and though far from being handsome, had an expressive intelligent countenance, and was a very cheerful and engaging girl.

All the chiefs that were expected being now assembled, I inquired of the king when the proposed voluntary cession of the island was to be confirmed. A short conversation immediately took place between *Tamaahmaah* and some of his counsellors then present; the result of which was, that as a *taboo-poory* was to commence on the evening of the ensuing Sunday, and would continue until Tuesday morning, they were unanimously of opinion, that it would be highly proper to embrace that opportunity of reconsulting the priests, that each might be fully satisfied with the propriety of the measure they were about to adopt. *Tamaahmaah* at the same time requested that I would attend him at the grand morai during the interdiction.

This was a reply that I did not altogether like, nor did I expect it, as they were all convinced how anxious I now was to take my departure. A final appeal to the priests, however, I was given to understand, could not be dispensed with; and as there was little probability of the party from Mowna Roa returning much before that time, I was induced to promise that I would comply with their wishes.

There appeared little reason to believe that the cession would not be made, although some previous ceremonies were still wanting, before they would be enabled to make the surrender in form, which at this time was fixed for the following Tuesday; immediately after which, I informed them I should sail with the land wind for Tyahtatooa[1] and Toeaigh;[2] to the former, for the purpose of more particularly examining the anchorage, and to the latter for the purpose of procuring such a further stock of refreshments as we could conveniently take; well knowing that we ought to place little dependance on the precarious supply that Mowee, Woahoo, or the rest of the islands to leeward might afford. The whole of the party did me the favor to say, that they would remain on board until we quitted Owhyhee.

I was very much concerned to find that my earnest endeavors to bring about a reconciliation, and to establish peace amongst these islands, had proved unsuccessful. The mutual distrust that continued to exist amongst the people of the several islands, which I had foreseen to be the greatest difficulty there was to combat, and which I had apprehended would be an insurmountable obstacle, had proved fatal to the attainment of this desirable object. Immediately on my arrival here, I inquired if my letter from Mowee had been received, and received an answer in the negative. But I was given to understand, that a small party from that island had arrived on the western side of Owhyhee, whose object was suspected to be that of seizing on some of the inhabitants there, for the purpose of taking them away, and of sacrificing them in their religious rites at Mowee; and some reports went so far as to assert that this diabolical object had been effected. On further inquiry, however, this fact appeared to be by no means established; as it was positively insisted on by some, and by others as positively denied. One circumstance, however, both parties agreed in, that of the people from Mowee having been under the necessity of making a hasty retreat. I could not understand that any chief was in the neighbourhood of the place where they had landed; and *Tamaahmaah* himself, either from a conviction that they had been unfairly dealt with, or that I should disapprove of the suspicious narrow policy that had influenced the conduct of his people on this occasion, was unwilling to allow that he had been made duly acquainted with their arrival, and was always desirous of avoiding the subject in conversation.[3]

After many attempts to fix his attention, I at length explained to him what was the result of my negociation with the chiefs at Mowee; and he then seemed to concur in opinion with me, that the party from Mowee who had landed on the western side of Owhyhee, could be no other than the embassy charged with my letter, and invested with powers to negociate for a general pacification.

[1] Kaiakekua Bay. Spelled 'Ti-ah-ta-tooa' previously. [2] Kawaihae Bay.

[3] Puget heard a different story, much to Kamehameha's credit, from Davis: 'Isaac informed me that the People of Mowee had landed at Tohassa [?] during our Absence & had Stolen some of the Indians for their Morai but Tomaihomaihaw...had strictly forbid any Retaliation being made, as he thought himself bound by the Promise he had made to Captain Vancouver not to go to Mowee.' – January 14.

It was some time before I was able to make myself thoroughly master of these circumstances; yet long before I had ascertained with any tolerable precision what was the state of the business, I was perfectly convinced that no overtures of this nature would be attended with success, and that nothing but by my passing backwards and forwards between the several islands in the manner before stated, would answer any good purpose; could I have done this, I entertained no doubt of accomplishing this desirable object; but neither our circumstances nor our time would admit of my engaging in this task, particularly at the present season of the year, when very boisterous weather usually prevailed amongst these islands, against which we should occasionally have been obliged to beat to windward. Our sails, rigging, and probably our masts, would necessarily have suffered in point of wear and tear, even should we have been so fortunate as to have avoided any material damage by accident; and as our stock of those essential articles, even with the supply we had received from port Jackson, which was very short of what I had requested, demanded the greatest œconomy and care to make them last, without subjecting us to unpleasant and even disastrous circumstances, during our progress in the unaccomplished part of our voyage; I was under the necessity of declining any further personal interference, notwithstanding that I was satisfied the happiness and tranquillity of many thousands might have been secured, at least for a time, could I have undertaken this important business.

This conviction did not fail to claim a great share of my attention; but the execution of the several important objects of our voyage that yet remained unfinished, and which were of an extensive nature, compelled me to give up all thoughts of secondary considerations. The completion of our business that appertained to the North Pacific Ocean, I had so far hopes of effecting in the course of the ensuing season, that I had not demanded the return of the Dædalus with a further supply of stores, nor indeed was it certain that such a supply could have been obtained from port Jackson; we had therefore to rely on the dispensations of Divine Providence, and our own care and frugality, for the accomplishment of the remaining part of our survey with the stores we had still remaining.

Tamaahmaah having become acquainted with our intended route from Karakakooa, and being watchful to embrace every opportunity by which he could continue his good offices, either for our present comfort, or our future welfare, ordered one of his principal domestics to depart immediately for Toeaigh; there to provide according to his directions such things as we stood in need of, and to have them in readiness for embarkation on our arrival.

After these, and other less important arrangements had been made relative to our departure, the king with his companions returned to the shore. About this time the gentlemen made their appearance from Mowna Roa, having descended from the mountains in a straight line to the sea shore, from whence they had returned by water; but had not this been their route, their journey hither would have occupied some few days more.[1] At first sight of the travellers I regretted the delay I had so recently consented to; but it was now too late to retract, especially as, on the most trivial occasions, I had made it a point to perform all promises made to these people with scrupulous punctuality. Two or three days, therefore, were not of sufficient importance to us to induce my breaking in upon the arrangements I had just made with *Tamaahmaah*; who would easily have discovered, that no new cause had arisen from any alteration in our plan; and I therefore determined to remain contented until Tuesday, when the restrictions of the *taboo* were to cease. This afforded an opportunity to some of the officers, whose attention to their several duties had confined them hitherto to the sea shore, to make a short excursion into the adjacent country.

The building of *Tamaahmaah*'s vessel was now so far advanced, that I considered its completion an easy task for his people to perform under the direction of Boid, who most probably had, by his attention to our carpenters, added some information to his former knowledge in ship-building. Her frame was completely fixed, and all that remained to be done was some part of the planking,[2] and fitting up her inside according to the taste and fancy of *Tamaahmaah*. Having no doubt but all this would be effected with little difficulty by themselves, on Saturday the 22d, our carpenters were ordered to repair on board with their tools. Besides the assistance I had afforded in

[1] Obviously annoyed by Menzies' late arrival, Vancouver makes only the briefest mention of the expedition, in which Mauna Loa was climbed for the first time by Europeans – possibly the first time by anyone, as the natives were reluctant to venture above the snow line. Menzies describes the trip in considerable detail in his journal. The party accompanied by Roohea, the chief delegated by Kamehameha to watch over them, travelled by canoe to a village near the southern tip of the island of Hawaii, and then followed a somewhat circuitous route overland that more than once tried Menzies' patience. They attracted much attention; at one stage 'what with men & women who followd us up the mountain through curiosity & our own attendants who carried bedding water and provisions of every kind for themselves & us we were very little short of a hundred people of the party.' The crowd thinned out rapidly when cold and snow were encountered. About the 11,000-foot level Heddington fell ill and Howell's shoes were so cut and torn that he had to turn back. The final ascent to the summit, on 16 February, was made by Menzies, Baker, McKenzie and a servant. With his barometer Menzies estimated the height to be 13,634 feet, very close to the true height of 13,680 feet. Botanizing was again disappointing: 'In this days march [14 February] we saw many strange looking plants different from any we had before observd, but very few of them being in flower or seed, it was not possible to make out what they were.' – 5 to 16 February.

[2] A note by Bell dated 16 February shows the urgency that Kamehameha attached to the building of the *Britannia*: 'The Boat Builders who had hitherto gone on pretty well were now at a Stand for Plank. In consequence of which Tamaihamaiha issued a Taboo against any man going on the water the next day, but ordered them up to the Hills to bring down Plank which had been there preparing, and as I walked through the Villages, not a man except the old and the maimed was to be seen.' On the 27th, as the *Discovery* was entering Kawaihae Bay, a seaman harpooned a porpoise, and the next day Menzies saw the natives 'busily employd in boiling down the porpoise...to make oile from it for painting the boat Britannia.'

building the hull of the vessel, I had furnished *Tamaahmaah* with all the iron work she would further require; oakum and pitch for caulking, proper masts, and a set of schooner sails, with canvass, needles, and twine to repair them hereafter. With respect to cordage, they had a sufficiency of their own manufacture for her rigging, schooner fashion, and every other necessary purpose.

Tamaahmaah was exceedingly well pleased, and thankful for our exertions; and it was extremely gratifying to my feelings to reflect, that such valuable opportunities should have offered for bestowing this gratification upon the king, and many essential benefits upon his people; all of whom were now well convinced, that these superior advantages were only to be obtained by the constant exercise of the same honesty and civility by which these had been secured to them on the present occasion.

Very little doubt can be entertained of the exalted pleasure *Tamaahmaah* would enjoy in the attainment, by honorable means, of so desirable an object as his new schooner; especially at those times, when his mind recurring to the virtuous causes that had given him so valuable a possession, he would naturally make a comparison between them and the criminal measures pursued by *Tamaahmotoo* for a similar acquisition; which he had no sooner possessed by treachery and barbarity, than he was deprived of it with indelible marks of infamy, and the loss of his reputation and character.

On the evening of Sunday the 23d, agreeably to my promise, I accompanied *Tamaahmaah* to the morai, and submitted to all the forms, regulations, and restrictions of the *taboo*. The ceremonies were similar to those I had before observed, though they were more concise, less formal, and attended by few persons.

I was not on this, as on the former occasion, purely an idle spectator; but was in some degree one of the actors. Whilst in the morning the principal ceremonies and prayers were performing, I was called upon to give my opinion on several matters that were agitated at one time by the king, and at others by the principal priests. Amongst these was the propriety of their remaining at peace, or making war against the other islands? The cession of the island; and if, by that voluntary measure, they would be considered as the subjects of Great Britain? Under this impression, in what manner ought they to conduct themselves towards all strangers, as well those who might visit them from civilized nations, as the inhabitants of the neighbouring islands? With these, and some other questions of less importance, I was very seriously interrogated; and I made such answers to each as was consistent with my own situation, and, as I considered, were most likely to tend in future to their happiness and tranquillity.

I was not prohibited in my turn from offering my suggestions, or demanding their attention to my requisitions. Anxious lest the object I had so long had in view should hereafter be defeated; namely, that of establishing a breed of sheep, cattle, and other European animals in these islands, which with so much difficulty, trouble, and concern, I had at length succeeded so far as to import in good health, and in a thriving condition; I demanded, that they should be *tabooed* for ten years, with a discretionary power in the king alone to appropriate a certain number of the males of each species, in case that sex became predominant, to the use of his own table; but that in so doing the women should not be precluded partaking of them, as the intention of their being brought to the island was for the general use and benefit of every inhabitant of both sexes, as soon as their numbers should be sufficiently increased to allow of a general distribution amongst the people. This was unanimously approved of and faithfully promised to be observed with one exception only; that with respect to the meat of these several animals, the women were to be put on the same footing as with their dogs and fowls; they were to be allowed to eat of them, but not of the identical animal that men had partaken, or of which they were to partake. Much conversation took place on these different subjects, when not otherwise engaged in functions of a religious nature; all these ceasing at sun-rise the next morning, I repaired on board, and found every thing in readiness for our departure.

In the forenoon of Tuesday the 25th, the king and queen, accompanied by *Terry-my-tee*, the king's brother; *Crymamahow*, half brother to the king, and chief of the district of Amakooa; *Kahowmotoo*, father to the queen, and chief of the district of Kona; *Kavaheeroo*, chief of the district of Kaow; *Tianna*, chief of the district of Poona; *Tamaahmotoo*, chief of the district of Koarra;[1] *Trywhookee*, half brother to the king, and our most faithful protector and purveyor at the encampment; all assembled on board the Discovery, for the purpose of formally ceding and surrendering the island of Owhyhee to me for His Britannic Majesty, his heirs and successors; there were present on this occasion besides myself, Mr. Puget, and all the officers of the Discovery.[2]

Tamaahmaah opened the business in a speech, which he delivered with great moderation and equal firmness. He explained the reasons (already stated) that had induced him to offer the island to the protection of Great Britain; and recounted the numerous advantages that himself, the chiefs, and the people, were likely to derive by the surrender they were about to make. He enumerated the several nations that since Captain Cook's discovery of these islands had occasionally resorted hither, each of which was too powerful for them to resist; and as these visitors had come more frequently to their shores, and their numbers seemed to increase, he considered that the inhabitants would be liable to more ill treatment, and still greater impositions than they had yet endured, unless they could be protected against such wrongs by some one of the civilized powers with whose people they had become acquainted; that at

---

[1] In modern spelling the five chiefs were: Kalaimanahu, chief of the district of Hamakua; Keeaumoku, chief of the district of Kona; Keaweaheulu, chief of the district of Kau; Kaiana, chief of the district of Puna, and Kameeiamoku, chief of the district of Kohala. Absent was the sixth of the island chiefs, Kamanawa, chief of the district of Hilo.

[2] Baker, Swaine, Whidbey and Menzies were present, according to Bell.

present they were completely independent, under no sort of engagement whatever, and were free to make choice of that state which in their opinion was most likely by its attention to their security and interests, to answer the purpose for which the proposed surrender was intended. For his own part he did not hesitate to declare the preference he entertained for the king of Great Britain, to whom he was ready to acknowledge his submission; and demanded to know who had any objection to follow his example. This produced an harangue from each of the five chiefs, all of whom had some ideas to offer on this important subject.

The warlike spirit and ambitious views of *Kahowmotoo* had long taught him to indulge the flattering hope, that on some future day he should be enabled to acquire the sovereignty of Mowee. This prompted him to state in a spirited and manly speech, that on their becoming connected and attached to so powerful a nation, they ought no longer to suffer the indignities which had been offered to their island, Owhyhee, by the people of Mowee; he also candidly enumerated the offences that Mowee had justly to complain of in return; but as these bore no proportion to her aggressions, he contended that she ought to be chastised, and that when a force for their protection should be obtained from England, the first object of its employment ought to be the conquest of Mowee;[1] after which the care of its government should be intrusted to some respectable chief, whose interest and inclination could be depended upon as being friendly towards Owhyhee.

Kavaheeroo, a chief of a very different disposition, content with the station he filled, and the comforts he enjoyed, looked forward with pleasure to the consequences that were likely to result from the adoption of the measure proposed; having no doubt of its tending to their future safety and protection, which had now become highly expedient in some way to effect, and of its being the means of producing a general pacification with their relations and friends, as he termed them, on the other islands.[2]

Tianna, after agreeing with *Kahowmotoo*, that Mowee ought to be chastised; and with *Kavaheeroo*, in the necessity of Owhyhee being protected; proposed that some persons, duly authorized for that purpose, should reside on shore by way of guards, and stated that a vessel or two would be requisite to defend them by sea. He very judiciously observed further, that so great a similarity

[1] Menzies gives an interesting variant. He understood that Tamaahmotoo (Kameeia-moku) stated that 'Taiteree King of the other Islands had at different times made four descents on Owhyhee, & that they had as yet made only one descent on his territories he therefore urged the justice of making three descents more, to be even with him, & when the event of these three descents were accomplished he should then rest satisfied.' – 25 February.

[2] Menzies noted that the existence of the *Britannia* was important, as she promised to provide a temporary solution to the problem of defence: 'it was urged by the King & others, that the Boat which our Carpenters had built for them, when equippd & riggd with the Cordage & Canvas that had been given them from both Vessels, would be the means of defending the Island & overawing their enemies from further attack.' – 25 February.

existed between the people of the four nations with whom they were already acquainted, but more particularly so between the English and the Americans, that in the event of their present surrender being accepted, and of a vessel being sent out for their protection, they should be doubtful as to the reality of such persons coming from England, unless some of the officers then present, or some of those on board the vessels with whom they were acquainted, and who they were convinced did belong to King George, should return to Owhyhee with the succours required. This appeared to him a measure of so much consequence that it could not be dispensed with, for otherwise, any of the distant nations, knowing they had ceded the island to the English government, might send to them ships and men whom they had never before seen, and who, by asserting they had come from England and belonged to King George, would deceive them into the obedience of a people against whom they should afterwards most probably revolt.

These were the prominent features in the several speeches made on the occasion: in every one of which their religion, government, and domestic œconomy was noticed; and it was clearly understood, that no interference was to take place in either; that *Tamaahmaah*, the chiefs and priests, were to continue as usual to officiate with the same authority as before in their respective stations, and that no alteration in those particulars was in any degree thought of or intended.

These preliminaries being fully discussed, and thoroughly understood on both sides, the king repeated his former proposition, which was now unanimously approved of, and the whole party declared their consent by saying, that they were no longer *Tanata no Owhyhee*, (i.e.) the people of Owhyhee; but *Tanata no Britannee*, (i.e.) the people of Britain. This was instantly made known to the surrounding crowd in their numerous canoes about the vessels, and the same expressions were cheerfully repeated throughout the attending multitude.

Mr. Puget, accompanied by some of the officers, immediately went on shore; there displayed the British colours, and took possession of the island in His Majesty's name, in conformity to the inclination and desire of *Tamaahmaah* and his subjects. On this ceremony being finished, a salute was fired from the vessels, after which the following inscription on copper was deposited in a very conspicuous place at the royal residence.

' On the 25th of February, 1794, *Tamaahmaah* king of Owhyhee, in council with the principal chiefs of the island, assembled on board His Britannic Majesty's sloop Discovery in Karakakooa bay, and in the presence of George Vancouver, commander of the said sloop; Lieutenant Peter Puget, commander of his said Majesty's armed tender the Chatham; and the other officers of the Discovery; after due consideration, unanimously ceded the said island of Owhyhee to His Britannic Majesty, and acknowledged themselves to be subjects of Great Britain.'[1]

[1] 'Two plates of Copper, on which was engraved the Cession of the Island were left here by Captn. Vancouver, one of which was to be nailed on a conspicuous Spot at this

Such a distribution of useful or ornamental articles was now made to the principal chiefs, their favorite women, and other attendants, as *Tamaahmaah* and myself esteemed to be suitable to their respective ranks and stations on this memorable occasion.

Thus concluded the ceremonies of ceding the island of Owhyhee to the British crown; but whether this addition to the empire will ever be of any importance to Great Britain, or whether the surrender of the island will ever be attended with any additional happiness to its people, time alone must determine. It was however a matter of great satisfaction to me, that this concession had not only been voluntary but general; that it had not been suggested by a party, nor been the wish of a few, but the desire of every inhabitant with whom we had any conversation on the subject; most of these having attended the external ceremonies, without shewing any other signs than those of perfect approbation; and the whole business having been conducted by the king and his advisers with great steadiness, and in the most serious manner, left me no doubt of the sincerity of their intentions to abide strictly by their engagement.

This transaction must ever be considered, under all the attendant circumstances, as of a peculiar nature; and will serve to shew that man, even in his rude uncultivated state, will not, except from apprehension or the most pressing necessity, voluntarily deliver up to another his legitimate rights of territorial jurisdiction.

With respect to astronomical observations whilst at Karakakooa, our attention had been principally directed to the rates and errors of the chronometers; these on being landed the 21st of January, 1794, shewed the longitude by Kendall's to be   205° 8' 45"

Arnold's No. 14,   204 26

Ditto 176,   204 1

The true longitude of Karakakoo being 204°,[1] shews their respective errors; by which Kendall's chronometer was at noon on the 19th of February, 1794, fast of mean time at Greenwich 3^h 30' 17" 59'''

And, by twenty-six days corresponding altitudes, was found to be gaining on mean time per day at the rate of   15 16

Arnold's No. 14, fast of mean time at Greenwich, as above,   3 25 49 59

And gaining on mean time per day at the rate of   21 12

Arnold's No. 176, fast of mean time at Greenwich, as above,   7 38 33 59

And gaining on mean time per day at the rate of   48 28

Bay, and the other near the King's residence at Whyatea. Two other plates of Copper for the Boat were also left, one to [be] nail'd on her Stern, mentioning by whom she was built, her dimensions &c.' – Bell, February. None of these plates is known to have survived.

[1] The correct position is long. 155° 56' W (204° 04' E).

Arnold's No. 82, on board the Chatham, fast of
mean time at Greenwich, as above,   8ʰ 25′ 53″ 59‴
And gaining on mean time per day at the rate of   35 25

The latitude, by twenty-one meridional altitudes of the sun, and three
meridional altitudes of the stars, varying from 19° 27′ 27″ to 19° 28′ 27″; and
differing 20″ from the mean result of the observations made in the month of
March, 1793, shewed by the mean result of both years observations, the
latitude to be 19° 28′ 2″.[1]

[1] Very close to the official reading, which is lat. 19° 28′ N.

CHAPTER III.

Quit Karakakooa—Visit Tyahtatooa and Toeaigh Bays—Some Description of the Anchorage at those Places—Examine the Northern Sides of Mowee, Woahoo, and Attowai—Observations on the Anchorage at Attowai and Onehow—Leave the Sandwich Islands.

NOTHING now remained to detain us in Karakakooa bay, the memorable spot where Captain Cook unfortunately fell a sacrifice to his undaunted and enterprising spirit. Notwithstanding it had, in that melancholy instance, proved fatal to one of the most illustrious navigators that the world ever produced, yet to us it had proved an asylum, where the hospitable reception, and friendly treatment were such as could not have been surpassed by the most enlightened nation of the earth. The unremitted attention in the superior classes, to preserve good order, and insure the faithful discharge of every service undertaken by the subordinate description of the people, produced an uniform degree of respect in their deportment, a cheerful obedience to the commands they received, and a strict observance and conformity to fair and honest dealing in all their commercial intercourse. Excepting in the instances of the table knives, the centinel's cartridge box, and a few others of little moment, occasioned, very probably, by our want of discretion in leaving irresistible temptations in their way, we had little to complain of; and such circumstances of this nature as did occur, ought only to be considered as reflections on the particular individuals concerned, and not as generally characteristic of the whole people.

All our friends were prepared to attend us; some were on board, and others were in their canoes, ready to follow the ship as soon as she got under sail. This was effected about three in the morning of Wednesday the 26th. Accompanied by the Chatham, we directed our course, with a light land breeze, close along the shore, toward Tyahtatooa bay;[1] the morning was delightfully pleasant, and the surrounding objects, whilst they attracted our attention, excited also our admiration. The country which, as we passed, rose with a gradual ascent from the sea shore, seemed to be in a high state of cultivation, and was interspersed with a great number of extensive villages; whilst our numerous companions on the surface of a serene tranquil ocean, fanned by a gentle breeze, to which some spread their sails, and the rest kept

[1] Kaiakekua Bay.

up with us by leisurely paddling along, added considerable beauty to the interesting scene, and exhibited, by this numerous population, that wealth which the improved state of this part of the island so strongly indicated. About eight o'clock we anchored in Tyahtatooa, bay, in 15 fathoms water, sand and rocky bottom.

According to Mr. Meares's account of Mr. Douglas's voyage, this place is represented as equal, if not superior, to Karakakooa, for secure anchorage; but to us it appeared in a very different point of view, as it is formed by a small bend only in the general direction of the coast, scarcely deserving the name of a bay.[1] Its northernmost point from us bore by compass N. 69 W.; the village called Ane-oo-ooa,[2] being the nearest shore, N. 30 E., about half a mile distant; and the point of Kowrooa S. 22 E. The station we had taken was as close to the land as we could with prudence lie, and the bottom, in all directions where we sounded, was a mixture of rocks and sand. A considerable swell rolled in from the westward, and by the beaten appearance of the rocks that chiefly composed the shore, this appeared to be in general the case; and for that reason not a very eligible resting place for shipping. It however possesses an advantage with respect to landing, superior to Karakakooa. This convenience is produced by the jutting out of two points; between these is a small cove, defended by some rocks lying before it, which break the violence of the surge, and render the communication with the shore very commodious.[3] The landing is on a sandy beach, before a grove of cocoa nut, bread fruit, and other trees, in the midst of which the village is situated. Towards the south part of this cove is a spring, which rose very rapidly from amongst some rocks that are generally covered with the sea water; but when this is low, which is sometimes the case, it is found to produce a stream of excellent fresh water; and there can be no doubt, by using proper means, that its current might be diverted, and made subservient to the domestic use of the neighbourhood, and to vessels refitting at Karakakooa, without their being under the necessity of submitting to the tardy process we were compelled to adopt; especially as the distance between the two places is only ten miles.

The southern base of mount Worroray[4] forms these shores. This mountain, with Mowna Kaah, and Mowna Roa, form each a large mass of elevated land,

[1] Meares refers to it as Tiroway Bay and states that it was 'superior in many respects to Karakakooa, the ground being extremely good, with not a spot of coral rock in any part of it: besides, vessels may lie at such a distance from the shore, that if the wind blows, they can clear the land with safety.' – *Voyages*, p. 355. The *Iphigenia* was in the bay on 3 March 1789. The abstract of her log gives the lat. of her anchorage as 19° 41′ N. Menzies gives the lat. of the *Discovery's* anchorage as 19° 38′ N. – February 26.

[2] This was the village from which Menzies had set out in January to travel overland and climb Hualalai. He relates that he embarked 'in one of the King's large double Canoes & proceeded along the shore to the Northward till we came to Taitatooa bay in the bottom of which we landed...at the village of Hannoora'. – January 16.

[3] This probably accounts for the good opinion of the natives, to whom ease of landing was important. They would not appreciate the problems of ships as large as the *Discovery*.

[4] Hualalai.

of which the island chiefly consists, though mount Worroray is the smallest.

Accompanied by *Tamaahmaah*, some of the officers, and several of the chiefs, I visited the royal residence at this place; which consisted of three of the neatest constructed houses we had yet seen; but not having been constantly inhabited for some time past, they were not in good repair. This habitation of the king, like that at Karakakooa, was in the neighbourhood of a grand morai, close to the sea side. The morai was the most complete structure of the kind, and kept in the greatest order and repair, of any that had fallen under our observation. It was decorated with several statues, or idols, carved out of the trunks of large trees, and meant to imitate the human form; but they were the most gigantic and preposterous figures that can be imagined.

Having satisfied our curiosity, we returned on board to dinner, which was purposely ordered of beef and mutton, to give all the chiefs an idea of the value of the animals I had imported, as articles of food; our party was numerous, and they unanimously agreed that both were excellent. The beef, though salted, seemed to have the preference in their opinion; the mutton was by most considered to be very similar in its taste to the flesh of their dogs, which they very highly esteem. The general opinion was taken by vote on the superior excellence of mutton to dog's flesh, and the preference was decided in favour of mutton, only by the casting voice of *Tamaahmaah*.

I was very anxious to quit this station, which is situated in latitude 19° 37½′, longitude 203° 54½,[1] lest the rocky bottom should damage our cables; but light breezes from the sea, succeeded by calms, prevented our moving until midnight, when, with a gentle breeze from the shore, we proceeded slowly along the coast to the northward.

In the forenoon of Thursday the 27th, we had a light breeze from the westward; with this we steered for the anchorage at Toeaigh,[2] but a strong current setting to the south-westward, we approached it very slowly; the weather however was fair and pleasant, and the objects about us were cheerful and entertaining, notwithstanding the adjacent shores were uninteresting, being chiefly composed of volcanic matter, and producing only a few detached groves of cocoa nut trees, with the appearance of little cultivation, and very few inhabitants. The deficiency of the population on shore was amply compensated by the number of our friends that accompanied us afloat in canoes of all descriptions; these still preserving the same orderly behaviour and cheerful good humour, our change of situation was scarcely perceivable, as the same sociability and friendly intercourse continued which had existed at Karakakooa.

As this evening was to be devoted to an appointed *taboo* that would continue until the morning of the 1st of March, the king and the rest of our friends went on shore for the purpose of attending their religious duties. The weather

[1] The correct position is lat. 19° 39′ N, long. 156° 00′ W (204° 00′ E).
[2] Kawaihae Bay.

in the evening being squally, with variable winds and alternate calms, gave me reason to believe it very probable that we should not reach our destination before it was dark; on intimating this to *Tamaahmaah*, he promised to have a light placed in such a situation, as would conduct us to it with safety.

It was not however until near four the next morning, Friday the 28th, that we gained soundings, when we anchored in 30 fathoms water, sandy bottom. After it was day-light we removed to the best anchorage in this bay, whose north-west point bore by compass N. 36 W. and the morai, N. 68 E.; this is a conspicious object, and a good leading mark to this anchorage; it is situated on a barren eminence to the southward of the village, and is to be kept in a line with a small saddle hill, on the eastern land descending from the higher parts, over the village of Toeaigh, on the north side of this spacious open bay. Its south point descending gradually from Worroray, and forming a low point, bore by compass S. 31 W.; within this point on the rising land are some elevated hummocks; the third of these, from the point forming a kind of saddle hill in a line with a low, projecting, black, rocky point, in the middle of the bay, bearing S. 22 W., is a further direction, and a cross mark for this anchorage; from whence the watering place lies S. 79 E., a mile and a half distant. The summit of Mowna-kaah also bore by compass S. 68 E.; Mowna Roa, S. 33 E.; and Worroray, S. 5 W. In this situation the depth of water was 25 fathoms, the bottom a stiff clay, and good holding ground; incommoded by the patch of rocky bottom, stated on our former visit to be at the depth of 10 fathoms only; but on a more minute search, this was now discovered to shoal suddenly, and the depth to decrease to 7, 4, and 3 fathoms, about the fourth of a mile to the south-westward of the station we had taken; and consequently to be a very great inconveniency to the roadstead, which at best, in my opinion, is but a very indifferent one; being intirely exposed to the north-west winds, and the western oceanic swell, which beats with great violence on the reefs that encompass the shores. These reefs stretch out a mile or upwards, leaving between them and the land a narrow channel, that affords comfortable and commodious landing for small boats and canoes; but the landing is at too great a distance from the place of anchorage to allow of protecting any debarkation from the ship.

The only circumstances that seem to render this a desirable stopping place, are the run of water, which however does not constantly flow; and the probability of procuring refreshments, from its contiguity to the fertile, and populous western part of the district of Koaarra,[1] and the plains of Whymea,[2] lying behind the land that constitutes this part of the sea coast.

The country rises rather quickly from the sea side, and, so far as it could be seen on our approach, had no very promising aspect; it forms a kind of glacis, or inclined plane in front of the mountains, immediately behind which the plains of Whymea are stated to commence, which are reputed to be very rich and productive, occupying a space of several miles in extent, and winding

---

[1] Kohala District.   [2] Waimea.

at the foot of these three lofty mountains far into the country. In this valley is a great tract of luxuriant, natural pasture, whither all the cattle and sheep imported by me were to be driven, there to roam unrestrained, to 'increase and multiply' far from the sight of strangers, and consequently less likely to tempt the inhabitants to violate the sacred promise they had made; the observance of which, for the time stipulated in their interdiction, cannot fail to render the extirpation of these animals a task not easily to be accomplished.

This day being devoted to their holy rites, the king, with all the provincial chiefs, remained in sacred retirement. The same cause operated to deprive us of the society of our other visitors, particularly the females, who are on no account permitted to be afloat on these occasions.

The next morning, Saturday, March the 1st, the king, with all our friends, were again about the vessels. In the course of the day a further proof of the liberality of *Tamaahmaah's* disposition was given, by his presenting us with near an hundred hogs of the largest size, and as great a quantity of vegetables as both vessels could well dispose of; with offers of a further supply if these were insufficient.

It was my intention to have sailed with the land wind in the evening, but *Tamaahmaah* pointing out that since Thursday his engagements on shore had totally deprived him of our society; first by his attendance on their religious ceremonies, and afterwards in procuring and sending us the supplies we required; and soliciting, at the same time, in the most earnest manner, that the last day should be dedicated to the enjoyment of each other's company, I was induced to remain the following day, to prove to him that there was no indulgence in my power, compatible with my duty, that I would not grant, in return for the friendship and regard he had on all occasions manifested towards us, and that in the most princely and unlimited manner.[1]

The succeeding day, Sunday the 2d, was consequently passed in receiving farewell visits, and making farewell acknowledgments to our numerous friends; who all expressed the high satisfaction they had experienced during our residence amongst them, and the deep regret they felt at our departure from the island; after which they were seen to steal away gently and reluctantly from a scene that had afforded them so many valuable acquirements, and so much pleasing entertainment. By sun-set nearly the whole group was dispersed in the several directions to which their inclinations or necessities

---

[1] Menzies tells a different story. He relates that Kamehameha 'askd Capt Vancouver at parting, to add to his other presents as much red cloth as would make him a Maro [loin cloth], a thing in great estimation at this time amongst the Chiefs, & would not require above half a yard of Cloth; this was refusd him, from what motives we know not, & he left the ship apparently in a huff. On his way to the shore he went with the Queen & John Young to take leave of his friends on board the Chatham, where he complaind of Capt Vancouvers stinginess, & told the story in a manner that induced the Commander of that Vessel [Puget] to present him with the last piece of red cloth he had. The refusal of a trifle of this kind, on such an occasion, cannot be viewed in a favourable light, when we reflect on the boundless generosity of this worthy prince towards us'. – March 3.

led. The occurrences of this day did not pass over without producing some impressions on our sensibility, from the repeated ardent solicitations that we would come back to them again, and from the undisguised sincerity of the wishes and prayers that were offered up for our future happiness and prosperity.

As our departure was to take place with the first breeze from the land, *Tamaahmaah* and his queen, unwilling to take leave until the very last moment, remained on board until near midnight, when they departed, with hearts too full to express the sensations which the moment of separation produced in each;[1] with them their honest and judicious counsellors Young and Davis returned to the shore. The good sense, moderation, and propriety of conduct in these men, daily increased their own respectability, and augmented the esteem and regard, not only of the king and all his friends, but even of those who were professedly adverse to the existing government, and who consequently were at first inimical to their interest.

As it was a great uncertainty whether we should or should not return again to these islands, I had given these two worthy characters their choice of taking their passage with me to their native country, or of remaining on the island in the same situation which they had so long filled with credit to themselves, and with so much satisfaction to the king and the rest of the principal people. After mature consideration, they preferred their present way of life, and were desirous of continuing at Owhyhee; observing, that being destitute of resources, on their return home, (which, however, they spoke of in a way that did honor to their hearts and understandings) they must be again exposed to the vicissitudes of a life of hard labour, for the purpose of merely acquiring a precarious supply of the most common necessaries of life; objects which,

---

[1] The departure was marred by some last-minute pilfering. 'I am sorry to observe that one of the Chiefs, in whom we had placed some confidence & who was amongst those we constantly admitted on board, was this day detected in pilfering some articles out of the Cabin, with which he made his escape on shore, & we were afterwards informd that three or four select friends of high rank amongst whom were Terimyty [Keliimaikai] the Kings brother, who was sufferd to remain on board the Chatham till the last moment, found means by the darkness of the night to carry off unnoticed half a dozen table knives, the breech pins belonging to the Swivels on the quarter deck & some other trifling articles, which were not missed till the day following.' Deeply disappointed, Menzies felt that these thefts were 'traits of various principles in their character which we cannot reconcile to their former behaviour, far less palliate or excuse,' and that it was 'but reasonable to conclude that their honesty hitherto towards us, has been the effect of fear, or the dread of punishment.' – Menzies, March 1. As the ship sailed slowly along the coast, Menzies notes that one odd item had been overlooked when Kamehameha was making his final departure from the *Discovery*: 'some straggling Canoes came off to us...& finding that the Kings spitting box had been left on board...we prevaild on one of them to carry it on shore to him...Tamaihamaiha was at times subject to considerable mucus expectoration, & whether from cleanliness or some superstitious notion of the priests we knew not, but a man generally followed him with a box to spit in, & as he had dispensed with his retinue some hours before he went ashore himself...the box had been forgot & left on board the ship.' – March 3.

for some years past, had not occasioned them the least concern. Nor was it probable that they would be liable hereafter to any sort of inconvenience in those respects; for, besides the high reputation, and universal good opinion they had acquired amongst all classes of the inhabitants, they were now considered in the light of chiefs, and each of them possessed a considerable landed property. Here they lived happily, and in the greatest plenty; and, to their praise be it spoken, the principal object they seemed to have in view was, to correct, by gentle means, the vices, and encourage, by the most laudable endeavors, the virtues, of these islanders; in this meritorious undertaking they had evidently made some progress, and there are reasonable grounds to believe, that, by steadily pursuing the same line of conduct, it will in time have a due influence on the general character of these people. From us they received every attention that could serve to raise them in the estimation of the natives; and such an assortment of useful articles for promoting their comforts, as it was in our power to afford.[1]

Our faithful shipmate *Terehooa*, who, to the last moment, conducted himself with the greatest integrity and propriety, was also left very advantageously situated under the protection of the king and his old master *Kahowmotoo*, with a large assortment of useful implements, and ornamental articles; and being firmly attached to Young and Davis, to whom he could be very useful, and who had it in their power to serve him in return, his future prospects in life seemed to have been much improved by his excursions in the Discovery, of which he seemed very sensible, and which he gratefully acknowledged.

Thus concluded our transactions at Owhyhee, to which we bade adieu about three in the morning of Monday the 3d of March, very highly indebted for our reception, and the abundant refreshments we had procured.[2] These essential comforts I should have entertained no doubt would, in future, have been administered to all visitors who should conduct themselves with common honesty and proper decorum, had we not left behind us a banditti of renegadoes, that had quitted different trading vessels in consequence of disputes with their respective commanders, who had resorted to this island since the preceding year, under American or Portuguese colours. Amongst them was one Portuguese, one Chinese, and one Genoese, but all the rest appeared to be the subjects of Great Britain, as seemed also the major part of the crew of

[1] When Vancouver returned to England he placed an advertisement in a London newspaper to inform relatives of Davis and Young that they were alive and well. Sarah Davis, Davis's sister, sent him a letter, now in the State Archives of Hawaii, begging him to come home, but, no doubt for the reasons Vancouver suggests, he stayed in the Islands.

[2] Menzies cites the supply of hogs as an example: 'The Discovery Chatham & Daedalus could not according to our estimation have taken less than a thousand Hogs between them during our stay, & the Lady Washington who was here five or six weeks before us & salted more than our three Vessels together, must have taken about four or five hundred, & yet there was no apparent scarcity of these Animals, which shews that this Island is by far the best of the group for Vessels to refresh at.' – 2 March.

the brig Washington, although they called themselves Americans. These latter persons, in the character of sailors, amounting to six or seven in number, had taken up their abode with different chiefs of some power and consequence, who esteemed these people as great acquisitions, from their knowledge of fire-arms; but as no one of them could produce any testimonials of their former good conduct, or even make out a plausible character for himself or his comrades, it is much to be apprehended they may be the means of creating intestine commotions, by inciting the jealousy, and furthering the ambitious views of the haughty chiefs, with whom they are resident. Their machinations to the prejudice of the existing government, however, will prove ineffectual, unless they should be able to elude the watchful attention of Young and Davis; who are both well aware of the danger they ought to be prepared to meet; and whose fidelity to *Tamaahmaah*, I had every reason to believe, was not of a nature to be shaken by the most flattering temptations.

That these apprehensions were well founded I could not entertain the least doubt; for soon after my arrival at Owhyhee, I received, by Young, a letter from Mr. William Brown, commanding the Butterworth of London, complaining heavily of a similar set of vagabonds, residing at Whoahoo and at Attowai, who had, at the latter place, taken up arms in support of an inferior chief, against the authority of *Taio* and *Titeeree*, the sovereigns of that island; and had so far forgotten their allegiance, and the rules which humanity, justice, and common honesty prescribe, as to concert, with the natives of Attowai, a plan for the capturing of an American brig, called the Hancock.[2] This was to have been effected by scuttling her under water, which would induce the crew to suppose she had sprung a very bad leak; when these renegadoes were to advise her being hauled on shore, for the purpose of saving from her as much as possible; and when in this situation she would be completely in the power, and at the disposal, of the natives. But, happily for those in the vessel, although she was near sinking, in consequence of a hole cut in her counter by some unknown hand, the rest of the diabolical scheme was detected before the contrivers had time or opportunity to carry it into execution, and by the exertions of the crew the vessel was saved.

Mr. Brown stated further, that by the bad advice, and far worse example, of these people, the natives of most of the leeward islands had arrived at such a degree of daring insolence, as rendered any communication with them from small vessels, or even anchoring near the shores, highly dangerous; and that he trusted it might be within the limits of my authority to take from these islands such improper and dangerous associates.

I represented in the strongest terms to *Tamaahmaah* all the bad consequences that were likely to result from those people remaining on Owhyhee; but no arguments could prevail upon him or the chiefs, to deliver them up. Their

---

[1] A Boston brigantine of 157 tons, commanded by Samuel Crowell. The attempt to seize the ship took place in 1791, when she called at the islands on her way to the Northwest Coast.

knowledge in the use and management of fire-arms, made their services of such importance, that it was evident nothing but compulsion would have any effect; and to have resorted to such a measure, in which I was by no means certain how far I should be justifiable, would necessarily have produced a breach, and destroyed that harmony which we had taken so much pains to establish, and care to preserve. In addition to which, these people were stated to possess landed property in the island, and to have conformed to the laws, both civil and religious. Nor had any specific charge been exhibited against the seven sailors living on Owhyhee, like that produced by Mr. Brown against those at Attowai and Woahoo.

With *Kavaheeroo* also resided a person by the name of Howell, who had come to Owhyhee in the capacity of a clerk on board the Washington; he appeared to possess a good understanding, with the advantages of an university education, and had been once a clergyman in England, but had now secluded himself from European society: so that with Young, Davis, and Boid, there were now eleven white men on the island;[1] but, excepting from these latter, I much fear that our Owhyhean friends will have little reason to rejoice in any advantages they will receive from their new civilized companions.

To Young and Davis I delivered such testimonials of their good conduct as I considered them fully intitled to, for the purpose of securing to them the respect and confidence of future visitors, who would be warned by them of the snares and dangers they were liable to, from the evil-disposed, civilized or savage inhabitants of the country.

The land wind blew faintly, and our progress from Owhyhee was so slow, that an opportunity was offered to a few small canoes from the shores of Koaarra to visit us as we passed; but we did not recognize any of the chiefs, or our former acquaintances. Towards noon the sea breeze reached us, with which we stood to windward, in order to pass to the north of the east point of Mowee; this engaged our time until afternoon on the following day, Tuesday the 4th, when we bore away along the north side of that island.

In this route we fell in with the south-east side of Mowee, near to the station

---

[1] Bell listed them as follows: 'Boyd came round, as did also a Portuguese Sailor that had been left here by a Vessel from Macao, and two other Sailors that had left Mr. Kendrick's Brig [the *Lady Washington*] in a State of ill health, – besides these people who all intended to remain on the Island, there were two other men who had also belonged to Mr. Kendrick's Brig, and a Gentleman of the name of Howell, who came out as a passenger from China in the Same Brig, – and two other Sailors that had left an American Vessel call'd the Hancock, Crowell, – making in all (including Young and Davis) Eleven white Men who intended remaining in the Island, and a most curious collection they were, for among them, were English, Irish, Portuguese, Genoaese Americans and Chinese.' January. Puget met Dinsdale, one of the men from the *Hancock*, and relates that 'under a pretence of Arrears of Wages... [he] engaged a Canoe and in the Night robbed that Vessel of some Skins and Small Guns and some Musquets. Such an audacious Act of Piracy must however here go unpunished and as the Islanders have not sufficient discernment to see through his Infamous Conduct only having heard his Story filled with *Cruelties* he is received as an injured and oppressed Person.' – 27 January.

where our survey had commenced the preceding year; and in beating round the western[1] part of the island, which does not terminate in a projecting point, but forms a large rounding promontory, we very anxiously looked out for the harbour mentioned by Captain King, as reported by the natives to exist in that neighbourhood; but nothing was seen that could warrant such a representation, excepting two small open coves, situated on each side of the eastern extremity of the island; these, answering all the purposes of the inhabitants with their canoes, probably induced them to suppose that such accommodations were all we required. Off this eastern extremity, which, according to our observations, is situated in latitude 20° 44½′, longitude 203° 58′,[2] and bearing by compass from the north-west[3] point of Owhyhee, N. 7 W. at the distance of nine leagues, lies a small islet, with some rocks between it and the shore.[4] To the north of this islet is a remarkably elevated hummock, rising almost perpendicularly from the sea, but gradually descending in a slope in land; it was covered with a pleasing verdure, and occupied by several houses, but destitute of trees or shrubs. The adjacent country, which was moderately elevated, presented a fertile appearance, and seemed to be thickly inhabited, as far back as the foot of those mountains that compose the eastern part of the island. As we passed this rounding promontory, some detached rocks were noticed lying about half a mile from the shore, along which we sailed at a distance from two to four miles, and found it a little indented, and chiefly composed of steep rugged cliffs.

The wind being light, enabled a few of the natives to visit us during the afternoon, but they had little with them to dispose of; in the evening they returned home, and at dark we hauled off the shore in order to preserve our station for continuing our survey. The next morning, Wednesday the 5th, we again stood in for the land, passing the deep bay that bounds the northern side of the isthmus,[5] which connects the two lofty ranges of mountains that form the island of Mowee. A very heavy surf beat on the low sandy shores of the bay, from whence a few of the natives, as ill appointed for barter as the former, paid us a visit.

From these people we understood that *Titeeree* was at Woahoo, and that *Taio* was at Morotoi; but that *Namahanna*, who in the absence of *Titeeree* had been left in charge of the government, accompanied by three or four other chiefs and some inferior people, were unfortunately in a house that contained the major part of the gunpowder *Titeeree* possessed, when it took fire and blew up. By this accident *Namahanna*, with two other chiefs and some of the people, had been killed, and all the rest had been very badly wounded. This house appeared, by their account, to have been appropriated by *Titeeree* as a

---

[1] 'eastern' not 'western'.

[2] Kauiki Head, in lat. 20° 45′ N, long. 155° 59′ W (204° 01′ E).

[3] 'north-east' not 'north-west'.

[4] Alau Island would seem to be the only possible identification; it is a mile and a half S of Kauiki Head.   [5] Kahului Bay.

magazine; that the accident had happened only a few days before our arrival, and that some of the persons who had been hurt had since died of their wounds.[1]

A fine breeze from the N.E. with clear and pleasant weather, brought us by noon up to the north-west point of Mowee. The observed latitude at this time was 21° 7', longitude 203° 23'.[2] The point bore by compass S. 8 W. distant four miles; off this lay an islet and some rocks, at a small distance from the shore, which is steep and cliffy. Having thus completed our intended survey of Mowee, we stood over, and brought to within about half a league of the north-east point of Morotoi,[3] in the expectation of seeing *Taio*; for whom, as well as for *Titeeree*, I had reserved some sheep, for establishing the breed in each of the islands. *Taio*, we had understood, resided somewhere hereabouts, and some of the natives who came off to us repeated this intelligence, but added that the day being *taboo poory*, it was impossible we should receive a visit from him.

We continued nearly stationary for three hours in the hope of obtaining some vegetables, but none were to be procured; at five we made sail, and as the Chatham the preceding year had examined the north side of this land, our course was directed for the north-east side of Woahoo; which, at day-light the succeeding morning, Thursday the 6th, bore by compass from W. to S. 27 W. and Morotoi, from S. 32 E. to S. 45 E. We continued our survey from what we had formerly examined on the southern part of this side of the island, and shortly after noon we passed its north point; which, according to our observations, is in latitude 21° 42½', longitude 202° 1';[4] the former being three miles further south, and the latter fourteen miles further west, than the situation of that point as laid down by Captain King; our present survey, however, corresponded with our former observations, as to the position of the south-east point of Woahoo; and made this side of the island four miles longer than Captain King's delineation, and agreed better with our estimated distance between Woahoo and Attowai. In every other respect our examination confirmed the remarks of Captain King; excepting, that in point of cultivation or fertility, the country did not appear in so flourishing a state, nor to be so numerously inhabited, as he represented it to have been at that time, occasioned most probably by the constant hostilities that had existed since that period.

My intentions were to have stopped near the run of water off which the Resolution and Discovery had anchored, called by the natives Whymea,[5] and

---

[1] Menzies learned that the accident had happened eight days before: 'The manner in which it happened as nearly as we could collect from their different stories of it, was by one of the Chiefs carelessly snapping a pistol near an open Calibash of Gunpowder, round which they were all setting, & by some accidental spark falling into it, the whole took fire, & blew them & the house up in a moment.' – March 4.

[2] Lipoa Point, in lat. 21° 02' N, long. 156° 39' W (203° 21' E).

[3] Cape Halawa, the NE point of Molokai.

[4] Kahuku Point, in lat. 21° 43' N, long. 157° 59' W (202° 01' E).   [5] Waimea.

rendered memorable by the fatal catastrophe that had awaited the commander and the astronomer of the Dædalus. Here I was in expectation of procuring an interview with *Titeeree*, who we had been informed was then in this neighbourhood; but learning from a few of the inhabitants, who visited us in a small, shabby, single canoe, that he was gone to Whyteete, and there being at this time a very heavy north-west swell that broke incessantly, and with great violence, on all the adjacent shores, to which, from their greatly exposed situation, they seemed very liable; and having also finished our survey, we quitted Woahoo, and directed our course towards the north-east part of Attowai,[1] which at day-light in the morning of Friday the 7th, bore by compass from N. 84 W. to S. 40 W. As we approached its shores, the same influence was felt from a northerly current, as we had before experienced; but the wind being to the southward, it did not prevent our passing to the north of the island, which, at noon, bore by compass from S. 75 W. to S. 25 E.; and the north-east extremity of the island, extending from the forked hill mentioned on our last visit hither, S. 13 E., distant three miles and a half. In this situation the observed latitude was 22° 15′, longitude 200° 36′. Here we rejoined the American brig Washington, which had sailed with us from Karakakooa, but had directed her course to the southward of the islands, for Whyteete in Woahoo, where she had remained five days. Amongst other articles that Mr. Kendrick had procured whilst there,[2] was eighty pounds weight of very fine bees wax, that had drifted by the sea on to the shores of that island, and had very recently been picked up by the natives; and I now understood that some pieces had also been procured from the natives of the other islands by Mr. Kendrick, who in a great measure confirmed the account contained in Mr. Brown's letter to me,[3] of the very improper conduct of the merchant seamen who had deserted, or otherwise quitted the vessels

[1] Kauai.

[2] Menzies records that Kendrick, who visited the *Discovery*, had bought 'from Taiteree a feather Cloak of nine feet deep & four & twenty feet wide in the spread at the bottom, the largest perhaps that ever was made at these Islands, for which he gave his two stern chasers mounted on their carriages.' – March 7. Sale of such a remarkable cape shows how eager the island chiefs were to acquire guns.

[3] It is surprising that Vancouver makes no mention of another letter from Brown that must have both interested and disturbed him. Menzies states that Kendrick 'shewd us a copy of a letter which Mr. Brown of the Butterworth left in Decr last with James Coleman at Waohoo, importing that Taiteree had in the most formal manner ceded to him that Island together with the four islands to windward, in consideration of some valuable presents he had made to the said Chief, & to render his claim more solemn & binding he had an instrument drawn up, which was signed by himself & four of his officers on the one hand & by Taiteree & four of his principal Chiefs on the other, after which he appointed James Coleman as resident on the Island of Waohoo in charge of his claim.' Nothing more is heard of this transaction, no doubt due to Brown's death in January 1795. In view of the scale upon which the sugar industry developed later in Hawaii it is interesting to find that Menzies also noted that 'Amongst other things which Mr. Brown left on the Island is a small Rand Sugar Mill, by the assistance of which Mr. Kendrick was enabled to make about 50 Gallons of good Molasses during his short stay.' – March 7.

to which they had belonged, for the purpose of residing amongst these
islanders. In this number were some whom he had formerly left at Attowai,
but he now seemed to be determined that they should no longer remain on
that island.

The wind during the afternoon was light and variable, consequently we
made little progress. In the course of the day we procured a small supply of
hogs, yams, and vegetables. At sun-set a small islet lying near the shore, and
situated from the north-east point of the island N. 55 W., six miles and a half
distant, bore by compass S. 33 W., about two miles from us, and the shores
of the island, which are alternately cliffs and beaches, bore from S. 50 E. to
S. 71 W.

The night was passed as usual in preserving our station, and in the morning
of Saturday the 8th, we again stood in for the land; about eight o'clock we
were off a small deep bay;[1] its east point lies from the above islet west, distant
four miles; this bay is nearly half a league wide, and about the same depth;
but being exposed to the violence of the north-westerly winds, and the oceanic
swell, is ineligible for shipping, and therefore we did not examine it further;
but continued our route with a fine breeze from the N.E. at the distance of
about two miles from the shore, passing some rocks and breakers, that extend
a small distance from the west point of the bay; where the coast of Attowai
assumes a very rugged and romantic appearance, rising suddenly to lofty
abrupt cliffs, that jet out into a variety of steep, rugged rocky points,
apparently destitute of both soil and verdure, but terminating nearly in
uniform even summits, on which, as well as in the vallies or chasms that were
formed between the points, were small patches of lively green that produced
a very singular effect. This sort of coast continued to the north-west point
of the island. As we approached this point, the regular trade wind being
intercepted by these lofty shores, we were retarded by light variable breezes,
and were frequently becalmed. At noon the observed latitude was 22° 12′,
longitude 200° 10½′. The island of Onehow[2] bore by compass from S. 34 W.
to S. 44 W.; Oreehooa,[3] S. 51 W.; and Attowai, from N. 78 E. to S. 9 E.;
its northwest point being the nearest shore, S. 37 E., distant three miles. From
this point the country assumed a very different aspect; it descended suddenly
from the mountains, and terminated in a low sandy shore, somewhat
diversified by eminences, and a few scattered habitations, but wearing a steril
and desolate appearance.

In the afternoon we were favored with a gentle northerly breeze, which
by sun-set brought us to the west point of the island, situated, according to
our observations, in latitude 22° 4′, longitude 200° 10′;[4] off which extends
a reef of rocks, about half a mile from the shore.

Having now completed the survey of Attowai, we met the regular trade

[1] Hanalei Bay.   [2] Niihau. Spelled Oneehow on Vancouver's chart.
[3] Lehua. Oreehoua on Vancouver's chart.
[4] Mana Point, in lat. 22° 02′ N, long. 159° 47′ W (200° 13′ E).

wind, with which we stood to windward for Whymea bay, in that island; where, at nine in the morning of Saturday the 9th, we anchored in 23 fathoms, soft bottom, and moored with a cable each way; the points of the bay bore by compass from N. 77 W. to S. 65 E.; the river S. 35 E., distant half a league. Here we again met the Washington; Mr. Kendrick, having beaten round the east end of the island, had arrived two days before us.

Our arrival was soon known, and we were early visited by many of our former friends and acquaintances. Amongst the number were the two young women I had brought from Nootka and settled here; during our late absence they had been treated with great kindness and civility, yet they were both very apprehensive that, on our finally quitting these seas, the attentive behaviour they had hitherto experienced would be discontinued. I however embraced the first opportunity of obtaining from all the principal chiefs the most solmen assurances of the contrary.[1]

We found *Enemo*, who had now changed his name to *Wakea*, still alive, and though in a somewhat better state of health than when we last left him, he was yet in a most deplorably emaciated condition.

Since our late departure, *Enemo* had attempted to acquire the supreme authority in the government of these islands, independent of *Titeeree* and *Taio*. To effect this object he had been assisted by Mr. Kendrick's people, and the rest of the European and American renegadoes; on whose support and knowledge in the use of fire-arms he had placed the greatest reliance, and had been induced to declare and consider his independency as certain. These proceedings soon reached the ear of *Titeeree*, who sent a chief and a party of men to inquire the cause of so sudden an alteration, and to know if it were countenanced by the chiefs and people of the island, amongst whom the regent had not been considered as very popular. But the intentions of these unfortunate people being supposed to be hostile to the interests or views of *Enemo*, they were met as they approached the shore, and, without any previous inquiry into the nature of their errand, were opposed by a small party of *Enemo*'s adherents conducted by the renegadoes, who, with their muskets drove them with great slaughter from the island, and pursued them in their flight until they left very few to relate the unfortunate issue of their embassy to *Titeeree*; and the untimely fate of those who had fallen, to their inquiring relations and friends. This melancholy event would not, most probably, have happened, had not these strangers advised and assisted in the perpetration of

---

[1] Menzies tells a quite different story: 'The eldest Taheemeerao had changed her name to Naunacottannee & told us that she livd with the Chief of Wymea as one of his wives. The other was still more fortunate, at least in point of consequence, for she became one of Ineemoh's wives. No part of their property they said was wrested from them, but according to the customs of the country, they were obligd to make presents to their Chiefs & Women of rank, & to their friends & relatives, by which the whole of their riches was soon dispersed, but by which means they became respected for their generosity & now livd comfortably & happy.' – March 9. At the time the girls were put ashore Menzies had predicted that their possessions would be dispersed in this way.

this diabolical and unprovoked barbarity; in extenuation of which they plead, that they were compelled to act this savage part in order to preserve the good opinion of, and keep themselves in favor with, the chief.

The Butterworth arriving at Woahoo shortly after the return of this unfortunate expedition, *Titeeree* solicited Mr. Brown to take him to Attowai for the purpose of effecting, in an amicable way, an accommodation with this rebellious chief. With this Mr. Brown complied, and after an explanatory interview on board his ship, all matters were compromised to the mutual satisfaction of both parties; and since that period the island has enjoyed tranquillity, though it still remained under the government of *Enemo* as regent.

But to return. We received an early visit from *Enemo* and *Tamooerrie*, accompanied only by a few chiefs, but by a great number of women, who were, for the most part, of some consequence, and attendants on his court. From the regent and prince I received a present of a few indifferent hogs, though, according to their assertions, they were some of the best on the island. The stock of these animals, they said, by the great demand from the trading vessels for them for some time past, had been much reduced; and judging from the small number that were brought for sale, we had no reason to discredit their information. A supply of vegetables was what we had principally depended upon procuring here, and in this expectation it appeared we were likely to be more successful; though the yams, by far the best species for sea store, were also very scarce.

During the afternoon the trade wind blew a very strong gale; it moderated for a few hours in the evening, but in the night was attended by heavy gusts from the N.N.E. A continuance of this weather, although it did not prevent, much retarded the natives, in their passage from the shore to the ships with the supplies we required, until the afternoon of the 11th; when it becoming more moderate, I paid my respects to the regent at his residence on shore, in consequence of an invitation to an evening amusement, which, from the description of it by the natives, was very different from those I had before attended.

Having been disappointed in seeing *Titeeree* or *Taio*, I took this opportunity of depositing with *Enemo* the breeding sheep I had intended for those chiefs; giving him to understand, that in proportion as they multiplied they were to be distributed amongst the other islands; and the produce of them were put under the same restrictions as I had exacted at Owhyhee; with all which, himself, and the chiefs then present, very seriously promised to comply.

On our arrival at the place of exhibition, we found the performers assembled, consisting of a numerous throng, chiefly of women, who were dressed in their various coloured clothes, disposed with a good effect. The entertainment consisted of three parts, and was performed by three different parties consisting of about two hundred women in each, who ranged themselves in five or six rows, not standing up, nor kneeling, but rather sitting upon their haunches. One man only advanced a few feet before the centre of the front row of the ladies, who seemed to be the hero of the piece, and, like a flugal man,[1] gave tone and action to the entertainment. In this situation and posture they exhibited a variety of gestures, almost incredible for the human body so circumstanced to perform. The whole of this numerous group was in such perfect unison of voice and action, that it were impossible, even to the bend of the finger, to have discerned the least variation. Their voices were melodious, and their actions were as innumerable as, by me, they are undescribable; they exhibited great ease and much elegance, and the whole was executed with a degree of correctness not easily to be imagined.[2] This was particularly striking in one part, where the performance instantly changed from a loud full chorus, and vast agitation in the countenances and gestures of the actors, to the most profound silence and composure; and instead of continuing in their previous erect attitude, all fell down as it were lifeless, and in their fall buried themselves under their garments; conveying, in some measure, the idea of a boisterous ocean becoming suddenly tranquillized by an instant calm. The great diversity of their figured dresses on this occasion had a particularly good effect; the several other parts were conducted with the same correctness and uniformity, but were less easy to describe. There appeared to be much variety and little repetition, not only in the acting of the respective sets, but in the whole of the three parts; the performers in which, could not amount to less than six hundred persons. This *hoorah* was completely free from the disgusting obscenity exhibited in the former entertainments, which I have before had occasion to notice. It was conducted through every part with great life and vivacity; and was, without exception, the most pleasing amusement of the kind we had seen performed in the course of the voyage.

The spectators, who were as numerous as at Owhyhee, were in their best apparel, and all retired very peaceably after the close of the performance, about the setting of the sun.

All our friends seemed to be much gratified with the applause we had bestowed, and the satisfaction we expressed at the great skill, dexterity, and taste of the performers. This entertainment was stated to be in compliment to the pregnancy of one of the regent's wives, and that it would frequently be repeated until she was brought to bed; which event was expected to take place in about three months.

In return for the amusement we had derived, we entertained the multitude after it was dark in our way, by a display of fire-works, which as usual were received with great surprize and admiration.

The weather being more settled, on the following day, Wednesday the 12th,

[1] Flugelman or fugleman: 'A soldier especially expert and well-drilled formerly placed in front of a regiment or company as an example and model to the others.' – OED.

[2] Menzies agreed: 'several pieces of vocal entertainment' were executed 'in a manner which greatly delighted us & excited our utmost astonishment at the regularity & studied elegance of the whole performance, which for grandeur & solemnity far surpassed any thing of the kind we had yet seen in the voyage.' – March 11.

we completed our water; and having procured a few hogs, with a tolerable
supply of vegetables, our intended departure was made known to the regent
prince and the rest of the chiefs; who, on receiving such presents as their
services had demanded or the occasion required, all took their leave (excepting
one or two who proposed to accompany us to Onehow) with every expression
of the most friendly regard and attachment, and with repeated solicitations
for our speedy return.

For the purpose of procuring a sea stock of yams, which we were given
to understand by the natives might be readily obtained at Onehow, we quitted
Attowai in the morning of the 13th,[1] and directed our course to that island.

By our several visits to Attowai, we had found that the roadstead of
Whymea was much confined in respect of safe anchorage; for although the
Discovery's cables had not been injured by a foul bottom, yet the Chatham,
in March 1792, when anchored in 30 fathoms water at only a convenient
distance to the north-west of the Discovery, on a bottom of soft mud, had
both her cables much fretted and damaged by the rocks at the bottom; and
not far to the eastward of our easternmost anchor was found also a patch of
rocky bottom, in some places not deeper than four fathoms, though surrounded
by a depth of from 30 to 40 fathoms.

Although a situation more convenient to the shore, in a less depth of water
and with a muddy bottom, might have been taken within the Discovery's
station, and is to be found by keeping the steep banks of the river not shut
in, but just a little open; yet, from the lurking patches of rocks that have been
found near the same sort of bottom, it is evident that great caution should be
observed to avoid those hidden dangers; which may serve to account for the
cables of former vessels having been cut through, without resorting to an
operation which appears to me incredible, and I believe impossible to have
been effected.

It had been positively asserted, and I doubt not as positively believed, that
the natives were capable of diving to the depth of 40 fathoms, and there cutting
through a twelve or fourteen inch cable; they have not only been suspected
and accused of accomplishing this task, but have been fired upon by some
whose cables have been supposed to be thus injured; an act not to be justified
by common humanity, or common sense. These people are however very
expert swimmers, and almost as dexterous as fish in the water, but their efforts
are chiefly confined to the surface, though some of them dive exceedingly
well, yet they are not capable of descending to such a depth, or of remaining
under water a sufficient time to cut through a cable.

One of the best divers of the country in *Tamaahmaah*'s estimation, I saw
endeavour at Karakakooa to recover a caulking iron that had been dropped
in 12 fathoms water; and in order to induce his utmost exertion, a great reward

---

[1] Heddington noted in his log on March 13 that 'The Time-piece [Arnold's chronometer
no. 82, in the *Chatham*] stopped, not being wound up.' Later he added: 'Set the Time-Piece
going', but Manby states that it was not set going until the 15th.

was offered to him if he succeeded; but after two unsuccessful attempts he was so tired and exhausted, that he was unable to make a third trial then, though he promised to renew his exertions the next day; the same reward was then again offered to him, but he could not be prevailed upon to make another effort, and the caulking iron remained at the bottom.

About two in the afternoon we anchored off the west side of Onehow, in 18 fathoms water, soft sandy bottom; the north-west point of the island bearing by compass N. 25 E., half a league distant; the nearest shore E.S.E., about a mile and a quarter; its west point S. 15 E.; Tahoorowa S. 43 W.; and the outer part of the reef that extends from the north-west point of Onehow, N. 8 E.

In the evening, Mr. Puget, whom I had directed to examine the north-west side of this island in the Chatham, joined us, and acquainted me that the Chatham was very crank.[1]

We had now accomplished our survey of the Sandwich islands; and as our expectations were disappointed in the promised supply of yams,[2] in the evening of Friday the 14th we took our leave of Onehow.

In the situation where we had anchored, our cables had not received any damage; but the Chatham, at anchor near us, hooked a rock under water, which engaged them some time, and was with difficulty cleared; after great danger of losing the anchor, as the cable was nearly chafed through by the rocks. It is here necessary to remark, that although this station has been the general rendezvous of the several vessels that have resorted hither, for the yams and other refreshments that Onehow once afforded, it is in all respects greatly inferior to the place of our anchorage on our former visit; the bottom here being at a greater depth, and very rocky, and the situation open, and exposed to all the violence of the north and north-west winds, and the swell of the ocean. The other situation is protected from this inconvenience, with the additional advantages of a less depth of water, and a clear bottom of good holding ground. It is not, however, quite so central for the inhabitants to bring the produce of the island to market; but this is of little importance, for when they have any to dispose of, the distance is not regarded by them.

At the anchorage we had just quitted, we left the Washington and an American ship called the Nancy; the latter had arrived only a short time before

[1] Menzies notes that 'several Tons of Iron were sent on board from the Discovery to ballast her, in order to enable her the better to withstand the boisterous weather in our Voyage to the Coast of America'. – March 14.

[2] Menzies calls the spot at which the ships anchored Yam Bay, but adds: 'there were none to be got on account of the dryness of the season & the heat of the sun, which had almost entirely destroyed their Crops & left the whole Island in a state of famine, that many of the inhabitants were obliged to remove to Atooi, & the lank emaciated appearance of those who remained on the Island, afforded a melancholy proof of the truth of this assertion'. – March 13. Hewett believed that the failure to secure a supply 'was partly in consequence of having a Chief on Board to assist in buying as I bought many [yams] in the Morning when no chief was stirring and even then they were hidden in the canoes till they were certain of having an opportunity of selling them undiscovered.'

our departure; and as it was natural to suppose that she must have recently
quitted the civilized world, her approach produced no small degree of anxiety
in the hope of obtaining some European intelligence. But we were disappointed
in these hopes, as those on board of her were as totally ignorant of transactions
there as ourselves, having been absent from New York twenty-two months;
during which time they had been principally engaged at Falkland's islands and
Staten land, in collecting seal skins and oil. Not being satisfied with their
endeavours to the southward, they had repaired hither to procure provisions
and refreshments, with the intention of proceeding afterwards to the coast of
North West America, in order to collect furs, which they understood were
to be had there; but, according to their own account, they neither knew what
were the proper commodities, nor were they possessed of any articles of traffic
for obtaining such a cargo from the inhabitants of the several countries.[1]

On sailing from Onehow, I appointed cape Douglas in Cook's river our
next place of rendezvous with the Chatham, in case of separation. There I
purposed to re-commence our survey of the coast of North West America;
and from thence to trace its boundary eastward to cape Decision, the point
which is stated to have terminated the pretended ancient Spanish discoveries.

Having ascertained satisfactorily that there was not any extensive navigation
eastwardly, between the 30th and 56th degrees of north latitude, on this side
of the American continent, I was led to believe, that if any such *did exist*, it
would most probably be found communicating with Cook's river, up which
I entertained no doubt of penetrating to a very considerable distance; and
should we not be able to complete our researches in the course of the present
season, we should at any rate, by this mode, reduce the unexplored part of
the coast within very narrow limits. And as the examination of Cook's river
appeared to me to be the most important, and I did not doubt would prove
the most laborious part of our task in the ensuring campaign, I was willing
not to lose any portion of the approaching season, but to avail ourselves of
the whole of it, for the sake of insuring, as far as was within our powers, a
certainty in the accomplishment of that object. For this purpose I wished to
be in readiness to commence the pursuit the instant the spring was sufficiently
advanced to render our endeavours practicable, and which was now likely to
be the case by the time we should reach that distance.

It was not much out of our way to ascertain the situation of a small island,
discovered in 1788 by the commander of the Prince of Wales, and by him
called Bird island, in consequence of its being the resort of vast flocks of the
feathered tribe;[2] and also to examine the neighbouring parts of the ocean,

---

[1] Nothing further seems to be known about the *Nancy*.

[2] The island is now called Nihoa. The *U.S. Coast Pilot 7* states that it was discovered
in April 1790 by Douglas in the *Iphigenia*, but this is incorrect. Menzies sorts out the
sequence of events: 'This Island was first discovered by us in the ship Prince of Wales
[Captain Colnett] in the year 1788 & on our return to the [Sandwich] Islands again in the
latter end of the same year, we questioned several of the Natives of Atooi & Oneehow
[Kauai and Niihau] concerning it, when all of them declard that they knew nothing of it,

where Captain Cook in his passage from Oonalashka to the Sandwich islands
in the year 1778 saw a shag, and other indications of the vicinity of land. For
these purposes, our course was first directed N.W. by N. in quest of Bird island,
under an easy sail, in order to allow the Chatham to come up with us, which
she did about midnight.

At day-light on Saturday the 15th we made all sail, and stood more to the
westward, surrounded by an immense number and considerable variety of
oceanic bords, consisting of the small black and white albatrosses, tropic, and
men of war birds; with boobies, noddies, and petrels of different kinds. In
the forenoon the wind at E.N.E. blew a fresh gale, and in consequence of some
of the back—stays giving way, we were obliged to reduce our sail; and as we
had but little cordage to replace such rigging, these defects became a
consideration of a very unpleasant nature in this early part of our summer's
expedition.

At noon the latitude observed was 23° 14', longitude 198° 42'; the former
was 14' further north than was shewn by our reckoning, and was nearly the
same distance to the north of the latitude assigned to Bird island; but as we
expected to find it further to the westward, though by some accounts we had
now passed its meridian, our course was directed to the south-west, and by
two in the afternoon it was seen bearing by compass W.S.W. about seven
leagues distant. About six in the evening we reached, and passed along
the southern side of, this very remarkable solitary island, or more properly
speaking, single rock, rising out of this immense ocean. Its greatest extent,
which was in a direction S. 74 W. and N. 74 E., did not exceed one mile;[1]
the uncouth form of its northern, eastern, and western extremities, against
which the sea broke with great violence, presented a most awful appearance,
rising perpendicularly from the ocean in lofty rugged cliffs, inaccessible but
to its winged inhabitants; on its southern side the ascent is not so steep and
abrupt; and near its western extremity is a small sandy beach, where in fine
weather, and with a smooth sea, a landing might probably be effected. At

& naturally enquired of us the size of it – the distance it was from them – & whether it
was inhabited?...Taio, King of Atooi expressed his design of sending some canoes to
explore it, on which account I then left with him a small pocket compass to guide their
way, as one of the Natives perfectly understood the use of it, from being with us on a
Voyage...& was on board when we discovered the Island. The Natives furnishing Mr
Douglas of the Ship Iphigenia next year with this information he made a point of making
this Island & settled its Longitude by Lunar observations with great precision as we find
by Meares Voyage, when he gives a very good representation of it in one of the plates
under the name Bird Island, and from the account which he afterwards gave the Natives,
of its diminutive size & inaccessible height to any other than the featherd tribe they
abandoned their design of visiting it'. – March 15. There is a rough sketch of the island
in Manby's log, March 16. Duncan sighted and named the island on 19 March 1789. For
the sketch of it made at the time see Meares, *Voyages*, p. 80. A note on a map of the Hawaiian
Islands published by the National Geographic Society reads: 'Uninhabited, but 12 fertile
acres were terraced and once intensely cultivated. Low platforms held ceremonial structures
where stone idols and artifacts of the ancient Hawaiians have been found.'

[1] The island is ·8 miles long and ·2 miles wide.

this place there was the appearance of a little verdure, though it was destitute of tree or shrub; every other part was apparently without soil, and consisted only of the naked rock. Its whole circumference does not exceed a league, and it is situated in latitude 23° 6', longitude 198° 8'.[1] When this rock was first discovered in 1788, there were on board the Prince of Wales some of the natives of Attowai, who expressed great surprize that there should be land so near to their islands (it lying from Onehow N. 51 W. at the distance of 39 leagues only) and of which not only themselves but all their countrymen were totally ignorant.

This intelligence was communicated on their return in the autumn of that year; and it excited in the active mind of *Taio* a strong desire to pay it a visit, to establish a colony there, and to annex it to his dominions; but on his being made thoroughly acquainted with its extent and sterility by the officers of that vessel, his project was abandoned. Those people however recognize it under the appellation of *Modoo Mannoo*,[2] that is, Bird island; and from its great distance from all other land, and its proximity to their islands, it seems to claim some distant pretensions to be ranked in the group of the Sandwich islands, of which we now took leave, pursuant to the determination already stated.

[1] Its position is lat. 23° 03' N, long. 161° 55' W (198° 05' E).
[2] Moka Manu, meaning Birds Island.

CHAPTER IV.

Quit the Sandwich Islands—Part Company with the Chatham—Indications of Land—See Tscherikow Island—Pass Trinity Isles—Proceed along the Coast—Enter and proceed up Cook's River.

HAVING bid farewell to the Sandwich islands on Saturday the 15th of March, our course was directed to the northward, with a fresh breeze from the N.E. by E.; but as the Chatham was some distance a-stern, the topsails were double reefed, and in the course of the evening the jib and stay-sails were taken in, under the idea that with such reduced sail the Chatham would soon overtake us; but as she did not make her appearance by ten at night, nor answer a false fire then burnt, the mainsail was hauled up, and we continued under the foresail and double reefed topsails only, in the hope of seeing our consort at day-light; but in this we were disappointed, and I was much at a loss to account for the cause that had produced our separation. It was a matter of extreme uncertainty what course would prove most likely to effect our meeting again, as it was not improbable that by the low sail we had carried during the night, she might have passed us unobserved, and was then a-head; this was as likely to have happened, as that some accident had occasioned her shortening sail, and that she was yet a-stern. The latter would probably have been announced by signal; under this impression we made the best of our way towards the coast of America, with the hope of rejoining our consort at the appointed rendezvous.[1]

The trade wind between N.E., E.N.E. and east, blowing a moderate gale, with squally and sometimes rainy weather, attended us until Friday the 21st, when towards midnight, having then advanced to the $35°$ of latitude, and in longitude $196\frac{1}{2}°$, it veered round by the east to the south, and on the next day, Saturday the 22d, it seemed to be fixed in the western quarter, accompanied with dark gloomy weather, and a very heavy sea from the north and N.W. which had been frequently the case since our leaving the islands.

But few of the black and white albatrosses, petrels, or others of the feathered tribe had attended us. In the evening the wind shifted to the N.N.E., where it continued with gloomy weather until Monday the 24th, when it fixed in the S.E., and blew a fresh gale with the same dark gloomy weather. A few

---

[1] 'Having parted Company with the Discovery the Commander opened the Rendezvous No. 6 and found Cooks River the appointed place for meeting.' – Manby, 17 March.

intervals of sunshine enabled us on the following day, Tuesday the 25th, to ascertain the latitude to be 39° 3', longitude 198° 46'; and the variation of the compass 19° 42', eastwardly. This was an increase in the variation far beyond our expectations; but as these were the first observations we had been enabled to make for this purpose since our departure from the Sandwich islands, it is probable the increase had been gradual to this station. Our climate was also greatly changed, the thermometer during the last week having fallen from 76 to 50; but the barometer having been unfortunately broken,[1] I had no means of ascertaining the other properties of the air. The southerly gale produced a smooth sea, and as towards night we approached the parallel where Captain Cook had noticed some indications of the vicinity of land,[2] we stood to and fro under an easy sail until the morning of Wednesday the 26th, when with a strong gale from the westward we passed about 15 leagues to the north-westward of the Resolution's track in the year 1778. Throughout the day the weather was clear, which enabled us to gain a distant view in all directions, but nothing was seen to intercept the horizon. The latitude at noon was 40° 45', which was extremely well ascertained by good observations. The longitude 200° 17' was deduced from altitudes of the sun, and from the chronometers both before and after mid-day, when the variation was found to be 15° 43' eastwardly. Few oceanic birds visited us in this situation. Two pieces of drift wood were passed this day, one piece appeared to have been a great length of time in the water, as it swam very deep, and was nearly covered with barnacles; the other was much more buoyant, and had on it but few of those shell fish. These were the only pieces of drift wood, and the only indications of the vicinity of land, seen by us between the Sandwich islands and the American coast. I was, however, afterwards informed by Mr. Puget, that in his passing these regions between the 37th and 39th degrees of latitude, about four degrees to the westward of our track, he saw, besides petrels and other oceanic birds, puffins, and a bird of the diver kind;[3] and

---

[1] 'When we got a little out from the Island of Oneehow we experienced a fresh breeze, accompanied with a disagreeable rough & high sea, which was the occasion of breaking the Marine Barometer in the Cabin – an irreparable loss during the remainder of the voyage.' – Menzies, 14 March.

[2] Cook wrote: 'In the Latitude of 42° 30', longt. 219° we began to see of the rock weed mentioned by Walters under the name of sea leek and now and then a piece of wood.' But he went on to remark on the scarcity of birds, and commented that had he 'not known that the continent of America was not far distant, from the few signs we had met with of the vicinity of land we might have concluded that there was none within some thousand leagues of us…' – *Journals*, III, p. 288. The reference was to Walter's account of Anson's voyage in which he noted that the Spanish galleons bound for Acapulco from Manila regarded the sea leek as a certain indication that land was near. See Glyndwr Williams (ed.), *Walter and Robins, A Voyage Round the World by George Anson* (London, 1974), p. 224.

[3] 'From the quantity of Birds about the Vessel we have Reason to suppose Land is not far distant. The Birds consisted of Albatrosses Shearwaters & Pettrells with Puffins and Sea Parrotts that are seldom seen 30 Leag[ues] from Land.' – Manby, 26 March. Puget's log for this period is missing.

that for a few hours, in the latitude of about 39°, the surface of the sea was remarkably smooth. Messrs. Portlock and Dixon also in their voyage, in two similar passages about the same latitude, and in longitude 206°, saw seals, puffins, and other indications, that induced them to think some undiscovered land was not far remote; but the weather being then, as it was also at the time of the Chatham's passing, very foggy, this fact could not be ascertained.[1] As such indications are by no means common in the North Pacific, they favor the conjecture that some land, though possibly of no very great extent, still remains unknown to Europeans in this neighbourhood.

With a fresh gale mostly from the western quarter, we proceeded rapidly to the north, and by the following Sunday, the 30th, reached the latitude of 50° 10′, longitude 205° 9′; the variation on the preceding afternoon was 16° 29′ eastwardly. The wind had been attended by a very heavy swell from the south-westward; the intervals of clear weather were of short duration, and in general it was very gloomy, with showers of rain succeeded by a fall of snow. The thermometer sunk to 35. In the course of the day some sea weed and some divers were observed; about the ship were also some albatrosses and sheer-waters. Our climate now began to assume a degree of severity that was new to us; on the next day, Monday the 31st, the mercury stood at the freezing point, and for the first time during the voyage the scuttle cask on deck was frozen.

After a few hours calm the wind settled in the N.E., attended with frost and snow until Wednesday, the 2d of April, when in latitude 55° 43′, longitude 204° 3′, it veered to the N.W., and blew so strong a gale that in the evening we were reduced to close-reefed topsails. The frost, with much snow and sleet, cased our rigging in ice; the thermometer stood at 26°. In the forenoon of Thursday the 3d a shag passed the ship, flying to the eastward, and about three in the afternoon, high land almost intirely covered with snow was discerned, bearing by compass N. by E. By seven in the evening this was plainly discovered to be an island, extending by compass from N. 2 W. to N. 32 W., at the distance of thirteen miles, with some detached rocks lying off its western extremity. In this situation the depth of water was 75 fathoms, sand and shelly bottom.

Although I did not consider this island as altogether a new discovery, yet as its situation had not hitherto been well ascertained, and as during the last three days our observations had been but indifferent, I thought it proper to pass the night in standing backward and forward, in order to gain a nearer view of it, and in the hope that the following day would be more favorable to our wishes for this purpose.

With the wind at N.W. blowing a moderate breeze, the mercury at 27, and extremely cold, we made all sail for the land the next morning, Friday the 4th, but in consequence of our having been set by a very strong current

---

[1] See Portlock, *Voyage*, p. 94; Dixon, *Voyage*, pp. 56–7.

to the S.W., we were so far distant, that it was near noon before we had passed
its southern point. We were fortunate in gaining excellent observations, which
at noon determined our situation to be in latitude 55° 48', longitude 205° 16';
this shewed a considerable error in our reckoning since the first day of the
month, the latitude being 22' further north, and the longitude 72' further east,
than had appeared by the log. The depth of water at this time was 23 fathoms,
fine black sandy bottom. The north-west point of the island bore by compass
N. 55 W. distant about two leagues; its eastern extremity, which is a low
rocky point, and was our nearest shore, S. 66 W. two miles; and its south
point, S. 30 W. about two leagues distant. In the point of view in which we
saw the south-west, southern, and eastern sides of this island, it appeared to
form a somewhat irregular four-sided figure, about ten leagues in circuit;
having from its western part, which is low and flat, and which had the
appearance of being insular, a remarkably high, flat, square rock, lying in a
direction S. 66 W., at the distance of two miles, between which and the island
is a ledge of smaller rocks. The centre of the island appeared by our
observations to be in latitude 55° 49', longitude 205° 4'.[1]

The season of the year greatly contributed to increase the dreary and
inhospitable aspect of the country; in addition to which it seemed to be intirely
destitute of trees or shrubs, or they were hidden beneath its winter garment of
snow, which appeared to be very deep about its south-eastern parts, consisting
of high steep cliffs; but on its western side, which was considerably lower, this
appearance was not so general. About its shores were some small whales, the
first we had noticed during this passage to the north. From the relative situation
of this island to the continent, I was inclined to believe it to be that which
Beering called Foggy island; but as Captain Cook gave that name to another
island not far distant to the westward, I have in honor of Beering's companion
Tscherikow, whose labors in the arduous task of discovery do not appear to
have been thus commemorated, called the island after him TSCHERIKOW'S
ISLAND.[2]

In our route from the Sandwich islands to this station it may be seen, that
whenever the winds would permit, our course was directed far to the
westward of the entrance into Cook's river, as delineated by that able
navigator. My reason for so doing, in the event of circumstances permitting,
was to fall in with those parts which Captain Cook was prevented from seeing
between Foggy cape and cape Trinity; as I much wished to ascertain whether
that space was occupied by land,[3] or whether it communicated with Smoky

---

[1] The island was Chirikof Island. The lat. given is correct but the long. would be about
155° 38' W (204° 22' E), about 27 miles W of Vancouver's position.

[2] Now spelled Chirikof Island. Beaglehole concluded that Vancouver was right in
identifying this as Bering's Foggy (Tumannoi) Island. Cook, *Journals*, III, p. 380n.

[3] Foggy Cape is the E end of Sutwik Island, which lies off the coast of the Alaska
Peninsula, and Cape Trinity is the S extremity of Kodiak Island. The broad approach to
the S entrance to Shelikof Strait, nearly 100 miles wide, lies between them.

bay, as has been represented in some late publications,[1] though in a manner not easily to be understood. The winds and weather had, however, been adverse to this design; and although the latter presented now a more favorable prospect, yet the wind, at N.W., blew in the very direction I wished to steer for that purpose. But as it was favorable for continuing along the exterior coast, and as we had already been greatly retarded in our general operations, by adverse winds and other untoward circumstances, I was induced to forego the object I had in view, lest similar inconvenience should continue to attend us, and cause delays that we could ill afford in the prosecution of our survey. These considerations induced me to make all sail, steering with the wind at N.N.W. during the afternoon to the N.E.; and having at six in the evening made our course good from noon, N. 65 E., 40 miles, Trinity island[2] was seen bearing by compass from N. 5 E. to N. 15 W., and another island from W. ½ N. to W. by S. The latter I took to be that which is laid down in Captain Cook's chart to the south-west of Trinity island. This land, although not noticed in Captain Cook's journal, was seen and passed on its southern side by the Discovery in that voyage,[3] which proves that the Resolution and Discovery could not have gone far to the north of Tscherikow's island, which was obscured at that time by thick foggy weather.

After sun-set, the wind veered more to the westward, and enabled us to

[1] Cook did not discover the existence of Shelikof Strait, which separates Kodiak Island (and Afognak Island N of it) from the Alaska Peninsula. Owing to poor visibility he concluded that its N entrance was only a bay, which Douglas, his editor, named Smokey Bay. Later Cook was similarly misled regarding the S entrance: 'There can be no doubt', he wrote, 'but that there is a continuation of the continent between Trinity Island [S of Cape Trinity] and Foggy Cape which the thick weather prevented us from seeing' – a sentence, Beaglehole notes, that 'is rather too confident a statement because if thick weather prevented a sight of the land, it also prevented a sight of divisions in the land.' – *Journals*, III, 381, n. Meares sailed through Shelikof Strait in the *Nootka* in August 1786, and Dixon noted this in his account of his interview with Meares in Prince William Sound in May 1787: Meares had 'found a passage into Cook's River' in which he met Russian settlers 'who informed him, that the land to the Eastward of the straight is called by them *Codiac*.' – Dixon, *A Voyage Round the World* (London, 1789), p. 155. Dixon shows the strait (unnamed) on his chart. In his companion volume of the same title and date Portlock also shows the strait on his chart with the note: 'Through this Strait the Snow Nootka went into Cook's River.' In his own *Voyages to the North West Coast of America* (London, 1790), Meares shows and names the strait on his chart and in his text refers to 'our passage through the straits, which we named Petrie's Strait, in honour of Wm. Petrie Esq. and found it brought us near that point forming Cook's River, distinguished by the name of Cape Douglas on Captain Cook's chart.' – p. xi. These were undoubtedly the 'late publications' to which Vancouver refers, and his refusal to accept their evidence reflects the deep distrust of Meares arising from his experience at Nootka.

[2] The Trinity Islands, two in number, as Vancouver soon suspected, are now named Sitkinak Island (to the E) and Tugidak Island. Cook seems to have seen only the former, which probably screened the strait that separates the two.

[3] Meaning that Vancouver saw it himself in 1778. It is mentioned in Cook's manuscript journal, but the sentence was deleted in the printed version available to Vancouver. Today there is no such island. Beaglehole comments on this mystery; see Cook, *Journals*, III, 378n. It is conceivable that a low island existing in 1794 could have been submerged later by earthquake action, as earthquakes are frequent in the area.

stand nearly for Trinity island, under our double-reefed-topsails; and at
midnight, having soundings at the depth of fifty fathoms, soft sandy bottom,
we plied until day-light under an easy sail, with soundings from 70 to 82
fathoms, fine sandy bottom. At day-light in the morning of Saturday the 5th,
we made sail, steering towards Trinity island, which bore by compass from
N. 6 W. to N.W., the main land beyond it stretching to the N.N.E.

With a moderate breeze, between N.W. and W.S.W., we drew in with
the land, and the weather being clear permitted us to notice three or four
mountains of considerable height, on the main land,[1] behind those that
bounded the sea-coast, all of which at first appeared to be covered with snow;
but as we approached the shores, the lower parts of the coast were found in
general to be free from snow, and considerably more so than Tscherikow
island. The frost which, since the 31st of March, had been very severe, now
gave way, and the thermometer rose to 35. At noon the eastern extreme of
Trinity island bore by compass S. 36 W., distant 13 miles; its north-west point
S. 42 W.; cape Trinity S. 77 W.; the land of Two-headed point[2] from N.
39 W. to N. 24 W.; and the northernmost land in sight N. 13 E. The observed
latitude 56° 40', longitude 207° 7½'. In the course of the morning, the
variation, by the surveying compass, was found to be 23° 30' eastwardly.

As we passed Trinity island, it appeared to be divided into two islands, with
several others of inferior size lying to the north, between them and the land
about cape Trinity. The east point of the easternmost is, according to our
observations, situated in latitude 56° 33½', longitude 206° 47';[3] and Two-
headed point, composing a small island that terminates to the north-east by
a low flat rocky point, in latitude 56° 54½', longitude 207° 5'.[4] Captain Cook,
in assigning the longitude to Trinity isles, which occupy an extent of about
six leagues in an east and west direction, does not designate any particular part,
but says they lie in latitude 56° 36', longitude 205°.[5] The longitude of the
east point of Trinity island, agreeably to the observations made that voyage
on board the Discovery, was 205° 53'; neither of which will be found to agree
with the longitude on this occasion, which was deduced from exceedingly
good observations, both before and after noon, and corrected by subsequent
observations.

Southwestward from Two-headed island the coast is low, and appears to
be compact; but immediately to the northward of it the shores descend
abruptly into the sea, appear to be much broken, and form an extensive sound,[6]
of which the flat rocky point may be considered as its south-west point of

[1] Actually on Kodiak Island. Like Cook, Vancouver thought at this time that it was
part of the mainland, but it appears as an island on his chart.
[2] Now Twoheaded Island, with 'two irregularly rounded peaks; the higher 1,838
feet... the lower 1,724 feet...' – U.S. Coast Pilot 9, p. 103.
[3] Cape Sitkinak, in lat. 56° 33' 45" N, long. 153° 52' 30" W (206° 07' 30" E).
[4] Its position is lat. 56° 54' N, long. 153° 35' W (206° 25' E).
[5] Cook, Journals, III, p. 377.
[6] The entrance to Sitkalidak Strait, which separates Sitkalidak Island from Kodiak Island.
A number of bays branch off it, notably Kaiugnak Bay and Three Saints Bay.

entrance; from this its north-east point, being low projecting land, lies N. 58 E. at the distance of three leagues.[1] The several branches that appeared to flow into the sound, seemed to wind toward the base of a connected range of high snowy mountains, which no doubt gave boundaries to their extent.

As we proceeded gently across the entrance of this sound with a light southerly breeze, we were visited in the afternoon by two of its inhabitants, a young man and a girl, in a small skin canoe,[2] who shewed that they had been acquainted with some European nation, by their having adopted our mode of salutation in bowing as they approached the ship, and by their coming on board without the least hesitation. We entertained no doubt of their having been so instructed by the Russians; and, if we understood them rightly, there were six persons of that nation then residing on shore in the sound. The man took his dinner without the least ceremony, drank brandy, and accepted such presents as were made him, but seemed to prefer snuff and silk handkerchiefs to every thing else.[3] Whilst he remained on board, which was about an hour, I endeavoured to learn from him the name which the natives give to this part of the coast, but could not gain any satisfactory information.[4] He clearly and distinctly counted the numerals in the languages of Oonalashka[5] and Prince William's sound, though these do not bear the least affinity to each other. From his general appearance, I was more inclined to believe him to be a Kamtschadale than a native of America or its adjacent islands. After their departure we were visited by a single Indian in a canoe, but he was not so familiar as the others; he paddled at a distance round the ship, and then returned to the shore. At seven in the evening we were becalmed within about two miles of the north-east point of the sound; when the depth of water was 24 fathoms, fine sandy bottom.

The weather continued fair, with faint variable winds, until midnight; at which time the wind fixed in the north-west quarter, and brought with it sleet and dissolving snow; thus the flattering prospect that had been presented, of a favorable passage to our destined station, was again obscured, and that we might not lose ground, we were obliged to ply against a heavy sea and a strong N.E. gale, which, on the forenoon of Sunday the 6th, reduced us to close-reefed topsails.

The gale between N.N.E. and east, varied a little in force and direction, and permitted us to gain some advantage. On the morning of Tuesday the

[1] Black Point, the S extremity of Sitkalidak Island.

[2] The first of the many kayaks the expedition would encounter. Most of them had only one manhole, but some had two. This was evidently one of the latter.

[3] Vancouver was unaware as yet that the Shelikov-Golikov Company had established the first permanent Russian settlement on Kodiak Island in nearby Three Saints Bay in 1784.

[4] Menzies' account differs on this point: 'These men [he states that there were two men in the canoe, not a man and a girl] gave us to understand that the part of the Coast abreast of us was called *Cadiak* [Kodiak].' – April 5.

[5] Unalaska, second largest of the long chain of islands, over 800 miles in length, W of the Alaska Peninsula.

8th we were within about a league of the coast, which appeared to be much broken; cape Barnabas[1] bore by compass S. 30 W.; the north point of a sound, of which the land adjoining to cape Barnabas forms its southern side, S. 57 W.;[2] the north point of another apparent sound, S. 69 W.;[3] a tract of land much lower than the coast in its vicinity, free from snow, and seemingly detached from the main land, from S. 80 W. to N. 29 W.; its nearest part W.N.W., about a league distant; a low projecting point, being the easternmost part of that which appeared to be the main land in sight, N. 16 E.;[4] and an island, from N. 26 E. to N. 32 E.[5] In this neighbourhood the land was more free from snow than that further to the south, occasioned most probably by the alteration in the temperature of the weather, as the mercury now stood at 40½, and gave us hopes that the severity of the winter season was at an end; this made me extremely anxious to reach our destined station, from whence the labours of the summer were to commence.

Our observations at noon shewed our situation to be in latitude 56° 58′, longitude corrected as before stated by subsequent observations, 208° 19′. The island then bore by compass N. 23 W.; and cape Barnabas appearing to lie in latitude 57° 10′, longitude 207° 45′, N. 81 W.[6]

The two following days being for the most part calm, though what little wind there was continued from the N.E. with thick misty weather, prevented our seeing much of the land until the evening of Thursday the 10th, when we tacked about a league from the north-east point of the above island, which appeared to be about two leagues in circuit, and its centre to be situated in latitude 57° 24′, longitude 208° 20′.[7] This island renders this part of the coast very remarkable, being the only distinguishable detached land of any magnitude north-eastward from Trinity isles.[8] Its north-west part projects in a low point towards the main land, from whence also a low flat point extends towards the island, forming a passage about half a league wide, to all appearance free from interruption. This island is not noticed in Captain Cook's chart or his journal, probably owing to the very foggy weather which prevailed when the Resolution was in its neighbourhood; it was however seen in that voyage from on board the Discovery, and then placed by me 5′ to the south of its situation deduced from the result of our present observations,

[1] The E extremity of Sitkalidak Island, named Cape St. Barnabas by Cook on 12 June 1778 (the day after St. Barnabas' Day). William Douglas named it Cape Hollings in 1788, but Cook's name, in simpler form, has survived.

[2] Left Cape. The 'sound' was Sitkalidak Strait, whose E entrance is between Cape Barnabas and Left Cape.

[3] Right Cape, the N point of the entrance to Kiliuda Bay, which is between Right Cape and Left Cape.

[4] Narrow Cape.   [5] Ugak Island.

[6] Its position is lat. 57° 09′ N, long. 152° 53′ W (207° 07′ E).

[7] Ugak Island, given no name in the text or on Vancouver's chart, is in lat. 57° 23′ N, long. 152° 16′ W (207° 44′ E).

[8] Vancouver was unaware that Twoheaded Point was on an island and that the very much larger Sitkalidak Island was detached from Kodiak Island.

which I have reason to believe are not liable to any material error.[1] The wind having fixed in the N.W. brought us clear weather, but we were obliged to stand from the coast, the northernmost part of which distinctly seen was cape Greville,[2] bearing by compass N. 50 W.; some rocks extending from the cape N. 42 W., and the above mentioned island, S. 20 W.

With the approach of the following day, Friday the 11th, the westerly breeze increased, and we passed rapidly to the north, though too far from the land to ascertain any thing with precision between cape Greville and cape St. Hermogenes;[3] had we been able to have steered for point Banks,[4] and from thence across Smoky bay,[5] some conclusion might have been drawn whether the land we had thus coasted along was composed of islands, or whether it was as Captain Cook had considered it, a part of the continent. I much regretted that I had it not in my power to become satisfied in this respect,[6] as the season had now put on a very favorable appearance, which rendered it important that not a moment should be lost in prosecuting the examination of this extensive opening. At noon cape Greville, the southernmost part of the coast in sight, bore by compass S. 28 W., the island of St. Hermogenes,[7] from S. 56 W. to S. 89 W.; the westernmost mountain seen over cape Douglas,[8] N. 81 W.; and the barren isles[9] N. 55 W. In this situation the observed latitude was 58° 14', and the longitude deduced from very satisfactory observations both before and after noon, 209° 25½'. From this authority cape Greville appeared to be in latitude 57° 34½', longitude 208° 26';[10] and the south extreme of the island St. Hermogenes, in latitude 58° 10½', longitude 208° 56'.[11] The variation in the afternoon was 21° 37' eastwardly.

These positions of longitude vary materially from those assigned by Captain

[1] Beaglehole comments: 'its sighting by the *Discovery*, and the reasonably accurate fixing of its latitude by Midshipman Vancouver, was much more remarkable than its being missed by the *Resolution*.' – Cook, *Journals*, III, 375n.

[2] The name is left blank in Cook's journal; 'Greville' was inserted in the handwriting of Cook's editor, Douglas. Cook, *Journals*, III, 375n.

[3] The NE point of Marmot Island. Cook named the cape under the impression that it was the feature to which Bering had given the name in 1741, but Bering's cape was probably much farther S. Black Point has been suggested. Cook, *Journals*, III, 358n.

[4] The N extremity of Shuyak Island. Cook states that 'Several Smokes' were seen on it, 'and on that account [it] was called *Smoky Point.*' Douglas, Cook's editor, changed the name in the text to Cape Banks, but on the engraved chart it is given its present name, Point Banks. Cooks, *Journals*, III, 359n.

[5] The N entrance to Shelikov Strait.

[6] By the time his charts were engraved Vancouver was aware that Kodiak Island and the islands N of it were islands, and they are so depicted on them.

[7] Now Marmot Island.

[8] On the mainland; the NW point of entrance to Shelikof Strait. Menzies notes that they saw 'two high snowy mountains near Cape Douglas'; they would be Mount Douglas (7,064 feet) and ('the westernmost') Fourpeaked Mountain (6,903 feet).

[9] Now the Barren Islands. The name was conferred by Cook and adopted by Vancouver.

[10] Its position is lat. 57° 35' 30" N, long. 152° 09' 30" W (207° 50' 30" E).

[11] Now Marmot Cape, in lat. 58° 10' N, long. 151° 51' 50" W (208° 08' 10" E).

Cook; but as similar differences occurred afterwards in other instances, I shall for the present decline making any comments on this subject.

With the wind chiefly at west, by Saturday the 12th at noon we were fast approaching the coast to the eastward of cape Elizabeth,[1] which then bore by compass N. 84 W.; the barren isles, from S. 55 W. to S. 34 W.; the northernmost part of the coast in sight, N. 26 E., and the nearest shore, N. 6 W., five or six miles distant; here we had soundings in 70 fathoms water, sandy bottom, and by an indifferent observation the latitude was 59°, longitude 209° 20'. The top of high water appeared to be at noon, as at that time no effect was felt from a tide; but immediately afterwards we were driven at a considerable rate to the eastward, until half past one, when, on a breeze springing up from that quarter, we steered for cape Elizabeth, and passed that promontory, and entered Cook's river[2] about half past five. The coast is composed of high land, before which lie three small islands[3] and some rocks; the cape is itself the largest, and the most western of these islands, which appeared to afford a navigable channel between them and the main land, nearly in an east and west direction; though between the cape and the middle island some low lurking rocks were discerned, which had the appearance of being connected with a cluster of rocks above the surface of the sea, lying from the cape S. 50 E., at the distance of three or four miles. To the south-west of the middle island is another cluster of rocks, both above and beneath the surface of the water.

The thermometer now varied between 40 and 45; and the snow, excepting in the deep chasms of the rocks, was melted to a considerable height on the sides of the hills, which being well wooded, assumed a far more cheerful aspect than the country to the southward. Spring seemed to be making so rapid a progress here, that we had every reason to indulge the hope of being able to carry our researches into execution, without any interruption from the severity of the season.

As I had determined to commence our survey on the western side of the river, as far up that side as the wind now at N.N.E. would permit us to fetch, we proceeded in quest of some convenient station for the ship, from whence two boat parties might be dispatched, the one to examine the shores southward to cape Douglas, the other to precede the ship in our route up the river.[4]

[1] At the W end of Elizabeth Island. It was discovered by Cook on 21 May 1778, the birthday of Princess Elizabeth, third daughter of George III.

[2] Now Cook Inlet. As will appear, Vancouver changed the name when it became known that it was not the estuary of a large river. A note by Douglas, Cook's editor, reads: 'Capt Cook having left a blank for its Name, by Lord Sandwich's Orders, it was named Cook's River.' Beaglehole notes that Cook did not leave a blank. 'He simply did not give the inlet a name.' – Cook, *Journals*, III, 368n.

[3] The Chugach Islands (Elizabeth, Perl and Chugach), near the S coast of the Kenai Peninsula, which forms the E shore of Cook Inlet.

[4] If the dating of his journal can be trusted, Menzies already suspected that they were about to explore an inlet and not a river: 'We here observd no discoloration of the Water

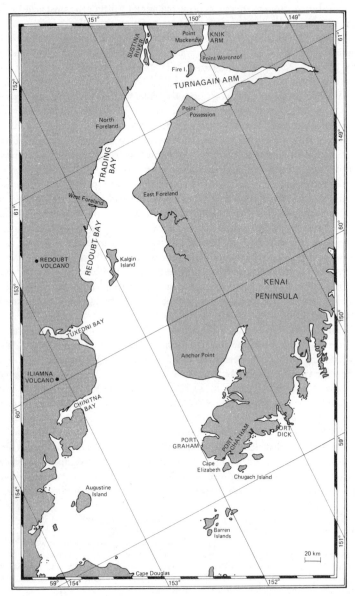

Figure 8. Cook Inlet. *Base map by Michael E. Leek.*

For the first time this season we noticed some flocks of wild geese, and could not avoid remarking, that they all flew to the southward, contrary to what might have been expected from the advanced state and mildness of the season; which, however, on Sunday morning the 13th, suffered a very material alteration, as the wind came to the N.E. and was attended by a sharp frost and a very heavy fall of snow. On leaving the eastern shore the depth of water gradually increased from 25 to 35 fathoms, fine sandy bottom in mid-channel, and then decreased again as we approached the western shore, which about six was indistinctly perceived through the falling snow; and being then in 20 fathoms water, we anchored until the weather should prove more favorable to our pursuit.[1] In this situation we remained, without being able to discern the adjacent shores, until the forenoon of Monday the 14th, when the western horizon became clear, and shewed us cape Douglas bearing by compass S. 9 E.; mount St. Augustin,[2] S. 9 W.; the northernmost land in sight N. 9 W.; and a low point, S. 31 W.; from whence the shores to the southward fell so far back to the westward, that we could only distinguish the summits of a range of lofty disjointed mountains intirely covered with snow, that seemed principally to occupy the space between that low point and cape Douglas, but at the same time gave the country an appearance in this point of view of being greatly divided by water. From thence to the northward, excepting a small open bay abreast of us with two rocks lying before its entrance, the shores appeared to be compact, and the surface of the country descending rather abruptly at first, admitted near the water-side a narrow border of low land; this was covered with wood, which continued to grow some distance up the sides of the mountains, which were very lofty and rugged, and above the line where vegetation ceased were wrapped in perpetual snow.

Whilst we had a clear and distinct view of every thing in the western quarter, the opposite side of the horizon was totally obscured from our sight by a dark misty haze. We had, however, by intervals of clearer weather, been enabled to form some idea of our situation, and of the coast to the south-westward, which I now considered as lying behind us; the broken and insular appearance of which gave me reason to expect the examination of it would be a laborious task, notwithstanding that the range of mountains that bounded our horizon, in that direction, admitted of a strong presumption that the whole might be closely connected by land, not sufficiently elevated to be visible at our remote distance.

As I concluded the Chatham could not be far behind, if she had not already

nor no casual signs or indications that would lead us to suppose we were even in the vicinity of land, had we not previously known it, far less in the entrance of a great River, in short it differd in no other respect from the entrances of those inlets we had already examined on the Coast but by its spacious appearance.' – 11 April.

[1] Vancouver's chart indicates that the anchorage was just S of Chinitna Bay.

[2] The smoking volcanic peak on Augustine Island. Named Mount St. Augustine by Cook on 26 May 1778, the day of St. Augustine of Canterbury. Spelled Augustine on Vancouver's chart.

preceded us; and as I had particularly directed that the survey should commence at cape Douglas, I had little doubt, on our meeting, that any thing would be left unexamined in that quarter; but should it so happen, that any further inquiry might be deemed necessary, and that we should be obliged to return by the same route, the summer season in that case would be more advanced and more favorable to our researches in that region, which is exposed to all the influence of the oceanic winds and waves, and in the present inclement weather would be a very hazardous undertaking in our open boats, the only means by which, from experience, I was confident this object could now be accomplished. To avoid, therefore, as much as possible, any delay, or misapplication of time, I determined to proceed up the river, keeping close along its western shore, and forthwith to pursue our investigation to its navigable extent.

Agreeably to this determination, being favored with the flood tide, although not a very rapid one, we steered to the northward until about three in the afternoon; when, on meeting the reflux, we anchored about a league from the western shore, in 20 fathoms water, soft sandy bottom. The latitude, by double altitudes, was 60° 1½′. The frost still continued; the wind was moderate, though variable, attended with a very heavy fall of snow, and an unpleasant swell from the S.E. These combined circumstances detained us at anchor until the next day, Tuesday the 15th, in the afternoon, when we took the advantage of the latter part of the flood-tide, but advanced only a few miles before the ebb obliged us again to anchor in 25 fathoms water, soft bottom. Here the western shore was bounded by lofty rugged mountains, between the bases of which and the water-side was a margin of low or moderately elevated wood-land country. Two small openings were observed, the northernmost, being the largest, appeared to be a sound, winding towards the foot of the volcano,[1] which, from its apparently close connection with the neighbouring mountains, probably gave the limits to its extent. These openings we left for the examination of Mr. Puget, not considering them sufficiently important to retard our progress, especially as the appearance of the atmosphere indicated a favorable change in the weather. The snow had ceased to fall, and, excepting some dark clouds between the N.N.E. and N.W. the sky and horizon were perfectly clear, and gave us, for the first time since Saturday night, a distant view of the southern parts of the eastern shore; the night, however, was attended with the severest frost we had yet experienced, the mercury fell to 23, and although the weather was clear and cheerful the next morning, Wednesday the 16th, yet the air was so excessively keen, that the sun's rays had no effect on the thermometer. We weighed about ten in the forenoon, with the flood-tide, and a light breeze from the N.W. and

---

[1] The smaller opening was Tuxedni Channel, which merges with the larger one, a broader but very shallow entrance to Tuxedni Bay, behind Chisik Island, which lies between the two. The bay runs inland for a dozen miles but is very shoal. The volcano referred to was the Iliamna Volcano (10,017 feet).

proceeded up the river; the mercury at noon had risen to 26°, the observed
latitude 60° 11', longitude 208° 23½', and the variation in the forenoon was
observed to be 23° 46' easterly, which I considered as too little, notwithstanding
that the observations were very carefully made. Our course was directed
between the western shore and the low island near it mentioned by Captain
Cook.[1]

Shortly after noon we were visited by three of the natives, each in a small
skin canoe, who without the least hesitation, made their canoes fast alongside,
and came on board with evident marks of being acquainted with European
manners, by their bowing very respectfully on coming upon deck.[2] They
made signs for snuff and tobacco, which, with some other trivial articles they
solicited, they seemed to be highly gratified by receiving, and expressed a
degree of modest concern that they had not any thing to offer in return. At
dinner they did not make the least scruple of partaking of our repast, with
such wine and liquors as were offered to them; though of these they drank
very sparingly, seeming to be well aware of their powerful effect.[3] The
weather was calm on their arrival; but towards the evening a light breeze
sprang up from the southward, and as they had but slightly secured their
canoes, the probability of their breaking adrift was pointed out to them. On
this they made signs to know if we were going up the river, and on their
being answered by the same means in the affirmative, they easily gave us to
understand that they wished to accompany us, and that their canoes should
be taken on board, with which I had no objection to comply.

With a boat a-head, sounding the depth of water from 13 to 17 fathoms,

[1] Kalgin Island. Referred to by Menzies as Channel Island.

[2] Menzies describes their clothing: 'They were well cloathed from head to foot with
long frocks of Racoon Skins; their hands were coverd with fur mittens, & their legs with
leather boots, so that they were well equippd to withstand the rigor of the Climate: They
had broad flat visages & wore their hair croppd short round the Nape of the Neck.' – March
16.

[3] It is difficult to identify with any certainty the natives met with in Cook Inlet. Gunther
points out that the inlet and Prince William Sound form a region 'of particular interest
because it is the meeting place of several cultures'. – Indian Life on the Northwest Coast, p.
182. A people akin to the Chugach Eskimo, who inhabited Prince William Sound, had
villages along the S coast of the Kenai Peninsula from Point Puget westward, and these
extended around the W end of the peninsula and up the coast of Cook Inlet as far as
Kachemak Bay. At one time, indeed, they may have occupied most of the inlet, but by
the time of Vancouver's visit the Tanaina, an Athapascan Indian people, had pushed
southward and seem to have reached Kachemak Bay not long before the Russians arrived
in the inlet. The Tanaina adopted much of the Chugach culture, including the kayak, which
adds to the problem of identification, which is complicated further by the Russian practice
of bringing natives from Kodiak Island, Unalaska and even Kamchatka to serve as sea otter
hunters. – See Frederica de Laguna, Chugach Prehistory. The Archaeology of Prince William
Sound, Alaska (Seattle, 1956), pp. 34–6. In July 1786 Portlock met a party of 25 Russians
accompanied by natives near Port Graham. He suspected that the latter 'were not natives
of this place, but brought here from Kodiak and Oonalaska, for the purpose of hunting'
and found this to be the case. – A Voyage Round the World (London, 1789), pp. 100, 104.

we continued our course until six in the evening, when the influence of the returning tide being stronger than that of the wind, we anchored in 15 fathoms water, sandy bottom. In this situation the mountains seen over cape Douglas bore by compass S. 5 E. distant 35 leagues; mount St. Augustin S. 6 W.; the north-east point of the most northern opening or sound,[1] S. 20 W. distant 19 miles; the Volcano,[2] S. 28 W.; a remarkably lofty mountain on the west shore,[3] S. 85 W.; the north extreme of the low island, in a line with another high distant mountain, N. 4 E.;[4] its nearest shore east, distant two miles; its south point S. 75 E. a league distant; beyond which the eastern shore was seen stretching to S. 41 E.; and the nearest part of the western shore N. 87 W. about four miles distant: this is a steep cliff moderately high; the shore on either side is a low flat beach, particularly to the northward, where the margin of low land is of a greater extent than we had noticed further to the southward, from the base of the mountains, which, so far as we were able to discern, are a connected and undivided barrier along the western side of the river. Our latitude at this anchorage was 60° 23½′, longitude 208° 33′. The night tide not serving our purpose, we waited the return of the flood on the following day, Thursday the 17th, but as that would not take place until about noon, I employed the morning by making an excursion to the island.

We landed with tolerable ease on the south point of what at high water forms a shallow bay, but at low tide is a flat of sand and mud, on which were lying innumerable large fragments of rock not attached to the spot on which they rested, but evidently brought and deposited there by the violence of the tide, or by some other powerful agency.[5] The globular form which most of them had acquired, with the smoothness of their surface, indicated their having been much subjected to a rolling motion. The island was in most parts covered with small pine and alder trees, but the snow that was lying very deep on the ground confined our walk to the beach, on which were lodged some small drift wood, and many large pieces of ice that seemed to have been there left by the tides that had flowed much higher than those which at that time prevailed; from hence we were induced to suppose that the frost had broken up, and that the severity of the then weather was a second visitation of winter. In the snow we saw the tracks of some small animals, and on the beach we

---

[1] Tuxedni Bay.   [2] The Iliamna Volcano.

[3] The Redoubt Volcano (10,198 feet).

[4] Mount Susitna (4,400 feet) or possibly South Peak (4,239 feet), which from Vancouver's viewpoint would be virtually in line with it.

[5] Under the heading 'Dangers' the U.S. Coast Pilot 9 comments: 'The shoals in Cook Inlet are generally strewn with boulders, which lie on the otherwise flat bottom, give no indication to the lead unless it strikes them, and are not marked by kelp. Most of those located by the survey were found by sighting them at low water. It was noted in places that the boulders rise as much as 30 feet above the general level of the bottom. As a measure of safety, it is considered advisable for vessels to avoid areas having depths no more than 30 feet greater than the draft.'

found some pieces of coal resembling the cannel coal. The ship proceeded at slack tide with a light breeze from the north-east, stood to windward, and having advanced about four miles from her last station in a direction N.N.E., I repaired on board.

The depth of water had now (about one o'clock) decreased to eight fathoms; in the expectation of finding a deeper channel we again stood towards the island; the soundings however soon decreased to six fathoms, and, immediately after, the ship grounded in 15 feet water; here she rested for a short time, then swung round, and again floated with a jerk, conveying the idea of her having rested on a round stone, similar to those found on the beach at the island. The depth soon increased, as we proceeded towards the island, to 15 fathoms, where we anchored to wait for the ebb tide, in order that we might return by the way we had come, as little advantage could be derived by persisting in a route so intricate and unpleasant. The shoal on which the ship had grounded is of some extent, it stretches to the northward, lies between six and seven miles from the main land, and is near a league from the west side of the island; where also a flat extends some distance into the river.

The object I had in view being now fully accomplished, in having ascertained that the western shore behind the island was compact, I determined to proceed immediately to the furthest extent of Captain Cook's researches, and from thence to carry my examination into execution as circumstances should direct. For this purpose, about seven in the evening, the weather being nearly calm, we weighed,[1] and committed ourselves to the influence of the ebb tide, a measure that in regions so unknown cannot be defended as being the most prudent; yet in services of this nature a very considerable degree of risk must frequently be encountered, or the accomplishment of particular objects would necessarily be prolonged to a very distant and indefinite period. The truth of this observation was very soon exhibited. By the time we had passed about a league in a direction S. 38 W. from the anchorage that we had quitted in the forenoon, we again suddenly found ourselves in a very shallow water, and were under apprehensions of being aground every instant, which, with the falling tide, must have been attended with very unpleasant, if not serious, consequences. Whilst in this irksome state, and at the moment when our depth had decreased to three fathoms, a light breeze of wind providentially sprang up, which rendered the ship manageable, and permitted us to steer to the eastward; our depth then soon increased to 7, and afterwards gradually to 30 fathoms. Having kept a south-westerly course until midnight, and at that time reaching no bottom with 40 fathoms of line, I concluded

[1] Menzies explains more clearly what was happening. After the ship floated off the rock 'An officer was sent in a boat to sound all round us, & on his report, it was determined to return back again out of this Channel the way we came into it & go up the other side of the Island: Accordingly in the evening we weighd & made Sail to the Southward'. – April 17. Cook had gone up the channel E of the island which Vancouver now proposed to follow.

we were far to the southward of the shoal laid down in Captain Cook's chart, as extending from the south point of the island.

For the purpose of taking the advantage of the flood tide, to assist our progress up the river, although we considered the shoal to lie far to the north of us, yet that we might run no risk we hauled gradually to the south and S.S.E., in order to pass it at some distance; this precaution, however, availed us little, for we had not advanced far before the depth of water was again under nine fathoms; and instantly decreasing to four, the ship struck with some degree of violence, occasioned by a very heavy swell from the ocean, that for some days past had been attendant on the flood tide. About one o'clock, having a fine commanding breeze from the N.E., we steered to the westward and S.W., but to no purpose, the tide having more influence on the body of the ship than the wind on her sails; in this very unpleasant predicament we remained nearly stationary for about an hour and an half, the ship frequently striking, and sometimes so heavily as to occasion constant apprehension lest the masts should come by the board, or some worse accident befall us. Every effort to get to the westward of the shoal proving ineffectual, we had no other alternative than to cross it if possible, by pursuing an opposite line of direction; this attempt however seemed to be full of danger, as its shallowest part appeared by the breakers to be at its eastern extremity, which had induced me to persevere so long in my endeavours to get to the westward. The attempt was made, and was happily crowned with a success far beyond my most sanguine expectations. After having got the ship's head to the eastward she struck but once more (though that was the most violent and alarming shock we had sustained) in crossing the shoal; the water soon after deepened to 10 and 15 fathoms, and we had the further satisfaction of finding that the ship made no water, nor were we able to perceive that she had in any other respect received the least damage.

We arrived in deep water just as the dawning of day enabled us to procure some angles, which shewed that we had passed the shoal about a league to the south-west of the south point of the island, and (by the appearance of the broken water in our passage) nearly over its middle, as it seemed to extend full a league further in that direction.[1] From the great variety in the soundings in passing over it, it should appear to be very uneven, as in several instances, when the ship struck violently, or when she rested on the ground, the depth by the lead line was frequently near four fathoms, and the rise and fall of the waves was by no means equal to this difference. It is not improbable that this shoal might have arrested some fragments of rocks similar to those before mentioned; and if so, it was infinitely more dangerous to contend with than a mere spit of sand, and renders our preservation a most providential event.

We continued to take advantage of the flood tide, and stood to windward until about seven the next morning, Friday the 18th, when on the ebb making, we anchored off the eastern side of the island, in 14 fathoms water, stony

[1] The shoal extends for about 16 miles S of Kalgin Island.

bottom, about a league from its shore; along which extends a continuation of the shoal about two miles from the island.

I should be wanting in justice to our Indian passengers, were I to omit stating their docility and respectful behaviour whilst they were on board; as also the anxiety they expressed for our safety, lest the vessel whilst striking should break to pieces; and the real satisfaction and happiness they exhibited on being given to understand that we were again in perfect security.

The weather now, though extremely cold, (the mercury standing at 25) was very cheerful, and afforded us an excellent view of the surrounding region, composed, at a little distance from the river, of stupendous mountains, whose rugged and romantic forms, clothed in a perpetual sheet of ice and snow, presented a prospect, though magnificently grand, yet dreary, cold, and inhospitable. In the midst of these appeared the volcano near the summit of which, from two distinct craters on its south-eastern side, were emitted large columns of whitish smoke;[1] unless, as was supposed by some on board, it was vapour arising from hot springs in that neighbourhood; but how far this conjecture was consistent with the severity of the climate at the top of that lofty mountain, is not within the limits of my judgment to determine

About ten in the forenoon, we were surprized by a much earlier return of the flood tide than we had expected, with which, and a light variable breeze, we directed our course to the northward. In the afternoon the wind blew a steady breeze from the N.N.W., which enabled us to reach the narrows by seven in the evening. On the return of the ebb we became again stationary in 17 fathoms water. Here the shores of the river were comparatively low, or only moderately elevated, jutting out into three remarkable steep cliffy points. These I distinguished by the names of the WEST, NORTH, and EAST FORELANDS;[2] the two former are on the western, and the latter on the eastern, shore; which, from the station we had taken, bore by compass as follow: the west Foreland, forming the south-west point of the narrows, S. 28 W., about four miles distant; the north Foreland N. 4 E.; and the east Foreland, forming the north-east point of the narrows, N. 76 E.

Here we were visited by two of the natives, in a small skin canoe, who understanding what reception their countrymen had met with, solicited the same indulgence; their canoe was accordingly taken in, and they were permitted to remain on board. One of these, whose name was *Sal-tart*, possessing some apparent superiority over the rest, presented me with some martin skins, and received in return some iron, beads, a few other trinkets,

---

[1] The Iliamna Volcano. 'Steam generally issues from fissures just below the summit and from one of the lower peaks on the southeast slope.' – *U.S. Coast Pilot 9*, p. 75.

[2] West Foreland and East Foreland are opposite one another. North Foreland is 25 miles above West Foreland. Cook gave these headlands no names, but John Gore, 1st Lieutenant of the *Resolution*, referring to the West Foreland, wrote: 'This Foreland I beg Leave to Call Nancy's, [after] a Favourite Female Acquaintance of your Humble Servant.' East Foreland is named Gore's Head on one of the charts of Cook's explorations, but Vancouver's names have obliterated both Nancy and Gore. Cook, *Journals*, III, p. 363n.

and a small quantity of snuff and tobacco, all of which he seemed to value very highly. These people appeared to be acquainted with the Russians, of whose language they seemed to speak several words; but our very confined knowledge of that, as well as our total ignorance of their native tongue, prevented our acquiring the information which, from the intelligent appearance of these very civil and well-behaved strangers, we might otherwise have been enabled to obtain.

The ebb tide ran at the rate of five miles per hour; and at half past one on Saturday morning the 19th, the flood returned with equal rapidity; and having by three o'clock increased with a velocity that the best bower cable was unequal to resist, it broke, and the buoy sinking by the strength of the current, the anchor and cable were irrecoverably lost. This was an accident that gave me very serious concern, since our stock of these important stores was already very much reduced. As it was now becoming day-light we proceeded up the river, with the flood tide and a light variable breeze in the northern quarter, attended with very severe weather; the mercury being at 18. We kept near the western shore to avoid being entangled with the shoal on which the Resolution had grounded,[1] and by that means lost much of the influence of the flood; so that on the ebb making about seven o'clock, we had not advanced more than two leagues. Here we again anchored in 13 fathoms water; the west Foreland by compass bearing S. 14 E., distant nine miles; the north Foreland N. 35 E. the east Foreland S. 61 E.; and the volcano S. 12 W. The observed latitude was 60° 51′, but we were not able to procure any observations for the variation.

Our Indian friends, who we had imagined were on their return from an excursion down the river at the time we met with them, now gave us to understand that their habitations were in this neighbourhood, on the western shore, and desired to take their leave; they departed, shewing a very high sense of gratitude for the kindness and attention with which they had been treated. Whilst on board they had behaved with a degree of modesty and decorum rarely found amongst men in a far more civilized state; and notwithstanding they had been constantly exposed to temptations, by articles lying in their way which were of the most valuable nature in their estimation, not the most trifling thing was missed, nor did their honesty in any respect suffer the least impeachment. They reposed the utmost confidence in our integrity, and considered themselves as much at home in our society, as if we had long been their most intimate friends. In short, if the conduct they exhibited during the time they passed with us, is to be received as their general national character, it indicates them to be a people unactuated by ambition, jealousy, or avarice; the passions which so strongly operate on the human species, to produce a constant dread and variance with each other, and stimulate to acts of oppression, violence and rapacity, as well on their nearest neighbours as the most distant strangers.

[1] The Resolution grounded on the Middle Ground Shoal, which is about 8 miles NNW of East Foreland. When the tide rose she floated off without having received any damage.

At low tide the shoal we purposed to avoid was seen from the mast-head to the north-eastward, between which and the western shore, on the return of the flood tide, about two o'clock our route was directed, with a fresh breeze from the N.N.W. which obliged us to ply, keeping nearer the shore than the shoal. The soundings from mid-channel towards the shoal were twenty fathoms and upwards, but towards the land the depth regularly decreased to 13 and 10 fathoms. The gale reduced us to double-reefed topsails and foresail, and was accompanied by so severe a frost, that the spray became instantly frozen and fell on the decks like sleet, or small particles of snow, and the water that was brought up with the lead-line, although in constant motion, cased it intirely with ice. On meeting the ebb tide in the evening, we anchored in 15 fathoms water, about two leagues to the north-eastward of the north Foreland, and about a league from the western shore. During the night a quantity of loose ice passed the ship, and in the morning of Sunday the 20th the wind blew a gentle breeze from the N.W., with intensely cold weather, the mercury standing at $7\frac{1}{2}$. Having both wind and tide in our favor, about three o'clock we proceeded towards the northern or main branch of the river,[1] but were soon alarmed by the appearance of a dry shoal in the direction of our course. This appearance was very unexpected, as we were then nearly pursuing the former track of the Resolution and Discovery, which could scarcely have passed such a shoal unnoticed. Many large lumps, like rocks of considerable size, were lying upon it, which at length induced me to believe, that what we had taken for a shoal would be found to be only a body of dirty ice. We had however contended sufficiently with dangers of this sort, and having understood that a Spanish officer had found the navigation of this extensive river intirely closed by shoals and sand banks, extending from side to side some leagues lower down than where Captain Cook had anchored,[2] I did not think it prudent to proceed until some examination should have taken place; especially as some of the crew were already frost-bitten, and in the event of our getting a-ground, the carrying out anchors, and other duties consequent upon such an accident, might expose others to the like inconvenience. For these reasons we again anchored, and after the sun had shone about three hours, I dispatched Mr. Whidbey in the cutter to ascertain the matter in doubt. About ten in the forenoon he returned, having gone several miles beyond where the shoal was supposed to have been seen, without meeting less than from 14 to 17 fathoms water. The appearance that had been mistaken for a shoal proved to be floating ice, which had been carried rapidly from the ship with the strength of the tide, and then disappeared, giving it, in the gray of the morning, the semblance of a shoal overflowed by the flood tide; this was manifested by the return of the next ebb, when, about noon, our horizon was encompassed in most directions with floating ice, of various shapes, magnitudes, and colours.

The weather was calm and serene, though intensely cold, and the ebb

[1] Knik Arm of Cook Inlet.
[2] The reference must be to the Fidalgo expedition of 1790.

tide obliging us to remain stationary, afforded a good opportunity for making such observations as were become requisite; by these the latitude was found to be 61° 10', longitude 210°;[1] and the variation in six sets of azimuths, by two compasses, shewed the mean result to be 29° 48' easterly, differing very materially from our last observations, notwithstanding that the two stations were not 30 leagues apart; the latter, however, I considered to be the most correct. In this situation the north Foreland bore by compass S. 28 W.; the nearest shore S. 74 W., about a league off; the island[2] lying before the river Turnagain,[3] N. 55 E.; the entrance of that river, N. 70 E.; point Possession,[4] N. 87 E.; and the volcano, S. 15 W. distant 32 leagues. Favored with the flood tide, and a southerly breeze, about three o'clock we resumed our course as beforementioned, and had soundings from 13 to 17 fathoms until seven in the evening, when we suddenly came into six and four fathoms; but on hauling a little to the south the water again deepened to six fathoms, in which we anchored. The west point of entrance into the northern branch of the river, by compass bore N. 48 E. five leagues distant; its east point, N. 55 E:; Turnagain island,[5] from N. 63 E. to east, and point Possession, S. 35 E. distant ten miles. Four large pieces of ice were aground to the north of us; and as we were about four miles to the north of Captain Cooks track, and a league to the south of the shoal laid down by him as extending from the northern shore, I considered the shoal we had anchored near to have been one that had escaped his notice.

The wind blew a strong gale in the night from the N.N.W. the weather was intensely cold, attended with a heavy fall of very small hard frozen snow, that prevented our seeing very far about us until the afternoon of Monday the 21st, when the weather clearing up about the time of low water, our situation was discovered to be about a quarter of a mile from an extensive dry shoal, bearing by compass from S. 74 W. to N. 54 E.; evidently connected with, and lying along the northern shore, of the river, which was at the distance of about five miles, and had the appearance, by the direction it took, of joining on to the west point of its northern branch. This left no doubt of its being the same shoal as that delineated in Captain Cook's chart, although

---

[1] The correct lat. was probably about 61° 08' N, or only about two minutes in error, but the long. was almost a full degree too far E. The *Discovery* was in about 150° 58' W (209° 02' E).

[2] Fire Island.

[3] Now Turnagain Arm, the E branch of Cook Inlet. Named the Turnagain River by Cook on 1 June 1778, when he decided to turn back and not pursue further the exploration of the inlet.

[4] The S point of entrance to Turnagain Arm; named by Cook on 1 June 1778: 'In the after noon I sent Mr King again with two armed boats, with orders to land on the northern point of the low land on the SE side of the River, there to desplay the flag, take possession of the Country and River in his Majestys name and to bury in the ground a bottle containing t[w]o pieces of English coin (date 1772) and a paper on which was in[s]cribed the Ships names date &ca.' – Cook, *Journals*, III, p. 368.

[5] Vancouver's name for Fire Island, at the entrance to Turnagain Arm.

by our observations both the shoal and its adjoining shore seem to lie some miles further to the south than is there represented.

The weather continuing to be fair, and having a commanding breeze from the N.N.W. we proceeded to the north-east along the edge of the shoal in soundings from 13 to 19 fathoms water, until about four o'clock, when the depth again decreased to six fathoms and a half. We stood towards Turnagain island, but not finding a deeper channel, we anchored,[1] in order to examine the passage before we should proceed further. On this service Mr. Whidbey was dispatched at day-light the next morning, Tuesday the 22d, with two boats, and he returned about noon, having found in the channel a depth of water from seven to seventeen fathoms, the deepest water being on the island side.

At four in the afternoon we weighed anchor, with the flood and a light westerly breeze; but our sails had not sufficient influence to act against the strength of the tide, which, in spite of every endeavor to the countrary, pressed us toward the shoals, forming the northern side of the channel; here the ship grounded for a short space of time, and again floated without occasioning us the least trouble; the wind from the westward becoming at this juncture somewhat more powerful, we hauled across the channel into seven fathoms water, where we again anchored, having now advanced as far as the passage had been examined.

A favorable change had this day taken place in our climate; the mercury in the thermometer had risen to 36, the weather was serene, the air comparatively mild, and we again flattered ourselves that a more temperate season was at length approaching.

The next morning, Wednesday the 23d, we discovered on the surface of the water innumerable large pieces of floating ice, which were drifted by the rapidity of the tide with great violence against the ship's bows, but fortunately they were not of sufficient magnitude to do us any injury. They however prevented the boats being hoisted out until eight o'clock, when Mr. Whidbey again proceeded in quest of a convenient station for the ship, within the entrance of the northern branch; this service engaged him until two in the afternoon, when he returned, and reported that from the ship's anchorage the depth of water had gradually increased to 10 and 15 fathoms, until he had reached the

---

[1] Some thought was evidently given to interrupting the survey and seeking a haven where the *Discovery* could wait for more favourable weather: 'Our sudden transition from the tropical regions to which our constitutions had been in some measure inurd, but ill fitted us to withstand such harrassing duty in this cold bleak & dreary country, we were therefore anxious to find some port, where we might take refuge & remain comfortably till the season broke up & the rigor of the Climate so far abated that we could commence our operations, for the frost was now so very intense, that a little before we got under way this morning the Thermometer was so low as 7°. At eight it was at 13° & at noon it rose no higher than 18° – the effect of which was that several of our people were frost bit in performing their duty on this & the preceeding day.' – Menzies, April 20. But no haven presented itself.

points of entrance,[1] between which he had found 20 fathoms, and within them from 26 to 10 fathoms, but this depth was by no means regular. He had then directed his researches some distance further up the branch than the boats from the Resolution and the Discovery had penetrated in the year 1778, and found all the shores round to the northward composed of compact low land; and unless the branch took a very sharp turn to the east or S.E. it had every appearance of terminating not many miles beyond the extent of his examination, in a spacious bason or harbour.

This account disappointed my expectations, as it was not easily reconcileable with the idea we had formed of the interior distance to which we should be led by the waters of this extensive opening. The presumption that our progress would speedily be stopped, became by this information very strong; but as that point remained yet to be proved, I was determined to persevere in my former intention, and weighing with the flood about five in the evening, we steered for the bason or harbour described by Mr. Whidbey; and which, although by his account capable of affording us protection and shelter against the winds or the sea, did not promise any very agreeable communication with the shore. Our progress was uninterrupted, and having about nine at night reached the limits of Mr. Whidbey's examination, we anchored near the eastern side of the harbour in seven fathoms water, black sandy bottom.

The weather was fair the next morning, Thursday the 24th, and at low tide a dry shoal was seen stretching from a high cliffy point to the northward on the eastern shore, where the river took an eastwardly direction.[2] This shoal seemed to be connected with the cliffy point, and to be some feet above water, forming as it were a ridge that extended towards the north-west or opposite shore, and was apparently united to that side also; at any rate, it was evident that if a channel did exist it could only be a very narrow one, and our curiosity became greatly excited by the appearances before us. For our satisfaction in this particular, and for the purpose of finding a more convenient station for the ship, and a supply of fresh water, I made an excursion after breakfast, accompanied by some of the officers.

We had not long quitted the ship, before we found a stream of excellent water on the eastern shore,[3] which, with little labour in clearing away the ice, could be very conveniently obtained. Our attention was now principally directed to a bay or cove, that seemed to be situated to the southward of the cliffy point before-mentioned,[4] where I entertained hopes of finding a commodious resting place for the ship, free from the inconvenience of the drifting ice, which seemed likely to occasion us much annoyance. On reaching

---

[1] Point Mackenzie on the N side of the entrance and Point Woronzof on the S. The entrance is about two miles wide.

[2] Beyond the point where the *Discovery* anchored Knik Arm (Vancouver's 'northern branch') is virtually filled with mudflats that are bare at low water. Channels and sloughs run through them, but none is more than a few fathoms in depth.

[3] Presumably the Eagle River.

[4] Eagle Bay, into the S end of which the Eagle River flows.

the south point of this bay, we observed near the edge of the steep cliffs that form it, some houses; these we visited, but found them scarcely more than the skeletons of habitations, that had apparently been some time deserted. The large ones were four in number, of a different shape and construction to any of the houses of the North West American Indians we had yet seen. One of these was twenty-four feet long, and about fourteen feet wide, built with upright and cross spars, had been covered in with the bark of the birch tree, and when in good repair must have been a very tolerably comfortable dwelling. Their shape resembled that of a barn, the sides perpendicular about nine feet high, and the top of the roof about four feet higher, which inclined uniformly from the sides until it met in the middle. Beside these there were two or three smaller tenements or hovels half under ground, and built more after the prevailing fashion of the native inhabitants of these regions.[1] This circumstance, in addition to the spars of which the larger houses were formed, having all been cut down by axes, and evidently by persons accustomed to such tools, induced us to suppose that this village had been the residence of a party of Russians, or some other European visitors, not only from the construction of the larger houses, but from the circumstance of these Indians not having yet been induced to make the least use of the axe, but universally preferring and using iron tools in the form of the knife or chisel.

From hence we proceeded to the examination of the bay. On sounding from point to point, the deepest water was not found to exceed from four to five fathoms, and this nearly at the top of the flood. And as the rise and fall of the tide according to our mensuration was not less than four fathoms, this part of the bay must necessarily be nearly dry at low water. After passing to the north of the high cliffy point to which at low tide the shoal had appeared to be united, we had for the space of a quarter of a mile nine and ten fathoms water, but on steering over towards the opposite or north-west shore the depth instantly decreased to four and three fathoms, and by keeping as nearly as we could judge on the shoal ridge seen from the ship, the depth was found to be from twenty to fourteen feet water, until within a little distance of the north-west side, when we had a few casts of seven and a half fathoms. At this time it was the top of high water neap tides.

Being unprovided for a more comprehensive survey, we left for future examination the width of these small spaces of deep water; as likewise the ascertaining whether this shoal constituted only a bar, and whether the extensive sheet of water to the E.N.E. became again navigable for shipping, and stretched to any remote distance in that direction. The general appearance of the country indicated the contrary, as the shores, in every direction in which we had seen them, had uniformly appeared to descend gradually, from the mountains to their termination at the water-side, in low flat land, apparently

---

[1] 'From this description' Gunther concludes that 'this probably was an Athapascan village, since the Athapascans used birch bark covering and built semiunderground houses as winter residences.' – *Indian Life on the Northwest Coast*, p. 201.

firm and compact; should these waters therefore penetrate beyond the limits of our view, their course must have been between interlocking points at no great distance from each other.

Our curiosity so far satisfied, we returned to the ship, not very well able to reconcile with each other the several circumstances that had thus fallen under our observation; namely, the rapidity and regularity of the tide forming equal intervals of flood and ebb, both of equal strength, and setting at the rate of three miles an hour; with the water, even at dead low tide, little, if at all, fresher than that of the ocean, although at the distance of near 70 leagues from the sea. These several circumstances could not be considered, notwithstanding the appearance of the shores, as indications of an early termination of this extensive opening on the coast.

The watering place to which I intended to resort lying to the south of our anchorage, we weighed with the latter part of the ebb, in order to place the ship as conveniently to it as the shores would admit; but in attempting this, the ship ran a-ground on a shoal that had escaped our observation, lying between our last anchorage and the shore. An anchor was immediately carried out, and on the return of the flood the vessel was hove off, without having received any apparent injury.

The next morning, Friday the 25th, Mr. Swaine was sent with a party to clear away the ice before the run of water, and prepare a convenient spot for the reception of the casks;[1] whilst another boat was employed in search of the most convenient anchorage for the ship. This being found about a mile to the southward of the run of water, we proceeded in the evening, took our station there, and moored with a cable each way in five fathoms depth at low water, soft bottom, composed of small loose stones, and fine black sand.[2]

[1] Recreation was not forgotten: 'in the same boat Mr Orchard & some others landed with their fowling pieces to take the diversion of shooting. They walkd along shore to a flat marsh at the bottom of the Bay [around the mouth of the Eagle River] to the Northward of us where they met with pretty good sport, & found in the skirts of the wood a habitation containing several natives both men & women who behavd very docile & friendly, & presented them with some furs.' – Menzies, April 25.

[2] All Vancouver's anchorages except this one are marked on his chart of Cook Inlet.

DUE DATE
